Data
Management

HANDBOOK
3RD EDITION

OTHER AUERBACH PUBLICATIONS

A Standard for Auditing Computer Applications, Martin Krist
ISBN: 0-8493-9983-1

Analyzing Business Information Systems, Shouhong Wang
ISBN: 0-8493-9240-3

Broadband Networking, James Trulove, Editor, ISBN: 0-8493-9821-5

Communications Systems Management Handbook, 6th Edition
Anura Gurugé and Lisa M. Lindgren, Editors, 0-8493-9826-6

Computer Telephony Integration, William Yarberry, Jr.
ISBN: 0-8493-9995-5

Data Management Handbook, 3rd Edition, Sanjiv Purba, Editor
ISBN: 0-8493-9832-0

Electronic Messaging, Nancy Cox, Editor, ISBN: 0-8493-9825-8

Enterprise Operations Management Handbook, 2nd Edition
Steve F. Blanding, Editor, ISBN: 0-8493-9824-X

Enterprise Systems Architectures, Andersen Consulting, 0-8493-9836-3

Enterprise Systems Integration, John Wyzalek, Editor, ISBN: 0-8493-9837-1

Healthcare Information Systems, Phillip L. Davidson, Editor, ISBN: 0-8493-9963-7

Information Security Architecture, Jan Killmeyer, ISBN: 0-8493-9988-2

Information Security Management Handbook, 4th Edition
Harold F. Tipton and Micki Krause, Editors, ISBN: 0-8493-9829-0

IS Management Handbook, 7th Edition, Carol V. Brown, Editor
ISBN: 0-8493-9820-7

Information Technology Control and Audit, Frederick Gallegos, Sandra Allen-Senft,
and Daniel P. Manson, ISBN: 0-8493-9994-7

Internet Management, Jessica Keyes, Editor
ISBN: 0-8493-9987-4

Local Area Network Handbook, 6th Edition, John P. Slone, Editor
ISBN: 0-8493-9838-X

Multi-Operating System Networking: Living with UNIX, NetWare, and NT
Raj Rajagopal, Editor, ISBN: 0-8493-9831-2

Network Manager's Handbook, 3rd Edition, John Lusa, Editor
ISBN: 0-8493-9841-X

Project Management, Paul C. Tinnirello, Editor, ISBN: 0-8493-9998-X

Effective Use of Teams in IT Audits, Martin Krist
ISBN: 0-8493-9828-2

Systems Development Handbook, 4th Edition, Paul C. Tinnirello, Editor
ISBN: 0-8493-9822-3

AUERBACH PUBLICATIONS

www.auerbach-publications.com
TO Order: Call: 1-800-272-7737 • Fax: 1-800-374-3401
E-mail: orders@crcpress.com

Data
Management
HANDBOOK
3RD EDITION

Sanjiv Purba
EDITOR

AUERBACH

Boca Raton   London   New York   Washington, D.C.

Cataloging-in-Publication Data is available from the Library of Congress

© 2000 by CRC Press LLC

Auerbach is an imprint of CRC Press LLC

No claim to original U.S. Government works

International Standard Book Number 0-8493-9832-0

Printed in the United State of America 1 2 3 4 5 6 7 8 9 0

Printed on acid-free paper

Contributors

HEDY ALBAN, *Freelance Writer, Cherry Hill, NJ*

BRUCE ANDERSON, *Independent Consultant, Toronto, Ontario, Canada*

MARY AYALA-BUSH, *Principal, Computer Sciences Corporation, Waltham, MA*

CHARLES BANYAY, *Manager, Deloitte & Touche Consulting Group, Toronto, Ontario, Canada*

JEFF BULLER, *Consultant, VISUAL Systems Development Group, Toronto, Ontario, Canada*

MICHELLE BURGESS, *Senior Manager, Deloitte & Touche Consulting Group, Toronto, Ontario, Canada*

JAMES CANNADY, *Research Scientist, Georgia Tech Research Institute, Atlanta, GA*

MARION G. CERUTI, *Scientist, Advanced C41 Systems, Engineering and Integration Group, Command and Intelligence Systems Division, Naval Command, Control, and Ocean Surveillance Center, RDT&E Division, San Diego, CA*

BOSCO CHEUNG, *Senior Consultant, Deloitte & Touche, Toronto, Ontario, Canada*

TIM CHRISTMANN, *Senior Consultant, Deloitte & Touche Consulting Group, Toronto, Ontario, Canada*

GARY CURDIE, *Systems Analys, Data Administration Group, TDIT, Toronto, Ontario, Canada*

JUDY DINN, *Manager, Deloitte Consulting, Toronto, Ontario, Canada*

LAURA DISISTO, *Training Leader, Canadian Imperial Bank of Commerce, Toronto, Ontario, Canada*

CHARLES DOW, *Practice Leader, Object-Oriented Technologies, Deloitte & Touche Consulting Group, Toronto, Ontario, Canada*

STEPHEN D'SILVA, *Senior Consultant and Technology Leader, Deloitte & Touche Consulting Group, Toronto, Ontario, Canada*

LEN DVORKIN, *President, Italex Consulting, Inc., Thornhill, Ontario, Canada*

JEFFERY FELDMAN, *Manager, Deloitte Consulting, Toronto, Ontario, Canada*

ELIZABETH N. FONG, *Computer Systems Laboratory, National Institute of Standards and Technology, Gaithersburg, MD*

JUDITH N. FROSCHER, *Principal Investigator, SINTRA Project, Naval Research Laboratory, Washington, DC*

YONGJIAN FU, *Professor, Computer Science, University of Missouri, Rolla, MO*

IDO GILEADI, *Manager, Deloitte & Touche Consulting Group, Toronto, Ontario, Canada*

VENKAT N. GUDIVADA, *Dow Jones, Jersey City, NJ*

KATHRYN A. HARVILL, *Computer Systems Laboratory, National Institute of Standards and Technology, Gaithersburg, MD*

JONATHAN HELD, *U.S. Navy, Monterey, CA*

ASHVIN IYENGAR, *Consultant, Object Technologies, Deloitte & Touche Consulting Group, DRT Systems, Toronto, Ontario, Canada*

DIANE JOHNSON, *Consulting Manager, Data Warehouse Service Line, Ernst & Young Consulting Services, Inc., Toronto, Ontario, Canada*

JOHN JORDAN, *Principal, Consulting & Systems Integration, Computer Sciences Corporation, Waltham, MA*

MARIE KARAKANIAN, *Senior Manager, Deloitte Consulting, Toronto, Ontario, Canada*

BONN-OH KIM, *Assistant Professor, Information Systems, Department of Management, University of Nebraska, Lincoln, NE*

PAUL KORZENIOWSKI, *Freelance Writer, Sudbury, MA*

TONY KRAJEWSKI, *Senior Consultant, Deloitte Consulting, Toronto, Ontario, Canada*

WALTER KUKETZ, *Consulting and Systems Integration, Computer Sciences Corporation, Waltham, MA*

CAROL L. LARSON, *Technical Writer and Desktop Publisher, Hillsboro, OR*

JAMES A. LARSON, *Senior Software Engineer, Intel Architecture Laboratory, Beaverton, OR*

RICHARD LEE, *Senior Consultant, Operations Reengineering, Deloitte & Touche Consulting Group, Toronto, Ontario, Canada*

PIERRE J. LEMAY, *Senior Consultant, Document Management, PJL Information Systems, Orleans, Ontario, Canada*

CONGHUA LI, *Manager, Deloitte Consulting, Toronto, Ontario, Canada*

PHILLIP Q. MAIER, *Member, Secure Network Initiative, Lockheed Martin Corporation, Sunnyvale, CA*

JACK MCELREATH, *Managing Partner, Consulting and Systems Integration, Computer Sciences Corporation, Waltham, MA*

LYNDA L. MCGHIE, *Director, Information Security, Lockheed Martin Corporation, Bethesda, MD*

MICHAEL K. MILLER, *Senior Data Architect, Worldwide Data Planning and Architecture, NCR Corp., Dayton, OH*

JAGDISH MIRANI, *Senior Product Manager, Data Warehousing, Oracle Corp., Redwood Shores, CA*

BRETT MOLOTSKY, *Lotus Notes Product Manager, Omicron Consulting, Philadelphia, PA*

ALI H. MURTAZA, *Senior Consultant, Data Warehousing Service Line, Deloitte & Touche Consulting Group, Toronto, Ontario, Canada*

BRIAN NICHOLLS, *Senior Manager, Deloitte Consulting, Toronto, Ontario, Canada*

ELISABETH OSTIGUY, *President, Emerson Communication Inc., Toronto, Ontario, Canada*

SRINIVAS PADMANABHARAO, *Consultant, Deloitte Consulting, Toronto, Ontario, Canada*

WILLIAM PEARSON, *Senior System Consultant and DB2 Database Administrator, Toronto, Ontario, Canada*

R. MICHAEL PICKERING, *Managing Consultant, Data Warehouse Practice, Oracle Consulting Canada, Toronto, Ontario, Canada*

SRIRAM PIDAPARTI, *Cargill Financial Services Corporation, Minnetonka, MN*

SANJIV PURBA, *Senior Manager, Deloitte & Touche Consulting Group, Toronto, Ontario, Canada*

LOIS RICHARDS, *Data Warehousing Project Manager, Dynamic Information Systems Corp., Boulder, CO*

CHARLES L. SHEPPARD, *Computer Systems Laboratory, National Institute of Standards and Technology, Gaithersburg, MD*

ANTONIO SI, *Assistant Professor, Department of Computing, Hong-Kong Polytechnic University, Hong Kong, China*

MANJIT SIDHU, *Independent Senior Manager, Deloitte & Touche, Toronto, Ontario, Canada*

MICHAEL SIMONYI, *Independent Consultant, Etobicoke, Ontario, Canada*

NANCY STONELAKE, *Senior Consultant, Deloitte & Touche Consulting Group, Toronto, Ontario, Canada*

MICHAEL J.D. SUTTON, *Director, Business Process and Document Management Services Group, Rockland, Ontario, Canada*

DAVID WADSWORTH, *Java Evangelist, Sun Microsystems, Toronto, Ontario, Canada*

DAVID C. WALLACE, *Professor, Applied Computer Science Department, Illinois State University, Normal, IL*

DOUG WARD, *Senior Manager, Deloitte Consulting, Toronto, Ontario, Canada*

JASON WEIR, *Technical Writer, DataMirror Corporation, Markham, Ontario, Canada*

RONALD A. WENCER, *Management Consultant, Toronto, Ontario, Canada*

JAMES WOODS, *Independent Consultant, Lewisville, TX*

DAVID YEO, PH.D., *Senior Business Solutions Specialist, Data Mining, SAS Institute (Canada) Inc., Toronto, Ontario, Canada*

YOUNGHOC YOON, *Associate Professor, Department of Information Systems, Virginia Commonwealth University, Richmond, VA*

MICHAEL ZIMMER, *Senior Data Administrator, Ministry of Health, Victoria, British Columbia, Canada*

Contents

SECTION XIII
DOCUMENT MANAGEMENT

SECTION XIV
INDUSTRY SPECIFIC AND PACKAGE SOLUTIONS

Introduction

DATA MANAGEMENT IS A MAJOR DRIVING FORCE IN THE ONGOING INFORMATION TECHNOLOGY (IT) REVOLUTION. Data comes in many formats, serves many uses, and passes through many corporate processes. The purpose of this book is to examine the essential art and science of data management. This handbook focuses on commonly asked questions such as the following:

- What is data? What is information?
- What is the relationship between data and processes?
- How do you build a data-centric global organization?
- Who owns the data in an organization?
- How do you connect heterogeneous data sources in distributed organizations?
- How are object technologies and business components used in data management?
- How are data models related to object or component models?
- What is a data-centric development methodology?
- How are the web and the internet leveraged to manipulate corporate data?
- How are business objects leveraged in the enterprise?
- How can organizations leverage the next generation of ERP solutions?
- How can business frameworks be leveraged across the organization?
- How to reuse data solutions?
- What are some of the anticipated future trends?

The scope of this handbook covers a full breadth of data management categories including strategy, methodologies, standards, techniques, database products, ERP solutions, data tools (e.g., modeling tools, database servers, conversion tools), data warehousing, data mining, the Internet, the World Wide Web, and future directions.

This handbook is written by experienced and acknowledged experts in the Information Technology (IT) field and in data management, and as such is a powerful tool for organizations of any size and industry.

NOTABLE VICTORIES

Data management has won significant battles over the past few years. Some of these are described here:

- Corporate data is widely perceived and protected as a corporate asset;
- Identification of specific data structures and elements by industry groups;
- The growth of data specific roles, such as data modelor, data administrator, and data analyst;
- An anticipated release of the next generation of the ANSI SQL standard;
- Data source connectivity to the Internet and World Wide Web;
- Relational database servers have not been replaced by object oriented databases, and in fact, appear to have proven their importance to the industry, at least into the next century. This has resulted in continued investments in database server technology;
- Large data warehouses and databases were once defined to be in the hundreds of megabytes range, grew to the gigabyte range, and are now characterized as having entered the terrabyte range;
- Dramatic increases in storage capacities;
- Improved system response times due to improved data access methods and tools;
- Investments in data development methodologies, frameworks, and techniques; and
- Continued popularity of modeling tools, conversion tools, and other data centric tools.

THE FORCES OF CHANGE

Data management has changed dramatically over the last few decades. There have been significant improvements in data storage, data access options, data protection, data security, and data distribution. Where data storage was once at a high premium, so much so that saving 2 bytes of data when storing dates caught on and spawned a billion dollar year 2000 problem, it is becoming increasingly inexpensive and easily available. The original 5¼" floppy disks were replaced by 3½" floppy disks and now routinely offer capacities of 3 GB or more. CD-ROMs can store 500 MB of data, and rumour has it that the next generation of CD-ROMs will store at least 10 times that amount.

There have been many challenges in the last few years to the traditional data management philosophies. Object oriented technology threatened to replace the importance of corporate data with objects that bundled processes and data together. Computer viruses started to become a data epidemic. Application programs became so large that traditional diskettes could no longer store them. At one time, talk of a Windows 95 release threatened to consume all the free diskettes available in the world. This created the demand for CD-ROMs (which has also swept the music industry). For the few readers who may not already know this, computers with sound cards running Windows 95+ can play music CDs right out of the box.

Large data stores have grown from the megabyte range to the terrabyte range. Most organizations are investing in their own data warehouses or data marts to support executive decision-making. This has supported the rapid growth of the data mining industry. Data stores are also connected to the Internet and the World Wide Web. This popularized multidimensional data stores, a new data modeling technique.

STRATEGIC ISSUES AND METHODOLOGIES

Data management is an enterprise-wide concern. While it is implemented at a technical level, several strategic issues must be resolved before data management initiatives can begin in most organizations. These include data ownership, data tools selection, building centralized data repositories, and defining corporate models. Data continues to be a valuable corporate asset in most organizations.

Data methodologies serve a useful function in many organizations. They are generally a part of a full lifecycle development methodology. Data methodologies are available in a number of delivery channels. They can be purchased from third parties, be bought as part of a modeling tool set, or built in-house, based on best practices. Development initiatives involving data management will benefit from leveraging data methodologies.

n-Tier Architecture, Client/Server Technology, and Components

What was once strictly called client/server technology, has over the last few years, been called many other names. Some industry professionals even describe client/server as an older architecture that is being replaced by newer architectures like "network architecture." But things are never straightforward in our profession.

Since the late 1980s, client/server technology essentially consisted of two tiers. One tier was a data tier that typically resided on a dedicated platform physically implemented on a database server (e.g., Sybase SQL Server, Microsoft SQL Server Oracle, Informix). Some business rules could be maintained in this layer. The user interface was the other tier, and it generally ran on a personal computer type of device. Business logic was also bundled with this layer. Fat client/server implementations were those that contained most of the business logic in the user interface tier. The data tier in this server only managed the applications data. Thin client/server implementations were those in which most of the business logic was moved into the data tier.

The 2-tier client/server model was popular, and relatively straightforward to implement. However, it had several drawbacks: (1) the client and the server tiers were tightly coupled, so they were essentially stuck with each other and were difficult to port; (2) the architecture did not scale well in term of users and system response time; (3) system management, which had been well enabled in the mainframe environment, was problematic in 2-tier architecture. 3-tier architecture was a response to some of these limitations.

In 3-tier architecture, the business logic is given its own tier, that can optionally run on a dedicated platform. This additional tier addresses many of the limitations posed by 2-tier architecture. In a 3-tier deployment, you generally have a thin client and a thin server (data tier). The business logic is encapsulated in the business logic tier. The Web-browser is arguably one implemetation of a 3-tier architecture. So, arguably, is network computing. n-Tier architecture is supported by component based development, which is expected to become significantly mainstream in the next few years. This is one area to watch closely in the new millenium.

Data Warehousing and Data Mining

Data warehouses have been around for a long time, but it was Inmon, who coined the term and made it a popular discipline. The entire purpose of data warehousing and data mining is to provide information, support decision making, and to alert the business of patterns that are detected. Data warehousing is also known as information warehousing. Data warehouses, which were once in the 100s of MB range have grown to terrabytes in size. Data warehouses support OLAP type processing, which offers decision support and what if analysis. It is also supported by a variety of tools and new modeling techniques (e.g., multidimensional database, metadata).

Data mining is a discipline that uses the information stored in a data warehouse to uncover important trends and information for the organization. Data mining can retrieve information that otherwise would go unnoticed.

Documentation Management

Document management satisfies an important requirement in data management. Where an organization has a requirement to store and retrieve complex datatypes, rich text, and blobs with a small set of access keys, document management offers advantages over the traditional relational or indexed databases. Document management is effective in storing large volumes of data that only requires access in a limited number of access keys. It can also include such tools as electronic forms, Lotus Notes, and Internet/Intranet solutions.

Industry Specific Solutions

The next few years are going to see the growth of industry based solutions that package data management and processes together. Package solutions have been available for decades, and are now entering what is commonly referred to as the second wave of ERP. This wave focuses on enhancing value received by organizations after implementing their ERP solutions. Organizations that are looking for new solutions, should consider purchasing such things as data models from a third party, before building them from the ground up. This will result in more industry specific data solutions, including models, applications, and processes. The growth of objects and components will also create an industry of reusable code.

THE FUTURE

The last few years in this industry have taught us a central truth about Information Technology. The pace of change in this industry is staggering and difficult to predict with any degree of certainty beyond two or three years. However, experience has also shown the continuing importance of data in this industry. No matter where it is, no matter how it's packaged, no matter how it's accessed, data will undoubtedly play a central role in the health and competitiveness of organizations well into the future.

Database management is in the process of radical changes coming from many different sources, including the following: faster data access, data on the Internet, stronger data protection, larger data stores, combinations of complex datatypes and traditional database servers, component based development, industry specific data models and solutions, new tools and databases, data mining, data migration, 64 bit processing, new operating systems, and more demanding data conversions.

GETTING THE MOST OUT OF THIS BOOK

Many authors have contributed their experiences, knowledge, and ideas in the chapters of this book. Each of them is a strong player in their respective niches. Taken as a whole, this handbook sweeps across many data management categories. It is divided into 16 sections, each focusing on a particularly useful aspect of data management. These sections are described here:

Section I, "Data Development Methodologies, Definitions, and Strategy," focuses on the full lifecycle and strategies issues relating to data management. This section defines criteria for selecting a data development methodology, defines an iterative database development methodology, defines an enterprise-wide data organization, defines commonly used database terminology, provides a framework for establishing enterprise-wide data standards, and focuses on several strategic issues relating to data management.

Section II, "Data Models and Modeling Techniques," investigates a variety of modeling techniques. This includes the traditional approaches to data modeling and process modeling that have created Online Transaction Processing applications (OLTP) all over the world. This chapter focuses on data models, component based modeling, process and data model integration, dimensional data modeling for data warehouses, and object-oriented techniques.

Section III, "Data Integrity and Quality," offers advice on ensuring the integrity of data and its quality. This section describes how to use database constraints, referential integrity, and data quality.

Section IV, "Data Administration, Security, and Operations," examines the operational aspects of administrating a database environment. This section describes data disaster recovery options, NT Domains, DBMS recovery procedures, change management strategies, and security controls and models.

Section V, "Data Migration, Conversion, and Legacy Applications," covers a topic that is exceedingly important in today's rapidly merging business environment. This section describes a case study for data conversion, legacy database conversion, and related conversion issues.

Section VI, "Database Server and Universal Server Technology," focuses on various examples and issues with these tools. This section describes database servers, universal data servers and complex data types. Performance improvements are also covered through examples of batch processing improvements and better indexing schemes. Specific examples include SQL Server and DB2.

Section VII, "Object Technology, Object Modeling, and Object Databases," covers the relationship and co-existence of object technology and data management. This section describes Microsoft Visual Basic's hot new releases improved data access methods. This chapter also covers component-based development, ActiveX, CORBA, Rational Rose, JavaBeans, Java, component architectures, and object wrapping.

Section VIII, "Distributed Databases, Portability, and Interoperability," examines issues related to distributed databases, portability, and interoperability. This section describes distributed database design, managing multiple distributed databases, mobile databases, and database gateways.

Section IX, "Data Replication," describes data replication through a variety of techniques and tools. The advantages and types of data replication that are available are also described in this section.

Section X, "Data and the Internet, Intranet, and the Web," describes the relationship of data management to the Intranet, Internet, and the World Wide Web (WWW). This section examines Lotus Notes and Intranets as corporate solutions. Other topics that are covered in this section include, publishing database information on the WWW, web-enabling data warehouses, and connecting data sources to the Web with minimal programming.

Section XI, "Data Warehousing, Decision Support, and OLAP," describes the different elements of this popular trend. This section defines a framework for enterprise data warehouse projects. This section also describes dimensional data modeling, contrasts relational models to dimensional models, and focuses on different aspects of OLAP.

Section XII, "Data Mining," focuses on several techniques for mining corporate data for valuable information. This section examines techniques, costs, and tools related to data mining initiatives.

Section XIII, "Document Management," describes the terms of reference for a document management project and compares DBMSs to document management applications.

Section XIV, "Industry Specific and Package Solutions," examines techniques for leveraging the increasingly popular trend of using package solutions or industry specific prints, as well as the next wave of ERP. This section describes how data management technologies can be used to improve several different industries. The section also describes how to integrate several different packages, such as BAAN and PeopleSoft.

Section XV, "LINUX Fundamentals," examines this popular new operating system, focusing on the development model, distribution model, application development, and database operations.

Section XVI, "Emerging Practices and Directions," examines topics such as E-commerce and ensuring call center data quality.

Sanjiv Purba

Section I
Data Development Methodologies, Definitions, and Strategy

EFFECTIVE DATA SOLUTIONS MUST START AT THE STRATEGIC LEVEL with an organization's executive. From here they must sweep across the organization touching all relevant departments, and incorporating diverse processes and tools. This section contains chapters to define how effective data solutions can be formalized and implemented across the organization. The cornerstone of this involves the selection and implementation of data development methodologies. Data development methodologies are a powerful tool that defines the activities and the deliverables produced in data related projects. In some cases, data development methodologies are a component of a larger, full cycle development methodology. This section contains the following 7 chapters:

Chapter 1, "Database Development Methodology and Organization," provides a framework for developing databases from the logical to the physical level in enterprises. The discussion in this section is independent of implementation tools. This chapter also discusses roles and responsibilities to support the database development methodology. The data development methodology is discussed in the context of a full lifecycle development methodology. This chapter also identifies features that should be considered when selecting or building a corporate data development methodology.

Chapter 2, "A Review of Database System Terminology," begins with a definition of data and then goes on to define various terms commonly used in data management, including data element, data item, schema, data administrator, repository, relational database system, attribute, record, federated database system, middleware, client/server, legacy data, migration, and integration.

1

Chapter 3, "Developing a Global Information Vision," describes how to provide a global perspective to information and data resources in an organization. This chapter defines a methodology, derived from actual success stories, for showing how a global vision can be constructed and implemented across the wider organization.

Chapter 4, "An Approach for Establishing Enterprise Data Standards," provides practical examples and categories for building a set of enterprise data standards. This chapter is assembled from actual project experiences to describe techniques that work, and as importantly, do not work, when trying to build and implement enterprise data standards. Suggestions for avoiding the common pitfalls experienced by organizations during this initiative are also provided in this chapter.

Chapter 5, "Enterprise Transformation and Data Management," discusses the benefits that can be realized from effective data management across the enterprise. Some of these include reduced duplication of data between different application and the consolidation of vendor information to negotiate large volume discounts from vendors.

Chapter 6, "Building an Integrated Customer Profile," shows how to develop an integrated customer profile that provides a comprehensive view of customers and their interactions in a typical business.

Chapter 7, "Divestiture IT Planning," provides a high level process and checklists for senior executives to use when planning divestitures. The chapter also identifies pitpalls and common dangers that are encountered in this process.

Chapter 1
Database Development Methodology and Organization

Sanjiv Purba

DATABASE DEVELOPMENT IS ONE OF THE FUNDAMENTAL OBJECTIVES of the data management function and certainly one of the end products of the process. In recent years, several trends have impacted the way that databases are built and the role they play in the overall organization. Some of these trends include data warehousing, object-oriented technology, E-commerce, and the emergence of very large databases (VLDBs). Other changes to the landscape include the popularity of complex data types (e.g., BLOBs, video), universal databases, and object databases. Despite these changes, the basis of many online transaction processing applications (OLTP) that run the business is still the relational database and the flat files. This fact is not going to change dramatically over the next few years. If anything, the relational database has proven its value as an enterprise enabler and, like the IBM mainframe, is here to stay for the foreseeable future.

This chapter defines a database development methodology and approach that has proven successful on a variety of projects, such as $100,000 to $15,000,000 budgets, mainframe, client/server, three-tier with OO, and package implementations. This approach promotes viewing methodologies as flexible frameworks that are customized for every specific instance. It allows data-oriented teams to use their personal insight and experience alongside the best practices embedded in the methodology. This chapter also defines organizational roles for a data-oriented environment.

0-8493-9832-0/00/$0.00+$.50
© 2000 by CRC Press LLC

BENEFITS

The complexity that is inherent in constructing relational database solutions can be reduced by using proven database development methodologies on projects. Methodologies are an excellent example of best practices and project lessons. Use of methodologies, therefore, reduces risk on development projects. Methodologies define activities and deliverables that are constructed in projects that were successful. Following these successful lessons can reduce project development time while increasing product quality. Furthermore, the use of methodologies simplifies the process of tracking project progress because there are clear benchmarks that can be reviewed by the project manager. Methodologies that offer templates/deliverables also allow a quickstart to the development process.

SELECTING A DATABASE DEVELOPMENT METHODOLOGY

Development methodologies with well-defined database development phases are commonly available in the marketplace. Some are freely available with modeling or project management tools, although others are found on the World Wide Web. Many of the larger consulting firms have developed proprietary methodologies based on their corporate project experiences and proven best practices. These can be purchased separately or they can be bundled with consulting/mentoring services retained from the firm. The following list identifies some of the features that should be included in any database development methodology that is being considered for deployment in an organization.

- *Linkage to a full lifecycle development methodology:* A full life-cycle methodology supports more than database development. The database development methodology chosen should either be a component of a larger full life-cycle methodology, or link seamlessly with one. Failure to do this could result in mismatched techniques or the development of deliverables that are not used.
- *Techniques:* Many popular development methodologies support a combination of techniques to streamline development of deliverables. The traditional waterfall approach involves producing deliverables in a sequential fashion. Deliverable B is not started until Deliverable A is completed and signed off. This approach, however, historically has proven to be slow on many projects of all sizes. As a result of this experience, a rapid application development (RAD) approach has gained popularity in the past 10 years. RAD produces deliverables in a much smaller timeframe than the older waterfall approach. Iteration and prototyping are cornerstones of most RAD approaches, as are teams that combine technical resources and users during the analysis and design phases of the project lifecycle. RAD has proven to be successful on smaller projects, but has been problematic on the larger ones due

to the complexity of the business requirements. A relatively new approach combines the best elements of both the waterfall and RAD approaches and has proven valuable on larger development projects.

- *Support:* A development methodology (or a database development methodology) is a product, whether an organization has paid for it or not. As such, it is important for the methodology to be supported by the vendor into the future. An unsupported methodology becomes obsolete in sort order. Some questions to ask the vendor include: "How much research is being conducted to improve the methodology?" "Is there a hotline for technical support?," and "When is the next release of the methodology being released?"

- *Price:* The price of the methodology should be considered in whole and in part and assessed against the value that is received. Consider the one-time cost, training costs, upgrade costs, yearly licence fees, costs per user, customization costs, hardware/software support costs, and costs for future releases.

- *Vendor:* Consider the stability and market share of the vendor providing the methodology. The vendor's references also should be checked to ascertain their support for clients. Vendors that are more stable and have more market share are more likely to improve their methodology with new techniques in the future.

- *Proven Success:* One of the surest ways of selecting a suitable methodology is to check the references of similar organizations that have used it successfully on development projects.

- *Electronic Availability:* The methodology should be available electronically through Lotus Notes, the Internet, or CD-ROM. It also should be available on paper. This makes the methodology widely available to those using it across the organization.

- *Templates/Deliverables:* Reusable templates and deliverables are a good source of best practices that provide the means for quick starting development projects. Many methodologies are demonstrated with these, but the templates/deliverables are not provided to customers. In such cases, it is valuable to try to negotiate the inclusion of templates/deliverables as part of the transaction. If the templates/deliverables still are not offered by the vendor, but the rest of the methodology is acceptable, a pilot project should be used to create reusable templates and deliverables for future projects to use. Although this may slow the pilot project down in the short term, subsequent projects will run more efficiently. It is also desirable to select a methodology architecture that allows additional templates and deliverables to be added to the database on an ongoing basis.

- *Linkages to newer architectures:* The methodology also should support linkages with modules that support data warehousing, object technology, E-commerce, and Web architectures. Flexibility in expanding the methodology directly or through deliverable linkages is desirable.

- *Ease of Learning and Use:* Methodologies that are easy to learn and use are more likely to be used on projects. Some methodologies are packaged with training courses from the vendor or other third parties.

It is not unusual to add to this list of features or to assign more weight to a handful of them because of their importance to a specific organization. Experience has shown that complicating the selection process does not necessarily improve the quality of the final selection. In fact, this can lead to wasted time and intense team debates or arguments that end in worthless stalemates. It is preferrable to build a short list of candidate methodologies by disqualifying candidates that are weak on one or two key features (e.g., not available electronically or purchase price is greater than $100,000). The short list then can be compared to maybe five or six of the features that are of key importance to the organization. It is useful to conduct a limited number of pilot projects that test the value of a methodology before making a final selection. It is also not unusual to pilot two different methodologies in a conference room pilot (CRP) to make a final determination. This process can take between 6 weeks and 6 months.

HIGH-LEVEL DATABASE DEVELOPMENT METHODOLOGY

This section defines a high-level methodology for database development. This methodology provides a good start for small to medium-size projects; however, a formal third-party methodology should be considered for projects that require more than 6 months of development effort. The activities discussed in this section are mapped to the standard project development framework, which consists of the following main phases: requirements, architecture, design, development, testing, implementation, and post-implementation. These phases can be conducted in parallel or sequentially depending on the exact nature of the methodology, and are restricted to database specific activities.

The subprocesses that are described in this section fit into a larger full life-cycle methodology that would address such activities as corporate sponsorship for the project, project plan definition, organization building, team building, user interface development, application design, technology selection, acceptance testing, and deployment. It is assumed that these activities are completed outside the database development methodology phases.

- *Define Business Requirements:* Business requirements are captured for any system development effort. The requirements also should be used to build the logical data model. They will feed such things as the number of entities, attribute names, and types of data stored in each attribute. These often are categorized by subject area.
- *Borrow or Create the Data Model:* With a solid understanding of the business requirements, it is a good idea to search the market for a data

model that can be purchased from a third party. This subsequently can be customized for the organization.

- *Build Logical Data Model:* The logical data model is built iteratively. The first view usually is done at a high level, beginning with a subject area or conceptual data model. Subsequent levels contain more detail. The process of normalization also is applied at this stage. There are many good books on normalization, so normal forms will not be covered. Foreign key fields and potential indexes also can be considered here. It is not necessary to build the logical data model for performance at this time, and physical considerations are left until a later process.

- *Verify the Data Model:* The logical data model is validated iteratively with users, the fields of the user interface, and process models. It is not unusual to make changes to the data model during this verification process. New requirements, which need to be fitted into the data model, also may be identified.

- *Build Data Architecture:* The data architecture is defined in the context of the physical data environment. Considerations, such as the database server, distribution, components, and partitioning, are considered in this step.

- *Build the Physical Data Model:* The logical data model is converted to a physical data model based on the specific database that is used. The physical data model will vary with the choice of database products and tools. The physical data model also contains such objects as indexes, foreign keys, triggers, views, and user-defined datatypes. The physical data model is optimized for performance and usually is denormalized for this reason. Denormalization can result in redundancy, but can improve system performance. Building the physical data model is not a one-stop process. Do not expect to build a final version of the physical data model on the first attempt.

- *Refine the Data Model:* The physical data model is refined continuously as more information becomes available, and the results of stress testing and benchmarking become available to the database development team. The logical data model also should be maintained as the physical data model is refined.

- *Complete Transaction Analysis:* Transaction analysis is used to review system transactions so that the physical data model can be refined for optimum system performance. Transaction analysis results are only meaningful after the business requirements and systems design are fairly solid. Transaction analysis produces statistics showing the access frequency for the tables in the database, time estimates, and data volumes.

- *Populate the Data:* After the database structure is established and the database is created, it is necessary to populate the database. This can be done through data scripts, applications, or data conversions. This can be an extensive set of activities that requires substantial data

mapping, testing, and parallel activities. It is expected that the details of this are included in the full life-cycle methodology.
- *Complete Testing:* Testing a database usually is done in the context of applications and is covered in the full life-cycle methodology. Some specific types of testing, such as stress testing, benchmarking, and regression testing, can be used to refine the performance of the physical data model. These require high volumes of data, testing tools, and distribution tools.

DELIVERABLES

Some of the important deliverables that are created from inception to the creation of a physical database are discussed in this section. It is useful to build a reference database that contains samples of each of these deliverables so that project teams know in advance what they are attempting to build.

- *Requirements Document:* This is the statement of the business requirements for the application being developed. This deliverable can contain narrative and any number of models or prototypes to capture and represent the business requirements.
- *Conceptual Model/Subject Areas:* This is a high-level view of the business subject areas that are within the scope of the data model (e.g., accounting, administration, billing, engineering).
- *Logical Data Model:* This contains entities, attributes, and business rules within the subject areas. The model also shows relationships between the entities. Key fields and foreign keys also can be identified in this model.
- *Transaction Analysis:* This is a list of transactions supported by the system, the entities (and possibly the fields) that are accessed by the transactions, and the frequency with which they are accessed. A create, read, update, and delete (CRUD) matrix is a useful input for helping with this analysis.
- *Physical Data Model:* This is a denormalized version of the logical data model that is optimized for performance under a specific technical environment and refined through the transaction analysis results. The physical data model usually is refined throughout a development cycle and is not finished until implementation. The physical data model contains physical objects such as tables, fields, indexes, foreign keys, primary keys, views, user-defined data types, and rules.
- *Object Model:* An object model supports the logical data model. This often serves as an intermediate layer between an object-based user interface and a relational back-end database.
- *Validation Model:* This is a cross-reference of models, such as process models, to the logical data model to prove its validity. It often includes

a mapping between the logical data model with a user interface and reports to identify gaps.

- *Conversion Strategy:* This is a statement of the strategy used to convert data into a new application. The level of detail can vary signficantly. This could be anything from high-level principles to detailed conversion scripts.

TOOLS

Modeling tools are critical for the database development process. There are a number of tools with various add-ons that can be used in this process. Modeling tools should offer support for both data models and process models. It also is becoming more useful for modeling tools to support object models or to link to other tools that do. Tools that support reverse-reengineering from physical databases to generate logical data model or scripts are useful for organizations that require extensive changes to data structures (possibly following a corporate merger).

There are many other tools that are useful in the database development process. Some of these include CASE tools, conversion tools, testing tools, and database server tools.

ORGANIZATION

When staffing a project that involves a data initiative, it is necessary to fill specific roles. The roles defined in this section are generally specific to the data initiative. These roles often are complemented by other roles in full implementation projects. Projects that have high object-oriented content skew the organization towards object-modeling skillsets.

- *Project Sponsor:* Projects should not be initiated or conducted without a senior project sponsor who is positioned to remove obstacles and ensure that the project team has the full support they require to be successful.
- *Project Manager:* The project manager is in charge of the entire project, including the data initiative.
- *Business User:* This person provides the business rules for the application, which are used to derive the entities and attributes necessary to save the data.
- *Business Analyst:* The business analyst provides a critical link between the business user and the data architect by understanding the business requirements and translating them into technical words.
- *Data Architect:* This person has the responsibility of defining the data architecture. This could be distributed, central, standalone, or integrated with a sophisticated overall architecture.
- *Data Analyst:* The data analyst works with the business analyst to build a consistent view of each element of the data. This person

understands the linkage between the business and the individual items of data.

- *Data Modeler:* This person works with the data architect to build a logical relational data model and also may get involved in transforming the logical data model into a physical data model.
- *Object Modeler:* The object modeler becomes involved in projects to build an object model, including messages and methods. This person also may be responsible for mapping the object model to the corporate data model.
- *Database Administrator:* This person implements the physical database, maintains and optimizes the physical environment, restricts access to the database by controlling privilege levels for users, offers advice to the development team for converting the logical data model to the physical data model, and holds the overall responsibility for running the database environment on a data-to-day basis.
- *Network Administrator:* The network administrator maintains the physical network, has the responsibility for maintaining the integrity of the physical environment that supports the data environment, and operates at the operating system level and the hardware level. For example, this person would add more physical disk to support larger databases.
- *Developer:* This person uses the database(s) for application development.

PITFALLS

Misuse or misinterpretation of how methodologies should be executed can result in signficantly negative impacts to project timelines. It is not unusual for organizations to use methodologies as process charts or recipes without streamlining any of the activities. This can result in a considerable amount of wasted time as deliverables or activities are produced without an understanding of how they are leading toward a solution. Methodologies should be adjusted for specific projects. Activities or deliverables that are not necessary should be dropped from the project plan.

Methodologies that are too complicated or difficult to learn and used frequently are avoided by project teams. There are some methodologies that may contain information for thousands of project contingencies. However, they require thousands of megabytes of storage or dozens of manuals to store. During tight project timeframes, such methodologies are sidelined quickly.

It is important to update methodologies over time. New project experiences and best practices should be included in the methodology at specific intervals.

CONCLUSION

Database development methodologies are a subset of full life-cycle methodologies. Project teams can access a third-party database development methodology or follow the high-level framework described in this chapter for database development. Database development methodologies also should support parallel development, iteration, high-user involvement, and be accompanied by a database of reusable templates or sample deliverables.

References

Deloitte & Touche Consulting Group Framework for Computing Solutions.

Maguire, S., *Writing Solid Code*. Microsoft Press, Redmond, WA, 1993.

Purba, S., *Developing Client/Server Systems Using Sybase SQL Server System 11.* John Wiley & Sons, New York, 1995.

Smith, P. N., *Client/Server Computing. 2nd. ed.,* Sams Publishing, Indianapolis, IN, 1994.

Willian, P., *Effective Methods for Software Testing*. John Wiley & Sons, New York, 1995.

Chapter 2
A Review of Database System Terminology

Marion G. Ceruti

MANY PUBLICATIONS, TECHNICAL MANUALS, AND MARKETING BRO-CHURES related to databases originated from sources that exhibit a wide variety of training, background, and experience. Although the result has been an expanded technical vocabulary, the growth of standards — particularly with regard to a comprehensive, uniformly accepted terminology — has not kept pace with the growth in the technology itself. Consequently, the nomenclature used to describe various aspects of database technology is characterized, in some cases, by confusion and chaos. This is true for both homogeneous databases and for heterogeneous, distributed database systems.

The state of imprecision in the nomenclature of this field persists across virtually all data models and their implementations. The purpose of this chapter is to highlight some areas of conflict and ambiguity and, in some cases, to suggest a more meaningful use of the terminology.

GENERAL DATABASE TERMS

What Does the Word *Data* Mean?

According to Webster, the word *data* is a noun that refers to things known or assumed; facts or figures from which conclusions can be inferred; information. Derived from the Latin word *datum*, meaning gift or present, data can be given, granted, or admitted, premises upon which something can be argued or inferred. Although the word *data* is most frequently observed, the singular form, *datum*, is also a real or assumed thing used as the basis for calculations.

The Department of Defense defines data as a representation of facts, concepts, or instructions in a formalized manner suitable for communication, interpretation, or processing by humans or by automatic means.

0-8493-9832-0/00/$0.00+$.50

The word *data* is also used as an adjective in terms such as *data set, data fill, data resource, data management,* or *data mining.* A data set is an aggregate of data items that are interrelated in some way.

Implicit in both definitions of data is the notion that the user can reasonably expect data to be true and accurate. For example, a data set is assumed to consist of facts given for use in a calculation or an argument, for drawing a conclusion, or as instructions from a superior authority. This also implies that the data management community has a responsibility to ensure the accuracy, consistency, and currency of data.

Data Element vs. Data Item

In an attempt to define database terms with a view toward practical applications, the Department of Defense (DoD) defines a data element as a named identifier of each of the entities and their attributes that are represented in a database. As such, data elements must be designed as follows:

- Representing the attributes (characteristics) of data entities identified in data models.
- According to functional requirements and logical (as opposed to physical) characteristics.
- According to the purpose or function of the data element, rather than how, when, where, and by whom it is used.
- With singularity of purpose, such that it has only one meaning.
- With well-defined, unambiguous, and separate domains.

Other definitions are that a data element is data described at the useful primitive level; a data item is the smallest separable unit recognized by the database representing a real-world entity.

What is clear from all these definitions is that there is considerable ambiguity in what these terms mean. The author proposes the following distinction between data element and data item:

> A *data element* is a variable associated with a domain (in the relational model) or an object class (in the object-oriented model) characterized by the property of atomicity. A data element represents the smallest unit of information at the finest level of granularity present in the database. An instance of this variable is a *data item*. A data element in the relational model is simply an attribute (or column) that is filled by data items commonly called the "data fill."

This distinction clarifies but does not preclude any of the other definitions.

What Is a Database?

The definitions for the term *database* range from the theoretical and general to the implementation specific. For example, K.S. Brathwaite, H. Darwen, and C.J. Date have offered two different, but not necessarily inconsistent, definitions of a database that are specific to the relational model. Darwen and Date build their definition on fundamental constructs of the relational model, and it is very specific to that model. Brathwaite employs a definition that is based on how databases are constructed in a specific database management system (DBMS).

These definitions are discussed in the next section on relational database terms. Actually, the term *database* can have multiple definitions, depending on the level of abstraction under consideration. For example, A.P. Sheth and J.A. Larson define database in terms of a reference architecture, in which a database is a repository of data structured according to a data model. This definition is more general than that of either Brathwaite or Darwen and Date because it is independent of any specific data model or DBMS. It could apply to hierarchical and object-oriented databases as well as to relational databases; however, it is not as rigorous as Darwen and Date's definition of a relational database because the term *repository* is not defined.

Similarly, P.J. Fortier et al., in a set of DoD conference proceedings, define a database to be a collection of data items that have constraints, relationships, and a schema. Of all the definitions for database considered thus far, this one is the one most similar to that of Sheth and Larson, because the term *data model* could imply the existence of constraints, relationships, and a schema. Moreover, Fortier et al. define *schema* as a description of how data, relationships, and constraints are organized for user application program access. A *constraint* is a predicate that defines all correct states of the database. Implicit in the definition of schema is the idea that different schemata could exist for different user applications. This notion is consistent with the concept of multiple schemata in a federated database system (FDBS). (Terms germane to FDBSs are discussed in a subsequent section.)

L.S. Waldron defines *database* as a collection of interrelated files stored together, where specific data items can be retrieved for various applications. A file is defined as a collection of related records. Similarly, L. Wheeler defines a *database* as a collection of data arranged in groups for access and storage; a database consists of data, memo, and index files.

Database System vs. Data Repository

Both of these terms refer to a more comprehensive environment than a database because they are concerned with the tools necessary for the management of data in addition to the data themselves. These terms are not mutually exclusive. A *database system* (DBS) includes both the DBMS software and one or more databases. A *data repository* is the heart of a comprehensive information management system environment. It must include not only data elements, but metadata of interest to the enterprise, data screens, reports, programs, and systems.

A data repository must provide a set of standard entities and allow for the creation of new, unique entities of interest to the organization. A database system can also be a data repository that can include a single database or several databases.

A. King et al. describe characteristics of a data repository as including an internal set of software tools, a DBMS, a metamodel, populated metadata, and loading and retrieval software for accessing repository data.

WHAT IS A DATA WAREHOUSE AND WHAT IS DATA MINING?

B. Thuraisingham and M. Wysong discussed the importance of the data warehouse in a DoD conference proceeding. A *data warehouse* is a database system that is optimized for the storage of aggregated and summarized data across the entire range of operational and tactical enterprise activities. The data warehouse brings together several heterogeneous databases from diverse sources in the same environment. For example, this aggregation could include data from current systems, legacy sources, historical archives, and other external sources.

Unlike databases that are optimized for rapid retrieval of information during real-time transaction processing for tactical purposes, data warehouses are not updated, nor is information deleted. Rather, time-stamped versions of various data sets are stored. Data warehouses also contain information such as summary reports and data aggregates tailored for use by specific applications. Thus, the role of metadata is of critical importance in extracting, mapping, and processing data to be included in the warehouse. All of this serves to simplify queries for the users, who query the data warehouse in a read-only, integrated environment.

The data warehouse is designed to facilitate the strategic, analytical, and decision-support functions within an organization. One such function is *data mining*, which is the search for previously unknown information in a data warehouse or database containing large quantities of data. The data warehouse or database is analogous to a mine, and the information desired is analogous to a mineral or precious metal.

The concept of data mining implies that the data warehouse in which the search takes place contains a large quantity of unrelated data and probably was not designed to store and support efficient access to the information desired. In data mining, it is reasonable to expect that multiple, well-designed queries and a certain amount of data analysis and processing will be necessary to summarize and present the information in an acceptable format.

Data Administrator vs. Database Administrator

The following discussion is not intended to offer an exhaustive list of tasks performed by either the data administrator (DA) or database administrator

(DBA), but rather to highlight the similarities and essential distinctions between these two types of database professionals. Both data administrators and database administrators are concerned with the management of data, but at different levels.

The job of a *data administrator* is to set policy about determining the data an organization requires to support the processes of that organization. The data administrator develops or uses a data model and selects the data sets supported in the database. A data administrator collects, stores, and disseminates data as a globally administered and standardized resource. Data standards on all levels that affect the organization fall under the purview of the data administrator, who is truly an administrator in the managerial sense.

By contrast, the technical orientation of the *database administrator* is at a finer level of granularity than that of a data administrator. For this reason, in very large organizations, DBAs focus solely on a subset of the organization's users. Typically, the database administrator is, like a computer systems manager, charged with day-to-day, hands-on use of the DBS and daily interaction with its users. The database administrator is familiar with the details of implementing and tuning a specific DBMS or a group of DBMSs. For example, the database administrator has the task of creating new user accounts, programming the software to implement a set of access controls, and using audit functions.

To illustrate the distinction between a data administrator and a database administrator, the U.S. Navy has a head data administrator whose range of authority extends throughout the entire Navy. It would not be practical or possible for an organization as large as the U.S. Navy to have a database administrator in an analogous role, because of the multiplicity of DBSs and DBMSs in use and the functions that DBAs perform.

These conceptual differences notwithstanding, in smaller organizations a single individual can act as both data administrator and database administrator, thus blurring the distinction between these two roles. Moreover, as data models and standards increase in complexity, data administrators will increasingly rely on new technology to accomplish their tasks, just as database administrators do now.

RELATIONAL DATABASE TERMS

Because relational technology is a mature technology with many practical applications, it is useful to consider some of the important terms that pertain to the relational model. Many of these terms are straightforward and generally unambiguous, whereas some terms have specific definitions that are not always understood.

17

A data set represented in the form of a table containing columns and rows is called a *relation*. The columns are called *attributes*, and the rows are called *tuples*.

Darwen and Date define a tuple to be a set of ordered triples of the form <A, V, v̲> where A is the name of an attribute, V is the name of a unique domain that corresponds to A, and v̲ is a value from domain V called the attribute value for attribute A within the tuple. A *domain* is a named set of values.

Darwen and Date also describe a relation as consisting of a heading and a body, where the heading is a set of ordered pairs, <A,V>; and the body consists of tuples, all having the same heading <A,V>. An *attribute value* is a data item or a datum.

In some respects, a relation is analogous to an array of data created outside a relational DBMS, such as in a third-generation language (3GL) program like C, FORTRAN, or Ada, in which the rows are called records and the columns are called fields. Waldron defines a *field* as a set of related letters, numbers, or other special characters, and defines a *record* as a collection of related fields.

The interchangeability of the terms *record* and *row* has been illustrated by some of the major DBMS vendors in the way in which they report the results of a query to the user. Earlier versions of commercial DBMSs indicated at the end of a query return message such as "12 records selected." Now, it is more common to see messages such as "12 rows selected" or "12 rows affected" instead.

Relation vs. Relation Variable

The correct manner in which the term *relation* should be used is according to the definition given previously, which specifically includes values v, from domain V. However, the term *relation* has not always been used correctly in the industry. Relation frequently is used as though it could mean either a filled table with data present (correct), or an empty table structure containing only data headers (incorrect). The confusion here stems from a failure to distinguish between a *relation*, which is a filled table with tuples containing attribute values, and a *relation variable* (or relvar), which is an empty table structure with only attribute names and domains from which to choose values. The values of a relation variable are the relations per se. This distinction becomes especially important when mapping between the relational and object-oriented data models.

Database vs. Database Variable

In a manner similar to the relation-relvar dichotomy, a *database variable* is different from a database per se. A database variable (or dbvar) is a named set of relvars. The value of a given dbvar is a set of specific, ordered pairs <R,r>, where R is a relvar and r (a relation) is the current value of that relvar, such that one such ordered pair exists for each relvar in the dbvar and that, taken together, all relvar values satisfy the applicable constraints (in particular, integrity constraints). A value of the dbvar that conforms to this definition is called a database. Some call this a *database state*, but this term is not used very often.

Database vs. DBMS

As all the examples discussed thus far indicate, not all database terminology is as unambiguous as "rows" and "columns." Incorrect understanding of the fundamental concepts in database technology can lead to inconsistent terminology, and vice versa.

DBMS Software Does Not Equal a Database. For example, databases frequently are described according to the DBMS that manages them. This is all well and good, as long as one realizes that references to an Oracle database and Sybase database refer to the databases that are managed using Oracle or Sybase software, respectively. Difficulty arises when this nomenclature results in the misconception that DBMS software is actually the database itself. The assumption that Informix, for example, is a database is as illogical as thinking that the glass is the same as the water in it.

Concept vs. Implementation in Relational Databases

Darwen and Date's definition of a database, as well as that of other database researchers (some of whom are mentioned by name in this chapter and others who are not), does not require the presence of a DBMS. Conceptually, it is possible to have a database without a DBMS or a DBMS without a database, although obviously the greatest utility is achieved by combining the two.

In the context of a specific DBMS environment, Brathwaite defines an IBM DB2 database as "a collection of table and index spaces where each table space can contain one or more physical tables." This definition is inconsistent with Date's definition because it allows for the possibility that the table spaces could be empty, in which case no data would be present. It is not clear that even relvars would be present in this case. That notwithstanding, if physical tables are present, Brathwaite's definition becomes an implementation-specific special case of Date's definition. (Substitute the word "must" for "can" to resolve the problem with Brathwaite's definition.)

Except in the case where the vendor has specified default table and index spaces in the DBMS code, the database and index spaces are not actually part of the DBMS per se. The DBA needs to create both the database space and the index space using the DBMS software.

DATABASE NORMALIZATION

The topic of *database normalization*, sometimes called *data normalization*, has received a great deal of attention. As is usually the case, database normalization is discussed in the following section using examples from the relational data model. Here, the terms *relation* and *table* are used interchangeably. However, the design guidelines pertaining to database normalization are useful even if a relational database system is not used. For example, B.S. Lee has discussed the need for normalization in the object-oriented data model. Whereas the intent of this section is to introduce the correct usage of normalization terminology as it applies to database technology, it is not meant to be an exhaustive exposition of all aspects of normalization.

What Is Database Normalization?

Strictly speaking, database normalization is the arrangement of data into tables. P. Winsberg defines normalization as the process of structuring data into a tabular format, with the implicit assumption that the result must be in at least first normal form. Similarly, Brathwaite defines data normalization as a set of rules and techniques concerned with:

- Identifying relationships between attributes
- Combining attributes to form relations (with data fill)
- Combining relations to form a database

The chief advantage of database or data normalization is to avoid modification anomalies that occur when facts about attributes are lost during insert, update, and delete transactions. However, if the normalization process has not progressed beyond first normal form, it is not possible to ensure that these anomalies can be avoided. Therefore, database normalization commonly refers to further non-loss decomposition of the tables into second through fifth normal form. Non-loss decomposition means that information is not lost when a table in lower normal form is divided (according to attributes) into tables that result in the achievement of a higher normal form. This is accomplished by placing primary and foreign keys into the resulting tables so that tables can be joined to retrieve the original information.

What Are Normal Forms?

A normal form of a table or database is an arrangement or grouping of data that meets specific requirements of logical design, key structure, modification integrity, and redundancy avoidance, according to the rigorous definition of the normalization level in question. A table is said to be in "X" normal form if it is already in "X-1" normal form and it meets the additional constraints that pertain to level "X."

In first normal form (1NF), related attributes are organized into separate tables, each with a primary key. A primary key is an attribute or set of attributes that uniquely defines a tuple. Thus, if a table is in 1NF, entities within the data model contain no attributes that repeat as groups. W. Kent has explained that in 1NF, all occurrences of a record must contain the same number of fields. In 1NF, each data cell (defined by a specific tuple and attribute) in the table will contain only atomic values.

Every table that is in second normal form (2NF) also must be in 1NF, and every non-key attribute must depend on the entire primary key. Any attributes that do not depend on the entire key are placed in a separate table to preserve the information they represent. 2NF becomes an issue only for tables with composite keys. A composite key is defined as any key (candidate, primary, alternate, or foreign) that consists of two or more attributes. If only part of the composite key is sufficient to determine the value of a non-key attribute, the table is not in 2NF.

Every relation that is in third normal form (3NF) must also be in 2NF, and every non-key attribute must depend directly on the entire primary key. In 2NF, non-key attributes are allowed to depend on each other. This is not allowed in 3NF. If a non-key attribute does not depend on the key directly, or if it depends on another non-key attribute, it is removed and placed in a new table. It is often stated that in 3NF, every non-key attribute is a function of "the key, the whole key, and nothing but the key." In 3NF, every non-key attribute must contribute to the description of the key. However, 3NF does not prevent part of a composite primary key from depending on a non-key attribute, nor does it address the issue of candidate keys.

Boyce-Codd normal form (BCNF) is a stronger, improved version of 3NF. Every relation that is in BCNF also must be in 3NF and must meet the additional requirement that each determinant must be a candidate key. A determinant is any attribute, A, of a table that contains unique data values, such that the value of another attribute, B, fully functional depends on the value of A. If a candidate key also is a composite key, each attribute in the composite key must be necessary and sufficient for uniqueness. Winsberg calls this condition "unique and minimal." Primary keys meet these requirements. An alternate key is any candidate key that is not the primary key. In BCNF, no part of the key is allowed to depend on any key attribute. Compliance with the rules of BCNF forces the database designer to store associations between determinants in a separate table, if these determinants do not qualify as candidate keys.

BCNF removes all redundancy due to singular relationships but not redundancy due to many-to-many relationships. To accomplish this, further normalization is required. Fourth and fifth normal forms (4NF and 5NF) involve the notions of multivalued dependence and cyclic dependence, respectively. A table is in 4NF if it also is in BCNF and does not contain any independent many-to-many relationships.

That notwithstanding, a table could be in 4NF and still contain dependent many-to-many relationships. A table is in 5NF if it is also in 4NF and does not contain any cyclic dependence (except for the trivial one between candidate keys.) In theory, 5NF is necessary to preclude certain join anomalies, such as the introduction of a false tuple. However, in practice, the large majority of tables in operational databases do not contain attributes with cyclical dependence.

What Are Over-Normalization and Denormalization?

Over-normalization of a table results in further non-loss decomposition that exceeds the requirements to achieve 5NF. The purpose of this is to improve update performance. However, most operational databases rarely reach a state in which the structure of all tables has been tested according to 5FN criteria, so over-normalization rarely occurs. Over-normalization is the opposite of denormalization, which is the result of intentionally introducing redundancy into a database design to improve retrieval performance. Here, the database design process has progressed to 3NF, BCNF, 4NF, or even to 5NF. However, the database is implemented in a lower normal form to avoid time-consuming joins. Because the efficiency of "select" queries is an issue in operational systems, denormalization is more common than over-normalization.

The first six normal forms (including BCNF) are formal structures of tables that eliminate certain kinds of intra-table redundancy. For example, 5NF eliminates all redundancy that can be removed by dividing tables according to attributes. Higher normal forms exist beyond 5NF. They address theoretical issues that are not considered to be of much practical importance. In fact, Date has noted that it is not often necessary or desirable to carry out the normalization process too far because normalization optimizes update performance at the expense of retrieval performance. Most of the time, 3NF is sufficient. This is because tables that have been designed logically and correctly in 3NF are almost automatically in 4NF. Thus, for most databases that support real-time operations, especially for those that have tables with predominantly single-attribute primary keys, 3NF is the practical limit. Note that a two-attribute relation with a single-attribute key is automatically in the higher normal forms.

DISTRIBUTED, HETEROGENEOUS DATABASE NOMENCLATURE

What Is a Distributed Database?

Date defines a distributed database as a virtual database that has components physically stored in a number of distinct "real" databases at a number of distinct sites.

Federated Database Systems vs. Multidatabase Systems. M. Hammer and D. McLeod coined the term *federated database system* to mean a collection of independent, preexisting databases for which data administrators and database administrators agree to cooperate. Thus, the database administrator for each component database would provide the federation with a schema representing the data from his or her component that can be shared with other members of the federation.

In a landmark paper ("Federated Database Systems for Managing Distributed, Heterogeneous and Autonomous Databases," *ACM Computing Surveys,* Vol. 22, No. 3, September 1990), Sheth and Larson define FDBS in a similar but broader architectural sense to mean a collection of cooperating but autonomous component database systems that are possibly heterogeneous. They also define a *nonfederated database* system as an integration of component DBMSs that is not autonomous with only one level of management, in which local and global users are not distinguished. According to Sheth and Larson's taxonomy, both federated and nonfederated database systems are included in a more general category called *multidatabase systems.* These multidatabase systems support operations on multiple-component DBSs.

Sheth and Larson further divide the subcategory of FDBS into two types: loosely coupled and tightly coupled FDBS, based on who creates and maintains the federation and how the component databases are integrated. If the users themselves manage the federation, they call it a *loosely coupled* FDBS; whereas, if a global database administrator manages the federation and controls access to the component databases, the FDBS is *tightly coupled.* Both loosely coupled and tightly coupled FDBSs can support multiple federated schemata. However, if a tightly coupled FDBS is characterized by the presence of only one federated schema, it has a single federation.

The term *multidatabase* has been used by different authors to refer to different things. For example, W. Litwin et al. have used it to mean what Sheth and Larson call a loosely coupled FDBS. By contrast, Y. Breitbart and A. Silberschatz have defined multidatabase to be the tightly coupled FDBS of Sheth and Larson. Sheth and Larson have described additional, conflicting use of the term *multidatabase.*

The terms *loosely coupled* and *tightly coupled* FDBSs have also been used to distinguish between the degree to which users can perceive heterogeneity in an FDBS, among other factors. In this system of nomenclature (devised by this author and M.N. Kamel), a tightly coupled FDBS is characterized by the presence of a federated or global schema, which is not present in a loosely coupled FDBS. Instead of a global schema, loosely coupled FDBSs are integrated using other software, such as a user interface with a uniform "look and feel" or a standard set of queries used throughout the federation, thus contributing to a common operating environment.

In this case, the autonomous components of a loosely coupled FDBS are still cooperating to share data, but without a global schema. Thus, the users see only one DBS in a tightly coupled FDBS, whereas they are aware of multiple DBSs in the loosely coupled FDBS. Here, the tightly coupled FDBS obeys Date's rule zero, which states that to a user, a distributed system should look exactly like a nondistributed system.

Given this manner in which to characterize an FDBS, a *hybrid FDBS* is possible for which some of the component DBSs have a global schema that describe the data shared among them (tightly coupled), but other components do not participate in the global schema (loosely coupled).

An Expanded Taxonomy. An expanded taxonomy is proposed to provide a more comprehensive system to describe how databases are integrated, and to account for the perspectives of both the data administrator and the users. Essentially, most aspects of Sheth and Larson's taxonomy are logical and should be retained. However, instead of using Sheth and Larson's terms for tightly coupled federated database and loosely coupled federated database, the terms *tightly controlled* federated database and *loosely controlled* federated database, respectively, should be substituted.

This change focuses on the absence or presence of a central, controlling authority as the essential distinction between the two. In this case, the terms *tightly coupled* and *loosely coupled* can then be applied to describe how the user, rather than the data administrator, sees the federation. Given this change, the coupling between components in a federated database will describe how seamless and homogeneous the database looks to the users and applications.

The expanded taxonomy can accommodate federated databases that differ widely in their characteristics. For example, if a tightly controlled federated database is tightly coupled, the global data administrator and the global database administrator have exercised their authority and expertise to provide a seamless, interoperable environment that allows the federation's users to experience the illusion of a single database for their applications and ad-hoc queries.

A tightly controlled federated database can also be loosely coupled, in which case the global data administrator allows the users of the federation to see some heterogeneity with respect to the component databases.

Both conditions are within the realm of possibility. However, a loosely controlled federated database is almost certain to be loosely coupled. This is because a loosely controlled federated database lacks a central authority capable of mediating disputes about data representation in the federated schema and enforcing uniformity in the federation's interfaces to user applications. A loosely controlled federated database is not likely to be tightly coupled.

Local or Localized Schema vs. Component Schema vs. Export Schema. A local or localized database generally starts as a stand-alone, nonintegrated database. When a local, autonomous database is selected for membership in a federation, a local schema is defined as a conceptual schema of the component DBS that is expressed in the native data model of the component DBMS.

When the local database actually becomes a member of a federated database, it is said to be a *component database*. The schema associated with a given database component is called a *component schema*, which is derived by translating a local schema into the common data model of the FDBS. An *export schema* represents the subset of the component schema that can be shared with the federation and its users.

Similarly, Date defines a local schema as the database definition of a component database in a distributed database.

Federated Schema vs. Global Schema vs. Global Data Dictionary. A federated schema is an integration of multiple export schemata. Because the distributed database definition is sometimes called the global schema, federated schema and global schema are used interchangeably.

A global data dictionary is the same as a global schema that includes the data element definitions as they are used in the FDBS. A data dictionary is different from a schema, or database structure specification, because a data dictionary contains the definitions of attributes or objects, not just the configuration of tables, attributes, objects, and entities within that structure.

It is especially important to include the data element definitions with the export schemata when forming a federated database in which multiple data representations are likely. Simply having a collection of database structures is insufficient to complete a useful federated schema. It is necessary to know the meaning of each attribute or object and how it is construed in the component database.

Middleware vs. Midware. In a three-tier client/server architecture designed to connect and manage data exchange between user applications and a variety of data servers, the middle tier that brokers transactions between clients and servers consists of middleware, which is sometimes called midware.

P. Cykana defines middleware as a variety of products and techniques that are used to connect users to data resources. In his view, the middleware solution is usually devoted to locating and finding data rather than to moving data to migration environments.

In addition, Cykana describes two options for middleware, depending on the degree of coupling between the user and the data resource. Loosely coupled middleware products allow flexibility in specifying relationships and mappings between data items, whereas tightly coupled middleware products allocate more authority to standard interfaces and database administrators. Each option has its advantages and disadvantages, as follows:

- *Loosely coupled middleware.* This type of middleware does not require the migration or legacy data structures to be modified, but it allows users to access multiple equivalent migration systems transparently with one standard interface. Its disadvantage is that it does not prevent multiple semantics and nonstandard structures.
- *Tightly coupled middleware.* This option represents a more aggressive strategy that combines applications program interface (API) and graphical user interface (GUI) technologies, data communications, and data dictionary design and development capabilities to provide distributed data access. Data standardization and reengineering are required.

The concept of loose and tight coupling to middleware is somewhat similar to, but also differs slightly from, the loose and tight coupling between data resources as discussed by Sheth and Larson and other researchers. In the case of middleware, the coupling occurs between software at different tiers or layers (between the middle translation layer and the data servers); whereas, in the case of an FDBS, the coupling occurs between data servers that reside at the same tier. (However, this difference does not preclude software that achieves the coupling between data servers from being located in the middle tier.)

G.V. Quigley defines middleware as a software layer between the application logic and the underlying networking, security, and distributed computing technology. Middleware provides all of the critical services for managing the execution of applications in a distributed client/server environment while hiding the details of distributed computing from the application tier. Thus, midware is seen in a critical role for implementing a tightly coupled FDBS.

Similarly, Quigley considers middleware to be the key technology to integrate applications in a heterogeneous network environment.

Database Integration vs. Database Homogenization. Many organizations in both industry and government are interested in integrating autonomous (sometimes called "stovepipe") databases into a single distributed, heterogeneous database system. Many terms describe the various aspects of this integration. The multiplicity of terminology occurs because of the many ways in which databases can be integrated and because of the many simultaneous efforts that are underway to address integration problems.

Because the degree to which database integration takes place depends on the requirements of the organization and its users, the term *integration*, as it is used in various contexts, remains rather vague. For people whose fields of expertise are outside the realm of database technology, it is necessary to hide the specific details of database system implementation behind midware layers and a user interface that together create the illusion of a single, unified database. By contrast, more experienced users with knowledge of multiple DBMS can function efficiently in an environment that preserves some distinctions between the database components.

Within all architectural options, *database integration*, in its broadest sense, refers to the combination and transformation of database components into a database system that is homogeneous on at least one level (e.g., the data level, the schema level, the program interface level, or the user-interface level). Such an integrated database system must satisfy the primary goals of interoperability between database system components, data sharing, consistent data interpretation, and efficient data access for users and applications across multiple platforms.

K. Karlapalem et al. describe the concept of *database homogenization* as the process of transforming a collection of heterogeneous legacy information systems onto a homogeneous environment. Whereas they do not define what they mean by the term *homogeneous environment*, they list three goals of database homogenization:

- To provide the capability to replace legacy component databases efficiently
- To allow new global applications at different levels of abstraction and scale to be developed on top of the homogenized federated database
- To provide interoperability between heterogeneous databases so that previously isolated heterogeneous localized databases can be loosely coupled

This definition of database integration explicitly includes multiple architectures and implementations; by contrast, the description of database homogenization is associated with loose rather than tight coupling of localized databases into a homogeneous environment. Sometimes the term *database normalization* is used incorrectly to mean *database integration*.

Interoperability vs. Interoperation. The conditions necessary for interoperability include:

- Interconnectivity via the necessary networking facilities
- Resolution of system heterogeneity
- Resolution of semantic heterogeneity
- Derivation and integration of schemata and views

There are three levels of heterogeneity, including platform heterogeneity, data model heterogeneity, and semantic heterogeneity. Excluding semantic heterogeneity, the term system heterogeneity is seen to be some combination of platform heterogeneity (e.g., different DBMS software and implementation) and data model heterogeneity (e.g., schemata, query languages, integrity constraints, and nullness requirements). Because Karlapalem et al. have already listed the integration of schemata as an item separate from system heterogeneity, system heterogeneity logically should refer to the differences between DBMS vendors, transaction processing algorithms, query languages, query optimization techniques, integrity constraints, and nullness requirements. If this definition is assumed for system heterogeneity, the necessary conditions for database interoperability listed above become sufficient conditions.

Similarly, computer system heterogeneity and data management system heterogeneity must be resolved as a requirement for interoperability among existing information systems.

The achievement of database interoperability simply supplies users and applications with the ability to interoperate in a common data environment. It does not guarantee that interoperation will occur. Database interoperation results when users and applications take advantage of a common, integrated environment to access, share, and process data across multiple databases.

Legacy Information System vs. Migration Information System. Autonomous systems that become candidates for integration into a more modern, global, and distributed system sometimes have been called migration systems. These systems are supported by migration information systems with migration databases.

The term *migration databases* indicates unambiguously that the database in question has been chosen to be included in some form of a modern database system, especially a distributed system such as an FDBS. By contrast, the term *legacy information system* has been used in two different ways.

At one extreme, some people use legacy information system and legacy database to be synonymous with migration information system and migration database, respectively. Others have referred to a legacy information system as if it were not a migration information system and is therefore deliberately excluded from the final integrated database configuration. This is the opposite extreme.

More commonly than in the extreme cases, a subset of legacy data is deemed important to the users of a shared data resource. This means that some or all of the data in a legacy information system may be migrated during a database integration effort. For example, Cykana describes steps in the data integration process that start with the movement and improvement of data and progress to the shutdown of legacy systems. Karlapalem et al. refer to the difficulty of migrating legacy information systems to a modern computer environment in which some difference is presumed to exist between the legacy system and the modern system.

The author recommends that the following terminology be adopted as standard:

> *Legacy data* and *legacy information system* should refer to the original data and original format, as maintained in the original, autonomous information system before any modification or migration to a new environment has occurred. *Migration data* and *migration information system* should be used to describe the subset of the legacy data and software that has been chosen to be included into a new (and usually distributed) information resource environment. When data and software are modified to accommodate a new environment, they should be called migration instead of legacy.

TERMS ASSOCIATED WITH SEMANTIC HETEROGENEITY

Semantic heterogeneity refers to a disagreement about the meaning, interpretation, or intended use of the same or related data or objects. Semantic heterogeneity can occur either in a single DBS or in a multidatabase system. Its presence in a DBS is also independent of data model or DBMS. Therefore, the terminology associated with this problem is discussed in a separate section.

Semantic Interoperability vs. Database Harmonization

The terms *database integration* and *interoperability* were discussed previously in a general context. For distributed, heterogeneous database systems to be integrated in every respect, semantic heterogeneity must be resolved.

Problems associated with semantic heterogeneity have been difficult to overcome, and the terminology to describe semantic heterogeneity has evolved accordingly. For example, R. Sciore et al. define semantic interoperability as agreement among separately developed systems about the meaning of their exchanged data.

Whereas the exact meaning of the term *database harmonization* is not clear, one can infer that the goal of database harmonization must be related to providing an environment in which conflicts have been resolved between data representations from previously autonomous systems. This definition further implies that the resolution of semantic heterogeneity is a prerequisite for database harmonization.

Although a more precise definition of database harmonization is needed, it appears to be related to the idea of semantic interoperability.

Strong and Weak Synonyms vs. Class One and Class Two Synonyms

A synonym is a word that has the same or nearly the same meaning as another word of the same language. Because a metadata representation will include more attributes (e.g., data element name, type, length, range, and domain) than ordinary nouns, it was necessary to consider various levels of similarity and therefore, levels of synonymy.

M.W. Bright et al. have described the concept of strong and weak synonyms. Strong synonyms are semantically equivalent to each other and can be used interchangeably in all contexts without a change of meaning, whereas weak synonyms are semantically similar and can be substituted for each other in some contexts with only minimal meaning changes. Weak synonyms cannot be used interchangeably in all contexts without a major change in the meaning — a change that could violate the schema specification.

This concept is similar to one (introduced by the author and Kamel) that states that there are two classes of synonym abstraction: Class One and Class Two. Class One synonyms occur when different attribute names represent the same, unique real world entity. The only differences between Class One synonyms are the attribute name and possibly the wording of the definition, but not the meaning. By contrast, Class Two synonyms occur when different attribute names have equivalent definitions but are expressed with different data types and data-element lengths.

Class Two synonyms can share the same domain or they can have related domains with a one-to-one mapping between data elements, provided they both refer to the same unique real-world entity. The concept of a strong synonym is actually the same as that of a Class Two synonym because both strong synonyms and Class Two synonyms are semantically equivalent and they can be used interchangeably because they have the same data element type and length. By contrast, the concept of a Class Two synonym includes (but is not limited to) the concept of a weak synonym because the definition of a weak synonym seems to imply a two-way interchange in some contexts. The main difference is that the interchangeability of Class Two synonyms is determined not only by semantic context, but also by the intersection of their respective domains, as well as their data types and lengths.

Class Two synonyms allow for a one-way, as well as a two-way, interchange in some cases, whereas the "each-other" part in the definition of weak synonyms seems to preclude a one-way interchange. For example, a shorter character string can fit into a longer field, but not vice versa.

SUMMARY

This chapter presents a review of the rapidly growing vocabulary of database system technology, along with its conflicts and ambiguities. The solutions offered address some of the problems encountered in communicating concepts and ideas in this field.

This effort is intended to be a first step toward the development of a more comprehensive, standard set of terms that can be used throughout the industry. More work is needed to identify and resolve the differences in interpretation between the many terms used in data administration, database development, database administration, database research, and marketing as they occur in industry, government, and academia.

ACKNOWLEDGMENTS

This work was created by a U.S. government employee in the course of employment and is therefore in the public domain.

Chapter 3
Developing a Global Information Vision

Tim Christmann

INTRODUCTION

INFORMATION TECHNOLOGY (IT) BUSINESS EXECUTIVES are experiencing increasing professional pressures as their organizations strive to become truly global. In an effort to leverage their resources around the world and serve global customers, companies are turning to information technology as a means of achieving these objectives. IT capabilities have evolved to the point where some would argue that IT can, for the first time, be a strategic enabler in helping a company become truly global. In order for IT to be a strategic enabler for a company on a global basis, all major IT investments must be aligned with the business goals and strategies of the organization. One step toward aligning IT investments with business objectives and strategies is to bring key business and IT leaders to a common understanding or vision of how information will enable the company's strategy and future competitive position in the marketplace.

What Does It Mean To Be "Global"?

In the age of economic globalization, it is not uncommon for companies to expand beyond domestic boundaries into foreign markets in search of new growth opportunities. If a company has operations around the world, does this make the company a "global business"? In short, the answer to this question is no. Being truly global involves mobilizing company resoures around the world and presenting a common face for the company's key stakeholders — customers, suppliers, shareholders, and employees.

What Is a Global Information Vision?

Let's start with what an information vision is not. It is not a statement conceived in the office of the CIO and posted above the door in the IT department. It is not about having the IT function achieve functional excellency through the use of leading edge technologies.

0-8493-9832-0/00/$0.00+$.50
© 2000 by CRC Press LLC

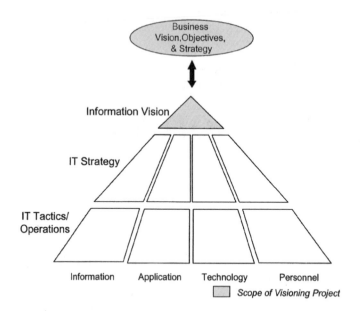

Exhibit 3.1. Information vision.

An information vision is a clear statement of how an enhanced information base will help the business achieve its strategic objectives. It is stated in business terms and contains a clear link to the competitive positioning of the business. A vision also indicates business outcomes that are recognizable by business and IT leaders alike.

As shown in Exhibit 3.1, within the IT decision-making hierarchy, the Information Vision provides a link between the business strategy and objectives and the IT strategy. Bringing the key business stakeholders to agreement on the Information Vision provides direction throughout the company on where IT investments should be focused to bring the most value to the company.

OBJECTIVES — "PAY-OFF IDEA"

Why Do You Need an Information Vision in Your Company?

There are a number of objectives that you should achieve as you facilitate the development of your company's information vision:

1. Raise the understanding at all levels in the company of how information and information technology can and will add value for the company.
   - Often executives see the enormous operational and capital expenditures for IT and wonder what value they are getting for their

money. They fear that deployment of technology solutions may be based on an underlying desire to have the latest technological innovation rather than the pure business value of the investment. Demonstrating the value of IT investments does not stop once an information vision has been established. However, developing an information vision does put into clear business terms how information does and will add value to the business.

- Do your business decision-makers think about information or IT when they are devising their business strategies? Business decision-makers often do not fully understand the capabilities of IT or do not think about how an enhanced information base can enable their business strategies. Engaging key business leaders in the exercise of developing a vision for information in the company will raise their level of awareness.

2. Promote better alignment of IT projects and the business objectives.

- How often do you hear about companies that have sizeable investments in state-of-the-art systems to improve an area or function that is not core to the business? Afterwards they often question how such an enormous investment of capital and human resources has actually changed the company's competitive position? By engaging key business and IT leaders in developing an information vision linked to clear business outcomes, a common understanding is reached with respect to where the value-adding opportunities exist for IT projects. Any project or opportunity not in line with the vision comes immediately under question.

3. Keep IT personnel focused on achieving an enhanced information base for the company rather than implementing new technologies for technology-sake.

- The visioning exercise creates a better focus on the "I" rather than the "T" in Information Technology. By focusing on information, it forces people to question technology investments that do not result in a sufficient improvement to the base of information that will enhance the company's competitive position.

4. Develop an understanding of how a common information vision can benefit the global units and the company as a whole — not just another head-office exercise.

- Often the words of a vision or mission mean little to those not directly involved in composing the statements. Especially if your company operates businesses around the world that have a certain amount of local autonomy, these units may offer some resistance if their interests have not been properly represented in developing the vision or they fail to realize how the vision improves the position of their business. For this reason, it can be beneficial to indicate how enhanced use of information will benefit the local units as well.

Phase 1: Assessment

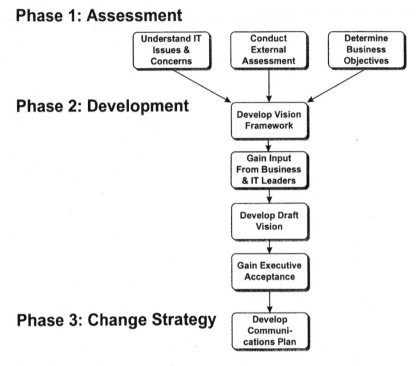

Phase 2: Development

Phase 3: Change Strategy

Exhibit 3.2.   The process for developing an information vision.

THE PROCESS

To develop an information vision effectively, it is important to understand that perhaps the greatest value is in the process of developing the Vision rather than in the words of the Vision itself. In order to gain the full value of this exercise, the right level of people in the organization, from both the business and IT community, must be involved in developing the Vision. Having the right people involved, especially from the business community, helps to ensure relevant content, organizational buy-in and business ownership. To ensure relevancy and ownership, the vision must be articulated using words that the business community understands, therefore the words themselves must come from key business leaders. Exhibit 3.2 outlines the process for developing a Global Information Vision. Exhibit 3.3 provides the Critical Success Factors for making this a reality.

PHASE 1: ASSESSMENT

If you already have a clear understanding of the current situation of information and information technology in the company then this phase can be condensed. However, it is important to note that there are distinct benefits

Exhibit 3.3. Critical Success Factors

The following points represent critical success factors in ensuring successful development of an information vision:

· The right level of sponsorship

It is important that this initiative be championed at the highest level in the organization in order to have the desired impact. An information vision should be viewed as an extention of the business strategy by stating how information will help the company achieve its business objectives. Therefore, a successful information visioning initiative will have a sponsor positioned at the same level in the company as the sponsor of a business strategy initiative. These initiatives might even be sponsored by the same individual.

· Involvement from key business leaders

The objectives of the visioning process are aggressive given that they often require the thinking and decision-making of management and staff throughout the company to be changed. One of the best ways to achieve buy-in from these people is to involve them as much as possible in the development process. Executive involvement is key. These people need to be involved to ensure that the vision is clearly aligned with the direction of the business. Also, their involvement lends credibility and importance to the initiative. Senior executives are often somewhat removed from decisions made at lower levels in the company, especially in a global company where decision-making is often decentralized. Therefore, it can be beneficial to have management involvement in the development process from various business areas and geographic regions. Choose representatives from the business areas or regions that are seen as critical to the business and individuals who are viewed as leaders in their respective areas.

· The right language

It is critical for the vision to be perceived as business owned and business led if the stated objectives are to be achieved. Therefore, the vision must be stated in business terms.

· Linked to business outcomes

Linking the vision to specific business outcomes helps people to understand exactly how improving the information base in the company results in business value, especially if they are not involved in developing the vision. It also may help to reveal in which areas IT projects may provide the greatest opportunity in terms of positioning information as a strategic enabler for the business.

---

in conducting a formal assessment to ensure that your understanding is complete.

As part of the assessment, there are three main questions that need to be answered:

1. What is the Current State of the IT?

The assessment phase provides an opportunity to gain a clear understanding of the current situation and bring to the surface any issues or concerns about the current state of information or information technology in the company. These issues or concerns represent not only areas of improvement, they may also represent significant barriers to changing the way people think about the ability of the information and information technology to add value to the business. The business community needs to know that their concerns are being heard. Soliciting input from key business leaders also provides a prime opportunity to begin developing buy-in and ownership for the Vision itself. It is also important to acknowledge past successes or progress that the company has made in IT projects. These successes are often not well known throughout the company and serve to boost the company's collective confidence in its ability to deliver business value through IT.

2. What are the Major External Forces or Pressures Facing IT?

If possible it is beneficial to understand how competitors in the same industry or companies with similar operations are using IT. Presenting this information may serve two purposes. First, if it is determined that competitors are further advanced in the way they are employing IT, it may serve as a strong imperative for change. Exploring how similar companies use IT to gain competitive advantage can also raise the level of education within the company, heightening awareness of what is possible.

In addition, it may be beneficial to articulate what the current possibilities are in IT today. People may ask, 'why does the company need a global vision about information?' It is important for people to understand that for the first time, global communications and real-time information sharing are possible and can deliver significant business value.

3. What are the Business Vision, Objectives, and Strategy?

This third question is perhaps the most important for a number of reasons. First of all, the information vision must be aligned with the vision of the company as a whole. Often the company vision is not explicitly stated or well understood. Therefore, it is important to conduct interviews with key business leaders to gain a clear understanding of where the business leadership intends to take the company in the future and what the critical success factors are for the company as a whole and its core business areas. Secondly, conducting interviews with key business leaders helps build ownership for the vision within the business community. People are more likely to champion the vision when they are part of its development. Finally, it is critical for the vision itself to be stated in business terms. Exhibit 3.4 provides an example of typical findings that may result from the Assessment Phase.

The Change Imperative

One of the most important outcomes of the Assessment phase is to build a clear understanding of the need for the company to change. The change imperative must be clearly articulated in terms of issues and challenges

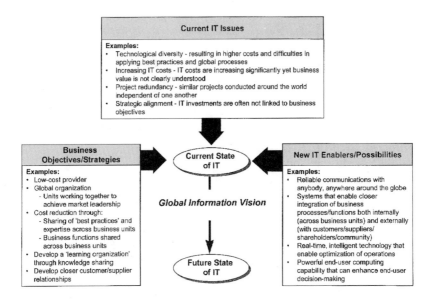

Exhibit 3.4. Typical findings from the assessment phase.

facing IT, changing business objectives and strategies, and the new IT capabilities that are available. It is important that the executive group understands the outcomes of the Assessment phase and to agree on the need for change.

PHASE 2: DEVELOPMENT

Different approaches may be used to develop the vision. Perhaps the most effective approach is to facilitate a group of key business leaders, including senior executives and key management personnel through each of the following steps. Although effective, this approach is often very difficult to execute especially if the key business leaders are situated around the world. It important to keep in mind that having active involvement from as many key business leaders as possible is critical to the success of the initiative. Therefore, if it is not possible to conduct steps 1 through 4 as one group, it may be necessary to break the group of targeted participants into smaller focus groups.

Step 1: Develop Vision Framework

Establishing a framework may not be essential but can be beneficial both in developing the vision and communicating it. A framework can provide an effective structure in which to organize ideas regarding how an enhanced information base can enable the business to achieve it's business

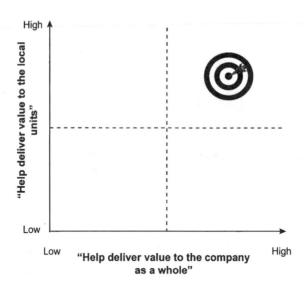

Exhibit 3.5.   Information vision framework.

objectives. The framework can also prove very useful in communicating how the vision can be linked to specific business outcomes. Exhibit 3.5 provides an example of a framework that could be used for a global company that is looking for ways to articulate how a common vision for an enhanced information base will not only improve the performance of the company as a whole, but also to improve the performance of the individual business units around the world.

Step 2: Gain Input from Key Stakeholders

Depending on the audience, different techniques can be used to gain input from key stakeholders. Often it is difficult to obtain extensive time with top executives. Therefore it may be beneficial to include specific questions during the executive interviews in the assessment phase that will provide insight into how enhanced information may better enable the business to achieve its objectives.

The following are examples of specific questions that could be used to facilitate input from the key business leaders:

- How can information help the company attain its vision?
- What information would make a difference in the various business units? For customers? For managers?
- What impediments exist today to using information to add value to the organization and to make a difference to the bottom line?

Exhibit 3.6. Examples of Business Outcomes from Developing an Enhanced Information Base

An enhanced information base will deliver value to the company as a whole by:	An enhanced information base will help to deliver value to the local units by:
• enabling optimization of operations between business units • enabling a learning organization through experience sharing • capturing knowledge about customer needs so that, whenever pertinent, it flows through the company's value chain • allowing the internal organization to be transparent to the customer around the world • enabling people to be more a part of the company as well as their local groups; people will then act in the common interest of global company rather than only in the interest of their own group at the expense of the others • decreasing complexity thereby decreasing costs and improving customer service • facilitating organizational change; reducing organizational boundaries; enabling the creation of virtual teams • increasing decision-making and implementation speed	• enabling optimization of operations within each business unit • capturing and exploiting innovative ideas and opportunities more quickly, more easily • tapping into global expertise for problem solving • tapping into global supplier options to reduce costs • improving operational stability, consistency and reliability • enabling production capacity optimization • increasing decision-making and implementation speed

Using the sample framework presented in Step 1, Exhibit 3.6 provides some examples of possible ways to add value or enable business strategies. These examples, when linked to the vision, provide clear business outcomes that may result from developing an enhanced information base.

Step 3: Develop Draft Information Vision

This step involves developing a simple statement that combines the strategic objectives and critical success factors of the business with the feedback that has been given regarding how the business could change as a result of having an enhanced information base. An example of this is shown in Exhibit 3.7.

How the draft Information Vision itself is assembled depends largely on the development approach that has been chosen. If all key business leaders are in one room then the words can be drafted by the group as a whole. If this approach is not possible, or if there is already general concensus among the participants on the business outcomes that can be achieved through an enhanced information base, the vision can be assembled and presented to the key business leaders for review and approval.

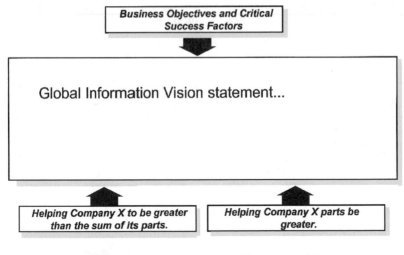

Exhibit 3.7.   Assembling the information vision.

Step 4: Gain Executive Acceptance

It is important that acceptance be given for the vision by the various business leaders involved in developing it. Once again, the vision must be business-owned and business-led. Acceptance will help to ensure that each of the leaders involved will serve as a champion for building an enhanced information base in their respective business areas or regions.

PHASE 3: CHANGE STRATEGY

A successfully executed Information Vision development process will generate a significant amount of awareness among key business leaders of how information can be a strategic enabler for the company. However, it is important to build on the momentum that has been achieved and have a plan for making all company management aware of the vision for how information will be leveraged to create business value. Do not make the mistake of relying on passive or informal communication methods. Instead, a detailed communication plan should be developed to ensure that all key stakeholder groups are aware of the vision. Exhibit 3.8 highlights a simple approach for developing a communication plan.

Key Messages

First you must identify the key messages that you wish the target audiences to hear and understand. Given the visioning process that has just been completed, typical messages would include:

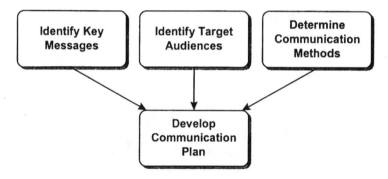

Exhibit 3.8.   Approach to developing communication plan.

- Business Vision and Strategy — pick key phrases that link directly to the Information Vision
- Information Vision — emphasize that the statement has been developed and approved by key business leaders
- Business Outcomes — state the business outcomes that can result from developing an enhanced information base are key to making people understand how the vision will change the business

Audiences

Generally, all decision-makers in the company should be made aware of the key messages coming out of the visioning exercise. For the purposes of the communication plan, it is important to specifically identify those audiences that will require targeted communications. Once these audiences have been identified, it is a worthwhile exercise to determine the roles of each group with regard to their use of information and IT and gain an understanding of their specific communication requirements. For example, some groups may simply need to be made aware of the key messages while others may need to incorporate this thinking into their decision-making. The level of communication required for a specific audience will dictate the method used.

Communication Methods

Typically, there are a variety of communication methods available within a company ranging from media tools, such as e-mail or company newsletters, to face-to-face communications, such as executive presentations. It may be necessary to create some specific communication opportunities to match the objectives of the visioning initiative. Compiling a list of the various methods available will help in developing the communication plan.

Developing the Communication Plan

Assembling the communication plan involves determining which methods will be used to communicate the key messages to the target audiences.

Conclusion and Next Steps

Once the Information Vision has been developed and the communication plan has been launched, you may ask yourself, "where to from here?" Once again, given the momentum established during the visioning exercise, it is important to build on this momentum. The following are typical initiatives or deliverables that may provide further value to your company.

Information Strategy. Building on the stated business outcomes from the visioning exercise, an information strategy would provide further detail regarding what the specific information requirements are to achieve these outcomes. The strategy would answer questions such as: What knowledge is critical to the success of the company? How can this knowledge be leveraged further? What are the key strategic and operational decisions in the company? What information would enable these decisions to be made more effectively? An information strategy also provides detail regarding where IT investments should be targeted to deliver the greatest value to the company.

Information Management Plan. Once people acknowledge that information is a valuable resource for the company, they will begin to realize the importance of managing this resource effectively. An information management plan identifies how key information will be defined, managed, delivered, and protected. The plan also identifies who will be responsible for defining, managing, delivering, and protecting key information.

Chapter 4
An Approach for Establishing Enterprise Data Standards

Sanjiv Purba

INTRODUCTION

STANDARDS EXIST IN SOME FORM OR OTHER in most organizations and tend to be wide reaching in establishing how work is performed and delivered within the environment. In the strictest sense, standards should thoroughly describe procedures and outcomes for all the events in an organization. The benefit of this is consistent communication within an organization and reliable deliverables. Implementing standards is a tricky business that can lead to an entirely different set of problems that can also jeopardize the health of the organization. Ideally, it would be best to simply borrow standards that have already been used successfully on similar projects and adapt them with minimal effort. Unfortunately, this is not possible in many real world cases, so another approach is required. As shown in Exhibit 4.1, simplicity is the key to successfully implementing enterprise data standards in most organizations.

Enterprise data standards are part of the larger, broader "enterprise development standards" category, which includes such topics as development approach, walkthrough procedures, and coding conventions. This paper focuses on establishing enterprise data standards. There are other types of standards in organizations (e.g., development standards), but these are outside the scope of this article. This distinction can sometimes be subjective; for example, consider the case of form naming standards. Is this a data standard or a development standard? For grouping purposes, I prefer to categorize it as naming convention standards. However, some

0-8493-9832-0/00/$0.00+$.50
© 2000 by CRC Press LLC

Standards are only useful if they are used.
Standards will only be used if they are understood.
Standards will only be understood if they are simple.
Standards will only be understood if the organization has bought into them.
The organization will buy into standards if they are simple, easily understood, and there is a stake in using them.

Exhibit 4.1. Guiding principles.

would prefer to stay pure and categorize it under the more general naming conventions in the development standards.

OBJECTIVES AND BENEFITS OF ENTERPRISE DATA STANDARDS

Data exists within organizations in a variety of formats, some of which include: documents, databases, flat files, paper documents, binary objects, voice, and video. Data is everywhere, and its value is in a constant state of flux, either being modified, deleted, changed, or manipulated in some way. All of this activity is supported by many human resources, both inside and outside the organization. Enterprise data standards support the objectives of bringing consistency and integrity across the organization based on the categories shown in Exhibit 4.2. This list is not exhaustive, but the categories that are identified are common across many organizations in a variety of industries and provide a good start for beginning this process.

The significant objectives and benefits of each of the categories defined in Exhibit 4.2 are described in this section, as they pertain to many organizations.

Architecture and Physical Environment Category

Objectives. This includes building a consistent technical data architecture including centralized databases, distributed database servers, and mobile databases. This also includes the physical storage of the data and associated data objects (e.g., indexes) and defines the methods for accessing the data in an n-tier environment from thin or fat clients using embedded SQL or remote procedure calls (RPCs). System management, change management, and version control tools are implemented to meet this objective based on procedures defined in the "Procedures Category."

Benefits. Provides a standard physical environment that is easier to support and enhance. Maintenance and support costs are also reduced. A standard architecture and physical environment also simplify application portability and interoperability.

Procedures Category

Objectives. This includes all the procedures required to support data for operational or development groups. This can include system management,

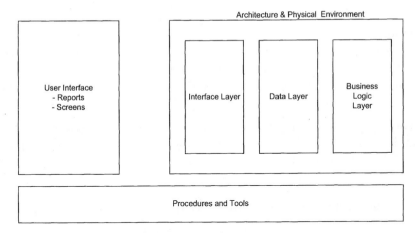

Exhibit 4.2.   Categories of enterprise data standards.

change management, and version control procedures. Included in this group are project naming standards (using tools like Microsoft Source-Save), module check in /check out procedures, support for multiple versions, and delta merging procedures.

Benefits. A significant benefit supported by this category includes the use of proven, consistent procedures for maintaining the integrity of the data environment. It also becomes easier to measure compliance with the standards processes.

n-Tier/Layers Category

Objectives. This category contains anywhere from one to *n* tiers, with three being the most common. The growing popularity of components will continue to increase the number of tiers. The predominant case includes three tiers, namely, user interface tier (or layer), data tier, and the business logic tier. The user interface tier is discussed in the next category. The *n*-tier category includes naming standards in terms of variable names, field names, data object names (e.g., tables, indexes, databases, user-defined datatypes, triggers, stored procedures), forms class libraries, and objects.

Benefits. There are significant benefits derived from standardizing in this category. Application modules are easier to read, build, and maintain. There is increased reuse of code and improved application portability and interoperability. This results in faster development and more accurate debugging. There is a reduced learning curve. The end result is improved product quality.

User Interface Category

Objectives. This category includes all types of user interfaces, including application screens and reports (both online and printed). The objectives in this category are to specifiy placement of data on screens or printed forms. Categories such as screen navigation are outside the scope of this topic.

Benefits. Standards in this category result in consistent look and feel for user screens and printed reports. Users know where to search for specific types of information. An example of this is an error line on a screen or the page number on a report.

CATEGORIES OF ENTERPRISE DATA STANDARDS

Enterprise data standards are required to support both operational and development groups within an organization. Operational groups include those who perform the company's business on a day-to-day basis. These groups require access to information, the ability to manipulate information, procedures, and forms of various kinds. Development groups are more project-focused, in that they are restricted by some sort of timelines and deliverables. These groups require many of the data standards required by the operational groups, but their demands go further. Since development groups get right into the architecture and plumbing of applications, they are dependent on how data is stored, accessed, and manipulated at the code level.

The exhibits that are included in this section provide subcategories for each category defined previously. Each of the subcategories should be considered in your organization and allocated standards. Exhibit 4.3 shows the subcategories for the Architecture and Physical Environment category.

Exhibit 4.4 shows the subcategories that are included in the Procedures category. Most of these are focused on protecting data (in databases or files) during the development cycle.

Exhibit 4.5 shows the subcategories for the *n*-Tier/Layers category. These are divided between the different tiers in the architecture model. This example covers the business logic tier and the data tier. The user interface layer is covered in Exhibit 4.6.

Exhibit 4.6 shows the subcategories for the User Interface category. There are two primary subcategories, namely user screens and reports.

PROCESS FOR DEFINING ENTERPRISE DATA STANDARDS

There are many approaches for defining enterprise data standards. Project experience has shown that the best approach for meeting the objectives

Exhibit 4.3. Architecture and Physical Environment Category

Subcategory	Comments
Data Partitioning	Position nonvolatile data near the client platforms that access it.
Physical Architecture	Data architecture for development, testing, and production.
Data Access	Call stored procedures from client platforms to update database table data.
	Use views to select information from database tables.
	Return minimum number of data rows to the client.
Locking	Assume optimistic locking approach instead of the pessimistic.

Exhibit 4.4. Procedures Category

Subcategory	Comments
Change Management Standards	All database objects should be created with SQL Scripts. The scripts should be saved in tools such as Microsoft SourceSave.
System Management Standards	New client platforms will be configured using Microsoft SMS with local data tables for static data values.
Version Control Standards	Check in/Check out, delta management.

identified earlier in this article is the early adoption of a simplified set of enterprise data standards that are easily understood and used across the organization. This is best achieved by starting with a set of proven standards from previous projects or from external vendors. For example, companies such as Microsoft, Forte, and Sybase all have publications that define standards to one degree or another. These can be readily found by searching the Websites of the vendors or phoning their marketing or technical departments. Exhibit 4.7 shows a high level view of a process that should be completed in your organization to define Enterprise Data Standards. This process has been defined through experiences on many small to large projects, and based on observations about what worked well and what did not work so well on the projects.

As shown in Exhibit 4.7, the "Borrow Approach" is the simplest to define or implement, which involves borrowing data standards from vendors, other successful projects, or organizations such as the American National Standards Institute (ANSI) or International Standards Organization (ISO) that define industry standards. A more complete list of organizations that define standards is provided at the end of this article. Such standards can be used on a small number of sample projects and finetuned into a consistent set of data standards for a wider audience. A review team consisting of a Senior Sponsor (e.g., VP or CIO) and a combination of business analysts, systems analysts, and developers can then finetune the data standards and expand them for the enterprise before deploying them.

Exhibit 4.5.   *n*-Tier/Layers Category

Subcategory	Comments
General Naming Conventions	All variables names must be in lowercase
	Variables names should be mneumonic and reflect the contents of the variable
	Variable names should not exceed 40 characters in length
	Variable names should start with an alphabetic letter (a–z)
	The remainder of the name can be any combination of letters or digits or the symbol (_). The underscore (_) is used to separate parts of a name
	Variable names cannot include embedded spaces
Table Names	Maximum length is 20 characters
	Use the singular form (e.g., customer instead of customers)
	Do not use abbreviations
	Do not use restricted words
Column Names	Preface column name with first two letters of the table name
Index Names	Always contain part of the first 5 letters of the table name
	Number them sequentially starting with '_1'
Rules	Preface rule names with the table name
Views	Do not include more than 4 tables in a view
Stored Procedures	Always comment your Transact-SQL code
	Use the 'SET NOCOUNT ON' option to minimize data traffic
	Avoid the use of NULLS
	Log errors using master error file
	Stored procedure names should not exceed 30 characters in length
Triggers	Delete triggers prefaced with "dl". Insert triggers are prefaced with "in"; update triggers are prefaced with "up"
	Rollback any transactions that result in data integrity errors or which violate referential integrity
Datatypes	All tables must have a timestamp field
	Use ANSI-92 compatible datatypes only
	Minimize the storage required by variables by using the smallest datatype available (e.g., tinyint instead of int)
	Improve performance by using numerics instead of strings
	Avoid variable length strings
	Build joins on columns that share compatible datatypes
	Avoid using NULLS

Exhibit 4.7 also shows another approach that involves "creating" the data standards because there are no satisfactory ones to be borrowed from another source. The key for making this approach a success is to begin with a framework that is similar to the exhibits shown previously. You will probably want to modify the subcategories in the tables, or even to merge or expand the number of tables that are shown. A champion in the organization, perhaps a business analyst, should then review other projects and define a standard for each subcategory (e.g., all variable names must be prefaced with their datatype, all databases will have

Exhibit 4.6. User Interface Category

Subcategory	Comments
Screens:	Include field sizes, field types, field objects
Help Screens	
Menu Screens	
Drop Down Menus	
Information Screens	
Transaction Screens	
Reports:	Include page headings, page footers, date,
Project Plans	page number, column headings, total
Status Reports	columns
Issue Logs	
Client Requests	Minimize number of SQL requests per transaction

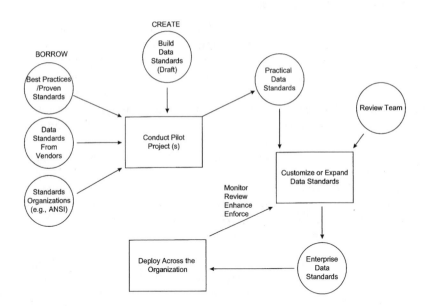

Exhibit 4.7. Process for defining enterprise data standards.

project names). It is unlikely that this first pass will be complete. The primary challenge is to establish a standards baseline and to begin using them. As in the "borrow" approach, one or more pilot projects are used to validate and enhance the data standards. In the "create" approach, it is likely that several projects will be required to define a satisfactory set of data standards.

There is a third approach that involves combining the "borrow" and "create" approaches. In this instance, standards organizations such as ANSI or ISO can be used to provide a first cut at the data standards. These are then customized as discused in the "create" approach.

Exhibit 4.7 shows that after the enterprise data standards have been prepared and signed off by the corporate sponsor, the next task is wide deployment. The manner in which this is done is critical for the successful adoption of the enterprise data standards. The first step here is to ensure that the data standards are readily available electronically or on paper. The next step is to communicate the importance, location, and procedures for using the data standards by both the operations and development groups. This message must be communicated to the organization by a senior sponsor, such as a CIO or VP, in order to maximize corporate buy in.

COMMON PITFALLS AND TRAPS

There are several common pitfalls and traps that can befall an organization trying to establish enterprise data standards. One of the obvious problems springs from the "enterprise" term itself. Many organizations view the use of this term to mean "broad consensus required" or "slow adoption". This can lead to several problems, not the least of which is that the standards require too much attention and time to implement, or are too cumbersome to learn, use, or understand. Such standards are usually put aside during tight project timeframes. Too many standards can be as bad as having too few standards. The surest way of ensuring that standards are not used is to spend a lot of time defining them and publishing them in a hundred plus page manual. It is preferable to spend a few days conducting research, and then having a small team publish a single digit page document defining the suggested data standards which are then immediately passed to project teams to test and refine in actual projects.

Another common problem involves the inaccessibility of enterprise standards. To be effective, the standards must be readily accessible to project teams at any time. Furthermore, the standards should also be readily usable. They must also be easy to duplicate. A useful method of achieving these is to use a combination of deployment strategies. A central data repository (e.g., a Website or a Lotus Notes database) can hold the enterprise standards. Project teams throughout the organization should have direct and remote access to the repositories. Reusable templates and deliverables (e.g., screen images) can also be included in the repositories to provide project teams with the ability to get started on their projects quickly. Paper-based, or CD-ROM-based, delivery of the standards and templates should accompany the electronic delivery modes.

MEASURING COMPLIANCE AND ENFORCING STANDARDS

During the pressure of development projects or unexpected operational emergencies, it is not uncommon for all standards, including data standards, to be suspended until the immediate problem is resolved. In some instances, this is acceptable in the short term. However, compliance is important in the long term, and several mechanisms should be used to measure and enforce this, as follows:

- Deliverable walkthroughs. Regular sessions should be scheduled to walkthrough and sign off on project deliverables to ensure that they comply with the published enterprise data standards. DBAs should be involved in this process;
- Audit. Infrequent audits of projects across the enterprise should be used to ensure ongoing compliance with the published standards. Resources on the audit teams can vary over time. A good size for the audit team is about three resources. It is a good idea to rotate resources on and off the teams over a period of time;
- Enforcement. Examples of noncompliance should be documented and the appropriate project manager(s) should be mandated to ensure that the standards are adhered to within a specific timeframe (e.g., one month); and
- Quality plan. Every project plan should be accompanied by a quality plan that includes the activities that will be followed by the project teams to ensure compliance with the standards.

TEN TIPS FOR GETTING STARTED

Many projects have shown that the following tips greatly simplify the process of establishing enterprisewide data standards:

1. Keep them simple;
2. Borrow, if possible, avoid creating;
3. Use samples from actual projects;
4. Make the standards readily accessible electronically;
5. Do not hesitate to modify enterprise data standards if a good argument is presented;
6. Use standards as reasonable guidelines;
7. Build early successes as showpieces;
8. Build data standard compliance right into the project plan or quality plan;
9. Never create standards in a vacuum;
10. Enforce the use of the data standards.

CONCLUSION

Enterprise data standards should be used by organizations that are building and maintaining nontrivial application systems. The key for establishing enterprise data standards is to keep them as simple as possible and to ensure that they are actually used on projects. It is recommended that standards be borrowed from third parties or vendors. Where this is not possible, it is recommended that a framework, such as the one included in this article, be used to build a first cut of the enterprise standards. These should then be validated in a few pilot projects before rolling them out to the enterprise.

LIST OF ORGANIZATIONS DEFINING STANDARDS

ISO	International Organization for Standardization (Global support)
OSF DCE	Open Software Foundation's (OSF) Distributed Computing Environment (middleware and enterprise standards)
POSIX	applications operating with OS. Deals with system calls, libraries, tools, interfaces, and testing
X/Open	European vendors and manufacturers
COSE	IBM, HP Santa Cruz Operation, Sun Microsystems, UNIX — application/OS implementations
CORBA	Object Management Group's Common Object Request Broker Architecture
IEEE	U.S. Standards body; works to get buy-in from ANSI
SQL Access Group	Call-Level Interface (CLI) and Remote Database Access (RDA)
ISOC	Internet Society. Internet standards and internetworking techniques

Chapter 5

Enterprise Transformation and Data Management

Richard Lee

GLOBALIZATION AND RAPID TECHNOLOGICAL CHANGE has forever changed the competitive landscape. There has been a great advance in information technology, and telecommunications that accelerate productivity and supply-chain integration. This rising sophistication, and expectations of customers around the world, has given rise to implications in the way companies manage processes and data.

Whether it is through the Internet, information kiosks, or some other means, there now exists the "virtual customer" who decides what, when, where, and how they will purchase goods and/or services. Customers have virtual access through "cyberspace" to products and services to which they previously could not gain access. Not only do customers now have access; they will demand products and services "online" and almost in "zero-time." Consequently, this will have dramatic effects on the way companies manage, process, and organize data. Organizations that traditionally retrieve and use "old data" to plan, forecast, and execute, will have a difficult time in meeting customers' needs in the future.

Leading organizations have shifted their focus from cost to growth strategies. These companies are building flexibility and rapid-response capabilities in their products and services. They are redesigning business processes, and leveraging technology to develop innovative, integrated solutions. Studies (conducted by Deloitte Consulting) conclude that the speed of adaptability to customers — not incumbency, size, or technological elegance — has become the chief determinant of success in the industry. In all regions and sizes of organizations, the ability to innovate and respond quickly to changing market conditions was cited as the most critical advantage. The most profitable companies recognize the power of 21st century customers and are adapting to a new customer value paradigm and proactively changing the basis of competition.

Organizations that collect, leverage, and utilize data effectively will have a distinct advantage over their competitors. Organizations that excel at data management will be more efficient at rolling out their key capabilities into new markets. Success depends on linking the organization's strategic objectives with data management. There must be clear strategic decision making for data sharing, and the appropriate infrastructure—both technical and non-technical. As well, organizations must address a number of issues including the mind-set to share data, the resources to capture and analyze the data, and the ability to find the right people and data.

IMPROVEMENT ON PROCESSES

Almost all enterprise transformations have involved some degree of reengineering, whether it has been minor incremental improvements to major dramatic change. Regardless of the degree of change, any transformation of an enterprise necessitates a reevaluation of the management of data.

Many enterprise transformations have improved processes through information technology integration and centralized data management. The advantage of integration allows a worldwide organization to run as a small business. Standardizing business processes all over the world with one system allows an organization to manage data in multiple languages and multiple currencies more effectively. Most IT managers cite that standardizing business processes is the primary advantage for integrating computer systems. Organizations also benefit by generation of better data through more effective utilization of resources. As well, the data that can be monitored through integrated systems allows an organization to know how it is actually producing, instead of knowing the forecasted or theoretical capacity of an operation. Once an integrated system is in place, it can also be less expensive to operate.

Finding Profits in Data

Companies must recognize the potential for utilizing data for profit. Improved processes, and integrated systems do not necessarily make enterprises more successful. To sustain growth and take advantage of the enterprise transformation improvements, companies are consolidating internal databases, purchasing market-research data, and retaining data longer in efforts to better focus their marketing efforts. To serve their customers better, organizations are analyzing behavioral characteristics of customers. If organizations can start tracking a customer's purchasing behavior, the kinds of things he or she likes and doesn't like, the organization can use the organization's data mining tools and data warehouses developed to target-market the customer. There would be a lot less "junk mail" and better deals that the customer really cares about.

However, building and managing data through centralized or decentralized databases is not an easy task. Many organizations have had difficulty in finding adequate tools to manage such an ordeal. Many IT departments have found that the tools required to manage these databases are inadequate, immature, and possibly nonexistent.

The business process should dictate the tools and data required for users to perform the responsibilities that enhance the enterprise. Business processes should be developed to maximize the value of the enterprise to customers, employees and shareholders. Identifying the correct tools and data translate into specific business goals that match the organization's unique objectives.

Critical Success Factors

Enterprise transformation not only impacts technical, and organization structures, but data structures as well. Companies must recognize the importance of managing information as an asset. Successful companies recognize the need to carefully manage their data as well as they manage other valued assets. Critical success factors include managing data from an enterprisewide basis, managing data quality, assigning data ownership and empowerment, and developing long-term data strategies to support the enterprise.

Managing Data from an Enterprisewide Basis. An effective approach to managing data on an enterprise scale is to transform data from a "functional-silo" view to a business-unitwide and enterprisewide view. The data should address not only functional areas, such as sales, financial, and products but also how their relationships with enterprise processes, such as marketing, finance, distribution, are mapped.

The culture of an organization usually dictates how data is distributed across its business units. A large multinational organization that has business units operating autonomously may have disparate technology architectures and distributed local databases. This environment provides more of a challenge than companies that have a strategy of centralizing data for current and detailed historical data, while allowing each business unit to retain corresponding summary data.

The purpose of an enterprise-view of data is to:

- Share data between multiple organizations or among business units that are critical to the enterprise.
- Identify and control data that have dependencies with other systems or subsystems.

- Improve the quality of data resources.
- Establish effective data change management processes that maximize the value of information while ensuring data quality.
- Minimize data duplication due to collecting, and processing information.
- Facilitate external partner data access and sharing.

Many companies can benefit from managing data on an enterprisewide basis. Data just sitting in a local database is just data. However, when data is shared on an enterprisewide scale, then other business units may be able to take advantage of that data. From a customer relationship perspective, when demographics and psychographics are added to customer data, the company can gain extensive knowledge about that customer. Business intelligence is gained when the results of a competitive analysis are added to base customer data. When this intelligence is utilized within the enterprise's planning process, it will result in value-added ways to manage and expand the customer base.

Managing Data Quality. One of the many benefits for improved data management through enterprise transformation is improved data quality through elimination of data duplication. Most companies have many individuals throughout different parts of the organization that enter data relating to a certain process or business function. Consequently, it is very difficult to identify the integrity of the various types of data that is entered.

Data error can be attributed to a number of factors including:

- Multiple data entries from multiple users.
- Lack of corporate standards.
- Data distributed across disparate sources and legacy systems.
- Data redundancy between different applications.
- Data entry errors.

An example of this was cited in an article in *"Automotive Manufacturing & Production,"* a first-tier automotive supplier, having seven divisions that shared some of the same vendors, but not the same vendor codes. Each division not only assigned a unique identification number to each of those vendors, each division also had its own descriptions for the components supplied by those vendors. Also, the seven divisions had a mix of legacy hardware platforms, software applications, and financial systems. To say the least, monthly roll-ups for divisional product sales, as well as component and supplier costs, were difficult for the parent company to obtain.

In order to improve quality of data, there have been a number of approaches utilized throughout industry. Companies have achieved improved labor time and cost by achieving gains in speed and accuracy of data entry. Directly related to this, is the higher degree of work satisfaction from staff, since the users will not have to re-key the information. As a result, companies that invest an amount up-front in improving labor and data entry processes will save an organization a substantial amount of effort and cost providing batch work solutions later.

Assigning Data Ownership and Empowerment. Enterprise transformation typically leads to a change of responsibility for users. As a result, it is very important for organizations to manage data effectively. A number of roles involved in creating and distributing data are important for effective data management. Roles have been identified in the *"Enterprise Data Management"* article as:

- *Business Process Owners:* The business process owner defines and maintains the processes and sub-processes across multiple business functions. Operational business processes may include market products/services, perform order management, procure materials/services, manage logistics and distribution, and provide customer support. Infrastructure business processes may include the following: perform financial management, manage human resources, manage information systems, and provide support services. Business process owners have the responsibility of evaluating and managing the proposed changes to data has on the impact of their business process.
- *Data Owner:* The data owner is usually a business-function manager that is responsible for the data resource. For example, a person in the finance department should own the tax-rate data. A data owner should be able to assess the validity of the data from a business point of view, and not necessarily a computer programmer. The data owners should drive and review proposed changes to the data and assess the impact on their own data.
- *Data User:* The data user is anyone that completes a simple, fill-in-the-field change to a data item. A data user tends to be a task-based role rather than a position, and can be anyone from a customer-support representative to a head of a plant temporarily changing the inventory capacity for a given item. Data entry should be performed under careful access, security, and data-validation controls.
- *Data Custodian:* The data custodian is a person that often resides in an information technology department or MIS providing services to several data owners. The data custodian is a person who actually manipulates the data structure for the data owner. Data custodians manage data dictionaries under change-control processes, implement proposed functional changes at the data level, and assess the broader impacts of proposed data changes. This role typically involves a combination of a database administrator, a data analyst, and an application-knowledgeable analyst.

Transforming enterprises usually occur through technology-enabled business processes. This transformation must include an in-depth knowledge of the enterprise's application, data, and technical infrastructure. Just as important as the technical infrastructure is the organizational infrastructure that must be in place. This includes a strong management committee that is involved in program management, selection committees, implementation teams, and on-going support teams.

In order to achieve a successful enterprise transformation, extensive training, education and overall project leadership are required. Resources must be both technically and business knowledgeable. Achieving an effective data management process during enterprise transformation is not easy, but it is essential to achieve the business improvements required in today's competitive economy.

Developing Long-Term Data Strategies to Support the Enterprise. Enterprises that undergo transformation look to improved data planning, and access through the use of appropriate methods, tools and technologies. Companies must learn to promote internally and externally the importance of data as a valuable resource and properly manage its creation, use, storage documentation, and disposition.

A survey conducted by *LAN Times* in *BusinessWeek*, 500 organizations found that a vast majority of the businesses have already implemented technology to provide intranet or browser-based access to corporate data. The major driving forces toward this internet or intranet based technology is the demand for mobile knowledge workers and the opportunities for revenue and efficiency by E-commerce. As a result, enterprises are now reformulating their data strategy to take advantage of the benefits of the Internet. Most companies have a long way to go, but are now looking at the most efficient ways to build database infrastructures and user-friendly, standardized access paths. The benefits are tremendous for enterprises looking to get useful information directly to the people, inside or outside the company, who need them most.

The Internet

The Internet provides companies with the ability to distribute data to end-users. Through consolidation and simplifying data on one universal client, companies can contact their customers and work with their business partners much more easily. The Internet makes it easier for companies to manage geographically distributed databases and organizations. Companies are now identifying ways to consolidate data onto a central server to allow access from users anywhere, with the proper data security, and integrity features in place.

Allowing customers to gain access to a company's database via the Internet provides many benefits to organizations. Customers can obtain information regarding billing, invoices, and their accounts via the Internet. Cost savings is just one of the reasons for companies managing their distributed databases via the Internet. According to the *LAN Times*, "A lot of organizations are interested in decentralizing the IT management operations because database administrators are so expensive. Rather than have a database administrator for each regional office, you can have one DBA team in the central office that can manage all the regional databases. The Internet will move that paradigm along because in the world of the Internet, physical location is more or less irrelevant."

The leading application for companies tends to be customer support followed by decision support, financial transactions, E-commerce, and EDI. Other internal uses are support for mobile employees, interactive intranet-based databases, and sales-force automation.

CONCLUSION

Enterprise transformation requires a robust strategy for enterprisewide data management. Managing data on an enterprisewide basis is increasingly crucial to running almost every aspect of today's business. Effective data management requires a combination of efficient processes, robust and flexible technology infrastructures, and skilled people. There is a growing need for enterprises to manage data on an enterprisewide base, through data ownership and empowerment while maintaining data quality. Companies are also developing long-term data structures to meet the business needs. The Internet is just one of the tools which enterprises are utilizing to manage their data.

References

Anonymous, "Data cleanliness is next to enterprise efficiency," *Automotive Manufacturing & Production*, Vol. 10, Issue 6, June 1998, p66.

Bartlett, Jeffrey, "Business needs driving data dependency," *LAN Times*, May 11, 1998, Vol. 15, No. 10, p15(1).

Caron, Jeremiah, "Access methods change it all.," *LAN Times*, May 11, 1998, Vol. 15, No. 10, p7(1).

Deloitte Consulting, Deloitte & Touche, "1998 Vision in Manufacturing" study, 1998.

Gibbs, Jeff, "The power of enterprise computing," *Internal Auditor*, February 1997.

Greenfeld, Norton, "Enterprise data management," *Unix Review*, February 1998.

Miller, Ed, "A solution approach to PDM," *Computer-Aided Engineering*, April 1998.

Moriarty, Terry, Swenson, Jim, "The data requirements framework," *Database Programming & Design*, April 1998 Vol. 11, No. 4, p13(3).

DATA DEVELOPMENT METHODOLOGIES, DEFINITIONS, AND STRATEGY

Mullin, Rick, "IT integration programmed for global operation," *Chemical Week*, Vol. 159, Issue 6, Feb. 12, 1997, p21–27.

Perez, Ernest, "Savings from data entry engineering," *Database*, Vol. 21, Issue 3, June/July 1998, p76–78.

Schwartz, Karen, D., "Distributed databases, distributed headaches," *Datamation*, June 1998.

Singh, Colin, Hart, Max, "Changing business culture: Information is the key," *Australian CPA*, Vol. 68, Issue 8, September 1998, p50–52.

Trussler, Simon, "The rules of the game," *Journal of Business Strategy*, Vol. 19, Issue 1, January/February 1998, p16–19.

Chapter 6
Building an Integrated Customer Profile

Brian Nicholls

ALMOST EVERY ORGANIZATION NOW CALLS ITSELF A CUSTOMER-CENTRIC BUSINESS. It is becoming clear that a company's ability to connect to its customers and truly understand their needs and wants is critical to survival in today's increasingly competitive business environment.

Equally important is the ability of a business to understand the value that each customer provides to them. Understanding a customer's value enables the business to devote the appropriate level of resources to not only acquiring but also retaining the customer. Spending too much to obtain a customer that is not profitable (or marginally profitable) is as unwise as not spending enough to keep a highly profitable customer happy.

Obtaining a good level of understanding of customers and the value that they bring is not an easy task. Companies have spent significant amounts of money and devoted years of effort to build up the required knowledge without achieving a truly comprehensive answer to the problem. For example, the major banks have been working on this challenge for several years, but it is still common to receive mailings from different parts of a bank (e.g., account statements, credit card bills, safety deposit box information) with different spellings for basic name and address information.

The focus of this chapter will be on the development of a customer profile that can be used as a basis for implementing effective customer-focused marketing, sales, and service strategies. The chapter will discuss the advantages and the challenges of developing a comprehensive customer profile, the key issues, and critical success factors to be considered, and suggests an approach for successful implementation.

THE CUSTOMER PROFILE

Before proceeding, let's take a moment to define what is meant by an integrated customer profile. Essentially, it is a logical data repository of all the information related to a company's customers and the various interactions with them from all areas of the business. It is accessible to all areas of the business with views that are specific to each area. The customer profile is a combination of physically replicated data and logical connections to data kept within production databases across the organization. Once the profile is in place, it can be made available to all access channels between a customer and the business. This includes Telesales, Branches, Internet, Voice, Automated Terminals, Fields Sales, Retail, and Video.

ADVANTAGES

There are many significant advantages to the business that can successfully implement an integrated customer profile. The most prominent of these is the ability to fully understand the customer base and use this knowledge to create effective strategies for retaining existing customers and obtaining new high value customers.

From a sales force perspective, the ability to draw on all relevant information for a given customer can be very powerful in planning a sales call or ensuring that service is provided quickly and effectively for existing customers. From a marketing perspective, the ability to extrapolate the characteristics of high value customers can help to prepare a strategy for successfully acquiring new customers that will also be high-value customers. From a service perspective, the profile will allow an organization to ensure that the appropriate level of service is provided to existing customers. In addition, the service organization will be able to perform cross-selling and up-selling of more services to customers.

As an example, suppose your business serves both the consumer and business markets. If you knew that a consumer market customer was also president of a business that was a significant business partner, you would likely want to provide that person with a higher level of service than you would for a consumer market customer with no other ties to your business. The integrated customer profile provides the information to ensure that the appropriate level of service is given.

Once a customer profile has been implemented, the business also has the ability to do extensive data analysis on its customers to further deepen and broaden this understanding. An effective data analysis effort will greatly augment marketing, sales, and service programs.

In addition, a natural byproduct of the effort to build a customer profile is that the data that has been kept for customers will by necessity be cleansed and consolidated. In some cases, many years of inattention to the validity of customer data can be overcome and business decisions can be taken with more confidence.

THE CHALLENGES

There is a significant technical challenge to building an integrated customer profile, but the most difficult aspects of the effort in any mid-size or large business are to overcome the organizational and political obstacles.

The primary one of these challenges is to obtain agreement on who owns the customer—and more importantly, who owns the customer data. The integrated customer profile will contain data from all organizational units within the company—marketing, billing, sales, and service. Data required for the customer profile will need to be obtained from systems within each of these organizational units and their systems. Since, in most organizations, there will be significant replication of customer data in these different systems it will be important to define which systems contain the current and accurate instances of the data that makes up the profile.

A related challenge is the need to be able to uniquely identify customers. Multiple systems containing customer information typically have multiple unique customer identifiers. Since the same customers can be held in multiple databases, consolidating all information for a customer and being able to match sets of customer data is a significant challenge in most organizations.

Organizationally, building an effective team to develop a customer profile requires cooperation across business units. Experts on customer data from the various "stovepiped" functional areas will need to be put on the team—which implies that these experts will need to be removed from other projects. The benefits to managers in the individual business units need to be clear for them to agree to assign staff to the customer profile project.

The strategy for building the customer profile requires careful consideration as well. It is usually impractical to replicate all data needed for the profile due to data volumes and volatility. At the same time, indices from the profile to existing legacy applications are impractical from a systems performance point of view. A very careful data modeling exercise is required to balance off the data replication versus the indexing strategies.

Another common challenge is the state of legacy applications and databases kept within them. Understanding what data is kept within each application, how often it is updated, the timing of its maintenance and the dependencies between different systems need to be clearly understood. In addition, the validity and reliability of data in legacy systems is always difficult to verify. Significant effort is usually required to map existing data and to build and execute data conversion and data clean-up programs.

KEY SUCCESS FACTORS

To offset the many challenges described above, the following strategies should be employed to minimize the risks associated with a customer profile creation project.

Sponsorship

To be successful, a strong sponsor who can cut across organizational boundaries to get things done is required. This sponsor needs to be committed to the project and must have the authority to solicit action from the affected functional areas of the business. Another key strategy is to build a steering committee that has representation from all affected functional units.

Scope Management

Controlling the scope of the project is critical to success. It is very easy to fall into the "analysis paralysis" trap and never actually build anything functional. To avoid this problem, an action orientation should be taken to define a narrow scope initial pilot to prove the concept and implement a practical solution for one business unit. The team should then aggressively manage to that limited scope. There should be one clearly defined user for the initial pilot and the needs of that one user should be the focus of initial development within the context of the larger design.

Flexible Rapid Development / Prototyping Approach

The customer-profile team should be biased towards building something quickly that can then be tested and tried in a production setting within a short period of time. One of the key goals should be to deliver some value to part of the organization quickly. Rapidly developing a pilot that can be tried in the field will increase the overall project's chances of success and will also provide evidence of progress that will assist in ensuring that funding for the project can be maintained as required.

Building the Right Team

The success of this project as with any other is dependent on having the right team in place and then giving them a clear direction. The team will need strong business requirements skills to not only ensure that business needs are being met but that there is a clear understanding of future needs as well to ensure that the design can be made flexible and scalable. In addition, strong technical expertise will be needed in three areas: the use of the middleware tools needed to access and extract data from legacy systems; the design and implementation of appropriate database models; and the legacy applications and their data. It should also go without saying that the team will need to be dedicated to the project to ensure results are delivered. Part-time team members will not be able to deliver results.

Issue Resolution Mechanism

A project of this nature that cuts across organizational boundaries will undoubtedly run into several serious issues. It is important to recognize this fact ahead of time and to install a comprehensive issue identification and resolution mechanism. This mechanism must be able to quickly deal with issues and the team must have access to someone with sufficient authority to make decisions that can resolve issues.

IMPLEMENTATION ACTIVITIES

A clear project approach and plan need to be developed. From an approach perspective, a guiding philosophy should be to think big and act small. In other words, the customer profile design should be developed with the big picture in mind so that there is flexibility in the profile to handle all of the business' needs. At the same time, the development should be structured so that small incremental pieces are put in place within the context of the wider design. This will enable the project team to provide value to the organization more quickly and build on success for a wider implementation.

A typical project plan for customer profile development should include the following activities:

- Define scope of overall project and for initial pilot.
- Clearly define assumptions.
- Define the functional requirements for the profile, including a clear definition of the customer data required and which group owns that data.
- Develop an inventory of current customer information and map the data flows currently in place, paying particular attention to the timing of these data flows.
- Complete the conceptual data model for the initial pilot.
- Evaluate and select the tools required:
  — Middleware
  — Connectivity
  — Presentation.
- Implement the tools required.
- Develop a strategy and detailed approach to implementation of the data structures; e.g., indexing vs. replication.
- Develop the programs and routines to access and convert customer data.
- Scrub and cleanse current customer data and populate the customer profile data structures.

- Thoroughly test all routines, plan and execute the pilot roll-out.
- Plan the next phase of the project.

Throughout the project, active and continual change management will be required. It will be necessary to ensure that the project sponsors remain committed and involved in the project and that all affected parts of the organization receive regular communication on project progress and impacts. Any changes in operating procedures also need to be managed throughout the process.

CONCLUSION

The path to the creation of a customer profile is a difficult one that requires a high level of executive commitment to overcome organizational barriers to success. The technical challenges are large but they can be managed by a practical approach that focuses on a series of incremental implementations. The challenges from a business impact and change perspective are more difficult to manage and therefore they should have the primary focus of the project manager.

Overcoming these difficulties is critical, however, for the development of an integrated customer profile has significant benefits for any organization that wants to be truly customer focused. The companies that build such a capability will have a true competitive advantage in the marketplace.

Chapter 7
Divestiture IT Planning

Tony Krajewski

WHEN DIVESTING A PORTION OF YOUR ENTERPRISE the easiest path is to hand over all your systems to the new entity. Although this may be the easiest, it may not be the best course of action and may prove more harmful than beneficial in the long run. There should at least, be some rigorous planning around why things are being done and not just because it is the path of least resistance.

Often a subset of an organization is divested because it was performing poorly in comparison to similar outside organizations. Because the competitors, market, and environment are different for the divested or sold firm than for the parent, we know that the business strategy of the divested business should not be exactly the same as the parent. The job of the new organization is to focus on winning against competitors in their own market. In the 1990s, senior IT practitioners know that the firm's information strategy enables the objectives of the business. What follows logically from this, is that the IT strategy for the parent cannot be used for the new entity. Where business strategies differ, IT strategies should differ.

IT PLANNING

An IT strategic plan represents the process of defining initiatives and allocating resources to maximize benefits to the enterprise. It tells people where IT is headed, how to get there, and how it is to be delivered in a common context that both business and IT professionals can understand and work from. The content of a strategic plan includes the current situation (where we are now), a vision (where to go), the strategy (how to get there), and implementation (what to do).

Recent research by Cognitech has shown that those organizations that perform IT planning are more likely to use IT effectively in their organization and are more likely to have higher profitability in their industry. In order to allow for those gains, the IT plan must be closely linked to the

0-8493-9832-0/00/$0.00+$.50

69

business objectives and processes and must be created with close interaction between business groups and IT planners. Creating that collaboration between business and IT can be difficult for traditional IT professionals who have grown up in the role of supporters to the business and not partners. The difficulties in developing productive IT and business collaboration is magnified when dealing with IT outsourcers.

A good IT plan mitigates project risk. Without the "IT Master Plan" no guidelines exist for applying governance procedures to ideas that affect a project or for prioritizing decisions. The divestiture IT project must be in the context of the new organization's IT strategy or it will fail to enable the objectives of the business. Without strict adherence to a plan, assumptions will drive the design and configuration of systems.

DIVESTING

IT departments in corporations that are divesting and creating smaller, less vertically aligned competitive organizations have a new and special responsibility to perform strategic planning. For years, leading up to the divestiture, the IT department in the parent corporation will have been dedicated to integrating the different components of the organization either through common systems or enterprise resource planning. When the divestiture occurs, the new organization will no longer use the business processes associated with a vertically integrated firm and should design their own processes in order to compete in their own markets. With a different focus and processes the information architectures of the new firm can not be defined by the old vertically integrated paradigm. Information flows, IT organization, information systems, cost structure and system scalability should all be different.

ORGANIZATIONAL PLANNING

Creating a new organization out of an old one can be a very difficult process that requires careful planning. The IT plan must ensure that it takes into account every aspect of the new organization to ensure that it achieves the right level of performance for the business.

IT planning for the new organization should:

- Define an IT governance model for clear responsibility, accountability, and authority.
- Define the right information for the industry and the firm to be competitive and define how the IT organization can create a competitive advantage.
- Create an IT organization that can support the systems created or purchased with defined metrics for performance.

OUTSOURCING MANAGEMENT

Often overlooked is the transition and management of the current outsourcer in a divestiture situation. This is another case where the status quo could be harmful. The divestiture is the CIOs opportunity to start from the ground up with the outsourcer and the internal IT management structure. The new organization's CIO must not take the outsourcer's new contract as set in stone. Research outside benchmarks for costs and service levels and reevaluate the performance metrics written into the service level agreement (SLA). The same metrics that mattered before may not be applicable. Often, pricing of IT services in the SLA is based on obscure allocation formula that encouraged a past strategy. Those kinds of prices should not be transferred to the new SLA. The areas that need improvement and the direction of the firm are in the IT strategic plan, the structure of the SLA should encourage the outsourcer to enable the new objectives and not those of the old corporation.

The internal staffing levels should be different than that of the parent, but should cost 3-7 percent of the total outsourcing deal. More importantly, once the CIO has chosen the staffing levels they must place them in an organizational framework that promotes the best price/performance out of the relationship. Just the right amount of supervision and planning, regardless of what occurred before or how much trust is built up with the outsourcer the CIO must remember that he can delegate responsibility for IT to the outsourcer but never accountability. (See Exhibit 7.1.)

A CASE STUDY

Recently, a large automotive manufacturer decided to divest a portion of its parts manufacturing organization. The new organization was to be a separate legal entity with its own systems and employees and continue to produce products two shifts a day through the transition. The solution was to "clone" most applications from the parent and give them to the now separate company. That solved the problem of what to do on day one, when the employees arrived for the first shift, but certainly didn't contribute to solving the organizations problem of being a poor competitor in the automotive parts market, the reason they were sold in the first place. They were hindered by large cumbersome systems that didn't reflect their new business strategy, industry sub-sector, or required flexibility.

The information available from the migrated systems was focused on building finished products and billing individual customers as opposed to sourcing raw materials, building parts and delivering to the JIT schedule of a demanding buyer. Over time, the parts manufacturer has slowly addressed their systems problems and competitive costs, but not before they were forced to sell half the plants they had bought. The problem in this

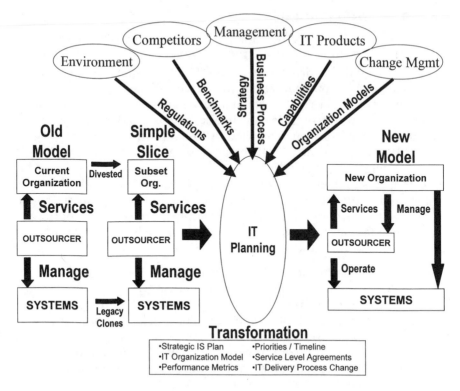

Exhibit 7.1.   Divestiture IT planning transformation model.

case was not poor systems. No one in the organization doubted that the inherited systems worked well for what they were designed to do. The problem lay in the new entity lacking the vision to create an IT strategy and conduct some rigorous planning to ensure that the IT strategy fit with the business objectives.

CONCLUSION

When a corporation divests a piece of its business, it should not automatically hand over the systems they used to manage their own organization. The divested firm will have a different business strategy than the parent and should therefore have a different IT strategy. The IT strategy should be clearly communicated alongside the business strategy and vision. Starting with IT governance and an organizational model the IT plan should drive down to information process flows, systems selections, outsourcing management and cost models. With a clear IT strategy, the divestiture plan should be a key enabler to getting the new organization to achieve their objectives. The IT strategy should be created and articulated before the divestiture planning and execution starts. The CIO of the new organization should not accept a jury rigged cloned set of systems from the parent but should start planning how they can use the transition period to progress towards making their organization competitive in the marketplace. The CIO must consider that the IT department will be benchmarked against its new competitors from the day it is divested and plan to be competitive from day one.

References

Lee, J., and Roberts, J., "How to Avoid IT Project Failure," Gartner Group, MDC-DF-04-8862, November 5, 1998.

Caldwell, Bruce, "GM's savings spree—automaker is halfway to planned $800M reduction in annual IT spending," *Information Week*, September 5, 1998.

Guptill, B., IT "Spending Levels: Keeping them in Context," Garnter Group 1998 IT Spending and IT Staffing Survey, Gartner Group, January 6, 1999.

Mehta Group, 3rd Quarter 1997 Trend Teleconference, "Panning for Outsourcing Gold or Improving Outsourcing ROI," Mehta Group, September 17, 1997.

Deloitte Consulting, Information Strategy Methodology, 1999.

Section II
Data Models and Modeling Techniques

DATA MODELS ARE THE CONCEPTUAL FOUNDATION OF DATA MANAGE-
MENT SOLUTIONS. They are used to capture business requirements and to
present them in a structured way that ultimately supports the development initiative. They are useful for communicating data design with users
and technical resources. They can also be used to sign-off on a formal contract with the business. Data models are also useful in object-oriented architecture, and can coexist and add value to object models. There are
many types of data models, modeling techniques, and syntax. There are
also an assortment of modeling tools and various types of implementation
tools. Data models capture one view of an organization. Other types of
models, such as process models, can capture different views. Taken together, the different models capture the logical essence of organizations. This
section contains seven chapters.

Chapter 8, "Evaluation of Four Languages Specifying Conceptual Database Design," examines different methods and syntax for building conceptual database designs.

Chapter 9, "Physical Database Design," logical database design, namely
building a physical database design.

Chapter 10, "Enabling Consumer Access to Business Databases," examines how to access business databases.

Chapter 11, "Well-Formed Entity Relationship Diagrams," shows how to
improve the content and quality of entity-relationship diagrams for infora-
tion modeling.

Chapter 12, "Component Design for Relational Databases," provides a
new twist on relational-to-object impedance matching also referred to as a
data-component approach in this chapter. This involves leveraging the advantages of having a component take responsibility for updating data while
providing relevant inquiry functions.

Chapter 13, "Integrating Process and Data Models in a Horizontal Organization," describes how process modeling and data modeling can be integrated in a horizontal organizaton. The chapter discusses the data-focused and process-focused approaches, and offers ways of integrating them into a single method. CASE tools are also reviewed in this chapter.

Chapter 14, "Data Warehouse Design: Issues in Dimensional Data Modeling," describes the multidimensional modeling concepts and techniques for designing information-rich data warehouses.

Chapter 8
Evaluation
of Four Languages
for Specifying
Conceptual
Database Designs

James A. Larson and Carol L. Larson

DATABASE ADMINISTRATORS (DBAS) NEED TO KNOW HOW TO DESCRIBE REAL-WORLD OBJECTS AND THEIR RELATIONSHIPS in a form that is both practical and meaningful to the database user and still be efficiently usable by the database management system. Defining a conceptual schema is important because it describes the objects in a database at an abstract level, which hides many of the low-level storage details. This article describes four conceptual database design languages from several perspectives and in sufficient detail so that a DBA, who must know the strengths and weaknesses of each design language, can use them to construct a conceptual schema that meets the needs of the database user.

DESIGN LANGUAGES AND CONCEPTUAL SCHEMAS

The conceptual schema describes data stored in a database to reflect a collection of real-world objects and relationships. It defines the names of objects in a database and the relationships in which the objects may participate. The conceptual schema also defines the constraints on the values of objects. These constraints are called business rules. Data in the database must obey all specified business rules. In order to define a conceptual schema, a database administrator may interview perspective users, examine existing and proposed reports and data screens, and consider existing and proposed applications to identify the contents of a conceptual

0-8493-9832-0/00/$0.00+$.50
© 2000 by CRC Press LLC

schema. A DBA describes the real-world objects, their relationships, and business rules using a special language called a conceptual database design language.

A conceptual database design language (CDDL) is a high-level language used by a DBA to describe a conceptual schema. In this article, the following four design languages will be evaluated:

- **English, or other natural languages,** are textual languages that the DBA and intended database users have in common. An example conceptual schema described in English is presented in Exhibit 8.1.
- **Entity-relationship diagrams** are a collection of graphical notations for describing conceptual schemas. First proposed by Peter Chen in 1976, they have become popular with many DBAs. A variation, called IDEF1X, was standardized by the military and is especially popular with defense contractors. Exhibit 8.2 illustrates entity-relationship diagrams for the conceptual schema shown in Exhibit 8.1.
- **SQL** is a formal computer language for creating and accessing a relational database. Exhibit 8.3 presents the SQL CREATE TABLE statements used to create a database that corresponds to the conceptual schema in Exhibits 8.1 and 8.2.
- **Relational diagrams** are a graphical notation that represents the objects and relationships expressed by SQL CREATE TABLE statements. Relational diagrams frequently appear in GUIs used by DBAs to define conceptual schemas for a relational database. Exhibit 8.4 shows the graphical notation describing the conceptual schema presented in Exhibits 8.1 through 8.3.

There are many other CDDLs, including the Universal Model Language (UML) and Bachman diagrams. However, the four languages identified above are the most popular with users of relational database management systems.

If the DBA designs the conceptual schema using notation other than SQL, it is necessary to convert the objects and relationships of the conceptual schema into the notation and format required by a relational DBMS. In most cases, the same software that DBAs use to create a conceptual schema can also be used to convert the schema into a relational database design.

The conceptual schemas shown in Exhibits 8.1 through 8.4 are designed to illustrate various features of the four design languages. However, the schemas do not contain all of the objects, relationships, and business rules of a real conceptual schema. Exhibits 8.1 to 8.4 illustrate that the same conceptual schema can be defined using any of the four popular CDDLs. Exhibit 8.5 presents the equivalent concepts and terminology used in entity-relationship diagrams and relational diagrams.

Exhibit 8.1.   Conceptual database design using English rules.

Every department has a name and budget.
No two departments have the same name.

Every employee has an employee identification, employee name, address, and social
   security number.
No two employees may have the same employee identification.
No two employees may have the same social security number.
Every employee must work in exactly one department.
Several employees may work in the same department.

Every project has a name, start date, and end date.
No two projects may have the same name.

Zero, one, or more employees may be assigned to a project.
An employee must be assigned to zero, one, or more projects.
An employee assigned to a project has a role.

Every dependent has a name and birthdate.
For a given employee, no two dependents may have the same name.
Some employees may have a policy that covers zero, one, or more dependents.
Each dependent must be covered by a policy of the employee for which they are listed
   as a dependent.

Every manager is also an employee.
Each manager has a bonus.

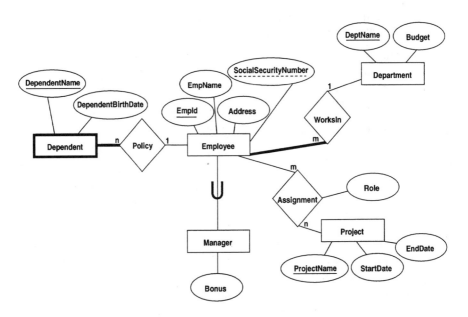

Exhibit 8.2.   Conceptual database design using entity-relationship diagrams.

Exhibit 8.3. Conceptual database design using SQL syntax.

CREATE TABLE Department	
(DeptName	INTEGER,
Budget	INTEGER,
PRIMARY KEY (DeptName))	
CREATE TABLE Employee	
(EmpId	INTEGER,
EmpName	CHAR(20),
Address	CHAR(40),
SocialSecurityNumber	INTEGER,
DeptName	INTEGER,
FOREIGN KEY (DeptName) REFERENCES Department,	
PRIMARY KEY (EmpId),	
UNIQUE (SocialSecurityNumber))	
CREATE TABLE Project	
(ProjectName	CHAR(20),
StartDate	DATE,
EndDate	DATE,
PRIMARY KEY (ProjectName))	
CREATE TABLE Assignment	
(EmpId	INTEGER,
ProjectName	CHAR(20),
Role	CHAR(20),
PRIMARY KEY (EmpId, ProjectName),	
FOREIGN KEY (EmpId) REFERENCES Employee,	
FOREIGN KEY (ProjectName) REFERENCES Project)	
CREATE TABLE Dependent	
(EmpId	CHAR (20),
DependentName	CHAR (20),
DependentBirthDate	DATE,
PRIMARY KEY (DependentName, EmpId),	
FOREIGN KEY (EmpId) REFERENCES Employee)	
CREATE TABLE Manager	
(EmpId	INTEGER,
Bonus	INTEGER,
PRIMARY KEY (EmpId),	
FOREIGN KEY (EmpId) REFERENCES Employee)	

This evaluation will first present examples of how each of the four languages represent frequently occurring logical data structure concepts. In effect, these examples are mini-tutorials showing how to use each of the four CDDLs. Following the examples, the four languages will be evaluated using several criteria.

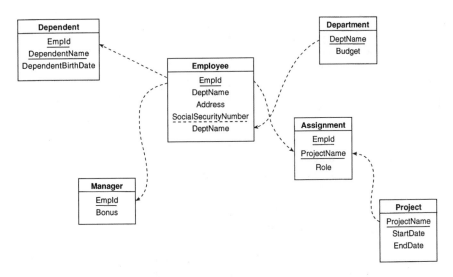

Exhibit 8.4.   Conceptual database design using relational diagrams.

Exhibit 8.5.   Equivalent concepts and terminology between entity-relationship and relational diagrams.

Entity-Relationship Concepts	Relational Concepts
Entity set	Table
Entity	Row of a table
Attribute	Column of a table
Unique identifier	Primary key, candidate key
One-to-many relationship	Foreign key constraint
Many-to-many relationship	Two foreign keys referencing a linking table
Partial participation	No NOT NULL declaration in a relationship for a foreign key
Total participation	NOT NULL declaration in a relationship for a foreign key
Weak entity	Primary key is a composite key containing the primary key of another table
Class hierarchy	Two tables have the same primary key, one of which is the foreign key of the contained table

EXAMPLE SCHEMAS USING FOUR DESIGN LANGUAGES

Entity Sets and Attributes

Basic to every conceptual database design language are the concepts of entity and entity set. An entity is a representation of a real-world person, event, or concept. For example, in Exhibits 8.1 through 8.4, the database may contain Employee entities Jones, Smith, and Lewis, and the Department entities Accounting and Sales. Each entity may take on a value for each of its attributes. An attribute is a characteristic of an entity. An Employee entity

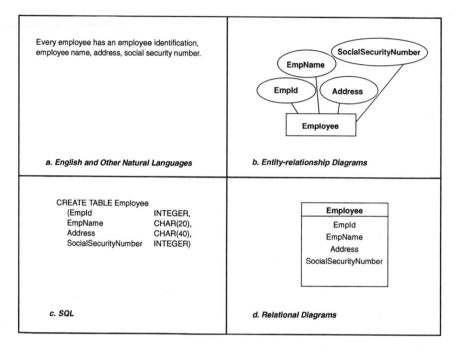

Every employee has an employee identification, employee name, address, social security number. *a. English and Other Natural Languages*	*b. Entity-relationship Diagrams*

CREATE TABLE Employee
    (EmpId   INTEGER,
    EmpName   CHAR(20),
    Address   CHAR(40),
    SocialSecurityNumber INTEGER)
 	
c. SQL
	d. Relational Diagrams

Exhibit 8.6. Entity sets and attributes.

may have values <13, Jones, Seattle, 999-99-9999> for attributes EmpId, Emp-Name, Address, and Social Security Number, respectively.

In order to organize the hundreds or thousands of entities in a database, entities with the same attributes are grouped together as entity sets. An entity set is a collection of homogeneous entities with the same attributes. In the example above, the entities Jones, Smith, and Lewis are members of the Employee entity set, while entities Accounting and Sales are members of the Department entity set.

Exhibit 8.6 shows the Employee entity set described using each of the four design languages. The English text describes the Employee entity set as having four attributes: Employee Identification, Employee Name, Address, and Social Security Number. The entity-relationship diagram represents the entity set as a rectangle labeled Employee with its attributes shown as ovals labeled EmpId, EmpName, Address, and Social Security Number. Attribute ovals are connected to the entity that they describe. The SQL CREATE TABLE statement describes the same entity set as a table consisting of four columns. The relational diagrams illustrate the Employee table by showing a box with table name Employee at the top and column headings EmpId, EmpName, Address, and SocialSecurityNumber at the bottom of the box.

Key Constraint

Exhibit 8.7 extends the entity set presented in Exhibit 8.6 to include the concept of a key constraint, which is used to enforce uniqueness among entities in an entity set. A key constraint specifies that no two entities in an entity set can have the same value for the key attribute. (A key is a subset of the attributes in the entity set.) In English, a constraint is specified by a sentence in the form of "No two <entities> may have the same value for <attribute>" or "<attribute> uniquely identifies <entity>." With entity-relationship diagrams, the attribute name of the unique identifier is underlined. In SQL, the clause PRIMARY KEY <attribute> identifies the unique identifier. With relational diagrams, the name of the unique identifier is underlined.

In the example shown in Exhibit 8.6, there are two key constraints — Employee Identifier and Social Security Number. That means there are two English sentences: one for employee and one for social security number. In the entity-relationship diagrams, multiple key constraints are illustrated by underlining each key attribute by a different type of line. Relational DBMSs

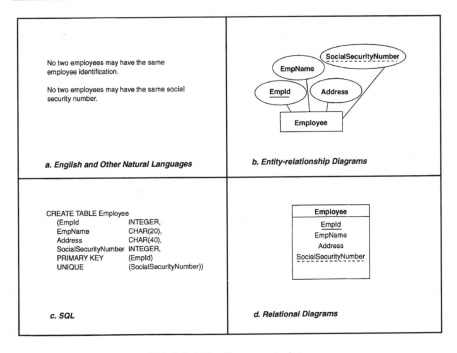

Exhibit 8.7. Key constraints.

require exactly one primary key. The remaining unique identifiers are called candidate keys. Each candidate key is declared with the UNIQUE clause in SQL. With the relational diagrams, each unique identifier is underlined with a different type of line, so they are not confused with other unique identifiers or the primary key.

One-to-Many Relationships

Exhibit 8.8 illustrates a one-to-many relationship between Department and Employee. A one-to-many relationship between entity sets A and B implies that zero or one A entity can be related to zero, one, or more B entities. In Exhibit 8, a single Department can be related to one or more Employee entities. Each entity participates in, at most, one relationship. One-to-many relationships are important because they describe how entities may relate to other entities. For example, a database containing Department and Employee entities alone fails to capture which employee works for which department. One-to-many relationships define these important types of associations.

With Exhibit 8.8, the English design language shows that one-to-many relationships are expressed with sentences, such as "Every employee may

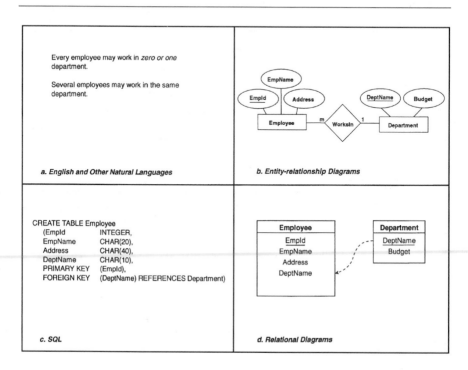

Exhibit 8.8.   One-to-many relationship with partial participation.

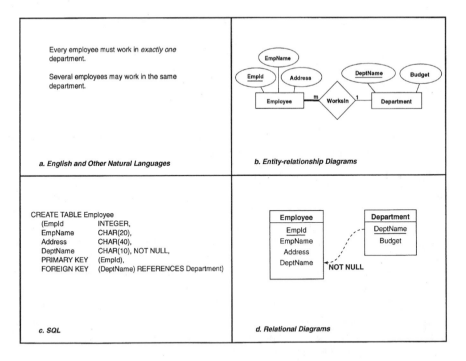

Exhibit 8.9.   One-to-many relationship with total participation.

work in zero or one department. Several employees may work in the same department." With entity-relationship diagrams, a one-to-many relationship is denoted as a diamond connecting two entity sets, with the "1" and "m" indicating the "one" and "many" entities in the relationship, respectively. The relationship name is shown inside of a diamond. In SQL notation, a one-to-many relationship is called a foreign key constraint. The DBA specifies the primary key of the "one" (or A) entity as a column in the table of the "many" (or B) entity. The value of this extra column in the Employee table identifies the Department entity for which the Employee works. A special clause, called a foreign key, describes a business rule that implies the only values of the DeptName column in the Employee table may be values in the Dept-Name column of the Department table. The relational diagram shows that the one-to-many relationship is represented by a dotted line from the primary key of the table representing the entity set A to the foreign key in the table representing entity set B. Thus, in this example, a dotted line goes from the DeptName column of the Department table to the DeptName column of the Employee table.

If the entities on the B side of the relationship exist without participating in a relationship, then entity set B is said to have partial participation in the relationship. Exhibit 8.9 shows a variation in a one-to-many relationship

**Exhibit 8.10. English wording for partial
and total participation.**

	One-side (A)	Many-side (B)
Partial	Zero or one	Zero or more
Total	Exactly one	One or more

where one of the B entities is required to participate in the relationship. This constraint often is referred to as total participation.

Exhibit 8.10 summarizes the English wording for partial and total participation of entities for both sides of a one-to-many relationship in the English CDDL. Total participation is denoted in entity-relationship diagrams with a thick line connecting the rectangle representing the entity — which must participate in the relationship — and the relationship diamond. In SQL, total participation is denoted by declaring the foreign key to be "NOT NULL." In Exhibit 8.9, the DeptName of the Employee is declared NOT NULL. This requires the Employee table to contain a value for the primary key of some Department record. This enforces the total constraint by requiring that each Employee works in some Department. As a comparison, Exhibit 8.9 shows that the DeptName of Employee has not been declared NOT NULL. This means that DeptName may be null, which in turn implies that the Employee does not work in any department. In relational diagrams, the words "NOT NULL" have been added near the relationship arrow to indicate total participation.

Many-to-Many Relationships

Exhibit 8.11 illustrates a many-to-many relationship between two entity sets. A many-to-many relationship implies that any number of entities from each of two entity sets can participate in a single relationship. Many-to-many relationships occur frequently in the real world. For example, pairs of entity sets — employees and projects, students and classes, and producers and suppliers — often are related by many-to-many relationships. There are two approaches for dealing with many-to-many relationships in the conceptual schema:

- Explicit representation, as presented in entity-relationship diagrams.
- Implicit representation by two one-to-many relationships, as shown in SQL notation and relational diagrams.

Using English, a DBA can describe a many-to-many relationship either:

- Directly, by specifying the participation of each entity set within the relationship; or example, one or more employees may be assigned to one or more projects.

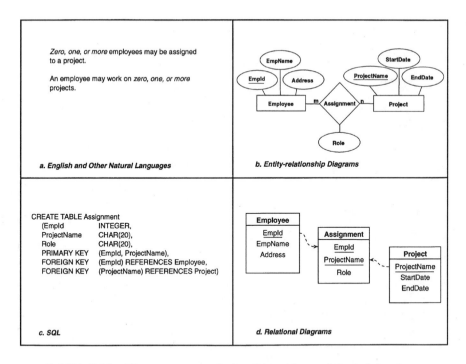

Exhibit 8.11. Many-to-many relationship with partial participation.

- Indirectly, by specifying two one-to-many relationships involving an induced entity set; for example, each employee is related to an Assignment, and each project is related to an Assignment.

In entity-relationship diagrams, an "m" or "n" is written on the sides of the diamond, which represents the many-to-many relationship. SQL always uses the indirect approach by using an induced linking table with two foreign keys.

As in one-to-many relationships, entity participation in many-to-many relationships can be partial or total. With English, the same words shown in Exhibit 8.10 can be used to specify partial or total participation in a many-to-many relationship. In entity-relationship diagrams, a thick line indicates total participation of entities with a relationship. Exhibit 8.12 presents a particular problem with SQL notation for a many-to-many relationship with total participation. SQL must use a TRIGGER command to specify the total participation constraint. Unfortunately, not all relational DBMSs support TRIGGER commands. Application developers who use these DBMSs must write applications to enforce total participation. Unfortunately, this makes applications more complex and difficult to write.

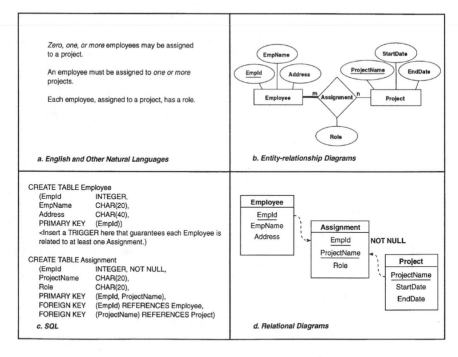

Exhibit 8.12.   Many-to-many relationship with total participation.

Weak Entities

Exhibit 8.13 presents a weak entity. A weak entity is an entity whose key values are unique among the entities participating within a single relationship, but not necessarily unique within the entire entity set. Weak entities occur when a compound attribute (an attribute containing multiple attributes) is replaced by an entity set and a relationship.

Two compound attributes — Dependent and EmpBirthDate — are illustrated in Exhibit 8.14. DBAs will seldom replace EmpBirthDate by an entity set related to Employee because BirthMonth, BirthDay, and BirthYear are not functionally dependent on one another. However, there is a functional dependency between DependentName and DependentBirthDate: given a Dependent's name, there is only one possible value for DependentBirthDate. Therefore, a DBA frequently can replace this compound attribute with a weak entity that participates in a total one-to-many relationship to Employee. (Note the similarity of this process to the process of normalization in relational database design.)

With the English CDDL in Exhibit 8.13, the DBA describes a weak entity that is related to another entity by a one-to-many dependent relationship.

88

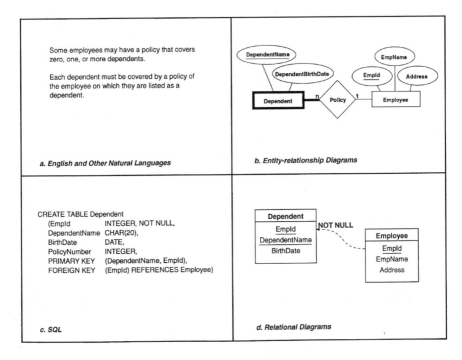

Some employees may have a policy that covers zero, one, or more dependents.

Each dependent must be covered by a policy of the employee on which they are listed as a dependent.

a. English and Other Natural Languages

b. Entity-relationship Diagrams

```
CREATE TABLE Dependent
    (EmpId              INTEGER, NOT NULL,
    DependentName   CHAR(20),
    BirthDate           DATE,
    PolicyNumber     INTEGER,
    PRIMARY KEY    (DependentName, EmpId),
    FOREIGN KEY    (EmpId) REFERENCES Employee)
```

c. SQL

d. Relational Diagrams

Exhibit 8.13.   Weak entities.

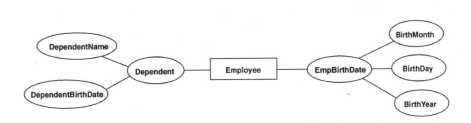

Exhibit 8.14.   Weak entity with compound attributes.

In the entity-relationship diagram, a thick line and a thick-lined rectangle denote the weak entity of the relationship. With SQL and relational diagrams, the primary key of the table corresponding to the weak entity is a combination of the key from the weak entity and the primary key from the related entity. The primary key from the related entity is also a foreign key.

Class Hierarchies

Exhibit 8.15 illustrates class hierarchy. A class hierarchy occurs when every entity in an entity set is also contained within another entity set. For

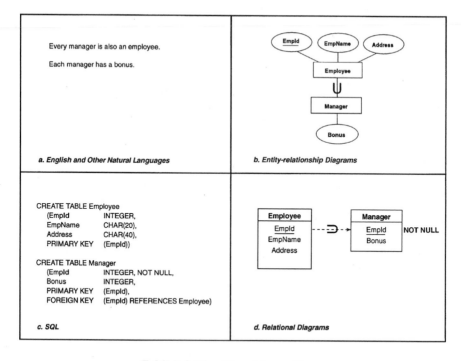

Exhibit 8.15.   Class hierarchies.

example, every Manager is also an Employee. In this example, the Manager entity has an extra attribute, Bonus, that regular employees do not possess. Class hierarchies have become popular because of their use in object-oriented modeling, so DBAs familiar with object-oriented modeling concepts have begun to use entity set hierarchies in entity-relationship diagrams. Class hierarchies are a convenient way to represent:

- Containment (every manager is also an employee).
- Common attributes (every attribute of Employee is also an attribute of Manager; in object-oriented modeling terminology, this is called inheritance).

In Exhibit 8.15, the terms "is a" or "is also a" indicate containment in the English CDDL. The terms "have" or "also have" indicate additional attributes of the contained entity set. Entity-relationship diagrams use a "contains" symbol " ." A line with a " " denotes a hierarchical relationship diagram with the " " opening toward the containing entity. In SQL and relational diagrams, two tables of a hierarchy share a common primary key, which is also a foreign key in the "contained" table.

Exhibit 8.16.   Summary of evaluation criteria for four conceptual database design languages.

	Conceptual Database Design Language			
Criteria	English	Entity-Relationship Diagrams	SQL	Relational Diagrams
Sufficiency	High	Medium	Medium	Low
Necessity	Low	Medium	High	High
Understandability and usability	Low	High	Medium	High
Consistency	Low	Medium	High	High
Software support	Low	Medium	High	Medium

Exhibit 8.15 also shows one way to represent class hierarchies using relational diagrams. The contained entity set (Manager) has a foreign key to the containing entity set (Employee) and additional attributes (Bonus) not associated with the containing entity set. In order to retrieve all attributes associated with Manager, the Manager table must be joined with the Employee table.

EVALUATION OF FOUR DESIGN LANGUAGES FOR SPECIFYING CONCEPTUAL DATABASE DESIGNS

Exhibit 8.16 summarizes various criteria used to evaluate conceptual database design languages.

Sufficiency

Sufficiency implies that the entire conceptual schema can be described using a design language. In other words, the CDDL has all of the constructs needed to completely and adequately describe the conceptual schema.

All of the CDDLs contain language to describe entity sets and their attributes, keys, foreign keys, weak entities, and class hierarchies. English rates high because it can be used to describe many constraints that cannot be described with the other conceptual database design languages. While entity-relationship diagrams cannot represent every possible rule, they can be used to specify many popular business rules. Entity-relationship diagrams are ranked medium. The SQL CREATE command must be augmented with TRIGGER commands to completely specify total participation of entity set within a many-to-many relationship. TRIGGER commands also enable DBAs to specify other business rules for which there is no corresponding notation in the entity-relationship and relational diagrams. Thus, SQL is ranked as medium. Relational diagrams do not have notation for TRIGGER commands, so they are given a low ranking.

Necessity

Necessity is defined to mean that each clause or concept of the design language is required to describe some conceptual schema.

Much of the syntax of English — and other natural languages — is not required to describe a conceptual schema. Therefore, it receives a low rating. Some DBAs feel that the entity-relationship diagrams contain too many concepts. Specifically, many-to-many relationships involving entity sets A and B can be replaced with a new, linking entity set related to each of A and B. Some DBAs argue that a one-to-many relationship set is itself unnecessary because it can be replaced by a foreign key constraint, as it is in SQL and relational diagrams. Likewise, the special hierarchical containment relationship can be replaced with a foreign key constraint. For this reason, entity-relationship diagrams are rated as medium. SQL and relational diagrams are rated high because of the small number of constructs, tables, keys, and foreign keys necessary to describe a realistic conceptual schema. None of these constructs can be removed from the conceptual database design language and still completely specify a conceptual schema.

Understandability and Usability

Understandability and usability mean that the conceptual schema is easy to learn, easy to understand, and easy to specify.

At first glance, English — or some other natural language — would appear to be easy because no training is necessary to use it. However, natural language sentences frequently can be vague and imprecise. Because of the ambiguity and misunderstandings inherent in English and other natural languages, English has a low rating. The understandability of SQL is rated as medium because users must carefully study the SQL descriptions in order to visualize the conceptual model it describes. Entity-relationship diagrams and relational diagrams receive a high rating because it is possible to comprehend the significant aspects of a conceptual schema by quickly examining the diagrams. Once again, the saying, "a picture" — or more appropriately in this context, a diagram — "is worth a thousand words," holds true. Some DBAs rate the understandability of entity-relationship diagrams above relational diagrams because the relationships reflect more of the diverse structures of the conceptual schema than does the table-orientation of relational diagrams. On the other hand, the structure of relational diagrams is familiar to relational DBMS users who may become confused when dealing with the relationships of the entity-relationship CDDL.

Consistency

Consistency means that two DBAs will use the same constructs to describe similar concepts. English receives a low rating because there may be nearly an infinite number of ways to describe each and every business rule. Entity-relationship diagrams are rated as medium because it is possible to describe many-to-many relationships as two one-to-many relationships. It is also possible to describe an attribute of an entity set A as a weak entity set that is related to A. SQL and relational diagrams are the most consistent because they describe just a single type of thing — a table. Therefore, SQL and relational diagrams receive a high rating.

Note that there might be more than one way to represent a collection of attributes as tables. For example, a single table may contain all of the attributes or multiple tables each may contain some of the attributes. DBAs frequently use the process of normalization to break apart a table that represents multiple entity sets and structure the attributes into multiple tables. Normalization occurs regardless of which CDDL is used. The concept of normalization is orthogonal to the concept of consistency discussed here. DBAs should perform normalization, regardless of which CDDL is used.

Software Support

Software support implies that software exists to enable DBAs to enter a conceptual schema into the DBMS. Check the conceptual schema for missing or redundant expressions, and automatically create a conceptual schema for a relational DBMS.

While text editors exist for entering text describing a conceptual schema using English or some other natural language, it is not possible for a text editor to check for missing or redundant descriptions. Nor is it possible to automatically generate a relational conceptual schema from a conceptual schema expressed in English. Therefore, English is rated low. SQL editors and compilers enable DBAs to enter and check the completeness and redundancy of conceptual schemas and to create a relational schema for use by a relational DBMS. SQL receives a high rating. Graphic editors enable DBAs to draw entity-relationship diagrams and relational diagrams. Some specialized graphic editors may even be able to check for missing or redundant objects. Because these editors are not available for all relational DBMSs, entity-relationship and relational diagrams are given a medium rating.

Many vendors of relational DBMSs also supply graphical editors to compose entity-relationship and relational diagrams that automatically convert the diagrams into SQL before being processed by a DBMS. These include:

- 4Keeps: A.D.Experts; Ann Arbor, MI; www.adexperts.com
- DataModeler: Iconix Software Engineering, Inc.; Santa Monica, CA; www.iconixsw.com
- EasyCASE, Database Engineer, and EasyEr: Visible Systems Corp.; Bellevue, WA; www.visible.com

- ER/Studio: Embarcadero Technologies, Inc.; San Francisco, CA; www.embarcadero.com
- ERWin: Logic Works Inc.; Princeton, NJ; www.logicworks.com
- SilverRun Professional: SilverRun Technologies, Inc.; Woodcliff Lake, NJ; www.silverrun.com

One more step is necessary to create a working database. The DBA must create a physical schema to describe the data structures and access paths that the DBMS will use to access a database. (When purchasing schema design software, it is important to select product offerings that also enable DBAs to specify the physical schema.)

RECOMMENDATION

Entity-relationship diagrams should be used to define conceptual schemas. These diagrams directly represent many-to-many relationships, weak entities, and class hierarchies. While the relational database equivalent of these constraints can be represented using SQL or relational diagrams, the understanding inherent in these structures is lost when they are converted to their relational counterparts.

It is best to use a tool, such as a graphic editor, to capture entity-relationship diagrams and to generate the equivalent SQL notation. This enables the DBA to easily update the entity-relationship diagrams and automatically generate the appropriate SQL to keep both the diagrams and the implemented schema synchronized.

If the entity-relationship design language is not suitable for the enterprise, then relational diagrams, followed by SQL, are recommended. English and other natural languages are not recommended because of their inherent vagueness and inconsistency.

Notes

The following sources are recommended.

Bachman, C. The Data Structure Set Model, *Proceedings of the ACM SIGMOD Debate on Data Models: Data Structure Set Versus Relational,* 1974. Edited by R. Rustin. Bachman diagrams were widely used to define schemas for hierarchical DBMSs.

Chen, P. The Entity-relationship Model: Towards a Unified View of Data, in *ACM Transactions on Database Systems,* 1(1), 9–36, 1976. The classic paper on conceptual database design languages that introduced entity-relationship diagrams.

Ramakrishnan, R. *Database Management Systems,* New York: WCB/McGraw-Hill, 1998. Chapter 14 provides an excellent tutorial of the entity-relationship conceptual database design specification language and how to map its constraints to SQL.

For a description of the Universal Modeling Language (UML), see: http://www.pfu.edu.ru/Tele-Sys/Calypso/Docs/Uml/html/ot/uml/technical_papers/index.html.

Chapter 9
Physical Database Design
James A. Larson and Carol L. Larson

CREATING A PHYSICAL DATABASE DESIGN CAN BE A COMPLEX AND DIFFI-
CULT TASK. This article presents a four-phase methodology for selecting
primary search keys and the corresponding files structure for each table,
determining how to support join operations, selecting secondary search
keys and appropriate supporting access methods, and identifying and supporting composite search keys and structures. The database administrator
(DBA) may need to fine-tune the physical database design as DBMS usage
requirements change.

STAGES OF A DATABASE LIFE CYCLE

Exhibit 9.1 illustrates the life cycle of a database that consists of several
stages leading to database usage. While Exhibit 9.1 presents each stage as
desecrate, in reality, DBAs frequently revisit and revise decisions made in
earlier stages as they proceed with later ones. Briefly, the individual stages
are:

- **Conceptual schema design.** The DBA interviews prospective users
  and considers the proposed database applications to create a conceptual schema design. The conceptual schema describes the entities
  and their relationships that will be represented in the database.
- **Relational schema design.** If the DBA designs the conceptual schema
  using notation other than the relational data model, then this stage is
  necessary to convert the objects and relationships of the conceptual
  schema into the notation and format required by a relational DBMS.
- **Schema refinement.** The DBA examines business rules describing the
  constraints on the data values in the database. The DBA structures the
  relational tables in such a manner that updating the tables will not result in update anomalies. However, if the database is never modified —
  as with data warehouses — or is seldom updated, then this stage can
  be skipped.

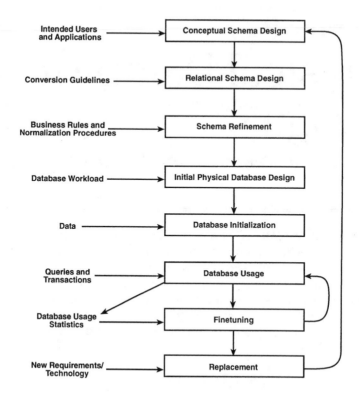

Exhibit 9.1. Life cycle of a database.

- **Initial physical database design.** The DBA examines the proposed database workload and determines how to physically represent each table in the database. The DBA also determines if extra indexes will be useful to make the DBMS more efficient as it processes the queries and transactions in the workload.
- **Database initialization.** The DBA uses utility programs to capture, reformat, and load data into the database.
- **Database usage.** Users submit queries and transactions to the database to obtain data needed to perform the users' every-day work functions.
- **Database fine-tuning.** As new uses for the database emerge, the workload will change. To optimize the execution of the DBMS with respect to the new workload, the database administrator should modify the initial physical database design by creating new tables, deleting existing indexes, creating new indexes, and modifying views.
- **Replacement.** There comes a time when the DBMS is not able to support new requirements of the enterprise in which it is used. New technology may enable new DBMSs to better serve the enterprise. When

the benefits of the new DBMS outweigh the costs of converting the old database to the new DBMS, the old DBMS is replaced and the database life cycle begins again.

INITIAL PHYSICAL DATABASE DESIGN METHODOLOGY

Creating the initial physical database design is an important stage in the database life cycle. The DBA determines the physical data structures for representing data so that the DBMS efficiently processes queries and transactions in the workload. The basic methodology for creating the initial physical database design consists of four phases:

1. For each table in the relational schema, determine the primary search key, determine the appropriate file structure, and choose the primary access method for accessing that file.
2. For frequently joined tables, determine how to support the join operation.
3. For each file, identify additional search keys and determine the appropriate physical structures for supporting them.
4. For each file, identify multi-attribute search keys and determine the appropriate physical structures for supporting them.

To illustrate each phase of the initial physical database design process, a simple relational database — which consists of two tables, Employee and Department — will be used. Exhibit 9.2 illustrates the relational schema for these two tables. The Employee table has four columns with the EmpId column as the primary key. The Department table has two columns with Dept-Name as the primary key. In addition, assume that the example workload consists of the six representative queries presented in Exhibit 9.3. A

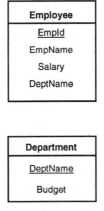

Exhibit 9.2. Example of a relational schema.

Exhibit 9.3.   Seven important queries and their relative frequency of execution.

Query Number	SQL Query	Relative Frequency of Query Execution
1	Select * from Department where DeptName = "Accounting"	25 percent
2	Select * from Department where DeptName = "Sales" or DeptName = "Production"	5 percent
3	Select * from Employee, Department where Budget = 200,000 and Employee.DeptName = Department.DeptName	15 percent
4	Select * from Department where Budget = 500,000	5 percent
5	Select * from Department where 100,000 < Budget and Budget < 500,000	15 percent
6	Select * from Employee where EmpName = "Jones"	20 percent
7	Update Employee	15 percent

representative query is a query that is representative of homogeneous class of queries. For example, Query 6 is representative of queries in the form:

```
Select <attribute list> from Employee where EmpName =
    <some name>
```

Also assume that while updates to the Employee table are 15 percent of the workload, updates to the Department table are not significant because they seldom occur.

With the relational schema and the anticipated workload in place, the DBA is ready to begin performing the four phases in the initial physical database design process.

Phase 1: Determine File Structures

Most DBMSs support three basic file structures: heap files, sorted files, and hashed files. Each of these structures organize multiple data pages. A data page is a unit of data that is transferred between disks and main memory and usually contains several database records. DBAs design physical databases so the number of data pages being transferred is minimized for frequently performed queries.

Two of the three basic file structures involve a search key. A search key is one or more columns of a table that are frequently used to access records of the file. Often, but not always, the most frequently used search key is the primary key of the table. DBAs design physical databases to efficiently access database tables using search keys. Some tables have multiple search keys. The most important search key is called the primary search key. The remaining search keys of a table are called secondary search keys.

It is important that the DBA understands the basic mechanisms of the three widely used file structures, as well as their strengths and weaknesses, so the database being designed will fit the needs of the users.

Heap Files. A heap file maintains an unsorted list of records in a file. Two popular approaches for implementing the Employee table as a heap file are illustrated in Exhibit 9.4. Heap files are implemented using a doubly linked list of data pages, each containing one or more records. For simplicity purposes, only the value of the EmpName search key is shown for each record. A new record can be inserted into any data page that has room to store the record, or a new data page can be inserted into the doubly linked list with the new record stored in the data page.

Alternatively, a directory contains pointers to every data page. A new record is inserted into any data page that has room to store the record, or a pointer to a new data page can be inserted into the directory with the new record stored in the new data page.

Heap files are efficient when every record in a file must be accessed. However, they are not efficient when retrieving a record with a specific value for the search key or retrieving records within a specific range of values for the search key. This inefficiency occurs because files must be scanned

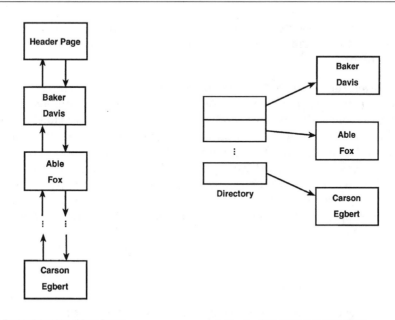

a. Doubly-linked List of Data Pages   b. Directory With Pointers to Data Pages

Exhibit 9.4.   Alternative heap file organizations.

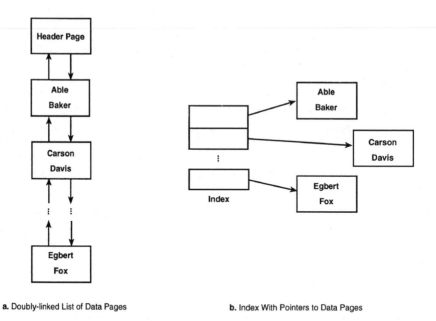

a. Doubly-linked List of Data Pages

b. Index With Pointers to Data Pages

Exhibit 9.5. Alternative sorted file organizations.

---

sequentially to locate any specific value or specific range of values. On the average, half of the records in a heap file must be accessed to locate a specific record.

Sorted Files. A sorted file maintains a list of records sorted by the values of the primary search key. The two approaches for implementing the Employee table with primary search key EmpName as a sorted file are presented in Exhibit 9.5. Again, for simplicity, only the value of the EmpName search key is shown for each record. When using the doubly linked list of data pages, a new record must be inserted into the appropriate data page so the sorted order of records is maintained. Alternatively, an index may contain pointers to every data page. Again, a new record is inserted into the appropriate data page so the sorted order of records is maintained. If there is no space for a new record in the existing data page, a new data page is created and linked into the appropriate position within the doubly linked list.

Sorted files are efficient when:

1. Records need to be accessed in the sequence of the search key. For example, if the Employee file is sorted by EmpName, then the sorted file would be efficient for the representative Query 6.

2. Records need to be accessed within a prescribed range of values of the search key. For example, if the Department file is sorted by Budget, then the sorted file would be efficient for Query 5. The DBMS would locate the first record with a value for Budget less than 100,000, then retrieve records sequentially from the sorted file until it encounters a record with a value for Budget equal to 500,000.

The DBA can use alternative tree structures to organize a sorted file. The Indexed Sequential Access Method (ISAM) was used for many years as a tree index structure, but has been replaced by the more popular B-tree and its variation, B+ tree. B+ trees are used because they are dynamically self-organizing. All searches of the B+ tree access the same number of internal branch points, even if the number of records in the indexed file grow. Exhibit 6a illustrates a B+ tree before an insertion, which results in the reorganized tree shown in Exhibit 6b. In the reorganized tree, the overall tree depth is increased with every leaf of the B+ tree guaranteed to be the same distance from the root of the tree.

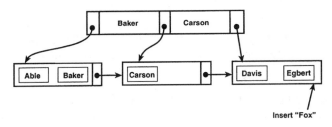

a. B+ Tree Before Inserting a Record for "Fox"

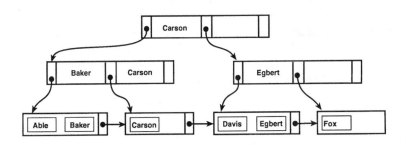

b. Reorganized B+ Tree After Inserting a Record for "Fox"

Exhibit 9.6.   B+ tree.

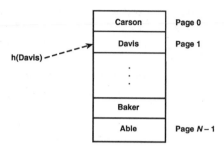

Exhibit 9.7.   Hashed file.

Hashed File. A hashed file enables access to any record given the value of its search key. In Exhibit 9.7, there are N pages in which data records can be stored. By performing a transformation — often called a hashing function — on the value of the search key, a page number is generated where the page number is in the range $[0, N-1]$. When the user inserts a record, it is stored in the page with the generated page number. When the user retrieves a record, the records stored in the page with the generated page number are retrieved.

Hashed files are efficient when retrieving records that match the selection criteria exactly. For example, consider the SQL request:

```
Select * from Department where DeptName = "Accounting"
```

Applying the hashing function to the value for "Accounting" would generate the page number for the data page containing the record for the department with DeptName = "Accounting," which would be retrieved quickly. Unfortunately, hashed files do not lend themselves to range searches, such as Query 5.

Choosing Primary Search Keys and File Structures. While a table may have multiple search keys, the primary search key is used to determine the file structure for the table. To choose a file structure for each table in a relational database, the DBA performs the following calculations: For each table in the relational database, examine the workload for queries and transactions that access the table. Let:

- HEAP be the sum of the weights associated with queries and transactions that scan the entire table.

For each potential search key, let:

- SORTED be the sum of the weights associated with queries and transactions that access the table in sequence by the search key or involve a range query involving the search key.

- HASHED be the sum of the weights associated with queries and transactions that access the table by matching values with the search key.

For each table, choose the search key with the largest value for HEAP, SORTED, or HASHED. This search key is the primary search key. Then choose the corresponding file structure to represent that table in the database.

For example, examining the queries presented in Exhibit 9.3, two search keys (DeptName and Budget) exist for the Department table and two search keys (EmpName and DeptName) exist for the Employee table. Exhibit 9.8 presents an additional analysis of Exhibit 9.3.

Exhibit 9.8.   Relational tables and search key analysis.

Table	Search Key	Use	Queries	Weight
Department	DeptName	Equality match	1, 2, 3	45
Department	Budget	Equality	3, 4	20
Department	Budget	Range	5	15
Employee	DeptName	Equality match	3	15
Employee	EmpName	Equality match	6	20

In the Department table, the DeptName search key is used more frequently than the Budget search key. The DBA chooses DeptName to be the primary search key for the Department table. Because the DeptName search key is always used for equality matches, the DBA selects a hashed file structure to represent the Department table.

In the Employee table, the EmpName search key is used more frequently than the DeptName search key. The DBA chooses EmpName to be the primary search key for the Employee table. Because EmpName is always used for equality matches, the DBA selects a hashed file structure to represent the Employee table.

Phase 2: Facilitate Frequent Joins of Two Tables

Joining of two tables is a potentially expensive operation that matches records from two tables with identical values for corresponding columns. In order to improve the efficiency of frequently executed joins, the DBA may elect to perform any of the three following tasks.

1. Denormalize the tables to be joined.
2. Build a hierarchical structure to facilitate the join.
3. Build an index to facilitate the join.

Denormalization. During the schema refinement stage in the database life cycle, the DBA examines the database tables to determine if they should be vertically partitioned into two or more tables to avoid update anomalies. This process, called normalization, can result in multiple tables replacing a single table. If two tables are frequently joined in the workload, the DBA might decide to denormalize them. Denormalization is the process of replacing multiple tables with a single table in the relational schema. During the initial physical database design stage, the DBA reexamines the decision to normalize and weighs the benefits of normalization, which avoids update anomalies, against the cost of performing frequent joins among the normalized tables.

As a general rule, if users always access two tables together, the tables should be denormalized by joining them into a single table. For example, suppose a DBA decides that a zip code functionally determines the city and state: given a value of zip code, there is one and only one possible value for city and one and only one possible value for state. In the schema refinement stage, the DBA normalizes the address table into two tables: one table containing the street address and zip code, and the second table containing the city, state, and zip code. However, the user always accesses the street address, city, state, and zip code at the same time. There should never be a record in the table containing the street address and zip code without a corresponding record in the table containing the street address, city, state, and zip code. In this case, the DBA should denormalize the two tables during step 2 of the initial physical database design phase.

Hierarchical Files. Table A is dependent on table B if table A is accessed only when table B is accessed. For example, suppose there is a third table, EmpDependent, that contains information about an employee's dependents. The EmpDependent table is dependent on the Employee table because no query ever accesses the EmpDependent table without also accessing the Employee table. Note that some employees may have no dependents, while others may have multiple dependents. The DBA determines that the Employee and EmpDependent tables should not be denormalized because there are many queries that access the Employee table without accessing the EmpDependent table.

Dependent tables are candidates for representation by hierarchical file structures. Exhibit 9.9 illustrates a hierarchical file structure that facilitates the joining of the Employee and EmpDependent tables. Each Employee record contains pointers to the records of dependents supported by the employee. The DBMS joins the Employee and EmpDependent records by accessing the Employee records one at a time. For each Employee record, the DBMS follows the pointers to retrieve the records of the employee's dependents. This results in an efficient join operation.

Indexes for Joins. Query 3 joins the Employee and Department tables and should be executed according to the following steps.

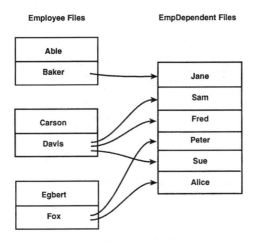

Exhibit 9.9. Hierarchical files.

1. Select the rows of the Department table where Budget = 200,000
2. Select the rows of the Employee table for which the value of Dept-Name matches the value of DeptName in one of the rows selected in step 1.

Step 2 executes faster if DeptName is a secondary search key of the Employee table.

Phase 3: Identify and Implement Secondary Search Keys

Secondary search keys are useful in two general situations:

1. Frequently executed queries involve conditions in which a column of a table matches a specific value and the column is not part of the primary search key. For example, in Query 3, Budget is a secondary search key for the Department table.
2. Frequently executed queries require that tables be joined on columns that are not part of the primary search key. In this case, Dept-Name in Query 3 is the secondary search key in the Employee table.

Either hashed indexes or tree indexes can be used to support secondary search keys. (Technically, hashing is not an index structure. But because it is used to provide fast access to individual records given a value of a search key, hashing is often used instead of a tree index.)

Hashed Index. A hashed index works basically the same way as a hashed file. A hashing function is applied to the value of the search key to calculate the number of the data page for the search key value. As illustrated in

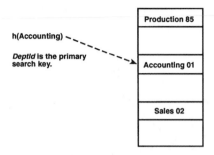

a. *DeptName* is the Primary Search Key Used for a Hashed File

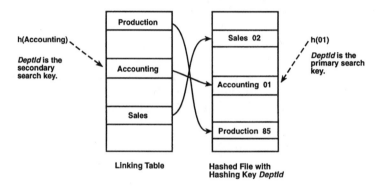

b. *DeptName* Search Key is Different from the Hashing Key of a Hashed File, which Requires a Linking Table

Exhibit 9.10.   Hashing search keys.

Exhibit 9.10a, if the search key is the same as the primary search key used for a hashed file, then no additional structure is needed. However, if the search key is different from the primary search key used for the hashed file as shown in Exhibit 9.10b, then a linking table is needed to relate the address calculated by the hashing function and the actual data page used by the underlying hashed file. Exhibits 9.10c and 9.10d show that a linking table is needed to relate the address calculated by the hashing function with the actual data page used by the underlying sorted or heap file.

Tree Index. Rather than using a function to calculate the data page address, a tree index can be used to map a value of a search key to a data page. The tree index does not require a linking table if the search key is the primary search key used to order the file. However, a linking table is

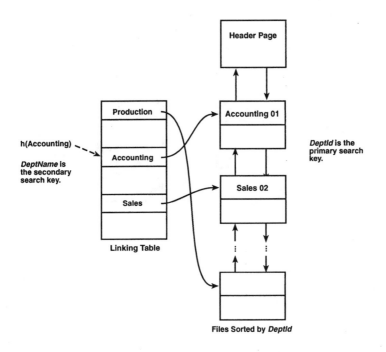

c. *DeptName* Search Key and a File Sorted by *DeptId* Require a Linking Table

Exhibit 9.10.   Hashing search keys (*continued*).

---

required if the file is a heap or hashed file, or if the secondary search key is different from the primary search key used to sort the file.

Hashed or Tree Index. The choice between using a hashed or tree index is determined by the number of matching requests as compared to the number of range requests. For example, consider Queries 4 and 5 from the workload in Exhibit 9.3:

- Query 4: Select * from Department where Budget = 500,000
- Query 5: Select * from Department where 100,000 < Budget and Budget < 500,000

Query 4 is an equality match on the Budget, while Query 5 is a range query over DeptName. The DBA should create an index on Budget to support the secondary search key Budget. Because Query 5 is executed more frequently than Query 4, the DBA should create a B+ tree rather than a hashed index to support the secondary search key DeptName because hashed indexes do not support range queries. A linking table will be needed because there already is an index file structure for Department.

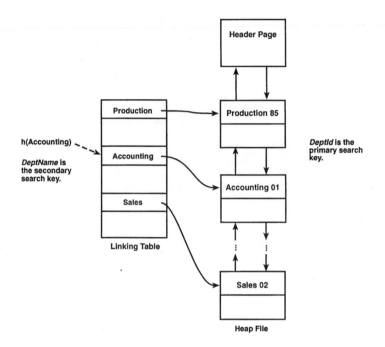

d. *DeptName* Search Key and a Heap File Require a Linking Table

Exhibit 9.10.   Hashing search keys (*continued*).

Phase 4: Build Composite Indexes

A composite index is an index built on a composite search key containing more than one field. Composite search keys can be useful if queries, such as the following, are executed frequently:

```
Select * from Project where 8/9/98 < StartDate and
     EndDate < 9/9/99
```

The DBA creates a composite tree index <StartDate, EndDate>. Then, the DBMS can use the index to locate addresses of records by examining one index structure. Exhibit 9.11 presents a composite index. The DBMS uses the composite index to locate projects quickly with 8/9/98 < StartDate and EndDate < 9/9/99.

An alternative approach is to create tree indexes on both the StartDate and EndDate. The DBMS can:

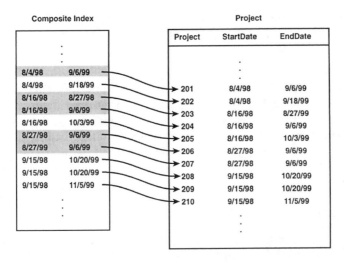

Exhibit 9.11. Composite index with highlighted data that satisfies the Condition 8/9/98 < StartDate and EndDate < 9/9/99

- use the StartDate index to create the set of addresses that satisfy 8/9/98 < StartDate
- use the EndDate index to create the set of addresses that satisfy End-Date < 9/9/99
- sort both sets and then identify addresses contained in both sorted sets
- finally, retrieve the records that satisfy both criteria

DATABASE FINE-TUNING

Physical database design is never complete as long as the database is in use. After the initial physical database design is complete, the DBA loads the database and users begin to access the data. When using a new DBMS, users will discover new methods of using data to facilitate their work tasks in ways the DBA did not anticipate. The DBA may find it necessary to modify the physical database design. In order to keep the DBMS working at near-optimal performance, the DBA needs to add and remove search keys, change index structures, and evolve the database. The DBA should monitor the DBMS activity to detect inefficiencies and take corrective action by modifying the physical data structures to reflect the new and unanticipated uses.

In many enterprises, DBMSs are accessed differently during different phases of their business cycle. For example, the DBMS maintaining student registration and grade information is accessed quite differently at the beginning of a term, in the middle of a term, and at the end of a term. The DBA should anticipate the changes in access during different processing phases and may adjust physical access structures accordingly.

Most major DBMS vendors provide a variety of performance-monitoring tools to assist the DBA in understanding how the DBMS is being used. Some of these tools and utilities are able to suggest changes to the physical database design and, with approval from the DBA, automatically implement those changes. However, the self-organizing DBMS is still in the distant future. Until then, the DBA will play a critical role in providing high performance for modern DBMSs.

CONCLUSION

In order to develop a good initial physical database design, the DBA must understand the anticipated workload of the DBMS, which includes the relative frequencies of queries and updates, as well as the properties of the various access methods and index structures available within the DBMS.

The DBA can use the four-phase procedure outlined in this article for designing an initial physical database. However, the method should be modified and extended appropriately to include any special data structures supported by the DBMS being used by the enterprise.

However, the DBA still is not finished after completing the initial physical database design. The DBA should monitor DBMS activity and modify the physical design when new queries and transactions adversely affect the DBMS performance.

Notes

Elmasri, R. and Navathe, S. *Fundamentals of Database Systems,* 2nd ed., Reading, MA: Addison-Wesley, 1994. Contains chapters on record storage and primary file organizations, index structures for files, and a short section on physical database design guidelines.

Ramakrishnan, R. *Database Management Systems,* New York: WCB/McGraw-Hill, 1998. Contains chapters on files, file organizations and indexes, tree-structured indexing, hash-based indexing, and physical database design and tuning.

Chapter 10

Enabling Consumer Access to Business Databases

James A. Larson and Carol L. Larson

MANY BUSINESSES DEPEND ON THE AVAILABILITY OF DATABASE INFORMA-
TION FOR CURRENT AND POTENTIAL CLIENTS. Airlines want current and
potential customers to access flight departure and arrival schedules.
Stockbrokers want clients to access stock quotes. Automobile dealers
want prospective buyers to access descriptions of new and used cars in
their inventory. Entertainment businesses want the public to access information about events and tickets. Other examples of database information
needed by consumers include customer account information, package delivery information, service call/time arrival information, college class
schedule information, and project schedule information.

Traditionally, consumers traveled to stores, markets, or other places of
business to obtain information about goods and to transact business.
Sometimes businesses approach consumers in the form of door-to-door
salesmen or telemarketing calls. In today's age of electronic communication, businesses and consumers can connect electronically to exchange information and save money.

To illustrate how new technologies deliver information to customers,
Exhibit 10.1 presents the Ajax Theaters movie schedule database, which
will be the basis for all examples in this article. This article describes and
evaluates four technologies that automate the delivery of information: interactive voice response (IVR) systems, conversational voice systems, database Web publication systems, and Internet agent-based systems.

INTERACTIVE VOICE RESPONSE SYSTEMS

Interactive voice response systems are widely used by customers to access an enterprise's data. An IVR system presents verbal menus to

0-8493-9832-0/00/$0.00+$.50
© 2000 by CRC Press LLC

Exhibit 10.1.   The Ajax Theaters database.

Theater	Title	First Show	Second Show	Third Show	Fourth Show
Central	Star Wars	2:00 p.m.	4:00 p.m.	6:30 p.m.	9:30 p.m.
Roxy	Star Wars	1:00 p.m.	3:45 p.m.	6:15 p.m.	9:15 p.m.
Roxy	Forest Gump	1:15 p.m.	4:15 p.m.	7:00 p.m.	9:30 p.m.
Roxy	Forest Gump	1:30 p.m.	4:30 p.m.	7:15 p.m.	9:45 p.m.
Grand	Star Wars	1:30 p.m.	4:00 p.m.	6:00 p.m.	9:00 p.m.
Grand	Indiana Jones	1:45 p.m.	4:30 p.m.	6:45 p.m.	9:15 p.m.
Grand	Gone With the Wind	11:15 a.m.	3:30 p.m.	7:45 p.m.	

consumers who, in turn, respond by pressing the buttons on their touch-tone telephones. For example, a consumer dials the Ajax Theaters database telephone number and is automatically connected to the IVR system. A prerecorded human voice presents menus to the consumer, such as "For the Central Theater, press 1; for the Roxy Theater, press 2; for the Grand Theater, press 3." The consumer might respond by pressing button 3 on the telephone keypad to select the Grand Theater.

Exhibit 10.2 illustrates the major components of an IVR system accessing a database. The dialog manager is responsible for generating menus presented to the consumer by the IVR software. The IVR system uses either prerecorded voice files or generates a synthesized voice from text using a text-to-speech (TTS) engine. The IVR software listens for the touchtones and converts the tones to digits, which are returned to the dialog manager. The dialog manager creates an SQL request and sends it to a relational database management system (DBMS). Based on the data returned from the DBMS, the dialogue manager generates the next set of menu options for presentation to the consumer. Exhibit 10.3 shows an example of a dialog between the IVR system and the consumer.

IVR systems require users to listen to menus and remember which telephone button to press. Because users generally dislike listening to verbal menu items and their corresponding buttons, some may memorize the menus to speed the process. This problem is overcome by conversational voice systems.

CONVERSATIONAL VOICE SYSTEMS

Some businesses are upgrading their IVR systems to conversational voice systems, where users respond by voice rather than by pressing the buttons on their touchtone telephone. With conversational voice systems, the consumer speaks the desired option without having to listen to the long list of menu options.

Exhibit 10.4 illustrates the major modules in a conversational voice system. The touchtone recognition engine in Exhibit 10.2 is replaced by an

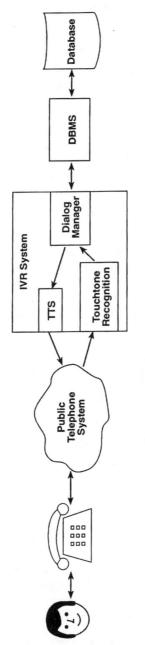

Exhibit 10.2. IVR system.

DATA MODELS AND MODELING TECHNIQUES

Exhibit 10.3.   Dialog between IVR system and consumer.

Dialog Manager to TTS:
> Present the message "Welcome to the AJAX Theaters. By pressing the touchtone keys on your telephone keypad, you can hear the movie titles playing at the theater of your choice. For the movies at the Central Theater, press 1; for the movies at the Roxy Theater, press 2; for the movies at the Grand Theater, press 3."

Consumer to touch recognition module:
> Press touchtone button 3

Dialog manager to DBMS:
> Select Title from AjaxTheaters where Theater = "Grand"

DBMS to dialog manager:
> **Title**
> Star Wars
> Indiana Jones
> Gone With the Wind

Dialog manager to TTS:
> Present the message, "For the show times of *Star Wars*, press 1; for the show times of *Indiana Jones*, press 2; for the show times of *Gone With the Wind*, press 3."

Consumer to touchtone recognition module:
> Press touchtone button 3

Dialog manager to DBMS:
> Select FirstShow, SecondShow, ThirdShow, FourthShow from AjaxTheaters where Theater = "Grand" and Title = "Gone With the Wind"

DBMS to dialog manager:

Title	First Show	Second Show	Third Show	Fourth Show
Gone With the Wind	11:15 a.m.	3:30 p.m.	7:45 p.m.	

Dialog manager to TTS:
> Present the message: "The show times for *Gone With the Wind* at the Grand Theater are at 11:15 a.m., 3:30 p.m., and 7:45 p.m."

automatic speech recognition (ASR) engine. As with the IVR systems, the consumer telephones the business and is connected automatically to the conversational voice system. Either a prerecorded human voice or a synthesized voice asks the consumer questions, to which the consumer responds with a word or phrase. For example, a conversational voice dialogue might proceed as described by the dialogue shown in Exhibit 10.5.

With conversational voice systems, consumers can say the option name without having to listen to the entire menu. Users may even say the answer

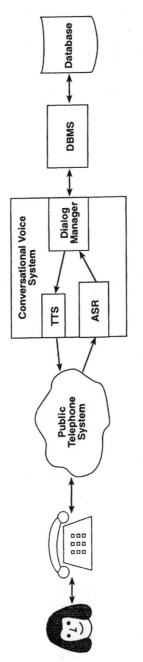

Exhibit 10.4. Conversational voice system.

Exhibit 10.5.   Conversational dialog.

Dialog manager to the TTS:

Present the message "Welcome to the AJAX Theaters. For which theater do you want information? The Central Theater, Roxy Theater, or Grand Theater?"

Consumer to the ASR:
"Grand" (The consumer can say "Grand" at anytime during or after the audio message from the conversational voice software.)

Dialog manager to DBMS:
Select Title from AjaxTheaters where Theater = "Grand"

DBMS to dialog manager:
Title
Star Wars
Indiana Jones
Gone With the Wind

Dialog manager to TTS:
Present the message "For which movie would you like show times — *Star Wars, Indiana Jones,* or *Gone With the Wind?*"

Consumer to the ASR:
"Gone With the Wind" (Again, the user can say the name of the movie at anytime during or after hearing the conversational voice system message. The user is not forced to listen to the menu options to determine which touchtone button to press.)

Dialog manager to DBMS:
Select FirstShow, SecondShow, ThirdShow, FourthShow from AjaxTheaters where Theater = "Grand" and Title = "Gone With the Wind"

DBMS to dialog manager:

Title	First Show	Second Show	Third Show	Fourth Show
Gone With the Wind	11:15 a.m.	3:30 p.m.	7:45 p.m.	

Dialog manager to TTS:
Present the message: "The show times for *Gone With the Wind* at the Grand Theater are at 11:15 a.m., 3:30 p.m., and 7:45 p.m."

before listening to the first menu item. This enables consumers to complete the conversation faster than with IVR systems.

DATABASE WEB PUBLICATION SYSTEMS

Rather than use a telephone that has no display, a consumer can use a computer to access a business Web site. The consumer types in or

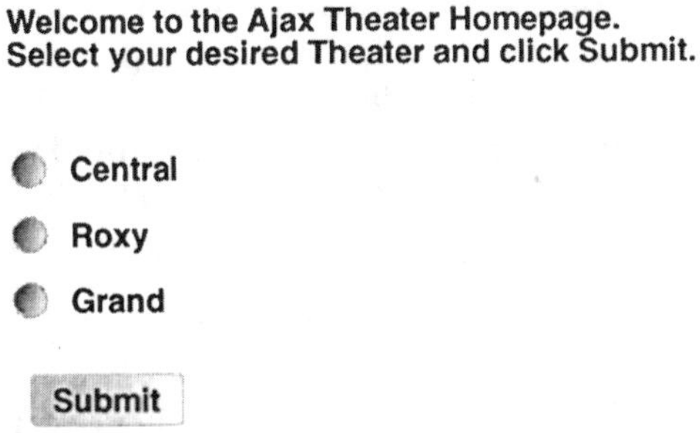

Welcome to the Ajax Theater Homepage.
Select your desired Theater and click Submit.

○ **Central**

○ **Roxy**

○ **Grand**

Submit

Exhibit 10.6.   Home Web page for the Ajax Theaters.

navigates to the URL address of the business. A Web page menu appears on the computer screen, from which the consumer selects an option by clicking a mouse. For example, a Web page for the Ajax Theaters is illustrated in Exhibit 10.6.

If the consumer selects the Grand Theater and clicks the SUBMIT button, then the Web page illustrated in Exhibit 10.7 is displayed.

Because of its visual nature, larger amounts of information can be presented to the consumer with the Web publication system faster than with the voice-oriented IVR and conversational voice systems; thus, time-consuming voice menus and verbal responses are avoided. Web pages also can present video and sound clips (sometimes called trailers) of currently playing movies. Consumers view a trailer by clicking on the movie title.

Before creating a Web page, the database administrator (DBA) determines whether the page should be static or dynamic. The information on a static page does not change when data in the database is modified, while information the consumer sees on a dynamic page reflects all updates applied to the database.

Welcome to the Grand Theater.
The movies currently showing are:

Title	First Show	Second Show	Third Show	Fourth Show
Star Wars	1:30 P.M.	4:00 P.M.	6:00 P.M.	9:00 P.M.
Indiana Jones	1:45 P.M.	4:30 P.M.	6:45 P.M.	9:15 P.M.
Gone With the Wind	11:15 A.M.	3:30 P.M.	7:45 P.M.	

Exhibit 10.7.   Web page for the Grand Theater.

Static Publication of Database Information. The DBA performs SQL commands to extract data from the database to be placed on the Web page. Next, the DBA inserts the appropriate HTML codes, which specify how to present the information to the user. For example, the HTML code for the information shown in Exhibit 10.7 is shown in Exhibit 10.8. The DBA can write the HTML codes manually; however, this tedious and time-consuming task can be automated.

Exhibit 10.8.   HTML code for Exhibit 10.5.

```
<html>

<body bgcolor="#FFFFFF">

<p>Welcome to the Grand Theater.<br>
The movies currently showing are:</p>
<p></p>

<table border="2">
        <tr>
                <td><strong>Title</strong></td>
                <td><strong>First Show</strong></td>
                <td><strong>Second Show</strong></td>
                <td><strong>Third Show</strong></td>
                <td><strong>Fourth Show</strong></td>
        </tr>
        <tr>
                <td><A HREF=StarWars><i>Star Wars</i></A></td>
                <td>1:30 P.M.</td>
                <td>4:00 P.M.</td>
                <td>6:00 P.M.</td>
                <td>9:00 P.M.</td>
        </tr>
        <tr>
                <td><A HREF=IndianaJones><i>Indiana Jones</i></A></td>
                <td>1:45 P.M.</td>
                <td>4:30 P.M.</td>
                <td>6:45 P.M.</td>
                <td>9:15 P.M.</td>
        </tr>
        <tr>
                <td><A HREF=GoneWiththeWind><i>Gone With the Wind</i></A></td>
                <td>11:15 A.M.</td>
                <td>3:30 P.M.</td>
                <td>7:45 P.M.</td>
                <td> </td>
        </tr>
</table>
</body>
</html>
```

While it is easy to create a static Web page, the page will not reflect updates to the database. Nor does a static Web page enable the user to interact with the database. For the user to interact dynamically with the database, the DBA creates a dynamic Web page.

Dynamic Publication of Database Information. Exhibit 10.9 illustrates the principal components of the dynamic publication of Web information. A common gateway interface (CGI) script is a program that runs on a database server. The CGI script performs four tasks:

- Accepts a user request for data.
- Constructs the appropriate SQL request.
- sEnds the SQL request to the relational DBMS for execution, which returns a table of resulting data.
- Generates the appropriate HTML code to display the information and accepts the resulting table from the DBMS.

Exhibit 10.10 displays an example of a Web-based system.

Web publication systems enable consumers to interact with a remote database using a graphical Web interface. Consumers select from displayed menus rather than listening to verbal menus. Because users scan displayed tables faster than listening to menus, the Web publication approach is usually faster than IVR systems. This approach may also be faster than conversational voice systems because the user only needs to recognize and select the desired option, rather than remembering and speaking the desired option. Agent-based systems combine the advantages of both the verbal-oriented IVR and conversational systems with the advantages of the visual Web-based systems.

INTERNET AGENT-BASED SYSTEMS

Exhibit 10.11 presents the principal modules of an agent system. An agent is a software module acting on behalf of its user by learning the consumer's habits and desires and by performing actions compatible with those habits and desires. The agent learns by recording the consumer's actions, analyzing those actions in a log, and deriving heuristics for performing future actions. For example, an agent records all accesses by the consumer, determines that the user frequently requests information about action movies, and generates a heuristic for accessing information about action movies.

Many software agents are written using Java, PERL, or some other machine-independent programming language. This enables the software agent to execute on a variety of computers. The software agent could reside within the Web server or within the consumer's PC. Because some

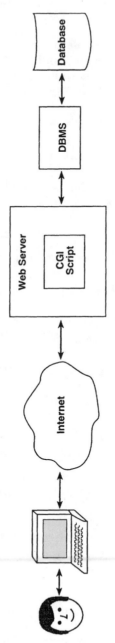

Exhibit 10.9. Dynamic Web publication system.

Exhibit 10.10.   A Web-based system.

CGI Script to Consumer:

Welcome to the Ajax Theater Homepage.
Select your desired Theater and click Submit.

● Central

● Roxy

● Grand

Consumer to CGI Script:
Click "Grand" radio button

CGI Script to DBMS:
Select Title from AjaxTheaters WHERE Theater = "Grand"

DBMS to CGI Script:

Theater	Title	First Show	Second Show	Third Show	Fourth Show
Grand	Star Wars	1:30 p.m.	4:00 p.m.	6:00 p.m.	9:00 p.m.
Grand	Indiana Jones	1:45 p.m.	4:30 p.m.	6:45 p.m.	9:15 p.m.
Grand	Gone With the Wind	11:15 a.m.	3:30 p.m.	7:45 p.m.	

CGI Script to Consumer

Welcome to the Grand Theater.
The movies currently showing are:

Title	First Show	Second Show	Third Show	Fourth Show
Star Wars	1:30 P.M.	4:00 P.M.	6:00 P.M.	9:00 P.M.
Indiana Jones	1:45 P.M.	4:30 P.M.	6:45 P.M.	9:15 P.M.
Gone With the Wind	11:15 A.M.	3:30 P.M.	7:45 P.M.	

consumers are concerned about the privacy of their Web interactions, the agent and its log are placed in the consumer's PC to guarantee privacy.

In addition to logging and analyzing the functions, the agent also manages the dialogue between the user and the database management system. An agent-based system integrates the voice dialogues of conversational interfaces using a text-to-speech engine and an automatic speech recognition engine with the visual data displayed as Web pages. The agent itself can be displayed on the consumer's monitor as an animated icon called an avatar, which acts like a master of ceremonies at a performance or a news anchor on a broadcast news program. The agent verbalizes the important aspects of each item displayed on the consumer's monitor. However, unlike

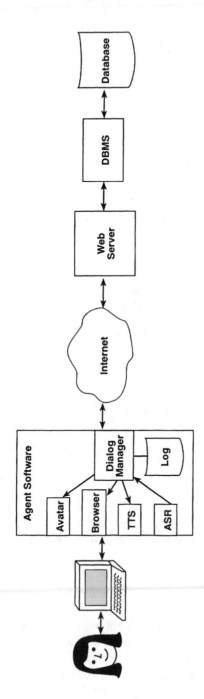

Exhibit 10.11.   Agent system.

a news anchor, the agent asks the consumer if the consumer wants additional information. The agent assists the user in browsing for the requested information and may suggest other information as well. For example, if the consumer recently watched several action films, the agent might suggest additional action films for consideration by the consumer.

Exhibit 10.12 displays a sample agent-based system dialogue.

Like Web-based systems, agent-based systems present visual menus to consumers, who can then quickly recognize and select desired options. In addition, Web-based systems use heuristics to simplify the process for the user by suggesting likely choices to the user.

EVALUATION AND COMPARISON

Exhibit 10.13 summarizes the strengths and weaknesses of the four technologies enabling consumers to access a database.

Potential Audience. The potential audience for IVR and conversational systems is high because over 95 percent of U.S. households have access to touchtone telephones. The prospective audience for Web access is medium because only about 20 percent of U.S. households have personal computers with Internet connections. The possible audience for a Web agent is lower still because only a portion of the households with Internet connections have sound capability on their computers.

Business Expense to Create. Creating IVR and conversational systems involves the purchase of special hardware to integrate the telephone with the data server. IVR and verbal dialogues also must be designed and tested carefully. Conversational dialogues are more difficult to create because they must constrain the consumer's responses to a small number of words or phrases that can be understood by an automatic speech recognition engine. On the other hand, creating dynamic Web pages containing database information is straightforward when using Web page creation tools. Unfortunately, tools for creating Web agents that are both visual and verbal are not yet widely available.

Consumer Acceptance. Consumers dislike IVR systems because they frequently require the consumer to listen to long verbal menus and remember which key on the telephone keypad to press. Instead, users generally prefer conversational systems because questions are answered quickly, without having to listen to the long verbal menus. Customers will prefer the visual menu options of the Web and Web-agent interfaces because they will be able to select options quickly. Most likely, the Web agent will become the most popular because consumers will be able to respond either by clicking or by speaking, whichever is more convenient.

Exhibit 10.12. Agent-based system dialogue.

Agent to the consumer's Web browser:

Welcome to the Ajax Theater Homepage.
Select your desired Theater and click Submit.

- ● Central
- ● Roxy
- ● Grand

Agent to TTS:
Present the message "Welcome to the AJAX Theaters. You usually ask for movies playing at the Grand Theater. Should I display this information now?"

Consumer to ASR:
"Yes."

Agent to DBMS:
Select Title from AjaxTheaters where Theater = "Grand"

DBMS to dialog manager:
Title
Star Wars
Indiana Jones
Gone With the Wind

Dialog manager to the consumer's Web browser:
Display the Web page showing the movies playing at the Grand Theater.

Dialog manager to TTS:
Present the message "Here are the movies playing at the Grand Theater. You usually prefer action movies. Do you wish to see the show times for *Star Wars* and *Indiana Jones*?"

Consumer to agent:
"Yes."

Dialog manager to DBMS:
Select Title, Select FirstShow, SecondShow, ThirdShow, FourthShow from AjaxTheaters where Theater = "Grand" and (Title = "Star Wars" or Title = "Indiana Jones")

DBMS to dialog manager:

Title	First Show	Second Show	Third Show	Fourth Show
Star Wars	1:30 p.m.	4:00 p.m.	6:00 p.m.	9:00 p.m.
Indiana Jones	1:45 p.m.	4:30 p.m.	6:45 p.m.	9:15 p.m.

Exhibit 10.12.   Agent-based system dialogue. (*continued*)

Dialog manager to consumer's Web browser:

Welcome to the Grand Theater.
The movies currently showing are:

Title	First Show	Second Show	Third Show	Fourth Show
Star Wars	1:30 P.M.	4:00 P.M.	6:00 P.M.	9:00 P.M.
Indiana Jones	1:45 P.M.	4:30 P.M.	6:45 P.M.	9:15 P.M.
Gone With the Wind	11:15 A.M.	3:30 P.M.	7:45 P.M.	

Dialog manager to TTS:
   Present the message "Here are the show times for *Star Wars* and *Indiana Jones*."

Exhibit 10.13.   Comparison of the four approaches

	IVR	Conversational	Web Access	Web Agent
Type of access	Hear and click	Hear and speak	See and click	Hear/see/click or speak
Potential audience	High	High	Medium	Low
Business expense to create/maintain	Low-medium	Medium	Low	High
Consumer acceptance	Low	Medium	Medium	High

RECOMMENDATIONS

IVR and conversational speech systems provide the greatest potential for consumers to access an enterprise's database. If already using an IVR system, an enterprise should consider upgrading to a conversational speech system. If an IVR system is not used, then a conversational speech system should definitely be considered. Although it is more difficult to implement, the acceptance of a conversational speech system among consumers is expected to be greater than that of the IVR system.

Database Web publication systems provide easy-to-browse facilities to an enterprise's database for customers with a Web-enabled computer. While Web agents promise improved consumer satisfaction, this has not yet been demonstrated. The success of visual-verbal agents on the Internet should be monitored. Consider converting the enterprise's Web pages to visual-verbal agents when the technology proves to be consistently useful.

Until the U.S. population has greater access to the World Wide Web, both conversational speech systems and Web pages are recommended. This enables most consumers to speak and hear information from a database via telephone, while consumers connected to the Internet can see and select information from the database.

DATA MODELS AND MODELING TECHNIQUES

RECOMMENDED READINGS

The following book describes technologies and management of call centers, including integration with IVR. Dawson, K. *The Call Center Handbook: The Complete Guide to Starting, Running, and Improving Your Call Center,* San Francisco, CA: Miller Freeman Books, 1998.

The following books explain how to write CGI scripts using two popular scripting languages — PERL and Java. Brenner, S. and Aoki, E. *Introduction to CGI PERL: Getting Started with Web Scripts,* Foster City, CA: IDG Books World-Wide, 1996.

Rahmel, D. *Server Scripts with Visual Javascript (Hands-On Web Development),* New York: McGraw-Hill, 1997.

The following book gives an overview of Microsoft's Web publishing tools. Chandak, R. *Web Programming with Microsoft Tools 6 in 1.* Indianapolis: Que Education & Training, 1997.

The enterprise's DBMS vendor should be consulted for Web-publishing tools compatible with the enterprise's DBMS.

RECOMMENDED WEBSITES

The following Web sites contain the telephone numbers with several demonstrations of conversational speech interfaces.

Applied Language Technology (ALTech), http://www.altech.com.
Nuance Communications, http://www.nuance.com.

This Web site contains demonstrations of 3-D graphical avatars that could be used as visualized agents:

Fluent Speech Technologies, http://www.fluent-speech.com.

Chapter 11
Well-Formed Entity Relationship Diagrams

James A. Larson and Carol L. Larson

THIS CHAPTER PRESENTS A DOZEN SIMPLE RULES that, if followed, remove much of the inexactness and ambiguity which can creep into entity-relationship diagrams. These rules fall into three categories:

- Syntactic rules to encourage the correct use of entity-relationship diagram graphical figures.
- Semantic rules to encourage a meaningful diagram representation of the data being modeled.
- Pragmatic rules to refine the diagram so it can be converted to a well-designed relational schema.

The entity-relationship approach is widely accepted as a useful technique for information modeling. The simplicity of the approach does not require detailed, formal specifications, which is one reason for its wide acceptance. However, this simplicity lends itself to inexactness and ambiguity, which may lead to confusion and inefficiencies within an implemented database.

To remove inexactness and ambiguities from entity-relationship diagrams, database administrators should follow the syntactic, semantic, and pragmatic rules presented in the chapter at both the beginning and the end of the database design process. By using the rules at the beginning of the design process, the database administrator (DBA) will create a more concise entity-relationship diagram. By using the rules as a checklist at the end of the process, the DBA will be able to recheck the newly designed diagram to improve conciseness and to remove remaining ambiguities.

However, before discussing the 12 rules, a short review of the elements of entity relationship diagrams are presented.

0-8493-9832-0/00/$0.00+$.50

BASICS OF ENTITY-RELATIONSHIP DIAGRAMS

Entity-relationship diagrams consist of graphical notations for describing conceptual schemas. First proposed by Peter Chen in 1976, they have become popular with many DBAs. A variation, called IDEF1X, was standardized by the military and is especially popular with defense contractors.

Entities and Entity Sets

Basic to every conceptual database design language are the concepts of entity and entity set. An *entity* is a representation of a real-world person, event, or concept. For example, the database may contain Employee entities Jones, Smith, and Lewis and the Department entities Accounting and Sales. Each entity may take on a value for each of its attributes. An *attribute* is a characteristic of an entity. An Employee entity may have values <13, Jones, Seattle> for attributes EmployeeId, EmployeeName, and Address.

In order to organize the hundreds or thousands of entities in a database, entities with the same attributes are grouped together as entity sets. An *entity set* is a collection of homogenous entities with the same attributes. In the example above, the entities Jones, Smith, and Lewis are members of the Employee entity set, while entities Accounting and Sales are members of the Department entity set.

A *key constraint* is used to enforce uniqueness among the entities in an entity set by specifying that no two entities can have the same value for the key attribute. A *key* is a subset of the attributes in the entity set. Exhibit 11.1 illustrates an entity-relationship diagram containing two entity sets, Employee and Department. Entity sets are denoted as rectangles, attributes are ovals, and key attributes are underlined. The key attributes of the Employee and Department entity sets are EmployeeId and Department-Name, respectively.

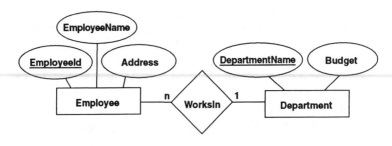

Exhibit 11.1. Entity-relationship diagram.

One-to-Many Relationships

A *one-to-many relationship set* between entity sets "A" and "B" implies that zero or one "A" entity can be related to zero, one, or more "B" entities. In the example above, a single Department may be related to one or more Employee entities. One-to-many relationship sets are important because they describe how entities may relate to other entities. For example, a database containing Department and Employee entities alone fails to capture which employee works for which department. One-to-many relationship sets define these important types of associations. Diamonds represent relationship sets in entity-relationship diagrams. In Exhibit 1, the WorksIn relationship set relates the entity sets Employee and Department. The small symbols "1" and "n" indicate a one-to-many relationship.

Many-to-Many Relationships

A *many-to-many relationship set* implies that any number of entities from each of two entity sets may participate in a single relationship. Many-to-many relationship sets occur frequently in the real world. For example, pairs of entity sets—employees and projects, students and classes, and producers and suppliers—often are related by many-to-many relationship sets.

The entity-relationship model has been extended over the years to include weak entities, class hierarchies, and aggregation, which has resulted in what generally is referred to as the *extended entity-relationship model*. For a description of these extensions, refer to any of several introductory database management system (DBMS) textbooks. The rules described below can be applied to either the basic or extended models.

RULES FOR BUILDING ENTITY-RELATIONSHIP DIAGRAMS

Database administrators should apply the following twelve rules as they specify entity-relationship diagrams. They also should apply these rules towards the end of the entity-relationship diagram design process, when the rules can be used as a checklist to make sure the diagrams are complete and precise.

Syntactic Rules

Syntactic rules describe how the graphical notation figures are combined to create an understandable diagram. Syntactic rules can be applied to an entity-relationship diagram without knowing much about the intended database. However, knowledge of the primitive entity-relationship figures is necessary. Syntactic rules are easy to apply by simply inspecting the entity relationship diagram. Many entity-relationship diagramming tools automatically detect semantic rule violations by highlighting the offending attributes, entity sets, or relationship sets to the database administrator. The software may automatically enforce other semantic rules. For example, it may be impossible for the database administrator to create an attribute without connecting it to an entity set or relationship set.

1. Each attribute is connected to exactly one entity set or one relationship set.

This rule guarantees that each attribute belongs to an entity set or relationship set. No orphan attributes are permitted. This rule also guarantees that no attribute belongs to more than one entity set. If the same attribute belongs to multiple entity sets, then it will have multiple copies within the database. This wastes disk space and, over time, may become inconsistent if one copy is updated without updating the other copies.

2. Each relationship set is connected to at least two entity sets.

When designing entity-relationship diagrams on paper, it is easy to specify one entity set of a relationship set and, then, forget to come back later to specify the remaining entity set.

3. Each entity set is indirectly connected to every other entity set in the diagram.

If the entity sets and relationship sets of a schema can be partitioned into two or more subsets so there is no connection between subsets, then the diagram might represent multiple schemas rather than a single, integrated schema. More likely, a relationship set or connection is missing from the diagram.

Semantic Rules

Semantic rules help the DBA to construct an entity-relationship diagram that captures the correct meaning and usage of the database. Unlike syntactic rules, knowledge of the database and its intended use is necessary to apply semantic rules.

4. Each attribute should have a unique name.

The names of attributes connected to the same entity set or relationship set should be unique so users can refer to each of the attributes by its name. However, attributes belonging to different entity sets and relationship sets occasionally have the same name. As illustrated in Exhibit 11.2, the attribute names can be made unique by appending the name of entity set or relationship set to which it is connected.

5. Each entity set should have a unique name.

Entity sets are treated as tables in relational databases. SQL requires that the names of tables be unique. Thus, the names of entity sets must be unique. As illustrated in Exhibit 11.3, when two tables are identified with the same name, the DBA should determine whether to make the names unique or combine the two entity sets.

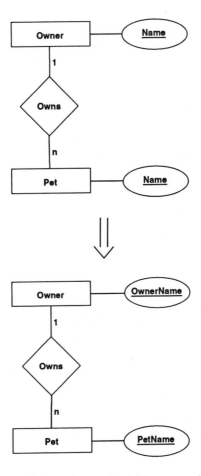

Exhibit 11.2. Each attribute should have a unique name.

---

6. Each relationship set, which connects the same pairs of entity sets, should have a unique name.

Exhibit 11.4 illustrates two relationship sets connected to the same pair of entities. Clearly, the names of the relationships should be unique so the user can understand the semantics of each relationship set. Another reason for making the relationship set names unique is because the relationship set name becomes part of the name for the key attribute of Department when the key attribute of Department appears in the Employee table in the corresponding relational schema.

Some database administrators require that names of all relationship sets be unique. However, it is often difficult for DBAs to think of unique names for similar types of relationship sets. For example, consider the

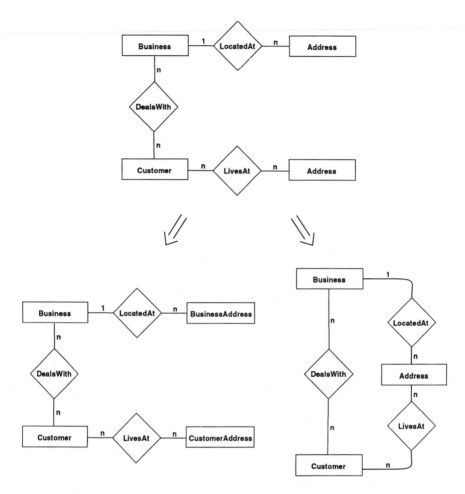

Exhibit 11.3. Each entity set should have a unique name.

---

relationship sets between Secretary and Employee, Scientist and Employee, Engineer and Employee, and Manager and Employee. In each case, the relationship set could be named "Is A." Identifying four different relationship names with each implying the same semantics as "Is A" obscures the semantics of the relationship sets.

7. No attribute may have multiple values.

Relational DBMSs do not allow a column of a table to have multiple values. The newer universal DBMSs do permit multiple values. However, until universal DBMSs become more widely used, it is best to remove multivalued attributes from entity-relationship diagrams.

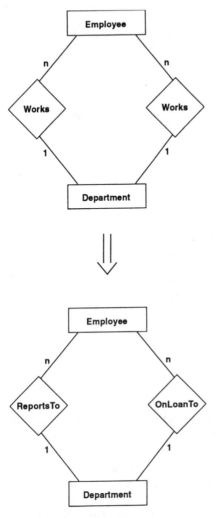

Exhibit 11.4. Each relationship set should have a unique name.

Database administrators frequently can identify multiple-valued attributes by observing that the noun used to name the attribute is itself plural. Exhibit 11.5 illustrates two approaches for removing multi-valued attributes. The first approach replicates the attribute a fixed number of times, each with a unique name. However, this may waste space if the number of values frequently is less than the number of attributes. It also limits the number of values that an entity may have. The second approach replaces the attribute with a new entity set and relationship set. This approach adds to the complexity of the diagram, but leads to a more flexible database because an entity can support an arbitrary number of attribute values.

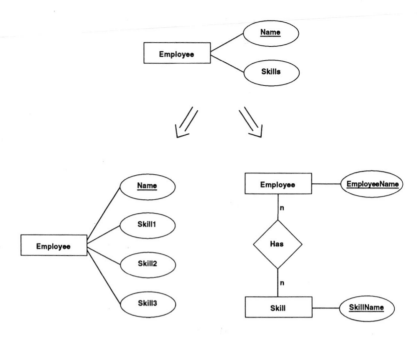

Exhibit 11.5.   No attribute may have multiple values.

---

8.   No entity set or relationship set may have a repeating group.

Exhibit 11.6 illustrates two approaches for representing a repeating group. The first representation merely lists the attributes belonging to a group of related attributes. The second approach indicates the grouping by showing the attributes of an attribute. Unfortunately, neither approach indicates whether or not the group of attributes repeats with multiple values for each attribute in the group. The database administrator must determine if the group repeats based on his/her understanding for the use of the database and its associated applications. Exhibit 11.6 illustrates how the repeating group of attributes becomes a separate entity set.

9.   The key attributes of an entity set functionally determine all of the values of other attributes connected to the entity set.

Database administrators familiar with the theory of relational schema normalization will recognize this rule as "normalize the database to avoid update anomalies." When dealing with entity-relationship diagrams, database administrators may want to normalize the entity sets to guarantee that each entity set represents a single class of entities.

Exhibit 11.7 illustrates an example of an unnormalized entity set, Pet. Many database administrators will intuitively recognize that Pet really represents two entity sets, Pet and Trick, and will create the two entity sets

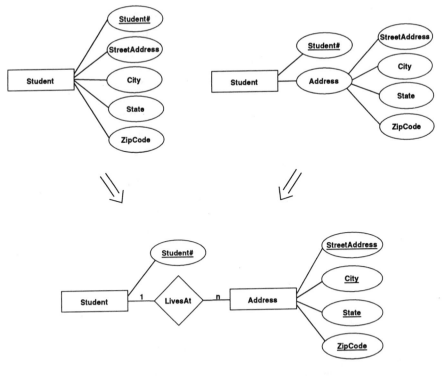

Exhibit 11.6.   No entity set may have a repeating group.

related by a new relationship set, Performs. The concept of functional dependency and the theory of normalization also can be used to partition the original Pet entity set into two new entity sets.

If a value of an attribute "A" *functionally determines* the value of attribute "B" whenever attribute "A" has value "x," then the value of attribute "B" must be "y." For example, Pet# functionally determines PetName and Trick# functionally determines TrickName. According to the rules of normalization, the key of an entity set must functionally determine each attribute of the entity set. Algorithms exist for converting entity sets into any of the various *normal* forms (second normal form, third normal form, Boyce Codd normal form, and so on) that partition an entity set into multiple entity sets. Most DBAs manually partition an unnormalized entity set into normalized entity sets by applying the following rule to each new entity set:

> Each non-key attribute of an entity set is functionally dependent upon the key of the entity set and nothing but that key.

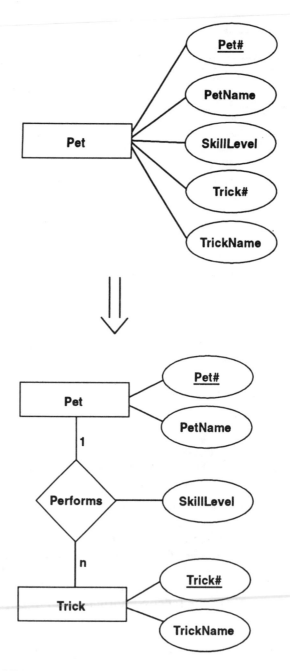

Exhibit 11.7. Normalize the attributes of each entity set.

Pragmatic Rules

Most commercial DBMSs support the relational model of data. Entity-relationship diagrams must be converted to relational notation before the DBMS can be used. *Pragmatic rules* make the conversion from entity-relationship notation to relational notation easier. Pragmatic rules differ from syntactic and semantic rules because a knowledge of how the database is to be used is necessary when applying these rules.

10. Remove redundant relationship sets.

Whenever a collection of entity sets and relationship sets are connected in a cycle, there is a potential for a redundant relationship. Exhibit 11.8 illustrates one such cycle which contains a relationship, Employees, that is redundant with the combination of the Within and WorksFor relationship sets. Employees is a redundant relationship set because it captures the same information as the two other relationship sets. The redundant relationship set should be removed to prevent inconsistencies from creeping into the database.

Rules 11 and 12 are useful if the entity-relationship diagram corresponds to a view within a relational DBMS. A *view* is a subset of a relational schema used by a special set of database users.

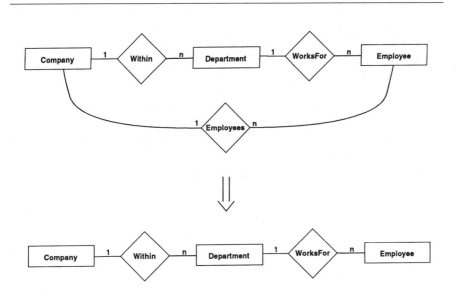

Exhibit 11.8. Remove redundant relationships.

11. Partition the entity set vertically if its attributes are accessed differently.

Usage information includes estimates about the frequency with which users will access an entity and the nature or type of access. Some DBAs resist considering usage information while designing the logical schema. Other database administrators feel that usage information impacts the logical design and, thus, include its use when designing logical schemas using the entity-relationship diagrams.

If different classes of users access different attributes of an entity set, consider partitioning the attributes of the entity set into two different entity sets. Exhibit 11.9 illustrates the Employee entity set with attribute Location (available to all users) and attribute Salary (available only to selected users). Because these attributes are accessed very differently, it makes sense to partition the Employee entity set into two entity sets, EmployeeLocation and EmployeeSalary.

12. Replace each many-to-many relationship set by two one-to-many relationship sets and a third entity set.

One of the advantages of the entity-relationship model is that it can represent many-to-many relationships directly, which is a capability missing from the relational data model. If the entity-relationship diagram is used only for representing the database concepts, and not for database design, then do not apply this rule.

One of the major steps in converting entity-relationship diagrams to relational schemas is to replace many-to-many relationships by two one-to-many relationships, as illustrated in Exhibit 11.10. Usually, the name of the many-to-many relationship set is used as the name for the new entity set. Some database administrators find it difficult to specify meaningful names for the two new one-to-many relationship sets. As a default, concatenate the names of the two related entity sets, then check for better relationship set names. In Exhibit 11.10, the entity sets "Man," "Woman," and "Marriage" would be concatenated to form the relationship set "ManMarriage" and "WomanMarriage." However, "Husband" and "Wife" are better relationship set names for this example.

ADDITIONAL TASKS

There are several other tasks that a DBA may perform to make an entity-relationship diagram more precise. Some database administrators prefer to make these specifications after the entity-relationship diagram has been converted to a relational schema.

Specify Business Rules

A *business rule* is a rule that describes valid values of attributes which are stored in a database. Examples include "A person's hire date must be

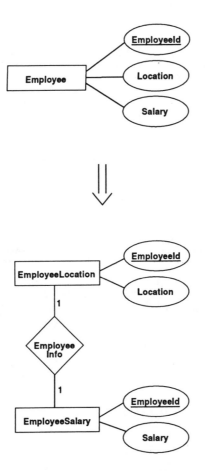

Exhibit 11.9. **Partition an entity set vertically if its attributes are addressed differently.**

greater than a person's birthdate" and "The valid values of the color attributes are 'green,' 'red,' and 'yellow.'" The graphical notation used to create entity-relationship diagrams can specify a wide variety of business rules, including cardinality, membership, and functional dependency constraints. However, there are many rules that cannot be specified by using graphical notation. Many database administrators write business rules next to the entity set containing the attributes involved in the business rule.

Specify the Meaning of Codes and Abbreviations

Some attributes will have values that are codes for the real values. For example, "1," "2," and "3" represent the colors "green," "red," and "yellow,"

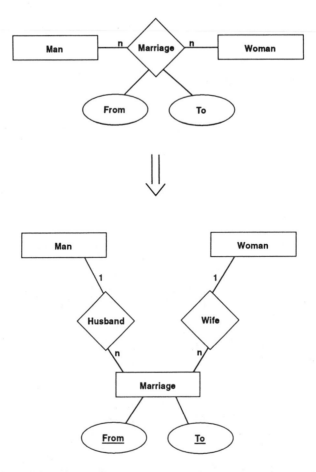

Exhibit 11.10. Replace N:N relationships by two 1:N relationships.

---

respectiely. If the code values are known, some DBAs write them next to their respective attribute.

Specify Data Element Information

Specify information about each attribute, such as its unit (feet, kilometers, and so on), its valid values, dates when the value is valid (e.g., grade point average does not reflect the results of the current quarter until two weeks after final grades are due), source of the data (person's birthdate comes from the person's application form), and office procedures for maintaining the data (the admissions office is responsible for entering the person's birthdate).

Whether or not a DBA records this additional information with the entity-relationship diagram or with the relational data model depends upon which model users will refer to the most. If the entity-relationship diagram will be the primary documentation for user reference, then it should include all additional information.

SUMMARY

Database administrators should apply these twelve rules as they design entity-relationship diagrams. The rules should also be reviewed at the end of the design process as a checklist to make sure that nothing was overlooked in the design of the entity-relationship diagram. The resulting entity-relationship diagram will be more correct, precise, and complete. The entity-relationship diagram also will be ready to convert into a well-defined relational schema with minimal effort and can be used as documentation to accurately describe the contents of the database. In summary, the twelve design rules are:

Syntactic Rules

1. Each attribute is connected to exactly one entity set or one relationship set.
2. Each relationship set is connected to at least two entity sets.
3. Each entity set is indirectly connected to every other entity set in the diagram.

Semantic Rules

4. Each attribute should have a unique name.
5. Each entity set should have a unique name.
6. Each relationship set, which connect the same pairs of entity sets, should have a unique name.
7. No attribute may have multiple values.
8. No entity set or relationship set may have a repeating group.
9. The key attributes of an entity set functionally determine all of the values of other attributes connected to the entity set.

Pragmatic Rules

10. Remove redundant relationship sets.
11. Partition the entity set vertically if its attributes are accessed differently.
12. Replace each many-to-many relationship set by two one-to-many relationship sets and a third entity set.

DATA MODELS AND MODELING TECHNIQUES

Recommended Readings

Chen, P. "The Entity-Relationship Model—Towards a Unified View of Data," *ACM Transactions on Database Systems* (1976).

Elmasri, R. and Navathe, S. *Fundamentals of Database Systems,* 2nd edition, Menlo Park, CA: Addison-Wesley, 1994.

Larson, J. and Larson, C. *Evaluation of Four Languages for Specifying Conceptual Database Designs.* New York: Auerbach Publications, 1999.

Ramakrishman, R. *Database Management Systems,* Boston, MA: WCB McGraw-Hill, 1998.

Chapter 12
Component Design for Relational Databases

Ashvin Iyengar

INTRODUCTION

COMPONENT-BASED OBJECT-ORIENTED ARCHITECTURES are becoming increasingly popular in building industrial strength applications. However, relational databases are not going to be replaced by object databases in the foreseeable future. This paper explores the ramifications of component-based designs on data management and offers strategies which could be deployed in the use of relational centralized databases with object-oriented component-based application architectures.

WHY RELATIONAL DATABASES ARE HERE TO STAY

From a pure application design perspective, object-oriented databases would be much more suitable for use with object-oriented component-based application architectures. However, the business realities are more complex and include the following considerations:

- Object-oriented databases are not mature enough to be entrusted with the job of managing large corporate data.
- It is more difficult to find professionals with experience in administration as well as the design of object-oriented databases.
- The vast majority of corporations are currently using relational databases to manage business information.
- Most current live applications have been designed and developed to work with relational databases.

MOVING TOWARDS A COMPONENT-BASED ARCHITECTURE STANDARD

The subject of object-oriented design and programming involving relational databases has been well explored. More often than not, the data model is constructed using pure relational database modeling techniques with little if any consideration for object-oriented design techniques. This necessitates the use of impedance matching techniques to allow object-oriented applications to interact with relational data models.

Application architectures are becoming increasingly component based to satisfy the need for flexible as well as manageable systems. The effort to move away from large monolithic applications has been underway for a number of years. This has resulted in the adoption of client-server based architecture as the *defacto* standard in the industry. However, with lack of proper design, client/server architectures became just as monolithic as mainframe applications and thus inherited all the maintenance problems associated with large monolithic applications. Object-oriented design techniques and multi-tiered architectures were adopted in order to solve this problem. Component design is a natural next step in the evolution of application architectures since it combines the principles of object-oriented design with multi-tiered application architecture. In addition, industry-wide acceptance of the incremental and iterative software development methodology over the old waterfall development methodology has provided an additional thrust towards component-based design.

Some of the other factors contributing towards making component-based application design the *defacto* standard are:

- The maturing of technologies like DCOM (distributed component object model) and CORBA.
- The plethora of new technologies encouraging the design and deployment of components over the Web (e.g., JavaBeans).
- The ability to design, develop, and deploy components using high level, widely used applications like Visual Basic.
- The potential for using third-party components along with in-house applications in order to fulfill specific needs (e.g., a professional third-party charting component).
- The resulting relative ease of component replacement.

BACKGROUND OF MULTI-TIERED ARCHITECTURES

The current thrust is towards the use of distributed, component-based application architectures. The ever-increasing need to deploy applications over the Web and the resulting security considerations have led to a n-tiered architecture, using, at the very least, three distinct tiers.

- Web server
- Application server
- Database server

Whereas, a number of studies have shown that pure object-oriented applications are difficult to design and develop and that the payoffs information technology (IT) executives had hoped for in terms of reuse are seldom realized, multi-tiered architecture is here to stay. Three-tiered architecture is, in fact, the industry standard and a wide variety of application development environments from Smalltalk to Visual Basic support and encourage the use of this standard architecture.

In general, a three-tiered architecture has the following layers:

- Interface layer
- Business layer
- Data layer

The driving force behind three-tiered architecture is the need to support both flexibility and robustness in applications. De-coupling the interface layer from the database offers the advantage of changes in the database that need not affect the interface layer directly, thereby isolating the effects of a change in either layer. The interface layer describes how the application interacts with the outside world. If the outside world is comprised of end users, then the interface layer refers to a user interface. Alternatively, if it is comprised of client applications, it refers to an application interface.

Arguably, the main payoff involved in object-oriented architectures is not reuse but rather change management. Effective change management is also the goal of three-tiered architectures. Since three-tiered architectures are easier to implement with object-based (if not object-oriented) systems, new life has been extended to object-based systems. In this article, a distinction is being made between object-oriented and object-based systems. Object-based systems implement classes and objects, but do not permit other aspects of object-oriented programming like inheritance and polymorphism. So whereas the three pillars of object-oriented programming can be said to be encapsulation, inheritance, and polymorphism, object-based programming concerns itself with mainly encapsulation.

A leading example of an object-based application development is Visual Basic. Visual Basic is to the client/server world what Cobol is to the mainframe world. Since classes in Visual Basic are implemented using DCOM (distributed component object model), it is extremely easy to develop and deploy components using Visual Basic.

An object-based component can be described as a set of objects collaborating to provide a common functionality and implementing a common interface. Thus, an object-based component improves the encapsulation aspect of object-based applications. By virtue of this it also increases the flexibility as well as robustness of an object-based application, since changes to the component are isolated.

It has already been argued that the main thrust towards three-tiered architecture is coming from a need for effective change management. Change management, as used in this paper, encompasses the concepts of flexibility and robustness. It has also been argued that object-based applications by virtue of their support for encapsulation are a natural choice for the implementation of business solutions with underlying multi-tiered architectures. Since a component-based architecture enhances the ability of multi-tiered architectures to deliver on its promise, it would be logical to conclude that component-based multi-tiered architectures are here to stay.

So the prevalent application development environment can be said to have the following features:

- Multi-tiered architecture
- Relational databases
- Object-based applications
- Component-based application architecture

APPLICATION ARCHITECTURE EXAMPLE

Now this chapter will take an example where a set of three tables provides a certain functionality (e.g., hold information pertaining to interest rates in a portfolio management system) and three discrete applications that interact with these three tables. It will start with a simple two-tiered application architecture example and note the problems in the chosen context.

Then it will move to a more object-oriented version of the same problem and again note the problems with the approach. Finally, it will illustrate a solution to the same problem using a data-component approach.

In Exhibit 12.1, Application A1 is responsible for displaying and maintaining information in M1 (the set of tables T1, T2, and T3 constituting a sub data model). Applications A2, A3 use the information in M1 to do their processing. Note that Application A1 interacts with all the tables in M1, whereas Applications A2, A3 interact with only T3.

The shortcomings of two-tiered applications have already been noted. In this case, the tight coupling between the applications and the data is obvious, and consequently, flexibility is severely compromised. Also, there are three different applications interacting with the same data and consequently, complexity is increased since a change in data storage/design would necessitate change to all the client applications.

To make this design more object-oriented, now move to Exhibit 12.2 which illustrates a three-tiered object-oriented architecture. Applications A1, A2, and A3 contain their own relational to object mapping layer (also known as impedance matching layer). Now consider that new business rules necessitate a change to M1. M1 is a sub data model corresponding to

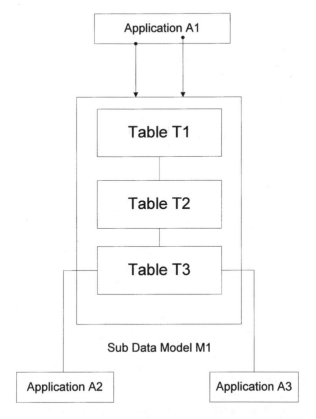

Exhibit 12.1. Two-tier application architecture.

functionality F1 (e.g., performance history of various investment options in a portfolio management system). If the new data model involves changing the way information is represented in T3, then all applications involving T3 (in this case Applications A1, A2, and A3) have to be updated. In addition to requiring duplication of effort this design increases the risk of application malfunction, since it is possible to miss updating an application which needs updating. Also note that even aside from complicating change management, this design involves duplication of effort in terms of data access as well as relational to object mapping.

In order to solve the above-mentioned problems, modify the design to produce a more object-oriented approach by introducing components. Exhibit 12.3 introduces a component C1 that encapsulates sub data model M1. This makes C1 a data-component. Consequently, to the methodology illustrated in Exhibit 12.3 is referred to as the data-component approach.

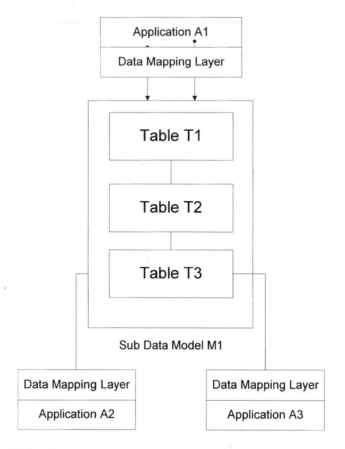

Exhibit 12.2. Three-tier application architecture with data-mapping layer.

ADVANTAGES/FEATURES OF THE DATA-COMPONENT APPROACH

The data-component approach, as illustrated in Exhibit 12.3, offers the following features and advantages:

- Applications do not access the tables directly but use the interface functions provided by the interface layer in C1.
- Satisfies an important OOD (object-oriented design) requirement: keep function and data together.
- Eliminates redundant data access as well as data mapping.
- Separates the GUI from the business logic — an important requirement of three-tier client server computing.
- Allows implementation of n-tiered architecture since C1 can be deployed on an application server.

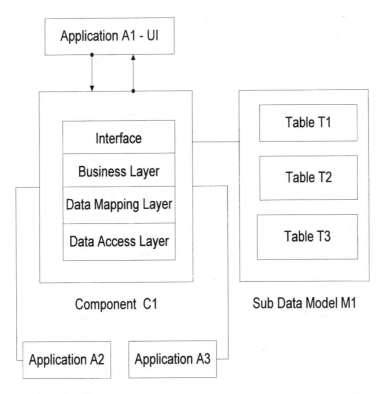

Exhibit 12.3. Application architecture example using data-component approach.

- Provides much better change management (which as elaborated before, is an even greater benefit of object-oriented development than reuse), since changes in the data model no longer affect client applications directly. The only time the client applications are affected is when changes to the data model/functionality affect the interface between C1 and the client applications.
- Allows implementation of multiple interface or different views of data thus adding a new twist to the classic MVC (Model View Controller) object-oriented architecture.
- Provides data source independence, since changing the source of the data will affect only the data access and data mapping layers of the component and the client applications will be insulated from any such change.
- Reduces the effort involved in allowing new applications to access the data.

DISADVANTAGES/LIMITATIONS OF THE DATA-COMPONENT APPROACH

The data-component approach as illustrated in Exhibit 12.3 has the following possible disadvantages or limitations:

- If used indiscriminately, this approach could lead to a proliferation of components thereby increasing the number of applications.
- Large applications using a large number of components could experience performance degradation, especially while loading the application.
- Each component will possibly have registration requirements, so the task of installing and distributing applications will be more complex.
- This approach deals primarily with discrete, non-overlapping use cases. Overlapping use cases will create additional complexities that have not been addressed in this approach.

DATA-COMPONENT GRANULARITY CONSIDERATIONS

To prevent proliferation of components, the granularity of the components can be increased. For example as shown in Exhibit 12.4, use cases U1 and U2 use sub data models M1 and M2 correspondingly.

Instead of having components C1 and C2 that correspond to use cases U1 and U2, if U1 and U2 are closely related, a single component C (with interfaces I1 and I2) can serve U1 and U2, as illustrated in Exhibit 12.5.

The same exercise of combining related use cases into components could be carried out through the application design space thereby bringing component proliferation under control.

IMPLEMENTATION OF THE COMPONENT-BASED DESIGN USING MICROSOFT'S ARCHITECTURE

Even though the component technology war between CORBA and DCOM is far from over, the fact remains that DCOM (in some form) has been around longer and is used widely in the industry. It also has, arguably, more opportunities to mature into a stable industrial strength technology. Consequently, Microsoft's DCOM platform is discussed in the implementation of the data-component approach illustrated in Exhibit 12.3.

In Microsoft's DCOM technology there are two main types of components:

1. ActiveX Exe
2. ActiveX DLL

The difference between the two types of components is that the ActiveX Exe is an out-of-process component while the ActiveX DLL is an in-process component. In-process components usually offer significantly better performance than out-of-process components. However, in-process components

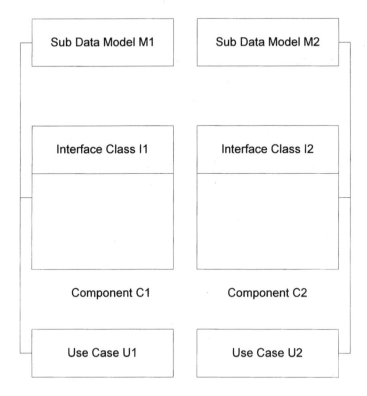

Exhibit 12.4. One-to-one component to sub data model example.

and their client applications must reside on the same physical machines. With out-of-process components there is no such restriction, therefore out-of-process components offer greater flexibility in terms of deployment at the cost of application performance.

The choice between in-process and out-of-process components would therefore depend on the physical architecture. Note that three-tier software architectures can be deployed using two-tier physical architectures. In a two-tier implementation, the database runs on a database server and the user interface layer as well as the business layer runs on the client desktops. This kind of implementation is also called fat-client, since most of the applications are deployed on individual workstations. Whereas this might be sufficient for a small shop, for larger shops, distribution as well as maintenance of all the various components on individual workstations can prove to be a daunting as well as error-prone task. For this reason, larger shops may prefer to implement a physical three-tier architecture which would involve client workstations interacting with an application server which in turn would

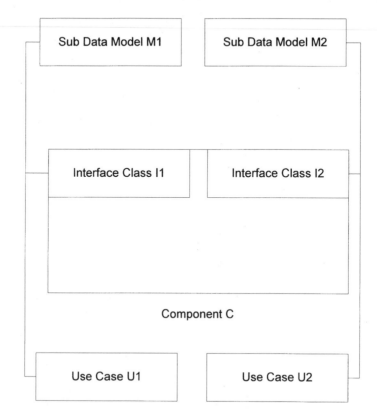

Exhibit 12.5. One-to-many component to sub data model example.

interact with a database server. While this approach alleviates some of the distribution problems inherent in the two-tier architecture, a new problem is created with multiple workstations accessing the same application on the application server concurrently. Clearly, it would be counter-productive to start up a new copy of the application for every workstation that needs it. Therefore, some sort of a queuing solution is inevitable. It is in this respect that the DCOM architecture is yet to mature. Microsoft's solution to the problem involves use of MTS (Microsoft's transaction server), but that may not be a universally viable solution for every situation.

It is also worth noting that even though it is technically easy to convert an ActiveX DLL to an ActiveX Exe, there are other considerations involved which might necessitate knowledge of the physical architecture in advance. The main consideration is network traffic. With out-of-process components, performance requirements usually dictate the use of fewer but longer messages, whereas with in-process components, frequencies of messages do not result in performance penalties.

If the generic architecture example illustrated in Exhibit 12.3 were to be implemented on a Microsoft platform, the following notes may apply:

- The interface layer of component C1 interfaces with Applications A1, A2, and A3. Since A2 and A3 are inquiry-only applications, they can share a common interface. So, we would have two interface classes, I1 and I2. I1 will implement the interface needed for A1 and I2 would implement the interface needed for applications A2 and A3. In some cases, classes I1 and I2 could be implemented in a separate ActiveX DLL. This has the advantage of providing de-coupling between the client and server applications. In practice, this has to be weighed against the cost of distributing this additional component. There will also be a minor performance penalty involved in separating the interface classes in a separate component, since an additional program will have to be loaded.

- Another factor to be considered while designing the interface layer is the number of parameters needed for the component to query and present the information. Assume for starters a method M1 in component C1, where the number of input parameters is n and the method returns only one value. A change in the input parameters would entail changing method M1 and therefore changing the interface. Therefore, except for trivial methods, it would make sense to encapsulate the data flowing between the component and its client applications, in classes. In this example a class C1M1 would contain all the input parameters as well as result values for method M1 in Component C1. M1 now would be passed a reference to object OC1MI (corresponding to class C1M1). With this approach, if method M1 were to need a new input parameter or need to return an extra result value, the interface would remain unchanged and changes would be restricted to class C1M1 and its usage.

- The business layer of the component should contain most of editing rules and the business logic. Including the editing logic in the business layer of the component goes a long way towards ensuring data integrity since applications that update the data maintained by the component have to use the interface layer of the component. Note that the business layer is not exposed directly to the outside world. External applications can only use the methods exposed by the interface layer, which in turn will interact with the business layer. Also, since the interface layer does not directly interact with the data layer of the component, the business layer has a chance to enforce its business rules and ensure logical integrity.

- The data layer of the component typically consists of two internal layers namely a relational to object mapping layer and a data access layer. The data access layer is responsible for the actual interaction with the database. The data mapping layer is responsible for mapping relational data into objects. Each record in a relational database is essentially an array of values. If a query returns more than one record (a

RecordSet in Microsoft-speak), then we are dealing with a two-dimensional array. The data-mapping layer typically converts a single record to an object and a RecordSet to a collection of objects. Also, for persistent data, the object in the data mapping layer must know how to access the objects in the data access layer in order to store updated data. It is also worthwhile noting that the data access layer could be implemented as a separate component in itself. That way multiple applications can use the data access layer to manage their interactions with the physical database.

Following are examples of the architectures discussed in this paper:

1. The business layer has classes B1 and B2 that correspond to the interface layer classes I1 and I2. B1 and B2 interact with classes R1,R2,...., RN which implement various business rules. B1 and B2 also interact with corresponding classes DM1 and DM2, which belong to the data mapping layer of the data layer. DM1 and DM2 in turn interact with classes DA1, DA2, and DA3, which access/update data in Tables T1, T2, and T3.
2. Instead of having separate classes B1 and B2, depending on the application, a single class B may suffice.
3. Again, depending on the application, a single class DA may provide the functionality provided by DA1, DA2, and DA3.
4. Note that DM1 and DM2 provide the business view of the data model and this case is basically driven by the choice of B1 and B2 as the business classes. Depending on the requirements, classes DM1, DM2, and DM3 could correspond to DA1, DA2, and DA3 or any other combination that makes sense.
5. Note that classes DM1 and DM2 could create and return a variety of objects. For example, object O11 might correspond to a specific record in the Table T1. Object O12 might correspond to a collection of records. Alternatively, O12 may be implemented as an object containing a collection of O11 objects. Similarly, objects O21 through O2N might correspond to Table T2. Alternatively, O21 through O2N might correspond to data linked between Tables T2 and T3 if appropriate.

The possibilities are endless. The examples listed previously illustrate some of the considerations that might come into play during the design of the component. To reiterate one of the main points in this article, effective change management, assume that a change is to be made to this design. Instead of accessing data in Tables T2 and T3 directly, applications must use a View instead. In this case, only relevant classes in the data access layer and maybe the data mapping layer will need to be changed. All other classes in the business and the interface layer of the component can remain unchanged. Also, the client applications using the component remain unaffected. Thus use of a multi-tiered component-based architecture has provided for flexibility (providing ease of change by restricting the area of change) as well as robustness (limiting the scope of the effect of change).

DATA-COMPONENT MINING

Data-component mining is the process by which an existing data model can be analyzed and broken up into sub data models with associated data-components. One approach to component mining is to study the data model to identify loosely coupled sets of entities. Each such set of entities can be called a sub-data model. Each such sub-data model is a good candidate for a component and more so if the sub-data model is used by more than one application. Use cases have become a standard way of defining requirements/functionality in object-oriented design. A list of existing as well as future use cases can also provide a valuable perspective during data-component mining design. Related use cases can be combined to help identify sub-data models and consequently corresponding data components.

For example, in a portfolio management system, analysis of the ERD (entity relationship diagram) of the data model might suggest that the set of entities containing historical performance data could constitute a sub-data model M1. Similarly, the set of entities pertaining to investment choices in a client's portfolio could constitute another sub-data model M2. There is now a potential use for two data components: C1 corresponding to model M1 (historical performance data) and C2 corresponding to model M2 (client's investment choices). Alternatively, it could start with use cases. For example, consider the following use cases:

- U1 — Provide inquiry of client's investment elections.
- U2 — Provide investment election change update/change.
- U3 — Provide inquiry of investment performance data.
- U4 — Provide update of investment performance data.
- U5 — Calculate portfolio values for a given client.

U1 and U2 deal with the same information (a client's investment choices). Similarly, U3 and U4 deal with the same information (investment performance data). U5 deals with the client's investment choices as well as investment performance data. Since investment performance data is independent of a client's investment choices, the entities in the data model corresponding to investment performance data, can be said to be loosely coupled with the entities pertaining to client investment elections. Therefore, investment performance data as well as client investment choices are both candidates for sub-data models with corresponding data components. The implementation of U5 would then involve use of both data components.

CONCLUSION

The data component approach to data management can be valuable in an environment involving object-oriented applications and relational databases. The primary advantage provided by this approach is ensuring that the application responsible for updating information is responsible for providing inquiry of the same information, thereby providing for superior change management. This approach can be used in any environment that allows development of component-based applications.

Chapter 13
Integrating Process and Data Models in a Horizontal Organization

David C. Wallace

INFORMATION SYSTEMS ARE CREATED TO HELP ACHIEVE THE GOALS AND OBJECTIVES OF THE ORGANIZATION by integrating them with information technology. Information technology is an extensive concept in which all the new technologies from fax machines to multimedia devices to new computer hardware and software are grouped. To be an effective part of an organization, individuals must understand and use information technology within the organization.

Therefore, an organization that wishes to be successful must first develop a strategic plan, which involves a systematic way of integrating information systems (IS) and information technology (IT). Currently, the IS field is focusing on developing both new methodologies and criteria for the evaluation and selection of appropriate methodologies. This is often completed without regard to new trends within the business and organization fields. When that happens, the new methodologies may not meet the needs of the business community and might produce systems that are flawed.

IS methodologies have largely ignored the recent trends within the business management area — the gap between research and practice. One of these major trends focuses on aligning organizational resources around essential processes, or *core processes*. This trend has been identified by F. Ostroff and D. Smith of McKinsey & Company as the horizontal corporation. M.A. Burns, Chairman of Ryder System Inc., states that the horizontal corporation concept is the wave of the future. From such large profit-centered organizations as General Electric, AT&T, Ryder, and Xerox to such small nonprofit organizations as the Police Department at Illinois

State University, there is a movement toward the horizontal organization. L.A. Bossidy, chairman of Allied Signal Inc., sees a significant increase in productivity as more organizations restructure themselves around this concept.

In this paradigm, the organization restructures its goals and objectives around the essential processes that define the organization's existence and sequential survival. The result is the flattening of the organizational structure into essential processes — eliminating the traditional hierarchy of bureaucratic divisions, departments, or sections. This allows both profit and nonprofit organizations to be more responsive to their clients or customers. The traditional goals of profitability, market share, and shareholders' satisfaction will not be identified as goals, but as natural outcomes resulting from the emphasis on tying goals to an organization's essential processes.

Integrating recent trends in the business organization field with an effective IS methodology is a critical success factor for an organization. For a profit-centered organization, this will often provide the means to achieve competitive advantages in the market by: enhancing existing products and services, developing new products and services, changing the existing industry and its characteristics, and creating new industries and markets.

For a nonprofit organization, the ability to stretch shrinking resources to meet the demands of its constituents is critical to its success. As budget dollars for local, state, and federal agencies are cut, these agencies still find themselves responsible for meeting the requirements of their charters. They will also need to integrate their IS structures around proven trends within the organization field to achieve their maximum productivity. Therefore, it is important to develop IS methodologies that integrate these recent trends.

THE HORIZONTAL CORPORATION

The horizontal corporation is an approach for all types of organizations — public or private, profit or nonprofit, corporate or sole proprietorships, large or small. The prerequisites for this approach are to redefine corporate goals around strategic actions that will improve the organization's competitiveness, efficiency, or other strategic actions defined by the organization. One important goal for any organization is to focus on improvement.

To meet the challenges of competitive domestic and international markets or the demands for shrinking funding dollars, organizations must constantly review and improve their operations. The organization must know its markets and customers thoroughly to know what it will take to satisfy them. For nonprofit organizations, shareholders include the people they serve and the funding sources on which they depend. Once these corporate goals have been clearly identified, the organization should be able to identify key objectives that will help them achieve these goals (e.g., customer and supplier satisfaction). These key objectives are measurable and identifiable for reach process and should contribute to the organization goals.

The next step requires the organization to identify its essential processes. These processes can be characterized by mission-critical applications or core processes. The applications focus on the very purpose or meaning of the organization (e.g., the identification of new markets and new customers, retention of existing customers, and other critical applications). The very purpose or meaning criteria can be answered by focusing on the actions necessary to accomplish the corporate goals. The key objectives identified in the previous step should provide insight into the identification of the essential processes. For example, customer satisfaction can be achieved through customer support, new product development, and sales and fulfillment. The next series of steps involves the actual restructuring of the organization.

Multidisciplinary Efforts

Once the essential processes have been identified, the organization will restructure itself around these processes. Each process will have a manager who helps facilitate the coordination and communication within the process and with other processes. Each process should link related tasks to yield a product or service to a customer or user. Careful attention should be given to the elimination of tasks that do not support, in some way, the related objectives of the process. Such tasks or activities are a waste of time and resources.

Training, evaluating, and paying employees should be linked to the accomplishments of objectives of the essential processes. Each process is responsible for all tasks needed to produce the end-product or service. This requires each process to be multidisciplinary (e.g., finance, marketing, production, accounting, or sales). The intent is to localize the necessary tasks for an essential process to streamline operations so that the organization can react quickly to changing conditions. Ideally, each task should harmoniously fit together with the next to generate the end result, thereby eliminating layers of bureaucracy that tend to increase costs and delay actions. All essential processes should harmoniously fit together to achieve all strategic goals of the organization.

By eliminating layers of administration and bureaucracy, each process can focus on accomplishing its objectives and becoming better able to meet the constant challenges of a changing market. The upper-level support departments provide additional expertise (e.g., legal, technical, and administrative). Core knowledge and expertise will be provided by the essential process. The main purpose of flattening the organization structure into horizontal layers of essential processes is to allow the organization to function more efficiently and quickly.

Traditional organizational structures require much coordination across department boundaries where such functions as sales, marketing, management, and accounting are often housed. The larger, more complex organizations would often experience long delays and information failure (e.g., lost or misdirected paperwork) as information was passed from one functional area or department to another. By localizing the necessary tasks into one process, the organization can provide a seamless effort in which the amount of information interchange is kept to a minimum, thereby reducing delays and information failures. Companies that have moved toward the horizontal corporate approach have been able to reduce response time significantly and improve overall operating performance.

The horizontal concept is illustrated in Exhibit 13.1. The essential processes operate on a horizontal level using the multidisciplinary efforts within each process to accomplish their objectives. Each process is not a standalone entity, but is integrated into part of an entire picture in which each part communicates and coordinates with each other part. Realistically, special expertise and strategic direction are needed to monitor changing conditions in the markets and environments in which the organization must exist.

These strategic considerations should be accomplished at a higher level. The more operational and managerial considerations would be held at the process level. Downsized support departments (e.g., finance, legal, accounting, and marketing) will exist at the higher level within the organization to provide the expertise needed by the processes. Strategic direction will be provided by a high-level department. The responsibility for this department will be to provide strategic planning and direction for the organization. Exhibit 13.1 illustrates the relationship between the essential processes and the higher-level support departments. The interactions between the processes, between the support departments, and between the support departments and the processes are shown with double arrows.

Information, and the systems that support its capture, transformation, and dissemination, are strategic to the survival of the organization. To support horizontal organization adequately, IS personnel must incorporate a methodology that supports the horizontal approach. Without recognizing the recent trends in organizational structure and adopting methods to facilitate their integration, information system resources will not gain full management support and may lose their major impact on the organization.

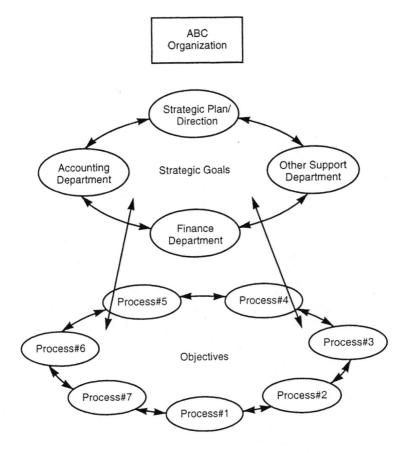

Exhibit 13.1. Horizontal organization structure.

IS METHODOLOGIES

Integrating IS throughout the organization is a key issue for senior management. Two popular methodologies that can be used to facilitate the integration of information systems within an organization are: a data-focused approach and a process-focused approach.

The Data-Focused Approach

The data-focused approach is currently the more popular methodology. Generally, data models are more stable reflections of how an organization uses data and establishes business rules within its various components. By focusing on the types of data and various attributes and classes they represent, a comprehensive, relational, or hierarchical model can be

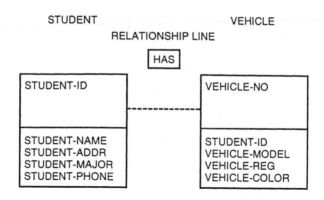

STUDENT   VEHICLE

RELATIONSHIP LINE

HAS

STUDENT-ID	VEHICLE-NO
STUDENT-NAME STUDENT-ADDR STUDENT-MAJOR STUDENT-PHONE	STUDENT-ID VEHICLE-MODEL VEHICLE-REG VEHICLE-COLOR

DATA MODEL

INCORPORATED BUSINESS RULES, BASED ON THE
DATA STRUCTURE AND RELATIONSHIP LINE:

1. A STUDENT IS UNIQUELY IDENTIFIED THROUGH STUDENT ID.
2. A VEHICLE IS UNIQUELY IDENTIFIED THROUGH VEHICLE NO.
3. A STUDENT MAY HAVE ZERO OR MANY VEHICLES.
4. A VEHICLE CAN ONLY EXIST IN BUSINESS IF IT IS ASSOCIATED WITH ONE STUDENT.
5. A VEHICLE CANNOT BE ADDED UNLESS IT IS IMMEDIATELY ASSOCIATED WITH ONE STUDENT.

Exhibit 13.2. Data model with associated business rules.

constructed to reflect their relationships within the organization. This model can serve to help simplify and reduce duplication of data, and validate business rules governing relationships and dependencies. Data-focused models are powerful tools for data administrators, but offer little help for senior executives in terms of IS planning unless they are properly presented (see Exhibit 13.2).

For nontechnical computer personnel, data-focused models are often very difficult to comprehend and implement within an organization. Many experienced IS managers and academics do not fully understand the data modeling process and the related topics of object orientation for developing information systems on the project level as well as on the corporate level.

The Process-Focused Approach

The process-focused methodology looks at IS as a series of related activities that transform data into information. The emphasis is on the processes or activities that comprise a particular information system. A model is generated to reflect the hierarchical relationships of information systems within an organization. Therefore, an information system like accounting can be broken into basic processes (e.g., accounts payable, accounts receivable, payroll, and general ledger).

These processes can be further decomposed into smaller processes. For example, payroll can include the following related processes: generating payroll, generating quarterly payroll reports, generating year-end payroll reports, and updating employee records. Each of these processes can further be decomposed into smaller, related processes. The end result is the hierarchical process structure. Exhibit 13.3 illustrates this hierarchical relationship between the processes.

Each process has a set of objectives that supports the objectives of the next higher level process that in turn support the overall goals of the organization. Therefore, each activity or process can be justified by the objectives and goals of the organization. An organization model can be created to facilitate the process of evaluating activities within each information system, and to establish an effective decision support system for management. The evaluation process could be used to identify activities that are not contributing to the goals and objectives of the organization, and either eliminate or modify them. A recent study indicates that the process-focused approach remains (or is being reinstated) as the preferred IS planning tool.

The next important step for the process-focused approach is to integrate it into a corporate structure. Recent studies have indicated that senior IS managers and senior corporate management are looking for information technology that can be elevated to the organizational level.

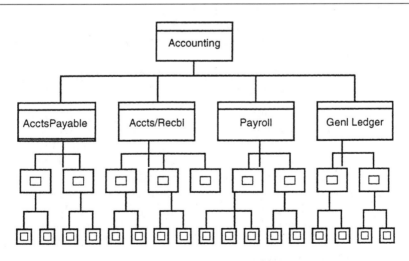

Exhibit 13.3. Simplified Information Systems structure.

Both process-focused and data-focused approaches have made significant effects on the project level where IS personnel have used each technique to develop information systems for specific applications. Yet, neither technique has made any significant effect on the corporate level. A methodology must be developed that can take the strengths of both process- and data-focused approaches and blend them into a corporate model — which can include the recent trends of the horizontal organization. This has been successfully accomplished in industry using the combination of the IDEF0 Activity Modeling and IDEF1X Data Modeling approaches, as well as through the Information Engineering Methodologies of J. Martin and C. Finkelstein.

INTEGRATING INTO THE HORIZONTAL ORGANIZATION

Integrating information systems technology into the corporate organizational structure requires the support of both senior management and lower-level personnel if it is to be successful. It must be a methodology that can be understood and communicated throughout the organization by both computer technical and noncomputer technical personnel to be effective. Since the horizontal organization concept uses multidisciplinary teams within each process, an effective IS methodology must be simple enough to communicate across disciplines and yet be effective in IS planning. Process-focused modeling relies on simple, easy-to-understand symbols that can be used across disciplines. This methodology must be easy and effective enough to be used by all levels within the organization.

Senior executives identified IS planning and information integration as a key issue for competition and survival in today's market. A process-focused methodology is compatible with modeling tasks and activities at the essential process level as well as strategic activities at the higher level. A process-focused approach has been recommended as an appropriate methodology for an organization structure. The data-focused approach is most appropriate for the data administrator. Therefore, an important consideration is to develop a methodology that can integrate the strengths of both process- and data-focused approaches within an organizational model.

With the growth in computer-aided modeling tools (e.g., CASE), the complex task of representing interrelated activities and their associated data components can be accomplished much more easily for both the process- and the data-focused methodologies. Detailed computer specifications can be generated to alleviate the problems of consistency at each level and between levels within each type of model hierarchy. The systems analyst must be very careful in choosing appropriate CASE tools to help facilitate the integration of process- and data-focused models. The CASE tool must be very easy to use and comprehensive enough to allow for easy integration between the two models.

164

Using Dynamic CASE Tools. The diagrams should have simple, easy-to-follow menus that allow the rapid development of each level of diagram. If the diagraming tool is difficult to use to create and modify different symbols, it becomes a more static tool with which systems analysts will tend to create models that they are reluctant to change. The tool should be aesthetically pleasing to view, and data flows should flow with arcs, straight lines, and right angles. Finally, the tool should be comprehensive enough to allow the systems analyst to move smoothly from the front-end stages (i.e., analysis and design) to the back-end stages (i.e., implementation and installation).

When users and systems analysts work with a CASE tool, the process should be a pleasing experience, thereby allowing the tool to be more dynamic or easily changeable. When the people who work with the model are glad that the model has been created and never have to touch it again, a static model has been created. If the model-creation process was a pleasing experience, they tend not to be bothered by changing it — this is a dynamic model. In the horizontal corporation, information systems change constantly as a result of changes in the competitive environment. Therefore, it is important that the model be a dynamic model capable of changing constantly.

By using simple, easy-to-understand symbols supported by a comprehensive data dictionary, a process model can be generated to represent detailed information processing as well as the more abstract decision-making at the higher level within the organization. The ultimate goal of integrating information systems methodologies into the horizontal organization is to develop a comprehensive organization model using a dynamic CASE tool that can handle constant changes. The major component of this model is a process-focused model supported by a data-focused model representing the higher-level support processes and the essential processes within the organization. This organization model can be used as a blueprint for the restructuring of the traditional hierarchical organization into the newer horizontal organization.

Data Structures. For organizations interested in developing a horizontal structure, the process-focused model can be used to reinforce and enhance communication, information flows, and coordination (i.e., exchanging of information) between the essential processes and the support departments. The data-focused portion of the integrated model supports the processes by ensuring that the data structures used (and perhaps created) by the processes are in their most logical formats. It will remove redundancy and simplify the actual data structures used within the organization.

Exhibit 13.4 represents the overview of this approach. In addition, more detailed discussions concerning process modeling techniques appear in

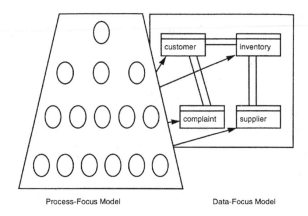

Process-Focus Model   Data-Focus Model

Exhibit 13.4. Simplified integration of process and data models.

McLeod's *Systems Analysis and Design: An Organization Approach* (The Dryden Press, 1994) and other comparable process modeling texts.

The arrows in Exhibit 13.4 illustrate the interaction or connection between the data structures in the process model and the data structure representation in the data model. Each access to a data structure in the process model is represented by either an object (e.g., customer) on the data model, or a relationship between objects (e.g., the connection between customer and inventory, or customer buys inventory). It is beyond the scope of this chapter to provide the detailed process of connecting the process-focused model to the data-focused model.

A possible connection can be established between the process and the data models. Once the process model has been developed, the principles of object orientation can be applied to the construction of a data model that will often provide better insight and use of existing data structures. If a particular data structure on the process model is not in its most logical format (redundancy with other data structures, transitive relationships or other problems associated related with data structures), the data model will show the changes and these changes will eventually be incorporated into the process model. Exhibit 13.5 illustrates the creation of a logical data structure model (entity-relationship diagram) and how it influences the changes in the process-focused diagram.

The original diagram accessed a complex data structure identified as a customer rental file. A normalization process generates a data model that in essence created three entities (i.e., customer, employee, and car) with relationships between the objects where customers rent cars and employees maintain cars. The final result is that the process diagram is modified by the data model. The data model is a quality control mechanism that

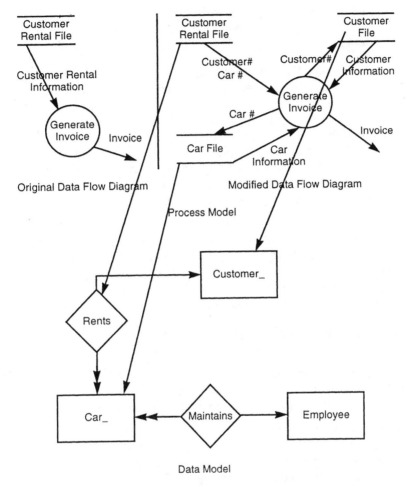

Exhibit 13.5. Relationship between data and process models.

ensures that the data used in the organization are in the most logical format. When that format is assured, data can easily be shared throughout the organization to improve both coordination and communication between the essential processes and the support departments on the higher level.

Data can also be easily maintained, thereby ensuring data integrity. It is the business rules in the activities or processes within the organization that establish the relationships between the various data objects. As the process model is applied to the entire organization, the data model is also extended to the entire organization (generally depicted by Exhibit 13.2). The end-product is an organization process model supported by an organization data model. The data administrator is responsible for maintaining the data model and coordinating with the various processes and support departments to ensure that changes in the process model are incorporated into the data model, subsequently modifying the process model.

Using the Internet. The Internet has grown at an astonishing rate over the past few years. Companies have been trying to integrate the Internet into their organizations to gain a strategic advantage with customers who now search the Internet for products and services. Developing applications of the Internet is an extension of the electronic data interchange (EDI) between customers and the company — except that the new EDI is open all year with customers all over the world. Now that companies can offer products or services that are bought over the Internet through the use of CGI programming techniques, the amount of overhead needed to maintain a sales operation has been dramatically reduced in may instances.

Understanding the relationship between home page development, CGI programming, network security, and Internet marketing strategies (such as listing the corporate home page on Yahoo, Lycos, WebCrawler, or Infoseek) is critical to the successful integration of Internet strategies into the process and data models of the organization.

CREATING A HORIZONTAL ORGANIZATION

To create a horizontal organization by integrating a process model and a data model, the organization will still have to identify the strategic goals of the organization and key competitive advantages (e.g., customer satisfaction and quality control issues) to achieve these goals.

These key competitive advantages will help the organization identify the core or essential processes necessary to achieve the goals. The next step is the restructuring of the organization. This involves establishing multidisciplinary teams centered around the essential processes. At this point, the teams will identify key objectives that will help them achieve the overall goals of the organization. Once the objectives have been identified, the essential process can be decomposed into several basic subprocesses that will allow the essential process to achieve its objectives. These subprocesses will often be multidisciplinary, involving accounting, finance, marketing, sales, production, and others.

After the essential processes and key subprocesses are identified, the organization should know what support departments are needed to provide more expertise for the essential processes. Of course, the standard support departments (e.g., legal, accounting, and other basic support functions) will probably be identified by both senior-level management and the essential processes. Each subprocess will be decomposed into smaller processes — each with its set of objectives (that support the objectives of its parent subprocess, as was mentioned earlier) — thereby creating a hierarchical information system model.

Again, the process of generating an IS model is not a disguise replacing one hierarchical structure with another. The process modeling concept is the identification of related activities or processes as a means of understanding the various multidisciplinary activities needed for incorporation into an essential process or support department. It shows how the activities within the organization interact, and not necessarily the lines of authority and responsibility often identified in the traditional hierarchical structure. Exhibit 13.2 shows the hierarchical nature of the process modeling method.

To facilitate the generation of an organization process model, a steering committee should be established at the highest level of the organization, to set such standards and guidelines as naming conventions for data elements and process identification. Each support department and essential process is responsible for developing its portion of the process model. Some overhead training will be needed to provide personnel involved in the development of the process model with basic information about process modeling. Experience has shown that a basic discussion (e.g., type of symbols, use of input data flows, processing, and output data flows) is necessary only to get nontechnical information personnel involved in the development process.

With the advance of group decision support systems (GDSS), a systems analyst can facilitate the decision-making processes used to generate the key objectives and the subprocesses. As each support department and essential process builds its respective model, the steering committee will provide guidance and coordination between all of these components. When each portion of the model (i.e., support departments and the essential processes) is completed, the steering committee will be responsible for bringing each portion together into an overall organization model.

Once the overall process model is created, the data administrator will be responsible for normalizing the data structures and subsequently for generating the data model. The series of steps used to generate the actual data model is beyond the scope of this chapter. But the general concepts of object-oriented analysis and design, along with the normalizing process, are used to generate this data model. Once the data model is completed, the process model must be modified to reflect the more logically created data structures. Exhibit 13.4 illustrates generally how data models on the project level change the process model. The same approach is used to develop data models on the organizational level and subsequent changes to the organizational level process models.

A CASE tool should be used to expedite the development of the subprocesses for the essential processes and for the support departments. The principles for selecting the appropriate CASE tool were discussed previously. In short, the CASE tool should be process oriented, with the ability to generate data models in support of the process models. The CASE tool should be powerful enough to handle complex organizations involving many levels. It should also be flexible enough to handle the dynamics of change. This decision must not be a trivial decision.

Building a dynamic process and data model is the salient consideration when deciding on an appropriate CASE tool. The methodology that supports the CASE tool is also important. The main point of this chapter is that the horizontal organization can be depicted by a process-focused model supported by a data model. Therefore, the use of a few simple, easy-to-understand symbols is necessary so that both technical and nontechnical IS personnel can use them appropriately.

Getting senior management to commit to a CASE tool and methodology is the underlying foundation of this approach. The use of the CASE tool must be a total effort by all personnel. The maintenance of the process model is the responsibility of each essential process and support department. With the help of the systems analyst component of each process, changes will be the constant force that drives the continual development of the process model. By incorporating users and IS personnel into the process model methodology, a common communication tool (e.g., CASE tool) can be used to help facilitate changes within the organization. Each person within the organization should be able to visualize his or her contribution to the organization and its goals by locating his or her process and its objectives in the process model.

SUMMARY

Incorporating the horizontal concept into today's organization is an important trend that will allow the organization to be more competitive in domestic and international markets for profit organizations and funding sources for nonprofit organizations. The horizontal organization will reduce the amount of bureaucracy that often generates information delays and failures. Organizations will need to be able to change quickly to meet the challenges of a volatile, competitive environment. IS methodologies should integrate recent trends to be successful and accepted by organizations. An effective approach would be to integrate the horizontal organization into an organizational process model supported by a data model. The process model should focus on the essential processes and the support departments in building its information system model.

The process model will help organizations move logically toward the horizontal organization by ensuring that the activities within each essential process and support department support the overall goals of the organization. The process model will also provide better coordination and communication throughout the organization by integrating the information used within it. The data model that supports the process model will ensure that the information is in its most logical format, thereby allowing the various components of the organization that need information to have it in a timely fashion. With the help of an effective, user-friendly CASE tool used as the common communication tool throughout the organization, the process model will become a dynamic tool for change.

Chapter 14
Data Warehouse Design: Issues in Dimensional Data Modeling

Jack McElreath

BEFORE BEGINNING A DISCUSSION OF THE METHODS OF MODELING INFORMATION IN A DATA WAREHOUSE, it is important to agree on the type of data to be stored in the warehouse and how the data differs from traditional operational data.

OPERATIONAL VS. DATA WAREHOUSE APPLICATIONS

Operational applications track business events (e.g., orders and payments) and the entities associated with those events (e.g., customers and products) from creation to completion. The status of each event is constantly updated, and the general objective of OLTP (online transaction processing) systems is to get the event processed and completed as soon as practical; processing usually means cost, and completion usually means revenue. Data is typically accessed at the detail level; individual records are read, updated, and replaced. Entities associated with the in-process events are constantly updated to reflect current attributes, and, generally, no history of an entity's prior status is maintained. Entities are usually retained while there is an open business event or likelihood of an incoming event.

Data warehouse applications capture completed business events and all associated information necessary for strategic analysis. Events are static (i.e., history cannot be changed) and held as long as they provide some historical significance. Data is typically accessed at aggregate levels; detail events are summarized across selected entities or categories. In general, the information retained for the entities related to completed events is

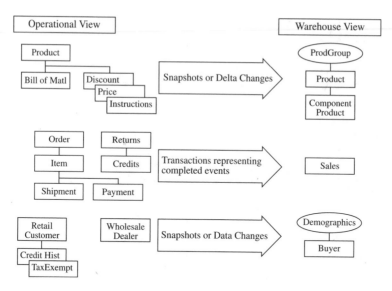

Exhibit 14.1. Operational and warehouse data models.

limited to that needed for aggregation or filtering of analytical queries; snapshots of entities may be needed to reflect the entity at the time of any associated events.

The operational model is process oriented and, often, application oriented; records and relationships support the flow of data from creation to completion. Warehouse models are analysis oriented and, ideally, subject oriented; records and relationships support the desired query aggregations. Data moves from the operational application to the warehouse but the data view — the model — should be quite different (see Exhibit 14.1).

Ideally, there should be little redundancy between the operational and warehouse databases. The completed events are purged from the operational database and moved to the warehouse on completion. The entities associated with the events have some necessary redundancy — the same product may be referenced on both active and historical events. However, redundancy should be limited to those entity attributes needed for both processing in the operational system and strategic analysis in the warehouse.

In practice, closed events must often be retained for some period in the operational system and, sometimes, in-process events must be recorded in the warehouse. For example, it may be impractical, inefficient, or undesirable to move the data real-time to the warehouse; it is often more efficient and less intrusive to extract and move the data periodically. It is also common to access recent history in the processing of active events (e.g., prior payment is shown on a new bill) and it may not be practical to cross over to a warehouse on a separate platform to retrieve this data. The goal, however, should be to avoid both of these cases to reduce the data inconsistency problems that accompany redundancy. The fastest way to destroy confidence in systems is to provide different answers to the same data questions because of redundant sources.

EXAMPLE OF EXPENDITURE ANALYSIS

To explore dimensional modeling issues, consider the example of a personal application for strategically analyzing expenditures. Most people certainly have an operational system to buy and pay for items, but many (including me) do not know where their money went, whether outgo matches income, or what their expenses should or will be in the future.

A data warehouse would certainly facilitate analysis. This simple personal application essentially has the same functional issues and analytical challenges as those encountered in any corporate warehouse; it is smaller in volume of data and users but no less complex. The technical issues increase with volume but the business issues and user views are just as difficult as they are in most large corporations.

An example assumes that the individual (me in this case) has an automated system for all cash outlays: purchases, payments, donations, and all other family expenses. This software can be used for all purchases and payments made by check, credit card, or cash to provide a monthly file (more likely a shoe box of illegible receipts) containing completed purchase and payment events. Information about each entity (e.g., stores, people, banks, and credit card issuers) associated with purchases and payments must also be made available to the warehouse. This includes snapshots of the relevant family members, products, and vendors.

Because the transaction volumes or usage patterns to be supported in the warehouse are unclear, I first select my hardware and software platforms. My spouse is currently controlling the operational systems using Quicken Version 1.0 running on a Compaq 286 portable. I think I will probably need a 200-MHz multimedia client hooked to a 64-bit UNIX server with a fiber Internet connection. I will also need software from Cognos, SAS, Oracle, Arbor, and ActiVision, which is easily obtainable from a local retailer. Spending too much time on infrastructure decisions is not worthwhile because the technology becomes obsolete in a few months anyway.

The advantage designers of smaller (in terms of data volume and number of users) warehouses enjoy is that there is probably no need to compromise functional requirements because of technical performance or capacity constraints. The line separating small from large data collections is constantly being raised; 20 years ago, we would become concerned at hundreds of thousands of records; 10 years ago, our concerns started at

1 million records; and today, concern is piqued at tens of millions of records and panic sets in at hundreds of millions. I would have predicted that billions of records would be routinely handled by the year 2000, but the date problems will implode the industry and make all else academic.

ADVANTAGES AND DISADVANTAGES OF DIMENSIONAL MODELING

The general conclusion evolving from the experts and tool vendors of data warehouse solutions is that for the purpose of schematically defining and analyzing historical information, dimensional modeling is preferable to the techniques used to model operational data (usually some form of entity-relationship or network diagram). Dimensional models are, in theory, simpler for users to understand and manipulate. Simplicity is both the benefit and the problem. It is difficult to model complex information with a simple technique. If the model is too complex, it will not serve users' needs; if it is too simple, it cannot answer tough questions.

Dimensional models are logical, not physical constructs; the underlying database for dimensional models is either relational or a multidimensional cube. It may also be necessary, based on the complexity of warehouse data, to employ different modeling techniques in the progression from the user view back to the data source, such as cube for the user, star model for the analyst, and entity relationship for the database administrator (see Exhibit 14.2). The ideal solution is to have the mapping capability to transparently transform the simpler user view to the complex physical data view,

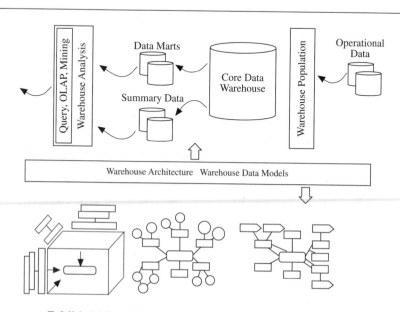

Exhibit 14.2. Warehouse architecture and data models.

efficiently and correctly. Unfortunately, data warehouse tools have not fully evolved to meet this need.

This shortcoming is the driving force behind the popularity of data marts — a mechanism to create a simple and focused subset of the more complex core warehouse. Their place in the warehouse architecture is also shown in Exhibit 14.2. If most user access can be satisfied from the custom view, then the complexities of the base warehouse are masked from the user. The problem with this approach is, of course, that as new requirements evolve, the party responsible for creating custom warehouse views (and this is seldom the user) must get involved in fulfilling new queries, potentially delaying information delivery.

Once the data warehouse is populated, the strategic user then forms complex aggregate views of this data to isolate trends and establish profound changes in the management or direction of the enterprise, which, in the case of our example, is the family. Individual events (e.g., a given purchase) are seldom of interest; more often, it is the aggregation of facts across selected dimensions (e.g., total spent on mail-order children's clothing in late summer). In general, individual events are provided only when some highlighted aggregate event must be exploded (i.e., drilled-down) to provide supporting detail. For example, once I have determined that I am spending excessively on sporting equipment, I might drill-down and discover that the purchase of the $500 titanium golf club was the major culprit.

DATA MODELS

In dimensional modeling, the numeric attributes of the event represent facts, such as quantity, cost, discount, and tax. People, places, times, things, and categories associated with the fact are shown as dimensions.

The Star Model

The star model (as shown in Exhibit 14.3) gets its name from the dimensions that radiate from central facts. An alternative explanation for the name could be that stars shed little light and even that light takes a long time to arrive; actually, stars, like data warehouses, emit a lot of light — it is just that so little ever reaches us.

The Snowflake Model

A snowflake model is an extended star model in which each dimension radiates aggregate categories (see Exhibit 14.4). These categories (sometimes called outboards) are what provide the richness of analysis within the data model. For example, we might ask how much is being spent by certain family members for clothing products to be used on family pets during the Christmas season. I believe these models are called snowflakes because they crystallize with infinite variety. However, in sufficient quantity,

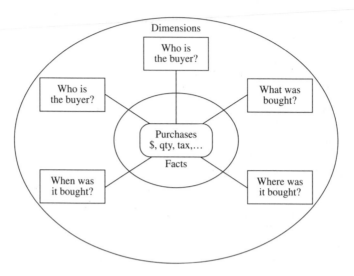

Exhibit 14.3.   The star model.

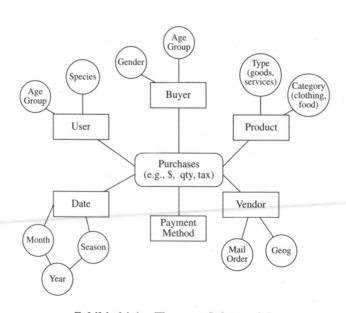

Exhibit 14.4.   The snowflake model.

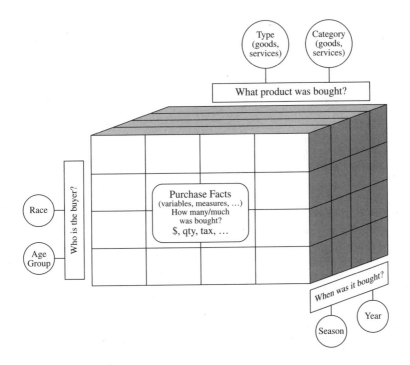

Exhibit 14.5. The cube model.

their beauty may be masked by the need to plow through them to make progress.

The Cube Model

Some vendors prefer to visualize the data as a cube — dimensions form the axes of the cube of facts; outboards are shown as hierarchies of each dimension. These multidimensional cube or hypercube models can be effective, but complex aggregations become difficult to envision, draw, or display on a two-dimensional surface. In Exhibit 14.5, purchases are analyzed at the intersection of three base dimensions (i.e., buyer, month, product); multiple purchases by the same buyer of the same product in the same month are conceptually summarized.

Dimensions may be rotated or eliminated in any requested view, such as drop product from the analysis and show purchases by buyer/ month with month on the vertical axis. Hierarchical groupings may be incorporated above each base dimension as outboards or snow- flakes. These result in a large number of additional aggregation possibilities, such as age group/month/product and year/product class/gender. It is

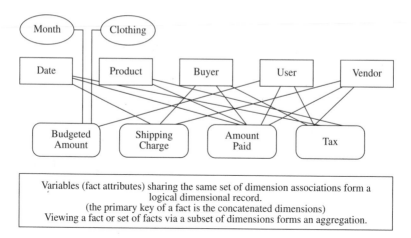

Variables (fact attributes) sharing the same set of dimension associations form a logical dimensional record.
(the primary key of a fact is the concatenated dimensions)
Viewing a fact or set of facts via a subset of dimensions forms an aggregation.

Exhibit 14.6.   Purist view of dimensional data.

clear that a relatively small number of dimensions and categories can result in many potential aggregations. The eight types across three dimensions in the exhibit provide more than 100 different permutations (approximately $2^8 - 1$). If we were to construct a six-dimensional cube with 13 outboards from the snowflake model in Exhibit 14.4, the possible aggregate permutations would exceed 100,000. Some of these aggregations are surely nonsensical or unnecessary; the trick is to match current and future user requirements to permissible aggregations and further determine which of these aggregations are to materialize statically (i.e., during the data load) versus dynamically (i.e., during the query).

A purist view of dimensional data would define each fact, or variable, separately and associate that variable with 1 to n dimensions (see Exhibit 14.6). A logical record would then consist of any variables sharing the same set of dimensions (including categories). An aggregated view would occur whenever a variable is viewed through a subset of existing dimensions. For example, tax and amount paid are part of a logical fact record because they have identical dimension associations. Budgeted amount is associated with user, month, and product group. A view of tax and amount paid through month/date, product group/product, and user would be a conceptual aggregation of all facts associated with only those dimensions. Budgeted amount could then be compared to actual expenditures at that level.

Database Management Systems

There is an evolving debate about whether online analytical processing (OLAP) modeling and implementation should be based on relational database management system (DBMS) products, multidimensional

DBMSs, or both (e.g., relational for atomic data, multidimensional for aggregations). Although valid arguments can be posed for both, the final outcome is based more on the success of individual DBMS products in providing aggregation capabilities that are flexible (in terms of ease of adding new facts and dimensions), efficient (in terms of acceptable response time), manageable (in terms of data quality), and easy to use (in terms of providing the user with understandable views of complex data).

Another major factor involves the dynamic versus static aggregation decisions and the ability to alter these choices as data usage evolves. Static aggregation would occur as data are loaded; dynamic aggregation would occur as the query is executed. Currently, relational products seem to have the lead in flexibility and efficiency for high volumes and multidimensional products in ease of use.

To meet the needs of complex data warehouses, dimensional models and the associated software tools must evolve to incorporate the following:

- Complex facts where a network of related events can be combined to form a single fact view.
- Complex dimensions containing subsets (including repeating groups) and supersets of data.
- Dimension-to-category associations that include many-to-many relationships (i.e., networks in addition to hierarchies).
- Recursive associations within categories.
- Temporal associations (i.e., point-in-time data).
- Business rules in data derivation.
- Effective aggregate navigation, or the ability to recognize presummarized data.

There are certainly other needs, but these directly affect the modeling of data.

DATA MODELING LEVELS

Data modeling should occur at four levels: conceptual, logical, physical, and technical.

The Conceptual Data Model

The conceptual data model is a high-level definition of the major entities, events, and associations required for the application being defined; it contains few, if any, attributes of the conceptual entities. For a data warehouse, the conceptual model should be subject oriented rather than application oriented, and use dimensions, facts, and categorizations rather than entities, events, and tables. Subject orientation means that data from separate operational applications (e.g., business expenses, donations, rentals, purchases, and budgets) should be consolidated into a single analytical subject (i.e., expenditures).

The Logical Data Model

The logical data model should define all entities/roles, events, categorizations, and relationships necessary to deliver the warehouse user requirements. The model is fully attributed and somewhat normalized. We have been taught that OLTP logical models are defined in third normal form, but the clarity of warehouse data is often improved by denormalizing some information (e.g., derived attributes, business rules, summary data, and data marts). The logical model should not be dictated or affected by the DBMS type (e.g., network, relational, multidimensional, and object) or product (e.g., Oracle, IMS, DB2, and Redbrick) chosen for implementation. In theory, one could convert from any DBMS to any other and use the logical model as a starting point for conversion.

The Physical Data Model

The physical data model is the phase in which the logical model is adapted to the major software and performance constraints of the DBMS, data and usage statistics, and intended processing platform. Physical design decisions are not usually transparent to the applications using the database. Ideally, the physical model mirrors the logical model.

It is more difficult to define the precise line between logical and physical design with warehouse models. Some examples of physical modeling steps include conversion of the dimensional model to a relational or multidimensional structure, data distribution or logical partitioning, entity and referential integrity methods, obvious denormalization needed for performance, and temporal data management options. In many cases, data summarization and creation of distributed custom warehouses are better handled in the logical modeling phase. The major question is whether these decisions involve the clarity of the user view of data (i.e., the realm of the logical model) or are dictated by performance issues or query/DBMS product shortcomings (i.e., the realm of the physical model).

The Technical Data Model

The technical data model incorporates the initial and ongoing tuning of the database, transparent to the applications using it. Indexing, bit maps, physical partitioning, and DASD space management are examples of technical modeling. This is the domain of the database administrator (a complete grasp of the subject usually occurs concurrent with the inability to function as a member of society at large).

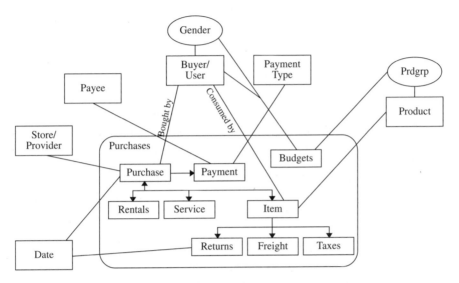

Exhibit 14.7. Expanded model of expenditure facts.

Model Expansion

If a dimensional model for the logical model is chosen, it is often necessary to simplify the data (and perhaps the user requirements) or explode complex components to incorporate essential network or hierarchical subsets of information. The warehouse in the family expenditures application is intended to track all expenditures, not just those for real products. What happens when the simple model must be expanded to incorporate payments for such items as services, health care, charity, and tolls? And, if one decides to include budgeted amounts for some dimensions, should returns and reimbursements be included? The model needed to fulfill the user requirements may begin to resemble Exhibit 14.6's depiction of the explosions of the individual components of the simple dimensional model. Many of these modeling decisions are subjective.

The star model may classify as expenditures a complex collection of components, depending on the type of purchase, method of payment, and the relationships to surrounding dimensions. In defining my family expenditures warehouse, I decided to incorporate all expenditures in a single fact set. I could have created separate fact tables for each class of expenditure — charity contributions, tax payments, highway tolls, and rentals — but any analysis across classes would have become impractical.

The extended model of expenditure facts in Exhibit 14.7 was created for several reasons, including the following:

- A single purchase can consist of multiple items (e.g., a VCR and a maintenance contract).
- The fact attributes can vary significantly between different expenditures (e.g., goods have quantities, services have hours, not all are taxed, and returns apply only to goods).
- A single purchase could involve multiple payments (e.g., part cash and part credit card, and installment payments).
- Relationships to dimensions may vary based on the type of component (e.g., buyers are associated with all purchases, users are optional and relate to the individual items).
- A single analysis may utilize many of the fact components (e.g., is the rate of returned purchases by female buyers of mail-order goods resulting in increasing freight costs?).
- Budgeted amounts will be created for some dimensions and categories.
- All the preceding are important for strategic analysis.

It may be possible to jam all this information into a single purchase fact by imbedding repeating groups and defining lots of attributes that are exclusive to a subset of records. In fact, this may have to be done during physical modeling if the software constraints or performance constraints leave no option. This model pollution should not be done, however, during logical design. The ideal is to provide software (i.e., query and DBMS) that can deal with complex data and transparently present that data in a simple customized view. Today, one is usually forced to simplify by restricting the core warehouse or by providing customized local repositories (i.e., data marts).

Dimensions can also become complex. Exhibit 14.8 shows a similar expansion of data for the producer associated with purchases. Provider types have both similarities and differences; stores selling goods may not have the same attributes or higher-level categorizations as other business or private entities providing charity, service, mortgage, or energy. The provider or payee associated with an expenditure could be a person (the plumber), a distributor (Walmart), a manufacturer (Nike), a church or synagogue, a municipal government, and on and on. One could increase the number of dimensions to include all distinct provider types as separate, mutually exclusive, entities, but this usually results in even more complexity and constraints. In general, it is better to consolidate into a single dimension role because it is easier to add a new type to an existing dimension than to add a new dimension to the model.

The following assumptions should be made about our strategic information needs for the provider dimension:

- The base provider describes all attributes common to every provider and serves as the focal point for most fact relationships: the supertypes (i.e., categorizations) above and subtypes (i.e., attributes

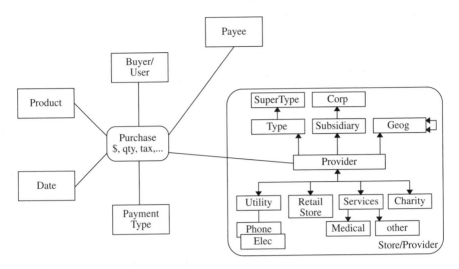

Exhibit 14.8. Expansion of data for store/provider associated with purchases.

exclusive to only some provider types) below. Subtypes may be squashed into the base component during physical design, but it is more informative to segregate them during logical modeling. Repeating groups, or arrays, of subtype data are especially messy and restrictive to imbed in the base entity (i.e., the utility company provides both gas and electricity).

- Some fact relationships may be firmly or optionally to a subtype or supertype rather than the base producer: for example, I donated to United Funds and not to individual member charitable organizations.
- Dimension categorizations must be established, each identifying subjective and objective criteria.
  - Are the categorization levels fixed or recursive? (For example, only permit two levels of corporate affiliations but permit variable levels of geography, such as city, state, country, and planet.)
  - Can a single producer concurrently belong to more than one member of a given category? (For example, producer is both Fortune 500 and pharmaceutical, each subjectively defined as a separate type in my model.)
  - Are the categorizations temporal? (For example, the producer has moved and, therefore, changed geographical affiliations. Do I have to remember the history to analyze older facts?)
  - These dimension categorizations are implemented as metadata in many of the OLAP tools; not only the schema (i.e., type to class), which is truly metadata, but the actual member values (e.g., meat and beverage records aggregate to food).

The ideal model, whether entity-relationship or dimensional, permits a simplistic view of dimensions and facts, transparently consolidating the complex underlying data as needed. For example, if I ask for the total spent on housing last year, it would be most effective if the request could be satisfied from presummarized data marts or from a myriad of detail composing that summary with no effect on the user view. The difficulties, of course, are that the consolidation can result in wrong or misunderstood results, and the DBMS and query software tools are somewhat limited in translating logical models to the supporting physical models.

Section III
Data Integrity and Quality

ENSURING DIRECT DATA INTEGRITY AND REFERENTIAL DATA INTEGRITY is a continuing concern for maintaining the value of application systems. This is true of both OLTP and OLAP based applications. Direct data integrity refers to the accuracy of individual items of data (e.g., 'rdd' is an incorrect spelling of 'red'). Referential integrity refers to the integrity of the relationship between items of data (e.g., invoice item records that belong to no invoices have no value). Decisions or activities that are based on corrupted data are pointless and can lead to monetary or material damages. From a quality standpoint, it is necessary to build procedures and processes that ensure data integrity and thus provide confidence about the accuracy of corporate data.

Data integrity and quality is an issue anytime there is a change to data. This includes insert, update, and delete operations against data repositories. In relational database(s), each of these operations must be executed in a specific order to ensure that the data is accurate during and after the operations are complete. For example, a cascading delete begins by removing records belonging to foreign keys. The primary key or parent record should be the last deletion in the operation. An insert of a logical record that consists of multiple physical records begins with an insert of the parent record, followed by inserts of the child records. This is opposite to the delete operation. Transaction processing is also relevant in this example. For example, if a cascading delete operation is interrupted (e.g., due to a power failure or a program failure), none of the records should be deleted. Those that were deleted before the interruption should be rolled back.

This section of the handbook reviews some common approaches for maintaining data and referential integrity in relational databases.

Chapter 15, "The Quality Vortex," examines the role that team members play in ensuring quality on projects.

Chapter 16, "What's Wrong with My Data," examines approaches for correcting "bad" data so that organizations can fully realize the potential of the systems that are being developed.

187

Chapter 17, "Programming Data Constraints Using Microsoft SQL Server," examines some of the commonly available contraints that can be attached to table columns at table creation time. These constraints are saved directly into the SQL Server data dictionary and automatically apply at runtime based on the occurrence of specific events. This information can also be applied to some versions of Sybase SQL Server tables because of the historical similarity between the Microsoft and Sybase products.

Chapter 18, "Referential Integrity for Database Design," defines referential integrity, describes its limitations with examples, and then proposes methods of overcoming its limitations. Attribute referential integrity is discussed as it applies to entity-relationship and relational data models.

Chapter 19, "Data Quality: An Architectural Solution," discusses the process of integrating data from multiple data sources into a data warehouse, while maintaining data quality. This chapter provides advice on resolving problems such as the existence of data from multiple data sources that are inconsistent, or data stores that utilize different data models. Such differences must be resolved when building a data warehouse.

Chapter 15
The Quality Vortex

Doug Ward

AN INFORMATION TECHNOLOGY PROJECT, ESPECIALLY A LARGE ONE, IS COMPLEX. Requirements must be gathered from people who often do not understand their needs. To convert these into a working solution requires the application of highly advanced technologies whose external projection of simplicity belies an awesome underlying complexity. Then these systems have to be implemented back into an environment where they are dependent on the same people who did not understand what they wanted in the first place, or were not part of the decision-making at all.

Obviously, for such an undertaking to be successful, there is the utmost need for superb project management. Any project management book, and indeed any business book, will devote pages to the importance of excellent management, be it on a project or in general day-to-day work. And any executive gearing up for a large Information Systems (IS) initiative would certainly put a great deal of effort into carefully selecting a skilled and experienced project management team.

Unfortunately, the same care is not usually taken with the selection of the more junior members of the team — the people who will actually do the hands-on work of designing, developing, and configuring the systems and technology deliverables. The average selection process consists of the reading of a résumé, followed by a brief interview. On many projects, the interview does not happen. Certainly, it is very rare for every programmer or analyst on a project to be thoroughly evaluated for their proposed role.

The reasons for this include assumptions that sound management will overcome any weaknesses, programmers can be trained on the job, and alternative programmers can be found easily. Lack of time to conduct detailed evaluations is also cited.

But the most common assumption is that the lower a person is in the project tree, the less influence that person has on the success of the project. This assumption is incorrect.

SELECTING AND MANAGING PERSONNEL

Consider the example in Exhibit 15.1 to illustrate the flaw in this thinking. A small Information Systems project included the following

0-8493-9832-0/00/$0.00+$.50
© 2000 by CRC Press LLC

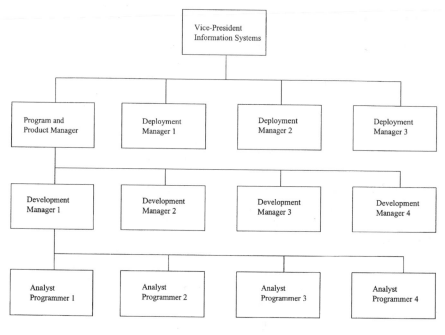

Exhibit 15.1. Organizational structure.

---

organizational structure under the Vice-President of Information Systems. The role of the development teams was to develop a suite of applications previously conceptualized by the product manager in conjunction with the users. A RAD approach was to be used; prototyping with the users for timeboxed periods, then coding each application based on a final, agreed prototype.

In development team 1, the development manager had four people under his control, an acceptable ratio that should have allowed him to fulfill his roles of customer liaison for prototyping, confirmation of specifications, systems integration, quality assurance, and assistance to his programming team.

Unfortunately, two of the programmers were not as experienced as they should have been. They consequently needed an unexpected amount of assistance from the development manager. As a result, the manager's own responsibilities suffered, including keeping a quality watch on the other two programmers. The latter two soon realized that they did not have to kill themselves to meet deadlines because the development manager was struggling to keep up with his own deadlines. So their quality deteriorated, and the development manager found himself fixing their quality problems in order to meet the strict quality requirements being thrust upon him by the product manager. And so the development manager was sucked down in a vortex created by his programmers.

Now being wrapped up in programming work, the development manager fell behind in his customer liaison and specification confirmation work. The product manager, being the representative of the customers, consequently found himself under fire. He was also the program manager, and it was clear that deadlines were starting to slip. So this manager spent time chasing the development manager, trying to direct the development effort so that deadlines and product requirements would be met. But in doing so, some of his other product management responsibilities were neglected, including the definition of requirements and management of vendors in other portions of the project. The vortex had trapped its next victim.

To meet certain deadlines, the product manager now had to ask the IS vice president to attend some meetings related to package evaluation. While the VP was there, the other company executives were getting angry because he was not available to provide them with strategic advice, which was his primary role in the firm. The vortex had reached right to the top of the project.

Not only had the vortex sucked down each layer of management from the bottom to the top of the project, it had also spread its influence over the rest of the project because every manager sucked in lost a degree of control over other portions under their responsibility. As mentioned earlier, this started at the bottom of the vortex when two programmers under-performed on quality because the development manager was too busy working with the other two programmers.

So, two under-experienced programmers took down an entire project, causing a nine-month schedule to run to 13 months — a 44 percent overrun.

And during this period, all the managers were killing themselves working late nights to try to keep the project on track, and the programmers were going home at 5 p.m. everyday. Just who was in charge anyway?

To the outsider, it appeared that the development manager was not performing — and was nearly replaced. If this had happened, it is quite likely that the problems would have continued because, obviously, the core problem had not been solved.

One could counter that if the development manager had been good at his job, he would have just removed the inexperienced programmers from the project and replaced them. There certainly is a place for such an action, but the Information Systems world is not so simple:

- Information Systems design and development is largely an intellectual job. Great strides are being made in the automation of this process; but currently, analysts and programmers still carry large portions of the developing application inside their heads. If they leave for any reason, the start-up cost and time of a replacement are significant.
- There is a worldwide shortage of competent Information Systems staff, currently exacerbated by the approaching year 2000 drawing large numbers of available resources for legacy system conversion and compliance projects.
- The shortage is allowing junior systems staff to go contracting, demanding inflated income, and moving on if they are dissatisfied with the working conditions. Dissatisfaction often extends to being required to deliver to a particular quality standard or project plan. In other words, if it is not fun, programmers move on to something else that is.

The scenario in the example described above is not unusual. This author has seen examples of the quality vortex on nearly every project he has worked in the last 17 years. A member of the team, who for some reason cannot be removed from his or her role, sucks down the rest of the project that is connected to his or her work.

How can such problems be avoided, or at least be recognized before they cause too much damage?

QUALITY MANAGEMENT PLAN

Like any vortex, one must break the vacuum at the *bottom* in order to stop it. This means that one must invest time and techniques in the people at the coalface of the project. For an Information Systems project, the following approaches should be considered.

- Carefully select the people who will actually produce the project's deliverables. These workers include the business analysts, technical architects, programmers, testers, trainers, production staff, etc. Examine each résumé with care. Conduct a full interview. Insist on, and follow up with, references from previous projects — one wants to weed out those people who did poor work or left the previous project early because they did not like to conform to standards. Conduct analytical tests that measure attributes such as ability to see a project through, desire to achieve quality results, intellect, ability to handle stress, teamwork, and others considered important for one's project teams.
- Spend time with them, one-on-one and in team briefing sessions, to ensure that they fully understand their roles, responsibilities, and deliverables. For each deliverable, clearly define its expectations of quality,

including tangible measures wherever possible. It is especially important that each person clearly understands where he or she fits within the larger team, and how dependent the project is on their work. Ensure that each person knows the consequences to the project if he or she does a poor-quality job. One would be surprised how many people are unaware of the problems they cause, and would stop causing them if only they knew about it.

- Give them any "top-up" training and coaching that they need to meet their expectations (if extensive training is required, then one should reconsider the role of the person). The training needs can be diverse, such as the use of new features in the latest version of a development language, techniques for personal time management, or coaching on how to work effectively in teams.

- Teach them to never knowingly pass on poor-quality work, and to never accept poor-quality work from anyone else. People will often take on the responsibility of repairing someone else's quality, believing they are doing what is right for the project. The converse is usually the case, because of the quality vortex. And the person who caused the quality problem may not even be aware of it, so one is not helping that person either. As a manager, one should create an environment where the project (or at least parts of it) stops for quality problems, allowing the whole team to assist in discovering the source of the problem and repairing it, never to happen again.

- Offer incentives for good quality. For example, give bonuses to teams that meet or exceed the quality expectations of their deliverables. But take care; the design of incentives is tricky and can lead to undesirable behavior. For example, teams are commonly rewarded for completing their work on time, which often leads to poor quality of the resultant deliverable as the team concentrates only on the deadline.

- At the beginning of the project, or at the beginning of any new team member's employment on the project, set a series of early deadlines to be achieved with a measurable deliverable. These can be as simple as a small module, a personal plan, a few screen layouts, or an entity-relationship diagram. There should be at least one deliverable per week, for at least four weeks. Then, ensure that the deadlines are achieved with the right quality. Investigate every missed deadline. There will always be good and valid reasons for a deadline, especially an early one, to be missed. But there is almost always some quality problem hidden within the reason — dig for it.

- Finally, if there is a person who continues to deliver poor quality, replace that person. And do it early, because of the intellectual content that IT projects have, so that the impact on project deadlines is not too severe (although it will never be as bad as keeping that person on the project).

The management process for all the above can be captured in the Project Quality Plan. At the beginning of the project, or a particular phase, prepare the quality plan for the work to be undertaken. There are many aspects to a quality plan, but the items below are particularly important in preventing a quality vortex.

- Define the major and interim deliverables, including the quality expectations of each. These range from simple sign-offs to more tangible measures such as numbers of allowable bugs. Be as specific as possible, as it makes it easier for the creators and the evaluators of the deliverables to assess whether quality has been achieved.
- For each deliverable, define the process, techniques, and tools to be used to ensure the desired quality expectations are achieved. Within this, define checkpoints to regularly measure whether quality is being achieved. Do not wait until the deliverable is ready for review before finding out that there have been problems during its creation. It is usually too late.
- Now that it is clear what deliverables are required and what work has to be done to achieve them, define the resources needed to do the work. Each role should be clearly identified, and should include comprehensive descriptions of the required education, training, and hands-on and management experience.
- Define a process for acquiring the resources, again with checkpoints for ensuring that the process is proceeding successfully. These would include requests for education and training certificates, reference checking, testing, or sign-off on responsibilities by the resources. It would also include the provision of orientation and training for the project at hand.
- Then do it! Follow the processes defined. If there are problems on the way, examine the source and update the quality plan so that the problems do not occur again.

There is normally a strong aversion to quality planning. At the beginning of a project, there is typically a rush to get things going and to show that something is being done, and people do not take time to plan. Customers are often not willing to pay for quality planning, as they see it as inherent in project management or in a methodology.

However, even if one has to pay for it oneself, it is well worth doing — because if one does not pay for it now, one will certainly pay for it later, and in much bigger amounts. Any first-year university student can refer to the reams of documentation on Information Systems projects, proving that it is much cheaper to prevent a problem than to fix it.

So, ask why there is no time to ensure the job is done right the first time, but there is time to do it again when the quality requirements are not achieved.

Also consider the effects of the quality vortex: should one spend money on recruiting extra managers to repair the quality problems that workers are causing, or whether the money is better spent on carefully choosing and rewarding the right workers in the first place? It is obvious to this author that the latter is cheaper and more effective.

Do not forget to make sure that one has great management. One still needs to ensure that the project is organized and controlled in the best way possible.

CONCLUSION

To summarize the effect of the quality vortex, good workers can make up for bad management; but poor workers will render helpless the best management in the world. So make sure to apply at least as much importance to the selection of your workers as you do to the selection of the management team. Look out for that quality vortex and cut it off at the bottom — before one gets sucked down into the spiral of inefficiency, poor quality, and missed deadlines that typifies the world of Information Technology projects.

Chapter 16
What's Wrong With My Data?

Jeffery Feldman

YOU HAVE PROBABLY HEARD THE EXPRESSION, "GARBAGE IN, GARBAGE OUT." A computer system utilizing the most technologically sophisticated architecture, elegant user interfaces, and intuitive report generation capabilities, can be rendered nearly useless if the data it relies upon is fundamentally flawed. While investigating and correcting "bad" data may be among the least glamourous tasks to perform, it is absolutely critical if organizations are to realize the full potential of the systems they have developed (often at a considerable cost in time, resources, and dollars).

This paper illustrates a variety of potential quality problems that could be present within the files and databases of any organization. These problems will be especially evident in older legacy systems, although not necessarily restricted to older systems by any means. Knowing the possible issues is the first step towards addressing them. Further steps would include taking action to correct the data, and (perhaps even more importantly) taking action to correct the processes that led to flawed data being stored in the first place. This paper focuses on describing those possible flaws.

WHY SHOULD I CARE?

Perhaps you are not quite convinced that data integrity should be a major concern, or at any rate not for the applications you are dealing with. After all, the existing systems are running just fine with the current data, aren't they? And any required data cleansing can be done at some point in the future, when time and resources become more available.

Well, maybe. Much depends on just how the data is being used, and on the organization's tolerance for risk. Let us say, for example, that the only use of the data is to support a company-internal management information system, and that about 5 percent of the data is known to be in error. A cost-benefit analysis that compares the effort required to correct the data vs.

0-8493-9832-0/00/$0.00+$.50
© 2000 by CRC Press LLC

the increased value of the system to its users might well conclude the 5 percent error rate is acceptable.

On the other hand, what if that error rate was actually 30 percent? Or what if the application in question was sending bills to your customers? It is unlikely that faulty data could be tolerated for long in either situation.

Just because existing systems can use a particular set of data, that does not necessarily imply ease-of-use for a new system — among other things, there may be a great deal of hard-coded logic in the old systems that allows them to bypass problems in the raw data. And there are a host of potential new problems once you start merging data from several different existing systems in order to feed your new system.

And postponing the cleansing effort is generally inadvisable. The initial data propagation/transformation efforts can require significant revision and re-execution. Considerable additional effort and cost may be needed to repair data, to make it accessible, and to prevent continued corruption. However, once the users have started to access the system, its credibility (and your own) are on the line. There may not be any funds available for continued work if the system's users are not satisfied with the initial release. And does time and additional resources ever *really* become easier to get onto a project at a "later date"?

Potential Impacts

Some potential impacts of unreliable data include the following:

- *Increased Cost of Database Marketing.* Poor quality data affects direct-mail, telemarketing, and marketing collateral costs. A large automobile manufacturer purged its customer files and cut direct-mail costs by U.S. $500,000 the first year, and lowered the costs of managing this data long term.[1]
- *Increased Operational Costs.* The time that resources must spend to detect and correct errors can be very significant. One estimate for the cost of poor data quality is 8 to 12 percent of revenue; for service organizations, a "good working estimate" might be 40 to 60 percent of expenses.[2] There is also a related negative impact on employee morale.
- *Lowered Customer Satisfaction.* Multiple mailings sent to the same customer can be annoying, they can cause the customer to question your enterprise's competence, and can harm the customer relationship. This is especially true if the information within a given mailing or statement pertaining to a customer is incorrect.
- *Reduced Use of System.* If the believability and/or the objectivity of the data comes into question, then the resulting poor reputation will cause reduced use of the system and underlying databases.[3] Considering the effort and cost of developing these systems, anything impairing their value or use is clearly counterproductive.

- *Risk to Health/Safety.* The quality of data in (for example) medical records is clearly of major importance, as the diagnosis and procedure must be recorded correctly. Other examples of critical systems include those controlling aircraft movement and traffic signals, chemical plants and nuclear reactors, jail security, and many others.

WHAT PROBLEMS MIGHT THERE BE?

Let us take the following as our working scenario: a new data warehouse is being constructed, and the data from several operational legacy systems/databases will be used to populate it. These legacy feeder systems will remain in production for some time. We are therefore concerned with the quality of the available data not only for the purpose of the initial load of our data warehouse, but also because any problems that currently exist will continue to contaminate our data until they are fixed. This is a hypothetical but common situation, and provides the context for further discussion.

Potential Problems

Missing Data

In Exhibit 16.1:

- Lee does not have a *Smoker* status code/flag, while Frank does not have a value in the *Sex* field. The degree to which either is an issue will depend upon whether they are mandatory fields or not. If one or the other is mandatory, how will you go about getting that information?
- Record 525 is not present. Does this indicate a deletion, or a problem with missing records in this particular file?
- Smith and Yu have a zero *Age*. Either they are less than a year old, or 00 is the default or dummy value given to the *Age* field. Do the business rules help you to determine which is which? If 00 is the dummy value, then this data is missing.
- There is another kind of missing data — data that is needed by the new application, but was not captured by any of the older feeding systems. If you are fortunate, it will be possible to derive the new value by manipulating the old data. Otherwise, the effort to capture and record new information can be considerable.

Exhibit 16.1. Example of missing data.

Identifier	Last Name	Sex	Age	Smoker
523	Smith	M	00	N
524	Jones	F	23	Y
526	Lee	M	42	
527	Frank		17	Y
528	Yu	M	00	N

Redundant Data with Inconsistencies

In Exhibit 16.2:

- Our hypothetical data warehouse draws information from both Files "A" and "B" (assume each has unique fields of interest not displayed in the above example). Because each file was developed and used separately by different divisions of the company, redundant information is stored. Which will you use as your primary source for those fields available from both?
- Note that the information for Jones is not consistent. Is it safe to assume that File "A" has more recent information, and therefore that Jones took up smoking at age 23? Regardless of the answer, how do we account for the difference in *Sex* for Lee?
- Data File "B" has a record 525 not present in File "A." Should we then merge the records from the two files to get a complete set? Or perhaps File "B" is out of date, and the record should have been deleted from File "B" as well? This is another illustration of inconsistency.

Exhibit 16.2.   Example of redundant data.

Data File "A"				
Identifier	Last Name	Sex	Age	Smoker
523	Smith	M	00	N
524	Jones	F	23	Y
526	Lee	M	42	
527	Frank		17	Y
528	Yu	M	00	N

Data File "B"				
Identifier	Last Name	Sex	Age	Smoke
523	Smith	M	00	N
524	Jones	F	22	N
525	Samuelson	M	54	Y
526	Lee	F	42	
527	Frank		17	Y

Different/Changing Business Rules or Logic

In Exhibit 16.3, our hypothetical data warehouse draws information from both Files "A" and "C":

- Notice that Lee's *Smoker* status is "Y" in File "C." This is a result of a business rule in the application logic which says "Unless the individual specifically indicates that they are a non-smoker, give them the smoker code." That rule is not present in the application producing File "A," causing the discrepancy.

- Is there disagreement on Smith's age between the two files? No, it's just that the dummy value for File "C" happens to be "99" rather than "00."
- Is File "C" missing more data for Frank than File "A"? Yes, but it's intentional — the logic for File "C" refuses to store values for *Age* and *Smoker* unless all mandatory fields (including *Sex*) are completed.
- Note that these types of inconsistency can appear within a single file just as easily as between files, if the business rules/application logic changes over time.

Exhibit 16.3. Example of different logic.

Data File "A"				
Identifier	**Last Name**	**Sex**	**Age**	**Smoker**
523	Smith	M	00	N
524	Jones	F	23	Y
526	Lee	M	42	
527	Frank		17	Y
528	Yu	M	00	N

Data File "C"				
Identifier	**Last Name**	**Sex**	**Age**	**Smoker**
523	Smith	M	99	N
524	Jones	F	22	N
525	Samuelson	M	54	Y
526	Lee	F	42	Y
527	Frank			

Missing/Non-Unique Primary Key

In Exhibit 16.4, our hypothetical data warehouse draws information from both Files "A" and "D":

- Data File "D" does not have the "Identifier" field, and in fact does not have a unique primary key. If we assume File "A" doesn't have the *First Name* field, then will you match record 523 with Fred Smith or with Sid Smith? Which File "D" record will you match record 528 with?
- At first glance, record 526 might seem an easy match. But can we really assume 536s Lee is the same person as File "D"s Tom Lee?
- The bottom line here is that the lack of a primary key can be a major obstacle to accessing the data you need, even when the data is present in the files themselves.

Exhibit 16.4. Example of primary key problems.

Data File "A"				
Identifier	Last Name	Sex	Age	Smoker
523	Smith	M	00	N
524	Jones	F	23	Y
526	Lee	M	42	
527	Frank		17	Y
528	Yu	M	00	N

Data File "D"				
Last Name	First Name	Department	Yrs Employed	Salary
Smith	Fred	40	2	50000
Smith	Sid	40	3	75000
Lee	Tom	30	3	60000
Yu	Robert	50	1	45000
Yu	Ted	30	6	80000

Non-Standardized and/or Multi-Element Fields

In Exhibit 16.5:

- Do all these people work for the same company? If there were 5,000 records to look at instead of just five, would you be able to identify the variations? Company names have not been standardized, and this is just a flavor of the possible result.
- In the *Name and Title* field there is an even worse lack of standards. Some titles are spelled out in full ("Vice President"), others are abbreviated ("Sr V.P.") Some names are accompanied by designations ("Mr."), others aren't. And do we include the department or division ("I.S."), or don't we?
- The positioning of the information in the *Name and Title* field is also inconsistent, with some last names first, some first names first, one title (marketing representative) preceding the name while the others follow the name, and so on.
- In fact, there are several individual elements contained within the *Name and Title* field, which is a large part of the problem. These elements include the First Name, Last Name, Initial (if any), Designation (e.g., Mr., Dr.), Title, the Department (e.g., I.S., Operations), and even in one case Degrees (B.Comm.)
- The individual elements within *Name and Title* are almost impossible to work with as they are now. Even a simple alphabetical report sorted by last name could be impractical. Clearly, separate fields for separate elements makes life much easier.

Exhibit 16.5. Example of non-standardized and multi-element fields.

Name and Title	Company
George Taylor, B. Comm., Vice President	DEC
Levi, Dr. Harold P. Sr V.P.	Digital Equipment
Marketing Representative Tim Hanlon	Digital
O'Leary Don, Operations	Digital Corporation
Mr. E. Rourke, Mgr I.S.	Dec Corp

Invalid Values

The constraints defining what constitutes a "Valid" value for any given field should be clearly defined within each database or file, as it will be different in every case, and can even change for the same field over time.

In Exhibit 16.6:

- If the only valid values for *Sex* are "M" or "F," then records 524 and 527 have invalid values. In the case of Jones, we know what was meant. In the case of Frank, however, the "N" might be a keystroke error, or it might mean "Not Known," or anything. Thus without the proper edits, coded values can easily become corrupted.
- Age should always be numeric, which makes Lee's age invalid as entered (what if we tried to add or subtract from it!) Also it is clear that Yu's age cannot be correct. The first problem illustrates that it is possible to get character data where numeric data is desired (and vice-versa), the second illustrates that without edits values can be entered outside of the acceptable range or domain for that field.
- Which Social Insurance Numbers are valid? Certainly Lee's and Yu's are not valid, and depending on our formatting rules Jones' may or may not be OK as is. Text fields are often the most difficult to validate, which is why when there is a choice (such as with SIN) it is generally better to look for alternatives.

Exhibit 16.6. Example of invalid values.

Identifier	Last Name	Sex	Age	SIN
523	Smith	M	00	143-476-987
524	Jones	Female	23	547198234
526	Lee	M	Forty-two	657-432-89
527	Frank	N	17	654-975-298
528	Yu	M	222	674-A27-897

Incorrect Values

In Exhibit 16.7, our hypothetical data warehouse draws information from both Files "D" and "E":

- Although the *Avg Salary* should have been the result of dividing the *Total Salary* by the *Total Staff*, somehow a mistake was made for Department 40, as 125000/2 = 62500, not 65000. Derived or calculated data can be in error within the same record, or file.
- Although the *Total* columns in File "E" were intended to sum the data of File "D," a calculation mistake was made in the *Total Years* (of experience) for Department 30 (should be 9, not 8). Thus derived or summary data in one file can also be incorrect based upon the data in a completely different file.
- These types of erroneous values can easily corrupt other results — For example, there may be a field in a third file containing the difference in average wages between men and women. Depending upon whether File "E" is used for source data (*Avg Salary*), the resulting calculation may be accurate, or not.

Exhibit 16.7. Example of incorrect values.

Data File "D"				
Last Name	**First Name**	**Department**	**Yrs Employed**	**Salary**
Smith	Fred	40	2	50000
Smith	Sid	40	3	75000
Lee	Tom	30	3	60000
Yu	Robert	50	1	45000
Yu	Ted	30	6	80000

Data File "E"				
Department	**Total Years**	**Total Salary**	**Total Staff**	**Avg Salary**
30	8	140000	2	70000
40	5	125000	2	65000
50	1	45000	1	45000

Referential Integrity Violations

Referential integrity is a constraint to ensure that relationships between rows of data exist, and in particular that one row of data will exist if another does (generally in different tables).

In Exhibit 16.8, our hypothetical data warehouse draws information from both Files "A" and "F":

- Although Data File "F" has *Identifier* as a key, unfortunately it is not unique, as can be seen from the two 523 rows. While under some circumstances this would boil down to a primary key issue (possibly combined with a missing, invalid, or redundant data issue), in this particular case it appears we should be consolidating the data in the two rows.
- There is no entry in File "F" corresponding to record 526 from File "A." This is a clear violation of referential integrity, as Lee must (at the very least) have a current-year salary recorded.
- Record 525 in File "F" has no corresponding entry in File "A," so just who is this a salary record for? This is an example of an "orphaned" record (does not have a "parent" record).

Exhibit 16.8. Example of referential integrity problems.

Data File "A"				
Identifier	**Last Name**	**Sex**	**Age**	**Smoker**
523	Smith	M	00	N
524	Jones	F	23	Y
526	Lee	M	42	
527	Frank		17	Y
528	Yu	M	00	N

Data File "F"				
Identifier	**Current Salary**	**Yr-1 Salary**	**Yr-2 Salary**	**Yr-3 Salary**
523	0	0	55000	45000
523	75000	65000	0	0
524	63000	58000	53000	50000
525	53500	48800	45000	42300
527	51800	47700	43500	40200
528	45000	45000	38500	37500

Special Case: Dates

Dates can be tricky to work with for a number of reasons:

- Many possible representations, including:
  - Multiple date formats (e.g., YYDDD, CCYYMMDD, DDMMYY)
  - Multiple internal storage options, depending on language, OS, etc.
  - Dates are often stored in pure numeric fields, or within text fields

- There are a large number of ways default or dummy dates have been established, some of which can be quite confusing:
  — Is 99365 (Dec 31, 1999) a dummy value, or a legitimate date?
  — How about 010101 (Jan 1, 2001)? 999999?
  — If your programs run across 000000 in the Year 2000, what action will they take? What action should they take?
- The Year 2000 itself will cause many of the existing dates and formats to become unacceptable, whereas up to now they may have worked just fine.
  — Two-digit years will need to be accompanied by two-digit century values, or
  — Some interim solution based (for example) on sliding date windows will need to be adopted, or
  — A business decision to accept the risks and potential consequences of inaccurate processing will need to be made by the enterprise.

Special Case: Addresses

Addresses can be complicated to work with because they routinely combine many of the issues we've described into just a few fields, with the resulting combination being particularly challenging to unravel and/or to correct. These problems can include:[4]

- No common customer key across records and files
- Multiple names within one field
- One name across two fields
- Name and address in same field
- Personal and Commercial names mixed
- Different addresses for the same customer
- Different names and spellings for same customer
- "Noisy" name and address domains
- Inconsistent use of special characters
- Multiple formats within disparate data files
- Legacy data buried and floating within free-form fields
- Multiple account numbers blocking a consolidated view
- Complex matching and consolidation
- Data values that stray from their descriptions and business rules.

CONCLUSION

Knowing your enemy is the first step towards defeating him. In this case the enemy is "bad" data, and this paper has illustrated several ways in which poor-quality data can be present in your files. The task for you, the reader, is to use the examples provided and apply them to your own specific systems and databases. Assess the severity of the situation, evaluate the cost-effectiveness or desirability of taking corrective action, and proceed accordingly.

Notes

1. Brethenoux, E. "Data Quality — The Missing Link in Data Mining." GartnerGroup (October 29, 1996).

2. Redman, T.C. The Impact of poor data quality on the typical enterprise. *Communications of the ACM* (February, 1998).

3. Strong, D.M., Lee Y.W., Wang R.Y. Data quality in context. *Communications of the ACM* (May, 1997).

4. "The Five Legacy Data Contaminants you will Encounter in your Warehouse Migration." White paper provided by *Vality Technology Incorporated*. Obtained from http://www.datawarehouse.com

Other helpful sources include:

Zimmer, M. Data conversion: doing it right the first time. *Handbook of Data Management 1999.* S. Purba, Ed. 1999. Auerbach Publications, Boca Raton, FL.

Customer Data Quality. White paper provided by *i.d.Centric*. Obtained from http://www. idcentric.com

Chapter 17
Programming Data Constraints Using Microsoft SQL Server

Sanjiv Purba

MICROSOFT® STRUCTURED QUERY LANGUAGE (SQL) SERVER was one of the first widely released database servers to support the functionality of coding data constraints directly inside the data dictionary itself — as far back as 1987 in colloboration with Sybase. These constraints are attached to tables or table fields with the ANSI '98 Data Definition Language (DDL) commands, "create table" and "alter table." This chapter provides examples of data scripts that will support the following:

- *Identity Constraints:* These constraints can be applied to a single column in a table so that the value in the field is incremented automatically when records are inserted.
- *Key Constraints:* SQL Server supports two types of key constraints, namely "Primary" key and "Foreign" key constraints. Primary key constraints ensure that duplicate records are not inserted into a table. Foreign key constraints ensure that records are not inserted into a table if a foreign key is missing.
- *Default Constraints:* Default contracts are associated with specific columns in tables. If a record is inserted into a table without a data value for a column that has an associated default constraint, the default value is saved in the column with the rest of the record. Default values can be overridden at insert time by a user-supplied data value.

CREATE TABLE CONSTRAINTS

The table creation script developed in the "Database Servers and Universal Servers" section did not take advantage of table constraints or related features. These are used to enforce table data integrity or to provide additional functionality that would otherwise need to be programmed at the client side or within stored procedures. There are several schools of thought regarding the use of these features. From a performance and practicality perspective, these constraints and features are highly useful. From a pure object-oriented perspective, they separate logic from data so that some classes are no longer pure. The author's preference is to make use of the constraints on a case-by-case basis. Constraints use the "sysconstraints" and the "sysreferences" system tables in the Microsoft SQL Server environment.

IDENTITY

A common requirement in transactional systems is to generate a sequential number for each row that is inserted into a table. Common application uses of this include ticket sales, new customers, new employees, and new invoices. Each new record is allocated a code value that is one greater than the previous record. Historically this was done in one of several ways. The first was to maintain an environment variable or a separate table that stored the last code value used. In high load transaction applications this did not work well because of constant locking contention against the table or variable as many users competed to read, lock, and update the value for the next user to retrieve. In such cases, a second method was used that preallocated ranges of numbers to different users or types of users. This reduced contention against single ranges of numbers by distributing users across a range of records. A third method was to use a SELECT command and a built-in function (e.g., MAX) to retrieve the highest number used in a table [e.g., SELECT @code_to_use = (max(code) + 1)]. Each of these offered advantages and disadvantages.

SQL Server's response has been the identity constraint. This feature is identified for a maximum of one column in a table at the time the table is created or altered. This column can be referred to with the logical name: IDENTITYCOL in SQL code that accesses the table. The syntax for allocating an identity constraint to a table column is as follows:

Syntax:

```
CREATE TABLE table_name
    IDENTITY (start, step)
```

Notes:

The "start" value is used for the first row. The "step" is the increment value added for the next insert.

Example:

This example builds a small user table to demonstrate creating a column with an IDENTITY feature. The example also extracts the inserted data from the "city_list" table.

```
USE address

go

DROP TABLE city_list

go

CREATE TABLE city_list

(

    city_code       int  IDENTITY (1000, 1),

    description     char(80)

)

go

/* You do not need to specify the IDENTITY column name
in an insert command. The city_code will begin with 1000,
and be incremented by 1 on every record insert. */

insert city_list

    (description) VALUES ("This is a description")

go

/* Insert a another record that will have a city_code of
   1001 */

insert city_list

(description) VALUES ("This is a description")

go

/* Display the results */

select * from city_list

go

/* use the logical name of the IDENTITY column to display
   the contents of the table */

select IDENTITYCOL, description from city_list

go
```

Normally, a value is not specified with the INSERT command for the column that is specified as an IDENTITY column. However, when rows are deleted or not successfully inserted, the number that is automatically generated by SQL Server is not recovered. This means that there can be gaps in the sequencing. In many applications this is not a problem. However, some business processes will use solid sequential series of numbers for auditing purposes. In this case, a gap in the sequential series may cause auditing problems. In such a case it is useful to locate the gaps and fill them in manually. The following sequence of commands does this. Notice the comments explain what is being attempted and what the results actually are

```
INSERT city_list

    (city_code, description)

    VALUES

    (2000, "this should not be accepted without a set
    command")

go
```

This command results in the following error message (unless the SET IDENTITY_INSERT is ON — in which case, add the two lines before the code: [1] SET IDENTITY_INSERT city_list off [2] go): "Attempting to insert explicit value for identify column in table 'city_list'." The following code corrects this error:

```
SET IDENTITY_INSERT city_list on

go

INSERT city_list

    (city_code, description)

    VALUES

    (2001, "this should be successfully inserted into the
    table")

go

SET IDENTITY_INSERT city_list off

go
```

KEY CONSTRAINTS

There are two basic key column constraints that can be applied to table columns with the CREATE TABLE and the ALTER TABLE commands, namely PRIMARY KEY and FOREIGN KEY. There can be no more than one PRIMARY KEY constraint for each table and no more than 31 FOREIGN KEY constraints for each table. The PRIMARY KEY constraint is used to enforce key column uniqueness in a table. When it is specified, two rows are not allowed to exist within the same table with identical primary keys. Once a column is specified as a PRIMARY KEY, it cannot be saved with a NULL value. Key constraints can be created with specific column names or as separate objects.

212

Primary Key Syntax:

```
CREATE TABLE table_name
(
  [column_list  datatype ...]  [PRIMARY KEY
  [CLUSTERED/NONCLUSTERED]]
)
```

OR

```
CREATE TABLE table_name
(
  [column_list  datatype ...],
  CONSTRAINT PK_constraint_name PRIMARY KEY
  [CLUSTERED/NONCLUSTERED] (column1, column2, ...)
)
```

Notes:

A clustered index is created by default on the column specified as PRIMARY KEY. At most, only one "column_name" can be associated with a PRIMARY KEY in one table.

Examples:

1. This example creates the "city_list" table, specifying the "city_code" field as an IDENTITY column and as a primary key column. This example also indicates that the column should generate a clustered index for the table. The example also extracts the inserted data from the "city_list" table.

```
USE address
go
drop table city_list
go
create table city_list
(
    city_code        int IDENTITY (1000,1) PRIMARY KEY
                     CLUSTERED,
    description      char(80)
)
```

```
go

create table city_list

(

    city_code           int IDENTITY (1000,1) PRIMARY KEY
                        CLUSTERED,

    description         char(80)

)

go

/* After parsing the code without errors into the address
database, insert a row into the table */

insert city_list

    (description)

values

    ("this is an example")

go
```

This insert batch can be executed recursively, adding a new record to the "city_list" table each time. Because the PRIMARY KEY field was created with an IDENTITY feature, a new code is generated starting at 1000 with the first insert. This allows each row to be unique. A join against two system tables, sysobjects, and sysindexes can be used to confirm that a clustered index was created in response to the primary key feature. As shown in the following code, an object ID joins the two tables together. In this example, the number of rows in the index is displayed. As an example, the insert code was executed four times, and then the join code was executed. The number of rows retrieved by the join is four. Another insert was then executed to insert a fifth row into the "city_code" table. The join showed that five rows were indexed.

```
select * from city_code

select a.id, b.rows

    from sysobjects a, sysindexes b

        where a.name = "city_list" and a.id = b.id

go
```

As an exercise, it is recommended that the reader adjust the create script for the "city_list" table so that the "city_code" column no longer has an IDENTITY attribute. The insert script also needs to be adjusted as follows: insert "city_list" ("city_code", description) values (2000, "this is a key"). The reader then should try to run the "insert" example twice. Notice that an error message "Violation of PRIMARY KEY constraint 'PK_city_list_5535A961' attempt to insert duplicate key in object 'city_list'. Command has been aborted." The "city_code" (in this case 2000) must be changed on every subsequent insert. As discussed in the application testing chapter, the IDENTITY feature is useful for creating a large number of data rows for stress testing and regression testing.

2. In this example, a PRIMARY KEY constraint is created using two columns as the key:

```
use address

go

drop table address

go

drop table city_state_code

go

create table city_state_code

(

    city            character (20),

    state           character (20),

    CONSTRAINT PK_citystate PRIMARY KEY CLUSTERED (city,
    state)

)  /* the PK represents primary key */

go
```

The FOREIGN KEY constraint is used to ensure referential integrity between related tables. SQL Server accepts up to 31 FOREIGN KEYs per table. A streamlined version of the command syntax for recreating a FOREIGN KEY on a table is as follows:

```
FOREIGN KEY Syntax:

CREATE TABLE table_name

)

    [column_name] FOREIGN KEY [columns] REFERENCES
    [reference_tables]

)
```

```
OR

    (

        [column_names     datatypes ....],

        CONSTRAINT contraint_name FOREIGN KEY [(column1,
        column2, ...)]

            REFERENCES [reference_tables(column1, column2,
            ...)]

    )
```

Notes:

FOREIGN KEY is validated with the table(s) identified in the REFERENCES part of the command.

Examples:

1. This example rebuilds two tables used earlier, customer and member_type, to demonstrate FOREIGN KEY and REFERENCES constraints. The original table generation scripts are modified in this example so that constraints are created with the tables. The "drop table" sequence is important in this example. The customer table, which references the "member_type" table, must be dropped first. Attempting to drop the "member_type" table first displays an error message.

```
USE address

go

drop table customer

go

drop table member_type

go

create table member_type

(

member_type          character(1) PRIMARY KEY,

description          character(30)

)

go

create table customer

(
```

```
customer_no              int  IDENTITY (1000,1) PRIMARY KEY
CLUSTERED,

last_name                char(30),

middle_initial           char(1),

first_name               char(30),

home_phone               char(15),

business_phone           char(15),

fax                      char(15),

email                    char(25),

preference               char(80),

member_on                datetime,

member_type              character(1) REFERENCES
                         member_type(member_type)

)
```

/* the member_type table should have a PRIMARY KEY to
support the REFERENCES constraint */

go

/* Insert data rows into the two tables. The reference
ensures that the member_type value in the customer table
occurs in the member_type table. */

insert member_type

    (member_type, description)

    VALUES

    ("O," "Open")

go

insert customer

    (last_name, middle_initial, first_name, home_phone,
business_phone,

     fax, email, preference, member_on, member_type)

    VALUES

    ("Okiet," "S," "Joe," "3499999999," "9999999999,"
"9999999999,"

     "okiet@tobos.com," "not known," "April 25 1997,"
"O")

go

2. In this example, an attempt is made to enter a customer record with a nonexistent "member_type". The constraint catches this error and does not allow the record to be used in the customer table. The error message: "INSERT statement conflicted with COLUMN FOREIGN KEY constraint 'FK_customer_member_...'. The conflict occurred in database 'address', table 'member_type', column 'member_type'. Command has been aborted." appears in response. Notice that the text of the message is descriptive and highly helpful in identifying the source of the error.

```
INSERT customer
    (last_name, middle_initial, first_name, home_phone,
    business_phone,
     fax, email, preference, member_on, member_type)
    VALUES
    ("Tom," "S," "Joe," "8889999999," "8889999999,"
    "8889999999,"
     "tom@tobos.com," "not known," "April 25 1996," "Z")
go
```

3. In this example, a FOREIGN KEY constraint is created for the address table to ensure that a valid city is being processed. The following example enhances this example to ensure that a valid city and state combination is being processed. This involves several steps. A PRIMARY KEY constraint must be created on the fields that are to be referenced in the "city_state_code" table. A FOREIGN KEY constraint must be created in the address table.

```
use address
go
drop table address
go
drop table city_state_code
go
create table address
(
customer_no         int,
address_code        char(1),
```

```
street1                char(25),
street2                char(25),
city                   char(20),
state_province         char(20),
country                char(15),
zip_pc                 char(10),


CONSTRAINT FK_address_city_state FOREIGN KEY (city)
                    REFERENCES city_state_code (city)
)
go
create table city_state_code
(
city                   char(20),
state                  char(20),
CONSTRAINT PK_citystate PRIMARY KEY CLUSTERED (city)
)
go
/* Test the FOREIGN KEY constraint */

INSERT city_state_code
(city, state)
VALUES
("New York City," "New York")
go
INSERT address
(customer_no, address_code, street1, street2, city,
state_province,
country, zip_pc)
VALUES
(2000, "S," "123 Joe Lane," "street 2," "New York City,"
"New York," "USA," "01")
go
```

4. In this example, the FOREIGN KEY constraint is modified to REFER-
   ENCE two columns in the code table. This also requires a change to
   the PRIMARY KEY CONSTRAINT to include to matching column
   fields as well.

```
use address

go

drop table address

go

drop table city_state_code

go

create table address

(

customer_no            int,

address_code           char(1),

street1                char(25),

street2                char(25),

city                   char(20),

state_province         char(20),

country                char(15),

zip_pc                 char(10),

CONSTRAINT FK_address_city_state FOREIGN KEY (city,
state_province)

                       REFERENCES city_state_code (city,
                       state)

)

go

create table city_state_code

(

city                   char(20),

state                  char(20),

CONSTRAINT PK_citystate PRIMARY KEY CLUSTERED (city,
state)

)

go
```

```
/* Test the FOREIGN KEY constraint */

INSERT city_state_code

(city, state)

VALUES

("New York City," "New York")

go

INSERT address

(customer_no, address_code, street1, street2, city,
state_province,

country, zip_pc)

VALUES

(2000, "S," "123 Joe Lane," "street 2," "New York City,"
"New York," "USA," "01")

go
```

Note: Testing the Constraints

The reader can test the multicolumn constraints by changing the values in some of the reference columns (e.g., change "New York" to "Texas" in the last example for the address record and attempt to insert the record). The multicolumn constraint traps this because there is no "New York City" and "Dallas" combination in the "city_state_code" table.

Note: Testing the Constraints

It is also possible to use triggers to enforce referential integrity instead of constraints. Constraints are processed before triggers and are conceptually easier to implement because the validation procedure is saved with the table creation code. Constraints, however, are limited to referencing tables in the current database. Triggers do not have this limitation.

DEFAULT CONSTRAINTS

In some of the INSERT scripts that were used earlier, some columns were filled with temporary data (e.g., "not known"). The CREATE/ALTER table commands provide a DEFAULT constraint that inserts a value into a field that is not passed a value.

Syntax:

The syntax for the DEFAULT CONSTRAINT command is as follows:

```
CREATE TABLE table_name
```

221

```
column1    datatype    DEFAULT (value),
column2    datatype    DEFAULT ('value'),
column3    datatype    DEFAULT value,
column4    datatype    DEFAULT 'value' ...
```

Examples:

1. In this example, defaults are assigned to the optional columns. Several insert commands demonstrate how the defaults are processed.

```
use address
go
drop table address
go
create table address
(
customer_no          int,
address_code         char(1)DEFAULT 'H',
street1              char(25),
street2              char(25) DEFAULT 'Street 2',
city                   char(20) DEFAULT 'New York City',
state_province       char(20),
country              char(15) DEFAULT 'USA',
zip_pc               char(10),
CONSTRAINT FK_address_city_state FOREIGN KEY (city,
state_province)
                     REFERENCES city_state_code (city,
                     state)
)
go
/* Enter some records into the address table and take
advantage of the defaults to save time and effort
entering the data */
```

```
INSERT address
    (customer_no, street1, state, zip_pc)
    VALUES
    (2000, "123 Hope Street," "New York," "10002")
go
/* Override the address-code column default within the
INSERT command */
INSERT address
    (customer_no, address_code, street1, state, zip_pc)
    VALUES
    (2000, "S," "123 Hope Street," "New York," "10002")
go
```

2. In this example, defaults are assigned to columns with various datatypes.

```
USE address
go
DROP TABLE deposit
go
CREATE TABLE deposit
(
customer_no      int,
amount           money        DEFAULT 0.00,
deposit_date     datetime     DEFAULT getdate(),
user_id          char (20)    DEFAULT 'Operator'
)
go
INSERT deposit
(customer_no, deposit_date) VALUES (1500, getdate())
go
INSERT deposit (customer_no) VALUES (1600)
go
```

CONCLUSION

This chapter provided scripts to add data constraints to table columns and tables. This included identity constraints, key constraints, and default constraints. The SQL scripts provide a baseline for reestablishing a database environment to the same point. This chapter also provided examples of SQL scripts that test the operation of the data constraints.

Chapter 18
Referential Integrity for Database Design

Bonn-Oh Kim

MAINTAINING THE INTEGRITY OF DATA is one of the most critical issues involved in designing in database systems. In relational database systems, there are four common integrity constraints:

- The key constraint, which states that the values of a primary key must be unique, so there should be no duplicate primary key values.
- Entity integrity, which indicates that a primary key of a relation cannot take null values.
- Referential integrity, which is a constraint to ensure the existence of a tuple of a relation that is referenced by a tuple in another relation.
- Semantic integrity, which states that data in the database systems should be consistent or semantically correct.

A relational database is commonly considered to have referential integrity if there are no unmatched foreign key values. This definition is incomplete because attributes other than a foreign key also require data consistency with other relations. It is also limiting when designing an entity-relationship (E-R) model or relational model because referential integrity is indirectly represented via the foreign key concept.

This chapter discusses attribute referential integrity (ARI), an expanded concept that allows referential integrity to be specified on any attribute of a relation. It also explains the specifications of the new referential integrity constraint on the E-R and relational models. Methods of enforcing the referential integrity constraint are also suggested.

Discussion of the integrity issues is restricted to the relational model, although other data models such as the network or hierarchical model share the same concerns.

THE COMMON DEFINITION OF REFERENTIAL INTEGRITY

Referential integrity in the relational model is defined in various ways. Some definitions assert that to maintain referential integrity, the database

0-8493-9832-0/00/$0.00+$.50
© 2000 by CRC Press LLC

225

must not contain any unmatched foreign key values; others assert that referential integrity is defined only between foreign and primary key relations. However, there is no theoretical reason to specify the referential integrity constraint only on the foreign key. Specifying referential integrity on any attribute of a relation should be possible.

In designing relational database systems, the E-R model can be used as a conceptual tool for specifying data requirements. This practice is widely accepted and supported by various computer-aided software engineering (CASE) tools.

In the E-R model, however, referential integrity is not explicitly represented, although it can be specified on a relationship among entity types. In the E-R model, referential integrity is implicitly represented on a relationship type between the participating entity types. It becomes explicit only after the E-R model is converted into the relational model. That is, referential integrity can be explicitly specified using structured query language (SQL) statements when creating tables.

LIMITS OF THE COMMON DEFINITION OF REFERENTIAL INTEGRITY

The commonly accepted definition of referential integrity is inadequate for representing the referential integrity constraint on attributes that are not a foreign key, as the following example illustrates.

A Sample Case: The Car Rental Company

A small car rental company wants to implement a database system for retaining information on vehicles and rental packages, represented by the objects VEHICLE and RENTAL_PACKAGE, respectively.

For VEHICLE, they would like to retain vehicle identification numbers (VehID#), makes (Make), and vehicle types (VehTypeName). Regarding RENTAL_PACKAGE, the package identification number (PackageID#), rates (Rate), and vehicle types (VehTypeName) need to be retained.

Information on vehicle types in both VEHICLE and RENTAL_PACKAGE should be consistent. RENTAL_PACKAGE is the primary source for information on the vehicle types. In other words, all the vehicle types shown in VEHICLE.VehTypeName should exist in RENTAL_PACKAGE.VehTypeName.

Exhibit 1 shows an E-R model for the above case. In the exhibit, the referential integrity constraint on VehTypeName between RENTAL_PACKAGE and VEHICLE is maintained by creating a new entity type (VEHICLE_TYPE) and two one-to-many relationships between VEHICLE_TYPE and RENTAL_PACKAGE, and VEHICLE_TYPE and VEHICLE.

Exhibit 18.2 shows a relational model converted from the E-R model in Exhibit 18.1. In these models, the referential integrity constraint of the

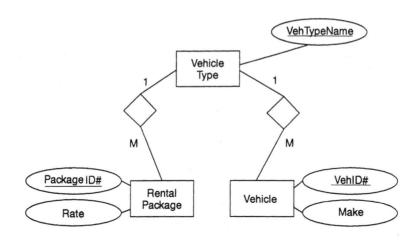

Exhibit 18.1.   An example of a conventional E-R model.

vehicle type information is maintained by specifying a foreign key on Ve-hTypeName on RENTAL_PACKAGE and VEHICLE, respectively.

Even though the models shown in Exhibits 18.1 and 18.2 appear to efficiently maintain referential integrity using the foreign keys, they actually incur unnecessary computational costs. That is, an entity type of VEHICLE_TYPE in Exhibit 18.1 and a relation of VEHICLE_TYPE in Exhibit 18.2 are created solely for maintaining and enforcing the referential integrity constraint of the vehicle type information.

Unless there is a need to retain more information (i.e., other attributes) in VEHICLE_TYPE, this way of implementing referential integrity is redundant and computationally expensive. Costs for creating and maintaining a unary relation (in the previous example, it is VEHICLE_TYPE) can be eliminated by directly defining the referential integrity between two relations (i.e., VEHICLE and RENTAL_PACKAGE). The following section discusses more direct and explicit representations of referential integrity to remedy this type of anomaly.

ATTRIBUTE REFERENTIAL INTEGRITY (ARI)

Referential integrity is an issue, not only in the context of referencing foreign keys and referenced primary keys. There is also a need to extend and generalize the concept of referential integrity beyond the current definition.

This section defines extended referential integrity and proposes a notation for the E-R model. Unlike the conventional definition of referential integrity, a foreign key is not a part of the definition. This expanded version of referential integrity is referred to as *attribute referential integrity.*

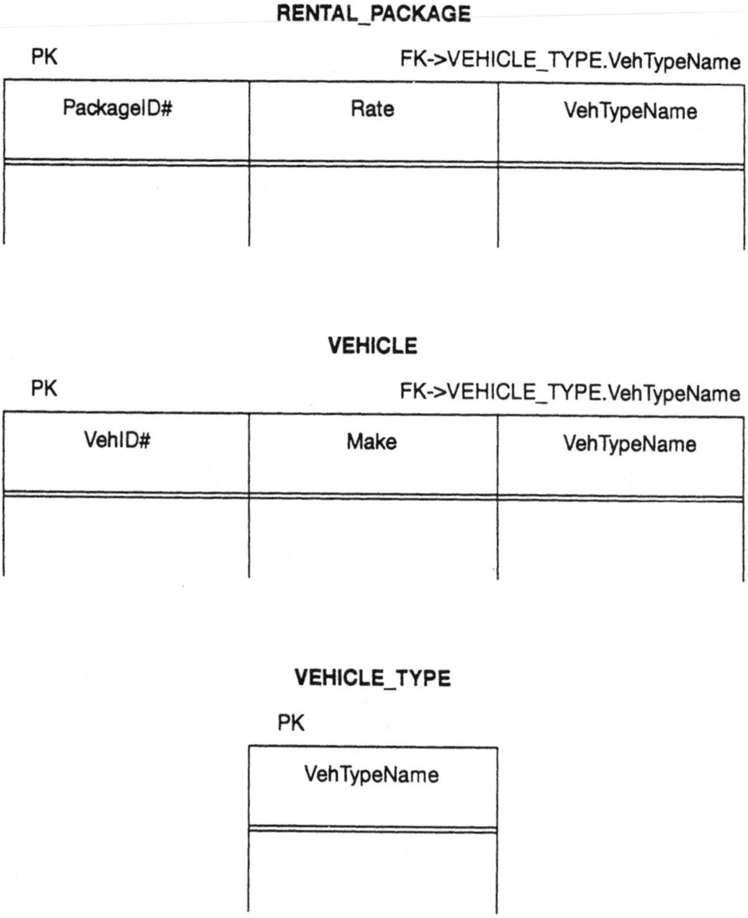

RENTAL_PACKAGE

PK   FK->VEHICLE_TYPE.VehTypeName

PackageID#	Rate	VehTypeName

VEHICLE

PK   FK->VEHICLE_TYPE.VehTypeName

VehID#	Make	VehTypeName

VEHICLE_TYPE

PK

VehTypeName

Exhibit 18.2.   A relational model generated from the E-R model in Exhibit 18.1.

Attribute referential integrity ensures that a value appearing in the referencing attribute of one relation appears in the referenced attribute of the other relation, where these two relations are not necessarily distinct, and referencing or referenced attributes can be a combination of multiple attributes. The following section provides the formal definition.

The Formal Definition of Attribute Referential Integrity

r1 (R1) and r2 (R2) are relations of a schema R1 and R2, respectively. A subset a of R1 is a referencing attribute referring to a referenced attribute b in relation r2 if it is required that for every tuple t1 in r1, there must be a tuple t2 in r2 such that t1[a] = t2[b]. Requirements of this form are called the

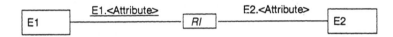

Exhibit 18.3. Proposed notation for attribute referential integrity.

---

attribute referential integrity constraint. This can be written as $\prod a_a(r1)\prod_a$ (r2), where $\prod$ is a projection operation in the relational algebra. For an attribute referential integrity constraint to make sense, either a = b or a and b must be compatible sets of attributes.

The E-R Model

Exhibit 18.3 shows a proposed notation for attribute referential integrity on the E-R diagram. RI in the small rectangle indicates that the participating entity types E1 and E2 contain the attributes whose referential integrity should be maintained.

On the line between the RI rectangle and the participating entity types, the referential relationship is represented (i.e., the referencing or referenced attribute is specified), where an underlined attribute represents a referenced attribute. As defined, the referenced attribute contains a superset of all values appearing in the referencing attribute.

Exhibit 18.4 shows an example of a new E-R model for the previous example. Unlike the first example, there is no need to create a new entity type solely for representing the referential integrity constraint. On the entity types RENTAL_PACKAGE and VEHICLE, the vehicle type attribute (VehType-

---

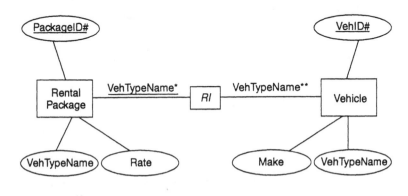

Key:
 * Referenced attribute
 ** Referencing attribute

Exhibit 18.4.   An example of the extended E-R model.

229

DATA INTEGRITY AND QUALITY

Name) is included instead of separately creating an entity type VEHICLE_TYPE as in Exhibit 18.1. On the lines emanating from the RI rectangle, a referenced attribute (RENTAL_PACKAGE.VehTypeName), and a referencing attribute (VEHICLE.VehTypeName), are specified explicitly; whereas, in Exhibit 11-1 this referential integrity is implicitly represented via the foreign key concept.

The Relational Model

The ARI constraint can be directly represented on the referencing attribute of a relation by specifying a referenced attribute of the other relation. A notation representing this is:

```
ARI(<referencing attribute>) Æ <referenced attribute>
```

For example, Exhibit 18.5 shows a set of relations generated from the E-R model shown in Exhibit 18.4 . By specifying the attribute referential integrity constraint directly on VEHICLE.VehTypeName , there is no need to create a new relation of VEHICLE_TYPE because no foreign keys are involved to specify the referential integrity constraints as in Exhibit 18.2. Instead, the referential integrity constraint on VehTypeName can be directly and explicitly specified on the referencing attribute, VEHICLE.VehTypeName , referring to the referenced attribute, RENTAL_PACKAGE.VehTypeName .

RENTAL_PACKAGE

PK

TermID#	Rate	VehTypeName

VEHICLE

PK   ARI->RENTAL_PACKAGE.VehTypeName

VehID#	Make	VehTypeName

Exhibit 18.5.   A relational model generated from the E-R model in Exhibit 11.4.

The conventional referential integrity constraint on the foreign key can be specified using SQL when defining a relation. In this relational model (or SQL based on it), there is no direct way of specifying the attribute referential integrity constraint. However, it can still be specified in the database designer's data dictionary and implemented using a procedural language. Future versions of SQL will include the specifications of the attribute referential integrity constraint on the non-foreign key attributes.

Following is the suggested syntax for specifying the ARI constraint:

```
CREATE TABLE <TableName>

    (<Attribute List> ; This attribute list must include
    the referencing attribute.

ATTRIBUTE REFERENTIAL INTEGRITY: <Referencing
Attribute>

REFERENCES <Referenced Attribute>)
```

The relational model shown in Exhibit 18.5 can be written as follows:

```
CREATE TABLE RENTAL_PACKAGE

    (TermID          #INT,

    RateDECIMAL      (3,1),

    VehTypeName      CHAR(20));

CREATE TABLE VEHICLE

    (VehID#          INT,

    Make             CHAR(20),

    VehTypeName      CHAR(20))

ATTRIBUTE REFERENTIAL INTEGRITY:

    (VehTypeName) REFERENCES RENTAL_PACKAGE
    (VehTypeName));
```

ENFORCING THE ARI CONSTRAINT

Enforcement of the referential integrity constraint on the foreign key can be conducted in three ways: restriction, cascading, and nullification (i.e., setting to a default value). The attribute referential integrity constraint can be enforced in a similar manner.

First, the delete or update operation on the referenced attribute can be restricted to the case where there are no matching values in the referencing attribute. Second, the delete or update operation on the referenced attribute cascades to delete or update the matching values in the referencing attribute. Finally, the referencing attribute value is set to null or a default value if a matching value in the referenced attribute is deleted or updated.

These three enforcement schemes are not, however, implemented in current database management systems (DBMSs). The attribute referential integrity constraint should be enforced by writing an application program on the database or attaching a procedure (i.e., trigger) to a referenced or referencing attribute.

SUMMARY

Specifying the attribute referential integrity has major advantages in database systems design. An E-R and relational model for a problem domain can be built compactly by dispensing with an entity type and a relation created solely for specifying the referential integrity constraint of a foreign key. Also, the referential integrity constraint of an attribute can be specified directly and explicitly without using foreign keys.

Using the attribute referential integrity concept, a referential semantic constraint can be explicitly represented in the E-R and relational models. In the current DBMS environment, this new integrity constraint can be implemented by writing an attached procedure on a referenced or referencing attribute. In the future, CASE tools and DBMSs will be able to represent the attribute referential integrity constraint.

Chapter 19
Data Quality: An Architectural Solution

Sriram Pidaparti

As CORPORATIONS EMBARK ON DATA WAREHOUSING EFFORTS, they are unearthing integrity and accuracy problems associated with the operational data. Another major challenge that has emerged is the integration of disparate operational data. This problem is characterized by inconsistent data models, disparate data structures, and poor quality of data that is fundamental to an organization — such as customer data, vendor data, and product data.

It is not uncommon to find a situation in which there are six different descriptions for the same product or four different data structures for customer name and address data. Such situations are common because of:

- Multiple transactional systems that have their own versions of the data stores (both structures and data), for example; different versions of customer data in order processing and billing systems.
- Package installations, business mergers, and acquisitions that incorporate new and different versions of data.
- Multiple instances of the same application used and extended differently in different geographies or departments.
- Different business units that have adopted their own definitions and standards for foundation databased on the belief that their business is different from the other business units.

Addressing these data quality issues at the enterprise architecture level is essential to finding an effective long-term solution. This chapter proposes that the corporate information factory be extended to include a construct called the foundation data store (FDS). The following sections define the foundation data store, describe how it fits into the corporate information factory, and suggest possible implementation approaches.

FDS OVERVIEW AND BENEFITS

Organizations have foundation data whether or not they design and implement it as a separate data store. Some organizations implement reference files/databases (also known in some companies as pillar databases, subject databases, and master databases) for foundation data. The foundation data store is a mechanism to formalize this practice into an architectural construct like the operational data store and data warehouse. The term *foundation data store* is used in this chapter because it appropriately reflects the architectural placement and importance of this data store.

The FDS contains relatively nonvolatile information that is traditionally found in a master file (e.g., customer data, vendor data, organization structures, and product data). This information can be viewed as a centrally maintained or authenticated data store that operational systems would use instead of creating and maintaining their own unique versions of the foundation data.

The information content of the FDS is based on standards for common data definitions, structures, and values. The commonality depends on how diverse an organization is; for example, the more diverse the organization, the less the commonality of data. An example of a high-level, entity-relationship (E-R) diagram for a foundation data store is shown in Exhibit 19.1.

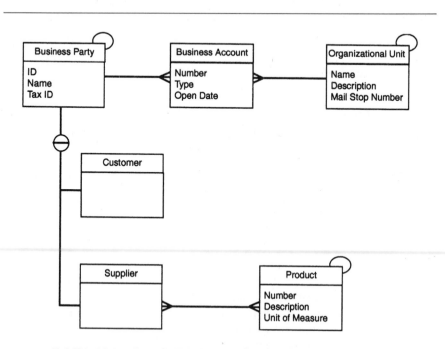

Exhibit 19.1.   Sample E-R diagram for foundation data store.

The FDS data model is only a part of the enterprisewide logical data model; otherwise, it would not contain all the entities and relationships. For example, an enterprise-level data model may have an associative entity called Order that connects the Customer and Product entities, but that entity belongs to the order processing transactional application data model rather than the foundation data model.

It is also possible that only certain attributes of an entity may belong to the FDS data model; for example, a business account balance does not necessarily have to be a foundation data attribute. The major entities of the foundation data store usually translate into dimensions in the informational processing world.

In addition to easier data integration and improved operational data quality, the foundation data store implementation offers the following benefits:

- Reduced effort in developing data warehousing applications because of easier integration of data.
- Better customer service because of data quality improvements.
- Cost savings because of centralized data maintenance and efficient external data vendor management.
- Improved decision-making because of more accurate information.
- More efficient transactional applications development because of reuse and avoidance of duplication of efforts.

FOUNDATION APPLICATION FRAMEWORK

The application or system that updates the foundation data store is primarily a data maintenance application. Therefore, it would not possess the complex processing logic of a transactional application such as an order processing system, production scheduling system, or trading system.

The framework shown in Exhibit 19.2 is a useful reference for administrators creating a new transactional application or reengineering a legacy

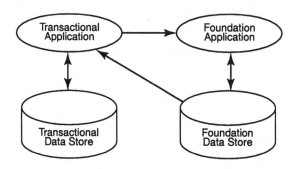

Exhibit 19.2. Framework for transactional and foundation applications.

	Transactional	Foundation
System Examples	Order processing system Billing system Equities trading system	Customer maintenance Product maintenance Vendor maintenance
Data Entity Examples	Order, invoice, shipment Payment, cash flow	Customer, product, vendor
Volatility	Very volatile	Relatively stable
Volume of Data	Large to very large	Small to large
Key Characteristic	Performance is most critical	Availability is most critical
Application Processing	Process/workflow intensive	Data intensive Mainly limited to table maintenance

Exhibit 19.3. Differences between transactional and foundation applications.

application. Architectural separation of foundation and transactional applications along with their data stores is recommended. The demarcation of update responsibilities is very clear — the transactional application updates its transactional data and the foundation application updates the foundation data store. Access to the foundation data store is critical to the transactional application. Administrators usually need to be able to join data within two data stores. Technology solutions such as gateways make this possible, even across heterogeneous database environments.

The foundation application should be a centrally developed application deployed in a distributed fashion. The purpose of the interaction between foundation and transactional applications, as shown in Exhibit 19.2, is not only to give the transactional application user access to the foundation application, but to make it appear seamless to the user. For example, to create a new customer entry while taking an order, the customer service representative does not have to log into the foundation application. Exhibit 19.3 shows the differences between transactional and foundation applications.

FDS AND THE CORPORATE INFORMATION FACTORY

Inmon, Imhoff, and Battas, in their book *Building the Operational Data Store* (New York: John Wiley & Sons, Inc., 1995), proposed a common architecture called the *corporate information factory* that includes the operational data store (ODS), data warehouse, and legacy applications (see Exhibit 19.4). They describe the flow of data within the corporate information factory as follows:

1. Raw, detailed data is put into the corporate information factory by means of data capture, entry, and transaction interaction with the older legacy applications.

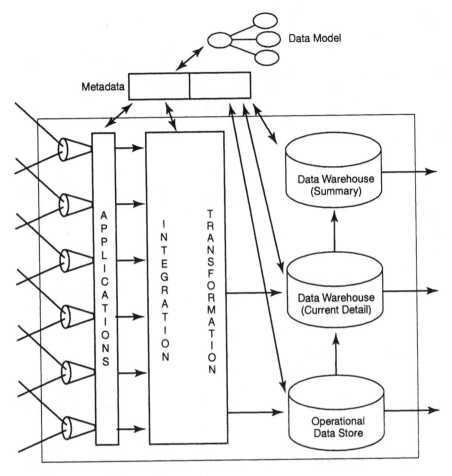

Note: Bulk storage not shown.

SOURCE: Inmon, Imhoff, and Battas, *Building the Operational Data Store* (New York: John Wiley and Sons, Inc., 1995).

Exhibit 19.4.   Corporate information factory.

2. The raw, detailed data are integrated and transformed and then passed into the operational data store or the current detail level of the data warehouse.
3. As the refined data passes out of the operational data store, this data goes into the current level of the data warehouse.
4. Once the refined data is summarized, the data passes from the current detail level of the warehouse into the summarized level of data in the data warehouse.

The corporate information factory can be extended to include the foundation data store as an integral architectural construct within the framework, as shown in Exhibit 19.5. The FDS functions as the official source (i.e., system of record) for an organization's foundation data. It maintains and supplies such data to transactional applications, the ODS, and data warehouse. The FDS also collects and conditions external data before that data can be used by an organization. The following sections discuss how the foundation data store relates to the other components of the corporate information factory.

Transactional Applications. Ideally, the transactional applications should not have their own versions of the foundation data, but should access the centrally maintained data store. In another possible configuration, the transactional application could make changes to a local copy of the central store, and the changes would be applied to the central store after authentication.

Integration and Transformation Layer. The implementation of the foundation data store makes the application component more integrated, which leads to a relatively simple and straightforward integration and transformation layer.

Operational Data Store. An ODS application usually uses the current version of the foundation data store. Therefore, ODS applications should be able to directly access the central foundation data store. An alternative is to replicate a subset of the central foundation data store into the ODS environment.

Data Warehouse. The major entities of the foundation data store become dimensions in a data warehouse. The data warehouse contains the historical snapshots of the foundation data store. The detail contained in the warehouse should reference the appropriate snapshot of the foundation data.

While doing comparative and trend analyses, users should be alerted if different summarization algorithms are used for different time periods. For example, if organizational hierarchy is one of the foundation data entities, the results of summarization would depend on the hierarchy that is used in the summarization process. Users should be given an option to view the history based on either the same hierarchy for all time periods or different hierarchies for different time periods.

Data Model. Design and implementation of the foundation data store should be based on a solid logical data model that is an integral part of an enterprise data model. In the case of foundation data, translation from the logical model to the physical design is relatively straightforward, unlike

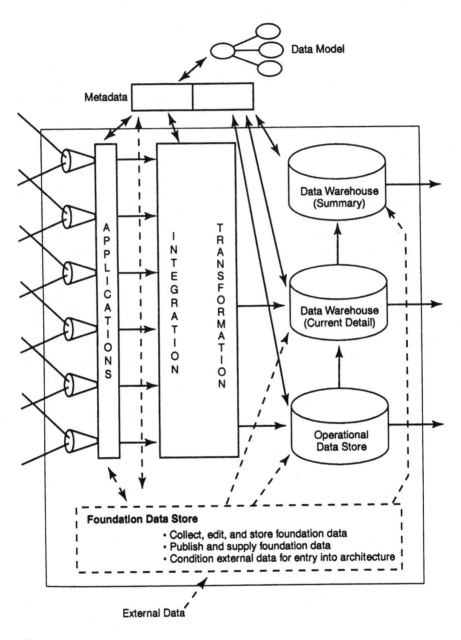

Notes: Bulk storage not shown.

For the sake of clarity, the flows from external data
to the other components of the architecture are not shown.

Exhibit 19.5. FDS as a component of the corporate information factory.

DATA INTEGRITY AND QUALITY

the design of data warehouse databases or transactional databases that may require a lot of denormalization or summarization.

Metadata. The metadata generated from the data model is used as a basis for the design of the foundation data store. One of the first steps in implementing a foundation data store is documenting the existing foundation data and developing the standards. Metadata is, therefore, a natural by-product of this process. In an organization that has an efficient FDS implementation, the data dictionary of the foundation database supplies a significant portion of the metadata.

External Data. There is a potential need for external data at all levels of the corporate information factory. For example, the data warehouse may contain external information to compare the historical performance of the organization with an external benchmark. Similarly, an order processing system may have electronic data interchange-related external data that is unique to that application.

Some of the external data that an organization uses is foundation information. Typical examples include financial product information from market data providers and name and address lists purchased from vendors. It is essential that the external data be conditioned to adhere to standards before that data is stored in the foundation data store.

External data should also be modeled and documented using the enterprise data model and metadata for it to be appropriately classified and integrated with the internal data in the data warehouse and other data stores.

FDS IMPLEMENTATION STRATEGIES

Implementing the foundation data store requires careful planning and commitment from all levels of an organization, including senior management, business user groups, and IS. The following sections discuss potential architectures for implementing the foundation data store.

Central Data Store with Direct Access. In this strategy, all the applications that require foundation data directly access a central data store. This technically simple solution provides the best data quality. However, it is vulnerable to performance problems and a single point of failure. In addition, this solution does not allow the creation of new foundation data or changes to be made to existing foundation data. Exhibit 19.6 shows a central data store with direct access.

Central Data Store with Replicated Copies. In this architecture, a subset of the central data store is replicated to allow local applications to access foundation data more rapidly. This solution provides better performance,

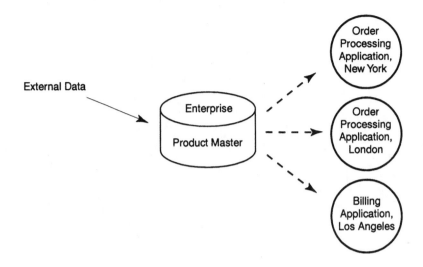

Exhibit 19.6. Central data store with direct access.

but is more complex technically and does not allow create and update functions to be performed. Exhibit 19.7 shows a central data store with replicated copies.

Central Authentication. Central authentication allows individual business units or local offices of an organization to create new foundation data and make changes to existing foundation data. The additions and changes are recorded locally in a database separate from the official replicated copy of the central store. The new and changed data is transferred to a cen-

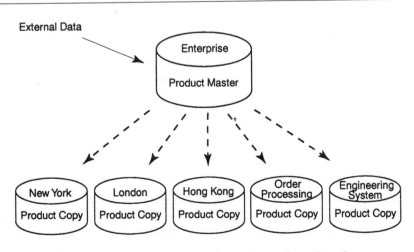

Exhibit 19.7. Central data store with replicated copies.

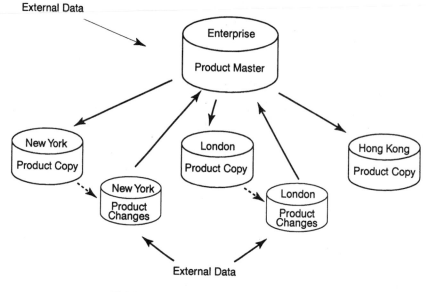

Exhibit 19.8.   Central authentication.

---

tral data store where the additions and changes are authenticated. The authenticated data are transmitted to all the users who requested it. This strategy reduces bottlenecks, but is the most complex technically. Central authentication is illustrated in Exhibit 19.8.

Consolidated Reference. This strategy is used primarily to implement consolidation standards for reporting and informational processing purposes (see Exhibit 19.9). Although it is a necessary step for data warehousing initiatives, it does not solve data quality problems in the operational systems.

Consolidated reference is a valid short-term strategy for organizations with urgent data warehousing project commitments and limited resources. A long-term solution to operational data problems, however, would be to implement the central foundation data store, which is the official source for the foundation data. Consolidated reference can be viewed as an intermediate step to implementing the foundation data store.

FDS IMPLEMENTATION FACTORS

An organization must choose the most appropriate implementation strategy based on its own context and situation. Although various factors influence FDS implementation in an organization, the solution depends on the organizational structure, number of database platforms, number of physical databases, number of geographic locations, and volume of data.

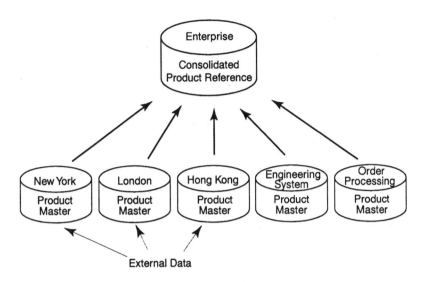

Exhibit 19.9.   Consolidated reference.

An organization with a decentralized management philosophy may prefer central authentication rather than a central store with direct architecture, as with an organization that does not have a very strong WAN infrastructure. A company that has several transaction systems on various DBMS platforms requires a well-planned technical architecture involving gateways and message queues.

Although it is desirable, it is not necessary to have the same implementation strategy for all of the foundation data. For example, for a particular organization, a central data store with direct access may be more appropriate for vendor data, whereas central authentication may be more appropriate for customer data.

SUMMARY

A foundation data store should be chosen based on organizational structure, number of database platforms, number of physical databases, number of geographic locations, and volume of data. Although it is more manageable, it is not necessary to implement the same strategy for all the foundation data. For example, a central data store with direct access may be more appropriate for vendor data, whereas central authentication may be more appropriate for customer data.

The foundation data store is presented as an architectural component of the corporate information factory. Finding the appropriate implementation strategy and addressing the data quality issues are critical to the long-term success of an organization's data warehousing initiatives.

Section IV
Data Administration, Security, and Operations

MANIPULATING DATA, WHETHER IT IS AT CREATE TIME, DELETE TIME, OR MODIFICATION TIME, IS AN IMPORTANT PART OF THE DATA MANAGEMENT CHALLENGE. The other significant challenge is the ongoing maintenance of the physical storage of the data and the operation of the tools that support the data. Data administration also includes system management, configuration management, and asset management tools and processes. Data must also be secured against viruses, unauthorized access, and corruption. Operations include the processes and procedures for maintaining data stores, regular backups, and data recovery procedures. This section contains five chapters that explore each of these topics.

Chapter 20, "Leveraging Checkpoint Processing," shows how to build check points into batch processes to allow jobs to be restarted in the event that processing problems are encountered. This is needed to allow batch jobs to complete in scheduled batch windows thereby allowing systems to become active and available to users at their scheduled times.

Chapter 21, "Managing Database Backup and Recovery," discusses how to invest in a sound databse backup and recovery process to protect corporate data. This involves examining the degrees of recoverability required by the business, fault tolerance alternatives, virus infiltration, and unauthorized tampering through the Internet.

Chapter 22, "Change Management Strategies for Data Administration," provides a non-technical overview of change management at the organizational level. This chapter describes how changes in an organization, such as downsizing, can affect the data management functions, and then discusses strategies for managing the data in the midst of such changes. In particular, data resource management principles are outlined for handling changes. Some of the behavioral as well as cost issues are also discussed.

245

Chapter 23, "Security Models for Object-Oriented Databases," describes how database administrators can address the unique security considerations of Object-Oriented systems. This chapter also focuses on the emerging security model.

Chapter 24, "Security Management for the World Wide Web," provides a solution set to leverage an organizations existing skills, resources, and security implementations in building an underlying baseline security framework for transacting corporate business over the Internet and the World Wide Web.

Chapter 20
Leveraging Checkpoint Processing

William Pearson

ON THE ROAD TO THE ENTERPRISE SERVER, following are a few reflections on lessons learned in the "glass house." I will introduce the concept of checkpoint restartability. Then, I will go on to explain how this can shave hours off of your batch window, just when you need it the most. Finally, I will show how you can apply checkpoint restart to any database management system (DBMS) such as DB2, ORACLE, SYSBASE or SQL server.

Murphy's Law proposes that anything that can go wrong, will, and usually at the worst possible time. For the manager of a support application, this usually means that the day begins sitting down to talk with a disheveled programmer. Now, given the 1990s dress code, your first clue that something went wrong during the night is not the faded T-shirt and blue jeans; nor is it the bags under the eyes, the five o'clock shadow, or even the extra large coffee mug clutched between white knuckles, has started weaving intricate patterns over your special report. No, it's the socks! They don't match—one of them is definitely black while the other is quite red.

The story is the old classic of heroic recovery where once again good triumphs over evil. It starts with a beep in the middle of the night and a 2:30 a.m. call to operations. Next comes the 45-minute drive to work, where, upon arrival, it only takes 15 minutes to analyze and resolve the problem (note the 'genius at work' logo on T-shirt). Then, 30 minutes to recover files to a prior run state. Finally, a long 1 1/2 hour wait to reprocess transaction records to get back to where the original ABEND occurred…only to discover a minor typo in the 'fix'; completely, understandable, under the circumstances. Fast forward 2 hours and 15 minutes to when the run finishes and your story's main character has just the time to buy a coffee and appear at your desk by 8:00 a.m.

DATA ADMINISTRATION, SECURITY, AND OPERATIONS

Global competition has ushered in a 7/24 world—your new Internet application is expected to run 24 hours a day, 7 days a week. Customers could be making online updates anytime from anywhere. Your nightly batch window has shrunk to zero. You do not have time for a 4-hour heroic delay to your 'daily' cycle. You do not have time to relive last night's adventure tale. If only the problem had been resolved quickly. If only there wasn't always a 30-minute recovery and a 1 1/2-hour reprocessing delay. Just imagine... you could be reading a short update via internal mail instead of listening to a blow-by-blow account of last night's epic drama, all the time wishing that the blinking red light on your phone, indicating a voice mail from your boss's boss, would go away!

Instigating a new closed-door policy will not solve this problem. Rather, I suggest that you start looking into making your programs Checkpoint Restartable. First, I will review some general principles. Next, using existing IMS Checkpoint/Restart functions as a starting base, I will go over the fundamental parts of taking checkpoints, using Save-Areas and performing a Restart. Then, I will review some basic principles to help you design with Restart in mind. Lastly, I will show you how to apply the above principles to any SQL Database Management System to bring Checkpoint Restartability to a programmer near you!

GENERAL PRINCIPLES

All programs should be transaction based. Simply put, this means that while a program's logic may read many tables, take locks, and update data, the complete process must be contained in a single 'unit of work.' A transaction manager then makes sure that all database updates processed in this unit of work are committed or rolled back together. This all or nothing approach is required to maintain data integrity.

An on-line program processes one transaction at a time and makes a commit decision at the end of each unit of work. We can say that it has a default checkpoint frequency of one. Batch programs should also be transaction based. Each input transaction represents a discrete unit of work. All processing for each input 'transaction' should be completed before continuing to the next one. The difference is that you can give batch programs a checkpoint frequency of 5, 50, or 50,000. For example, one of your 'nightly' batch programs takes 2 hours to process 500,000 input transactions. Your DBA recommends a checkpoint frequency of 50,000. If the program were to ABEND after 90 minutes, it would have successfully taken 7 checkpoints, one approximately every 12 minutes. The last one would have occurred after 84 minutes. Up to this point, 350,000 units of work would have been successfully committed. The last 6 minutes of work, approximately 25,000 transactions, would be rolled back. Under this scenario, let us pick up our story just after the original ABEND occurred.

It still takes the programmer 45 minutes to arrive and 15 minutes to fix the problem. This time, however, zero time is spent on database recovery because all updates are valid. Moreover, the second ABEND, due to that typo in the programming fix, occurs after only about 6 minutes. Again, potential updates are rolled back. Thus, 22 minutes later, the program is past the problem. By the time the hero has mailed you a short problem report, the batch cycle has completed. It is still night, so your tired programmer returns home.

IMS CHECKPOINT/RESTART FUNCTIONS

In the above story, there is a conspicuous usage of a black box labeled, "a miracle happens here." In the following paragraphs, I will attempt to demystify this box by reviewing the basic functions that allow checkpoint restart to work.

Checkpoint Frequency

Usually, a simple Control Card interface serves to supply this value to your program. It allows you to control the number of input transactions that a program processes between commit points. The value should be easy to change as estimating the frequency is not an exact science. For example, 50,000 is too high if your program only processes an average of 40,000 transactions each run. On the other hand, 1 is too small.

Recommendation: Talk to your DBA about checkpoint frequency. As a rule of thumb, I suggest a minimum of 10 checkpoints per run and/or an average elapse time between checkpoints of less than 15 minutes.

Checkpoint Call

This is where your program commits all IMS database, DB2 table and sequential file (GSAM) updates. All locks held by your DBMS are released. All data is written to disk or tape. Save areas are copied to the log. Conversely, in the case of a program ABEND, a roll back call should be performed to undo all updates, release all locks and make sure that no data is written to disk.

At the end of the 'unit of work' for each input transaction, your program should update a transaction counter and compare the current value to the checkpoint frequency number. Upon reaching the checkpoint frequency, your program may make a checkpoint call and reset the transaction counter to zero.

Recommendation: Do not take a checkpoint, unless your program can restart from there. For example, if your input transactions are driven by an SQL FETCH then make sure that your program has just crossed a break

249

point from which the process can be restarted. After all, the program must be able to reopen this CURSOR exactly where it left off.

Save-Areas

Under IMS, a checkpoint call may contain up to seven Save-Areas. Each one may represent a 01 level in Working Storage several thousand bytes long. It allows you to save several fields or several blocks of data by writing the information to the IMS log dataset. Upon restart, the system retrieves the data from the log and places it back into these specified data areas. Thus, your program can save more data than you should ever need.

Recommendation: Only save the minimum amount of data. I have known some misguided individuals who liked to save their program's entire working storage. Please use some common sense. After all, you designed the program to completely finish processing one transaction before proceeding to the next one, so what data needs to be kept?

Here are four suggestions:

- Always keep the Checkpoint ID and counter. This permits your program to write out checkpoints sequentially. While IMS expects this, it is also reassuring to anyone double checking last night's batch run report. It is also useful during testing to show that save-areas work.
- Keep the Run date that your program displays on any reports. After all, if the date suddenly changes on page 21 of a report, users will assume that the entire results must be wrong! (You may skip this one, if your program obtains this value from a control card.)
- Do not save the Checkpoint frequency. Upon restart, your program should always re-input this value from the control card. This is just in case you decide to change it during the run.
- The transaction records driving the batch process, frequently, come from a sequential file. In this case, the IMS RESTART command automatically repositions the sequential (GSAM) file upon restart. However, if the process driving your program is either IMS GN calls or DB2 FETCHs then this reposition is not done. You must add code to your program to save the key field data needed to reposition itself. For IMS, I also recommend adding a qualified GU call in the Restart paragraph to actually reposition the IMS database. For DB2, your existing OPEN CURSOR statement should work. However, this assumes that the WHERE clause in the FETCH's DECLARE statement contains greater than and/or less than logic to use the saved key field data in order to effectively reposition the CURSOR.

That is it...unless the program is maintaining a list of summary totals by branch, by region, by division. In this case, you must save the summary field area(s) so that, upon restart, your program may continue to add more data to these values.

Restart Call

This should be the first IMS call in your program. It serves to determine whether to continue processing as a normal (cold start) or to restart the program from a post ABEND state (warm start). Following the call, your program should test for SPACES in the Checkpoint ID field. If found then a normal start is performed. If not, then a restart is done. Regardless of which logic path is chosen, the majority of your program's initialize logic should be always followed. For example, control card files for Checkpoint frequency should be opened and read. Initialization of working storage area done. Transaction control flags set. There are, however, a few items that require your consideration.

Normal Start Paragraph

1. Initialize the Checkpoint Id field, for example **PCIP0000**. IMS expects your program to take unique checkpoints. Follow your company standards. For example, we use an 8-byte field, made up of a 4-byte character name and a 4-byte counter field. Your program updates the counter field by one before it takes each checkpoint. Thus, it is possible to restart the program back at any of the checkpoints that have been taken. Of course, you would normally want to restart at the last checkpoint.
2. Initialize any Save-Area fields. This is where you get the date field, set any summary fields to zero. If the transaction records driving your batch process come from a DB2 Fetch, make sure that any host fields used in the SQL DECLARE's WHERE clause to guarantee repositioning during a restart are set to appropriate low-values.
3. If the transaction records driving the batch process come from a sequential file then you must access this file as an IMS GSAM databases. You want to use IMS because the RESTART call automatically repositions GSAM databases.

   In COBOL, this means replacing the usual READ and WRITE commands with IMS GN and ISRT calls. The file should also be deleted from the FD section, etc. Please note that GSAM databases do not need to be explicitly opened. However, if you wish to insert this code, do so here.
4. Sequential output files, such as report files, must also be accesses as IMS GSAM databases. This is because IMS automatically repositions GSAM databases during a restart. Again, GSAM databases do not need to be explicitly opened.

Restart Paragraph

1. The IMS Restart call returns the Checkpoint Id value used to restart, for example: PCIP0007. Before the program takes the next checkpoint, it updates the counter field by one. During each Checkpoint call, IMS automatically displays the Checkpoint ID as well as the system date and time. This is a simple way to confirm that restart logic is processing as expected.

2. Do not initialize any Save-Area fields. The restart call automatically retrieves the data from the log and updates these fields. You may need to make sure that the program properly sets up any SQL Fetch criteria used to guarantee repositioning during a restart from data previously stored in saved fields.

3. The system automatically opens and repositions both input and output sequential files (GSAMs only) to the correct relative byte address as of the checkpoint.

4. Your program is responsible for reopening DB2 cursors and repositioning any IMS databases. Once again, since the processing path of secondary database calls should be dictated by data in the transaction record, no special coding considerations should be required.

Sample Program Flow

See Exhibit 20.1 for a sample program flow.

DESIGN CONSIDERATIONS

We covered all the main points. You have added restart and checkpoint logic to your program and converted the sequential input and two report files to use GSAM calls. Well, you are not quite done! There is one final design consideration. Your program's main processing loop has shifted from inside the program to that of submitting the entire job. That's correct. You must include the job's JCL in your design and make sure that your checkpoint/restart scenario is bullet proof. I recommend that you walk through the job's JCL and make sure that is restartable. For instance, upon restart, would your output report file be deleted and reallocated? Thereby, losing all the data written during processing of the first 350,000 records as per our previous example. Would generation dataset file indicators need to be changed? Does the JOB run two separate programs? If so, how would you restart if the second one abends?

Secondly, I recommend that you actually test the restart logic, as follows:

1. Perform a sample test run to a successful completion. Then, back up the output report files.

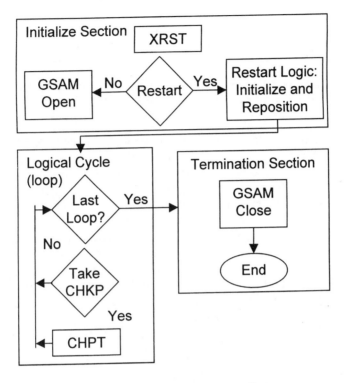

Exhibit 20.1. Sample program flow.

2. Refresh the test environment and begin the sample test run. This time force an ABEND by canceling the program.
   N.B. — you may need to reduce the Checkpoint frequency to an arbitrary low value such as 2 in order to produce sufficient checkpoints.
3. Restart your program and let it run to a successful completion. Check to see if the Checkpoints correctly picked up where they finished. Compare the output files to those of the first sample run; they should be exactly the same!

Do's and Don'ts

- Test an ABEND — most programmers assume that their program works. Make sure that they have forced an ABEND and done a successful restart. You would be surprised at the number of typos that can be caught.
- Remember to test restarting the JOB from the top; 3:00 a.m. is not the time to expect people to restructure JCL to restart in the proper sequence.

- Set a single consistent Restart policy. I know of a case where two checkpoint/restart programs run in a single JOB. The second program failed. Upon restart, the first program ran successfully again. (Alas, it was not the payroll system.)

Recommendation: All jobs should be restartable by just submitting them again. (Of course, you may have to change the JCL to provide the system with the checkpoint id indicating the correct restart point.)

- File Allocation: Make sure that all output files have DISP=OLD. This means that they are exclusively reserved for use by your program. It also means that you will not attempt to reallocate them during a restart. Allocate report files in a different job. The last thing that you need is to have an important report file deleted and reallocated during a restart.
- Do not write directly to a +1 version of a Generation Dataset. Once again, upon restart, a +1 G.D.G. would refer to a different dataset. Instead of changing all +1 to +0 just before a restart, I recommend that you write to a simple sequential file. You can use IEBGENER utility to back it up to a +1 G.D.G. in a following step after the program has successfully completed. There are other approaches that would work just as well.

APPLYING CHECKPOINT RESTART TO ANY SQL BASED DBMS

You want to use Checkpoint/Restart in all your batch programs. But, you don't have IMS. Nor do you have a vendor tool. However, you do have an SQL database management system (DBMS) such as DB2, ORACLE, SYSBASE or SQL SERVER. In this case, I propose the following "magic-box" solution. It requires the use of 2 new tables; one to record Save-area data and a second table to record output file records.

```
CREATE SAVE_AREA_DATA TABLE
PROGRAM_NAME                    8 CHARACTER,
CHECKPOINT_ID                   8 CHARACTER,
DATE_CHPT_TAKEN                 DATE,
TIME_CHPT_TAKEN                 TIME,
SAVE_FIELD_AREA_ID              SMALL INT,
SAVE_FIELD_DATA                 VARCHAR;

CREATE OUTPUT_FILE_DATA TABLE
PROGRAM_NAME                    8 CHARACTER,
FILE_DDNAME                     8 CHARACTER,
RECORD_COUNTER                  INTEGER,
RECORD_DATA                     133 CHARACTER;
```

Generic Restart

1. IMS accepts the Checkpoint ID via an existing input parameter string. In a generic solution, you may simply supply this value via a new control card. A DUMMY entry or SPACES would indicate a normal start while an actual Checkpoint Id would mean a restart.

2. In the program's Restart section, add logic to FETCH save-areas and move the data retrieved into the correct working storage areas using the SAVE_FIELD_AREA_ID as a key.

3. Input file repositioning — add logic to open sequential file and perform a read loop until you reached the last input record as indicated by a count field in the save-area.

   Add counter field updates to input I/O logic and store value(s) in save-areas.

4. Output file repositioning. I propose avoiding repositioning by replacing sequential file WRITE statement with SQL INSERTs to the OUTPUT_FILE_DATA table. Upon restart, your program may be continuing to INSERT output records as rows in the OUTPUT_FILE_DATA table. Upon completion of all transactions, your program may retrieve the data from the table and write the records out to a flat file.

   A generic program could be written to FETCH the output file records, write them to a sequential file and then delete them. This program would run as a following step after the successful completion of the main program.

Generic Checkpoints

1. Change the CHKP call to an SQL COMMIT. This will release all locks and write data to disk.

2. Add logic to INSERT records into the SAVE_AREA_DATA table, making sure that each save-area has a different SAVE_FIELD_AREA_ID.

3. If required, add logic to make sure that the value of the input record counter field is placed into a save area.

CONCLUSION

Getting your super programmers to adopt checkpoint restart may turn out to be your biggest challenge. Have them try it at least once. Then, if they still enjoy fumbling for socks in the middle of the night, you could indicate that you appreciate a quick recovery much more than a time-consuming effort of epic proportions.

Now that your team has successfully adopted Checkpoint/Restart, you can spend the morning concentrating on reducing the next major bottleneck—the 45 minutes wasted in travel time. Clearly, on call staff should bunk in at their desk!

Chapter 21
Managing Database Backup and Recovery

Michael Simonyi

INTRODUCTION

Management of the corporate database is arguably one of the most mismanaged areas in information technology today. Database technology has evolved from historical glass-house foundations of the past into the point-and-click implementations that come right out of the box today. Where databases and systems were once carefully designed, implemented, and deployed, they are now installed, loaded, and deployed without regard to basic effective design. This article addresses the concepts necessary to formulate a method to protect, back up, and, in the event of failure, recover perhaps the most important aspect of a business — its database. Without proper preparation, planning, and testing, an entire database infrastructure can become the target of lost devices, indexes, degraded backup mechanisms, and corrupted data.

HIGH AVAILABILITY VS. RECOVERABILITY

There are important differences between database availability and recoverability. Database availability can be a driving factor to recoverability, but it does not guarantee recoverability. Database availability is the measurement of production uptime and physical access to production data in a networked environment. In contrast, database recoverability refers to the ability to recover a database successfully in its entirety. Recoverability is a measurement of how accurate and lengthy the process of recovering from partial or total failure can be. The difference lies in the application of backup tools used in conjunction with high-availability tools. The redundancy of high-availability systems in an environment can directly relate to a higher grade of successful backups for the database environment as well as the supporting systems. In this article, a database environment is

0-8493-9832-0/00/$0.00+$.50

defined as the database, connecting middleware, and application front-end screens. These technologies are used to complement each other to offer accuracy, reliability, and stability.

METHODS OF DATA PROTECTION

The common methods of data production include the following: (1) tape; (2) mirroring (RAID 0); (3) data guarding (RAID 5); (4) duplexing; (5) partitioning; (6) replication; and (7) clustering. Each of these are explained further in this section.

Before investigating these different methods available for protecting a database environment, this article discusses the business requirements for data recoverability and availability. For example, if a database, in the event of failure, would place individuals in a life-threatening situation or would place the organization into financial chaos and eventual closure, then it is necessary to implement all available methods to become 100% fault tolerant. However, if a failure would be merely an inconvenience, then a simple tape backup procedure may suffice. Most organizations seek the middle ground.

Tape Backup

Tape backup should form the foundation of a corporate backup strategy because of its ease of use and low cost. In order for the tape backup mechanism to be useful it must be well designed and tested regularly. At a minimum, backups should be performed on a daily basis and not less than weekly. If possible, the entire database(s) should be backed up on a daily basis. The database transaction logs should be backed up during and after business hours, or whenever feasible to minimize the risk of lost data.

Mirroring

Mirroring or RAID 0 provides for duplicate sets of data on two separate hard disk drives, a primary and a secondary. This is also known as a master–slave configuration. For each logical write operation there are two physical write operations to the hard disks. This scenario protects against failure of an individual or set of drives. If either the primary or secondary drive fails, the data on the surviving drive allows for system recovery. In most situations, this option is ideal for protection of the database transaction logs. However, it does not offer protection against multiple simultaneous failures.

Data Guarding

Data guarding or RAID 5 has the ability to stripe redundant data across multiple drives (minimum three) in an array. The striping of data protects against a single drive failure in the array. When an array loses a drive, the system still functions by using the redundant data found on the surviving drives. There are two types of RAID 5 available today, namely, software- and hardware-based RAID 5. Hardware RAID is the more desirable implementation method because it was designed with drive failures in mind. Extending the tolerance level of a RAID 5 system can then be achieved by mirroring or duplexing drive arrays. This type of extension allows for whole drive arrays to fail without impacting the system

Duplexing

Duplexing is similar to mirroring except that in a duplexed configuration separate controller cards manage each drive or sets of drives. In essence, duplexing is Raid 0 with an additional layer or redundancy. The second disk controller cards remove a single point of failure that is exhibited in a standard mirroring (Raid 0) configuration.

Partitioning

Partitioning is the ability to deploy a database system across multiple servers where each server houses a different portion of the overall database. Should a server go down, only the component running on that server becomes unavailable. In this scenario the database can continue to function normally, provided applications are written to handle these types of situations. Additional protection can be achieved by employing RAID 0, RAID 5, or duplexing to minimize system downtime further.

Replication

Replication offers the ability to publish the contents (complete or portions thereof) of a database to another or multiple servers in an environment. The technique is similar to partitioning; however, to employ replication requires sophisticated application transaction logic to be used effectively. Replication allows for the mirroring of database transactions to be replicated in a secondary database at the central site or in a distributed location. Ideally, all transactions should be processed at a central database and the transactions should be replaced to the other subscribing sites. This eliminates the difficulty that becomes inherent with transaction logic of the traditional two-phase commit that fails as a result of hardware failures.

Clustering

Clustering is the ability of a group of *n* servers to share or cooperate with each other in utilizing common resources. Clustering allows systems to monitor each other and, in the advent of failure, transfer processing to their counterpart. Clustering is a very reliable method for maintaining a fault tolerant and highly available systems environment; however, vendors approach clustering differently. It is recommended that organizations examine their application architecture and processing requirements prior to selecting a clustering strategy and infrastructure.

Each of these individual methods can be used in tandem with each other to build a graded level of fault tolerance and high availability. Again, as with any other technology, the system requirements dictate the configuration and detail that is ultimately required. In most cases the higher the required tolerance, the more methods that are included in the solution.

Batch Cycles

The size and complexity of the database environment determines the most suitable backup cycle. A small site can afford the luxury of daily full database and transaction log backups. A medium-sized site must perform a mix of backups of full database and transaction log backups on daily and weekly cycles. A large site requires multiple staggered sets of backups and transaction logs on a daily basis with weekly and even monthly cycles backing up segments of the database to achieve a full database backup.

Transaction logs should be backed up at least once during the day. However, this depends on the transaction flow of the database. A low-volume online transaction processing (OLTP) database may only require a single transaction log backup at the end of a business day, before or after any additional processing is enacted on the data. In the case of high-volume OLTP processing environments, the backup of the transaction log may require hourly backups. It will be necessary to gauge the transaction flow of the environment to determine the backup schedule of the transaction logs.

Sample backup schedules for small, medium, and large sites are shown in the tables given in Exhibit 21.1. With each scenario outlined above, the robustness of the hardware also impacts the backup schedule of an organization. Since most organizations cannot afford to replace hardware on an as-needed basis, different backup schedules may need to be adopted over time, for different pieces of hardware.

ACCURACY OF BACKUPS

Although data backups are important, equally important is the need to determine the accuracy of the data prior to backup and the ability to guarantee the restoration of the contents of the backup into the original database or backup database system. The accuracy or consistency of the backup is paramount for recoverability. Should inconsistent data or data structures be stored onto the backup media, any attempt to restore them will most likely render the database inoperable or, worse, introduce inconsistent data into the production environment that may unknowingly place the organization at risk.

Exhibit 21.1. Sample backup schedules for small, medium, and large sites

Time	Mon	Tues	Wed	Thurs	Fri	Sat	Sun
Schedule for a Small Site for Database Less Than 10GB							
12am	DB Check	DB Check	DB Check	DB Check	DB Check	DB Check	DB Check
1am		Full DB	Full DB	Full DB	Full DB		
5pm	Tlog	TLog	Tlog	TLog	TLog		
9pm	Purge Log	Purge Log	Purge Log	Purge Log	Purge Log		
Schedule for a Medium Site for Databases Greater Than 10GB but Less Than 100GB							
12am	DB Check	DB Check	DB Check	DB Check	DB Check	DB Check	DB Check
1am						Full DB	
5pm	Tlog		Tlog	TLog	TLog		
9pm	Purge Log		Purge Log	Purge Log	Purge Log		
Schedule for a Large Site for Databases Greater Than 100 GB							
12am	DB Check	DB Check	DB Check	DB Check	DB Check	DB Check	DB Check
1am	DB Seg 1	DB Seg 2	DB Seg 3	DB Seg 4	DB Seg 5	DB Seg 6	DB Seg 7
5pm	Tlog	TLog	Tlog	TLog	TLog	TLog	TLog
9pm	Purge Log	Purge Log	Purge Log	Purge Log	Purge Log	Purge Log	Purge Log

Times noted are for clarity only.

DB Seg refers to a portion or segment of the database to be backed up. Each segment or portion of the database in conjunction with the transaction logs will provide for a full database backup at any point in time.

Most databases on the market today provide built-in tools that provide some level of data integrity checking that verifies that internal data structures are intact and tables, indexes, and page linkage is consistent. Any warnings or errors reported for these utilities should be acted upon at once. Failure to act on these messages can render a database inoperable and, depending on when the problem surfaced, can cause a loss of data. The following pseudoimplementation provides an approach to handling a database backup.

Generic Backup Stream

Perform a data integrity check on the contents of the database.

    1.1. Have inconsistencies been found in the database?
        1.1.1. Send alert to DBA and Operations staff, write events to log file.
        1.1.2. Halt backup stream. (Problem resolution takes place at this point.)
        1.1.3. Reestablish backup stream after problem has been resolved.
    1.2. Database is free of defects.
        Begin backup stream.
        Verify completion status.
        Notify operations and DBA of backup completion.

Incremental Backups

Incremental backups are something that should only be performed if it is not possible to complete a full backup during the allotted time frame or backup window. Incremental backups extend the time required for restoring the contents of a database in the event of a failure. Although unavoidable in huge database environments where incremental backups are the mainstay, they should still be staggered in such environments.

Backing Up in a Distributed LAN/WAN Environment

Backing up a distributed database in the LAN/WAN environment can be a nightmarish challenge. Time zones and production uptime in differing geographical areas can affect a reliable and accurate backup. If the data volumes are small and maintainable, it will be possible to coordinate backups and replication over the WAN. Some thought should be given to using redundant WAN links so as not to affect other communications over primary WAN links. If data volumes are extremely high or if the network spans the globe, it may become practical to build a hot site for this type of environment. Whether the site is built and maintained internally or through third-party vendors is purely academic. The rationale is to provide a site for conducting business transactions should the primary production facilities fail. The site should mirror the current production facilities at all times. It can be updated by replication or by use of tape media. Such a site should also be tested on a regular basis to ensure accuracy and guarantee the ability to continue business if failure encroaches upon the production systems (see Exhibit 21.2).

Administration Tools

As mentioned previously, most products on the market ship together with some sort of administration tool sets to maintain and administer database environments. These tools can be either GUI based or Command line based, and, at a minimum, the following tasks should be included in the process: user management, DDL scripting, data import and export, database consistency, device management, data recovery, and security utilities. Some database vendors also provide additional utilities in the areas of hierarchical storage management (HSM), database cluster management, and online statistics monitoring tools. If a database does not provide for a specific level of administration, there are many third-party products available on the market that can complement most database environments.

Areas to Protect

There are three basic areas of a database that must be protected: the data, of course, being the blood of the system; the catalogs, which are the skeleton of the system; and the transaction logs, which are the heart of a database because they detail all the events that have transpired against the data since the last full backup.

The transaction logs are considered paramount for any database system, especially after a database failure. Without the ability to maintain a readable copy of the transaction logs, any failure in the database places the data at extreme risk. For example, suppose a database is backed up fully once a week on Friday nights. During the week, the transaction logs are written onto the hard disk. If the hard disk that holds the transaction log fails on a Thursday, and no prior backup of the transactions logs has taken place, the database will only be recoverable to the last point of full backup — the preceding Friday.

The database catalogs, as described above, act as the skeleton for the database. They detail the structure of the physical database. The catalogs must be rigorously maintained. Each and every change to the database modifies the catalog. The catalog has two facets to it: the system catalog and the user database catalog. Each has it own specialized backup requirements.

The system catalog defines the database environment, including the disk drives, database devices, configuration, log-on privileges, tuning parameters, and device load points. This catalog must be backed up after every change because it affects the entire database environment. Any changes to the system catalog that are lost will seriously impair the ability

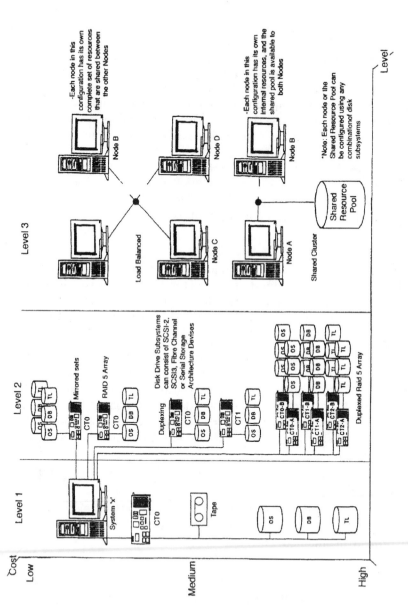

Exhibit 21.2. Types of protection.

to recover a database. In addition to having a backed-up system catalog, a paper-based reproduction of the system catalog can be beneficial for audit purposes or if the need ever arises to restore an older database backup on a system prior to the installation of a new RAID array. As hardware is added to the system, database load points will vary. This can have undesirable effects when loading an older version of a database back onto the server.

The user database catalog, on the other hand, is the definition of the user database. It contains all the details regarding the tables and indexes used in the physical implementation of the database and must be kept under strict observance. It should follow a strict change control process and must be backed up after each and every change to the database using a version control system. A failure to backup the database catalogs will result in loss of data if the database must ever be reloaded from flat files. The database catalog, sometimes referred to as a schema, is the blueprint of the database, the foundation of the database. It must be kept up-to-date, and its path of evolution must be able to be retraced.

The data, of course, as the lifeblood of the database and the reason for its existence, must also be safeguarded. The data should be backed up on a daily basis, if time permits, but no less than once a week. Backups should be restored from time to time to verify the validity of the backup and its state. There is no point in performing a backup if it is not tested periodically. What may have been restorable last year may not be restorable now. Also, recoverability from tape backups must be carefully tested.

Levels of Protection

Each of the individual methods provides a level of afforded protection. The base level of protection and last line of defense for a system failure should be a tape backup. This is deemed the last line of defense, as it is the slowest of all methods to get the system back into operation when disaster strikes. The highest level is a hybrid system. Exhibit 21.3 demonstrates the varying levels of recovery and associated costs.

Exhibit 21.3. The varying levels of database recovery and associated costs

Method	Level	Cost	Downtime
Tape (mandatory)	Low	Low	Hours
Mirroring	Medium	Low	Minutes to hours
Duplexing	Medium	Low	Minutes to hours
Data guarding	High	Medium	Minutes
Partitioning	Medium	High	Minutes to hours
Replication	High	High	Minutes
Clustering	Very High	Very High	Seconds to minutes
Hybrid combinations	Extremely High	Extremely High	Seconds

The application of each method will dictate the level of availability in the system and the degree of time required in recovering from a failure. For example, in a partitioned system the database is distributed between many separate servers. Should one of the servers go down, only a portion of the database becomes unavailable. Its cost is relatively high as there are many servers deployed and it is set up in a modular fashion. Each server then employs its own recovery mechanism.

In defining the level of protection needed to meet particular needs these questions should be asked:

- Can the company run without the database for an extended period of time?
- Are customer relationships risked if the database is unavailable?
- If the system becomes unavailable, is human life at risk?

If the answer is yes to any one of the above questions, some form of high availability solution will be needed to meet the needs. As mentioned previously, a tape backup should form the foundation of any backup strategy. Use the decision tree in Exhibit 21.4 to help guide the requirements for the backup strategy.

Virus Protection

Although a database system is usually well protected against direct virus attacks, the database should be well secured from the rest of the computing environment. This usually means protecting the database by placing it on a dedicated system, making sure that the only way of reaching the system is via administrative tools, the deployed middleware, or operating system-related administrative tools.

Even with a well-secured database, similar precautions will need to be taken on the front-end systems, as well. Virus-checking utilities should be deployed at the end user client workstations, and at any point in the environment where data will be fed into the database. Of course, this depends on the types of data being stored in the database. If binary large objects (BLOBs) are allowed to be inserted into documents, applications, or images that a virus can attach to, it may be necessary to implement additional levels of virus protection.

Internet and Intranet Firewalls

Database vendors are pursuing the ability to allow corporate data to become extensible to the Web if it is not already there. Most databases provide for this by using extensions to the middleware or database interface, providing extended data types in the database or providing plug-ins to the database. This presents the problem of how to ensure that no one can gain direct access to a corporate database. By implementing hardware/software

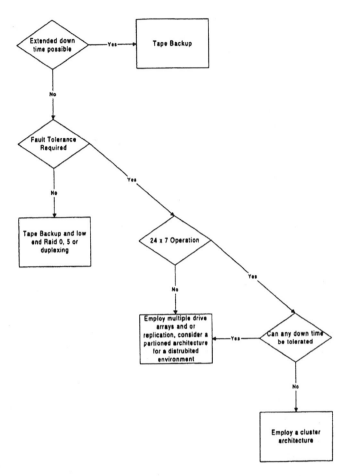

Exhibit 21.4.   Decision tree for selecting desired level of protection.

firewall combinations and proxies, it is possible to segregate the database carefully from the publicly exposed portion of a network. This allows construction of unidirectional paths into and out of the database that cannot be easily compromised.

CONCLUSION

In the author's experience, there is never too much protection, only too little. Having a well-thought-out backup-and-recovery procedure in place will save time, money, and embarrassment when things go wrong. All of the topics examined within the body of this article detail methods that can be used to safeguard corporate databases or any other system, for that matter. Readers should pick and choose the pieces that best suit their needs when building a fail-safe environment.

Chapter 22
Change Management Strategies for Data Administration
Michael K. Miller

AS COMPANIES DOWNSIZE, RIGHTSIZE, AND BECOME LEANER IN ORDER TO BE MORE COMPETITIVE, stronger focus must be placed on all staff organizations to determine if they add value. Amid organizational change, a window of opportunity also exists to establish data resource management (DRM) principles within the entire organization. Companies guided by a strong DRM function in establishing an infrastructure to support client/server business systems have the flexibility to respond to rapidly changing business conditions and use all their information resources in the struggle for profitability.

PREPARING THE FOUNDATION FOR RESPONDING TO CHANGE

The data management function may need to answer questions about the value of expending resources on managing the information resource. Many strong forces exert pressure on any organization — technological change, societal change, competition, economic realities, layoffs associated with downsizing and rightsizing, and changing and conflicting management priorities. In combination, these forces create an atmosphere of upheaval. The first thing to determine is which forces are effecting change. Then DRM can determine how it can assist in achieving the change, while at the same time realizing the goals of information sharing.

Depth of Commitment

It is important to plumb the depths of commitment to the data management function and the degree to which the information management mindset has pervaded the corporate psyche. Information about how past DRM initiatives have fared and the degree of difficulty associated with obtaining resources and funding will assist in charting a strategy for increasing and

0-8493-9832-0/00/$0.00+$.50
© 2000 by CRC Press LLC

maintaining the commitment. It is sometimes necessary to reiterate the basic justification for the data management function every time there is a management change.

During downsizing efforts, all business departments are examined to see if they add value. Savvy professionals have an ear to the ground and maintain the right connections to the financial organization in order to recognize potential threats. If an organization, such as DRM, is not prepared to meet the forces of change, it can quickly be swept away with the rising tide of corporate downsizing in order to save money.

Rate of Change

The speed and proportion of changes dictate the urgency of the response. Therefore, the long- or short-term nature of planned changes should be studied. If the organization is strapped financially, it will probably require much more financial justification to get the DRM effort funded. The ability to demonstrate a past record of successes becomes critical for continued existence.

Objectives Setting

Sailors use fixed points from which to chart their course. Data management professionals must also be able to refer to clear landmarks, such as management directives, policies, charters, industry authorities, and common sense.

The guiding light should be the long-term vision of an information utility that allows anyone to have access to the right information at the right time. With this information, DRM sets goals and objectives that are in harmony with the business but that also align with the long-term objectives of information sharing.

Human Nature and the Fear of Change

One of the most intractable problems when trying to change an organization, a direction, or a policy is basic human resistance to change. Many people have difficulty recognizing the value in changing from a comfortable situation to an unsure one. Politics is also ever-present during any human endeavor and must be addressed.

People are often fearful to take steps that are outside the mainstream and thus are afraid to lead. Human nature is an obstacle that must be reckoned with when devising any strategy or program for change.

A conscious effort must be made to understand the pressures that create fear and anxiety among employees during times of change. Usually, people are afraid of losing their livelihood and this reaction creates a defensive mentality that can be counterproductive. People's concerns need to be addressed honestly and forthrightly with the best information available in order to end false rumors. Employees should also be engaged in planning for changes and encouraged to continue with productive activities so they retain a sense of value to the corporation.

Sure Ways to Fail

Lack of Mission or Direction. When there is a lack of direction within an organization, a condition of drift sets in. This leads to busywork and a lack of value being produced. During times of crisis, there is no question as to what department should be eliminated.

No Perceived Value. When business people are looking for ways to trim the budget, they look first at those organizations and people who are not adding value. Even in a case where a data management group is adding value, the group may not have made its contribution apparent to business management. Management's perception is just as important as reality.

Going on the Defensive. When people feel threatened by change, there is a natural defense mechanism that produces a reaction of "circling the wagons" against attackers. This creates hostility and, more importantly, a lack of productivity.

Territorial Issues. Turf wars and a parochial attitude are destructive during times of change. These destructive behaviors divert people's attention away from achieving goals that are valuable to the organization; instead, people focus on nonproductive activities designed to protect their territory.

Inability to Change. When faced with a choice between a status quo situation and total uncertainty, it is only natural that most people will choose the status quo. When, however, the fear of change becomes crippling to the point that the organization cannot move forward, the resultant stagnation and subtle resistance can hamper a successful transition.

Being Self-Centered Instead of Customer-Centric. When humans become fearful, they tend to think about self-preservation and can easily defeat their own best interest. When change is imminent, it is critical to focus on adding value and benefit to the corporation. If the DRM group is crippled by inaction brought on by fear and self-preservation, it will be easy for upper management to trim the group as an unnecessary expense.

Ignoring Human and Culture Issues. Those involved in planning for change must not fail to put human and culture issues at the forefront of consideration. When planning for any kind of technological or organizational change, definite measures must be taken to address the natural human reactions. Plentiful communication, education, and employee participation must be built into the structure of the plan for change.

Failure to Respond to Emerging Technology. In a society where new technology emerges nearly every day, the DRM professional must be responsive. This is another opportunity to ride the wave of change and institutionalize sound information management principles. Business users of information expect to have their information stored in multimedia formats with quick access. DRM must respond with multimedia-capable data bases of information that are Web enabled. Because business users find the World Wide Web easy to access, this becomes an avenue to entrench the data management function as the group that supplies the quality data — when and where it is needed.

Determining the DRM Function's Value

A very important way to counteract the forces of change is to know the value of your function. Throughout the life of the DRM function, ample attention should be paid to the value that the organization adds toward achievement of business objectives. Thus, it is important to establish ways of determining and measuring that added value.

Data management professionals should make every effort to quantify the value of their efforts and document this value. Then, when the latest management fad strikes, DRM will have a solid backlog of documented savings and bottom-line effects to demonstrate to management.

Metrics

Establishing solid metrics for DRM is an elusive goal. Many of the benefits of managing information are intangible and consequently difficult to measure and defend. The effort should be made, however, and the effort should consider the full lifecycle of data — not only logical modeling, but also the monetary effects of storing redundant, conflicting data. Cost savings that DRM can contribute, and the relative difficulty in quantifying them, are outlined in Exhibit 22.1.

Cost Avoidance

One of the areas that can be quantified is in the area of avoiding costs. Through construction of common databases within a client/server infrastructure, it is possible to avoid the expense of building redundant data bases. Development costs can be easily quantified based on a company's rich experience; plans to build these databases can be identified through examination of long-range systems plans.

An example of cost avoidance through reuse of existing standard data definitions is presented in Exhibit 22.2. When a company wants a new

Exhibit 22.1. **Ways of quantifying cost savings.**

IRM Impact	Type of Value Gained	Difficulty to Quantify
Less analyst time in requirements gathering	Cost avoidance	Moderate
Less business analysis time in gathering decision support information from disparate data sources	Cost avoidance	Moderate
Fewer redundant databases constructed and maintained	Cost reduction	Easy
Fewer human resources needed for accounting and financial analysis	Cost reduction	Easy
More accurate information about customers	Revenue generation	Difficult
Web-enabled access to standard data	Revenue generation	Moderate

system or data base, analysis time is required of both IT and business people. For an average requirements-gathering workshop, there could be two analysts and seven business people. Empirical evidence within the IT organization should enable DRM analysts to make an approximation of the number of person-hours it takes to define one data entity together with its

Exhibit 22.2. **Cost avoidance through reuse of existing standard data definitions.**

Workshop Participant	Person-hours	Comments
Business analyst team	13.0	Includes analyst time before, during, and after the analysis workshop
Data administrator (DA)	3.0	Included DA documentation, consulting, and analysis time
Business expert	7.0	Includes 7 business experts working for one hour in an analysis workshop
Total analysis hours	23.0	
Loaded cost per hour	70.00	Conservative estimate considering all the costs pertaining to a profession
Total cost per entity	1610.00	

associated attributes. A conservative figure of 2 hours may, for example, be used for defining business entities. As a repository of existing data definitions grows and is used on successive projects, a greater proportion of the analysis work is already completed when the project starts; therefore, analysis time can be avoided.

True Cost Savings

Another savings classification is actual bottom-line savings that affect the profit-loss statement. Through implementation of common systems with common databases, it is possible to reduce personnel headcount substantially. Through effective data management, measures of physical data, redundancy, and inaccuracy can be reduced. This results in reduced cycle time, reduced headcount, and greater employee satisfaction.

The spreadsheet shown in Exhibit 22.3 uses actual cost savings of redundant database elimination, reduced IS headcount, and reduced staff analysis time for management reporting. It also figures a conservative 1 percent increase in sales revenue as the result of having integrated, quality customer information.

Defining "Real" Business Contribution

What would be the result if there were no data management organization? How does data management help achieve business objectives? When data management professionals begin to think about their role in hard-dollar terms, it provides a fresh perspective.

Data management professionals can tend to pursue academic questions and theories if they are not tightly focused on helping business achieve solid results. There are many different projects that require attention, but in this area, management needs to be ruthless in maintaining focus on those DRM activities that actually have an impact on the business.

The perception of value must reflect how the rest of the company views DRM's efforts. Others may not be aware that the data management group's efforts pay off in terms of dollar savings, greater productivity, increased data integrity, and better decision support. They may only see the data management group as a standards and policy-producing body that has no real value. When DRM management understands how its staff is perceived, then it is possible to craft a response that addresses any deficiencies.

DRM must be tied solidly to achievement of business objectives. No one must be allowed to think of DRM as solely a staff function. To do this, the DRM group should create an objectives chart for themselves and for others to view. All DRM activities should be measured against this chart to determine their true value. If a proposed activity cannot be clearly tied to a

Exhibit 22.3. Customer information environment cost savings.

Customer Information Environment Actual Cash Flow USD 000 12-Feb-96	1996	1997	1998	1999	2000	2001	2002	TOTAL
Capital								
Hardware	(1,800)	(100)	(50)					(1,950)
Software Basic	(70)	(30)	(30)					(130)
TOTAL Capital	**(1,870)**	**(130)**	**(80)**	**0**	**0**	**0**	**0**	**(2,080)**
Nonrecurring Expense								
Extracts and Interfaces	(459)	(459)	(75)	(55)	(30)	(30)	(30)	(1,138)
Implementation	(40)	(40)	(40)	0	0	0	0	(120)
Training and Travel	(10)	(10)	(10)	0	0	0	0	(30)
Miscellaneous								0
TOTAL Nonrecurring	**(509)**	**(509)**	**(125)**	**(55)**	**(30)**	**(30)**	**(30)**	**(1,288)**
Recurring Expense								
Third-Party Source of Data	(1,075)	(1,075)	(1,075)	(1,075)	(1,075)	(1,075)	(1,075)	(7,525)
IS Administration Headcount	(500)	(500)	(500)	(250)	(250)	(250)	(250)	(2,500)
S/W Maintenance (15% of Software)	0	0	0	0	0	0	0	0
TOTAL Recurring	**(1,575)**	**(1,575)**	**(1,575)**	**(1,325)**	**(1,325)**	**(1,325)**	**(1,325)**	**(10,025)**
Incremental Savings								
Redundant Data Base Development	200	600	900	1,200	1,500	1,800	2,100	8,300
Management Reporting-Staff Analysis	2,000	2,000	2,000	2,000	2,000	2,000	2,000	14,000
Manual i/f user/ISS headcount	0	153	1,025	2,100	2,100	2,100	2,100	9,578
Increased Revenues (1% Sales)	10,000	35,000	70,000	70,000	70,000	70,000	70,000	395,000
TOTAL Savings	**12,200**	**37,753**	**73,925**	**75,300**	**75,600**	**75,900**	**76,200**	**426,878**
Depreciation								
Hardware	0	(487)	(487)	(487)	(487)	0	0	(1,948)
Software Basic	0	(25)	(25)	(25)	(25)	0	0	(100)
Software Application	0	0	0	0	0	0	0	0
TOTAL Depreciation	**0**	**(512)**	**(512)**	**(512)**	**(512)**	**0**	**0**	**(2,048)**
Cash Flow Before Tax	9,821	36,602	73,208	74,733	75,058	75,870	76,170	421,462
Taxes 35% on Non-Cap	(4,092)	(12,856)	(25,651)	(26,157)	(26,270)	(26,555)	(26,660)	(148,240)
Total After Taxes	5,729	23,746	45,557	48,576	48,788	49,316	49,511	273,222
Add Depreciation	0	512	512	512	512	0	0	2,048
TOTAL cash flow after tax	**5,729**	**24,258**	**48,069**	**49,088**	**49,300**	**49,316**	**49,511**	**275,270**
NPV 13%	**158,979**							

corporate objective, then it should be placed at the bottom of the priority list (see the following table).

DRM initiative	Corporate objective
Scalable data warehouse	Know our customers
Metadata standards	Corporate efficiency
Enterprise databases	Reduce expenses

Sharpening Long- and Short-Term Outlooks

Data management professionals must be a combination of business strategist and database administrator. They provide the foresight and drive to implement the vision of sharing information throughout the enterprise, whether it is private business or government. They help define the vision for the business person and plot a road map for implementation for the systems developers and network experts.

At all top-flight companies, the business leaders or top executives have a clearly communicated vision. In support of a vision, objectives must also be clearly enunciated by a company's managers. For every company objective, DRM must be able to provide the leadership and direction for attainment of that objective in the information area; DRM does that by establishing principles by which information is managed, processes are reengineered, applications are designed, and by creating an organization that supports the roles and responsibilities of sound information management.

As business leaders outline their business strategies, data management professionals must become a partner with business management in reaching those objectives. All business managers will support the people who help them realize their goals. One of the most effective strategies for assisting managers to meet their objectives is to focus on short-term, incremental deliverables. DRM must be resourceful and flexible enough to adapt its techniques and procedures to reach business goals.

BUILDING STRATEGIC ALLIANCES

Wherever there are people, there are politics. It is important to understand that politics is a fact of life and then determine a constructive approach for dealing with it. Often, any number of people may be attempting to advance their own agendas and goals. Where these goals are constructive for the corporation, DRM can seek to work with people with different agendas and advance the cause of information management.

Building Influence

Within any human organization, there are always individuals who have more influence on the group than do others. The data management group must seek to win the confidence of the rest of the organization by focusing on results, having well-researched solutions to problems, exhibiting a firm grasp of business issues, and by addressing the target group's true concerns. As the DRM solution over time benefits the long-term health of the organization, DRM will become increasingly influential.

Moving with the Movers and Shakers

Movers and shakers are those individuals within an organization who make things happen. People who are placed in responsibility over important projects, managers of successful departments, and others could all be potential allies or champions of DRM efforts. Contacts with these individuals should be cultivated and harnessed.

In addition, informal channels of communication such as the grapevine and rumor mill should be used to advantage, both as a source of information about coming changes and a means of communicating positive information.

Participating in Cross-functional Projects

Data management professionals should seek to be involved in every cross-functional team or special project team that is formed. By knowing what management priorities are, DRM can then focus limited resources on helping those projects succeed.

This will make DRM participation come to be regarded as a critical success factor. Data management professionals are generally well-seasoned business people as well as technology experts. Whenever business people are looking for help, DRM analysts should be presenting themselves as solution providers, offering their services as a fully integrated part of the business.

Being First to Market with the Value

Most organizations are faced with a constantly changing landscape filled with new problems. What was important yesterday is no longer remembered today. DRM groups typically have too few professionals and must therefore allocate their resources to high-visibility projects that provide answers to current problems. For example, to deliver the value in a timely fashion, the scalable data warehouse is a primary vehicle. The DRM group must devote resources to defining and maintaining the metadata so that new information may be made available to business users as soon as possible.

Promoting DRM's Contribution

There is an old saying that a little yeast spreads through the entire loaf of bread dough. The management of information is a critical success factor for a company's success. Only by spreading the DRM gospel before every possible audience will the message begin to sink in and become a way of thinking for the average business person or systems developer.

All leaders face opposition. It can come from old-line programmers, political climbers, budget-conscious managers, or people who simply do not understand the importance of managing the information resource. Opposition sends many people out of meetings muttering under their breath and complaining to their co-workers later. Instead, these events should be viewed as opportunities to make a clearer case to convince opponents and win them over with the quality and thoroughness of your approach.

In every organization, there are many opportunities to promote beneficial programs. Meetings, internal seminars, newsletters, and brochures are just a few. Constant exposure to DRM concepts and principles will eventually result in the program being ingrained in the corporate culture. Why do consumers know certain brands of products more than others? It is because of constant advertising and exposure. DRM can apply the same concepts.

Of course, the first and most important focus of the DRM group should be to drive toward real, measurable, visible results. Often, however, there is a tendency to believe that successes are self-apparent to the rest of the organization when in fact they are not. Successes must be publicized in a method that will ensure that the right people understand the value of data management.

DRM should have its own well-publicized Web site. On this site, there should be quick access to data standards, data warehouse information, data architecture, and other valuable information that is geared to business people's access to information. People will also find the Web site interesting if the DRM professionals each have their own home page with their pictures and personal information.

GAINING AND KEEPING MANAGEMENT COMMITMENT

There is one thing that business management usually understands, and that is the bottom line. It is critical for the DRM group to have prepared its value calculations and to have documented the worth of its contribution.

Quantifying the Costs of Redundant Data and Customer Dissatisfaction

W.E. Demings often asked the question, "How much is a satisfied customer worth?", and the companion question, "How much damage can a dissatisfied customer do?". This point needs to be brought home to managers — that the costs of improper information management are multiplying every hour in terms of lost productivity, dissatisfied customers, and poor decision-making. The costs of maintaining conflicting data on disparate systems and developing multiple interfaces to merge systems, not to mention staff analysis hours to try to make sense of the data, are staggering.

One of the most difficult tasks faced by the data management professional is to put a price tag on the cost of redundant data and processing. The costs of doing business the wrong way must be emphasized when dealing with business management. When a customer gets the runaround from company personnel because they do not have good information, there is a cost associated with that event. It is beneficial to assemble a list of war stories of dissatisfied customers that can be documented. It is then possible to attach a cost to each of these stories, show how better information could have prevented the situation, and come up with a solution. Here, the DRM group can never be seen as an adversary or critic.

With constant exposure to DRM principles of sound information management, business managers will begin to understand that their success is inextricably linked with having quality information at their and every worker's fingertips. For example, increased profitability is often cited as a business objective. DRM has an impact on this objective because managing information has the effects of:

- Reducing IS resources
- Building better information about customer sales
- Reducing cycle time
- Reducing multiple storage, development, and interface costs

A DYNAMIC MIGRATION PLAN

Dynamic means changeable, and that is exactly what DRM plans need to be. One of the main data management functions is to create a plan for migrating to a new information environment and to guide the organization to that goal. During times of change, the plan needs to be altered to meet the altered needs of the corporation. Exhibit 22.4 displays the goals of the migration to an enterprise data-sharing environment.

Organization

There are several organizational models for DRM, most of which can be effective, depending on the people who staff the model. The data management organization needs to be structured so as to support the business in the most effective way. One key aspect is that whatever the scope of information sharing is, it is critical that the data management function is situated in the organization so that it spans that entire scope.

Architecture

A data architecture for the entire company is somewhat less subject to change as organizations shift. Subtle adjustments may be necessary, however, and should be part of the migration plan. Exhibit 22.5 shows how an architecture is at the center of the data planning environment to support the migration to the vision state.

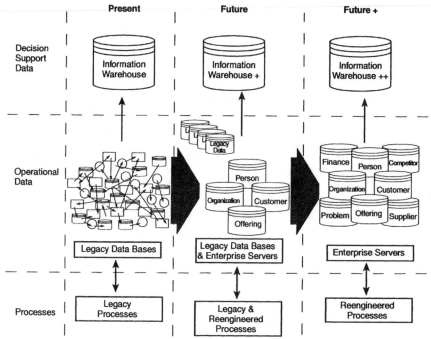

Exhibit 22.4.   Goals of migrating to a data-sharing environment.

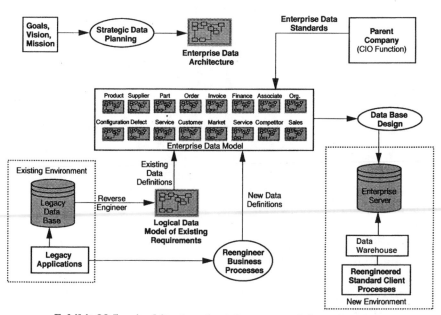

Exhibit 22.5.   Architecture is at the center of data planning.

ARCHITECTURE IS AT THE CENTER OF DATA PLANNING

People and Skills

As organizations change, there is an ebb and flow of personnel requirements. Skills, requirements, and people need to be matched regularly to meet the shifting requirements. It may be beneficial for data management professionals to rotate out into a business function for a couple of years to broaden their experience.

Participation in industry conferences, courses, books, and membership in professional organizations are all means of keeping skill sets at the cutting edge. It is also very important to hone nontechnical skills that are often forgotten — skills such as interpersonal relations, negotiating, and presenting.

Education must be addressed at every level of the DRM organization. Data management professionals need to develop their set of skills to cover a broad range of business and technology issues. Web-enabled access to data standards is now a prerequisite. DRM professionals should develop intranet expertise. The DRM group is also responsible for educating end-users, managers, and systems developers in the importance of sound information management.

Because DRM professionals need to be part visionary, part cheerleader, part technologist, part business person, they must be flexible and adaptable. People who cannot make this transition need to be allowed to find other career opportunities. Pessimists and cynics cannot make a strong contribution in the discipline.

Infrastructure

Data management professionals should participate in infrastructure planning in order to guide a migration to an environment that will support massive decision-support, parallel-processing data base engines, enterprisewide communications capabilities, and easy user access. DRM professionals should be visionaries concerning the future use of data and information. That is why the data warehouse infrastructure should be scalable — able to grow with the need for information without becoming obsolete. It is not only the data warehouse engine that must be sized for future growth, but also the bandwidth and infrastructure for providing Web access to all potential users in the company. There is nothing that turns users off quite like being unable to get rapid response time to critical information.

The focus is on getting quality information to the right person at the right time. The infrastructure should be planned so as to be independent of organizational structures.

DRM Process

Forward-thinking companies are structuring their activities according to a process management scheme instead of a stovepipe functional orientation. The DRM group should be deeply involved in defining the company's process architecture and its own part in that framework. In a process architecture, core processes are defined together with supporting processes. DRM should be a prominently displayed supporting process along with other activities like architecture management, financial management, and technology.

SUMMARY

Several critical success factors are necessary ingredients for success. The DRM program and strategy should be aimed at addressing the four Cs — confidence, competence, commitment, and consistency — and building them into the organization.

Human Issues Are More Important than Technical Ones

In the final analysis, if change is to be instituted in a culture, it will be the human issues that either make or break the effort. Advanced technologies, faster computers, and friendly GUI interfaces are a small piece of the puzzle. The human issues must be studied, understood, and planned for when attempting to change culture, organization, or systems.

At the same time that new responsibilities for DRM employees are defined and new behaviors are expected, the reward and bonus system must be altered to reward the performance that is desired. If people have no incentive to change, it will be next to impossible to effect a true cultural shift. By changing the reward system, however, people will be motivated by their own interests to act in the desired way.

FOCUS ON RESULTS, NOT THEORIES

DRM management must never allow the organization to stray from results-producing activities to academic ones. Analysts have the tendency to gravitate toward theory and abstraction, but this can result in the DRM group being viewed as counterproductive and useless.

Chapter 23
Security Models for Object-Oriented Databases

James Cannady

OBJECT-ORIENTED (OO) PROGRAMMING LANGUAGES AND OO ANALYSIS AND DESIGN TECHNIQUES influence database systems design and development. The inevitable result is the object-oriented database management system (OODBMS).

Many of the established database vendors are incorporating object-oriented concepts into their products in an effort to facilitate database design and development in the increasingly object-oriented world of distributed processing. In addition to improving the process of database design and administration, the incorporation of object-oriented principles offers new tools for securing the information stored in the database. This chapter explains the basics of database security, the differences between securing relational and object-oriented systems, and some specific issues related to the security of next-generation OODBMSs.

BASICS OF DATABASE SECURITY

Database security is concerned primarily with the secrecy of data. Secrecy means protecting a database from unauthorized access by users and software applications.

Secrecy, in the context of database security, includes a variety of threats incurred through unauthorized access. These threats range from the intentional theft or destruction of data to the acquisition of information through more subtle measures, such as inference. There are three generally accepted categories of secrecy-related problems in database systems:

- The improper release of information from reading data that intentionally or accidentally was accessed by unauthorized users. Securing databases from unauthorized access is more difficult than controlling access to files managed by operating systems. This problem arises from the finer granularity that is used by databases when handling files, attributes, and values. This type of problem also includes the violations to secrecy that result from the problem of inference, which is the deduction of unauthorized information from the observation of authorized information. Inference is one of the most difficult factors to control in any attempts to secure data. Because the information in a database is related semantically, it is possible to determine the value of an attribute without accessing it directly. Inference problems are most serious in statistical databases, where users can trace back information on individual entities from the statistical aggregated data.

- The improper modification of data. This threat includes violations of the security of data through mishandling and modifications by unauthorized users. These violations can result from errors, viruses, sabotage, or failures in the data that arise from access by unauthorized users.
- Denial-of-service threats. Actions that could prevent users from using system resources or accessing data are among the most serious. SYN flood attacks against network service providers are an example of denial-of-service threats in which a barrage of messages is sent to the server at a rate faster than the system can deal with them. Such attacks prevent authorized users from using system resources.

Discretionary vs. Mandatory Access Control Policies

Both traditional relational database management system (RDBMS) security models and object-oriented database models make use of two general types of access control policies to protect the information in multilevel systems. The first of these policies is the discretionary policy. In the discretionary access control (DAC) policy, access is restricted based on the authorizations granted to the user.

The mandatory access control (MAC) policy secures information by assigning sensitivity levels or labels to data entities or objects. MAC policies are generally more secure than DAC policies and they are used in systems in which security is critical, such as military applications. However, the price that usually is paid for this tightened security is reduced performance of the database management system. Most MAC policies also incorporate DAC measures as well.

SECURING AN RDBMS VS. OODBMS: KNOW THE DIFFERENCES

The development of secure models for object-oriented DBMSs obviously has followed on the heels of the development of the databases themselves. The theories that currently are being researched and implemented in the security of object-oriented databases also are influenced heavily by the work that has been conducted on secure relational database management systems.

Relational DBMS Security

In traditional RDBMSs, security is achieved principally through the appropriate use and manipulation of views and the SQL GRANT and REVOKE statements. These measures are reasonably effective because of their mathematical foundation in relational algebra and relational calculus.

View-Based Access Control

Views allow the database to be divided conceptually into pieces in ways that allow sensitive data to be hidden from unauthorized users. In the relational model, views provide a powerful mechanism for specifying data-dependent authorizations for data retrieval.

Although the individual user who creates a view is the owner and is entitled to drop the view, he or she may not be authorized to execute all privileges on it. The authorizations that the owner may exercise depend on the view semantics and on the authorizations that the owner is allowed to implement on the tables directly accessed by the view. For the owner to exercise a specific authorization on a view that he or she creates, the owner must possess the same authorization on all tables that the view uses. The privileges the owner possesses on the view are determined at the time of view definition. Each privilege the owner possesses on the tables is defined for the view. If, later on, the owner receives additional privileges on the tables used by the view, these additional privileges will not be passed onto the view. To use the new privileges within a view, the owner will need to create a new view.

The biggest problem with view-based mandatory access controls is that it is impractical to verify that the software performs the view interpretation and processing. If the correct authorizations are to be assured, the system must contain some type of mechanism to verify the classification of the sensitivity of the information in the database. The classification must be done automatically, and the software that handles the classification must be trusted. However, any trusted software for the automatic classification process would be extremely complex. Furthermore, attempting to use a query language such as structured query language (SQL) to specify classifications quickly becomes convoluted and complex. Even when the complexity of the classification scheme is overcome, the view can do nothing more than limit what the user sees — it cannot restrict the operations that may be performed on the views.

GRANT AND REVOKE PRIVILEGES

Although view mechanisms often are regarded as security freebies because they are included within SQL and most other traditional relational database managers, views are not the sole mechanism for relational database security. GRANT and REVOKE statements allow users to grant privileges selectively and dynamically to other users and subsequently revoke them if necessary. These two statements are considered to be the principal user interfaces in the authorization subsystem.

There is, however, a security-related problem inherent in the use of the GRANT statement. If a user is granted rights without the GRANT option, he or she should not be able to pass GRANT authority on to other users. However, the system can be subverted by a user by simply making a complete copy of the relation. Because the user creating copy is now the owner, he or she can provide GRANT authority to other users. As a result, unauthorized users are able to access the same information that had been contained in the original relation. Although this copy is not updated with the original relation, the user making the copy could continue making similar copies of the relation and providing the same data to other users.

The REVOKE statement functions similarly to the GRANT statement, with the opposite result. One of the characteristics of the use of the REVOKE statement is that it has a cascading effect. When the rights previously granted to a user subsequently are revoked, all similar rights are revoked for all users who may have been provided access by the originator.

Other Relational Security Mechanisms

Although views and GRANT/REVOKE statements are the most frequently used security measures in traditional RDBMSs, they are not the only mechanisms included in most security systems using the relational model. Another security method used with traditional relational database managers, which is similar to GRANT/REVOKE statements, is the use of query modification.

This method involves modifying a user's query before the information is retrieved, based on the authorities granted to the user. Although query modification is not incorporated within SQL, the concept is supported by the Codd-Date relational database model.

Most relational database management systems also rely on the security measures present in the operating system of the host computer. Traditional RDMBSs such as DB2 work closely with the operating system to ensure that the database security system is not circumvented by permitting access to data through the operating system. However, many operating systems provide insufficient security. In addition, because of the portability of many newer database packages, the security of the operating system should not be assumed to be adequate for the protection of the wealth of information in a database.

Object-Oriented DBMS Characteristics

Unlike traditional RDBMSs, secure object-oriented DBMSs (or OODBMSs) have certain characteristics that make them unique. Furthermore, only a limited number of security models have been designed specifically for object-oriented databases. The proposed security models make use of the object-oriented concepts of:

- Encapsulation
- Inheritance
- Information hiding
- Methods (in the OO paradigm, an object contains data and methods; methods are the components that act on the data and provide user access to the data. It helps to think of methods as functions from the structured programming environment.)
- The ability to model real-world entities

The object-oriented database model also permits the classification of an object's sensitivity through the use of class and instance. When an instance of a class is created, the object automatically can inherit the level of sensitivity of the superclass. Although the ability to pass classifications through inheritance is possible in object-oriented databases, class instances usually are classified at a higher level within the object's class hierarchy. This prevents a flow control problem, where information passes from higher to lower classification levels.

Object-oriented DBMSs also use unique characteristics that allow these models to control the access to the data in the database. They incorporate features such as flexible data structure, inheritance, and late binding. Access control models for OODBMSs must be consistent with such features. Users can define methods, some of which are open for other users as public methods. Moreover, the OODBMS may encapsulate a series of basic access commands into a method and make it public for users, while keeping basic commands themselves away from users.

Proposed OODBMS Security Models

Currently only a few models use discretionary access control measures in secure object-oriented database management systems.

Explicit Authorizations

The ORION authorization model is probably the best OODBMS discretional access control security model available today. ORION permits access to data on the basis of explicit authorizations provided to each group of users. These authorizations are classified as positive authorizations because they specifically allow a user access to an object. Similarly, a negative authorization is used specifically to deny a user access to an object.

The placement of an individual into one or more groups is based on the role that the individual plays in the organization. In addition to the positive authorizations that are provided to users within each group, there are a variety of implicit authorizations that may be granted based on the relationships between subjects and access modes.

Data-Hiding Model

A similar discretionary access control secure model is the data-hiding model proposed by Dr. Elisa Bertino of the Universita' di Genova. This model distinguishes between public methods and private methods.

The data-hiding model is based on authorizations for users to execute methods on objects. The authorizations specify which methods the user is authorized to invoke. Authorizations only can be granted to users on public methods. However, the fact that a user can access a method does not mean automatically that the user can execute all actions associated with the method. As a result, several access controls may need to be performed during the execution, and all of the authorizations for the different accesses must exist if the user is to complete the processing.

Similar to the use of GRANT statements in traditional relational database management systems, the creator of an object is able to grant authorizations to the object to different users. The creator also is able to revoke the authorizations from users in a manner similar to REVOKE statements. However, unlike traditional RDBMS GRANT statements, the data-hiding model includes the notion of protection mode. When authorizations are provided to users in the protection mode, the authorizations actually checked by the system are those of the creator and not the individual executing the method. As a result, the creator is able to grant a user access to a method without granting the user the authorizations for the methods called by the original method. In other words, the creator can provide a user access to specific data without being forced to give the user complete access to all related information in the object.

Other DAC Models for OODBMS Security

Rafiul Ahad has proposed a similar model that is based on the control of function evaluations. Authorizations are provided to groups or individual users to execute specific methods. The focus in Ahad's model is to protect the system by restricting access to the methods in the database, not the objects. The model uses proxy functions, specific functions, and guard functions to restrict the execution of certain methods by users and to enforce content-dependent authorizations.

Another secure model that uses authorizations to execute methods has been presented by Joel Richardson. This model has some similarity to the data-hiding model's use of GRANT/REVOKE-type statements. The creator of an object can specify which users may execute the methods within the object.

A final authorization-dependent model emerging from OODBMS security research has been proposed by Dr. Eduardo B. Fernandez of Florida Atlantic University. In this model the authorizations are divided into positive and negative authorizations. The Fernandez model also permits the creation of new authorizations from those originally specified by the user through the use of the semantic relationships in the data.

Dr. Naftaly H. Minsky of Rutgers University has developed a model that limits unrestricted access to objects through the use of a view mechanism similar to that used in traditional relational database management systems. Minsky's concept is to provide multiple interfaces to the objects within the database. The model includes a list of laws or rules that govern the access constraints to the objects. The laws within the database specify which actions must be taken by the system when a message is sent from one object to another. The system may allow the message to continue unaltered, block the sending of the message, send the message to another object, or send a different message to the intended object.

Although the discretionary access control models do provide varying levels of security for the information within the database, none of the DAC models effectively addresses the problem of the authorizations provided to users. A higher level of protection within a secure object-oriented database model is provided through the use of mandatory access control.

MAC Methods for OODBMS Security

Dr. Bhavani Thuraisingham of MITRE Corp. proposed in 1989 a mandatory security policy called SORION. This model extends the ORION model to encompass mandatory access control. The model specifies subjects, objects, and access modes within the system, and it assigns security/sensitivity levels to each entity. Certain properties regulate the assignment of the sensitivity levels to each of the subjects, objects, and access modes. To gain access to the instance variables and methods in the objects, certain properties that are based on the various sensitivity levels must be satisfied.

A similar approach has been proposed in the Millen-Lunt model. This model, developed by Jonathan K. Millen of MITRE Corp. and Teresa Lunt of SRI/DARPA (Defense Advanced Research Projects Agency), also uses the assignment of sensitivity levels to the objects, subjects, and access modes within the database. In the Millen-Lunt model, the properties that regulate the access to the information are specified as axioms within the model. This model further attempts to classify information according to three different cases:

- The data itself is classified.
- The existence of the data is classified.
- The reason for classifying the information also is classified.

These three classifications broadly cover the specifics of the items to be secured within the database; however, the classification method also greatly increases the complexity of the system.

The SODA Model

Dr. Thomas F. Keefe of Penn State University proposes a model called Secure Object-Oriented Data Base (SODA). The SODA model was one of the first models to address the specific concepts in the object-oriented paradigm. It often is used as a standard example of secure object-oriented models from which other models are compared.

The SODA model complies with MAC properties and is executed in a multilevel security system. SODA assigns classification levels to the data through the use of inheritance. However, multiple inheritance is not supported in the SODA model.

Similar to other secure models, SODA assigns security levels to subjects in the system and sensitivity levels to objects. The security classifications of subjects are checked against the sensitivity level of the information before access is allowed.

Polyinstantiation

Unlike many current secure object-oriented models, SODA allows the use of polyinstantiation as a solution to the multiparty update conflict. This problem arises when users with different security levels attempt to use the same information. The variety of clearances and sensitivities in a secure database system result in conflicts between the objects that can be accessed and modified by the users.

Through the use of polyinstantiation, information is located in more than one location, usually with different security levels. Obviously the more sensitive information is omitted from the instances with lower security levels.

Although polyinstantiation solves the multiparty update conflict problem, it raises a potentially greater problem in the form of ensuring the integrity of the data within the database. Without some method of simultaneously updating all occurrences of the data in the database, the integrity of the information quickly disappears. In essence, the system becomes a collection of several distinct database systems, each with its own data.

CONCLUSION

The move to object-oriented DBMSs is likely to continue for the foreseeable future. Because of the increasing need for security in distributed processing environments, the expanded selection of tools available for securing information in this environment should be used fully to ensure that the data is as secure as possible. In addition, with the continuing dependence on distributed data, the security of these systems must be integrated fully into existing and future network security policies and procedures.

The techniques that ultimately are used to secure commercial OODBMS implementations will depend in large part on the approaches promoted by the leading database vendors. However, the applied research that has been conducted to date also is laying the groundwork for the security components that in turn will be incorporated in the commercial OODBMSs.

Chapter 24
Security Management for the World Wide Web

Lynda L. McGhie
Phillip Q. Maier

COMPANIES CONTINUE TO FLOCK TO THE INTERNET in ever-increasing numbers, despite the fact that the overall and underlying environment is not secure. To further complicate the matter, vendors, standards bodies, security organizations, and practitioners cannot agree on a standard, compliant, and technically available approach. As a group of investors concerned with the success of the Internet for business purposes, it is critical that we pull our collective resources and work together to quickly establish and support interoperable security standards; open security interfaces to existing security products and security control mechanisms within other program products; and hardware and software solutions within heterogeneous operating systems which will facilitate smooth transitions.

Interfaces and teaming relationships to further this goal include computer and network security and information security professional associations (CSI, ISSA, NCSA), professional technical and engineering organizations (I/EEE, IETF), vendor and product user groups, government and standards bodies, seminars and conferences, training companies/institutes (MIS), and informal networking among practitioners.

Having the tools and solutions available within the marketplace is a beginning, but we also need strategies and migration paths to accommodate and integrate Internet, intranet, and World Wide Web (WWW) technologies into our existing IT infrastructure. While there are always emerging challenges, introduction of newer technologies, and customers with challenging and perplexing problems to solve, this approach should enable us to maximize the effectiveness of our existing security investments, while bridging the gap to the long awaited and always sought after perfect solution!

0-8493-9832-0/00/$0.00+$.50
© 2000 by CRC Press LLC

Security solutions are slowly emerging, but interoperability, universally accepted security standards, application programming interfaces (APIs) for security, vendor support and cooperation, and multiplatform security products are still problematic. Where there are products and solutions, they tend to have niche applicability, be vendor-centric or only address one of a larger set of security problems and requirements. For the most part, no single vendor or even software/vendor consortium has addressed the overall security problem within open systems and public networks. This indicates that the problem is very large, and that we are years away from solving todays problem, not to mention tomorrows.

By acknowledging todays challenges, bench-marking todays requirements, and understanding our "as is condition" accordingly, we as security practitioners can best plan for security in the twenty-first century. Added benefits adjacent to this strategy will hopefully include a more cost-effective and seamless integration of security policies, security architectures, security control mechanisms, and security management processes to support this environment.

For most companies, the transition to "open" systems technologies is still in progress and most of us are somewhere in the process of converting mainframe applications and systems to distributed network-centric client-server infrastructures. Nevertheless, we are continually challenged to provide a secure environment today, tomorrow, and in the future, including smooth transitions from one generation to another. This article considers a phased integration methodology that initially focuses on the update of corporate policies and procedures, including most security policies and procedures; secondly, enhances existing distributed security architectures to accommodate the use of the Internet, intranet, and WWW technologies; thirdly, devises a security implementation plan that incorporates the use of new and emerging security products and techniques; and finally, addresses security management and infrastructure support requirements to tie it all together.

It is important to keep in mind, as with any new and emerging technology, Internet, intranet, and WWW technologies do not necessarily bring new and unique security concerns, risks, and vulnerabilities, but rather introduce new problems, challenges and approaches within our existing security infrastructure.

Security requirements, goals, and objectives remain the same, while the application of security, control mechanisms, and solution sets are different and require the involvement and cooperation of multidisciplined technical and functional area teams. As in any distributed environment, there are more players, and it is more difficult to find or interpret the overall requirements or even talk to anyone who sees or understands the big picture. More people are involved than ever before, emphasizing the need to communicate both strategic and tactical security plans broadly and effectively throughout the entire enterprise. The security challenges and the resultant problems become larger and more complex in this environment. Management must be kept up-to-date and thoroughly understand overall risk to the corporations information assets with the implementation or decisions to implement new technologies. They must also understand, fund, and support the influx of resources required to manage the security environment.

As with any new and emerging technology, security should be addressed early in terms of understanding the requirements, participating in the evaluation of products and related technologies, and finally in the engineering, design, and implementation of new applications and systems. Security should also be considered during all phases of the systems development lifecycle. This is nothing new, and many of us have learned this lesson painfully over the years as we have tried to retrofit security solutions as an adjunct to the implementation of some large and complex system. Another important point to consider throughout the integration of new technologies, is "technology does not drive or dictate security policies, but the existing and established security policies drive the application of new technologies." This point must be made to management, customers, and supporting IT personnel.

For most of us, the WWW will be one of the most universal and influential trends impacting our internal enterprise and its computing and networking support structure. It will widely influence our decisions to extend our internal business processes out to the Internet and beyond. It will enable us to use the same user interface, the same critical systems and applications, work towards one single original source of data, and continue to address the age-old problem: how can I reach the largest number of users at the lowest cost possible?

THE PATH TO INTERNET/BROWSER TECHNOLOGIES

Everyone is aware of the staggering statistics relative to the burgeoning growth of the Internet over the last decade. The use of the WWW can even top that growth, causing the traffic on the Internet to double every six months. With five internal Web servers being deployed for every one external Web server, the rise of the intranet is also more than just hype. Companies are predominately using the web technologies on the intranet to share information and documents. Future application possibilities are basically any enterprisewide application such as education and training; corporate policies and procedures; human resources applications such as a résumé, job posting, etc.; and company information. External Web applications include marketing and sales.

For the purpose of this discussion, we can generally think of the Internet in three evolutionary phases. While each succeeding phase has brought with it more utility and the availability of a wealth of electronic and automated resources, each phase has also exponentially increased the risk to our internal networks and computing environments.

Phase I, the early days, is characterized by a limited use of the Internet, due in the most part to its complexity and universal accessibility. The user interface was anything but user friendly, typically limited to the use of complex UNIX-based commands via line mode. Security by obscurity was definitely a popular and acceptable way of addressing security in those early days, as security organizations and MIS management convinced themselves that the potential risks were confined to small user populations centered around homogeneous computing and networking environments. Most companies were not externally connected in those days, and certainly not to the Internet.

Phase II is characterized by the introduction of the first versions of database search engines, including Gopher and Wide Area Information System (WAIS). These tools were mostly used in the government and university environments and were not well known nor generally proliferated in the commercial sector.

Phase III brings us up to todays environment, where Internet browsers are relatively inexpensive, readily available, easy to install, easy to use through GUI frontends and interfaces, interoperable across heterogeneous platforms, and ubiquitous in terms of information access.

The growing popularity of the Internet and the introduction of the Internet should not come as a surprise to corporate executives who are generally well read on such issues and tied into major information technology (IT) vendors and consultants. However, quite frequently companies continue to select one of two choices when considering the implementation of WWW and Internet technologies. Some companies, who are more technically astute and competitive, have jumped in totally and are exploiting Internet technologies, electronic commerce, and the use of the Web. Others, of a more conservative nature and more technically inexperienced, continue to maintain a hard-line policy on external connectivity, which basically continues to say "NO."

Internet technologies offer great potential for cost savings over existing technologies, representing huge investments over the years in terms of revenue and resources now supporting corporate information infrastructures and contributing to the business imperatives of those enterprises. Internet-based applications provide a standard communications interface and protocol suite ensuring interoperability and access to the organization's heterogeneous data and information resources. Most WWW browsers run on all systems and provide a common user interface and ease of use to a wide range of corporate employees.

Benefits derived from the development of WWW-based applications for internal and external use can be categorized by the cost savings related to deployment, generally requiring very little support or end-user training. The browser software is typically free, bundled in vendor product suites, or very affordable. Access to information, as previously stated, is ubiquitous and fairly straightforward.

Use of internal WWW applications can change the very way organizations interact and share information. When established and maintained properly, an internal WWW application can enable everyone on the internal network to share information resources, update common use applications, receive education and training, and keep in touch with colleagues at their home base, from remote locations, or on the road.

INTERNET/WWW SECURITY OBJECTIVES

As mentioned earlier, security requirements do not change with the introduction and use of these technologies, but the emphasis on where security is placed and how it is implemented does change. The company's Internet, intranet, and WWW security strategies should address the following objectives, in combination or in prioritized sequence, depending on security and access requirements, company philosophy, the relative sensitivity of the companys information resources, and the business imperative for using these technologies.

- Ensure that Internet- and WWW-based application and the resultant access to information resources are protected and that there is a cost-effective and user-friendly way to maintain and manage the underlying security components, over time as new technology evolves and security solutions mature in response.
- Information assets should be protected against unauthorized usage and destruction. Communication paths should be encrypted as well as transmitted information that is broadcast over public networks.
- Receipt of information from external sources should be decrypted and authenticated. Internet- and WWW-based applications, WWW pages, directories, discussion groups, and databases should all be secured using access control mechanisms.
- Security administration and overall support should accommodate a combination of centralized and decentralized management.
- User privileges should be linked to resources, with privileges to those resources managed and distributed through directory services.
- Mail and real-time communications should also be consistently protected. Encryption key management systems should be easy to administer, compliant with existing security architectures, compatible with existing security strategies and tactical plans, and secure to manage and administer.

- New security policies, security architectures, and control mechanisms should evolve to accommodate this new technology; not change in principle or design.

Continue to use risk management methodologies as a baseline for deciding how many of the new Internet, intranet, and WWW technologies to use and how to integrate them into the existing Information Security Distributed Architecture. As always, ensure that the optimum balance between access to information and protection of information is achieved during all phases of the development, integration, implementation, and operational support lifecycle.

INTERNET AND WWW SECURITY POLICIES AND PROCEDURES

Having said all of this, it is clear that we need new and different policies, or minimally, an enhancement or refreshing of current policies supporting more traditional means of sharing, accessing, storing, and transmitting information. In general, high-level security philosophies, policies, and procedures should not change. In other words, who is responsible for what (the fundamental purpose of most high-level security policies) does not change. These policies are fundamentally directed at corporate management, process, application and system owners, functional area management, and those tasked with the implementation and support of the overall IT environment. There should be minimal changes to these policies, perhaps only adding the Internet and WWW terminology.

Other high level corporate policies must also be modified, such as the use of corporate assets, responsibility for sharing and protecting corporate information, etc. The second-level corporate policies, usually more procedure oriented typically addressing more of the "how," should be more closely scrutinized and may change the most when addressing the use of the Internet, intranet, and Web technologies for corporate business purposes. New classifications and categories of information may need to be established and new labeling mechanisms denoting a category of information that cannot be displayed on the Internet or new meanings to "all allow" or "public" data. The term "public," for instance, when used internally, usually means anyone authorized to use internal systems. In most companies, access to internal networks, computing systems, and information is severely restricted and "public" would not mean unauthorized users, and certainly not any user on the Internet.

Candidate lower-level policies and procedures for update to accommodate the Internet and WWW include external connectivity, network security, transmission of data, use of electronic commerce, sourcing and procurement, electronic mail, nonemployee use of corporate information and electronic systems, access to information, appropriate use of electronic systems, use of corporate assets, etc.

New policies and procedures (most likely enhancements to existing policies) highlight the new environment and present an opportunity to dust off and update old policies. Involve a broad group of customers and functional support areas in the update to these policies. The benefits are many. It exposes everyone to the issues surrounding the new technologies, the new security issues and challenges, and gains buy-in through the development and approval process from those who will have to comply when the policies are approved. It is also an excellent way to raise the awareness level and get attention to security up front.

The most successful corporate security policies and procedures address security at three levels, at the management level through high-level policies, at the functional level through security procedures and technical guidelines, and at the end-user level through user awareness and training guidelines. Consider the opportunity to create or update all three when implementing Internet, intranet, and WWW technologies.

Since these new technologies increase the level of risk and vulnerability to your corporate computing and network environment, security policies should probably be beefed up in the areas of audit and monitoring. This is particularly important because security and technical control mechanisms are not mature for the Internet and WWW and therefore more manual processes need to be put in place and mandated to ensure the protection of information.

The distributed nature of Internet, intranet, and WWW and their inherent security issues can be addressed at a more detailed level through an integrated set of policies, procedures, and technical guidelines. Because these policies and processes will be implemented by various functional support areas, there is a great need to obtain buy-in from these groups and ensure coordination and integration through all phases of the systems' lifecycle. Individual and collective roles and responsibilities should be clearly delineated to include monitoring and enforcement.

Other areas to consider in the policy update include legal liabilities, risk to competition-sensitive information, employees' use of company time while "surfing" the Internet, use of company logos and trade names by employees using the Internet, defamation of character involving company employees, loss of trade secrets, loss of the competitive edge, ethical use of the Internet, etc.

DATA CLASSIFICATION SCHEME

A data classification scheme is important to both reflect existing categories of data and introduce any new categories of data needed to support the business use of the Internet, electronic commerce, and information sharing through new intranet and WWW technologies. The whole area of

Exhibit 24.1. Sample data protection classification hierarchy

	Auth.	Trans. Controls	Encryption	Audit	Ownership
External Public Data				(X)	X
Internal Public Data				(X)	X
Internal Cntl. Data	X	X	(X)	X	X
External Cntl. Data	X	X	X	X	X
Update Applications	X	X		X	X

nonemployee access to information changes the approach to categorizing and protecting company information.

The sample chart in Exhibit 24.1 is an example of how general to specific categories of company information can be listed, with their corresponding security and protection requirements to be used as a checklist by application, process, and data owners to ensure the appropriate level of protection, and also as a communication tool to functional area support personnel tasked with resource and information protection. A supplemental chart could include application and system names familiar to corporate employees, or types of general applications and information such as payroll, HR, marketing, manufacturing, etc.

Note that encryption may not be required for the same level of data classification in the mainframe and proprietary networking environment, but in "open" systems and distributed and global networks transmitted data are much more easily compromised. Security should be applied based on a thorough risk assessment considering the value of the information, the risk introduced by the computing and network environment, the technical control mechanisms feasible or available for implementation, and the ease of administration and management support. Be careful to apply the right "balance" of security. Too much is just as costly and ineffective as too little in most cases.

APPROPRIATE USE POLICY

It is important to communicate management's expectation for employee's use of these new technologies. An effective way to do that is to supplement the corporate policies and procedures with a more user-friendly bulletined list of requirements. The list should be specific, highlight employee expectations and outline what employees can and cannot do on the Internet, intranet, and WWW. The goal is to communicate with each and every employee, leaving little room for doubt or confusion. An Appropriate Use Policy (Exhibit 24.2) could achieve these goals and reinforce the higher level. Areas to address include the proper use of employee time, corporate computing and networking resources, and acceptable material to be viewed or downloaded to company resources.

Exhibit 24.2. Appropriate Use Policy

Examples of unacceptable use include but not limited to the following:

1. Using Co. equipment, functions or services for non-business related activities while on company time; which in effect is mischarging;
2. Using the equipment or services for financial or commercial gain;
3. Using the equipment or services for any illegal activity;
4. Dial-in usage from home for Internet services for personal gain;
5. Accessing non-business related news groups or BBS;
6. Willful intent to degrade or disrupt equipment, software or system performance;
7. Vandalizing the data or information of another user;
8. Gaining unauthorized access to resources or information;
9. Invading the privacy of individuals;
10. Masquerading as or using an account owned by another user;
11. Posting anonymous messages or mail for malicious intent;
12. Posting another employee's personal communication or mail without the original author's consent; this excludes normal business e-mail forwarding;
13. Downloading, storing, printing or displaying files or messages that are profane, obscene, or that use language or graphics which offends or tends to degrade others;
14. Transmitting company data over the network to non-company employees without following proper release procedures;
15. Loading software obtained from outside the Corporation's standard company's procurement channels onto a company system without proper testing and approval;
16. Initiating or forwarding electronic chain mail.

Examples of acceptable use includes but is not limited to the following:

1. Accessing the Internet, computer resources, fax machines and phones for information directly related to your work assignment;
2. Off-hour usage of computer systems for degree related school work where allowed by local site practices;
3. Job related On-Job Training (OJT).

Most companies are concerned with the Telecommunications Act and their liabilities in terms of allowing employees to use the Internet on company time and with company resources. Most find that the trade-off is highly skewed to the benefit of the corporation in support of the utility of the Internet. Guidelines must be carefully spelled out and coordinated with the legal department to ensure that company liabilities are addressed through clear specification of roles and responsibilities. Most companies do not monitor their employee's use of the Internet or the intranet, but find that audit trail information is critical to prosecution and defense for computer crime.

Overall computer security policies and procedures are the baseline for any security architecture and the first thing to do when implementing any new technology. However, you are never really finished as the development and support of security policies is an iterative process and should be revisited on an ongoing basis to ensure that they are up-to-date, accommodate new technologies, address current risk levels, and reflect the company's use of information and network and computing resources.

There are four basic threats to consider when you begin to use Internet, intranet, and Web technologies:

- Unauthorized alteration of data
- Unauthorized access to the underlying operating system
- Eavesdropping on messages passed between a server and a browser
- Impersonation

Your security strategies should address all four. These threats are common to any technology in terms of protecting information. In the remainder of this chapter, we will build upon the "general good security practices and traditional security management" discussed in the first section and apply these lessons to the technical implementation of security and control mechanisms in the Internet, intranet, and Web environments.

The profile of a computer hacker is changing with the exploitation of Internet and Web technologies. Computerized bulletin board services and network chat groups link computer hackers (formerly characterized as loners and misfits) together. Hacker techniques, programs and utilities, and easy-to-follow instructions are readily available on the net. This enables hackers to more quickly assemble the tools to steal information and break into computers and networks, and it also provides the "would-be" hacker a readily available arsenal of tools.

INTERNAL/EXTERNAL APPLICATIONS

Most companies segment their networks and use firewalls to separate the internal and external networks. Most have also chosen to push their marketing, publications, and services to the public side of the firewall using file servers and web servers. There are benefits and challenges to each of these approaches. It is difficult to keep data synchronized when duplicating applications outside the network. It is also difficult to ensure the security of those applications and the integrity of the information. Outside the firewall is simply *outside*, and therefore also outside the protections of the internal security environment. It is possible to protect that information and the underlying system through the use of new security technologies for authentication and authorization. These techniques are not without trade-offs in terms of cost and ongoing administration, management, and support.

Security goals for external applications that bridge the gap between internal and external, and for internal applications using the Internet, intranet, and WWW technologies should all address these traditional security controls:

- Authentication
- Authorization
- Access control
- Audit
- Security administration

Some of what you already used can be ported to the new environment, and some of the techniques and supporting infrastructure already in place supporting mainframe-based applications can be applied to securing the new technologies.

Using the Internet and other public networks is an attractive option, not only for conducting business-related transactions and electronic commerce, but also for providing remote access for employees, sharing information with business partners and customers, and supplying products and services. However, public networks create added security challenges for IS management and security practitioners, who must devise security systems and solutions to protect company computing, networking, and information resources. Security is a CRITICAL component.

Two watchdog groups are trying to protect on-line businesses and consumers from hackers and fraud. The council of Better Business Bureaus has launched BBBOnline, a service that provides a way to evaluate the legitimacy of on-line businesses. In addition, the national computer security association, NCSA, launched a certification program for secure WWW sites. Among the qualities that NCSA looks for in its certification process are extensive logging, the use of encryption including those addressed in this chapter, and authentication services.

There are a variety of protection measures that can be implemented to reduce the threats in the Web/server environment, making it more acceptable for business use. Direct server protection measures include secure Web server products which use differing designs to enhance the security over user access and data transmittal. In addition to enhanced secure Web server products, the Web server network architecture can also be addressed to protect the server and the corporate enterprise which could be placed in a vulnerable position due to served enabled connectivity. Both secure server and secure web server designs will be addressed, including the application and benefits to using each.

WHERE ARE YOUR USERS?

Discuss how the access point where your users reside contributes to the risk and the security solutions set. Discuss the challenge when users are all over the place and you have to rely on remote security services that are only as good as the users' correct usage. Issues of evolving technologies can also be addressed. Concerns for multiple layering of controls and

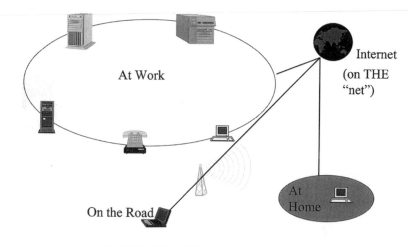

Exhibit 24.3. Where are your users?

dissatisfied users with layers of security controls, passwords, hoops, etc. can also be addressed (Exhibit 24.3).

WEB BROWSER SECURITY STRATEGIES

Ideally, Web browser security strategies should use a network-based security architecture that integrates your company's external Internet and the internal intranet security policies. Ensure that users on any platform, with any browser, can access any system from any location if they are authorized and have a "need-to-know." Be careful not to adopt the latest evolving security product from a new vendor or an old vendor capitalizing on a hot marketplace.

Recognizing that the security environment is changing rapidly, and knowing that we don't want to change our security strategy, architecture, and control mechanisms every time a new product or solution emerges, we need to take time and use precautions when devising browser security solutions. It is sometimes a better strategy to stick with the vendors that you have already invested in and negotiate with them to enhance their existing products, or even contract with them to make product changes specific or tailored to accommodate your individual company requirements. Be careful in these negotiations as it is extremely likely that other companies have the very same requirements. User groups can also form a common position and interface to vendors for added clout and pressure.

You can basically secure your web server as much as or as little as you wish with the current available security products and technologies. The tradeoffs are obvious: cost, management, administrative requirements, and time. Solutions can be hardware, software and personnel intensive.

Enhancing the security of the web server itself has been a paramount concern since the first Web server initially emerged, but progress has been slow in deployment and implementation. As the market has mushroomed for server use, and the diversity of data types that are being placed on the server has grown, the demand has increased for enhanced Web server security. Various approaches have emerged, with no single *de facto* standard yet emerging (though there are some early leaders — among them Secure Sockets Layer [SSL] and Secure Hypertext Transfer Protocol [S-HTTP]). These are two significantly different approaches, but both widely seen in the marketplace.

Secure Socket Layer (SSL) Trust Model

One of the early entrants into the secure Web server and client arena is Netscape's Commerce Server, which utilizes the Secure Sockets Layer (SSL) trust model. This model is built around the RSA Public Key/Private Key architecture. Under this model, the SSL-enabled server is authenticated to SSL-aware clients, proving its identity at each SSL connection. This proof of identity is conducted through the use of a public/private key pair issued to the server validated with x.509 digital certificates. Under the SSL architecture, web server validation can be the only validation performed, which may be all that is needed in some circumstances. This would be applicable for those applications where it is important to the user to be assured of the identity of the target server, such as when placing company orders, or other information submittal where the client is expecting some important action to take place. Exhibit 24.4 diagrams this process.

Optionally, SSL sessions can be established that also authenticate the client and encrypt the data transmission between the client and the server for multiple I/P services (HTTP, Telnet, FTP). The multiservice encryption capability is available because SSL operates below the application layer and above the TCP/IP connection layer in the protocol stack, and thus other TCP/IP services can operate on top of a SSL-secured session.

Optionally, authentication of a SSL client is available when the client is registered with the SSL server, and occurs after the SSL-aware client connects and authenticates the SSL server. The SSL client then submits its digital certificate to the SSL server, where the SSL server validates the clients certificate and proceeds to exchange a session key to provide encrypted transmissions between the client and the server. Exhibit 24.5 provides a graphical representation of this process for mutual client and server authentication under the SSL architecture. This type of mutual client/server

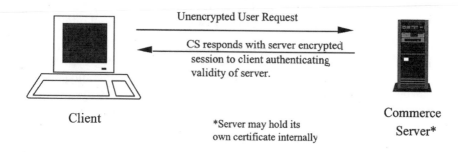

Unencrypted User Request

CS responds with server encrypted session to client authenticating validity of server.

Client

*Server may hold its own certificate internally

Commerce Server*

Exhibit 24.4. Server authentication.

authentication process should be considered when the data being submitted by the client are sensitive enough to warrant encryption prior to being submitted over a network transmission path.

Though there are some "costs" with implementing this architecture, these cost variables must be considered when proposing a SSL server implementation to enhance your web server security. First of all, the design needs to consider whether to only provide server authentication, or both server and client authentication. The issue when expanding the authentication to include client authentication includes the administrative overhead of managing the user keys, including a key revocation function. This consideration, of course, has to assess the size of the user base, potential for growth of your user base, and stability of your proposed user community. All of these factors will impact the administrative burden of key management, especially if there is the potential for a highly unstable or transient user community.

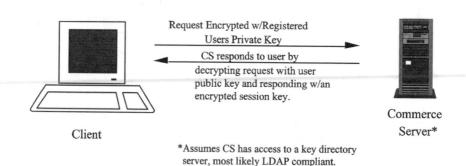

Request Encrypted w/Registered Users Private Key

CS responds to user by decrypting request with user public key and responding w/an encrypted session key.

Client

Commerce Server*

*Assumes CS has access to a key directory server, most likely LDAP compliant.

Exhibit 24.5. Client and server authentication.

The positive considerations for implementing a SSL-secured server is the added ability to secure other I/P services for remote or external SSL clients. SSL-registered clients now have the added ability to communicate securely by utilizing Tenet and FTP (or other I/P services) after passing SSL client authentication and receiving their session encryption key. In general the SSL approach has very broad benefits, but these benefits come with the potential added burden of higher administration costs, though if the value of potential data loss is great, then it is easily offset by the administration cost identified above.

Secure Hypertext Transfer Protocol (S-HTTP)

Secure Hypertext Transfer Protocol, (S-HTTP) is emerging as another security tool and incorporates a flexible trust model for providing secure web server and client HTTP communications. It is specifically designed for direct integration into HTTP transactions, with its focus on flexibility for establishing secure communications in a HTTP environment while providing transaction confidentiality, authenticity/integrity, and nonrepudiation. S-HTTP incorporates a great deal of flexibility in its trust model by leaving defined variable fields in the header definition which identifies the trust model or security algorithm to be used to enable a secure transaction. S-HTTP can support symmetric or asymmetric keys, and even a Kerberos-based trust model. The intention of the authors was to build a flexible protocol that supports multiple trusted modes, key management mechanisms, and cryptographic algorithms through clearly defined negotiation between parties for specific transactions.

At a high level the transactions can begin in a untrusted mode (standard HTTP communication), and "setup" of a trust model can be initiated so that the client and the server can negotiate a trust model, such as a symmetric key-based model on a previously agreed-upon symmetric key, to begin encrypted authentication and communication. The advantage of a S-HTTP-enabled server is the high degree of flexibility in securely communicating with web clients. A single server, if appropriately configured and network enabled, can support multiple trust models under the S-HTTP architecture and serve multiple client types. In addition to being able to serve a flexible user base, it can also be used to address multiple data classifications on a single server where some data types require higher-level encryption or protection than other data types on the same server and therefore varying trust models could be utilized.

The S-HTTP model provides flexibility in its secure transaction architecture, but focuses on HTTP transaction vs. SSL which mandates the trust model of a public/private key security model, which can be used to address multiple I/P services. But the S-HTTP mode is limited to only HTTP communications.

INTERNET, INTRANET, AND WORLD WIDE WEB SECURITY ARCHITECTURES

Implementing a secure server architecture, where appropriate, should also take into consideration the existing enterprise network security architecture and incorporate the secure server as part of this overall architecture. In order to discuss this level of integration, we will make an assumption that the secure web server is to provide secure data dissemination for external (outside the enterprise) distribution and/or access. A discussion of such a network security architecture would not be complete without addressing the placement of the Web server in relation to the enterprise firewall (the firewall being the dividing line between the protected internal enterprise environment and the external "public" environment).

Setting the stage for this discussion calls for some identification of the requirements, so the following list outlines some sample requirements for this architectural discussion on integrating a secure HTTP server with an enterprise firewall.

- Remote client is on public network accessing sensitive company data.
- Remote client is required to authenticate prior to receiving data.
- Remote client only accesses data via HTTP.
- Data is only updated periodically.
- Host site maintains firewall.
- Sensitive company data must be encrypted on public networks.
- Company support personnel can load HTTP server from inside the enterprise.

Based on these high-level requirements, an architecture could be set up that would place a S-HTTP server external to the firewall, with one-way communications from inside the enterprise "to" the external server to perform routine administration, and periodic data updates. Remote users would access the S-HTTP server utilizing specified S-HTTP secure transaction modes, and be required to identify themselves to the server prior to being granted access to secure data residing on the server. Exhibit 24.6 depicts this architecture at a high level. This architecture would support a secure HTTP distribution of sensitive company data, but doesn't provide absolute protection due to the placement of the S-HTTP server entirely external to the protected enterprise. There are some schools of thought that since this server is unprotected by the company-controlled firewall, the S-HTTP server itself is vulnerable, thus risking the very control mechanism itself and the data residing on it. The opposing view on this is that the risk to the overall enterprise is minimized, as only this server is placed at risk and its own protection is the S-HTTP process itself. This process has been a leading method to secure the data, without placing the rest of the enterprise at risk, by placing the S-HTTP server logically and physically outside the enterprise security firewall.

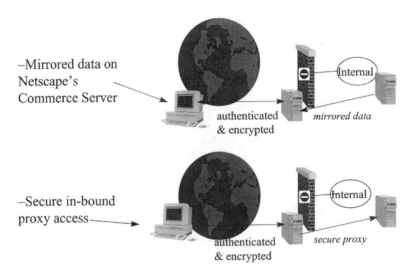

-Mirrored data on
Netscape's
Commerce Server

authenticated
& encrypted

mirrored data

-Secure in-bound
proxy access

authenticated
& encrypted

secure proxy

Exhibit 24.6. Externally placed server.

A slightly different architecture has been advertised that would position
the S-HTTP server inside the protected domain, as Exhibit 24.7 indicates.
The philosophy behind this architecture is that the controls of the firewall
(and inherent audits) are strong enough to control the authorized access
to the S-HTTP server, and also thwart any attacks against the server itself.
Additionally, the firewall can control external users so that they only have
S-HTTP access via a logically dedicated path, and only to the designated S-
HTTP server itself, without placing the rest of the internal enterprise at
risk. This architecture relies on the absolute ability of the firewall and S-
HTTP of always performing their designated security function as defined;

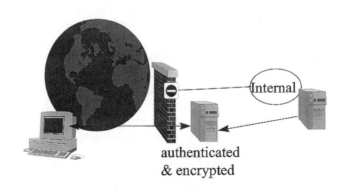

authenticated
& encrypted

Exhibit 24.7. Internally placed server.

otherwise, the enterprise has been opened for attack through the allowed path from external users to the internal S-HTTP server. Because these conditions are always required to be true and intact, the model with the server external to the firewall has been more readily accepted and implemented.

Both of these architectures can offer a degree of data protection in a S-HTTP architecture when integrated with the existing enterprise firewall architecture. As an aid in determining which architectural approach is right for a given enterprise, a risk assessment can provide great input to the decision. This risk assessment may include decision points such as:

- Available resources to maintain a high degree of firewall audit and S-HTTP server audit.
- Experience in firewall and server administration.
- Strength of their existing firewall architecture.

SECURE WWW CLIENT CONFIGURATION

There is much more reliance on the knowledge and cooperation of the end user and the use of a combination of desktop and workstation software, security control parameters within client software, and security products all working together to mimic the security of the mainframe and distributed application's environments. Consider the areas below during the risk assessment process and the design of WWW security solution sets.

- Ensure that all internal and external company-used workstations have resident and active antivirus software products installed. Preferably use a minimum number of vendor products to reduce security support and vulnerabilities as there are varying vendor schedules for providing virus signature updates.
- Ensure that all workstation and browser client software is preconfigured to return all WWW and other external file transfers to temporary files on the desktop. Under no circumstances should client server applications or process-to-process automated routines download files to system files, preference files, bat files, start-up files, etc.
- Ensure that JavaScript is turned off in the browser client software desktop configuration.
- Configure browser client software to automatically flush the cache, either upon closing the browser or disconnecting from each Web site.
- When possible or available, implement one of the new security products that scans WWW downloads for viruses.
- Provide user awareness and education to all desktop WWW and Internet users to alert them to the inherent dangers involved in using the Internet and WWW. Include information on detecting problems, their roles and responsibilities, your expectations, security products available, how to set and configure their workstations and program products, etc.

- Suggest or mandate the use of screen savers, security software programs, etc., in conjunction with your security policies and distributed security architectures.

This is a list of current areas of concern from a security perspective. There are options that when combined can tailor the browser to the specifications of individual workgroups or individuals. These options will evolve with the browser technology. The list should continue to be modified as security problems are corrected or as new problems occur.

AUDIT TOOLS AND CAPABILITIES

As we move further and further from the "good old days" when we were readily able to secure the "glass house," we rely more on good and sound auditing practices. As acknowledged throughout this chapter, security control mechanisms are mediocre at best in today's distributed networking and computing environments. Today's auditing strategies must be robust, available across multiple heterogeneous platforms, computing and network based, real-time and automated, and integrated across the enterprise.

Today, information assets are distributed all over the enterprise, and therefore auditing strategies must acknowledge and accept this challenge and accommodate more robust and dicey requirements. As is the case when implementating distributed security control mechanisms, in the audit environment there are also many players and functional support areas involved in collecting, integrating, synthesizing, reporting, and reconciling audit trails and audit information. The list includes applications and applications developers and programs, database management systems and database administrators, operating systems and systems administrators, local area network (LAN) administrators and network operating systems (NOS), security administrators and security software products, problem reporting and tracking systems and helpline administrators, and others unique to the company's environment.

As well as real-time, the audit system should provide for tracking and alarming, both to the systems and network management systems, and via pagers to support personnel. Policies and procedures should be developed for handling alarms and problems, i.e., isolate and monitor, disconnect, etc.

There are many audit facilities available today, including special audit software products for the Internet, distributed client server environments, WWW clients and servers, Internet firewalls, e-mail, News Groups, etc. The application of one or more of these must be consistent with your risk assessment, security requirements, technology availability, etc. The most important point to make here is the fundamental need to centralize distributed systems auditing (not an oxymoron). Centrally collect, sort, delete, process, report, take action and store critical audit information. Automate any and all steps and processes. It is a well-established fact that human beings cannot review large numbers of audit records and logs and reports without error. Today's audit function is an adjunct to the security function, and as such is more important and critical than ever before. It should be part of the overall security strategy and implementation plan.

The overall audit solutions set should incorporate the use of browser access logs, enterprise security server audit logs, network and firewall system authentication server audit logs, application and middle-ware audit logs, URL filters and access information, mainframe system audit information, distributed systems operating system audit logs, database management system audit logs, and other utilities that provide audit trail information such as accounting programs, network management products, etc.

The establishment of auditing capabilities over WWW environments follows closely with the integration of all external WWW servers with the firewall, as previously mentioned. This is important when looking at the various options available to address a comprehensive audit approach.

WWW servers can offer a degree of auditability based on the operating system of the server on which they reside. The more time-tested environments such as UNIX are perceived to be difficult to secure, whereas the emerging NT platform with its enhanced security features supposedly make it a more secure and trusted platform with a wide degree of audit tools and capabilities (though the vote is still out on NT, as some feel it hasn't had the time and exposure to discover all the potential security holes, perceived or real). The point, though, is that in order to provide some auditing the first place to potentially implement the first audit is on the platform where the WWW server resides. Issues here are the use of privileged accounts and file logs and access logs for log-ins to the operating system, which could indicate a backdoor attack on the WWW server itself. If server-based log are utilized, they of course must be file protected and should be off-loaded to a nonserver-based machine to protect against after-the-fact corruption.

Though the server logs aren't the only defensive logs that should be relied upon in a public WWW server environment, the other components in the access architecture should be considered for use as audit log tools. As previously mentioned, the WWW server should be placed in respect to its required controls in relation to the network security firewall. If it is a S-HTTP server that is placed behind (Exhibit 24.4) the firewall then the firewall of course has the ability to log all access to the S-HTTP server and provide a log separate from the WWW server-based logs, and is potentially more secure should the WWW server somehow become compromised.

The prevalent security architecture places externally accessible WWW servers wholly outside the firewall, thus virtually eliminating the capability of auditing access to the WWW server except from users internal to the enterprise. In this case, the network security audit in the form of the network management tool, which monitors the "health" of enterprise components can be called upon to provide a minimal degree of audit over the status of your external WWW server. This type of audit can be important when protecting data which resides on your external server from being subject to "denial of service" attacks, which are not uncommon for external devices. But by utilizing your network management tool to guard against such attacks, and monitoring log alerts on the status or health of this external server, you can reduce the exposure to this type of attack.

Other outside devices that can be utilized to provide audit include the network router between the external WWW server and the true external environment, though these devices are not normally readily set up for comprehensive audit logs, but in some critical cases they could be reconfigured with added hardware and minimal customized programming. One such example would be the "I/P Accounting" function on a popular router product line, which allows off-loading of addresses and protocols through its external interface. This could be beneficial to analyze traffic, and if an attack alert was generated from one of the other logs mentioned, then these router logs could assist in possibly identifying the origin of the attack.

Another possible source of audit logging could come from "back end" systems that the WWW server is programmed to "mine" data from. Many WWW environments are being established to serve as "front ends" for much larger data repositories, such as Oracle databases, where the WWW server receives user requests for data over HTTP, and the WWW server launches SQL_Net queries to a back end Oracle database. In this type of architecture the more developed logging inherent to the Oracle environment can be called upon to provide audits over the WWW queries. The detailed Oracle logs can specify the quantity, data type, and other activity over all the queries that the WWW server has made, thus providing a comprehensive activity log that can be consolidated and reviewed should any type of WWW server compromise be suspected. A site could potentially discover the degree of data exposure through these logs.

These are some of the major areas where auditing can be put in place to monitor the WWW environment while enhancing its overall security. It is important to note that the potential placement of audits encompasses the entire distributed computing infrastructure environment, not just the new WWW server itself. In fact, there are some schools of thought that consider the more reliable audits to be those that are somewhat distanced from the target server, thus reducing the potential threat of compromise to the audit logs themselves. In general, the important point is to look at the big picture when designing the security controls and a supporting audit solution.

WWW/INTERNET AUDIT CONSIDERATIONS

After your distributed Internet, intranet, and WWW security policies are firmly established, distributed security architectures are updated to accommodate this new environment. When planning for audit, and security control mechanisms are designed and implemented, you should plan how you will implement the audit environment — not only which audit facilities to use to collect and centralize the audit function, but how much and what type of information to capture, how to filter and review the audit data and logs, and what actions to take on the violations or anomalies identified. Additional consideration should be given to secure storage and access to the audit data. Other considerations include:

- Timely resolution of violations.
- Disk space storage availability.
- Increased staffing and administration.
- In-house developed programming.
- Ability to alarm and monitor in real time.

WWW SECURITY FLAWS

As with all new and emerging technology, many initial releases come with some deficiency. But this has been of critical importance when that deficiency can impact the access or corruption of a whole corporation or enterprise's display to the world. This can be the case with Web implementations utilizing the most current releases which have been found to contain some impacting code deficiencies, though up to this point most of these deficiencies have been identified before any major damage has been done. This underlines the need to maintain a strong link or connection with industry organizations that announce code shortcomings that impact a sites Web implementation. A couple of the leading organizations are CERT, the Computer Emergency Response Team, and CIAC, Computer Incident Advisory Capability.

Just a few of these types of code or design issues that could impact a sites web security include initial issues with the Sun JAVA language and Netscapes JavaScript (which is an extension library of their HyperText Markup Language, HTML).

The Sun Java language was actually designed with some aspects of security in mind, though upon its initial release there were several functions that were found to be a security risk. One of the most impacting bugs in an early release was the ability to execute arbitrary machine instructions by loading a malicious Java applet. By utilizing Netscape's caching mechanism a malicious machine instruction can be downloaded into a user's machine and Java can be tricked into executing it. This doesn't present a risk to the enterprise server, but the user community within one's enterprise is of course at risk.

Other Sun Java language bugs include the ability to make network connections with arbitrary hosts (though this has since been patched with the following release) and Java's ability to launch denial of service attacks through the use of corrupt applets.

These types of security holes are more prevalent than the security profession would like to believe, as the JavaScript environment also was found to contain capabilities that allowed malicious functions to take place. The following three are among the most current and prevalent risks:

- JavaScripts ability to trick the user into uploading a file on his local hard disk to an arbitrary machine on the Internet.
- The ability to hand out the user's directory listing from the internal hard disk.
- The ability to monitor all pages the user visits during a session.

The following are among the possible protection mechanisms:

- Maintain monitoring through CERT or CIAC, or other industry organizations that highlight such security risks.
- Utilize a strong software distribution and control capability, so that early releases aren't immediately distributed, and that new patched code known to fix a previous bug is released when deemed safe.
- In sensitive environments it may become necessary to disable the browsers capability to even utilize or execute Java or JavaScript — a selectable function now available in many browsers.

In the last point, it can be disturbing to some in the user community to disallow the use of such powerful tools, because they can be utilized against trusted Web pages, or those that require authentication through the use of SSL or S-HTTP. This approach can be coupled with the connection to S-HTTP pages where the target page has to prove its identity to the client user. In this case, enabling Java or JavaScripts to execute on the browser (a user-selectable option) could be done with a degree of confidence.

Other perceived security risks exist in a browser feature referred to as HTTP "Cookies." This is a feature that allows servers to store information on the client machine in order to reduce the store and retrieve requirements of the server. The cookies file can be written to by the server, and that server, in theory, is the only one that can read back their cookies entry. Uses of the cookie file include storing user's preferences or browser history on a particular server or page, which can assist in guiding the user on their next visit to that same page. The entry in the cookies file identifies the information to be stored and the uniform resource locator (URL) or server page that can read back that information, though this address can be masked to some degree so multiple pages can read back the information.

The perceived security concern is that pages impersonating cookies-readable pages could read back a users cookies information without the user knowing it, or discover what information is stored in their cookie file. The threat depends on the nature of the data stored in the cookie file, which is dependent on what the server chooses to write into a user's cookie file. This issue is currently under review, with the intention of adding additional security controls to the cookie file and its function. At this point it is important that users are aware of the existence of this file, which is viewable in the Macintosh environment as a Netscape file and in the Win environment as a cookies.txt file. There are already some inherent protections in the cookie file: one is the fact that the cookie file currently has a maximum of 20 entries, which potentially limits the exposure. Also, these entries can be set up with expiration dates so they don't have an unlimited lifetime.

WWW SECURITY MANAGEMENT

Consider the overall management of the Internet, intranet, and WWW environment. As previously mentioned, there are many players in the support role and for many of them this is not their primary job or priority. Regardless of where the following items fall in the support infrastructure, also consider these points when implementing ongoing operational support:

- Implement WWW browser and server standards.
- Control release and version distribution.
- Implement secure server administration including the use of products and utilities to erase sensitive data cache (NSClean).
- Ensure prompt problem resolution, management, and notification.
- Follow industry and vendor discourse on WWW security flaws and bugs including CERT distribution.
- Stay current on new Internet and WWW security problems, Netscape encryption, JAVA, Cookies, etc.

WWW SUPPORT INFRASTRUCTURE

- WWW servers accessible from external networks should reside outside the firewall and be managed centrally.
- By special approval, decentralized programs can manage external servers, but must do so in accordance with corporate policy and be subjected to rigorous audits.
- Externally published company information must be cleared through legal and public relations departments (i.e., follow company procedures).

- External outbound http access should utilize proxy services for additional controls and audit.
- WWW application updates must be authenticated utilizing standard company security systems (as required).
- Filtering and monitoring software must be incorporated into the firewall.
- The use of discovery crawler programs must be monitored and controlled.
- Virus software must be active on all desktop systems utilizing WWW.
- Externally published information should be routinely updated or verified through integrity checks.

In conclusion, as information security practitioners embracing the technical challenges of the twenty-first century, we are continually challenged to integrate new technology smoothly into our existing and underlying security architectures. Having a firm foundation or set of security principles, frameworks, philosophies and supporting policies, procedures, technical architectures, etc. will assist in the transition and our success.

Approach new technologies by developing processes to manage the integration and update the security framework and supporting infrastructure, as opposed to changing it. The Internet, intranet, and the World Wide Web is exploding around us — what is new today is old technology tomorrow. We should continue to acknowledge this fact while working aggressively with other MIS and customer functional areas to slow down the train to progress, be realistic, disciplined, and plan for new technology deployment.

Section V
Data Migration, Conversion, and Legacy Applications

ALL THE CHAPTERS IN THIS SECTION ARE OF INCREASING RELEVANCE TO THE IT INDUSTRY due to the globalization of many corporations and the continuing mega-mergers. This results in the need to reengineer business processes, consolidate the organization, and to consolidate the data sources. This is done through data migration, conversions, and by building bridges to legacy applications.

Data migration refers to the process of migrating or transferring data from one source to another over a project development lifecycle. Conversion generally refers to a one way movement of data. Data conversion involves several steps. Data mapping involves identifying relationships between data items in one system to the data items in another system. The quality of the data being converted must always be determined with extensive user involvement. Data can be corrupt or may require translation to other values. Data scrubbing is a process used to correct the data as or after it is converted. It is imperative to build control reports to keep a running audit trail of any data conversion cycle.

Legacy applications contain most of the data in the world. This involves trillions and trillions of bytes of data. At the first emergence of client/server architecture, projects relied heavily on converting legacy data for the new systems to leverage. The last few years have seen the emergence of data gateways and bridges that accept standard ANSI SQL type requests to access legacy data in the legacy applications and to return this to other applications.

This section contains four chapters with the following focuses:

Chapter 25, "Data: Everchanging and Eternally the Same," examines common types of data change that occur within organisations so that teams can focus on finding rules and information that is used to maintain data integrity over time and through data conversion cycles.

Chapter 26, "A Practical Example of Data Conversion," looks at opportunities for categorizing data conversions in order to remove much of the fear, apprehension, and stagnation that face many data conversion projects. The approach that is defined includes iteration and strong controls. With the number of corporate acquisitions, mergers, and system replacements, it is expected that data conversions are going to become even more common in the industry.

Chapter 27, "Legacy Database Conversion," describes planning activities that the data center manager can undertake to identify and reduce risks associated with converting legacy, nonrelational data to a relational format.

Chapter 28, "Data Conversion: Doing it Right the First Time," describes common problems with data, outlines steps for performing a successful conversion, and suggests methods for correcting errors detected during conversion.

Chapter 25
Data: Everchanging and Eternally the Same

Bruce Anderson

ONE OF THE CONSTANTS IN DATA PROCESSING IS THAT DATA CHANGES — vales, obviously, but also the attributes and relationships. Over time, the nature of the business changes, so data attributes follow: new systems are installed, and data must be converted; companies merge and data from disparate sources must be integrated; branch offices can often make creative interpretations of data rules. An initiative is started to create an Enterprise Data Warehouse. All of these events constitute data *changes* in the sense of this article.

All data stores have *views*. (Note: this term is being used here in a much more generic and intuitive way then a data management language *view*). Some views are embedded in a database management system. Some views are embedded in complex SQL under some sort of centralized control. Some views are embedded in programs or suites of programs under centralized control; e.g., standardized inventory reports from IT. Some views are embedded in programs, SQL or (worst of all) spreadsheets which are user built and maintained. Some DBMSs attempt to capture the business rules (i.e., the semantics) of the data in ways such as cardinality rules, foreign keys, referential integrity. Data warehouses and repositories allow for metadata with more sophisticated descriptors of what the underlying data mean. *The core problem is that, ultimately, data means whatever the end user/decision-makers choose to make them mean or assume they mean.* There are many business rules embedded in those SQL queries; those suites of programs running against a sequence of 76 flat files; those user maintained programs and queries; and those innumerable spreadsheets that finance keeps separate from centralized data stores.

In other words, the business rules/semantics/"what the data means" are never really stored in a fully reusable manner. Many of those rules are hidden away. The repository people are trying hard to migrate as much of the semantics as possible into a repository. We are not there yet, and (so far) there is no obvious "light at the end of the tunnel" suggesting that all of the semantics of a data store can ever be captured in a broadly re-usable way. The object-oriented people are trying hard to get us to migrate the business rule into a hierarchy of objects (Model-View-Controller). Again, we are not there yet, and again, there is no light at the end of the tunnel. Yet another way of expressing this is to say that **much of the meaning of the data is hidden in the programs**.

One way of appreciating this reality is to explore what it means to say that a program or system is "old," "obsolete" or "legacy." A critical piece of why this can happen, even in the face of all good intentions, good people and good management is that the business rules are hidden away amongst millions of lines of PL/1 or COBOL or C code, and no one remembers what they are. One of the prime motivations to senior management for funding the replacement of systems is to force staff to re-derive the enterprise's business rules. With any luck, this time around, a larger proportion of the business rules will be captured in a more explicit form than the last attempt — making business change quicker, easier, and less costly. A key reason why table driven systems such as SAP are achieving such market penetration is that they promise to capture a large fraction of the business rules in tables rather than code.

THE WINDS OF CHANGE — WHAT KINDS OF CHANGE/MISMATCH CAN HAPPEN?

We will explore three categories of change to underlying data in this chapter: (1) two data sources are merging — one has information about 'X' and the other does not; (2) one data source groups data codes data values one way, and another groups them differently; and (3) there are business rule differences between the data sources. In all cases, by understanding the kinds of change, it is easier to describe the existing options for dealing with them. In many cases, some forethought can prevent or mitigate problems.

The Case of the Missing Attribute

The simplest sort of difference is a missing attribute. For example, an insurance company decides to start tracking education level of insureds; while building the data staging process for a data warehouse, you discover that one division tracks the customers zip code while another does not. In each case, you are faced with a decision to make or delegate upwards. The data is missing from part or all of the available information over a period of time. The problem arises when someone wants to see continuity of data over time.

The only appropriate systems response here is sensible expectation management. There are not many options for this one, and most managers inherently appreciate that if they did not collect the information in the first place, you cannot subsequently show it to them.

THE SHELL GAME — LOSING DATA BETWEEN THE SUMMARIES

The second sort of change or mismatch stems from what I call "non-atomic" data. For example, take age (see Exhibit 25.1). There are several ways to represent age:

- *By capturing the birth date/start date*—an "atomic" representation of age. It allows the age of the person or thing to be calculated not only as of the capture date, but for any other date as well. Atomic data presents no problems for change over time, conversion or integration since the data is at a fine a level as it can be represented. Note that it is possible to quibble with even this definition: for items that are very short-lived, the exact time of start may be critically important—e.g., the exact time that a long distance phone call began.
- *By capturing the explicit age in whatever units are appropriate (e.g., years, months, days, hours)* — this could be atomic under one set of business rules and not under another. If, for example, the age were captured in years in one system, but new rules required age in months, we have a conversion/integration problem. Also, unless the date at which the age was captured is known, ages may not be comparable.
- *By capturing a code for the age range (e.g., under 25, 26 to 35, 35 to 50, over 50)*—definitely not atomic. This concept becomes important whenever certain types of change rear their ugly head. For example, one insurance company categorized motorcycles as "up to 250cc's" and "greater than 250cc's." The second company categorized them as "up to 100cc's," "100cc's to 450cc's" and "greater than 450cc's." When the companies merged, they had a difficult time sorting out records to develop combined actuarial results (critically important to business planning as larger sample size gives greater validity).

Other examples of non-atomic data are:

- Total sales by region (regions can be re-shuffled)
- Codes representing distance from a fire hydrant (ranges can be changed)
- Average annual income (without keeping the actual amounts)

For the mathematically inclined, the situation we are describing here arises when two different homorphic mappings are applied to the two sets of data and the underlying (atomic) data is deleted. In other words, the mappings should be views of the underlying data but the views have been

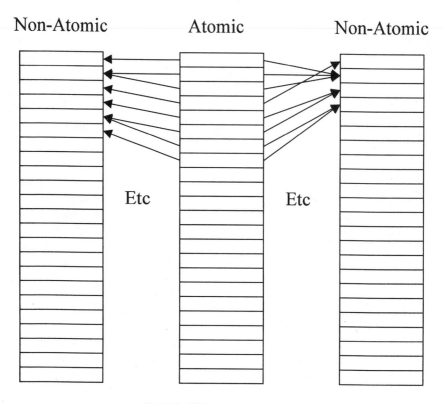

Exhibit 25.1.   Atomic data.

kept and the underlying data discarded. As long as you have the underlying data, new views can easily be generated. Without it, life is not so simple.

Lesson 1: If you are at the planning stages, **always keep the underlying atomic data — even if management is adamant about not wanting it**. (You can always present codes as views of the atomic data). If it is too late for that, you may still have some options.

- If the atomic data is still available in electronic form, and it has appropriate identifying keys, then it should be possible to simply restore it. This is likely to be feasible and cost effective unless there is an issue of sheer magnitude. I have personally been on both sides of the decision for this category. In all cases, management made the call based on weighing the cost of restoring the data vs. the short-term benefit. Lesson: once you get into this problem, it is very difficult to sell the long-term benefits of correcting the problem.

- If the atomic data is still available but not in electronic form, if the appropriate identifying keys are available, then it should be possible to manually restore it. This may or may not be feasible, depending on the volume and complexity of the data and the business value of restoring it. Conversions of reasonable magnitude are often done manually — but that is the **whole** conversion, not the work to add a missing attribute. If there is any significant volume of data involved, it is likely to be very difficult to justify this sort of effort.
- If the atomic data is still available in any form, but the identifying keys are either missing or suspect, then this boils down to two options:
  - "Guess:" This includes any mechanism for allocating the data in the term "guess" including using suspect keys.
  - "Give up:" Admit to the stakeholder that there is either no way to reconstruct the data or no way to justify the cost of reconstructing it with any degree of accuracy.
- If the atomic data is not available, but the views are close, then in some special circumstances, it may be feasible to do some form of statistical reconstruction. This is not a rare thing — various categories of overhead expense are frequently allocated down to more detailed levels based on a variety of business rules — e.g., headcount, square fottage, and gross sales. Warning: make sure that this option is clearly understood at the highest management level that will be depending on the data, as it will not be real.
- If the atomic data is not available and the views are not close to the original, then accept reality and promise to keep atomic data in your next design.

In summary, there are four ways of dealing with the situation:

- Load the atomic data in the first place.
- Restore the missing data, either electronically or manually.
- Approximate the missing data (and make sure to document very carefully the accuracy of the approximations and the circumstances in which they may be misleading).
- Accept the fact that you are not going to be able to deliver the missing data.

Keep in mind that someone will be disappointed or misled if you end up with options 3 or 4. Further, someone may make expensive business decisions based on the data that they see — not realizing that it is incomplete or misleading. Make sure that you go to significant lengths to communicate to that person or persons that the data differs from reality in important ways.

A large insurance company once decided to reorganize itself into cleaner product lines. Independent insurance brokers typically come close to breaking even on the straight commissions they are paid, and make their profit on the profit sharing bonuses that most insurers pay annually. The fee paid is based on the profitability of the brokers business. It is calculated based on a complex formula that uses results in several categories over multiple years. The problem arose when the company decided to re-state each broker's historical results based on the new and cleaner definition of product lines, without having first re-stated all the basic data. There were many situations where it was not clear from historical data which of the new, cleaner product lines a piece of business belonged.

Using the analysis I've presented above, this project faced not one, but two of the core data problems: The underlying data was missing an attribute (the one that identified which of the new product lines any give historical transaction belonged to). In turn, the broker historical profitability data — a summarized view of the company transaction data — was a non-atomic summary whose definition needed to be changed. Had anyone on the project team clearly understood this situation at the time, the results might have been more pleasant. The actual results were that a massive overtime effort was undertaken to (1) re-stating the current transaction data and (2) approximate the historical data. There were two major gaps: (1) the historical data was actually re-stated a year later, so the "badness" of the approximation was then easily measured; and (2) since no one at the time clearly understood the impact of the approximations, no one could clearly communicate to the executive how good or bad the approximation was. Common sense caught a lot of bad approximations as checks were about to go out the door, but the cost was still considerable.

This anecdote points out two realities: (1) even though the categorization of data mismatches seems simple on first reading, it can be quite complex when applied to a real world situation; and (2) no matter how clever one is, it is easy to lose sight of the swamp when the alligators are closing in.

BUSINESS RULE MISMATCHES

The bigger the organization, the more energy it will take to get these sorted out. The more history an organization has, the worse the business rule matches are likely to be.

To read the marketing brochures of information warehouse providers is to wax rhapsodic in a reverie of total information availability — every fact and facet of the business instantly available at executive fingertips, all relationships neatly sorted, and all data readily comparable with other data. So if the technology is here, why isn't the dream a reality?

My answer: **business rule mismatches**. Remember that there are fairly explicit directly data related business rules like cardinality and referential integrity. There are also all those "other" nuances of data interpretation

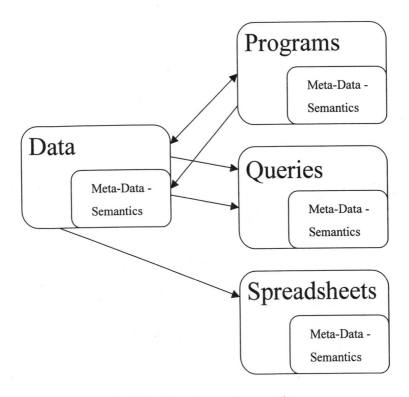

Exhibit 25.2. Data and semantics.

that are imbedded in all those queries, spreadsheets and programs that are lurking out there (see Exhibit 25.2).

Here is a good example that will cause lots of telco problems in the next few years. There is a historical association between NPA-NXX (known to most people as "area code" and "exchange") and a geographic location. The NXX normally corresponded with a physical structure called a frame. In fact, in the past, if you knew someone's NXX (exchange) in an urban area you could tell the general neighborhood they lived in. In the thousands upon thousands of programs that have been written to handle Telco billing and provisioning, the assumption about that connection has been so deeply embedded as to be hardly detectable. The same assumptions have been embedded in hundreds of file and database designs. This is still important for two reasons: (1) someone has to know where the "end of the wire" is; and (2) someone has management responsibility for managing the frame at the "end of the wire."

Yet, technology has advanced. There are remote switches which allow large businesses, governments and universities to maintain the same NXX across what used to be NXX boundaries. With competition came Equal Ease of Access rules, local number portability, and in some areas, overlay — which means that two NPAs (area codes) can co-exist and overlap in the same geographic area.

The most obvious data mismatch here will be a missing attribute — the identity of the physical frame or frame location that represents the "end of the wire."

There are also more subtle impacts. Consider the situation where a planner depends on a query that measures working lines, and makes a prediction when the next major investment will be required on communication feeder routes. The planner enters the code number of the "Frame," but the calculations done by the query have a hidden anomaly that still assumes the old NXX to frame relationship. As a result, the planner is presented with a distorted projection that has the appearance of correct data, but the resulting decision could be tragic!

Other data "land mines" arise as a result of changing data relationships that have not been anticipated in the data manipulation/transformation code. Even the simple addition of a new product can produce unexpected results if the existing transformation code was not designed to dynamically adjust to new codes (or someone forgets to update a product–matching list).

In addition to the problems that stem from hidden or invisible business rules, there are subtle (and not-so-subtle) problems that crop up all the time when users or programmers violate an existing, but hidden rule. Senior managers are particularly adept at this as they will tend to ignore all of the subtle exceptions to normal business flow and relationships as they search for the big picture. This results in views which portray conflicting information. This leads senior management to no end of headaches, and leaves a bad taste about the "reliability" of systems. IT usually gets the blame.

Query "land mines" are not limited to incorrect data relationships. Problems frequently arise from assumptions made in the query code. Clients often wrongly assume that all attributes are data-filled, and then make wrong decisions on what they believe to be a complete answer. For example, when the planner needs to know how many customers are eligible for a new location-sensitive service, they must not rely entirely on postal codes that may or may not be data-filled. Often, this problem can be mitigated by weighing factors computed from the percent of populated data.

In another example, a client assumed that a join between the Circuit table and the Customer table would give them a list of all customers affected by the rearrangement of a high-capacity fiber optics cable. Unfortunately, the query was coded as a conventional (inside) join, resulting in the omission of switched circuits from the planning (i.e., circuits without a dedicated customer).

CONCLUSION

Data may just be strings of 1s and 0s, but the value of that data is the combination of the data and the meaning hidden in the data, data relationships, queries, interpretive programs, and the hidden assumptions of the people who use the data. Changes and mismatches occur over time as rules change, as the business rules change, as entities merge and separate and as regulations and generally accepted principles change. This article has identified the places where the **meaning** of the data is hidden, and the structure of how changes and mismatches come into being.

There are three types of mismatch: missing attributes, non-atomic data, and business rule changes. Data practitioners need to work aggressively towards gaining control of these mismatches — through central control and through making business rules explicit.

- *Lesson 1:* if you are at the planning stages, always keep the underlying atomic data — even if management is adamant about not wanting it.
- *Lesson 2:* You cannot provide an enterprise view without (central) enterprise control.
- *Lesson 3:* The more explicit you make the business rules the easier it will be for business consumers of data to validate them on an on-going basis — and thus make your life easier.
- *Lesson 4:* No matter how explicit you make the business rules, you'll have to rewrite the systems every 10 years or so to force staff (both business and IT) to rethink them all.

Chapter 26
A Practical Example of Data Conversion

Charles Banyay

CONVERSION, THE WORD IS ENOUGH TO DIM THE ENTHUSIASM OF MOST SYSTEMS DEVELOPERS. The word instills fear in some, trepidation and loathing in others. Regardless of the nature of the project with which she/he is involved, if there is any conversion effort involved, the reaction is the same. Exclude it from project scope! Let someone else do it! Although some might suspect that there may be some religious connotation here, and rightly so, the topic of this chapter is not converting from one religion to another. Nor is the topic software conversion, although this would be closer to the mark. This chapter deals with the various forms of the conversion of data.

Even if the project promises to be primarily development and/or implementation, which is usually the dream of most developers. Even if it involves some of the latest state-of-the-art technology, the word conversion immediately throws a pall over all the luster and glitter, and hopes of an interesting endeavor. Most systems implementations involve some form of conversion. When the software changes, the data model or the data itself often changes with it.

For some reason, conversions have come to be associated with the mundane, boring, and tiresome aspects of systems implementation. Most developers would consider conversion efforts as boring, tiresome, and devoid of interesting challenges, when compared to the implementation of state-of-the-art technology.

This is a misconception in many instances. Conversion efforts can be as challenging as any state-of-the-art technology. They can exercise the most creative abilities of technology professionals. An entire chapter probably could be devoted to discussing the possible reasons behind the general lack of enthusiasm for the conversion effort. This chapter, however, will focus on examining the following:

0-8493-9832-0/00/$0.00+$.50
© 2000 by CRC Press LLC

- Different types of conversion efforts that one encounters during systems implementation projects.
- The taxonomy of the conversion effort.
- Common pitfalls that can have rather detrimental effects on the overall effort if one is not aware of them and does not take the necessary precautions before hand.

CLASSIFYING DATA CONVERSIONS

There are a number of different ways to classify a data conversion. One of the most common ways is to classify it by what is involved in the conversion effort. This could be one or more of the following:

- Converting from one hardware platform to another, e.g., a host system upgrade (on PCs this is done on a matter-of-fact basis almost daily).
- Converting from one operating system to another, e.g., UNIX to NT.
- Converting from one file access method to another, e.g., converting from an indexed or flat file structure into a DBMS.
- Converting from one coding structure or format to another, e.g., from EBCDIC to ASCII.
- Converting application software such as upgrading versions of an application or replacing one application with another as in replacing an outmoded payroll application with a state-of-the-art pay benefits system.

One of the most common pitfalls of conversions is to combine into one conversion effort a change of too many variables, e.g., changing hardware, operating system(s), file access method(s), and application software all at once. Sometimes this cannot be avoided. Ideally, however, as few as possible of the variables should be changed at once. With only one variable changing, error detection and correction is the simplest. Any problem can be attributed to the change of the single variable and, thus, can be rectified by analyzing the single variable. With combinations and permutations, the effort increases exponentially.

Unfortunately, as often happens in life, the ideal state is the exception. In general, it is a rare conversion that does not have some combination of the above variables changing at once. The taxonomy of each, however, can be explored individually, as can most of the pitfalls. Some combinations will have unique pitfalls simply due to the combination of changes in variables.

CHANGE IN HARDWARE

In general, the simplest conversion is upgrading hardware, assuming that all of the other variables remain constant, i.e., operating systems, file access method, coding structure and format, and application software. This can be illustrated best in the PC world. PCs have been upgraded with relative ease continuously from one configuration to another for the past 10 years. As long as the operating system does not change the upgrade in hardware usually involves nothing more than copying the files from one hard disk to another. This migration of files usually is accomplished with the assistance of some standard utilities. Using utilities rather than custom-developed software lowers the amount of effort involved in ensuring that the files have migrated successfully. Most utilities provide fairly good audit trails for this purpose. Even files on the same floppies can be used in a 286, 386, 486, or Pentium machine. Data on floppies does not require any conversion.

In environments other than personal computers, the same simplicity of conversion generally holds true. Upgrading from one configuration of mainframe to another is relatively easy. Changing configurations of a minicomputer, such as from one AS/400 to a more powerful configuration of the same or from one HP/3000 to a more powerful HP/3000, generally does not require significant effort. These kinds of conversions generally are imperceptible to the users and are done without much involvement from the user community. There usually is no requirement for any user testing or programmer testing. This cannot be said for the more complex conversions such as changes in the operating system.

MIGRATING FROM ONE OPERATING SYSTEM TO ANOTHER

Changes to the operating system are generally more complicated from a conversion perspective, than changes to hardware. The complexity, however, is usually more pronounced at the application software rather than the data level. There is considerable insulation by the operating system of the application software and associated data from the hardware. In general, there is little to insulate the application software from the operating system. Object-oriented approaches are slowly changing this fact, but for now it is safe to say that a change in operating system requires a more complex conversion effort than a change in hardware.

For individuals who primarily have limited their involvement with technology to the WINTEL world, conversion complexity due to changes in operating system may come as a surprise. In the WINTEL world one generally can change from DOS to Windows 3.x to Windows 95 (or higher) with little or limited problems. In fact, most users do this on a regular basis. This may imply that changes in operating system are as simple as changes in hardware. This is a misconception. The people at Microsoft® and to a limited extent at Intel have spent innumerable hours to ensure that there exists a degree of compatibility between these operating systems that does not exist in any other environment.

Even in the WINTEL world this compatibility is breaking down. As the move to NT accelerates this is becoming evident. Users moving to NT have discovered that many of their favorite software programs are not functioning as they would like them to, or the programs are not functioning at all.

Although some form of conversion effort usually is involved when operating systems are changed, the changes in operating system more definitely impact the application software than the data. The impact on any of the data is usually from indirect sources such as from a change in one of the other variables such as data format or file access method. Different operating systems may support only different data coding structures and/or different file access methods.

CHANGES IN FILE ACCESS METHOD

It is not often that one changes a file access method while leaving the operating system and the application system the same. The general reasons for doing this would be suspect unless the current file access method was being abandoned by whomever was providing support. Another valid reason for changing file access method may be if a packaged application system vendor released a new version of their application. This new version may offer a new data architecture such as an RDBMS. There may be valid reasons, such as better-reporting capability using third-party tools, for upgrading to this new version with the RDBMS. For whatever the reason, a change in file access method usually requires some form of change in data architecture.

A simple illustration of this change in the underlying data architecture would be in converting a flat file sequential access method to an indexed file access method. Some form of indexing would have to be designed into the file structure resulting in a change in the underlying data architecture. A more complex example would be in changing from a sequential access method to a database management system.

This change at the minimum would involve some degree of data normalization and a break up of the single segment or record structure of the file. The resultant change in data architecture would be quite substantive. This type of conversion generally is not simple and requires a comprehensive conversion utility. In the case where it is a packaged application being upgraded, the vendor probably would provide the conversion utility. In the case where a custom-developed application is being converted, the conversion utility probably would have to be custom-developed as well.

In either case, the tasks are straightforward. All of the data must be converted. Every record must have a corresponding entry or entries in some table or tables. Each field in the source file needs to be transferred to the target database. Field conversion is not required. There is only a limited degree of selection involved. The conversion utility is run against the source data to create the target data store. Often there are a number of intermediate steps. Different tables or segments of the database may be created in different steps. The resultant data is verified at each step. Taking a step-by-step approach, one can minimize the number and extent of the reruns of the conversion. This is another example of minimizing the number of variables that can change at once.

There are a number of approaches to ensuring that the resultant data store has the required integrity. These approaches are identical to the ones used to ensure the integrity of data that is converted due to a change in the application software.

The extent of the effort depends on the degree of reliability that is required. The effort has an obvious cost. The lack of data integrity also has a cost. A financial system requires a high degree of data integrity. It can be argued that the data controlling the operation of a nuclear power station requires even a higher degree of integrity.

MIGRATING FROM ONE APPLICATION SYSTEM TO ANOTHER

Changing or upgrading applications always requires converting data from the old to the new application. These conversions are generally the most complex and require the most effort.

One of the first steps in the conversion process is to decide which is the driving application. What is most important in the conversion process? Being exhaustive in converting the data in the old application or ensuring that the new application has the required fields that it needs to operate effectively. This may not be intuitively obvious. This is not to imply that the decision as to which data to convert is at the whim of the person designing the conversion programs.

There is always a base amount of data that must be converted. Many old applications, however, accumulate various codes and indicators over the years that either lose meaning over time or are particular to that application and are not required in a new application. This situation is more particular to operational applications such as payroll, materials management, etc. When converting data in an operational application, the emphasis is on converting the minimum amount of current data for the new application to fulfill its role and be able to operate. The data requirements of the new application drive the conversion design.

Record-keeping applications on the other hand, such as document management systems and pension administration systems need to retain almost all of the information within the current database. These applications generally hold a tremendous amount of history that needs to be retained. Recordkeeping applications as a rule require that the emphasis be on being exhaustive in converting all of the information within the current database. The data requirements of the old application drive the conversion design.

DATA MIGRATION, CONVERSION, AND LEGACY APPLICATIONS

Generally speaking converting operational applications is considerably easier than converting recordkeeping applications. Populating fields necessary for the operation of a particular piece of software can be done in various ways. New information required for the effective operation of the new application, which is not available from the old application, can be collected from other repositories. This is generally the most time-consuming and complex way of meeting the data requirements of the new application. On the one extreme of the conversion continuum is the possibility of disregarding the old application completely and satisfying the data requirements of the new application by collecting the data from original sources. This approach is particularly useful when the data integrity of the old application is very suspect.

New information also can be provided as defaults based on other data, which are available from the old application. For example, in classifying employees for payroll purposes, give each employee the same classification based on the department where they work. In some instances new information can be fudged if the new data are not critical to the output required. For example, if source medium for an invoice is a required field in a new accounts payable application and it is not a current business requirement to keep source medium, then it could be assumed that all invoices are on paper and the information fudged with that indicator.

Being exhaustive and ensuring that all of the data in an old application are converted to a new application, as a rule, is more complex than meeting the data requirements of a new application. The complexity is not just in the conversion. The old application must be analyzed much more thoroughly to ensure that all of the data are understood and put into proper context. The converted data must be screened much more thoroughly to ensure that everything has been converted appropriately and is in the proper context within the new application. In addition there are still the data requirements of the new application to consider.

Converting historical information often requires shoehorning existing data into fields that were not designed for that data. Very often field conversions are required. For various reasons there may be an array of information in the old application, for which there is only one field in the new application. Pension administration systems are notorious for this. For example, it is not uncommon to have numerous pension enrollment dates depending on the prior plans of which an individual was a member. The new application, especially if it is not sophisticated, may provide only one pension enrollment date.

Acquisitions, mergers, and changes in union agreements and government legislation can cause havoc with historical recordkeeping systems. These then result in a nightmare of a conversion when one of these applications needs to be converted to a new application system. A very common experience is that the conversion routines often approach the complexity of artificial intelligence applications. These are the conversions that tax the abilities of even the most experienced developers. These conversions are also the ones that are potentially the most interesting and challenging to complete.

Once the driving application is determined, the next decision, which is basic to any conversion, is whether an automated conversion is the most effective way of transferring the data to the new application. In certain instances an automated conversion may not be possible. For example, if the source data architecture or the data format is not known and cannot be determined, and there is no export utility provided by the application, then it would be very difficult to develop an automated conversion utility. In certain instances it is simply not cost-effective to develop an automated conversion utility. If the volume of source data is relatively low and the complexity of the data requires conversion routines approaching the complexity of artificial intelligence routines, then a manual conversion effort may be more cost-effective.

The next conversion decision that must be made is how to get the data into the new application. For some reason many application system designers never think of the initial population of their application with the relevant data. It is as if this was supposed to occur by magic. There are four basic ways of populating the new application. In order of relative complexity these are

1. Using a bulk load facility if one is provided by the target application.
2. Generating input transactions into the new application if the application is transaction-based and the format of the transactions is known.
3. Real-time data entry through key stroke emulation.
4. Creating the target database so that it is external to the application.

Bulk load facilities often are provided by most packaged application system vendors. If a bulk load facility is not provided, then the vendor often provides the necessary APIs in order that a bulk load facility can be developed. Bulk load facilities are the most effective tools with which to populate a new application. The bulk load facility generally provides the necessary native edit and validation routines required by the application, while providing the necessary audit capabilities with which to determine the degree of success of the conversion.

If a bulk load facility is not provided and cannot be developed from vendor-provided APIs, then the next best thing is to generate the transactions which ordinarily would be used to enter data into the system. In this way the data is cleansed by the application-provided routines, and one is ensured that the resultant data has the required integrity from the application perspective and is appropriately converted. This approach generally requires multiple conversion routines, possibly one per transaction type and multiple iterations of the conversion as the transactions are loaded.

If neither of the previous methods for converting the data is available, then one can explore using key stroke emulation as a method of entering the data. There are numerous key stroke emulation or screen scraping utilities available that can assist in this endeavor. The trick here is to generate flat files from the source application and then to assemble screens of information that ordinarily are used by the application for data entry. The application is in essence fooled into behaving as if a client was communicating with it for data entry.

There are some technical limitations or challenges with this approach. With large volumes of information, multiple clients with multiple client sessions may have to be established. This is dependent on the efficiency of the client application. The slower the client application and the higher the volume of data, the greater the number of clients who need to operate simultaneously. The more client sessions the higher the risk of malfunction. Auditing this type of conversion effort is usually quite challenging. The audit process needs to be very thorough to ensure that all of the data is converted. As with the previous approaches to conversion, by using this process one is still assured that the data that does make it to the new application have been validated and edited by the application-provided routines.

As a last resort, if it is determined that none of the above alternatives are feasible or available, then one can attempt to use the following approach. The tool of last resort is to convert the data from the source application by constructing the target database from outside the application. In the past, when applications and application data architectures were relatively simple, i.e., a flat file structure, this approach was used quite frequently. The trick here is that the conversion designer must have an intimate knowledge of the application design and underlying data architecture and the context of the data. With a simple application and a simple data architecture, this is not a daunting requirement. With today's complex application packages, however, this approach is almost not supportable. For example, creating the application database for an SAP implementation outside of the application would be out of the question.

Once the decision is made as to which approach to use for the conversion, the actual conversion routines need to be written and tested just like any piece of application code. There usually is no user testing required at this point. When the routines are ready and thoroughly tested the time comes for the actual conversion. This is the trickiest part of the entire effort. It is rare to have the luxury of ample time between running the conversion and certifying the resultant database for live operation. The planning of the actual conversion, checking the resultant database, and certifying the data must be planned with military precision.

Checking the data usually is done using multiple independent audit trails at least providing the count of data records converted and some hash totals on certain fields. The amount of effort expended is usually commensurate with the cost and impact of an error. The users of the data must be involved and have the final sign-off. Whatever audit trails are used, the results and associated statistics must be kept in archives at least for the first few years of operation of the new application. A copy of the source database used for the conversion also should be archived together with some application code that can access the data for reporting purposes. If questions with regard to the conversion process arise at a later date, then one has something to go back to for verification.

After a successful conversion, the last step involves decommissioning the old application. This sounds much simpler than it actually is. It is not unusual; in fact, it is often absolutely mandatory that the old and the new applications be run in parallel for some specified time period. Weaning users from the old application can sometimes be a major challenge. That, however, is not a subject for a chapter on conversions, but is more in the realm of change management.

CONCLUSION

As the preceding discussion illustrates, conversions are not as boring and lacking in challenges as most professionals assume. Neither are conversions as frightening as they are made out to be. Most systems implementations involve some form of data conversion. When the software changes, the data model or the data itself often changes with it. Conversion software design and development can challenge the most creative juices of the most skilled developers. Conversions can be interesting and fun. Keep this in mind the next time you hear the word "conversion."

Chapter 27
Legacy Database Conversion

James Woods

THE MATERIAL PRESENTED IN THIS CHAPTER AIDS THE DATA CENTER MANAGER in planning the move to a relational database system. Encompassing more than the traditional information (e.g., table normalization and project organization), the chapter examines managerial, political, and other considerations and identifies and discusses the more technical considerations.

Before any project is begun, certain questions must be answered. Why is the organization going to a relational database? What are the benefits that managers hope to gain? Now, if the list of benefits comes solely from the vendor's representative, the organization may not get a complete and accurate representation of what is to be gained. Instead, managers need to consider what new capabilities mean specifically to the way the organization does business; for example, how the new system will make it easier or faster to do business, thereby lowering overhead.

One of the things to be considered is the capabilities of the old system as opposed to the capabilities of the new. If the abilities of the new system are drawn as a circle or a set, and the abilities of the old system are likewise drawn, the two should have an area where they overlap, representing the union of the two sets. If project managers target this union to be the result of the conversion, they are losing many of the advantages of the new system. The most desirable objective, therefore, is to gain the whole second set, rather than just the union of those sets. Project managers should not limit the new system by thinking only in terms of the old system.

The legacy system was thought of in terms of applications. The new system should be thought of in terms of models. There is a paradigm shift involved. The most severe shift is to be expected at the technical level. As far as the end user is concerned, there should not be a great difference in the content of the information at the first stage. There certainly may be after the initial conversion because, at that point, it will be possible to implement the wonderful features that have been talked about for years but were never cost-effective to add.

341

0-8493-9832-0/00/$0.00+$.50

Generally, one of the benefits of moving to a modern database system is the facility of the tools. They are better, faster, and more complete. COBOL, for example, may indeed be the mainstay of business because of the legacy systems, but it is not more powerful than a visually oriented diagramming tool that will automatically set up the users' screens, filter the data, and so forth.

PRECONCEPTIONS AND MISCONCEPTIONS

The announcement of an implementation of a legacy-conversion project gives rise to certain predictable reactions within an organization, and the data center manager needs to be aware of the preconceptions members may hold. Two common expectations are

- There will be no problems with the new system, or at least the new system will present fewer problems than historically encountered with the legacy system. Human nature is such that staff will expect the new system to be without challenges. Everyone hopes to move from the old patched system to the new improved system, one that will not have any problems. This, however, is seldom the case. Whereas the likelihood is that the new system will offer many advantages over the old system, those advantages do not exhibit themselves without effort.
- The new system will be more efficient. On the contrary, database performance very well could be lowered when performing the same tasks using a relational system. A database that must make access path decisions at query time is inherently slower than a system that is preconfigured only to retrieve data in a particular way; such decision-making takes time. However, if a computer hardware upgrade also involved is in the conversion project, the increased demand for central processing unit (CPU) cycles is more than compensated for by the increased power of the new machines. The data center manager should note that if the organization is changing only database systems rather than changing database systems as well as moving to a new, more powerful computer platform, users most likely could suffer a performance hit for at least part of the system, perhaps even a major part. This, of course, depends on the efficiency of the existing system. A broad rule is that generalized solutions cost more CPU cycles than specific solutions do. The system does, however, gain great flexibility in return for the additional CPU cycle cost.

To identify and isolate the potential problem areas, the safest route is to perform benchmarks for both the old and new systems. In fact, many organizations make it a condition of sale. The managers can choose samples of transaction data and run them on both systems. At least one of the sample sets should be large because the response of a database system is seldom linear. Managers also should be sure to include critical applications in the benchmark set. These are the applications that must fly in order for the new system to be a success.

BEYOND NORMALIZATION

Any thorough textbook on relational databases outlines clear instructions on applying standard normalization rules to nonnormalized data. (Normalization refers to a procedure used to ensure that a data model conforms to standards that have been developed to avoid duplication of data and to minimize create, update, and delete anomalies of data. Normalization involves the decomposition of a large relation into smaller relations; this process generally improves data integrity and increases the effectiveness of a database system's long-term maintenance.) Textbook instructions on applying normalization rules generally do not cover some of the difficulties that can be encountered in the conversion of a legacy system. The information content must be reverse-engineered from the legacy database, at which point the actual normalization can begin. The exceptions that almost never are examined within the textbooks fall into two categories:

- The Data-Definition Shift. The definition of the data originated at one point in the system's history in one form and has evolved into another. One reason is that the data usage is subject to change over the course of many years. For example, what used to be a facility location may now be labeled "Material Storage Location." This type of shift has important ramifications when deciding how to represent this data in a relational database.
- Incognito Data. In this situation, the data's name is not necessarily indicative of its function. It is, instead, a statement of the data's original intent. In fact, the name of a data item reflects the understanding of the programmer involved at the time that the first program using that data was written.

DATA REDUNDANCY

On occasion, the conversion process uncovers two or more items of data that conflict. Possibly, they have different names, but they serve similar functions. Under the old system, these two or more items do not come into contact, but they may in the new. The function of each piece of data must be understood clearly before a correct model of that data can be made in the relational database.

Summary Data Redundancy

Many systems store summary data because the cost, in terms of time/CPU cycles, is too high to perform the calculations in real time.

However, this stored summary data may not match the actual counts or sums. This causes a difficult and embarrassing situation: The first report on the new system does not balance with the report on the old system. This can be distressing because if the new system is correct the old system has been wrong for an undetermined amount of time. In any case, the summary data should be discarded in favor of direct calculations from the database.

Data Conflicts

It is not unusual to have redundant data conflict. For example, in one system, the vendor record was duplicated for each product line that was supplied by that vendor. There was a bug in the update program that caused the system to update the records of only the active products. During the conversion project, when the data was brought over, sometimes one of the old records was picked up and the demographic data was taken from there. There must be a standard decision reached to apply to all redundant data within the system as to which data will be considered true. The other data must be discarded during the transfer. However, the data center manager should be advised that this could cause the users to see differences between their old reports and new.

HISTORICAL ERROR TRACKS

A scenario common to organizations going through a conversion project is the existence of hidden, damaged data. What very often has happened is that at one time in a company's history an error occurred in an update program; the program was fixed, and the data was corrected. However, some of the damaged data still lingers in the system. It actually may never show up in user reports, but it will stop the new systems' data transfer cold because it violates the very rules that were culled from the program that was supposed to guard that data.

The precaution is simple: Programs must be audited; so must data. For example, a certain field is supposed to contain the groupings of letters INC or SER, which indicate the type of record. Before any transfer attempt is made, a simple program should be written to look at all the records, including historical records if they are to be transferred to the new database, to ascertain that indeed those are the only two codes embedded in the data.

If the database involved employs dictionaries, staff members can use them as a source for the data item name and function, depending on how well the code has been documented. However, if the legacy file or database system does not have a centralized dictionary, then staff members are dependent on the program code to provide the name and function and thereby the implied function of the data item.

AVOIDING HIDDEN PITFALLS

The larger the number of programs and the more extended the lifetime of the system, the more likely it is that the data items involved conflict in intent and purpose and perhaps even form and function. At this point, it might be time to start thinking about the planning of the conversion. Even though the legacy system is presumably well-understood and the relational database is thought to be well-understood, no manager should assume that the translation from the legacy system to the relational database will be the simple matter of applying normalization rules to the legacy system.

The first assumption that leads to numerous problems is that the current staff understands the intricacies of the legacy system. Unless their numbers include at least a few members who originally helped to build the system, the assumption should be otherwise. Each staff member working on the conversion has a specific, applications-oriented view of the data, as opposed to a systemwide view, and the conflicts and the anomalies that staff members in systems development have lived with and accommodated within the application code over the years will not be able to be tolerated easily within the new system. The situation calls for a solution to be found, finally.

The second assumption is that relational databases are well-understood. In academic and theoretical circles, this is a true assumption. It is not, however, necessarily true of the organization's staff, and this staff must be able to support the system. Sending them to the vendor's school is a starting point, but it is not a finish line. They must understand relational databases, but they also must see the need and understand the benefits for the organization.

THE COMPONENTS OF THE CONVERSION PROCESS

The conversion is not a technical process; rather, it is a managerial process with major technical components. The following sections describe two key considerations in the project.

Defining Documentation

Certain preliminary decisions have been made, so the project has been defined loosely. For example, the organization is determined to move to a relational database; managers have chosen which database is to be the replacement system, and a clear picture of the current system has been created. The staff training has been arranged for and the project is set to go in a couple of months. At this point, what is the procedure?

The first step is to document the current legacy system. If the system has inadequate documentation, the project will be besieged by last-minute surprises during the conversion process and while bringing up the new system. If the system is overdocumented (if, indeed, such a thing is possible), the project will be assured of no surprises and a smooth transition. Therefore, logic would dictate that if the staff does err, they should err on the side of too much documentation.

The term documentation requires some definition because what the manager means by documentation and what the programmer means are not necessarily the same thing.

To the programmer, documentation means materials that answer such questions as, "When I get ready to make an application that asks for the insured's middle name, what data item, in what file, will give it to me?" and "Is there an index on that item?"

What managers mean when they ask for documentation is material that answers such questions as, "When I ask you to modify a particular application, is there some documentation that you can use to find out what that application currently does and what the factors are that will be involved in your modification of that process?"

What end users mean when they ask for documentation, of course, is how they "drive" that application. In the context of this chapter, users could include either the end user for terminal systems or the operator for batch systems.

At least three different definitions exist for documentation. For the purposes of the conversion, the term actually refers to a combination of all three, to some degree. Technically, yes, the programmer-level documentation must be complete. The interrelationships that the manager wants must be completely documented. The user information, however, does not need to be complete for the purposes of the conversion, but it still needs to be noted and understood.

One of the determinations to make in the labyrinth of management decisions for a conversion effort of this type is estimating the desired degree of impact on the current organization and end users? Questions to consider are as follows: Will applications look the same? Will they act the same? It may be a highly desirable motive, politically and even sociologically, to keep the impact as small as possible. However, minimizing the effects is not a desirable goal, technically. That would mean the project simply is putting new milk in an old bottle, limiting the benefits of the new system by trying to make the system appear as it always did.

One of the things that users usually insist on, of course, is accurate paper reports. Those reports have, over the years, become a definition of their work. Even though there has been much crowing about the benefits of the paperless office for some time now, it has not materialized yet. This does not mean, however, that the office has to be one or the other, entirely based on paper reports or entirely paperless; it is not an all-or-nothing kind of deal. The new system can reduce the amount of paper and still come out way ahead, and the biggest deterrent to being able to achieve great savings in information acquisition and turnaround is the end user who emotionally may be tied to the reports. It has been their private database; they have been able to mark it up, highlight it, and in general own it. Now, all of a sudden, the new system threatens to take that away from them, and the new database is in a magic box that the end user does not know how to access yet.

Managers must sell the benefits of online information as opposed to printed information. It is to the corporation's benefit to head in this direction, as many of the modern database systems are oriented toward online information retrieval, as opposed to printed information. True, the new system can be created to replicate the old reports, but this approach misses one of the major benefits of an online database.

DATA HISTORY IN THE NEW SYSTEM

Legacy systems typically have a particular way of trapping the data's history. Some remove the record, or a copy of it, to another file. Others record the history within the record itself. A relational database, however, is designed to model the current data flow. It is a model of the current data within the organization. The model reflects the data as it is rather than as it was. Usually, the plan should be to trap the information in a number of historical tables, which must be designed at the outset.

CONCLUSION

In general, time for planning is crucial. Conversions succeed or fail in the planning stage. The management challenge most often is seen as technical, but there are many areas to manage in such an endeavor. The technical planning is a critical activity, but so are managing expectations of the new system, selling the capabilities of the new system, and providing a plan to implement those capabilities into company strategic tools that help put the organization ahead of the competition.

There has never been a conversion that was over planned; however, many have not been planned in sufficient detail to succeed.

Chapter 28
Data Conversion: Doing it Right the First Time

Michael Zimmer

WHEN SYSTEMS DEVELOPERS BUILD INFORMATION SYSTEMS, they usually do not start with a clean slate. Often, they are replacing an existing application. They must always determine if the existing information should be preserved. Usually the older information is transferred to the new system — a process known as data conversion.

Data conversion can involve moving data from flat file systems to relational database management systems (RDBMS). It also can involve changing from systems with loose constraints to new systems with tight constraints.

This chapter focuses on laying the groundwork for successfully executing a data conversion effort the first time around. It is assumed in this chapter that data modeling is being done and that relational database technology is employed. At the logical level, the terms *entity set, entity,* and *attribute* are used in place of the terms *file, record,* and *field.* At the physical level, the terms *table, row,* and *column* are used instead of *file, record,* and *field.* The members of IS engaged in the data conversion effort are referred to as the data conversion team (DCT).

COMMON PROBLEMS WITH DATA

The difficulties of a data conversion effort almost always are underestimated. Usually the conversion costs many times more than originally anticipated. This is invariably the result of an inadequate understanding of the cost and effort required to correct errors in the data. Usually the quality of the existing data is much worse than the users and development team anticipate.

Problems with data can result from missing information and mismatches between the old model (often only implicit) and the new model (usually explicitly documented). Problems also result if the conversion effort is started too late in the project and is under-resourced. The most common sources of problems are data quality and incomplete data.

Costs and Benefits of Data Conversion

Before embarking on data conversion, the data conversion team should decide whether data really needs to be converted and if it is feasible to abandon the noncurrent data. Starting fresh is an option.

The customers may decide that the cost to preserve and correct old information exceeds the benefit expected. Often, they will want to preserve old information, but may not have the resources to correct historical errors. With a data warehouse project, it is given that the data will be converted. Preservation of old information is critical.

The Cost of Not Converting

The DCT first should demonstrate the cost of permitting erroneous information into the new database. It is a decision to be made by user management.

In the long run, permitting erroneous data into the new application usually will be costly. The data conversion team should explain what the risks are to justify the costs for robust programming and data error correction.

Costs of Converting

It is no easier to estimate the cost of a conversion effort than to estimate the cost of any other development effort. The special considerations are that there may be a great deal of manual intervention, and subsequently extra programming, to remedy data errors. A simple copy procedure usually does not serve the organization's needs. If the early exploration of data quality and robust design and programming for the conversion routines is skimped on, IS generally will pay for it.

STEPS IN THE DATA CONVERSION PROCESS

In even the simplest IT systems development projects, the efforts of many players must come together. At the managerial and employee levels, certain users should be involved, in addition to the applications development group, data administration, database administration, computer operations, and quality assurance. The responsibilities of the various groups must be defined clearly.

In the simplest terms, data conversion involves the following steps:

- Determining if conversion is required
- Planning the conversion
- Determining the conversion rules
- Identifying problems
- Writing up the requirements
- Correcting the data
- Programming the conversion
- Running the conversion
- Checking audit reports
- Institutionalizing

Determining if Conversion is Required

In some cases, data does not need to be converted. IS may find that there is no real need to retain old information. The data could be available elsewhere, such as on microfiche. Another possibility is that the current data is so erroneous, incomplete, or inadequate that there is no reason to keep it. The options must be presented for the clients so that they can decide.

Planning the Conversion and Determining the Conversion Rules

Once the DCT and the client have accepted the need for a conversion, the work can be planned in detail. The planning activities for conversion are standard in most respects and are typical of development projects.

Beyond sound project management, it is helpful for the DCT to keep in mind that error correction activities may be particularly time-consuming. Determination of the conversion rules consists of these steps, usually done in sequence:

- Analyzing the old physical data model
- Conducting a preliminary investigation on data quality
- Analyzing the old logical data model
- Analyzing the new logical data model
- Analyzing the new physical data model
- Determining the data mapping
- Determining how to treat missing information

Analyzing the Old Physical Data Model

Some published development methods imply that development starts with a blank slate. As a result, analysis of the existing system is neglected.

The reverse engineering paradigm asserts that the DCT should start with the existing computer application to discern the business rules. Data conversion requires this approach for data analysis. The DCT can look at old documentation, database definitions, file descriptions, and record layouts to understand the current physical data model.

351

Conducting a Preliminary Investigation of Data Quality

Without some understanding of data structures for the current application, it is not possible to look at the quality of the data. To examine the quality of the data, the DCT can run existing reports, do online queries and, if possible, quickly write some fourth-generation language programs to examine issues such as referential, primary key, and domain integrity violations that the users might never notice. When the investigation is done, the findings can be documented formally.

Analyzing the Old Logical Data Model

When the physical structure of the data is understood, it can be represented in its normalized logical structure. This step, although seemingly unnecessary, allows the DCT to specify the mapping in a much more reliable fashion. The results should be documented with the aid of an entity-relationship diagram accompanied by dictionary descriptions.

Analyzing the New Physical Data Model

The new logical model should be transformed into a physical representation. If a relational database is being used, this may be a simple step. Once this model is done, the mapping can be specified.

Determining the Data Mapping

This step is often more difficult than it might seem initially. Usually, the exceptions are one old file-to-one new file, and one old field-to-one new field.

Often there are cases where the old domain must be transformed into a new one; an old field is split into two new ones; two old fields become one new one; or multiple records are looked at to derive a new one. There are many ways of reworking the data, and an unlimited number of special cases may exist. Not only are the possibilities for mapping numerous and complex, in some cases it is not possible at all to map to the new model because key information was not collected in the old system.

Determining How to Treat Missing Information

It is common when doing conversion to discover that some of the data to populate the new application is not available, and there is no provision for it in the old database. It may be available elsewhere as manual records, or it may never have been recorded at all.

Sometimes, this is only an inconvenience — dummy values can be put in certain fields to indicate that the value is not known. In the more serious case, the missing information would be required to create a primary key or a foreign key. This can occur when the new model is significantly different from the old. In this case, the dummy value strategy may be appropriate, but it must be explained fully to the client.

Identifying Problems

Data problems only can be detected after the old data structure is fully understood. Once it is determined what the new model will look like, a deeper analysis of the issue can be done.

A full analysis of the issue includes looking for erroneous information, missing information, redundancies, inconsistencies, missing keys, and any other problem that will make the conversion difficult or impossible without a lot of manual intervention. Any findings should be documented and brought to the attention of the client. Information must be documented in a fashion that makes sense to the client.

Once the problems have been identified, the DCT can help the client identify a corrective strategy. The client must understand why errors have been creeping into the systems. The cause is usually a mixture of problems with the old data structure, problems with the existing input system, and data entry problems that have been ongoing. It may be that the existing system does not reflect the business properly. The users may have been working around the system's deficiencies for years in ways that violated its integrity. In any case, the new system should be tighter than the old one at the programming and database level, should reflect the business properly, and the new procedures should not result in problems with usability or data quality.

Documenting the Requirements

After the initial study of the conversion is done, the findings should be documented. Some of this work will have been done as part of the regular system design. There must also be a design for the conversion programs, whether it is a one-time or an ongoing activity. First-time as well as ongoing load requirements must be examined.

Estimates should include the time necessary to extract, edit, correct, and upload data. Costs for disk storage and CPUs also should be projected. In addition, the sizing requirements should be estimated well in advance of hardware purchases.

Correcting the Data

The client may want to correct the data before the conversion effort begins or may be willing to convert the data over time. It is best to make sure that the data that is converted is error-free, at least with respect to the formal integrity constraints defined for the new model.

If erroneous information is permitted into the new system, it probably will be problematic later. The correction process may involve using the existing system to make changes. Often, the types of errors that are encountered may require some extra programming facilities. Not all systems provide all of the data modification capabilities that might be necessary. In any case, this step sometimes can take months of effort and requires a mechanism for evaluating the success of the correction effort.

Programming the Conversion

The conversion programs should be designed, constructed, and tested with the same discipline used for any other software development. Although the number of workable designs is unlimited, there are a few helpful rules of thumb:

- The conversion program should edit for all business rule violations and reject nonconforming information. The erroneous transactions should go to an error file, and a log of the problem should be written. The soundest course is to avoid putting incorrect data into the new system.
- The conversion programs must produce an audit trail of the transactions processes. This includes control totals, checksums, and date and time stamps. This provides a record of how the data was converted after the job is done.
- Tests should be as rigorous as possible. All design documents and code should be tested in a structured fashion. This is less costly than patching up problems caused by a data corruption in a million record file.
- Provisions should be made for restart in case of interruption in the run.
- It should be possible to roll back to some known point if there are errors.
- Special audit reports should be prepared to run against the old and new data to demonstrate that the procedures worked. This reporting can be done in addition to the standard control totals from the programs.

Running the Conversion

It may be desirable to run a test conversion to populate a test database. Once the programs are ready and volume testing has been done, it is time for the first conversion, which may be only one of many.

If this is a data warehouse application, the conversion could be an ongoing effort. It is important to know how long the initial loads will take so that scheduling can be done appropriately. The conversion then can be scheduled for an opportune cutover time. The conversion will go smoothly if contingencies are built-in and sound risk management procedures are followed. There may be a number of static tables, perhaps used for code lookup that can be converted without as much fanfare, but the main conversion will take time.

At the time planned for cutover, the old production system can be frozen from update or run in parallel. The production database then can be initialized and test records removed (if any have been created). The conversion and any verification and validation routines can be run at this point.

Checking Audit Reports

Once the conversion is finished, special audit reports should be run to prove that it worked, to check control totals, and to deal with any problems. It may be necessary to roll back to the old system if problems are excessive. The new application should not be used until it is verified that the conversion was correct, or a lot of work could be lost.

Institutionalizing

In many cases, as in data warehousing, conversion will be a continuous process and must be institutionalized. Procedural controls are necessary to make sure that the conversion runs on schedule, results are checked rigorously, rejected data is dealt with appropriately, and failed runs are handled correctly.

DATA QUALITY

A strategy to identify data problems early in the project should be in place, though details will change according to the project. A preliminary investigation can be done as soon as the old physical data model has been determined. It is important to document the quality of the current data, but this step may require programming resources. Customers at all levels should be notified if there are data-quality issues to be resolved. Knowledge of the extent of data-quality problems may influence the user's decision to convert or abandon the data.

Keeping the Data Clean

If the data is corrected on a one-time basis, it is important to ensure that more erroneous data is not being generated by some faulty process or programming. There may be a considerable time interval between data correction and conversion to the new system.

Types of Data Abnormalities

There may be integrity problems in the old system. For example, there may be no unique primary key for some of the old files, which almost guarantees redundancy in the data. This violation of entity integrity can be quite serious.

To ensure entity integrity in the new system, the DCT will have to choose which of the old records is to be accepted as the correct one to move into the new system. It is helpful for audit routines to report on this fact. In addition, in the new system it will be necessary to devise a primary key, which may not be available in the old data.

Uniqueness

In many cases, there are other fields that also should be unique and serve as an alternate primary key. In some cases, even if there is primary key integrity, there are redundancies in other alternative keys, which again creates a problem for integrity in the new system.

Referential Integrity

The DCT should determine whether the data correctly reflects referential integrity constraints. In a relational system, tables are joined together by primary key/foreign key links. The information to create this link may not be available in the old data. If records from different files are to be matched and joined, it should be determined whether the information exists to do the join correctly (i.e., a unique primary key and a foreign key). Again, this problem needs to be addressed prior to conversion.

Domain Integrity

The domain for a field imposes constraints on the values that should be found there. IS should determine if there are data domains that have been coded into character or numeric fields in an undisciplined and inconsistent fashion. It should further be determined whether there are numeric domains that have been coded into character fields, perhaps with some non-numeric values. There may be date fields that are just text strings, and the dates may be in any order. A common problem is that date or numeric fields stored as text may contain absurd values with the wrong data type entirely.

Another determination that should be made is whether the domain-coding rules have changed over time and whether they have been recoded. It is common for coded fields to contain codes that are no longer in use and often codes that never were in use. Also, numeric fields may contain out-of-range values. Composite domains could cause problems when trying to separate them for storage in multiple fields. The boundaries for each sub-item may not be in fixed columns.

There may be domains that incorrectly model internal hierarchy. This is common in old-style systems and makes data modeling difficult. There

356

could be attributes based on more than one domain. Not all domain problems will create conversion difficulties, but they may be problematic later if it cannot be proven that these were preexisting anomalies and not a result of the conversion efforts.

Wrong Cardinality

The old data could contain cardinality violations. For example, the structure may say that each employee has only one job record, but in fact some may have five or six. These sorts of problems make database design difficult.

Wrong Optionality

Another common problem is the absence of a record when one should be there. It may be a rule that every employee has at least one record of appointment, but for some reason 1% of old records show no job for an employee. This inconsistency must be resolved by the client.

Orphaned Records

In many cases, a record is supposed to refer back to some other record by making reference to the key value for that other record. In many badly designed systems, there is no key to refer back to, at least not one that uniquely identifies the record. Technically, there is no primary key. In some cases, there is no field available to make this reference, which means that there is no foreign key. In other cases, the key structure is fine, but the actual record referred back to does not exist. This is a problem with referential integrity. This record without a parent is called an orphan.

Inconsistent Redundancy

If each data item is determined fully by its key, there will be no undesirable redundancy, and the new database will be normalized. If attempts at normalization are made where there is redundant information, the DCT will be unable to make consistent automated choices about which of the redundant values to select for the conversion.

On badly designed systems, there will be a great deal of undesirable redundancy. For example, a given fact may be stored in multiple places. This type of redundancy wastes disk storage, but in some cases may permit faster queries.

The problem is that without concerted programming efforts, this redundant information almost certainly is going to become inconsistent. If the old data has confusing redundancies, it is important to determine whether they are due to historical changes in the business rules or historical changes in the values of fields and records.

The DCT also should determine whether the redundancies are found across files or within individual files across records. There may be no way to determine which data is current, and an arbitrary choice will have to be made. If the DCT chooses to keep all of the information to reflect the changes over time, it cannot be stored correctly because the date information will not be in the system. This is an extremely common problem.

Missing Information

When dealing with missing information, it is helpful to determine whether:

- The old data is complete.
- Mandatory fields are filled in.
- All necessary fields are available in the files.
- All records are present.
- Default or dummy values can be inserted where there is missing information.

Date Inconsistencies

When examining the conversion process, it is helpful to determine whether:

- The time dimension is represented correctly.
- The data spans a long enough time period.
- The data correctly reflects the state of the business for the time at which it was captured.
- All necessary date fields are available to model the time dimension properly.
- Dates are stored with century information.
- Date ranges are in the correct sequence within a given record.
- Dates are correct from record to record.

Miscellaneous Inconsistencies

In some fields, there will be values derived from other fields. A derived field might be computed from other fields in the same record or may be a function of multiple records. The derived fields may be stored in an entirely different file. In any case, the derived values may be incorrect for the existing data. Given this sort of inconsistency, it should be determined which is correct — the detail or the summary information.

Intelligent Keys

An intelligent key results from a fairly subtle data-modeling problem. For example, there are two different independent items from the real world, such as employee and department, where the employee is given a key that consists in part of the department key. The implication is that if a department is deleted, the employee record will be orphaned, and if an employee changes departments, the employee key will have to change. When doing a conversion, it would be desirable to remove the intelligent key structure.

Other Problems

Often other problems with the old data cannot be classified easily. These problems involve errors in the data that cannot be detected except by going back to the source, or violations of various arcane constraints that have not been programmed as edit checks in the existing system. There may be special rules that tie field values to multiple records, multiple fields, or multiple files. Although they may not have a practical implication for the conversion effort, if these problems become obvious, they might falsely be attributed to the conversion routines.

THE ERROR CORRECTION PROCESS

The data correction effort should be run as part of a separate subproject. The DCT should determine whether the resources to correct the data can be made available. A wholesale commitment from the owners of the data will be required, and probably a commitment of programming resources as well. Error correction cannot be done within the context of rapid applications development (RAD).

Resources for the Correction Effort

Concerning resources for the correction effort, the best-case scenario would ensure that:

- Resources are obtained from the client if a major correction effort is required.
- Management pays adequate attention to the issue if a data-quality problem is identified.
- The sources of the problem will be identified in a fair and nonjudgmental manner if a data-quality problem is identified.

Choices for Correction

The effort required to write an edit program to look for errors is considerable, and chances are good that this will be part of the conversion code and not an independent set of audit programs. Some of the errors may be detected before conversion begins, but it is likely that many of the problems will be found during the conversion run.

Once data errors are discovered, data can be copied as is, corrected, or abandoned. The conversion programs should reject erroneous transactions and provide reports that explain why data was rejected. If the decision is made to correct the data, it probably will have to be reentered. Again, in some cases, additional programming can help remedy the problems.

Programming for Data Correction

Some simple automated routines can make the job of data correction much easier. If they require no manual intervention, it could be advantageous to simply put them into the main conversion program. However, the program may require that a user make the decision.

If the existing data entry programs are not adequate for large-scale data correction efforts, some additional programs might have to be written for error repair. For example, the existing system may not allow the display of records with a referential integrity problem, which are probably the very records that need correction. Custom programming will be required to make the change.

SPECIFYING THE MAPPING

Often, crucial information needed for the conversion will be missing. If the old system can accommodate the missing information, it may be a matter of keying it in from original paper records. However, the original information may not be available anymore, or it may never have been collected. In that case, it may be necessary to put in special markers to show that the information is not available.

Model Mismatches

It can be difficult to go from an non-normalized structure to a normalized structure because of the potential for problems in mapping from old to new. Many problems are the result of inconsistent and redundant data, a poor key structure, or missing information. If there is a normalized structure in the old system, there probably will not be as many difficulties. Other problems result from changed assumptions about the cardinality of relationships or actual changes in the business rules.

Discovered Requirements

The requirements of a system almost never are understood fully by the user or the developer prior to construction of the system. Some of the data requirements do not become clear until the test conversions are being run. At that point, it may be necessary to go back and revisit the whole development effort. Standard change and scope control techniques apply.

Existing Documentation

Data requirements are rarely right the first time because the initial documentation is seldom correct. There may be abandoned fields, mystery fields, obscure coding schemes, or undocumented relationships. If the documentation is thorough, many data conversion pitfalls can be avoided.

Possible Mapping Patterns

The mapping of old to new is usually very complex. There seems to be no useful canonical scheme for dealing with this set of problems. Each new conversion seems to consist of myriad special cases. In the general case, a given new field may depend on the values found in multiple fields contained in multiple records of a number of files. This works the other way as well — one field in an old record may be assigned to different fields or even to different tables, depending on the values encountered.

If the conversion also requires intelligent handling of updates and deletes to the old system, the problem is complicated even further. This is true when one source file is split into several destination files and, at the same time, one destination file receives data from several source files. Then, if just one record is deleted in a source file, some fields will have to be set to null in the destination file, but only those coming from the deleted source record. This method, however, may violate some of the integrity rules in the new database.

It may be best to specify the mapping in simple tabular and textual fashion. Each new field will have the corresponding old fields listed, along with any special translation rules required. These rules could be documented as decision tables, decision trees, pseudo code, or action diagrams.

Relational Mathematics

In database theory, it is possible to join together all fields in a database in a systematic manner and to create what is called the "universal relation." Although this technique has little merit as a scheme for designing or implementing a database, it may be a useful device for thinking about the mapping of old to new. It should be possible to specify any complex mapping as a view based on the universal relation. The relational algebra or the relational calculus could be used as the specification medium for detailing the rules of the mapping in a declarative fashion.

DESIGNING THE CONVERSION

Before starting to design a computer program, reentering the data manually from source records should be considered as a possibility.

Special Requirements for Data Warehousing

Data warehousing assumes that the conversion issue arises on a routine, periodic basis. All of the problems that arise in a one-time conversion must be dealt with for an initial load, and then must be dealt with again for the periodic update.

In a data warehouse situation, there most likely will be changes to source records that must be reflected into the data warehouse files. As discussed previously, there may be some complex mapping from old to new, and updates and deletes will increase the complexity greatly. There will have to be a provision for add, change, and delete transactions. A change transaction often can be handled as a paired delete and add, in some cases simplifying the programming.

Extra Space Requirements

In a conversion, it will be necessary to have large temporary files available. These could double the amount of disk space required for the job. If it is not possible to provide this extra storage, it will be necessary to ensure that the design does not demand extra space.

Choice of Language

The criteria for programming languages is not going to be too different from that used in any other application area. The programming language should be chosen according to the skills of the IS team and what will run on the organization's hardware. The most appropriate language will allow error recovery, exception handling, control totals reporting, checkpoint and restart capabilities, full procedural capability, and adequate throughput.

Most third-generation languages are sufficient, if an interface to the source and target databases or file systems is available. Various classes of programs could be used, with different languages for each. For example, the records may be extracted from the old database with one proprietary product, verified and converted to the new layout with C, and input into the new database with a proprietary loader.

SQL as a Design Medium

The SQL language should be powerful enough to handle any data conversion job. The problem with SQL is that it has no error-handling capabilities and cannot produce a satisfactory control totals report as part of the update without going back and requerying the database in various ways.

Despite the deficiencies of SQL as a robust data conversion language, it may be ideal for specifying the conversion rules. Each destination field could have a corresponding SQL fragment that gave the rules for the mapping in a declarative fashion. The use of SQL as a design medium should lead to a very tight specification. The added advantage is that it translates to an SQL program very readily.

Processing Time

IS must have a good estimate for the amount of elapsed time and CPU time required to do the conversion. If there are excessive volumes of data, special efforts will be required to ensure adequate throughput. These efforts could involve making parallel runs, converting overnight and over weekends, buying extra-fast hardware, or fine-tuning programs.

These issues are not unique to conversions, but they must not be neglected to avoid surprises on the day of cutover to the new system. These issues are especially significant when there are large volumes of historical data for an initial conversion, even if ongoing runs will be much smaller.

Interoperability

There is a strong possibility that the old system and the new system will be on different platforms. There should be a mechanism for transferring the data from one to the other. Tape, disk, or a network connection could be used. It is essential to provide some mechanism for interoperability. In addition, it is important to make sure that the media chosen can support the volumes of data and provide the necessary throughput.

Routine Error Handling

The conversion routine must support sufficient edit code to enforce all business rules. When erroneous data is encountered, there might be a policy of setting the field to a default value. At other times, the record may be rejected entirely.

In either case, a meaningful report of the error encountered and the resultant action should be generated. It will be best if the record in error is sent off to an error file. There may be some larger logical unit of work than the record. If so, that larger unit should be sent to the error file and that transaction rolled back.

Control Totals

Every run of the conversion programs should produce control totals. At a minimum, there should be counts for every input record, every rejected record, every accepted record, and every record inserted into each output file or table. Finer breakdowns are desirable for each of these types of inputs and outputs. Every conversion run should be date- and time-stamped with start and end times, and the control report should be filed after inspection.

RECOVERY FROM ERROR

Certain types of errors, such as a power failure, will interrupt the processing. If the system goes out in the middle of a 20-hour run, there will have to be some facility for restarting appropriately. Checkpoint and restart mechanisms are desirable. The operating system may be able to provide these facilities. If not, there should be an explicit provision in the design and procedures for dealing with this possibility. In some cases, it may be necessary to ensure that files are backed up prior to conversion.

Audit Records

After the data has been converted, there must be an auditable record of the conversion. This is also true if the conversion is an ongoing effort. In general, the audit record depends on the conversion strategy. There may be counts, checksums (i.e., row and column), or even old vs. new comparisons done with an automated set of routines. These audit procedures are not the same as the test cases run to verify that the conversion programs worked. They are records produced when the conversions are run.

CONCLUSION

Almost all IS development work involves conversion of data from an old system to a new application. This is seldom a trivial exercise, and in many projects it is the biggest single source of customer dissatisfaction. The conversion needs to be given serious attention, and the conversion process needs to be planned as carefully as any other part of the project. Old applications are fraught with problems, and errors in the data will be common. The more tightly programmed the new application, the more problematic the conversion.

It is increasingly common to make the conversion part of an ongoing process, especially when the operational data is in one system, and the management information in another. Any data changes are made on the operational system and then, at periodic intervals, copied to the other application. This is a key feature of the data warehouse approach. All of the same considerations apply.

In addition, it will be important to institutionalize the procedures for dealing with conversion. The conversion programs must be able to deal with changes to the operational system by reflecting them in the data warehouse. Special care will be required to design the programs accordingly.

Section VI
Database Servers and Universal Server Technology

DATABASE SERVERS ARE AN IMPORTANT COMPONENT OF THE CLIENT/ SERVER APPLICATION MODEL. Database servers typically reside on a server platform running on top of a 32+ bit operating system, such as Windows NT, UNIX, AIX, or MVS. They service applications which also run on client platforms running 16 bit or 32 bit operating systems. The client/server model supports a continuum of architectures ranging from "thin server-fat client" to "fat server-thin client," and anywhere in between. The "thin" and "fat" terminology refers to the amount of processing or business logic residing on the client or the server. In a thin client model, the application interface resides on the client platform and captures or displays information to the user. The data is transferred to the fat server where the business processing occurs. In a fat client model, the user interface still captures and presents data to the user, however, the processing also occurs on the client platform. In this model, the thin server acts as a data repository with minimal or no processing. Between these extremes, the business processing can be apportioned between the client and server platforms. The next generation application model extends the basic client/server model by including a web-browser on the client platform. Although this model offers many advantages over the strictly thin/fat client/server model, the role of the database server is just as important. It is still the guardian of corporate data.

At a high level, a database server consists of the following components: a data repository, a database engine consisting of a query parser and optimizer, relational database compatibility, SQL (SEQUEL) dialect, database extensions and a security framework. Distributed database servers allow components to be invoked remotely. One of the major enhancements of database servers over traditional databases is the programmable database engine. This integrates an SQL dialect with database extensions to maintain applications within the database server repository. Applications running on client platforms can invoke applications stored within the database server in this architecture. This provided dramatic improvements to client/server applications by moving processing logic to the database server platform, thus reducing data transfer volumes over local area networks and wide area networks. The database extensions or enhancements provide the capability of writing powerful applications that imbed SQL commands with procedural constructs. In the future, procedural constructs are expected to be supported through standard languages such as JAVA and C++. Microsoft is also expecting to incorporate Visual Basic script into many of their products, including SQL Server. Such moves will allow components or applets to be distributed and redistributed freely across different technical requirements. Currently, the database extensions are, in essence, proprietary.

Chapter 29, "Using DB2 for OS/390 Stored Procedures," examines the syntax and approach for writing stored procedures in DB2.

Chapter 30, "Microsoft SQL Server: Key Transact-SQL Features," focuses on the common elements of the Transact-SQL dialect that allows SQL Server to be the world's first programmable database server. The constructs in this section provide the reader with the tools to write sophisticated database objects, such as stored procedures, views, and triggers.

Chapter 31, "Selecting Universal Data Server Technology," examines the features offered by Universal Data Servers as compared to database servers. Universal-data servers extend relational-data servers to support new data types. Database administrators, information-processing managers, information technologists, and long-term planners will find this article useful in solving management problems involving new types of data.

Chapter 32, "Managing Complex Data Types: Middleware, Universal Database Servers, and Object-Oriented Data Servers," examines some of the additional data types that have grown in popularity over the last few years. This section examines four mechanisms: data extraction, middleware, universal data servers, and object-oriented data servers for supporting complex data types compound and multimedia. The features, strengths, and weaknesses of each mechanism are summarized. These four mechanisms represent four points of a long-term migration strategy to support the data management of complex data types.

Chapter 33, "Creating Effective Batch SQL Jobs," examines techniques in coding batch SQL routines to build highly reliable and well-performing jobs.

Chapter 34, "The Advanced Art of Indexing," describes the developments and challenges of indexing. The chapter states that efficient retrieval is especially important for decision support applications, which often lack appropriate indexing techniques. Various indexing techniques such as B-Trees, bit-maps, and inverted files are analyzed.

Chapter 29

Using DB2 For OS/390 Stored Procedures

Gary Curdie

A DB2 STORED PROCEDURE IS A PROGRAM ON THE HOST (MAINFRAME) that is invoked by another program on any platform using an SQL call as opposed to a regular program call. The Stored Procedure program can be written in several languages, such as COBOL, Assembler, PL/I, C, and C++ (note that all examples given in this article are in COBOL). The calling program can be written in any language that can issue an SQL call statement (this can also include many development tools, such as Powerbuilder).

A Stored Procedure consists of a series of DB2 operations plus other logic to manipulate the data that is required by the calling program as indicated by the call request. While the data most commonly used would be DB2 data, it can access anything a regular program can (some of these accesses can be quite cumbersome). The accesses, although most commonly a read, can be any of the standard read, add, update, or delete operations.

The Stored Procedure program can call other programs, as any program can, using regular calls, but cannot issue an SQL call itself.

Stored Procedures were introduced to DB2 for OS/390 with Version 4. The capabilities were quite limited at that time, to only being able to pass back and forth a parameter list, and all modules would have to be statically linked. In this version, its use is somewhat limited.

Version 5 of DB2 enhanced Stored Procedures significantly, adding the much requested and needed result sets for passing back, and allowing modules to be static.

Rumor has it that Version 6 of DB2 will introduce several other significant changes to Stored Procedures.

WHY USE A STORED PROCEDURE?

The main reason one might use a Stored Procedure is to reduce communication resource requirements between a client and a host. With a Stored

0-8493-9832-0/00/$0.00+$.50
© 2000 by CRC Press LLC

Procedure, only one communication to the host is required to execute a series of SQL commands, instead of one communication per command. In addition, there will only be one authorization check required, to check if the client is authorized to execute the Stored Procedure, as opposed to a check for each table access. Both these items mean an improvement in execution time for the process. Note that while use of a Stored Procedure can provide performance improvements, there is overhead involved in executing a Stored Procedure that can nullify the performance improvements, and potentially hinder performance. The general guideline (from IBM) is that if four or fewer DB2 accesses are required, performance improvements should not be expected from the use of a Stored Procedure.

By calling a Stored Procedure rather than executing the DB2 calls remotely, all DB2 accesses are isolated in a central location. This gives more control over the data accesses being done, in that they can be tuned for optimal performance, and can be run as static SQL, giving a consistent access to the data. This is significant because many PC development tools (such as Powerbuilder) and some mainframe tools perform DB2 accesses using dynamic SQL, meaning that the access path is redetermined each time the access is done, and there is no guarantee that the access generated for the SQL is efficient.

Look at an example of the differences between doing a similar operation with a Stored Procedure or by just executing the SQL statements individually. For the example, the Client Procedure requires that data be retrieved from a table, and from that, an update to another table must be done, followed by an insert into yet another table.

When a Client Procedure calls a Stored Procedure, an authorization check is done to see if the Stored Procedure can be used; and if so, a communication to the Stored Procedure is sent, passing a parameter list. The Stored Procedure will execute the **SELECT, UPDATE,** and **INSERT** statements that are required, with the **SELECT** and **UPDATE** using an optimal access path to get at the data that was ensured through the efforts of the developer of the Stored Procedure and his DBA when the Stored Procedure was bound. On completion of execution, the Stored Procedure sends a communication message back to the Client Procedure, passing back a parameter list, and possibly making available a result set for access. Through this process, one obtains one authorization check and two communication messages between the client and the host.

When a Client Procedure tries to execute the three SQL statements directly, for each of the **SELECT, UPDATE,** and **INSERT** commands to be executed, an authorization check must be done to see if that statement can be executed, a communication is sent to the host to pass the required information as to what DB2 should do, and a communication is sent back to the

Client Procedure, providing the output and an SQLCODE from the execution of the DB2 instruction. Here, one has three authorization checks and six communications between client and host. Because the usual bottleneck in client/server applications is the time required for communications, it is fairly obvious that using a Stored Procedure can reduce the number of communications and, therefore, can reduce the execution time of the application. In addition, because the SQL statements will be executed dynamically (most of the time), the access paths are determined at execution time, and depending on the DB2 catalog statistics that are active at time of execution, it is possible that a less than optimal access path may be selected.

HOW DOES A STORED PROCEDURE WORK?

A Stored Procedure receives a parameter list from the calling program, and returns a parameter list and possibly one or more result sets to the calling program. The fact that it can return result sets differentiates it, in one way, from a normal called program. Note that this feature is only available as of DB2 Version 5.

Stored Procedures run in the DB2 Stored Procedure Address Space (SPAS). Any program that a Stored Procedure calls must also run in the SPAS. All programs with DB2 usage that run in the SPAS require attachment to DB2 via the DB2 remote Call Attachment Facility (CAF). For a COBOL program, this requires the use of a special precompile option that indicates that for any communication with DB2, CAF will be used instead of the regular TSO attach. This means that any program that is run as a Stored Procedure cannot be run as a regular program, because the wrong attachment facility would be used.

DB2 must be told that a program is a Stored Procedure. This is done by having it defined to the SYSIBM.SYSPROCEDURES DB2 catalog table. This gives DB2 various information about the Stored Procedure, including the input/output parameters and the number of result sets to be returned. This only applies to the Stored Procedures themselves, and not to all programs that run in the SPAS.

HOW TO CODE A STORED PROCEDURE IN COBOL

Communication Area

Communication with a Stored Procedure should be through a communication area defined in the linkage section. It is recommended that the communication area be defined in a copybook that could also be used by any program that might call the DB2 Stored Procedure. This looks exactly the same as it would if the Stored Procedure was a regular called program module. The communication copybook should look something like:

```
01 STATS-INPUT-INFO PIC X(44).
01 STATS-INPUT-INFO-BKDN REDEFINES STATS-INPUT-INFO.
05 STATS-TEAM-NAME PIC X(40).
05 STATS-YEAR-ENDING PIC 9(04).
01 STATS-OUTPUT-INFO PIC X(87).
01 STATS-OUTPUT-INFO-BKDN REDEFINES STATS-OUTPUT-INFO.
05 STATS-LEAGUE PIC X(04).
05 STATS-SEASON PIC X(09).
05 STATS-STATUS-CODE PIC S9(04) COMP.
88 STATS-STATUS-OK VALUE ZERO.
88 STATS-INVALID-INPUT VALUE +200.
88 STATS-UNEXPECTED-SQLCODE VALUE +900.
05 STATS-SQLCODE PIC S9(04) COMP.
05 STATS-SQLERRMC PIC X(70).
05 STATS-SQL-ACTION PIC X(08).
88 STATS-SELECT-ACTION VALUE 'SELECT '.
88 STATS-OPEN-CSR-ACTION VALUE 'OPEN CSR'.
...
05 STATS-SQL-OBJECT PIC X(18).
88 STATS-TEAM-TABLE VALUE 'TEAM'.
88 STATS-CSR-BATTING VALUE 'CSR_BATTING'.
...
```

This copybook should be used in the Linkage Section as follows:

```
LINKAGE SECTION.
EXEC SQL INCLUDE STATSPRM END-EXEC.
```

The input/output parameters for the Stored Procedure are specified by the procedure division statement. This statement should look like:

```
PROCEDURE DIVISION USING STATS-INPUT-INFO
STATS-OUTPUT-INFO.
```

Input parameters are not required (just the call itself might be sufficient to trigger some sort of operation). Output parameters are also not required; however, it is recommended to at least have a Status Code and SQL error fields to pass back information as to how successful the execution of the Stored Procedure was. Note that the various parameters can be passed as group items, as is done in the example (the 01 levels), or as individual parameters. There is a limit of 3000 bytes as to the length of the definition of the parameter list. Using the group level will ensure this is not a problem and make things like the CALL parameter list, both in the Stored Procedure and the client program, easier to manage. However, it could require more work by the client program to separate out the various fields. Use should be determined by one's requirements.

Reusable and Reentrant

It is desirable for a Stored Procedure to be both reusable and reentrant. To make a Stored Procedure reusable and reentrant:

- Define the appropriate parameters to SYSPROCEDURES (described later).
- Validate all input parameters.
- Initialize all output parameters.

STORED PROCEDURE RESULT SETS

Result sets are a feature introduced to Stored Procedures in Version 5. A DB2 select statement can retrieve zero, one, or many rows of data. A result set allows one to pass back multiple rows of data to a client program in an area external to the normal communication area. This is a major advantage. It eliminates the need to define a huge storage area with large arrays to return multiple rows of data, and avoids the size limits on call parameters. In addition, for client tools that can handle multiple rows as a set type retrieval (as opposed to a COBOL program that can only deal with one row at a time), this greatly simplifies their processing.

Returning a Result Set

A Stored Procedure has the ability to return one or more result sets to the calling program outside of the communication area. A result set is created via a special DB2 cursor that uses the WITH RETURN option. This would look like:

```
EXEC SQL
    DECLARE CURSOR CSR_BATTING WITH RETURN FOR
    SELECT PLAYER, AB, R, H, 2B, ...
    FROM BASEBALL_BATTING
    WHERE TEAM = :TEAM-NAME
    AND SEASON = :SEASON
    AND LEAGUE = :LEAGUE
    ORDER BY PLAYER
    FOR FETCH ONLY
END-EXEC.
```

Most DB2 cursor options are available for use, including WITH HOLD.

To create the result set, a DB2 OPEN CURSOR is issued in the Stored Procedure. The FETCHes and CLOSE cursor will be done in the calling program. If one issues a FETCH in the Stored Procedure, it will reduce the number of rows returned in the result set by one (only unread rows are returned in the result set). If a CLOSE is executed, no result set will be returned.

If the potential exists for the Stored Procedure to be called by a program that uses checkpointing, the result set cursor should be declared with the WITH HOLD option. This will prevent the result set from being lost when a checkpoint is issued.

A Stored Procedure can return more than one result set. All that is required for each result set is to have a cursor defined and left open, as was described earlier. In addition, the Stored Procedure does not have to return the same number of result sets every time it is used.

A Stored Procedure that returns a result set(s) also returns the communication area.

COMMIT AND ROLLBACK

A DB2 COMMIT cannot be executed in a Stored Procedure. The COMMIT should be executed in the calling program (or it can be automatically executed by setting a parameter in the Stored Procedure definition to the DB2 catalog).

While a COMMIT cannot be executed, a DB2 ROLLBACK can. This will not actually execute a rollback, but will put the whole process in a must rollback state, which will require the calling program to execute a rollback. This should be used to back out all changes made during the execution of the Stored Procedure if a problem arises that would invalidate the changes made.

HOW TO CODE A COBOL PROGRAM TO CALL A STORED PROCEDURE

Communication Area

A COBOL program that calls a Stored Procedure should use the communication area defined for it. This means using the same copybook that was created with the Stored Procedure. It should be included (EXEC SQL INCLUDE) in the Working-Storage Section (as opposed to the Linkage Section used in the Stored Procedure).

Output Indicator Variable

An output indicator variable can be used (and should be if possible) when calling a Stored Procedure. What this does is limit the size of the information passed to the Stored Procedure to only be the input parameters. Both input and output parameters are returned by the Stored Procedure. This can improve performance because the less information passed to the Stored Procedure, the more efficient the communication will be.

The output indicator should be defined like:

```
77 STATS-OUT-INDICATOR PIC S9(04) COMP.
```

To make use of the indicator, a value of –1 should be moved to it prior to making the Stored Procedure call, and the indicator will be used in the call statement (see subsequent examples of how to initiate an SQL CAL).

Calling a Stored Procedure

A Stored Procedure program is called using an SQL Call statement instead of a regular program call. The values of the input and input/output parameters in the communication area are set to what is to be passed to the Stored Procedure, and the call is issued. If an output indicator variable is to be used, it should be set to –1 (as described previously).

The call to the Stored Procedure, using the communication area and output indicator variable described earlier, would look as follows:

```
EXEC SQL
CALL STATSERV (:STATS-INPUT-INFO
, :STATS-OUTPUT-INFO
INDICATOR :STATS-OUT-INDICATOR)
END-EXEC.
```

where STATSERV is the name of the Stored Procedure.

On return from the Stored Procedure, there are two possible SQLCODEs that can be expected: 000 and +466. Any other SQLCODE that is returned indicates that there was a problem with the call to the Stored Procedure, and should be dealt with appropriately.

A 000 SQLCODE indicates that the call to and return from the Stored Procedure was successful, and the Communication Area was returned. This does not indicate that the Stored Procedure executed properly — only that the communication worked properly. Any return code that might come back from the Stored Procedure needs to be checked to see if it executed properly, and if not, it should be handled appropriately. It should be noted that if a result set(s) is expected to be returned, 000 is not a valid SQL-CODE, as this indicates no result sets were returned.

A +466 SQLCODE indicates that the call to and return from the Stored Procedure was successful, the Communication Area was returned, and one or more result sets are available for retrieval. As with a 000 SQLCODE, there is a need to check passed back return codes. If result sets were not expected, +466 is not a valid SQLCODE.

RETRIEVING KNOWN RESULT SETS

The following process outlines how to retrieve a result set where it is known what result set is being retrieved and what columns are being passed back.

The first step in the retrieval of a result set after the SQL CALL has successfully completed is to determine the address (pointer) of the result set(s) that is to be retrieved. This address will be assigned to a variable known as a locator variable. This locator variable will be defined in Working-Storage as:

```
01 WS-STATS-LOC-BATTING USAGE SQL TYPE IS
RESULT-SET-LOCATOR
VARYING.
```

Note that locator variables must be defined as level 01 variables. The name used for a locator variable can be anything. There can be more than one locator variable defined in a program.

To get the appropriate value assigned to the locator variable(s), an **ASSOCIATE LOCATORS** command is executed. It would look like:

```
EXEC SQL
ASSOCIATE LOCATORS (:WS-STATS-LOC-BATTING
, :WS-STATS-LOC-PITCHING)
WITH PROCEDURE STATSERV
END-EXEC.
```

The locator values are assigned in the order that the cursors were opened in the Stored Procedure. If there are less result sets returned than the number of locator variables given, the remaining locator variable(s) will be assigned a value of zero. This example indicates that there are probably two results sets being returned.

Each Stored Procedure call that returns result sets would need its own **ASSOCIATE LOCATORS** command issued, and there should be at most one per Stored Procedure call.

Once the locator variables have been associated with the result sets, a cursor needs to be defined for each result set to retrieve them. This is done by using an **ASSOCIATE CURSOR** command, and would look like:

```
EXEC SQL

ALLOCATE BATTING-CRSR CURSOR

FOR RESULT SET :WS-STATS-LOC-BATTING

END-EXEC.
```

BATTING-CRSR is the name that is assigned to the cursor. Note that this cursor name does not have to be the same name as is used by the related cursor in the Stored Procedure being called.

Defining a cursor to retrieve a result set is different from defining a regular cursor in that a different command (**ALLOCATE CURSOR** instead of **DECLARE CURSOR**) is used, and it must be executed in the Procedure Division after a value has been assigned to the host (locator) variable (as opposed to the Declare, which can be done in Working-Storage or anywhere in the Procedure Division as long as it is executed prior to the Open Cursor).

Once the cursor for the result set is allocated, to retrieve the rows, all that is required is to execute FETCH statements, as would be done with any cursor, until a non-zero SQLCODE is returned. Note that an OPEN CURSOR is not required, as this, effectively, has been executed in the Stored Procedure.

Retrieving an Unknown Number of Result Sets

It is possible that the Stored Procedure might not always return the same number of result sets, and the calling program will have no way of knowing until after the Call to the Stored Procedure completes.

The first and most straightforward possibility is that, depending on some criteria, the Stored Procedure might sometimes return N result sets, and sometimes N+M results sets where the first N are the same ones as in the first scenario. In this situation, the coding of the Associate Locators would be to assign locator values for the maximum number of result sets possible (N+M). Then the program would retrieve from all the result sets until one is found with a zero locator variable. This approach will only work if the result sets are always opened in the Stored Procedure in the same order.

The other possibility is that, as well as having a varying number of result sets being returned, what these result sets are, and what Stored Procedure cursors they are related to, is not known either. In this case, a slightly different approach must be used.

To determine the various cursors that are opened by a particular call to a Stored Procedure, a DESCRIBE PROCEDURE statement must be executed after the Call. This would look like:

```
MOVE +9 TO WS-MAX-NO-OF-SETS.

EXEC SQL

DESCRIBE PROCEDURE STATSERV

INTO :WS-PROCEDURE-SQLDA

END-EXEC.
```

This puts the information about the result sets returned from the Stored Procedure into the SQLDA. The SQLDA was previously used in DB2 with the DESCRIBE statement, so that the number of columns, their names, and their definitions could be varied in a cursor FETCH. This concept has been extended for use with the DESCRIBE PROCEDURE to vary the number and names of result sets being returned from a DB2 Stored Procedure.

In this example, the value assigned to WS-MAX-NO-OF-SETS (the maximum number of result sets that might be returned from the Stored Procedure) will enable the WS-PROCEDURE-SQLDA area to receive all the needed information. Without the assignment of a value to WS-MAX-NO-OF-SETS, no information identifying the cursors opened by the Stored Procedure will be returned.

A sample layout for an SQLDA for use with DESCRIBE PROCEDURE is:

```
01 WS-PROCEDURE-SQLDA.

05 FILLER PIC X(12).

05 WS-MAX-NO-OF-SETS PIC S9(04) COMP.

05 WS-NO-RESULT-SETS PIC S9(04) COMP.

05 WS-RESULT-SET OCCURS 1 TO 9 TIMES

DEPENDING ON WS-MAX-NO-OF-SETS.

10 FILLER PIC X(04).

10 WS-RESULT-SET-LOCATOR POINTER.

10 FILLER PIC X(04).

10 WS-CURSOR-NAME.

49 WS-CURSOR-NAME-LNGTH PIC S9(04) COMP.

49 WS-CURSOR-NAME-CHAR PIC X(18).
```

The information that is put in the SQLDA includes:

- WS-NO-RESULT-SETS contains the number of result sets returned for the Stored Procedure.
- Each occurrence of WS-RESULT-SET (up to the value of WS-MAX-NO-OF-SETS) represents one of the result sets in the order the related cursors were opened in the Stored Procedure, and for each:
  - WS-CURSOR-NAME contains the name of the related cursor in the Stored Procedure.
  - WS-RESULT-SET-LOCATOR is the locator value for the result set that is normally determined using an ASSOCIATE LOCATORS statement.

Note that the names of the individual fields are irrelevant, and can be called anything that is desired. However, the layout of the area must be defined in this manner (the FILLERs are place holders for fields in the SQLDA that are not used for this purpose).

This allows the processing of result sets to be done like:

```
MOVE +1 TO INDX-CURSOR.

PERFORM UNTIL (INDX-CURSOR > WS-NO-RESULT-SETS)

OR (ERROR-FOUND)

EVALUATE WS-CURSOR-NAME-CHAR (INDX-CURSOR)

WHEN 'BATTING'

PERFORM RETRIEVE-BATTING-STATS

WHEN 'PITCHING'

PERFORM RETRIEVE-PITCHING-STATS

...

WHEN OTHER

handle error

END-EVALUATE

ADD +1 TO INDX-CURSOR

END-PERFORM.
```

Once the cursors to be retrieved from have been determined, the locator variables must be assigned for each cursor. In this situation, the **ASSOCIATE LOCATORS** command is not used, but instead the WS-RESULT-SET-LOCATOR field (a pointer variable) is assigned to the locator variable. This requires two things: redefining the locator variable appropriately and assigning the WS-RESULT-SET-LOCATOR field to it. To do this, the locator variable(s) should be defined as:

```
01 WS-LOCATOR-1 USAGE SQL TYPE IS

RESULT-SET-LOCATOR

VARYING.

01 WS-LOCATOR-1-PTR REDEFINES WS-LOCATOR-1 POINTER.
```

and the value would be assigned by:

```
SET WS-LOCATOR-1-PTR TO WS-RESULT-SET-LOCATOR
    (INDX-CURSOR).
```

Once the values have been assigned to the locator variables, retrieval works as usual with the **ALLOCATE CURSOR**commands, and then the FETCHing of the cursors.

Retrieving a Result Set with Varying Columns

This is a much more complex situation, and should be avoided if possible.

It is possible that the Stored Procedure might not always return the same columns in a result set. This could mean that it returns a different number of columns, or even a completely different set of columns. This would only be the case if the cursor to create the result set was defined on a dynamically prepared SELECT statement where the columns retrieved are determined by some criteria. Note that this is different from having two cursors defined to select from the same table, but return different columns. For the latter situation, the previously mentioned technique would be used to retrieve indeterminate result sets.

To determine the various columns that are returned in a result set by a particular call to a Stored Procedure, a DESCRIBE CURSOR statement must be executed after the ALLOCATE CURSORcommand. As with the DESCRIBE PROCEDURE statement, DESCRIBE CURSOR makes use of the SQLDA, and looks like:

```
MOVE +21 TO WS-MAX-NO-OF-COLUMNS.

EXEC SQL

DESCRIBE CURSOR BATTING_CRSR

INTO :WS-CURSOR-SQLDA

END-EXEC.
```

This puts the information about the columns returned in the result set from the Stored Procedure into an SQLDA. In this example, the value assigned to WS-MAX-NO-OF-COLUMNS (the maximum number of columns that might be defined for the result set) will enable the WS-SQLDA area to receive all the needed information. Without the assignment of a value to WS-MAX-NO-OF-COLUMNS, no information identifying the columns of the result set will be returned.

A sample layout for an SQLDA for use with DESCRIBE CURSOR is:

```
01 WS-CURSOR-SQLDA.

05 FILLER PIC X(12).

05 WS-MAX-NO-OF-COLUMNS PIC S9(04) COMP.

05 WS-NO-COLUMNS PIC S9(04) COMP.

05 WS-COLUMN OCCURS 1 TO 21 TIMES

DEPENDING ON WS-MAX-NO-OF-COLUMNS.

10 WS-COLUMN-TYPE PIC S9(04) COMP.

10 WS-COLUMN-LENGTH PIC S9(04) COMP.

10 FILLER PIC X(08).

10 WS-COLUMN-NAME.

49 WS-COLUMN-NAME-LNGTH PIC S9(04) COMP.

49 WS-COLUMN-NAME-CHAR PIC X(18).
```

The information that is put in the SQLDA is:

- WS-NO-COLUMNS contains the number of columns returned for the result set
- Each occurrence of WS-COLUMN (up to the value of WS-SQLD) represents one of the columns in the order they were selected for the result set, and for each:
  - WS-COLUMN-NAME contains the name of the column being retrieved in the result set
  - WS-COLUMN-TYPE contains a code for the data type of the column (what these codes mean are in the SQL Reference, Appendix C)
  - WS-COLUMN-LENGTH contains the length attribute for the column.

After determining what columns have been retrieved, only FETCHing the data from the result set remains to be done. While determining what columns have been retrieved is not difficult, the problem in retrieving the rows is that, in its normal form, a FETCH statement has static variables. This means that a separate FETCH statement must be defined for every possible combination of columns that can be returned, and logic to determine which one will be used must be coded. Hopefully, this is a manageable number.

There is a way of having variable columns in a FETCH using the SQLDA, as can be done when using a normal DESCRIBE statement on a cursor. This technique could also be applied to a FETCH for a DESCRIBE CURSOR situation.

GETTING A STORED PROCEDURE RUNNING

Compiling

As with any DB2 program, to create a running load module for a Stored Procedure, the program must be precompiled, compiled, and linked.

For a Stored Procedure, this procedure differs for Version 4 and Version 5.

The precompile of a Stored Procedure in Version 5 is slightly different from a regular DB2 program. The option ATTACH(CAF) must be in the precompiler parameter list. This informs DB2 that when the attach call is made by the program to DB2, it will use the CAF attach module, DSNALI, to do the attachment, rather than the regular TSO attach module, DSNELI. The precompile for Version 4 is just a normal precompile, as this parameter does not exist in Version 4.

The compile should use options that define the Stored Procedure to be reentrant and reusable. In addition, for Version 4, the compile must specify that the program's allocation is not dynamic; whereas, in Version 5, it should be specified as dynamic (this is not a requirement in V5, just a recommendation). Note that the IBM V5 manual still specifies that the module must not be dynamic, but that is not true; this author currently runs Stored Procedures defined as dynamic.

The link should also define the Stored Procedure to be reentrant and reusable, and have AMODE=31 and RMODE=ANY. In addition, for V4, one must link in the Call Attach Module to allow the module to use the correct attachment to DB2. The extra parameter mentioned in conjunction with the precompile for Version 5 alleviates this requirement. The additional link card should be: INCLUDE SYSLIB(DSNALI).

Binding

A Stored Procedure requires only a package bind. Since it is, by definition, a called program, there is no plan defined for it. If a Stored Procedure calls other programs to do all the DB2 work for it (i.e., there is no SQL in the Stored Procedure itself), a package is not required for the Stored Procedure program; however, all the called programs that contain SQL will require one.

Any program that calls a Stored Procedure, whether on the same system or off on some other platform, must have a package created for it on the system that the Stored Procedure is running on. If on another system, a DB2 remote bind would be done. In addition, if the calling program is attaching to DB2 for OS/390, it will have to have a plan created for it that will include the Stored Procedure (and any programs it calls), possibly with a LOCATION indicated, in the package list.

Authorization

In order to be able to execute a Stored Procedure, the user must be authorized, either implicitly or explicitly, to execute the Stored Procedure's package and the packages of any other programs that it will call during its execution.

To execute a Stored Procedure, EXECUTE authority must be granted to the user for the Stored Procedure's package (if there is one), and for the packages of all programs that the Stored Procedure calls. This is done in one of two ways: (1) by granting EXECUTE on the calling program's plan (if the calling program runs under OS/390), which implicitly grants EXECUTE on each of the packages in its package list; or (2) by granting EXECUTE on the necessary packages (if no plan exists for the calling program), including the package that is created for the calling program on the system that the Stored Procedure runs on.

In addition, all normal communication security checks must pass before the Stored Procedure can be executed.

SYSPROCEDURES

A Stored Procedure is identified to DB2 by inserting a row into the SYSIBM.SYSPROCEDURES table. This row tells DB2 that the program is a Stored Procedure, what collection ID it runs in, how many result sets can be returned from it, etc. Exhibit 29.1 provides a list of all the columns in SYSPROCEDURES, and what they can or should be set to.

Note that the names given to the parameters in this definition do not have to be the same as those used in either the Stored Procedure or the calling program, but the field definitions (length, type, etc.) must be the same. For the given example, represents the length of the parameter. Parameters do not have to be defined as CHAR, and even in the case of the given example, if the parameter is greater than 256, it would have to be defined as VARCHAR. This is just a recommended approach to defining the parameters. For a more complete description of how to define the parameter list, see the *Application Programming and SQL Guide,* Section 6.2.3.1.2.

Exhibit 29.1. Columns in SYSPROCEDURES.

Column Name	Contents
PROCEDURE	The name of the Stored Procedure
AUTHID	Blank unless there is a requirement to restrict use of the Stored Procedure to a specific authid
LUNAME	Blank unless there is a requirement to restrict use of the Stored Procedure to a specific Logical Unit
LOADMOD	The name of the Stored Procedure
LINKAGE	Blank nulls not allowed in the input parameters
	N nulls allowed in the input parameters
	It is recommended to leave this blank unless there are specific requirements not to
COLLID	The COLLID of the package associated with the Stored Procedure
LANGUAGE	Programming language of Stored Procedure
ASUTIME	0
STAYRESIDENT	Y unless there are specific reasons for not having the program stay resident in memory after its completion, in which case a blank would be specified
IBMREQD	N
RUNOPTS	ALL31(ON),BE(4K,,),CH(OFF),NODEBUG,LIBS(4K,,), STAC(,,ANY,),STO(,,,4K),H(,,ANY)
PARMLIST	Whatever the defined input and output parameters are; based on the example of a CA, this will be of the format: PARMIN CHAR (??) IN, PARMOUT CHAR (??) OUT
RESULT_SETS	The maximum number of results sets that can be returned by the Stored Procedure at any point in time; if no result sets are being returned, this should be 0
WLM_ENV	Blank; this and the next would be different if running the Stored Procedure under WLM on OS/390
PGM_TYPE	M, indicating it is to be run as a main program
EXTERNAL_SECURIT Y	N, unless using some external security
COMMIT_ON_RETUR N	N

Of course, only a person with authority to, can insert rows into SYSPRO-CEDURES. This will usually be restricted to someone with SYSADM or DBAADM.

START AND STOP PROCEDURE

To make a new Stored Procedure active, a DB2 **START PROCEDURE** command must be issued.

If the Stored Procedure program is changed, and has been copied to the SPAS specified load library, there is a possibility that the changed version will not be used immediately. This would occur if the Stored Procedure had been defined as reusable (as is recommended). If this is the case, there is a possibility that the load module is active in memory (it is not deleted when use of it completes), and the new version will not be used until such a time as it becomes necessary for the system to load the program into memory again. A problem is liable to happen in this scenario because it would be difficult to keep the package timestamp synchronized with that of the version of the load module currently executing (since which version is executing cannot be determined at a point in time). If a synchronization error (the two timestamps do not match) occurs, the first SQL statement executed within the Stored Procedure would receive a –805 SQLCODE.

To get around the potential timestamp problem, remove the program from memory by issuing a DB2 –STOP PROCEDURE command (to deactivate the Stored Procedure), followed by a –START PROCEDURE command (to reactivate it). Then when the Stored Procedure is executed, it will be required to be loaded into memory, meaning that the new version of the program will be picked up; and as long as a package bind has been done for the new version of the program, there will be no timestamp problem.

CONCLUSION

DB2 Stored Procedures are a useful tool for improving performance of a client application that has to retrieve data from DB2 for OS/390. This is done by minimizing the number of communications between the client and the server, and by ensuring an optimal, consistent access to the data.

DB2 Stored Procedures are still very much a work-in-progress for IBM. This means that from release to release, there can still be fairly significant changes to how Stored Procedures work. In Version 5, result sets (the most important use of Stored Procedures in this author's opinion) were introduced, and the compile process changed to allow for Stored Procedures to be defined as dynamic modules. Rumor has it there will be more noticeable changes in Version 6 (although not as significant as those introduced in Version 5). Therefore, care should be taken when developing procedures for using Stored Procedures, as they might have to change from release to release. In addition, if there is a requirement to retrieve multiple rows of data (think result set), it is probably better to wait until you have Version 5.

Chapter 30
Microsoft SQL Server: Key Transact-SQL Features

Sanjiv Purba

THIS CHAPTER EXAMINES SOME OF THE USEFUL TRANSACT-SQL COM-MANDS AND DATABASE OBJECTS that support the development of substantial application modules that are saved inside the Structured Query Language (SQL) Server data dictionary. These include views, stored procedures, triggers, and column constraints (e.g., primary, foreign, and identity). This chapter provides streamlined syntax for creating and manipulating common Transact-SQL database objects to allow the reader the opportunity to learn them in this primer. The list of Transact-SQL features covered in this chapter includes the following:

- *Joins:* This is an ANSI SQL-compliant feature that is used to join multiple SQL Server tables to produce result sets, which are themselves user tables. For example a table of names and addresses can be joined to produce a result set containing name plus addresses. There are several different types of joins, including equi-join and outer join.
- *Subqueries:* Subqueries are similar to joins in terms of their end product. Subqueries are used to produce result sets from a group of SQL Server tables based on variable subqualifiers. For example, "for all employees living in Boston, find the ones that wear red hats."
- *Views:* Views offer a mechanism for accessing multiple physical tables based on a single logical view. Security and permissions can be allocated to the view to control the types of access users of the view have pertaining to the underlying physical tables. Views hide the physical complexity of a database structure from the users accessing the data.

- *Stored Procedures:* Stored procedures were once an extension to the basic SQL Dialect standard. As such, their implementation method varies from database server to database server. For example, both Oracle and Sybase support stored procedures. However, the syntax and implementation of these are not identical — meaning that stored procedures cannot be transferred seamlessly from one tool to the other. This severely restricts their portability and interoperability. However, they offer many advantages that make them highly popular. Microsoft SQL Server and Sybase SQL Server, due to their common ancestry, have similar implementations of stored procedures. Stored procedures support complex programming logic (e.g., if, while, execute commands) that can be leveraged to build sophisticated programs that are invoked from the data server's data dictionary.
- *Triggers:* Triggers are a special kind of stored procedure that automatically are invoked whenever predefined events occur on specific tables. These events can be identified and trapped by the developer. Triggers often are used to maintain referential integrity in a database. For example, selling a product to a customer can fire a trigger to decrement the onhand quantities of that product and perhaps place a new order to the supplier — all from the same trigger.

JOINS

The Relational Data Model is based on mathematical set theory. Each table in a database can be viewed as a mathematical set and, as such, mathematical operations are used to manipulate them. One of the most common operations involves joining two or more tables to create temporary or virtual tables. A join operation across a group of tables relies on foreign key fields in each of the tables involved in the operation and a SELECT command to retrieve the results into the new table. Several types of joins are supported by the ANSI Standard, but this chapter focuses on one of the more commonly used ones, namely the "Equi-Join." In this type of join, a column field in Table A is joined with a field in Table B. The fields are not required to have identical names, but they must have compatible data types. An equi-join operation returns a set that combines rows from Table A and Table B that have matching values in the key/foreign key columns. A join can support more than two tables, however. Due to physical performance reasons the practical guideline is to use between six and eight tables, with a desired limit of four or less. Join operations that involve more than about eight tables become very difficult to maintain from a programming complexity, as well as from a performance perspective. The result set of a join operation can contain all the fields in the matching records or a reduced set of fields, as identified in the JOIN command itself.

An equi-join requires an exact match between columns in separate the tables. The natural join involves two tables in the FROM clause of a SELECT statement without a WHERE clause so that all rows are matched with all other rows in the tables involved in the natural join. The outer join involves the situation where a value in table A does not have a matching key record in the second table. In the equi-join, such a record would be dropped from the result set. In the outer join the result set contains all the records in the equi-join result set plus the records that do not have matches in the remaining tables. There are many practical applications of this. For example, suppose that Table A is a list of depositors and Table B is a list of their deposits. An equi-join selects only depositors who have made deposits. An outer join selects depositors who have made deposits and depositors who have not made deposits yet.

Some other common examples where equi-joins are useful include the following:

- Join two tables, one containing a code for a person's job title as well as the person's name, and the other table being a code table. The resulting set displays the person's name and the actual job description.
- Join three tables, two as in the previous example, and a third one containing all the different addresses corresponding to a person's year-around requirements.

Although equi-joins are a powerful tool for extracting ordered information from relational tables, they have a performance overhead that must be considered and possibly offset through smarter programming techniques. Some methods for doing this include the order of the tables in the join clause, the presence of indexes on the columns specified in the join command, and the number of records in the tables involved in the joins. Badly constructed joins literally can lock up the SQL Server and make it virtually inaccessible to production users.

A simplified syntax for performing an Equi-Join on any number of tables is shown in the following:

Syntax:

```
SELECT [alias.]column_list

    FROM table1 alias1, table2 alias2 ....

        WHERE selection_clause
```

Examples:

```
1. SELECT a.first_name, a.last_name, b.description

    FROM customer a, member_type b

        WHERE a.member_type = b.member_type

    go
```

```
2. SELECT a.first_name, a.last_name, b.description,
       c.address_type, c.street1, c.city
   FROM customer a, member_type b, address c
       WHERE a.member_type = b.member_type AND
           a.customer_no = c.customer_no
   go
```

SUBQUERIES

Subqueries and joins can produce equivalent data result sets in many common cases. Subqueries generally are nested in the WHERE or HAVING clauses of Data Manipulation Language commands, such as SELECT, UPDATE, INSERT, and DELETE. This section provides examples of subqueries that utilize both the EXISTS and the IN keywords. The syntax for a subquery is shown here:

Syntax:

```
SELECT column_fields FROM table_list
    WHERE [EXISTS/IN] (selection_clause)
```

Examples:

```
1. /*****************************************************/
   In this example, the subquery returns a true/false to the
   WHERE clause when customer_no exists in the address
   table and has an address_type of "R."
   /*****************************************************/
   SELECT first_name, last_name, home_phone
       FROM customer
           WHERE EXISTS (SELECT * from address
               WHERE customer_no = customer.customer_no
               AND address_code = "R")
   go
2. /*****************************************************/
   The IN command word can limit the scope of the set.
   /*****************************************************/
   SELECT first_name, last_name, home_phone
       FROM customer
           WHERE customer_no IN (SELECT customer_no from
   address
               WHERE address_code = "R")
   go
```

VIEWS

Views provide a mechanism for accessing one or more tables in a relational database without requiring knowledge of the physical details of how the tables are organized. Views are useful in the following situations:

- Simplifying user access to data by providing non-SQL users with a convenient method of accessing data that they require, however it is organized.
- Combining multiple table under a common object name.
- Implementing a security layer to restrict user access to relevant column names only.

Creating a view is similar to creating a user table in that a view object is created for the default database. This means that the view is actually a physical object. Running views causes a new user table to be built as a result of filtering table columns through the restrictions of the view. Views are identified uniquely with object names within a database. A view must be dropped before a view with the same name can be updated or recreated in that database. Once a view is created, it can be used as a user table name with the SELECT command. Views do not support triggers.

A simplified syntax for the CREATE VIEW command is the following:

Syntax:

```
CREATE VIEW owner.viewname [column_list]
    AS select_clause
```

A simplified syntax for the command to drop a view from a database is as follows:

Syntax:

```
DROP VIEW owner.viewname
```

A simplified syntax to execute a view after it is created is as follows:

Syntax:

```
SELECT [*/column_names] from view_name where
search_clause
```

Unlike many other SQL Server commands, view objects are created in the default database only.

Examples:

1. Create a view for a user who only requires a subset of fields in a table. Use a DROP VIEW command to drop the view before trying to create it to support iterative execution of the CREATE VIEW command. This code can be entered interactively or through an executed script file.

```
DROP VIEW customer_contacts
go

CREATE VIEW customer_contacts
AS
    SELECT first_name, last_name, home_phone,
business_phone
        FROM customer
go

SELECT * FROM customer_contacts
                    /* retrieves all the columns in the
view */
go

SELECT first_name from customer_contacts
go
```

2. In this example, a view is created to join two tables. This example demonstrates how views can be used to simplify database access by users. Instead of learning to write joins or other complex queries, users use a view name as a virtual table to retrieve their data. However, using views is not free. Someone in the data organization needs to be charged with the responsibility for building and maintaining views for the user community. This often turns into a full-time job. The caretaker of the views must understand the business application.

```
DROP VIEW customer_type
go

CREATE VIEW customer_type
AS
    SELECT a.first_name, a.last_name, b.description
        FROM customer a, member_type b
            WHERE a.member_type = b.member_type
go

SELECT * FROM customer_type
                /* retrieves all the columns in the view */
go
```

STORED PROCEDURES

Stored procedures are an innovation of Sybase SQL Server and Microsoft SQL Server and were an important contribution to the first programmable database server product widely released in 1987. They quickly proved their value in distributed client/server applications and SQL Server (which was essentially the same product in both the Sybase and Microsoft versions until 1995) quickly gained market share. Sales people from the competitor dataserver products found many IS directors asking them a simple question, "Does your product support stored procedures?" For a time, the answer was "no", so SQL Server started to be the product of choice in many industries. Stored procedures are now an integral part of many database servers, including Oracle. Stored procedures also support reuse, security, and software distribution.

Stored procedures can be written inside or outside the SQL Server environment, but they are stored directly in SQL Server system tables, including both sysobjects and sysmessages. Stored procedures themselves are a combination of SQL Data Manipulation Language (DML), Data Definition Langauge (DDL), Data Control Language (DCL), and Transact-SQL. SQL, by itself, does not support repetitive program flows and conditional structures. Transact-SQL provides this enhancement to the basic SQL dialect. The combination of all these command structures enables stored procedures to support programs that are as sophisticated and complex as 3GL and 4GL languages.

Stored procedures are constructed in several steps. A stored procedure can be written using a text editor in the operating system environment, or can be written directly into the SQL Server system tables using the SQL Server Query Analyzer (previously SQL/w) or the SQL Server Enterprise Manager. These are the most common methods of writing and saving stored procedures. Other methods also exist. For example, a stored procedure can be written using a third generation language (e.g., C programming language) with embedded SQL Server. However, this latter method has performance implications that make it less desirable than the other methods in many cases. This method also creates a fat client and a thin server, which creates a high network load for client/server applications. In the case where a stored procedure is written into an operating system file using a text editor, the stored procedure must be parsed into an SQL Server database using ISQL or one of the other methods of invoking SQL commands in the SQL environment. The parse procedure is sometimes called a "compile" procedure, but this is not a true compile in the 3GL sense in that an object module is not created. Rather, the parse procedure interprets the code in the stored procedure and returns error messages if there are syntactical logical errors (e.g., a reference to a database object that does not exist). If the stored procedure commands are interpreted successfully, the entire code belonging to that stored procedure is saved into the default database system tables.

Because stored procedures are created and stored as database objects, it is necessary to drop them before they are created. The basic syntax for writing a stored procedure is as follows:

Syntax:

```
CREATE PROC[EDURE] proc_name

(

    @parameter              datatype,

    @parameter_list         datatype

)

AS

DECLARE local_variable          datatype,

    local_variable_list         datatype


Transact SQL Statements


RETURN return_code

go
```

A comprehensive list of Transact SQL statements are supported within stored procedures including SQL commands and built-in functions. Stored procedures also can call nested stored procedures or call themselves recursively. Stored procedures are dropped from a database using the following syntax:

Syntax:

```
DROP PROCEDURE proc_name

go
```

Stored procedures that successfully are compiled into the database system tables can be executed using the following command syntax:

Syntax:

```
EXECUTE proc_name [parameters]

go
```

When working with stored procedures, two names are relevant. The first name is the operating system file name that contains the script for the stored procedure. The second name is the stored procedure name that is saved in the sysobjects table. The operating system file name is *stexple1.sql*. The stored procedure name is *stexample1*.

Examples:

1. The following example creates a stored procedure in the default database under the object name *stexample1*.

```
/*---------------------------------------------------*/
/*--Code below this line is saved into stexple1.sql--*/
/*---------------------------------------------------*/
/* Filename: stexple1.sql */


/* drop the stored procedure*/
DROP PROC stexample1
go    /* test this procedure without the go. Does it
still work? */


CREATE PROC stexample1
AS
    SELECT 'this is a stored procedure'
    RETURN 0 /* return a 0 code to the calling routine */
go


/*---------------------------------------------------*/
/*--Code above this line is saved into stexple1.sql--*/
/*---------------------------------------------------*/


/* Execute the stored procedure by entering the
following command(s) in the MS SQL Server Query
Analyzer, a batch file, or through an isql session */


stexample1
go
```

Stored procedures (and other objects like views and triggers) are compiled into several system tables within the default database. The text is stored in syscomments under an ID. Several system procedures can retrieve the code for a stored procedure and save it in an ASCII operating system file for modification and recompilation. The sysobjects system table contains header information for all database objects including stored procedures.

2. The following stored procedure inserts one record into the "member_type" code table:

```
/* Filename: stinsert.sql */

/* drop the stored procedure if it exists. */
IF EXISTS (select name from sysboects where name =
"insmember")
BEGIN
    select "stored procedure found"
    DROP PROC insmember
end
go


CREATE PROC insmember
(
    @member_type      char (1),
    @description      char (30)
)
AS
    /************************************/
    /* Include data validation tests here */
    /************************************/
    INSERT INTO member_type
    (
        member_type,
        description
    )
    VALUES
    (
        @member_type,
        @description
    )
```

```
/**************************************************/
/* Test for insert error and take appropriate
action */
/**************************************************/
RETURN 0 /* return a 0 code to the calling routine */
go


/**************************************************/
/* Execute the stored procedure and enter the parameters
in*/
/* the order they are expected by the proc —
member_type*/
/* first and description second*/
/**************************************************/
insmember "B," "Book Collector"
go

insmember "A," "AAAA" /* insert another member_type */
select * from member_type
                /*display the contents of the member_type
table*/
go
```

SQL Server displays a success message if the command was successful (e.g., "The command(s) completed successfully"). To review the results of the insert, use the command format: "select * from member_type." Trying to execute the stored procedure without the correct number or data types of the parameters displays appropriate error messages and the insert is not completed. In fact, SQL Server displays meaningful information to identify the missing parameters.

3. The following stored procedure updates the description for an existing "member_type":

```
/* Filename: stupdate.sql */


/* drop the stored procedure if it exists. */
IF EXISTS (select name from sysobjects where name =
"updmember")
    DROP PROC updmember
go
```

```
CREATE PROC updmember
(
    @member_type        char (1),
    @description        char (30)
)
AS
    /*****************************************/
    /* include data validation tests here */
    /*****************************************/
    UPDATE member_type
    SET description = @description
        where member_type = @member_type

    if @@rowcount < 1 /* no rows were affected */
        print "no record found to update" /* raiseerror
        here */
    else
        print "record updated"
    RETURN 0 /* return a 0 code to the calling routine */
        go


/**********************************************************/
/* Execute the stored procedure and enter the
parameters in*/
/* the order they are expected by the proc — member_type
first*/
/* and description second*/
/**********************************************************/
updmember "B," "Book/Magazines"
go


select * from member_type
go
```

4. The following stored procedure deletes a record from the "member_type" code table based on a "member_type":

```
/* Filename: studelete.sql */


/* Drop the stored procedure if it exists. */
IF EXISTS (select name from sysobjects where name =
"delmember")
DROP PROC delmember
go


CREATE PROC delmember
(
    @member_type      char (1)
)
AS
    DELETE member_type
        WHERE member_type = @member_type


    /*************************************************/
    /* Test for insert error and take appropriate
    action*/
    /*************************************************/
    if @@rowcount < 1 /* no rows were affected */
        print "no record found to delete" /*raiseerror
        here*/
    else
        print "record deleted"
    RETURN 0 /* return a 0 code to the calling routine */
go


/*************************************************/
/* Execute the stored procedure and enter the parameters
in*/
/* the order they are expected by the proc — member_type
only*/
/*************************************************/
delmember "A"
go
```

5. The following stored procedure inserts two records into the address database into the tables: customer and address tables. This example demonstrates issuing a nested procedure call.

```
/* Filename: stins2.sql */


/* Drop the stored procedure if it exists */
IF EXISTS (select name from sysobjects where name =
"inscustomer")
    DROP PROC inscustomer
go


/* Drop the stored procedure if it exists */
IF EXISTS (select name from sysobjects where name =
"insaddress")
    DROP PROC insaddress
go


/************************************************/
/* Create the inscustomer stored procedure */
/************************************************/
CREATE PROC inscustomer
(
    @customer_no          int,
    @last_name            char(30),
    @middle_initial       char(1),
    @first_name           char(30),
    @home_phone           char(15),
    @business_phone       char(15),
    @fax                  char(15),
    @email                char(25),
    @preference           char(80),
    @member_on            datetime,
    @member_type          character(1),
    @address_code         char(1),
    @street1              char(25),
    @street2              char(25),
    @city                 char(20),
    @state_province       char(20),
    @country              char(15),
    @zip_pc               char(10)
)
AS
```

```
DECLARE
@return_code  int /* variable names must begin with @ */


/***********************************/
/* Include data validation tests here */
/***********************************/


INSERT customer
(
    customer_no,
    last_name,
    middle_initial,
    first_name,
    home_phone,
    business_phone,
    fax,
    email,
    preference,
    member_on,
    member_type
)
VALUES
(
    @customer_no,
    @last_name,
    @middle_initial,
    @first_name,
    @home_phone,
    @business_phone,
    @fax,
    @email,
    @preference,
    @member_on,
    @member_type
)
```

```
/*****************************************************/
/* Test for insert error and take appropriate action */
/*****************************************************/


/* Call stored procedure to insert address record */
EXECute @return_code = insaddress @customer_no,
@address_code, @street1, @street2, @city,
@state_province, @country, @zip_pc


/******************************************************/
/* Inspect return_code, test for error and take
appropriate*/
/* action*/
/******************************************************/


RETURN 0 /* return a 0 code to the calling routine */
go


/*********************************************/
/* Create the insaddress stored procedure */
/*********************************************/
CREATE PROC insaddress
(
        @customer_no            int,
        @address_code           char(1),
        @street1                char(25),
        @street2                char(25),
        @city                   char(20),
        @state_province         char(20),
        @country                char(15),
        @zip_pc                 char(10)
)
        AS
```

```
/****************************************/
/* include data validation tests here */
/****************************************/

INSERT address
(
    customer_no,
    address_code,
    street1,
    street2,
    city,
    state_province,
    country,
    zip_pc
)
VALUES
(
    @customer_no,
    @address_code,
    @street1,
    @street2,
    @city,
    @state_province,
    @country,
    @zip_pc
)

/*****************************************************/
/* Test for insert error and take appropriate action */
/*****************************************************/

RETURN 0 /* return a 0 code to the calling routine */
go
```

```
/*************************************************/
/* Execute the stored procedure and enter the
parameters in*/
/* the order they are expected by the proc.*/
/*************************************************/
inscustomer 3000, "Flanders," "T," "Marsha,"

    "9998888888," "9899899999," "9999998888,"

    "mflanders@tobos.com," "European & Vegetarian Cook
Books,"

    "Mar 1995," "1,"

    "H," "567 Aeta Rd," " ", "Dallas," "Texas," "USA,"

    "10001"

go
```

6. The following stored procedure updates two records in the address database inside the tables: customer and address tables. This example demonstrates a nested procedure call.

```
/* Filename: stupd2.sql */


/* drop the stored procedure if it exists. */
IF EXISTS (select name from sysobjects where name =
"updcustomer")

    DROP PROC updcustomer

go


/* drop the stored procedure if it exists. */
IF EXISTS (select name from sysobjects where name =
"updaddress")

    DROP PROC updaddress /* drops all triggers with the
table */

go
```

```
/*******************************************/
/* Create the updcustomer stored procedure */
/*******************************************/

CREATE PROC updcustomer

(

    @customer_no          int,
    @last_name            char(30),
    @middle_initial       char(1),
    @first_name           char(30),
    @home_phone           char(15),
    @business_phone       char(15),
    @fax                  char(15),
    @email                char(25),
    @preference           char(80),
    @member_on            datetime,
    @member_type          character(1),
    @address_code         char(1),
    @street1              char(25),
    @street2              char(25),
    @city                 char(20),
    @state_province       char(20),
    @country              char(15),
    @zip_pc               char(10)

)

AS

    DECLARE

    @return_code int/* variable names must begin with
    @ */
```

```
/****************************************/
/* Include data validation tests here */
/****************************************/
UPDATE customer
    SET
        last_name        = @last_name,
        middle_initial   = @middle_name,
        first_name       = @first_name,
        home_phone       = @home_phone,
        business_phone   = @business_phone,
        fax              = @fax,
        email            = @email,
        preference       = @preference,
        member_on        = @member_on,
        member_type      = @member_type
            WHERE
                customer_no = @customer_no


/*********************************************************/
/* Test for update error and take appropriate action */
/*********************************************************/


/* Call stored procedure to update address record */
EXECute @return_code = updaddress @customer_no,
address_code, @street1, @street2, @city,
@state_province, @country, @zip_pc


/*********************************************************/
/* Inspect return_code, test for error and take
appropriate*/
/* action*/
/*********************************************************/


    RETURN 0 /* return a 0 code to the calling routine */
go
```

```
/******************************************/
/* Create the updaddress stored procedure */
/******************************************/


CREATE PROC updaddress
(
    @customer_no        int,
    @address_code       char(1),
    @street1            char(25),
    @street2            char(25),
    @city               char(20),
    @state_province     char(20),
    @country            char(15),
    @zip_pc             char(10)
)
AS

    /***************************************/
    /* include data validation tests here */
    /***************************************/
    UPDATE address
    SET
        address_code    = @address_code,
        street1         = @street1,
        street2         = @street2,
        city            = @city,
        state_province  = @state_province,
        country         = @country,
        zip_pc          = @zip_pc
            WHERE
                customer_no = @customer_no
```

```
/************************************************/

/* test for update error and take appropriate
action*/

/************************************************/

RETURN 0 /* return a 0 code to the calling routine */
go



/**************************************************/

/* execute the stored procedure and enter the
parameters in*/

/* the order they are expected by the proc.*/

/**************************************************/

updcustomer 3000, "Flanders," "T," "Marsha,"

    "9998888888," "9899899999," "9999998888,"

    "mflanders@tobos.com," "Asian & Vegetarian Cook
    Books,"

    "Mar 1995," "1,"

    "H," "87 Rhodes Rd," " ", "Dallas," "Texas," "USA,"

    "10001"

go
```

7. The following stored procedure deletes a logical customer record. This requires two tables to be processed for the deletion, namely, customer and address.

```
/* Filename: stdel2.sql */



/* drop the stored procedure if it exists. */

IF EXISTS (select name from sysobjects where name =
"delcustomer")

    DROP PROC delcustomer

go
```

```
/********************************************/
/* Create the delcustomer stored procedure */
/********************************************/
CREATE PROC delcustomer
(
    @customer_no        int
)
AS
    DECLARE
    @return_code        int /* variable names must begin
                            with @ */
/************************************/
/* include data validation tests here */
/************************************/


DELETE address
    WHERE customer_no = @customer_no


/****************************************************/
/* inspect return_code, test for error and take
appropriate*/
/* action*/
/****************************************************/
DELETE customer
    WHERE customer_no =@customer_no
    /****************************************************/
    /* inspect return_code, test for error and take
    appropriate*/
    /* action*/
    /****************************************************/


    RETURN 0 /* return a 0 code to the calling routine */
go
```

TRIGGERS

Triggers are another SQL Server innovation and a solid feature of the programmable database server. All triggers are stored procedures, but not all stored procedures are triggers. Triggers essentially are stored procedures that are activated by specific events on a table and, hence, use essentially the same system tables as stored procedures. (Triggers use the sysprocedures table.) These events include the following at the table level: *insert a row*, *update a row*, and *delete a row*. Triggers also can be created to fire when specific columns are updated. The guidelines provided for stored procedure creation and maintenance through scripts also apply for triggers. Triggers are created in the current database, but they can access objects in any database within the same SQL Server. There are several reasons to use triggers in an application: (1) referential integrity, (2) cascading operations (inserts/deletes), (3) code reuse, (4) transaction rollbacks, and (5) simplified module development. A trigger is fired by a specified event on a table or a table column. The trigger has access to two trigger tables, namely, *inserted* and *deleted*, before the trigger completes. Insert operations use the inserted trigger table. Delete operations use the deleted trigger table. Update operations use the inserted and deleted trigger tables. These tables are referenced with these specific names, inserted and deleted in the command section of triggers.

It is important to realize that triggers have had a performance overhead since SQL Server first emerged in the marketplace. This overhead performance has been reduced with the release of faster CPU chips and will continue to decline with the release of streamlined SQL Server modules in the future. Before designing a large number of triggers, it is important to benchmark the use of a few triggers to ensure that the application response time is sufficient to meet requirements.

The process for creating and using triggers is similar to that of stored procedures. The difference lies in the execution process. Triggers are not executed explicitly with EXEC command, as stored procedures, but rather they are fired by events occurring against triggers applied to the table. There are some limitations on triggers, including (1) apply to a single table as specified in the syntax; (2) can be nested to 16 levels; (3) cannot contain certain types of commands, such as DROP, ALTER, permissions, update statistics, CREATE, and LOAD. SQL Server has several features to stop trigger infinite loops (e.g., a trigger inserting a record into a table firing an update trigger on the same table firing the update on the same table and so on). The first is the nested level limit and the second is that a trigger does not fire itself. A streamlined syntax for creating triggers is as follows:

Syntax:

```
CREATE TRIGGER owner.trigger_name

    ON owner.table_name

    FOR [INSERT/UPDATE/DELETE]/[INSERT/UPDATE]

    AS

        [IF UPDATE (column_field) [AND/OR
column_field(s)]]

        commands
```

The "sp_configure" system procedure can be used to set nested triggers to change the default nested level value. In addition to the limitation that some SQL commands cannot be used inside triggers, environment variable values also are changed during the trigger. When inspecting an environment variable, do so before the variables are changed by commands inside the trigger. The values of the environment variable are local to the trigger.

Examples:

1. Create a trigger to fire when a customer record is deleted as a final warning to the user.

```
use address

go

drop trigger trdelete_customer

go


CREATE TRIGGER trdelete_customer

ON customer

FOR DELETE

AS

    IF @@rowcount < 1

        /* no records were located by the deletion
        criteria */

        PRINT ("Customer not found. No records deleted")

    ELSE

        PRINT ("Customer Deleted. Save screen image to
        undelete customer.")

    go
```

```
/* Ensure that the trigger was parsed successfully into
the database */

select * from sysobjects where name =
"trdelete_customer"

go
```

Use a join to retrieve the text associated with the trigger from the sys-comments table. Execute the following join using the Microsoft SQL Server Query Analyzer utility.

```
SELECT a.type, b.text

    FROM sysobjects a, syscomments b

        WHERE a.name = "trdelete_customer" AND

            a.id = b.id

go
```

This join displays the following results in the "Results" tab of the Microsoft SQL Server Query Analyzer:

```
type                    text

----                    -----------------------------------

TR                      create trigger trdelete_customer


ON customer

FOR DELETE

AS

    IF @@rowcount < 1

        PRINT ("Customer not found. No records deleted")

    ELSE

        PRINT ("Customer Deleted. Save screen image to
        undelete customer.")
```

The row associated with the table that fires the trigger is updated in the sysobjects table. The following SQL commands display the modified column containing the ID of the delete trigger that was created previously. Notice that the SQL code also displays the columns for other triggers (e.g., insert, update) that could be created for the table as well. Notice that the "deltrig" column in the sysobjects systems table contains the ID of the trigger selected by the join with the syscomments table.

410

```
select name, id, deltrig, instrig, updtrig, seltrig
    from sysobjects where name = "customer"


select a.type, a.id, b.text
    from sysobjects a, syscomments b
        where a.name = "trdelete_customer" AND a.id =
        b.id
```

Test that the trigger fires when a customer is deleted.

```
delete customer
    where customer_no = 3000
go
```

Note: Table objects within a database are identified within the sysobjects system table. The type column can be used to identify the type of object that a particular row is representing. Some of the common codes are

- S — system procedure
- V — view
- U — user table
- P — stored procedure
- TR — trigger

Using this information, the SELECT command can be used to identify all the objects belonging to a particular type, e.g., SELECT * FROM sysobjects WHERE type = 'P' (to locate all the stored procedures in the default database).

CONCLUSION

This chapter provided the syntax and examples for manipulating some of the commonly used database objects or features offered in SQL Server's Transact SQL dialect. Each of these objects or features form the foundation of modern database servers and three-tier client/server development. It is expected that their value will not diminish in the future, despite the constant changes to technology. Joins and subqueries are used to create virtual tables based on multiple physical tables and user-supplied qualifiers. Views are used to remove the physical complexity of accessing multiple relational tables. Stored procedures are used to build complex modules that are saved in SQL Server's data dictionary and can be executed remotely by clients. This provides a number of advantages: (1) reduced data transferrance on the LAN, (2) simplified change management, (3) modularization of business logic, and (4) module sharing. Triggers, a special type of stored procedure, also were examined in this chapter. Triggers are attached to tables or columns in tables. They automatically are invoked when specific events occur on the tables or columns. Triggers are a tool for enforcing referential integrity on a set of tables.

Chapter 31
Selecting Universal Data Server Technology

James A. Larson
Carol L. Larson

THE PROBLEM

RELATIONAL DATABASE SERVERS are used to store and access the data of an enterprise. This data is highly structured and organized into *relations* consisting of *tuples* and *domains*. In this chapter, the more familiar terms of *tables* consisting of *rows* and *columns* will be used. The elements of each table column are simple data types such as integers, floating point numbers, short character strings, or dates. However, relational databases store only a fraction of the information important to an enterprise. Much of the information necessary to an enterprise does not lend itself to be represented as simple data types in tables. This information is in the form of:

- Text — Memos, reports, messages, and documents
- Images — Diagrams, illustrations, and pictures
- Audio — Voice messages, audio recordings, and recorded music
- Video — Television commercials and news segments, taped interviews and focus groups, recorded movies, and television programs

Until recently, relational databases could not deal with these data types, leaving enterprises to use manual systems to manage nontabular forms of information.

THE CHALLENGE OF UNIVERSAL DATA SERVERS

Recently, database management system vendors have introduced extensions to relational data servers that store, retrieve, and, in some cases, search nontabular data types. These systems are called object-relational, extended relational, multimedia, and universal data servers. Frequently,

Exhibit 31.1. Four new data types and their storage requirements

New Data Type	Uncompressed Size	Typical Compressed Size	Typical Compression Factor
Text	3.3 KB/page	1.2:1	2.6 KB/page
1280 × 1024 Image with 24 Bits of Color	3.9 MB/image	4:1	1.0 MB/image
High-Quality Audio	176 KB/sec	4:1	44 KB/sec
640 × 480 Video at 30 Frames/Sec	49.1 MB/sec	50:1	1 MB/sec

the term *universal data server* is used to indicate that a relational data server has been extended to support a variety of new data types.

A universal database falls somewhere between a relational database and an object-oriented database. A relational data server contains tables with values (but not pointers) in each column. A universal data server contains tables where some of the columns contain pointers (addresses) to files stored outside of the table. These files contain large or complex data types. An object-oriented data server contains objects consisting of fields, some of which may be large or complex data types. Although an object-oriented data server need not be structured as a table, it may still support SQL requests.

New Data Types

Traditional document management systems manage text and image documents. Usually, text and image documents are augmented by a set of descriptors similar to tables containing fields describing documents. However, most document management systems do support extensible data types. There is little chance that they can be extended to support audio, video, or other new data types such as date and time, unit conversions, and time series.

Exhibit 31.1 shows four new data types and the storage requirements for information represented using these formats. Even with compression, these data types require significant amounts of disk storage.

Data Storage

How can a relational data server support new data types? One approach is to store each new data type as an element in a relational table. However, these data types are large, may overflow the memory buffers of traditional relational data servers, and are not easily displayed as table elements on the users monitor. Another approach is to divide the data type into smaller chunks and store each chunk as an element in a relational table, and the data server reconstructs the data type from its chunks before presenting the data type to the user. Most relational data server vendors have used yet another approach and have extended their systems by placing physical pointers directly into their relational tables that reference files containing the new data type.

For example, the file names, résumés, and pictures of employees are elements of the relational data table. Users retrieve and update the rows of the table, which includes changing the pointers in the Résumé or Picture column to reference new files. There are, of course, operations to retrieve and present file contents, so users can read résumés and view the pictures of employees.

Searching and Indexing

Relational databases enable users to search on any column of a table. Because it may be expensive to fetch each referenced file into main memory, characteristics about the new data type also are represented in the table. Whenever a table contains a pointer to a new data type, the table also contains attributes about the new data type such as its type, size, date stored, and temporal length (for audio and video data types). These attributes can be searched by using traditional SQL requests. These new data type attributes are derived automatically by the database server. However, none of the attributes describes the information content of the referenced file.

For some data types, information about the content can be extracted automatically. For example, automatic procedures exist for extracting keywords from text. Next, the keywords are placed into the columns of tables. Users may include these keywords as part of their SQL requests. However, extracting keywords is difficult for new data types. Speech recognition algorithms convert spoken audio into text; then, keywords can be extracted from the text. Because of accuracy problems, the algorithm may not be able to extract all significant keywords. In the future, artificial intelligence vision algorithms may be able to examine images and video files and infer attributes about their content. Today, with the exception of text, attributes about the content of a file must be extracted manually.

Most traditional relational data servers use B-trees and/or hashing as indexing mechanisms. New data types often require new data organizational mechanisms. For example, R-trees are useful for organizing the contents of two-dimensional data types. Organizational techniques will emerge for each new data type.

Extensions

It is impossible for data server vendors to anticipate all possible new data types which users might require. Instead, database administrators

415

Exhibit 31.2. Examples of new data types and their extensions

New Data Type	Cross-Industry	Industry-Specific
Multimedia	Text	Medical: MRI, PET, EKG or ECG
	Image	Law Enforcement, Security: Fingerprints
	Audio	Radio: Sound Bites, Preprogrammed Music
	Video	Television: News Tapes, Commercials
Complex	Unit Conversion	Medical: Hourly Blood Pressure Readings
	Date and Time	(Time Series)
		Oil Exploration: Location of Oil Fields (Geo-positioning Data)

may extend their universal data servers to support the storage and manipulation of new data types. These extensions enable

- Storage of new data types using an efficient storage organization.
- Indexing techniques to support data access.
- Presentation of the new data type.
- Manipulation of specific data types (for example, graphic images may be rotated, enlarged, or shrunk; audio files may be compressed, decompressed, and converted between .au and .wav formats).
- Query optimization for queries involving new data types.
- Stored procedures for the enforcement of business rules and constraints which affect the new data types (if a new data type is stored as a file in a file system separate from the universal data server, then mechanisms should be installed into the file system to prohibit deleting files without also deleting pointers to the new data type from within the universal database).
- Application programming language extensions for the manipulation of the new data types.

A cottage industry will emerge to provide extensions to popular universal data servers for new data types. Exhibit 31.2 lists some of the new data types for which extensions have been built.

Although many of the extensions support cross-industry data types, such as text, image, audio, and video, other new data types have been implemented. New data types for date and time and unit conversion (meters from feet, pounds sterling from American dollars) also have been created. A geo-spatial data type pinpoints an object anywhere on Earth's surface. Time series is a new data type consisting of a sequence of values, where each value is associated with a calendar index. Examples of new time series are a sequence of monthly weight measurements or a sequence of monthly expenditures. Other new data types that aggregate tabular data types will certainly be implemented in the future.

JUSTIFYING AND SELECTING A UNIVERSAL DATA SERVER

The two major criteria for switching to a universal data server are

- Requirement 1: The enterprise needs data types not supported by traditional relational data servers.
- Requirement 2: The new data types must be integrated with existing data types.

Requirement 1 recommends that an enterprise truly needs new data types, not that new data types would be nice to have. New data types can be justified by explaining how the enterprise can be more competitive by using the new data types. For example, enterprises producing consumer catalogs may need a database containing text, illustrations, and photographs of products. Extending their product description database to include illustrations and photographs would enhance their catalog usage, especially if the catalog is placed online via the World Wide Web. Other areas benefiting from new data types include the following:

- Office information — Memos, reports, letters, and documents.
- Medical information — X-rays, magnetic resonance imagings (MRIs), positron emission tomographies (PETs), and electrocardiograms (EKGs or ECGs).
- Engineering information — Engineering drawings, blueprints, and load and stress limits.
- Library information — Encyclopedias, histories, dictionaries, biographies, other reference works, archival collections, and literature.
- Geographic information — Satellite images, maps, weather information, geologic data, and census data.
- Training and education — Readings, exercises, workshops, and tests
- Museums — Art, music and recordings, history, science, and sports.

Requirement 2 recommends that new data types be integrated with existing databases. This requirement improves two types of integration — user integration and computational integration. With user integration, users easily access traditional old and new data types together. In the online catalog example, users access pictures of a product and its cost at the same time. With computational integration, old and new data types share the same organizational and indexing mechanisms. Optimization algorithms analyze queries involving both old and new data types. Mechanisms enforcing business rules and constraints apply to both old and new data types.

In addition to supporting the definition and processing of new data types, a universal data server should support all the features and functions of relational data servers. Schema design, data entry, backup and recovery, transaction commit and rollback, security, and the specification and

Exhibit 31.3. DBMS vendors and their universal database servers

DBMS Vendor	Product Name	Web Page
IBM	DB@Universal Database 5.0	www.ibm.com
Informix	Informix-Universal Server	www.informix.com
Microsoft	Microsoft SQL Server 6.5	www.microsoft.com
Oracle	Oracle Universal Server	www.oracle.com
Sybase	Adaptive Server	www.sybase.com
UniSys	Osmos Object-relational Database	www.unisys.com; www.osmos.com
Unidata, Inc.	Universal Object Server	www.unidata.com

enforcement of business rules are all features supported by relational data servers and also should be supported by universal data servers. As shown in Exhibit 31.3, most leading relational data server vendors have announced universal database server products that are upgrades or extensions of their current relational data servers.

Each of the vendors shown in Exhibit 31.3, along with its partners, continue to enhance its respective universal data servers by implementing additional new data types. If its products do not support the data types currently used by the enterprise, the vendor's partners may provide extension software supporting the needed data types. If not, new data types can be created and installed by designing and implementing the extensions noted above in the Extensions subsection.

Universal data servers may support other new features in addition to extensible data types. Some vendors introduce features in their universal data servers which are available in the products of their competitors. In general, universal data servers support additional transaction and concurrency control capabilities, reporting capabilities, and query features. Database administrators should consider all features of a universal data server to determine if and when a switch should be made to a universal data server. From a pragmatic viewpoint, it is wise to upgrade to a universal data server provided by the vendor of the users current relational database server — the new universal data server from the old vendor will provide more backward compatibility and require less migration effort than would selecting a universal data server from a different vendor.

MIGRATING TO A UNIVERSAL DATA SERVER

Three factors affect the amount of effort required to migrate data to a universal data server:

1. How much analog data is to be migrated and in which digital form should the data be represented?
2. How many values of the required index fields must be extracted manually from the digitized data rather than extracted automatically?

3. How much information about relationships must be generated manually rather than extracted automatically from the data?

Converting from Analog to Digital Form

Most universal data servers manage digitized data only. This enables the data to be stored, retrieved, transferred, and presented to users via common digital hardware and software.

Paper documents must be scanned to digitize their contents. Audio and video analog information must be processed by a digital signal processor (DSP) for conversion to a digital format. Although there may be some manual activities involved with these processes, such as feeding pages into a scanner or inserting cassettes into a tape drive, software and hardware perform the actual conversion automatically.

Some digital forms may be more convenient than others for digital processing. For example, an ASCII representation of text is more convenient than a bitmap of the same text. Optical character recognition converts images of text into ASCII bit strings with accuracy greater than 95%. Speech recognition algorithms convert audio speech into ASCII text provided that the source contains only a single voice at a time with little background noise. Unfortunately, vision algorithms do not exist that can reliably convert images and video captured via a camera into useful ASCII text strings.

Extracting Values for Index Fields

Universal data servers maintain data about data types in such a way that queries about the data types are processed without retrieving and examining the data types. Some values of these fields can be generated automatically. An example is the automatic calculation of the length of an audio clip and the size of a text string. However, values of index fields describing the content of a data type are another matter. If the data type is an image or video, the user must examine the data type and enter the field value. If the data type is text, it may be possible to extract the value from the text using text manipulation routines. As an example, software routines examine the text to extract keywords. By using more-advanced text-processing routines, it may be possible to detect themes by searching for words frequently related to specific themes. For example, Oracles ConText™ is able to examine a text string and extract relevant keywords and themes.

Extracting Relationships between Data Types

Automatically extracting relationships may be possible if the data types have index fields containing values that can be compared with each other. For example, if both a résumé data type and a picture data type have social security fields, then matching values in the respective social security fields implies that an equivalence relationship exists between the two data types.

419

Such value-based relationships are identified easily. Sometimes relationships can be established by combining two existing relationships. If a savings account and a checking account have the same value for social security number and the checking account and an address file entry have the same name, then the address from the address file is also the address of the owner of the savings account. However, care should be taken to make sure that bogus relationships are not inferred. For example, there is no relationship between a person and a cow if the birth-date field of a person data type and the birth-date field of a cow data type have the same value.

There may exist useful relationships among data types that are not evident by examining the values of their respective index fields. These relationships must be identified and entered manually.

A database administrator may be tempted to minimize the number of index fields and relationships of data types just to make the migration to a universal data server easier. However, queries may be more expensive for the universal data server to process if relevant index fields and relationships are missing. On the other hand, maintaining index fields and relationships between data types that are seldom used in queries is an unnecessary expense. It is the job of the database administrator to design the database carefully to contain the appropriate index fields and relationships.

CONCLUSION

A universal data server should not be used unless an enterprise can truly benefit by using the new data types. Migration to a universal data server should be considered only if it solves a specific enterprise problem, enables users to be more productive, and gives an enterprise a competitive edge over its competitors. In order to minimize conversion costs and efforts, it is wise to purchase a universal data server from the DBMS vendor currently used by the enterprise.

Recommended Reading

Campbell, R., Object-relational databases: the key players, *Databased Web Advisor*, 15(8), 28–35, 1997.

Davis, J. R., Extended relational DBMSs: the technology, Part 1, *DBMS*, 10(7), 42–49, 1997.

Davis, J. R., Universal servers: the players, Part 1, *DBMS*, 10(8), 75–86, 1997.

Stearns, T., Adapting to a new universe, *Information Week*, 652, 73–79, 1997.

Recommended Websites

See the Web pages for the individual universal data server vendors listed in Exhibit 31.3.

Chapter 32

Middleware, Universal Data Servers, and Object-Oriented Data Servers

James A. Larson
Carol L. Larson

RELATIONAL DATABASE MANAGEMENT SYSTEMS are used widely to store and access an enterprise's data. The data elements managed by relational DBMSs are simple data types such as integers, floating point numbers, short character strings, and dates. However, relational DBMSs do not manage complex data types that may be important to an enterprise. Complex data types include multimedia data types such as text, images, audio, and video, and compound data types such as dates and time series. Until recently, relational DBMSs could not deal with these data types, which left enterprises with file systems or manual systems to manage their nonrelational forms of information.

Different enterprises have different requirements for complex data types. Some enterprises need multimedia data types, some need compound data types, and some need both. Although many enterprises depend heavily upon relational database technology, others rely primarily on file systems, and still others rely on manual procedures to manage noncomputerized multimedia data. It is doubtful that a single mechanism can satisfy these differing requirements.

THE CHALLENGE OF COMPLEX DATA TYPES

Exhibits 32.1 through 32.4 illustrate four different mechanisms for dealing with complex data types. To illustrate the differences among the four approaches, a simple medical information system containing three types of data will be used.

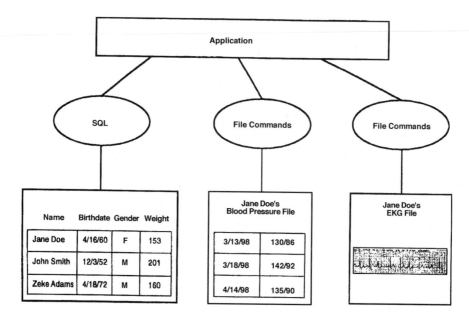

Exhibit 32.1.   Data extraction mechanism.

Relational data includes the patient's name, unique identifier, address, date of birth, height, and weight. Typically, this information is stored in a Patient Information table managed by a relational DBMS. In an object-oriented DBMS, the information is contained within the Patient object.

Compound data includes daily blood pressure readings taken over several weeks. For the data extraction and middleware mechanisms, this information may be stored as a file consisting of several records, each containing the <date> and <reading> values. With a universal data server, the information is stored as a single data type called a time series consisting of a sequence of <date, reading> pairs. In an object-oriented data server, the information is represented as a Blood Pressure sub-object of the Patient object.

Multimedia data includes the electrocardiogram (EKG) of the patient's heartbeat. With the data extraction, middleware, and universal data server approaches, the EKG is stored as a bit map in a file. In the object-oriented data server mechanism, the EKG is represented as an electrocardiogram subobject of the Patient object.

Of course, a real medical database would have much more information than illustrated in each exhibit, but the examples will serve to illustrate the differences among the four mechanisms. For this discussion, assume that all data reside on the same computer.

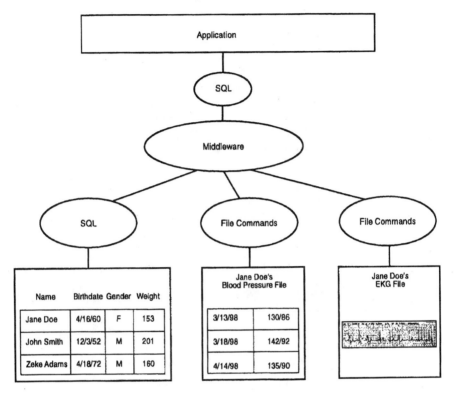

Exhibit 32.2. Middleware mechanism.

The issues of distributed data are complex and beyond the scope of this article. Please see *Software Architectures for Distributed DBMSs in a Client/Server Environment* by J. A. Larson and C. L. Larson (Auerbach Publication, in press) for more information.

MECHANISMS SUPPORTING COMPLEX DATA TYPES

The first two mechanisms illustrated in Exhibits 32.1 and 32.2 enable applications to access existing data structures without migrating data to new types of servers.

Data Extraction

In Exhibit 32.1, applications extract and integrate data from a relational database and a file system. To access relational information about Jane Doe, the application issues an SQL request to the relational DBMS, which returns the Patient Information about Jane Doe by accessing the Jane Doe Blood Pressure and EKG files. The application then merges and formats the information before presenting it to the user.

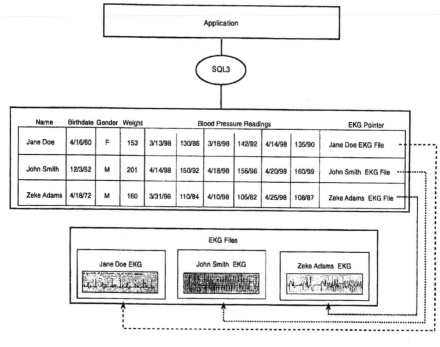

Exhibit 32.3.   Universal data server.

Middleware

With this approach, commercial middleware acts on behalf of the application to extract multimedia data from files and data from a relational data server. As shown in Exhibit 32.2, the application first issues an SQL request to the middleware, which passes it on to the relational DBMS, which in turn accesses the database and returns the Patient Information about Jane Doe. Next, the application issues SQL requests to the middleware, which converts the SQL request into file accesses applied to the file system and then returns the Jane Doe Blood Pressure file and the Jane Doe EKG file to the application. The application is responsible for merging the data from the database and the files before presenting it to the user.

A special type of middleware, called gateways, enables users to formulate requests in a language that is converted by the middleware to another language for processing. For example, when the application submits a request using SQL, the middleware translates the request to the format required by the underlying data server. Example gateways include the following:

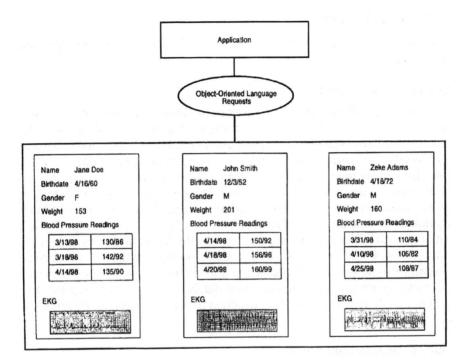

Exhibit 32.4. Object-oriented data server.

- CrossAccess Data Delivery System from Cross Access Corporation. This system translates DB2 SQL to IMS, IDMS, Model 204, and file systems.
- EDA/SQL from Information Builders Incorporated. This software translates SQL into nonrelational data commands.
- OLE DB and Open Database Connectivity (ODBC) from Microsoft Corporation. These application program interfaces (APIs) and associated implementations enable applications to access many relational data servers, file systems, and other data sources.
- DB2 DataJoiner from IBM. DB2 DataJoiner is a translator that converts SQL requests into the format required by nonrelational data sources. It also performs other functions, including cross database joins and data conversions. Unlike most gateways, it has an optimizer to optimize queries involving data from multiple sources.

Gateways enable applications to access existing data sources without migrating the data to a new type of data server.

NEW DATA SERVERS

DBMS vendors have introduced two new data servers to manage complex data types.

Universal Data Server

Exhibit 32.3 illustrates a universal data server, which contains extensions to relational data servers that store, search, and retrieve complex data types. These systems are called object-relational, extended relational, multimedia, and universal data servers. The term universal data server is used frequently to indicate that a relational data server has been extended to support a variety of new data types. The application issues an SQL request to the universal data server, which returns Jane Doe's Patient Information, including the Blood Pressure complex data type, to the application. The universal data server uses pointers in the EKG column to access the bitmap containing Jane's EKG from the file system. Unlike the data extraction and middleware mechanisms, the universal data server integrates data from the file system and the universal database before returning the integrated results to the application, which in turn formats it and presents it to the user.

Object-oriented Data Server

As shown in Exhibit 32.4, this server stores, retrieves, and searches complex data types. In the object-oriented data server, the complex data types are called objects; they contain data to which the user may apply object-specific functions. Some objects may be similar to tables in relational DBMSs, and other objects may be complex data objects containing multiple nested subobjects. In the medical example, the object-oriented data server retrieves the Patient object for Jane Doe, as well as subobjects EKG and Blood Pressure. The application formats and presents the information to the user.

MECHANISM SELECTION AND EVALUATION CRITERIA

The four mechanisms differ in the features they support and are summarized in Exhibit 32.5.

Programming Language Support

When using data extraction, middleware, or universal servers, application programs use an Application Program Interface (API) to open a database, submit a request, and retrieve the results. These approaches do not support a programming language that accesses the database directly. However, applications written in an object-oriented language, such as C++ or Java, access objects in an object-oriented data server directly. Object-oriented data servers enable programmers to access the database using

Exhibit 32.5. Comparison of mechanisms

	Mechanism			
Criteria	Data Extraction	Middleware	Universal Data Servers	Object-Oriented Data Servers
Programming language support	No	No	No	Yes
Extensible data type support	No	No	Yes	Yes
User-defined functions	No	No	Yes	Yes
Integrated backup and recovery	No	No	Yes	Yes
Automatic optimizers	No	No	Yes	Yes
SQL access	No	Yes	Yes	Yes
Multimedia access	Yes	Yes	Yes	Yes

the programming language without using special I/O commands, such as read and write.

Extensible Data Type Support

With the extracted and middleware approaches, programmers must implement new data types in the application and map the new data types to the data types supported by the underlying data sources. These tasks are taken over by database administrators for the universal and object-oriented data servers. For the universal data servers, database administrators define new data types by defining their representation, storage structure, and access methods using SQL 3. (Although SQL and SQL2 both describe tables, SQL3 describes tables and other complex data types that may be nested.) For object-oriented data servers, database administrators use an object-oriented language to define new data types.

New Functions

Part of defining a new data type is defining new functions involving the new data type. In the extracted and middleware approaches, programmers implement these new functions as part of the application. For universal and object-oriented data servers, database administrators define new functions to operate on the new data types. These functions can enforce business rules on the data, implement new functions required by application programs, and optimize queries.

Integrated Backup and Recovery

With the data extraction and middleware approaches, there is no integrated backup and recovery for both the file system and database. However, both universal and object-oriented data servers provide automatic backup and recovery mechanisms so that the entire database can be backed-up and restored.

427

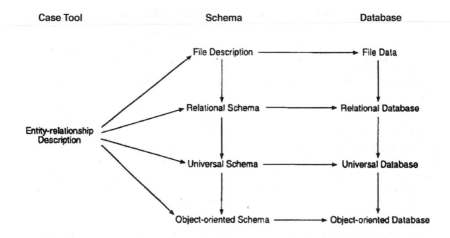

Exhibit 32.6. Mappings and conversions among schemas and databases.

Automatic Optimizers

For the data extraction and middleware approaches, the application programmer must code all optimizations directly into the application. Any global query optimization also must be done by the programmer. With the universal and object-oriented data servers, the database administrator specifies optimization procedures for execution by the data server. These optimization procedures are reused by each request submitted to the server.

SQL Access

Although the extraction approach includes a relational DBMS that supports SQL requests, all accesses by applications to the file system must be expressed using traditional file I/O commands. The remaining three mechanisms support SQL requests for accessing all data. With the middleware approach, the middleware translates SQL requests into file I/O commands. The universal data server accepts and executes SQL requests against all data. Objects in most object-oriented data servers can be viewed as tables and, thus, support SQL requests. In addition, object-oriented servers also support requests expressed using an object-oriented language. These requests may include data type-specific functions.

Multimedia Access

All of the mechanisms support access to complex data types.

MIGRATING SCHEMA AND DATA

Exhibit 32.6 illustrates data models and databases involved in the conversion from files to relational or universal servers and, finally, to object-oriented data servers. Many enterprises use CASE tools to develop conceptual models of the enterprise's data. For example, several CASE tools use the entity-relationship modeling technique to represent the enterprise's data and a database schema for a relational or universal data server. Other CASE tools generate object-oriented syntax for creating object classes for an object-oriented data server.

When migrating from files to relational or universal data servers, file descriptions must be converted into relational schema. Some CASE tools are able to accept file descriptions and generate SQL syntax for creating equivalent relations. However, most database administrators perform this step manually.

When migrating to a universal server, most relational schema do not need to be converted; however, some schema may need to be extended to describe new media and complex data types. CASE tools should be used to modify the enterprise's conceptual schema and, then, to generate a revised relational schema. If the CASE tool does not support media or complex data types, the database administrator may need manually to modify the SQL generated by the CASE tool to incorporate these new data types into the relational schema.

When migrating from relational or universal servers to object-oriented servers, the database administrator must decide whether to model existing data as relations or as more complex objects. To minimize changes to existing applications, most data remain modeled as relations. However, some data should be modeled as objects, especially the new media and compound data types that provide the motivation for switching to an object-oriented data server. Some CASE tools generate either relational or object-oriented schema, which enable the database administrator to avoid manually converting a relational or universal schema into an object-oriented schema. If the enterprise does not have such a CASE tool, then the database administrator must generate object-oriented schema for all new data and existing relational data.

After the schema are in place, the database administrator must populate the new data server with data from the old files and/or databases. This involves writing conversion software that extracts data from the source files or databases, changes the format to conform to the new data schema, and inserts the data into the new data server. Any new data also must be captured and entered into the new data server. This conversion software may be quite complex when migrating from files into relations, especially when integrating data from multiple files. The conversion software is quite simple when converting relations from a relational or universal data server into relations in an object-oriented data server. Capturing and loading new media and compound data into the object-oriented data server may, however, be quite complex. Most database server venders provide conversion software to assist database administrators when migrating data to a new server.

RECOMMENDATIONS

The four mechanisms represent four steps of a migration path from independent relational data servers and file systems (which are integrated by applications that extract data) to integrated object-oriented data servers (which perform the most data management functions). For enterprises requiring complex data types, the long-term goal is clearly to employ an object-oriented data server. The other approaches can be used as intermediate stepping stones before migrating to an object-oriented data server.

If only a handful of applications require complex data types, the data extraction approach is preferred because it provides no disruption for legacy applications.

The middleware approach adds SQL support, which may be desirable for end users who are able to use GUI interfaces to generate SQL requests to all of the data. This positions the data for later upgrade to universal data servers, which support SQL directly.

Universal data servers provide integrated data management support for the new data types, as well as integrating them with the traditional tables of relational data systems. For relational data servers users, this is a reasonable alternative because most major relational data server vendors support universal data servers. The upward migration from relational to universal data servers is straightforward, if the enterprise does not switch vendors.

The object-oriented data server promises to provide the most features and functions. However, some experts feel that object-oriented data servers do not provide performance superior to the relational data servers with their optimizers. In time, the optimizers of object-oriented data servers will improve just as optimizers for relational data servers have improved over the past 10 years. Universal data servers appear to be in a safe holding pattern, providing access to complex data types, until object-oriented data servers provide the features and performance required by users.

Recommended Reading

Barry, D. K., *The Object Database Handbook : How to Select, Implement, and Use Object-Oriented Databases,* John Wiley & Sons, New York, 1996.

Cattell, R. G. G., *Object Data Management: Object-Oriented and Extended Relational Database Systems,* Addison-Wesley, Reading, MA, 1991.

Chamberlin, D., *DB2 Universal Database : IBM's Object-Relational Database Systems,* Morgan Kaufman Publishers, San Francisco, 1988.

Colonna-Romano, J. and Srite, P., *The Middleware Source Book,* Digital Press, Burlington, VT, 1995.

Finn, M., Use OLE DB to Integrate Your Data, *Databased Web Adv.,* Nov. 1997, 64–66.

Francett, B., Middleware on the March, *Software Mag.,* April 1996, 71–76.

Goddard, D., How Middleware Can Help Your Enterprise, *Databased Web Adv.,* May 1996, 100–107.

Larson, J. A. and Larson, C. L., *Designing an Integrated Data Server,* Auerbach Publication No. 22-01-95 (1997).

Larson, J. A. and Larson, C. L., *Migrating Files to Relational Databases,* Auerbach Publication No. 22-01-29 (1996).

Larson, J. A. and Larson, C. L., *Software Architectures for Distributed DBMSs in a Client/Server Environment,* Auerbach Publication (TBA 1998).

Larson, J. A. and Larson, C. L., *Why Universal Data Servers,* Auerbach Publication (TBA 1998).

Loomis, M. E. S. and Chaudhri, A. B., Eds., *Object Databases in Practice,* Prentice-Hall, Upper Saddle River, NJ, 1997.

Making Connections Across the Enterprise: Client-server Middleware, *DBMS,* January 1993, 46–51.

Recommended Websites

For more information about the products mentioned in this chapter, see the following Web pages:

Cross Access Corp. (Cross Access Delivery System), Oakbrook Terrace, IL, http://www.crossaccess.com/

IBM DB2 DataJoiner: http://www.software.ibm.com/data/datajoiner/

IBM Home Page: http://www.ibm.com/

Information Builders Inc. (EDA/SQL), Two Penn Plaza, New York, NY 10121-2898, 212.736.4433, Fax 212.967.6406, http://www.IBI.com/

Microsoft Corporation, Redmond, Washington, http://www.microsoft.com/

Microsoft Open Database Connectivity (ODBC), http://www.microsoft.com/data/odbc/

Microsoft OLE DB, http://www.microsoft.com/data/oledb/

Chapter 33
Creating Effective Batch SQL Jobs

Len Dvorkin

INTRODUCTION

THE RECENT ARRIVAL OF MATURE RELATIONAL DATABASES, powerful enough to handle mission-critical functions, has provided systems developers with the ability to perform complex processing in a much simpler way than traditional data repositories and languages previously afforded.

This power, however, has represented a double-edged sword when combined with traditional programming approaches and style. When complex business requirements are combined with the power of Structured Query Language (SQL), the result can be code that is syntactically correct, but runs poorly or not at all at production-level data volumes.

This problem commonly occurs during the creation of online transaction processing (OLTP) systems, when a frequently encountered scenario has developers coding and testing an application in a test environment, certifying it as ready for production, and watching it fail with a higher number of users, more data, etc. Fortunately (or unfortunately), this type of failure generally manifests itself directly and clearly, in the form of an online function that stops working, or that only performs slowly.

A more subtle trap relates to batch processing in SQL. Most significant DBMS-based systems have batch components to support them. These components include:

- Internal processing: using data from tables in the system to update other tables within the system.
- Data loading: updating the system's database with data from other systems.
- Data extraction: creation of tables or flat files for use by an outside system.
- Reporting: collection of data from within the system in order to present it for user review.

These components are not as "flashy" as their online cousins; however, they have the potential to seriously impact a system if they are not created and managed correctly. And batch routines are here to stay — the power represented by relational databases does not exempt mature systems from requiring tasks to run automatically and unattended, separately from any online components.

Most of the recurring problems in batch SQL are also frequently encountered when creating SQL for online purposes — after all, the language is the same. However, given the usual purposes of batch SQL, certain traps tend to manifest themselves with annoying frequency, even when coded by experienced developers. This chapter describes principles and techniques that represent good practice when designing any SQL job, but seem to be forgotten or left out more often when the batch environment is concerned. (See Exhibit 33.1.)

SQL CODING PRINCIPLES

Joins

A common operation in batch SQL involves combining data coming from multiple tables that have a relationship to each other. These may be a series of transaction tables coming from different sources, or a single transaction table with several foreign keys that need to be referenced.

In these cases, it can be hard to resist the power of SQL's ability to join database lookups across multiple tables. Although careful design of queries can result in a tightly tuned, fast-performing join, most databases use rules coded in an internal optimizer to examine a query and develop the plan that will guide the database engine in processing the query. In complicated joins, it is not uncommon for the database optimizer to make an unexpected decision on the join order and turn what should be a simple query into a large, slow-running database killer.

For example, assume that a report extract is needed for a table with four foreign keys to code tables. As a join, this could be coded as follows:

```
INSERT INTO report_table
SELECT t.column1,
    t.column2,
    a.description,
    b.description,
    c.description,
    d.description,
    <other columns>
```

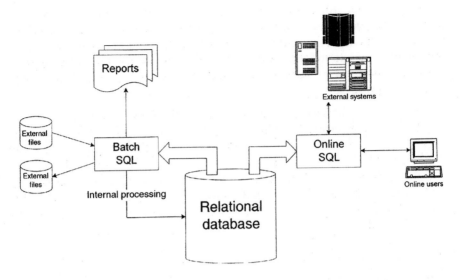

Exhibit 33.1.   Common functions of online and batch SQL.

```
FROMtransaction_table t,
    code_table1 a,
    code_table2 b,
    code_table3 c,
    code_table4 d
WHERE t.code_a = a.code
AND t.code_b = b.code
AND t.code_c = c.code
AND t.code_d = d.code
AND <other conditions>
```

Under low-volume conditions, or under high-volume conditions when the database statistics are current and the database's query optimizer is working effectively, this query will run well. The first table to be examined will be transaction_table, and code values found there will be used to reference the required code tables.

Sometimes, though, a large number of *where* clauses or a significant change in database volumes can confuse the optimizer, resulting in disastrous query plans (building the result set in the above example from one of the code tables, for instance).

In a batch SQL job, developers are generally not worried about shaving seconds off of transactions. They are much more interested in predictable, arithmetic increases in performance time directly related to database table volumes. (There are exceptions to this statement — some systems have a very restricted batch processing time window within which their processing must be completed. However, the techniques in this article can be used to reduce the server load of a given batch job, or to permit multiple jobs to run concurrently, potentially fixing these "batch window squeeze" situations.) To that end, splitting the single multitable join into separate queries involves a relatively small performance penalty in exchange for a predictable overall runtime. For instance:

```
loop for each qualified record in transaction_table:
    SELECT :col1 = t.column1,
        :col2 = t.column2,
        :code_a = t.code_a,
        :code_b = t.code_b,
        :code_c = t.code_c,
        :code_d = t.code_d,
        <other columns>
    FROM transaction_table t
    WHERE <other conditions>
    SELECT :description_a
    FROM code_table1
    WHERE code = :code_a
    SELECT :description_b
    FROM code_table1
    WHERE code = :code_b
    SELECT :description_c
    FROM code_table1
    WHERE code = :code_c
    SELECT :description_d
    FROM code_table1
    WHERE code = :code_d
    INSERT INTO report_table
    VALUES (:col1,
        :col2,
        :description_a,
        :description_b,
        :description_c,
        :description_d,
        <other columns>)
    end loop
```

At the cost of a few extra lines of code, the five-table join in the first example becomes a bulletproof routine with predictable performance under virtually all conditions of data volume or database statistics.

Note that the number of required database lookups in the previous code has not changed from the more complicated example, leaving only a small net extra cost in separate processing of the SQL statements. If these statements are running inside the database engine (in a stored procedure, for instance), the overhead becomes even smaller.

Declarations and Initializations

The top section of any routine should contain declarations of any variables that will be used in the job. If a data value is likely to be changed during testing or after the job is running in production, consider changing it to a "constant" variable. This makes it easier to read and maintain the code. Similarly, table columns containing code values are easier to deal with if their code values are stored in constants. Consider the example below:

```
declare :MIN_DOLLAR_VALUE float = 10.0
declare :SALE char(1) = "S"
declare :RETURN char(1) = "R"


<other processing>


SELECT sum (trans_value)
FROM trans_table
WHERE trans_value > :MIN_DOLLAR_VALUE
AND trans_type = :SALE
```

Read Once, Write Once

Depending on the specific driver program type and database implementation being used, the cost of an SQL table hit is easily 10 times or more expensive than processing a simple logic statement. However, many batch programs are profligate in their use of table access statements. In the following example, a single row in a source table is read once for its index value, a second time for a lookup value, and a third time for other information needed to write to an output table:

437

```
loop for each qualified record in transaction_table:
    SELECT :index_field = t.index_field
    FROM transaction_table t
    WHERE t.transaction_date = <today>


    < processing of the record >


    SELECT :transaction_type = a.type_description
    FROM transaction_table t,
        code_table1 a
    WHERE t.index_field = :index_field
    AND t.type_code_a = a.type_code_a


    < other processing of the record >


    INSERT INTO report_table
    SELECT t.column1,
        t.column2,
        :transaction_type,
        <other columns>
    FROM transaction_table t
    WHERE t.index_field = :index_field
end loop
```

When examining this program structure, developers often explain that this is a straightforward approach to satisfying the program's requirements — what is wrong with it? They may be influenced by the method in which a traditional/hierarchical data store is read, where the first access to a record brings all of its data directly into a program cache, and subsequent access to fields on the record are virtually "free" reads of local memory.

However, this is certainly not the case when discussing database access. Each time the (same) row in a table is referenced in a select statement, a nontrivial amount of database work must take place. Most database implementations will cache the affected data row in its local memory pages after the first read, preventing hard disk access in subsequent reads. However, the overhead cost of parsing the statement, determining a query path, supporting a join, identifying the desired row, determining that it is resident in memory, etc., is still significantly higher than that of a simple reference to a local variable in the program's memory space.

This routine can be rewritten with minimum effort to access each table only once, retrieving all columns that will be required in this select statement and saving them locally for use later in the process:

```
loop for each qualified record in transaction_table:
    SELECT :index_field = t.index_field,
        :type_code_a = type_code_a,
        :column1 = column1,
        :column2 = column2,
        <other columns>
    FROM transaction_table t
    WHERE <conditions>


    < other processing of the record >


    SELECT :transaction_type = a.type_description
    FROM code_table1 a
    WHERE a.type_code_a = :type_code_a


    < other processing of the record >


    INSERT INTO report_table
    VALUES (:column1,
        :column2,
        :transaction_type,
        <other columns>
end loop
```

An analogous situation can occur when writing an output record. Rather than adopting a simple structure that first inserts a skeleton of a new output row, and then updating elements of the same row during processing, the column data to be inserted can be saved in local variables and inserted in a single SQL statement.

Indexes

The optimizers in today's database engines have matured tremendously compared to those of several years ago. For ad hoc, complex queries, it is now often possible to rely on the optimizer to determine the optimum query path that should be taken to minimize a query's runtime.

However, even the best optimizers cannot be used as a safety net for all queries. If a database's internal table statistics are not up-to-date, for instance, many optimizers will choose poor query plans or even switch to table scans with sometimes disastrous results. This problem can be avoided, to some extent, by regularly running an "update statistics" routine that recreates internal table data volume and distribution statistics. However, in cases where the volume or type of data is changing frequently in a table, even daily or weekly updates of table statistics may not be adequate to guarantee the use of a desired index.

For that reason, good defensive coding practices take the approach that "it's nice to have a database optimizer, but let's not leave anything to chance." Every query on a table of nontrivial size should be examined, with particular attention to ensuring that its where clauses correspond to an existing index. If an appropriate index does not already exist in the database, it should either be added to the table or, if this is not practical, consideration should be given to redesigning the query.

An extremely common development scenario has normally careful developers designing batch jobs without consideration of indexes ("After all, we won't have any users sitting at their desks waiting for this job to finish tonight."), testing the jobs under low-data-volume conditions and verifying their correctness, and then watching in horror as the batch job run time grows steadily under regular data volume conditions.

There may be some exceptions to this principle; for example, when an entire table is being read and processed using a cursor, direct sequential access can be faster than involving any indices. But, in general, every database access in the routine should be explicitly designed to use a predefined index. If this is done, then overall job performance may grow geometrically in proportion to the volume of data being processed, but the time should be manageable and predictable from the start.

Transaction Commitments

One of the common design tradeoffs in batch routines involves decisions concerning committing transactions. As in other aspects of the batch routines, the developer approaches adopted in the construction of online routines do not always correspond well to the design requirements of a batch routine.

Within a transaction block, either all updates are applied to the database, or none of the updates are applied. This makes the approach to determining whether a transaction is required for an online SQL routine (and, if so, what its scope should be) a relatively simple exercise. The programmer simply identifies the logical unit of work, in terms of database changes, which may not be left partially complete in case of data or database problems.

The logical extension of this concept to batch routines would be to place a transaction block around every set of inserts and updates that comprise a single block of work. The problem with this straightforward approach is that the impact of processing individual transactions blocks in a routine reading of an input table of, say, 20,000 rows, can seriously affect the database's performance and logging.

A compromise approach to transaction design in batch routines involves grouping together a larger number of individual input records into a single transaction, and repeatedly beginning and committing transactions when that number of input records has been processed. The following example groups input records into batches of 500 for the purpose of transaction processing:

```
declare :counter int = 0
declare :MAX_RECORDS_IN_COMMIT int = 500


BEGIN TRANSACTION


loop for each qualified record in transaction_table:
    SET :counter = :counter+1
    if :counter = :MAX_RECORDS_IN_COMMIT
        COMMIT TRANSACTION
        BEGIN TRANSACTION
    end if
        <process record>
    end loop


COMMIT TRANSACTION
```

Some experience is necessary to determine the best number of rows to include in a single commit block, because this decision depends on the specific database implementation and environment. Establishing this number as a local constant or parameter to the routine (as in the previous example) is an effective way to make it easily tunable based on actual experience.

Note that if the batch routine will be running while online users are working on the system, the MAX_RECORDS_IN_COMMIT value should be kept relatively low to avoid locking an excessive number of rows or pages needed by other processes.

If the input records are not being deleted or flagged in a specific way when they are processed, transaction parameters can be used in conjunction with transaction diagnostic messages to facilitate restartability of the routine. They allow a person responding to a problem encountered when running the routine to determine quickly and accurately how much data had been processed successfully before a problem occurred. In this way, steps can be taken to reset the input source and restart the job without incurring the risk of missing or double-processing input data.

Data All in a Row

Most batch routines, either as part of a recurring loop or as a one-time operation, must read data and conduct processing based on that data. The "read once, write once" approach discussed in this article applies here — the aim is to select data from tables as few times as possible. This may mean storing data in local variables, or organizing the routine in order to defer executing the select statement until all required selection criteria have been established.

If the source data is read in a loop, there are several useful techniques available to "walk through" the qualifying rows.

Cursors. Cursors support a single selection of input data, and one-by-one processing of the results. Depending on the database implementation, it may not be practical to use cursors when the number of input rows is large.

Ascending Key Read. This method stores a starting key position and repeatedly reads additional records with larger key values. This method is most simple when the routine can count on the existence of a sequential key in the source table. If that key is indexed properly, this can also be a very efficient way to read the table rows:

```
declare :current_key int
SET :current_key = <appropriate starting value>

loop:
    SELECT <columns>
    FROM trans_table
    WHERE trans_key = :current_key

    if <no rows found>
        exit loop
    else
        SET :current_key = :current_key + 1

    <process the selected row>
end loop
```

Read and Delete. This is appropriate for cases when the data in the input table does not need to be saved after the routine is complete. This is implemented simply by deleting the rows from the source table as they are processed.

This approach is most suitable for cases where a flat file needs to be processed in a database. The batch jobstream can first transfer the flat file data into a temporary table, and then invoke the batch routine to process the records one by one. If a problem halts the batch routine in midstream, it should be automatically restartable with the (presumably) smaller input table, which would contain all unprocessed rows.

Reading a table using this approach can be highly efficient, especially in database implementations that allow the programmer to specify a row retrieval limit in its syntax (for instance, the "set rowcount 1" statement in SQL Server). With this restriction in place, the read can be a simple, nonindexed select statement that permits the database to retrieve the first physical record encountered with no need to refer to indices or complicated query plans.

The program structure for this approach is somewhat similar to the previous example:

```
loop:
    <restrict selection to 1 row>
    SELECT :key_field = key_field,
        <other columns>
    FROM trans_table
    <remove the single-row restriction>

    if <no rows found>
        exit loop

    <process the selected row>

    DELETE trans_table
    WHERE key_field = :key_field
end loop
```

Read and Flag. This is very similar to read and delete, but is used when the input table must be kept intact after being processed. Rather than deleting each input row as it is processed, a status flag is set in one of its columns indicating that it has been used and should therefore not be picked up on the next loop iteration:

```
declare :PROCESSED char(1) = "P"

loop:
    <restrict selection to 1 row>
    SELECT :key_field = key_field,
        <other columns>
    FROM trans_table
    WHERE processing_status != :PROCESSED
    <remove the single-row restriction>

    if <no rows found>
        exit loop

    <process the selected row>

    UPDATE trans_table
    SET processing_status = :PROCESSED
    WHERE key_field = :key_field
end loop
```

GENERAL PRINCIPLES

Consistency

In many development environments, database routines seem to often suffer from a lack of structure, design, and clean formatting. This is perhaps due to the ease with which they can be coded, and the relatively relaxed formatting restrictions of most SQL implementations. When compared to regular 3GL or 4GL processing code, many database routines are characterized by few (or nonstandard) comments, inconsistent indentation, and capitalization of keywords, resulting in an erratic look and feel. Batch routines, because they tend to be longer and more complex, are particularly impacted by this lack of consistency.

Although there are many standards that could be described as clear, this article does not attempt to define a single "best" one. The important thing is to choose a standard and stick with it for all SQL routines in a system. This coding discipline generally pays for itself many times in reduced overall maintenance time in the long term.

In addition to these cosmetic issues, an objective of clarity can lead a structured development shop to convert complex batch routine syntax into simpler statements, even if this involves a small cost in terms of performance. For example, even if a complex table join has been tested and verified to be correct in all circumstances (including tests under high-volume conditions), it can be worthwhile to review the performance and coding cost involved in splitting it into separate but more simple queries. If this cost is not excessive, it will almost certainly be recovered with interest when the routine needs to be modified because of system problems or new business requirements.

Diagnostics

If a batch routine is running without a user sitting at a screen waiting for its completion, it is very tempting to build it with a minimum of inline diagnostics. Sometimes, a small set of control totals may be generated and saved as part of the job run, but batch routines are commonly built without even that level of output.

Although it is true that there is little need for detailed diagnostics when a job is working correctly, their lack is felt most deeply in the most stressful situations — when problems manifest themselves. In a typical real-life scenario, the complex batch job runs for several months without problems and then, due to some unforeseen data input scenario, starts producing incorrect results. The support staff designated to investigate the problem is faced with a sometimes daunting task of diagnosis and repair, often complicated by less-sophisticated debugging tools for the database environment.

To speed up diagnosis and resolution of these problems, a relatively small amount of developer time and batch job runtime can be applied to producing diagnostic messages directly from the batch routine. A simple but comprehensive approach involves issuing two types of diagnostic messages: control diagnostic messages and transaction diagnostic messages.

Control Diagnostic Messages. These act as milestones along the road of a batch routine. If one section becomes slow or fails to work, then the offending section should be immediately obvious by referencing the control diagnostics. These could read, for instance, as follows:

ddMMMyyyy hh:mm:ss ... Routine "process_transactions" started
ddMMMyyyy hh:mm:ss ... Beginning to process input rows from
   trans_table
ddMMMyyyy hh:mm:ss ... Processed 1000 input rows
ddMMMyyyy hh:mm:ss ... Processed 2000 input rows
ddMMMyyyy hh:mm:ss ... Processed 3000 input rows
ddMMMyyyy hh:mm:ss ... Processed 4000 input rows
ddMMMyyyy hh:mm:ss ... 4692 input rows processed
ddMMMyyyy hh:mm:ss ... Beginning generation of report_table
ddMMMyyyy hh:mm:ss ... Generation of report_table complete, with
   2456 adds and 1205 changes

The level of detail and wording can depend entirely on development shop standards, as long as they satisfy their primary purpose — to facilitate quick identification of the likely location of problems.

Transaction Diagnostic Messages. These support a more detailed look at the data being processed by the batch routine. Their existence acts as a record of the data processed, and can be used to quickly answer questions like, "Why didn't product #5682 get reset last night?" or "Why do the sales to customer #7531 appear twice on this morning's reports?"

Transaction diagnostics can represent quite a large quantity of data and, for that reason, they are generally overwritten on a daily or, at least, weekly basis. Using the same example just shown, they could look like this:

ddMMMyyyy hh:mm:ss ... Routine "process_transactions" started
ddMMMyyyy hh:mm:ss ... Beginning to process input rows from
   trans_table
ddMMMyyyy hh:mm:ss ... Processing product #14, status "A"
ddMMMyyyy hh:mm:ss ... Sales record: Sold 50 units to customer #5532
   at $45
ddMMMyyyy hh:mm:ss ... Sales record: Sold 14 units to customer #5532
   at $48

ddMMMyyyy hh:mm:ss ... Returns record: Returned 12 units from customer #5532 at $43

ddMMMyyyy hh:mm:ss ... Processing product #18, status "A"

ddMMMyyyy hh:mm:ss ... No sales records found

ddMMMyyyy hh:mm:ss ... No returns records found

ddMMMyyyy hh:mm:ss ... Processing product #22, status "D"

ddMMMyyyy hh:mm:ss ... Skipping discontinued product

ddMMMyyyy hh:mm:ss ... Processing product #23, status "A"

ddMMMyyyy hh:mm:ss ... Sales record: Sold 10 units to customer #5532 at $2.50

ddMMMyyyy hh:mm:ss ... Sales record: Sold 12 units to customer #18006 at $2.75

ddMMMyyyy hh:mm:ss ... Sales record: Sold 985 units to customer #34925 at $2.60

... and so on

If applicable (or necessary), control diagnostics and transaction diagnostics can be combined into a single output file. The emphasis here is not on a cosmetically fancy report layout — rather, the point should be to produce useful diagnostic information that can be referenced when results of the batch process are in question and details of its processing are needed.

If disk space is not adequate to generate transaction diagnostics on a regular basis, the routine can be coded to issue them only when an input "debug" parameter is set. In normal situations, the debug parameter would be turned off. When specific problems arise and there is a need to trace the routine's running more carefully, the parameter would be turned on. By coding the parameter into the routine from the start, production diagnostics can be turned on and off months or years later without changing a single line of code.

Affecting Other Batch Jobs

In many cases, batch processes will be scheduled for times when there are no online users accessing the database. In these cases, using the power of SQL to access many rows in a single statement can have the dual advantages of simplicity and speed. For example, to copy details from today's transactions to a reporting table, the statement

```
INSERT INTO report_table
SELECT t.column1,
     t.column2,
     <other columns>
FROM transaction_table t,
WHERE t.transaction_date = <today>
```

can certainly be very effective (assuming an appropriate index on the transaction date field).

However, it is very important to realize that in most database implementations, even a single statement like this one places an implicit transaction on all data accessed in its select statement. This lock ensures that either the entire selection is made and inserted into the destination table, or none of it is.

This means that all rows selected by the query are locked for its duration. If the table and/or number of rows being affected is large, this has the potential to freeze any online users or other batch jobs attempting to access the locked records (or pages, depending on the database implementation of locking).

Running this type of query during the day — to create an ad hoc report, for example — is often responsible for frustrating calls to the help desk, where online users report intermittent freezing of their systems in no discernible or reproducible pattern.

The same phenomenon can occur if multiple batch jobs are scheduled concurrently by system administrators. In the worst case, two batch jobs can fall into a deadlock situation where each is holding resources needed by the other.

To avoid this trap, the most important point is to remember that "you are not alone." If query speed and simplicity is paramount, then designers and database/system administrators must be very conscious of the database access contained in these routines and consciously schedule them in such a way to preclude conflicts.

If robustness of the system is important enough to accept a small speed penalty in running the routine, then a walkthrough approach can produce the same ultimate results as the single query, but without locking tables or inflicting performance penalties on other users or processes sharing the database:

```
loop for each qualified record in transaction_table:
    SELECT :col1 = t.column1,
        :col2 = t.column2,
    <other columns>
    FROM transaction_table t
    WHERE t.transaction_date = <today>
    INSERT INTO report_table
    VALUES (:col1,
        :col2,
        <other columns>)
end loop
```

CONCLUSION

Many problems in batch SQL jobs can be avoided by developing and applying a good set of SQL programming instincts. These instincts comprise rules of thumb that sometimes represent simple common sense, but in other cases are not in the natural toolkit of a developer coming from other technology platforms.

However, applying an "ounce" of prevention in the design and construction phases of a project's batch SQL components can easily pay back several "pounds" of savings in future maintenance efforts.

Chapter 34
The Advancing Art of Indexing

Lois Richards

DESPITE THE ENORMOUS SUMS OF MONEY SPENT on client/server, data warehousing, LAN technology, UNIX systems, and PC access tools, the job of delivering information to end-users in an efficient manner remains difficult. With all the new technology and computing power now available, why are IS departments still struggling to answer this fundamental need? More important, is a solution at hand?

IN THE BEGINNING, THERE WAS DATA

In retrospect, it seemed so simple. Of course, data was there to be used. The problem was that traditional systems were designed for record keeping. Data gathering was the priority, not data dissemination. The end-user, however, was unaware of this barrier.

Finance departments were the first to see the benefit of the summary reports and analyses. Marketing departments were not far behind in asking for reports on their customers and prospects. Inventory management, manufacturing, engineering, personnel ... soon all departments could see the need for access to the data in these computerized corporate storehouses.

THEN THERE WERE USERS: THE REIGN OF THE 4GL

What evolved was the decision support system (DSS). DSS applications may access just the back-end or legacy systems, may include data warehousing, or may encompass an enterprisewide client/server information system. Decision support applications all require extensive access to corporate data stowed in the coffers of the computer system. Whether the database is a relational or other file structure, these decision support inquiries contribute to analyses of the selected data or display of the selected data in reports. In addition, the users submitting these inquiries insist on consistent, immediate response. IS must respond to these demands.

Whenever tackling any daunting task, most practitioners undertake the most obvious issues first. Thus, when it came to providing enterprisewide data access, the most prominent roadblock was getting users onto the system with the appropriate levels of security and programs to access the data they needed.

In the 1980s, such companies as Information Builders, Cognos, and Uniface launched the first revolution in end-user access by selling fourth-generation language (4GL) development tools. Fourth-generation languages made it possible to develop new applications in a fraction of the time required by conventional programming techniques. Meanwhile, PCS were gaining favor in the corporate world. Terminal emulation software sold by the thousands — then millions — as the proliferation of PCS became the new way to get access to the corporate system.

These new applications and terminal emulation techniques allowed a multitude of users to directly access data in corporate systems. The decision support system for the organization's knowledge worker was on its way. Granted, the access was usually reserved for either the data-entry level technician who used the system to enter, update, and delete information, or the hearty few who were confident enough to manipulate the applications. But the revolutionary step of allowing users directly on the system had taken place. The idea of interactive data access had become the norm. Users requested access to data immediately — online!

LET THERE BE UNIVERSAL ACCESS: CLIENT/SERVER AND NETWORKS

Throughout the 1980s and early 1990s, millions of users were brought online. Databases grew larger while the number of users who accessed them and the frequency of their access continued to expand. Even as users were clamoring for more, organizations were failing to see the return they had expected from their investments in technology.

Even though these new applications allowed access to corporate data, it was in a rigid, predefined manner that protected system resources. Users who were not comfortable with a character environment, or who did not take the time to learn the cryptic commands and data layouts, still needed to depend on the IS department for their data needs. Information could still take weeks to get if it differed from the preestablished reports. Individual access was limited to one system at a time. Access to multiple data sources on various hosts from the same terminal was virtually impossible.

The next step was inevitable. The obvious choice to many was to marry the now-pervasive PC and its user-friendliness with the power of the corporate system. By the early 1990s, most corporations began developing some form of client/server system to increase efficiency and end-user access.

Client/server systems answered, at least temporarily, the next level of end-user access issues. The point-and-click interfaces of Windows and Macintosh systems made interacting with the data far easier. Users no longer had to memorize command sequences to get in and out of applications and databases. They could perform queries and create reports on the fly, and download data directly into the PC. Advances in network technology made it possible to have access to any number of corporate systems from the same PC or workstation.

With client/server connections, middleware connectivity tools, and networking, IS has solved the second hurdle of providing universal access: users are online and can request information through a relatively intuitive graphical environment. Fast access to information through online inquiry, analysis, and reporting remains a crucial factor if today's knowledge workers are to get their questions answered and work completed. But, as with most elements of progress, this new access has brought with it another dilemma — performance.

THE PERFORMANCE DILEMMA

Unfortunately, there appears to be one indisputable constant: fast is never fast enough.

As users point-and-click their way to the data they need, both users and IS now dread the infamous QFH ("query from hell"). Perfectly reasonable business questions such as "How many customers in the northeast region bought our product last quarter at the promotional price?" can bring even the most powerful server with millions of records to its knees — and all other users along with it. Because of this slow response time, interacting with the data is clumsy at best and impossible at worst.

Without question, CPU-intensive tasks, such as engineering and scientific applications, have seen dramatic increases in speed. In addition, the CPU-intensive tasks required in data base applications, such as sorting, are considerably faster. With CPU speeds increasing and the cost per millions of instructions per second (MIPS) dropping, it might appear that the solution to transaction and analysis bottlenecks experienced in most database applications has been met. Unfortunately, this is not true.

The reason is that most database applications benefit only modestly from higher-speed CPUs. Typically, the inability to resolve user queries comes from the application being disk I/O-bound rather than CPU-bound. The CPU is busy reading the data from disk in order to answer, or process, the request. Two basic strategies have emerged in an attempt to solve the performance dilemma:

- Limit the number, type, or timing of the queries that can be done through the client/server system.

- Pull the analytical/historical data into a data warehouse, so that the queries do not affect online production performance.

DSS inquiries and reports require access to large amounts of data, even when only a small subset of records is of interest. Consequently, placing limits on queries is generally unsatisfactory for all involved. The time required to accomplish the DSS request depends on disk throughput rather than CPU speed. While CPU speeds continue to increase and disk capacities see great gains, the transfer speeds (disk I/O) have only made incremental gains. So, users continue to be frustrated about the limits that are set, and IS is again put in the position of "policing" access to data.

Offloading data into a data warehouse only shifts the problem from one data structure to another. The assumption made with moving the data into a query-focused database is that the data warehouse, unlike a production system, does not require the same response times. Knowledge workers must wait hours, and sometimes days, for information they need.

The solution is to reduce the amount of disk I/O required to get the job done. In database applications, this means minimizing the amount of I/O needed to select and retrieve a desired subset of records for display or reporting. With this in mind, indexing becomes one of the most important aspects of any decision support system.

INDEXING — THE FUTURE IS NOW

Decision support applications require users to query, analyze, and report data. As data structures increase in size (millions and billions of records of data), the ability to meet the need to query, analyze, and report on data becomes burdensome — even for a super-powered computer. Whether a DSS application is in the conceptual stage or already developed, the issue of making data easily and immediately accessible to users will always be a challenge. Indexing provides a way to realize optimal benefits with minimal investment in new technologies or equipment.

Sophisticated indexing is the most effective way to reduce the disk I/O required to retrieve a subset of data. With advanced indexing techniques, record selections by any criteria are accomplished using few disk reads. As a result, complex selections from large databases execute in seconds.

Not the New Kid on the Block, But Effective

Data file structures offer several ways to access data. Foremost among them, sequential searches, or table scans, match data to the user's criteria. This technique requires access to every record and, consequently, large disk I/O. If available, an index can expedite this process by decreasing the number of reads.

B-Tree Indexing. The native indexes in relational databases such as Oracle, Informix, Sybase, and other relational database management systems (RDBMSs) use a B-tree structure that allows partial key retrievals, sorted retrievals, and concatenation of columns. B-tree indexing has been effectively used for years but has several drawbacks, including:

- *Limited to single attribute.* There is no efficient way to combine multiple criteria to narrow a search through thousands and millions of records.
- *Limited to support of full key values in left-to-right sequence.* Users must enter the search criteria in the same order the data was entered, in order to attain the most efficient search.
- *Limited to exact match of criteria to data stored.* Again, users must be aware of how the data was entered.

Several RDBMSs also have a "hashed" key capability, which is fast but not flexible. Hashed indexes require a full key lookup and a perfect match, including upper or lower case letters, spaces, and punctuation.

Though indexing has been around for as long as the computer file, there have been great advances in indexing technology. Specialized indexes provide new and improved solutions to the high-performance needs of decision support data access. Advanced indexing can deliver true interactive DSS query capabilities to the knowledge worker.

Bit-Map Indexing. One advanced indexing technology is bit-map indexing. Bit-map indexing represents each unique value in the underlying file structure as an array of bits, setting the bits ON or OFF. This indexing structure can provide high-speed index-only processing.

Bit-map indexing has been targeted to be most effective for low cardinality data (i.e., data with few unique values, such as male/female, yes/no, or coded data). Its weakness, however, is in its limitation to high cardinality data (i.e., data with many varying values, such as text data, name fields, and descriptive fields). The more varying the data, the more bit-maps that must be created and maintained.

There is a focus on positioning bit-map indexing as the indexing solution for the data warehouse. This approach often assumes that the data is static (i.e., lower index maintenance) and that the underlying data can be off-loaded (i.e., lower online disk utilization).

Inverted File Indexing. Another advanced indexing technology is inverted indexing. Inverted indexes store pointers to the database as data, and the data from the database as keys. Inverted file indexing maintains indexes to all values contained in an indexed field.

455

Inverted indexing delivers the broadest range of function and flexibility for ad hoc data access and analysis. Users can obtain truly interactive access to data across the enterprise.

Inverted indexes expedite fast, ad hoc searches of previously undefined queries. Inverted file indexing allows users to find information based on any combination of qualifying criteria. Regardless of where the criteria occur in a field, query results process in seconds — without serial reads or sequential index.

An Example. For example, a user wants to know, "How many customers in the northeast (NE) region bought a product last quarter at the promotional price?" The traditional index, or B-tree, could quickly identify all the NE region customers, but would be of no use to also select those that bought in the last quarter at a particular price. To find those records, the processor must retrieve the NE region customer records from disk and evaluate each one for the remaining criteria. If the initial selection yields a large result — say, several hundred thousand records — the processor must physically retrieve every record. Next, it must evaluate the transaction date and amount fields for a match to the query criteria. Furthermore, B-tree indexes are required to scan records byte-by-byte. They can be of no use when searching for records where the selection criteria is buried within the record, such as an appended product code or first name in a name field listing lastname-firstname.

In contrast, inverted file indexes sort and store all values in indexed fields. If a table contains sales data with records 1, 5, 13, 22, and 70 representing the NE region, an inverted index would contain NE with pointers to records 1, 5, 13, 22, and 70. They select records almost instantly by simply scanning the index files for the appropriate values and comparing the record IDs for the shared values — the kind of computation a computer excels at doing. This process takes place at the index level. Inverted indexes augment the relational database to provide the high-performance data access that native B-trees cannot.

RELATIONAL INDEXES VERSUS INVERTED INDEXES

Relational databases offer great retrieval capabilities and flexibility, allowing users to access the data in whatever way they need — unfortunately, it is often at the cost of performance. Though structured query language (SQL) contains syntax for the addition and deletion of indexes, no syntax is included to refer to an index in a query. Therefore, indexed searches are controlled by the RDBMS and, if available, an optimizer.

When a user submits a query, the RDBMS determines how to resolve the query, choosing an index, if defined, to improve performance. Without an index, a sequential search or table scan will be used. The more complex the query, the greater the likelihood of a table scan, because of the limitation that B-tree indexes provide a single key access. If a query encompasses more than one column, only one B-tree can be used, even if every column in the query is indexed. The optimizer then "weighs" which column of a multicolumn query will generate the smallest result. All other columns in the query are evaluated through a table scan.

Inverted file indexing offers a far more efficient method to access data in an ad hoc decision support environment. Inverted file indexes, in contrast to native B-tree indexes, sort and store all values contained in an indexed field. Since most of the work is being done at the index level, the inverted index will prequalify records before they are actually read. Queries are resolved instantaneously by simply scanning the index files for the appropriate values that meet the selection criteria. In addition, inverted file indexes provide a count of the records that qualify before records are retrieved.

An inverted file structure also provides greater capabilities and flexibility than B-tree indexes. Users can enter queries in any combination to identify records that contain them, without concern for query performance. In multicolumn queries, the index of one column is compared to the index of another column. No database records are being accessed. The result of a multicolumn query is a list (or address) of the records that qualify — fast and efficiently.

Exhibit 34.1 compares the functionality of relational access methods and inverted indexing. A subsequent section discusses in more detail the advanced features of inverted indexing.

USING INVERTED FILE INDEXES WITH APPLICATIONS

Only a handful of vendors offer advanced indexing that works on various standard databases and file structures. A wide variety of applications — online production systems, decision support, data warehousing — can use these indexes to support a variety of database structures.

Inverted indexes do not change the existing structure in any way, nor do they involve installing some other proprietary database. Consequently, an IS organization can implement one indexing strategy across multiple hardware and database platforms. As a database changes, so do the indexes. Therefore, it is possible to synchronize indexes in real time or on a regular schedule (e.g., nightly or weekly).

Inverted file indexing can be integrated into applications in a variety of ways. Application programming interfaces (APIs), Open DataBase Connectivity (ODBC), and callable objects are just a few methods for transparently delivering advanced indexing to business applications.

Exhibit 34.1. Access method comparison.

Search Techniques Access Methods	Sequential Scan	Relational Key	Inverted Index
Keyword Searches	Yes	-	Yes
Partial Key Searches	Yes	Yes[1]	Yes
Progressive Searches (drill-throughs)	-	-	Yes
Multiple Key Combinations	-[3]	Yes[2]	Yes
Automatic Qualifying Count	-	-	Yes
Case Insensitivity	-	-	Yes
Position Insensitivity	-	-	Yes
Pre-Joined Indexes	-	-	Yes
Relational Logic (equal to/greater/less than)	Yes	Yes	Yes
Boolean Logic (and/or/not)	Yes	Yes	Yes
Soundex	-	-	Yes
Excluded Words	-	-	Yes
Concatenated Keys	-[3]	Yes	Yes
Composite Keys	-	-	Yes
Grouping of Columns	-	-	Yes
Batch Indexing	-	-	Yes

[1]Inverted indexing provides partial keyword lookups, whereas partial lookups with a relational index must start with the leftmost byte of the column.
[2]Inverted indexing performs a lookup on each indexed column in combination, whereas only one relational index can be read then the records are scanned for matches on the others.
[3]Inverted indexing and relational indexes can perform lookups on a combination of columns. A sequential scan can obtain the same net effect, with time.

Note: Hashed keys were omitted because of their limited functional capabilities, although they are the optimal when users have a full-key exact match.

INVERTED INDEXING

What do users and IS practitioners achieve through inverted indexing? Inverted indexing provides information retrieval capabilities superior to relational indexes. Both users and IS benefit from the added functionality and enhanced performance gained. Users can freely inquire into the corporate data stores while IS need not worry about problematic queries.

Flexible Retrievals

In addition to the tremendous speed advantages that inverted indexing provides, it delivers great flexibility to users in the ways they can search and query data. Users can intuitively search through data, finding records in a way that is obvious and logical. Users are not limited by computer query languages and constructs. Some of these intuitive search capabilities include keyword searches, multiple criteria iterative searches, and qualifying counts.

Keyword Searches. A keyword is any word or value surrounded by spaces or punctuation. Each word or value (keyword) in a column is indexed separately, so that keyword searches perform a fast, efficient lookup on a value that occurs anywhere in a column. Keyword searches are ideal for descriptive data, free-form text, dates, and numeric data, allowing users to find records using words (or strings) that appear anywhere in the indexed column.

In contrast, native relational indexes, B-trees, support searches on full key values in left-to-right sequence. A name field, for example, may contain the last name, followed by the first name (SMITH, JOHN). To efficiently find customer JOHN SMITH, a user must know that SMITH precedes JOHN. A B-tree index on this name field would be useless if users only knew the first name (JOHN) in the record they were searching for. The only alternative is a sequential scan of all the data rows to find an embedded value and do a pattern match.

Progressive Searches and Multiple Key Combinations. Keyword searches can combine multiple keywords against one or more columns. This capability allows users to progressively search, or iteratively "drill through," and refine their queries to contain only that subset of data needed. Users can select and analyze the data in many different ways without incurring the overhead of retrieving the rows.

Relational databases using SQL do not inherently provide a progressive search capability. Since B-trees are limited to a single attribute, there is no efficient way to combine multiple criteria to narrow your search through thousands or millions of rows of data. The user must enter all the selection criteria up front in one SELECT statement. If the user wants to modify just one component of the selection criteria, or just continue to narrow the search, the user must resubmit the query.

For example, a user submits a query to retrieve on SMITH. If this query qualifies a million records, this may not exactly be the data needed. If the user then needs to either narrow or widen the search, he must submit another retrieval, such as JOHN OR JIM SMITH.

Qualifying Counts. Another feature of keyword searches is the automatic return of qualifying counts. These counts tell users how many rows qualified for the current search criteria. Instant qualification counts provide feedback to the user on how many records fit a given query, before accessing the underlying database. The search can be further qualified, expanded, or discarded if the results are unsatisfactory, without touching the database itself.

The qualifying count eliminates wasteful sequential reads of massive tables that select no records, or searches that accidentally select almost the whole table. This type of search capability is extremely valuable for applications where minimizing the CPU overhead is important. In a client/server environment, the qualifying count is especially critical in managing network traffic loads. Imagine the impact of an SQL query that inadvertently selects most of a 1-million row table.

B-trees incur additional overhead in order to return a count of qualified records. A qualifying count requires retrieval and tabulation of the underlying data.

Case and Position Insensitivity. Inverted index keyword searches are both case and position insensitive. Users can quickly find the rows that meet their selection criteria wherever the keyword appears and regardless of whether the value is in upper case, lower case, or a combination of both.

B-trees typically require an exact match to the stored data. If a name was entered as SMITH, JOHN, but users searched for Smith, John, they would not find the record. To perform the most efficient index search, the retrieval criteria must exactly match the value in the database, including upper or lower case letters, spaces and punctuation, and the order entered.

An inverted index lets users index and find records regardless of the data's format. Users can easily find "SMITH," whether it was entered as "Smith," "SMITH," or even "sMith." In addition, because inverted indexing is nonpositional, a retrieval using "JOHN OR JIM AND SMITH" will find any of the following names:

JOHN SMITH   John jim smith   SMITH, JOHN   Smith, Jim JOhn

Multidimensional Capabilities. With inverted indexing, users can enter a combination of keys to invoke a multiple index query. This capability allows users to easily and quickly query any number of criteria across one or more columns, across one or more tables. Thus, true multidimensional function is delivered without the added maintenance and limitations of multidimensional databases.

For example, consider a SALES-HISTORY database whose PRODUCT and CUSTOMER tables have inverted indexes on STATE, PRODUCT, DATE, and STATUS. Users can enter any combination of values for a retrieval. A sample retrieval could be: PRODUCT = "ABC OR XYZ," DATE = "95*," STATUS = "Shipped," and STATE = "CA." The inverted indexes on STATE, PRODUCT, DATE, and STATUS invoke a search across multiple indexes, without retrieving the individual data records.

Most RDBMSs can use only one index per SELECT statement. Even if there are indexes on more than one column, the RDBMS uses only index.

An option in relational databases is to concatenate the columns into one index to provide a keyed retrieval.

Moreover, RDBMSs require a different index definition for each component combination. To retrieve any combination of five columns in a table, a large number of relational indexes (5 factorial, or 120) would be needed. Inverted indexing can provide greater functionality with just five indexes defined. Multidimensional databases attempt to address multiple column, high-performance querying, but they have met maximum dimension constraints (up to 10 dimensions) and require additional maintenance (both design and star-schema management).

Prejoined Indexes. Inverted indexing allows the indexing of columns from more than one table or file to be combined into a single index. This "prejoining" of the indexes yields fast, optimized cross-table joins for searches that span more than one table.

For example, users could search for all the customers in a particular city and state (from CUSTOMERS table) who ordered a particular product (from PRODUCT table) within a date range (from ORDERS table). The intersection is performed at the index level, rather than incurring the overhead of large table joins and excessive data I/O.

Because each index in an RDBMS is separate and cannot be prejoined, cross-table joins are notoriously slow, especially on large tables. The best the user can do is key the desired columns in both tables and the common column. Even then, the data is intersected by doing a keyed read on one table, joining to the second table, reading all the related rows, and selecting the rows that meet the second criteria. The alternative is to do a parallel sort and merge. The method the optimizer chooses, however, may not be the most efficient.

Some relational databases try to make retrievals faster by allowing clustered indexes or data clusters, which refers to the physical placement of related rows contiguously on disk. This approach reduces the amount of I/O to read the rows, but the fact remains that more rows are read than meet all the selection criteria. Inverted index retrievals remain the more efficient and flexible option.

Various Search Operations. With inverted file indexing, users can combine various operations to define their search criteria. These operations include relational logic (equal to, less than, greater than), Boolean logic (AND, NOT, OR), and ranges (TO). In addition, a "sounds-like" feature (also known as Soundex) allows phonetic searches on data. Commonly used for name searches, a phonetic search allows users to find, for example, "SMITH" even when spelled "SMYTHE."

Users can easily carry these operations across keyword indexes, in one or more tables, to access data across the enterprise without concern of data navigation or performance constraints.

RDBMSs support most of these operations, except a sounds-like functionality. Still, the more complex the users' criteria, the greater the exposure to poor performance.

Excluded Words. Inverted indexing allows users to designate noise words — words such as "the" or "an" that are typically useless for retrieval — to be excluded from indexing. This feature reduces the amount of time it takes to load indexes and reduces the amount of storage space that indexes require.

RDBMSs are unable to exclude values from indexing.

Composite Keys. A composite key is a virtual key that allows the redefinition of one or more existing columns. Users can easily create indexes from entire fields or parts of fields. For example, a user can break an ACCOUNT-NUMBER column into its components — DIVISION, DEPARTMENT, NATURAL ACCOUNT — without duplicating the data. In addition, composite keys can reorganize the bytes of a column into a new key. An example would be rearranging a MMDDYY date column to YYMMDD.

RDBMSs do not allow composite keys. They require an index to be comprised of an entire column, in its existing order, or a combination of columns.

Grouping of Columns. Grouping is a powerful feature that lets users index several keyword indexes in one index, thus providing the flexibility to query several similar columns at one time. Say, for example, ADDRESS1, ADDRESS2, and ADDRESS3 contained various address information, including city, state, and country. By grouping these three columns, the index treats them as one logical key or retrieval unit. Users can easily retrieve on city, state, or address information, regardless of which column the data was entered into.

RDBMSs do not have a grouping capability.

PERFORMANCE BENCHMARKS

In summary, inverted file indexes allow a variety of sophisticated search techniques: full keyword searches (e.g., find all customers with the word "Mark" somewhere in the company name), multidimensional searches (e.g., find all customers with the word "Mark" somewhere in the company name that has done business with the company in the last 6 months), range searches (e.g., find all records with transactions between June and December), Soundex (e.g., find all records with any word that sounds like Mark [Marc] in the company name), plurality, synonym searches, and searches

Exhibit 34.2. Performance comparison of a query with and without inverted indexes.

Query Performance / Data File Structure	Without Inverted Indexes	With Inverted Indexes
Oracle	33 minutes	1.6 seconds
Sybase	35 minutes	1.9 seconds
Informix	34 minutes	1.8 seconds
Rdb	36 minutes	1.7 seconds
Digital RM	42 minutes	2.5 seconds

that ignore differences in capitalization. In addition, inverted file indexes can deliver performance improvements of as much as 1000% on multiple selection searches, allowing retrievals that might otherwise take minutes or even hours to be completed in seconds.

Benchmarks were performed against various data file structures, including relational and flat file. In this case, a query performed on a 1-million record database needed to find all customers in Texas who ordered in the previous month. This query required a cross-table join, based on a free-format address field in the CUSTOMER file and a date range in the ORDER file. The results are shown in Exhibit 34.2 and demonstrate that inverted indexing can guarantee consistent performance enhancements for an organization's data access requirements.

SUMMARY

In the rush to serve the constantly expanding demands of knowledge workers, businesses have created a complex environment for IS to develop and maintain enterprisewide data access services. Parallel processing, multidimensional servers, and partitioning are all brute-force methods proposed to address data access performance and query flexibility. Alternatives that minimize I/O and maximize memory processing may deliver the best performance for the price. Inverted file indexing may be a relatively simpler and cost-effective solution for many businesses. These multiple keyword indexes allow users to perform ad hoc queries with minimal impact to online systems. Users are also able to construct complex queries quickly. In addition, by providing feedback to the user on the size of their request before data is retrieved, client/server network traffic is minimized.

Inverted indexing leverages investments in existing hardware and software, allowing for the integration of new technologies while protecting much of the application developed. Inverted indexes provide the broadest range of flexibility for providing true data access across the enterprise. Sometimes, simple is better.

Section VII
Object Technology, Object Modeling, and Object Databases

OBJECT TECHNOLOGY COMBINES PROCESS AND DATA INTO ENCAPSULAT-ED OBJECTS. Object technology leverages data in many formats, from pure object data stores to hybrid databases. Object technology is supported by a suite of object modeling methodologies, tools, procedures, and databases. This section contains eight chapters that focus on different aspects of object technology:

Chapter 35, "Getting the Benefits of Inheritance in Visual Basic" provides an approach for leveraging inheritance-like operations using Visual Basic.

Chapter 36, "Data Access Using Microsoft Visual Basic 5.0+," compares and contrasts the different data access methods available in Visual Basic Version 5.0+. This includes RDO, ADO, and DAO. This version of Visual Basic has a strong degree of object orientation. Coupled with Microsoft Transaction Server (MTS) and ActiveX, Visual Basic is well on the way to becoming a strong component based toolkit.

Chapter 37, "Component Based Development," discusses the opportunities available to organizations to leverage component based development for shorter implementation schedules and code reuse. Component based development is expected to fuel a strong trade of reusable components from vendors and corporations over the next few years.

Chapter 38, "Developing ActiveX Internet Server Components with Visual Basic and Rational Rose," examines, using object-oriented analysis and design techniques with Rational Rose 98 to design robust component based systems that can be implemented quickly and easily in Visual Basic 5 and deployed in an internet server based architecture.

Chapter 39, "A Technical Primer for Getting Started with JavaBeans," provides examples for creating components through JavaBeans. This chapter provides examples for creating and compiling a JavaBean class.

Chapter 40, "JavaBeans and Java Enterprise Server Platform," examines the Java programming language and its interaction with data repositories. JavaBeans are the component object model for the Java platform. It's architecture is explored in this chapter. Enterprise JavaBeans, which offers support for legacy systems and extended enterprise services are also discussed in this chapter.

Chapter 41, "Distributed Objects and Object Wrapping," contrasts current and future trends in distributed object architectures, specifically Open Software Foundation's (DCE) and the Object Management Group's CORBA.

Chapter 35
Getting the Benefits of Inheritance in Visual Basic

Nancy Stonelake

OBJECT-ORIENTED PROGRAMMING AND OBJECT-ORIENTED ANALYSIS AND DESIGN HAVE ENTERED THE MAINSTREAM, however, the level of the object-paradigm support varies among languages. Polymorphism and inheritance are fundamental concepts in the object paradigm, but not all languages support both mechanisms. We will exam different techniques for implementing inheritance in languages that support polymorphism, but not inheritance. We will look at Visual Basic as an example of such a situation.

Inheritance plays several key roles in an object oriented language. People have a natural tendency to group objects in classes or taxonomies. This promotes the idea of a simpler model of the real world. Within these taxonomies we expect similar attributes and behavior amongst objects from the same class. Inheritance in object oriented languages acts as a reuse mechanism, with objects from lower levels in the hierarchy directly accessing methods from higher level classes. The code is written in a single place. This impacts construction and maintenance time and effort. Construction time is decreased since the code is written and tested only once. Error detection is facilitated since the code will only occur in one place instead of several. This also allows us to affect change across a broad spectrum when high-level behavior changes, or a code fix must be made, without duplicating our efforts in multiple places. This idea of code sharing does not have to be limited to a single application, but may occur across applications, compounding its benefits. Inheritance enforces a consistent interface, so that lower level classes are called and perform in the same manner as higher level classes. This allows us to use subclasses interchangably in situations where we are unsure of what subclass to expect. A consistent interface increases developer productivity, since new functionality will be added in a cumulative rather than conflicting manner. Inheritance helps us exploit the "black-box" aspect of encapsulated objects. We can expand on a class through subclassing, without knowing all the implementation details of the superclass.

How do we handle languages that do not support the concept of inheritance and still achieve these benefits? In languages that do not support inheritance, such as Visual Basic, there are two basic alternative methods for mimicking inheritance:

1. Implementing inheritance by using composition
2. Using interfaces

These alternatives may also be used for multiple inheritance.

The class hierarchy is based on two fundamental relationships that we can refer to as IS-A and HAS-A. The IS-A relation describes inheritance whereas the HAS-A relation describes containment.

The IS-A relation refers to a class of objects which are a specialization of another class of objects. For example, a collie is a dog. Inheritance does not limit the fact that all dogs are not collies, but all collies must be dogs. Inheritance for specialization is the most common type of inheritance relation, however, inheritance may also occur for specification, construction, generalization, extensions, limitation, variance and combination (Budd). Specification ensures a common interface so that multiple classes implement the same methods. Construction allows us to reuse methods that perform the same functionality but have context specific names. Generalization allows us to override the behavior of existing classes to create a more general type. Extension adds functionality by building upon existing classes. Limitation restricts the behavior of a subclass. Variance allows us to connect two classes that are not taxonomically related, but share similar properties and behavior. Combination describes the joining of multiple superclasses to create a subclass with a combination of behaviors (Budd).

The HAS-A relation refers to a class of objects containing another (or the same) class of objects. For example a dog has a leg. Other classes may have a leg property, horses for instance. In fact, different instances may contain the same instance, as in the case of multiple people having the same address.

Replacing inheritance with containment impacts the design and construction phases, however it does not impact analysis. During the high-level design phase we should determine the class hierarchy independent of the language of implementation. Exhibit 35.1 shows a simple class hierarchy in UML notation, where the class "child" will have the use of the method "parentMethod( )" and an attribute "parentAttribute."

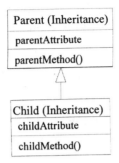

Exhibit 35.1.   A simple class hierarchy in UML notation.

The necessity to convert a logically inherited class to a class using composition should be determined at the low-level design phase, after the choice of the language for implementation has been made. To convert an inheritance relation to composition in our low-level design, we need to replace the inheritance relation with an aggregation relation, as shown in Exhibit 35.2. Note that the child is the client of the aggregation and the parent is the supplier; that is the child class contains the parent. The parent implements the code for executing the method.

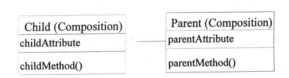

Exhibit 35.2.   Replacing the Inheritance Relation with an Aggregation Relation.

From this configuration, some decisions must be made on how to access the contained parent. The first mechanism we may use is:

```
aChild.parent.parentMethod()
```

The second mechanism involves adding the parent methods to the child class (see Exhibit 35.3) and calling them from within the child class method. The child class delegates the message to the parent. The child class may contain additional code to be executed, either before or after the parent method is called.

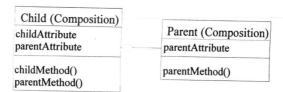

Exhibit 35.3. Adding the Parent Methods to the Child Class.

Our second technique is to convert the inheritance relation of Exhibit 35.4 to an interface. An interface is a contract to support a set of methods. An interface determines a minimal set of what an object will do, but it does not dictate how it will do it. Classes implementing an interface are free to contain additional methods and attributes. In the design model we create an interface that acts as the parent, and a child class that realizes or implements that interface. On implementation, all the code for executing the method will be contained in the child class.

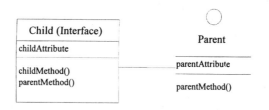

Exhibit 35.4. Converting the inheritance relation.

Let us examine both these methods from the implementation point of view. We will use a class "Dinosaur" and its subclass "Carnivore," for meat-eating dinosaurs, as depicted in Exhibit 35.5.

Exhibit 35.5. Class "Dinosaur" and its subclass "Carnivore."

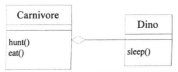

```
'Dinosaur class
Public Sub sleep(ByVal hours As Integer)
    'Debug.Print "dino sleeping ... for " & hours & vbCrLf
End Sub
```

```
'Carnivore class
Private mvardino As dino

Private Sub Class_Initialize()
    'create the msubcar object when the carnavore class is created
    Set mvardino = New dino
    Debug.Print "init dino"
End Sub

Public Property Get subcar() As subcar
    Set subcar = mvardino
End Property

Public Property Set subcar(vData As subcar)
    Set mvardino = vData
End Property

Public Sub sleep(ByVal sleep As Integer)
    mvardino.sleep (sleep)
End Sub

Public Sub hunt(ByVal hunt As Integer)
    'search for food
    'is it food?
    'if food found chase
    'if caught eat else search for food
    Debug.Print "carn hunt" & vbCrLf
End Sub
```

Exhibit 35.6. Using the Composition option.

Implementing this using the composition option gives us Exhibit 35.6, while the interface method produces Exhibit 35.7. Only the essentials of the class are provided.

Note that in the containment method an instance of Dino is contained in the instance of Carnivore. The Dino instance is created when the Carnivore instance is created. Lazy initialization may also be used, where we create the Dino instance when we require it. The sleep( ) method is accessed by using message passing where the carnivore passes the message to its member "Dino" to execute it.

In the interface method the class directly implements the code for the sleep method, and it is executed directly by the class.

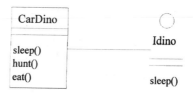

```
'Abstract interface class Idino
Public Sub sleep(ByVal hours As Integer)
End Sub
```

```
'Carndino
Implements Idino

Public Sub Idino_sleep(ByVal hours As Integer)
    'Debug.Print "carndino sleeping ... for " & hours & vbCrLf
End Sub

Public Sub hunt(ByVal hunt As Integer)
    'search for food
    'is it food?
    'if food found chase
    'if caught eat else search for food
    Debug.Print "carn hunt" & vbCrLf
End Sub

Public Sub eat(ByVal food As String)
    ' eat food, add energy to animal and health score
    Debug.Print "carn eating ..." & food & vbCrLf
End Sub
```

Exhibit 35.7. The Interface Method.

So what are the advantages and disadvantages of these two methods? Examining design, Exhibit 35.8 summarizes the reason for inheritance that the containment and interface methods support.

Exhibit 35.8. Containment and Interface Methods summary.

Type	Containment	Interface
Specialization	Yes	Yes
Specification	No	Yes
Construction	Yes	No
Generalization	No	Yes
Extension	Yes	Yes
Limitation	No	No
Variance	No	Yes
Combination	Yes	Yes

472

Inheritance for specialization is supported by both methods. We abstract out the common methods into the contained class or the interface. Specification is supported and is clearly the purpose of an interface. There is no value in containing a "parent" class, when inheriting for specification, unless the execution of the methods in the parent can be reused in multiple children. Construction can be implemented by containment, implementing context specific names in the child class and delegating messages to the parent class. Generalization is not supported by containment, as it eliminates the advantages of containing the subclass. It should be noted that this technique is primarily used in situations where the inheritance hierarchy is fixed and cannot be remodeled or altered. Both techniques permit extension, as neither technique limits the addition of methods to the child class. Neither technique can restrict the behavior of a subclass, so limitation is not supported. Variance is best supported by interfaces, as interfaces have no requirement to be taxonomically related. Containment can be used for variance if the behavior of the child classes is sufficiently similar so that the parent code can be reused in multiple children. Containment and interfaces both support inheritance for combination, as multiple parents may be contained, and there is no limit on the number of interfaces that may be supported. In this case, it may be advantageous to mix the two techniques, depending on the specific requirements of inheritance for each parent class.

From a more abstract modeling view, neither of these options neatly models our natural view of the world. Interface hierarchies can be as complex as class hierarchies but fortunately design tools allow us to elegantly track these. The Visual Basic Object Browser allows for the easy viewing of object parts, but has no way of tracking interfaces or their implementors.

On implementation, we looked at some physical characteristics and found that the two methods produced executable files of similar size. A more complex example may be required to identify differences. It is expected that where a parent class has many children the executable size will be smaller using the containment method, since the main body of code need only appear once. There was a difference in execution time, with the composition method slower than the interface method. This could be attributed to the extra call in the composition method (delegating to the parent), and it should be noted that the interface method is fastest if the receiver object is not first cast to the interface.

There are other concerns besides execution time, including term code maintenance. Only the composition option provides the benefits of inheritance in the reuse of code and the single point for change. Each class that implements an interface has it own unique code for a method, so the same error may be repeated in multiple places, especially if cut and paste development occurs. If the method reciever is not cast to the interface, the interchangability of subclasses is eliminated. This will impact long term maintenance, especially as new subclasses are added.

CONCLUSION

Two methods have been provided which will allow the VB programmer to enjoy some of the benefits of inheritance. Each project must evaluate its long-term goals to determine which method is best for the given situation. The designers and developers need to evaluate the reasons for subclassing, execution speed and size and maintenance goals of the project using the guidelines provided above, in order to determine a course of action that will benefit the organization over the long term.

References

Budd, Timothy, (1991) An Introduction to Object-Oriented Programming, Addison Wesley-Publishing Company.

Chapter 36
Data Access Using Microsoft Visual Basic 5.0+

Stephen D'Silva

THE FUNDAMENTAL AND VITAL PART OF ANY BUSINESS IS DATA both within and without the organization. Data within the organization can provide insights into the performance of the company, and data from outside can enable organizations to be cooperative and competitive. Information technology (IT) plays a very important role in the analysis and presentation of data besides offering other benefits. This is accomplished by computer-based applications, developed and customized using the many development tools available in the market. One of the more popular tools being used to develop business applications is Microsoft® Visual Basic.

Data in many organizations resides in databases such as Microsoft Access, Microsoft SQL Server, Sybase SQL Server, Oracle, DB2, Informix, and Ingres. This chapter provides methods and techniques that are available to the Visual Basic developer to access data residing in these databases.

BASIC DATA ACCESS INTERFACES

The following paragraphs describe the basic database interface options available to a developer. These options provide a very low-level interface to the database and, therefore, are not usually the ones that are used by most developers. They compensate, however, for programming difficulty with excellent database access performance. Higher-level interfaces are now available that provide ease of developing data access components with varying levels of performance. These interfaces will be discussed in the next section. Exhibit 36.1 illustrates the connection between the data access interfaces, the databases, and the client application.

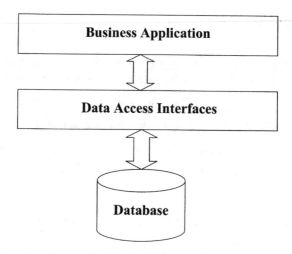

Exhibit 36.1. Connection between the data access interfaces, databases, and client application.

NATIVE DATABASE DRIVERS

A few years ago data from database servers could be accessed only by using the native drivers that the database vendors provided for their product. These usually consisted of APIs (Application Programming Interfaces) that included database libraries and, for remote access, network libraries. The developers then would program the database connectivity interface to their applications using these APIs. This method proved to be tedious and time-consuming and had the following disadvantages:

- The database connection interface usually had to be written in the programming language that was used to write the API.
- There was a tight coupling between the APIs and the application program and, therefore, changes in the API could produce errors due to incompatible function calls.
- The application was tied to a database; therefore, if the database were changed, major changes would be required in the application. This resulted in the organization being tied to a single vendor.

The advantage with this approach was performance, as the APIs were fine-tuned to the database.

FILE-BASED AND ISAM DATABASE INTERFACES

Data that has been saved as text or in proprietary data formats in files can be accessed using file input/output (I/O) operations. The Indexed Sequential Access Method (ISAM) is a binary format that was used by the file-based databases to speed up data retrieval. Because most of the ISAM databases used proprietary formats, data access was possible only by using specific data access drivers. The Joint Engine Technology (JET) was developed as an attempt to standardize file and ISAM data access. JET loads ISAM drivers to facilitate communication with ISAM databases in various formats.

MICROSOFT ODBC (OPEN DATABASE CONNECTION)

For the Microsoft Windows platform, Microsoft developed the ODBC standard. This standard was based on the premise that applications needed to be developed using a more general interface to the database and a loose coupling model.

ODBC translates common ODBC SQL and API calls into a format recognizable by an SQL database server. The database connection was established by using a data source specification entry in the ODBC configuration file. The ODBC configuration for the data source included parameters such as database name, database drivers, user ID and password.

The advantage with this method was that it broke down the application-database dependence. This, however, affected the data access performance. ODBC certainly provided a standard and general method to access data residing on SQL databases, thereby reducing the database access task to writing SQL statements.

OLE DB

OLE DB is Microsoft's latest attempt to provide a common interface for all data storage formats such as relational database formats and other unstructured data formats like documents and graphic sources, regardless of location or type. The OLE DB specification is a set of interfaces that expose data from both structured and unstructured data sources using the Microsoft Component Object Model (COM). OLE DB acts as a COM wrapper around the data source, whether the data is in ISAM or SQL format. Clients are not intended to call OLE DB directly because it is a low-level interface to a data source. OLE DB will be the standard to access all types of data formats just as ODBC was for SQL data formats.

OLE DB goes beyond simple data access by partitioning the functionality of a traditional relational database into logical components. There are three main categories of components built on the OLE DB architecture: data consumers, data providers, and service components.

Data consumers are applications that need access to a broad range of data. These include development tools, languages, and personal productivity tools. An application becomes OLE DB-enabled by using the OLE DB API to talk to data.

Data providers make their data available for consuming. They may do this by natively supporting OLE DB or they may rely on additional OLE DB data providers. If a data provider is a native OLE DB provider, an application can talk to it directly, via OLE DB. There is no need for additional drivers or software.

A data provider that natively does not support OLE DB relies on an intermediary in the same way that ODBC data sources rely on ODBC drivers.

The OLE DB Provider for ODBC enables applications to use OLE DB to talk to relational data via ODBC. This means that one can use OLE DB today to get to all of the same data he or she currently uses ODBC to access. ODBC remains the ideal technology for accessing SQL databases, and the OLE DB Provider for ODBC ensures that one can continue writing high-performance database applications.

OLE DB provides a base-level data access functionality: the managing of a tabular rowset.

Service components provide additional functionality such as query processing or cursor engines. A query processor allows SQL queries to be constructed and run against the data source. A cursor engine provides scrolling capabilities for data sources that do not support scrolling.

So for example, if wanting to query Microsoft SQL Server data, one would not need a service component because SQL Server has both a query processor and cursor engine. However, to query a Microsoft Internet Information Server log file one would either build or buy a component that provided querying capabilities for text files.

High-Level Data Access Methods

As mentioned earlier, the high-level data access methods are the ones that developers use to access the database. Though the performance gets reduced, these methods provide the best of both worlds. Exhibit 36.2 illustrates the different access methods available to the Microsoft Visual Basic developer. These access methods are discussed in detail along with sample code in Visual Basic.

DATA ACCESS OBJECTS (DAO)

DAO is the COM interface to Jet. It is best-suited for use with Microsoft Access, FoxPro, or Dbase files. DAO also will connect ODBC-compliant databases. The current version is Microsoft DAO 3.5 Object Library, which also provides support for remote data sources. Exhibit 36.3 is the DAO object model. The DAO is the most mature object-based interface for developers and provides optimal performance with ISAM databases; however, it is being de-emphasized and will be replaced by newer access methods.

478

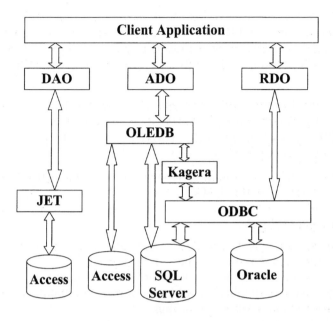

Exhibit 36.2.   Access methods available to Microsoft Visual Basic Developer.

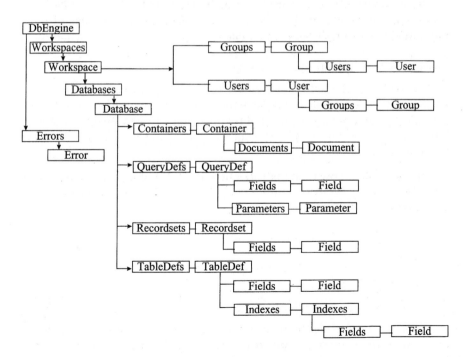

Exhibit 36.3.   The DAO object model.

ODBCDirect is a feature of DAO that allows for a more direct access to ODBC. When opening ODBC sources through ODBCDirect, the DAO object model separates from the Jet engine. This approach is useful when a combination of ISAM and ODBC data sources are referenced in the same application.

To use DAO in Visual Basic the application first must have a reference to the DAO object library, which currently is Microsoft DAO 3.5 Object Library. Without this an error will be received when an attempt is made to declare the necessary object variables.

The following paragraph describes some of the more useful and commonly used objects within DAO.

The Workspace Object

The workspace object is used for setting environment information such as user names and database engines. This object does not have to be created as it automatically is provided. However, it must be created when used with a secured database or when the settings for database are not the same as the default workspace settings.

The Database Object

The database object represents the database that is to be opened and accessed. The database object's methods and properties are used to manipulate data within the open database.

The Recordset Object

A recordset is the data that is returned in response to a query to a database. The recordset object manages the recordsets created with DAO. The recordset object defines a group of records that can be viewed or manipulated. Only one record can be the current record in the recordset containing more than one record.

The example below demonstrates how the DAO objects are used to access data from a database source using both the Jet and the ODBCDirect methods.

```
'Declare as Workspace Object
Dim oWrkSpace As Workspace
'Declare a database object
Dim oMyDatabase as Database
'Declare a recordset object
oRSet as recordset
'Create workspace object for Jet
```

```
Set oWrkSpace = CreateWorkspace("", "admin," "",
dbUseJet)
'Open the database
oMyDatabase = oWrkSpace
OpenDatabase("c:\anza\registration.mdb")
'Open a recordset
set oRSet = oMyDatabase.OpenRecordset("Select * from
students," _
    dbOpenDynaset, dbReadOnly)


' Add code to process the data records
'

'Close the objects
oRSet.Close
oMyDatabase.close
```

For ODBCDirect the above code will be as follows:

```
'Declare as Workspace Object
Dim oWrkSpace As Workspace
'Declare a recordset object
oRSet as recordset

'Declare a connection object
Dim oConnect as Connection

'Create workspace object for ODBCDirect
Set oWrkSpace = CreateWorkspace("", "admin," "",
dbUseODBC)

'Connect to database using ODBCDirect method
Set oConnect = oWrkSpace.OpenConnection("", , , _
"ODBC;DATABASE = registration; UID=sa, PWD=;DSN=ANZA")
'Open a recordset
set oRSet = oConnect.OpenRecordset("Select * from
students," _
    dbOpenDynamic)


'

' Add code to process the data records
'
```

```
'Close the objects
oRSet.Close
oMyDatabase.close
oWrkSpace.close
```

REMOTE DATA OBJECTS (RDO)

Remote Data Objects (RDO) provides an object layer over the ODBC API. In other words, the RDO provides the performance gains of the ODBC API. RDO allows access to databases from any 32-bit platforms such as Windows 95 and Windows NT using ODBC data sources. RDO provides significant performance and flexibility when accessing remote database engines.

RDO can be used to execute stored procedures and queries that return multiple recordsets. The number of rows that are returned by a query can be limited, and all messages and errors generated by the remote data source can be monitored. Finally RDO supports asynchronous and synchronous operations for data access, and has its own object hierarchy as shown in Exhibit 36.4.

RDO support is available from the Visual Basic 5.0 Enterprise development version. To use RDO in Visual Basic the application first must have a reference to the RDO object library, which currently is Microsoft Remote Data Object 2.0.

The following paragraphs describe some of the objects within RDO.

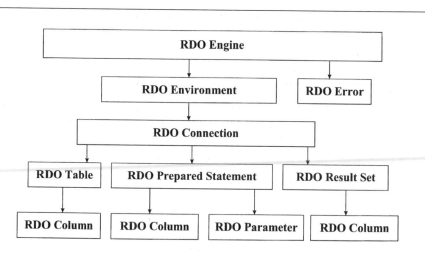

Exhibit 36.4. The Remote Data Object (RDO) hierarchy.

The Connection Object

The connection object in RDO represents a connection to the database. It is similar to the database object in DAO. The connection object requires the environment object that automatically is provided by the RDO.

The Resultset Object

A resultset object represents the results returned from a query. Result objects are created using the OpenResultSet method of the connection, query, or table objects, namely, rdoConnection, rdoQuery and rdoTable respectively.

The following example demonstrates data access using RDO:

```
'Declare Connection object
Dim oConnect As rdoConnection

'Declare Result set object
Dim oRSet As rdoResultset

'Declare SQL string variable
Dim sAQL As String

'Instantiate a connection object
Set oConnect = New rdoConnection

'Connect to Database
With oConnect

.Connect = "DSN=ANZA;UID=sa;PWD="
.EstablishConnection
End With

'Format SQL Statement
sSQL = "Select * from students"

'Send query and get result set
Set oRSet = oConnect.OpenResultset(sSQL, rdoOpenKeyset,
rdConcurReadOnly)
'
' Add code to process data
'
' Close Data objects
oRSet.Close
oConnect.Close
```

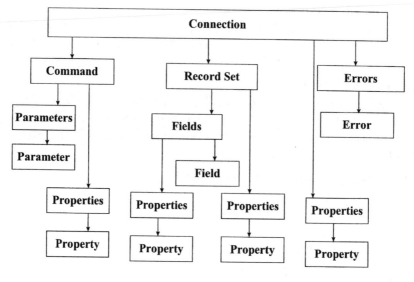

Exhibit 36.5.   The ActiveX Data Objects model.

ACTIVEX DATA OBJECTS (ADO)

ActiveX Data Objects (ADO) represents the future of data access methods and is a fundamental component of Universal Data Access.

ADO is an extensible programming model providing an interface to OLE DB. It is designed to access databases of various types and uses independent data service providers to access specific data.

ADO is COM-based; therefore, any application or language capable of working with COM objects can use it. Active Server Pages for the Internet written using Visual Basic Scripting Language can use ADO. Exhibit 36.5 shows the ADO object model.

Unlike the situation with DAO or RDO, when using ADO the data access code does not have to work its way through the object hierarchy. Instead of referencing the Workspace object and then a database, ADO can make direct reference to a recordset.

To use ADO in Visual Basic the application first must have a reference to the ADO object library, which currently is Microsoft OLE DB ActiveX Data Objects 2.0 Library.

The following code snippet creates a simple connection to an SQL Server database using ADO:

```
'Declare and instantiate a recordset object
Dim oRSet As New ADODB.Recordset


'Execute query using open method of recordset object
oRSet.Open "Select * from Students," "DSN=ANZA;UID =
sa;PWD="
'Print Lastname from rows returned by query
Do Until oRSet.EOF
    Print oRSet!LastName
    oRSet.MoveNext
Loop
Close recordset object
oRSet.Close
```

SELECTING WHAT TO USE

This chapter has covered ADO, ODBC, RDO, and DAO with Microsoft Jet. Which should be used today?

Use ADO if ...

Starting an application today. Take a look at using ADO. If it meets one's needs, it makes sense to use it in your Visual Basic, Access, and Office applications. It will be simpler to convert from today's ADO to tomorrow's ADO than to write to RDO/DAO now and convert to tomorrow's ADO. Use ADO if using Active Server Pages with IIS. ADO ships with IIS and was designed to work very well with IIS.

Use DAO if ...

There is a need to access Microsoft Jet or ISAM data or to take advantage of Microsoft Jet features such as compacting and repairing databases, replication, or DDL through the objects. One should use DAO if he or she has an existing application that uses DAO with Microsoft Jet and wants to convert the application to use ODBC data, while achieving better performance.

Use RDO if ...

Accessing ODBC data and desiring the most functionality. ADO today has most of the features of RDO, but not all of them. In the future ADO will be a superset of RDO.

485

Exhibit 36.6.   Suggested Data Access Methods

Data Access Method	Use Case
ADO	• Creating a new application • Developing applications using Active Server Pages with IIS • Need high performance
DAO	• Data access primarily to Microsoft Jet and ISAM databases • Need specific JET database features in application • Converting existing application using DAO with JET to use ODBC data
RDO	• Accessing ODBC data and require most functionality • Need high performance

When to Use What

Exhibit 36.6 provides a description of what access method may be used in a given situation.

Feature Comparison

Exhibit 36.7 presents a comparison list of major features found in ADO, DAO, and RDO.

Exhibit 36.7.   Major features of ADO, DAO, and RDO

Feature	ADO 1.5	DAO 3.5	RDO 2.0
Asynchronous connection	Yes	No	Yes
Asynchronous query execution	Yes	Yes	Yes
Batch updates	Yes	Yes	Yes
Error handling	Yes	Yes	Yes
Disconnected recordsets	Yes	No	Yes
Events on column/field	No	No	Yes
Events on connection	No	No	Yes
Events on engine	No	No	Yes
Events on resultset/recordset	No	No	Yes
Events on query	No	No	Yes
Threadsafe	Yes	Yes	Yes
Free-threaded	Yes	No	No
Return value parameters	Yes	Yes	Yes
Independently created objects	Yes	Yes	Yes
MaxRows property on queries	Yes	Yes	Yes
Queries as methods	Yes	No	Yes
Return multiple recordsets	No	Yes	Yes
Efficient Microsoft JET database access	No	Yes	No
Compatibility from Microsoft JET to SQL Server	No	Yes	No

Universal Data Access

Universal Data Access is Microsoft's strategy for providing access to information across the enterprise. Today, companies building database solutions face a number of challenges as they seek to gain maximum business advantage from the data and information distributed throughout their corporations. Universal Data Access provides high-performance access to a variety of information sources, including relational and nonrelational and an easy-to-use programming interface that is tool- and language-independent. These technologies enable corporations to integrate diverse data sources, create easy-to-maintain solutions, and use their choice of best-of-breed tools, applications, and platform services.

Universal Data Access is based on open industry specifications with broad industry support and works with all major established database platforms. Universal Data Access is an evolutionary step from today's standard interfaces, including ODBC, RDO, and DAO, and extends the functionality of these well-known and tested technologies.

The Microsoft Data Access Components enable Universal Data Access. These components include ActiveX Data Objects (ADO), Remote Data Service, (RDS, formerly known as Advanced Database Connector or ADC), OLE DB, and Open Database Connectivity (ODBC).

PROGRAMMING THE DATA SERVICES OBJECTS

With all the data access methods discussed, the common denominator is data access. The differences are many, some of which are the ease or difficulty in programming, object or procedural models, and performance. Other nontechnical but very important factors are when these access methods were introduced and also the time lapsed between the introductions of any two given data access methods. Though these are nontechnical factors, they are very important when it comes to application support within an organization.

Take the case of an organization developing applications using ODBC API to access data. A few months later, with the introduction of RDO offering an easier programming approach and a comparable performance factor, it would be appropriate for developers to move to the newly introduced data access method. This produces a problem to maintain applications depending on different standards. The situation gets worse when the vendor decides to discontinue support for an older data access method. This ordeal is typical and has been faced by many organizations, but the trend to provide newer and better access methods still continues with an increasing frequency.

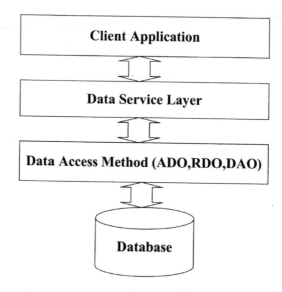

Exhibit 36.8.   Adding the data service layer.

To take advantage of the newer and better access technologies and still be in a position to effectively manage and maintain applications, there needs to be a fundamental change in the way software is designed and built. The key phrase is independence through loose coupling. What this means is designing and building software that will have no dependence or a very low level of dependence on services or products that have the potential to change or be replaced by newer products.

The answer lies in creating an additional layer, which lies sandwiched between the business application being developed and the vendor-specific data access method. Exhibit 36.8 illustrates this approach.

This layer will be called "the data services layer" as this is a service that normally is provided in-house as part of the application development infrastructure — similar to a function library for frequently used functions.

In an object-oriented programming environment, this layer could exist as classes with methods that include all the required data access functionality. An example of this class and methods that form the data access services layer is listed in Exhibit 36.9.

The applications will instantiate objects from this data services class and then invoke methods to get results from a query or insert, delete, and update records. The application will not have any knowledge of or dependence on a vendor-specific data access method. The data access service

Exhibit 36.9.   Classes and their methods

Method Name	Description
	Class Name: CdataAccess
OpenRecordSet	Opens a recordset with stored procedure as a parameter
Execute	Executes SQL statements
BeginTrans	Begins a transaction for a batch
CommitTrans	Commits a transaction
RollbackTrans	Rolls back a transaction

Method Name	Description
	Class Name: CrecordSet
MoveNext	Moves pointer to the next record

Properties	Description
Columns	Column Names
EOF	End of File (Record) indicator

layer will contain code to access data using a vendor-specific data access method.

The major advantage with this approach is when newer and better data access methods become available; the only part that will require change will be the data access services layer. No change will be required to any application built using this approach.

OBJECT-ORIENTED DATABASE ACCESS

A lot of data accessed today are stored in flat-file databases navigated with hierarchical pointer-based systems and in tables in relational databases connected by keys. Data are accessed using languages that are usually proprietary. The type of data usually simple and not difficult to manage.

However, this situation is changing rapidly. Some types of data today and in the future will be enormous and complex. We will need to access and organize audio, video, compound documents, geographic information, and other data types. The traditional SQL-based relational database systems are unable to address the type of complex data mentioned previously.

The object-oriented approach has addressed programming issues such as representing business entities as objects. But data still are not stored as objects. Usually there is a data translation layer that converts object data from the application to a relational format and vice versa. This introduces performance problems and data representation issues. Data are represented in the form of complicated relationships using joins. Storing a complex data type in an RDBMS is like disassembling a car before garaging it.

The answer lies in object-oriented database management systems (OODBMS). OODBMS are centered around the concepts of persistence storage meaning that classes, attributes, and instances of objects can be represented within a database in the same way that they are represented in an object-oriented programming language.

This technology is available today vendors such as Object Design Inc., Versant, Gemstone, Objectivity, O2 are marketing OODBMS products.

CONCLUSION

This chapter covered various methods offered by Visual Basic 5.0+ to access data, including ADO, ODBC, RDO, and DAO with Microsoft Jet. Each of these technologies has its place and offers advantages and disadvantages. Microsoft's latest advancement in remote data access is offered in OLE DB, which supports access to a wide variety of data sources, both relational and nonrelational.

Chapter 37
Component-Based Development

Nancy Stonelake

INTRODUCTION

COMPONENT-BASED DEVELOPMENT is being touted as the solution to the latest software crisis. What is it and how true is the hype? The objectives of this article are shown in the following list:

- To define component-based development.
- To describe its benefits and weaknesses.
- To examine the basic architecture and popular component models.
- To examine alternatives and component-based developments in conjunction with current technology and data management.
- To examine some of the challenges facing IT shops that want to move to a component approach.

DEFINITION

Component-based development differs from traditional development in that the application is not developed completely from scratch. A component-based application is assembled from a set of preexisting components. A component is a software bundle that performs a predefined set of functionality with a predefined API. At its simplest level, a component could be a class library or GUI widget; or it may be as complex as a small application, like a text editor; or an application subsystem, like a help system. These components may be developed in house, reused from project to project and passed between departments. They may be purchased from outside vendors who specialize in component development, or bartered between other companies in similar lines of business.

Components can be divided into two broad "types," namely: business components and framework components. Business components encapsulate knowledge of business processes. They may be applied in a vertical industry sector, such as banking, or in a cross-industry standard business function like accounting or E-commerce. Framework components address specific software architecture issues like the user interface, security, or reporting functions.

BENEFITS

How is component-based development better than traditional development practices? If we compare developing enterprisewide applications to auto manufacturing, current application development is like machining each part from scratch pretty much for every automobile being assembled. This is time consuming and expensive, when most of the parts are the same or similar in configuration. Henry Ford revolutionized manufacturing by standardizing parts and having workers specialize in small aspects of construction. Component-based development works on the same principles and reaps similar benefits.

Due to the similarity between all software applications, using components can reduce design time. Almost all applications have some security system, error handling, and user help functionality. Why are we wasting our time deciding how to provide help to users when the real question is what level of help users need? Components can provide framework solutions that can be tuned to our business requirements. This has the additional benefit of allowing us time to focus on the business logic, which is the key to fulfilling requirements.

Implementation time is reduced because components are already built. Additional coding may be required to integrate the component into the system, but the required functionality is already there.

These two main facts have additional implications. Since components are prebuilt, testing time is reduced. Components are already unit tested; they only require integration testing within the application. Overall, with components we require less design, development, and testing resources. This means we need fewer people with highly specialized and hard-to-find skill sets and we can leverage the people we have to do the things needed in the application.

Additionally, the cost of developing the components can be leveraged over many buyers. Since we acquire components from other departments in the company and pass our components onto them, they share in the costs. Vendors sell to multiple users and they all share in the development and maintenance costs. Component developers can afford to have designer/developers devoted to each component over its lifecycle and these resources can become specialists in the component piece.

WEAKNESSES

Component development is an immature industry. This has several effects and implications, primarily: limited vendors, products, and skilled human resources.

At this time there are limited choices in component vendors and company stability may be an issue. While there is a stable set of GUI component vendors, the offerings in true business components are limited. The lack of availability also limits competitive advantage. If all our competitors are using the same business logic, are we doing anything better than they are or are we just matching the pace? Product stability is also an issue. It is important that the API of a component remain constant otherwise we may incur heavy maintenance costs when integrating new product releases.

Component-based development requires a different approach to software development and there are few people who have actually done it. It requires people who can discern what parts of an application may be useful to other applications and what changes may need to be made to support future applications. In other words, you need a good designer/architect with a good crystal ball. To successfully reuse components you must have designers/implementers who are familiar with the component library, so they don't spend all their time looking for components that don't exist. They must also be able to adapt components to fulfill the requirements.

In addition, there must be supporting corporate strategies to promote reuse. No benefit is gained by crafting components that remain unused. Designers and developers need some impetus to change and the resources to support component development must be provided. This means taking the time to develop and locate components and promoting awareness of their availability.

BASIC ARCHITECTURE

Component architecture is based on locating components where they can best serve the needs of the user. This must account for several factors. Speed, processing power, and accessibility. One possible architecture is shown in Exhibit 37.1.

GUI widget components sit on the client, however business logic may be required locally for complex applications, or on the server for transactional applications. These components can be placed wherever the architect sees fit. Component-based development does not provide an architecture so much as it permits good architectural choices to be implemented.

In distributed environments components can follow the CORBA or DCOM models. Components can be wrapped as CORBA objects or have a CORBA object interface. This makes them accessible through an ORB, permitting ready distribution. Alternatively, components can conform to the COM model and be distributed using the DCOM specifications. While these two distribution models can interwork, that is beyond the scope of this discussion.

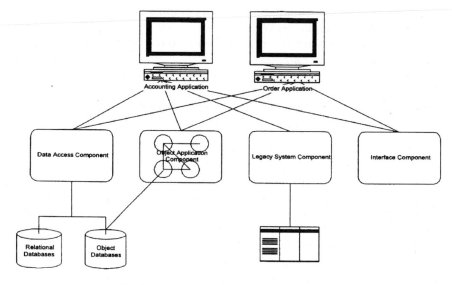

Exhibit 37.1.   Component architecture.

A component architecture can be described as a service-based architecture, like in the SELECT Perspective, where components act as the interface to a "service" which is a black box encapsulation of a collection of related functionality which is accessed through a consistent interface. Services are shared among applications to provide the application functionality. The system is then distributed according to business requirements, rather than software limitations.

COMPONENT TYPES

As mentioned previously, different components address different areas of functionality. These can be divided into framework components and business components. Framework components can be further broken down into data access components, user interface components, and subsystem components. Business components include business logic components and application components. These groupings allow us to place components based on the best configuration for our environment.

Data access components handle database interaction, including creation, deletion, query, and update. While data access components generally access a relational database, components can also access flat files, object databases, or any other persistent storage mechanism. This allows us a mechanism to change the back end data storage without impacting the delivered applications. It also allows us to deliver the same application using different databases with minimal change. The data component is replaced to suit the new environment.

User interface components handle user interaction and define the look and feel of the application. Separation of this component allows us to change the interface so that applications can take on the look and feel of the deployment environment. This helps to reduce training time by offering the user a consistent paradigm across applications.

Subsystem components provide functionality like error handling, security, or user help. They allow for standardization across applications.

Business logic components encapsulate the policies of a business. By separating them from general application or data logic, we can easily change applications to reflect changing business policies, such as offering discounts to large customers, or recommending complementary products.

Application components are small applications that contribute to the functionality of a larger piece, for example text editors. Application components include legacy applications that are wrapped to provide a standard interface for interaction with other components or use within applications.

COMPONENT MODELS

Currently there are two primary component models: JavaBeans and ActiveX. These two models can interact over bridges or by wrapping one as the other.

JavaBeans is the component model for the Java programming language. Because Beans are written in Java they run on any platform. A Bean may implement any functionality but it must support the following features: introspection, customization, events, properties, and persistence. JavaBeans are intended to be integrated with visual development environments and they should have some visually customizable properties, although they may not have a visual representation themselves.

ActiveX is based on the Component Object Model (COM) and was developed by Microsoft. While ActiveX has been a proprietary technology, Microsoft plans to transition it to an industry standards body. ActiveX enables developers to embed event driven controls into Web sites by optimizing the COM model for size and speed. While ActiveX components implemented in different languages can interact, ActiveX components are compiled into platform specific formats. The most common ActiveX implementation is for "Windows-Intel," limiting ActiveX to a Microsoft environment.

The OMG is currently in the process of defining a distributed component model based upon the Object Management Architecture. This will define a

CORBA component and make integrating CORBA Components significantly easier.

COMPONENTS, OO, CLIENT SERVER, AND NETWORK COMPUTING

Component-based development has its roots in object-oriented technology and client/server development and can act as an enabler for network computing.

Components extend object technology and object methodologies. Like objects, components should be developed in an iterative, incremental fashion. Components must be identified from existing applications and reworked to apply to new applications. Components and objects incorporate the idea of encapsulation and black box accessibility. With components, as with objects, we are not concerned with how a service is performed internally, only that it is performed correctly. Components are refinements of objects in that the API is defined in a language-independent standard. Components, like objects, communicate through industry standard middleware: CORBA or DCOM. This middleware acts as a layer of abstraction, so that components can be called in the same fashion, regardless of their function. This further hides the component's implementation, whereas direct object communication can rely on implementation specific calls.

Components act as service bundles, relying on tightly coupled object or legacy applications to implement their functionality. Components are then loosely coupled to form applications.

Components can be used to develop stand-alone applications or assembled in a traditional client/server fashion, with components providing server functionality like database access or client functionality on the user interface. Additionally, components allow us to move one step beyond. Components are designed to provide a limited service, and so allow for a true separation of the interface, business logic, and persistence. This allows them to be assembled in a multi-tier relationship and locate the components/tiers in the best place to run them.

Components can also enable network computing. Network computing allows for dynamic deployment, execution, and management of applications. Network computing architectures feature cacheable dynamic propagation, cross-platform capabilities, automatic platform adjustment, and runtime context storage. Since components are small units of work they are easily cacheable. Components written in Java using the JavaBeans specification are cross-platform and ActiveX components can run on any Microsoft friendly platform. Components can be dynamically managed; running on whatever server is appropriate given the current load.

ALTERNATIVES

As shown, component technology can work with client/server and network computing architectures, as well as object-oriented development.

The primary alternatives to component-based development are traditional "from scratch" development and package implementation.

Component-based development is superior to "from scratch" in that we anticipate reduced design, development, and testing time, with a lower bug ratio, since components are prebuilt and pretested. We spend our time developing new components that are missing from our library, and crafting and testing the links between components.

Component-based development is superior to package implementations in its flexibility. We have more control over what features are included based on our needs; additionally we can change those features as our needs change.

CHALLENGES

It looks as if component based development is a good thing. It saves time and money. How can we use components effectively in our own development environments? We will examine several areas: design, component acquisition, implementation, and maintenance.

Remember the idea behind component-based development is to free up our resources to concentrate on finding solutions for business problems. This can take us down several alleys. We may have to make a paradigm choice. If the application needs to be distributed or if the components are developed in multiple languages, we will have to decide whether to use DCOM or CORBA. The environment the application will run in and the available components will influence this choice. When working in an all Microsoft environment DCOM is the obvious choice. Where heterogeneous operating systems are used CORBA is a better choice.

Acquiring components has its own challenges. If they are to be acquired from internal sources, channels for reuse have to be set up. This means components have to be described in a way that other departments can use them easily. There must be a mechanism for publishing their availability; and accounting systems must reflect the costs of component development and recapture on reuse. In short, the whole corporate structure may have to change.

Purchasing components has other problems that may be influenced by corporate culture. While the ideal is that components can be replaced at will, the reality is that an application may become dependent on a component. Corporations may not desire this dependence. When purchasing components the financial stability of the provider company and the product stability must be considered. Will the product be supported in the future, and will its functionality and API remain consistent. Resources must be allocated to identify suitable components, evaluate the risk and future considerations that may impact their use.

Integrating components into an application presents challenges to developers and project managers. If the component is a class library, the object model will be affected. Library considerations can affect the subclass relationship. There may be conflicts between releases if you override methods in a subclass or make extensions to the purchased library.

Components also require good configuration management. You may not just be dealing with your own code releases, but also with the code releases of vendors, and your releases will impact users of your components. Code releases should be scheduled so downstream users can schedule regression testing. Vendor releases should be integrated into the application release and should undergo full regression testing. While there will be a lag time, efforts to keep everyone on the same release should be made, otherwise the releases may diverge into separate products. This will lead to confusion about what the component should do and require additional maintenance resources.

Another issue for project managers is developer resentment. Many developers feel that code that is not developed in-house is not as good as their own code. In addition, there is the old hacker mentality of trying to get into the guts of the component, instead of using the interface. This will make integration of vendor supplied software updates more difficult because the component has lost its "black box" functionality. Staff that can act as advisors on component use are required. The advisors will work with the development teams to recommend components for use on specific projects and harvest new components. Rotating development staff through the advisory positions will build knowledge about the component library and development process and help in identifying functionality that is used across development teams.

Finally, there are long term maintenance considerations. If a component is developed in-house, who is responsible for maintaining it? Is it the developer of the component, or the user who may require modifications to apply it? Organizational change may again be necessary. A software library, with its own dedicated staff, is a good solution to this problem. The library staff is responsible for maintaining the components and managing potential conflict between multiple users. For purchased components, maintenance is also an issue. Vendors may be slow to correct problems, and you may find yourself maintaining the component and feeding the fixes back to the vendor. Even with prompt vendor response, the component must be regression tested and fed into the release schedule.

CONCLUSION

In conclusion, component-based development offers an environment that can facilitate multi-tier architecture and allow a true separation of data, business logic, and user interface. It has the potential to increase developer productivity and lower costs but it is not an approach without risk. The advantages must be weighed against the risks over the entire software lifecycle.

References

ActiveX FAQ, Microsoft Corporation, 1996.

Allen, Paul and Frost, Stuart, *Component-Based Development For Enterprise System: Applying the SELECT Perspective,* Cambridge University Press and SIGS Books, 1998.

Austin, T., *Is Network Computing Just a Slogan?* Gartner Group, 1997.

Hamilton, Graham (Ed.), *JavaBeans API Specification Version 1.01,* Sun Microsystems, 1997.

Natis, Y., *Component Models Move to the Server,* Gartner Group, 1997.

Smith, D., *Microsoft Bolsters ActiveX: Developers Should Use Caution,* Gartner Group, 1996.

Chapter 38

Developing ActiveX™ Internet Server Components with Visual Basic and Rational Rose

Jeff Buller

THE POPULARITY OF COMPONENT-BASED SOFTWARE has increased steadily over the last few years. Server-side component software is a natural fit for Internet applications because it provides a reliable mechanism for packaging, deploying, and maintaining middle-tier services designed to encapsulate complex business rules. Microsoft's COM/ActiveX™ distributed object technology has emerged as an industry standard for component-based development. With the release of Visual Basic 5, Microsoft® has simplified the task of creating fully functional ActiveX components almost literally to a point-and-click operation.

Visual Basic 5 is an object-based language, which means that ActiveX components can be designed and constructed using object-oriented techniques. With any such object-oriented design process, it is important first to design an object model that will validate the key abstractions and object interfaces necessary to implement components correctly. Rational Rose 98 provides an excellent environment for modeling ActiveX components and is integrated fully with Visual Basic 5 to enable code generation and round-trip engineering.

This chapter discusses the benefits and uses of ActiveX server-based components, component creation with Visual Basic 5, object-oriented modeling techniques that can be used with Rational Rose 98, and finally component deployment considerations.

ActiveX COMPONENTS

Microsoft defines a component as "a discrete unit of code built on ActiveX technologies that delivers a well-specified set of services through well-specified interfaces. Components provide the objects that clients request at run time."

ActiveX is the result of the continuing evolution of Microsoft's distributed object technologies. The component concept was introduced with VBX controls in Visual Basic 3. The next advance came in the form of OLE custom controls (OCX's) with the release of Visual Basic 4. ActiveX components are a more efficient implementation of OLE controls that use resources more efficiently, incorporate more efficient communication protocols, and offer improved compatibility across operating environments. Many of these refinements are the direct result of making ActiveX components more compatible with the Internet environment.

The ActiveX component infrastructure is based on the Microsoft Component Object Model (COM) which Microsoft defines as:

> "an open architecture for cross-platform development of client/server applications based on object oriented technology. Clients have access to an object through interfaces implemented on the object. COM is language neutral, so any language that produces ActiveX™ components can also produce COM applications."

Components based on COM can leverage the benefits of object-oriented technology, including encapsulation and reuse. Components are accessed through well-defined object interfaces, which means that clients need not be concerned with the implementation details of a component to benefit from the services it has to offer. Furthermore, COM interfaces are discovered dynamically by the client, which adds to their flexibility and ease of use. Finally, COM is designed to be language neutral. This is the basis for making COM an industrywide standard where distributed COM objects can interact, regardless of the language with which they have been developed. This is already largely the case: Visual Basic applications, for example, can interact seamlessly with COM components developed in C++, PowerBuilder, Delphi, and Visual J++, to name a few.

COMPONENTS FOR INTERNET APPLICATIONS

The main prerequisite to using server-based ActiveX components in an Internet application is an application server that supports the COM interface. Examples of COM-compliant server applications include Active Server Pages, Hahtsite, and Jaguar. Many of these Internet application servers provide a programming environment for developing code that will execute in the application server environment in response to an HTTP request.

This server-based code usually is designed to generate HTML dynamically or access a database.

Through COM interface support, these server-side programming environments have direct access to instantiate and interface with ActiveX server components. Hahtsite, for example, provides a Visual Basic programming environment, which supports the CreateObject() function for creating component object instances. Once the component object has been instantiated it can be used in the same manner as a built-in object.

ActiveX server-based components provide an excellent mechanism for encapsulating complex business rules and services on an Internet server. In this configuration, much of the application logic resides on the server, the client/front-end function is reduced mainly to data capture and display. Thin clients are ideal in an Internet environment because they improve browser compatibility and performance. A centralized component-based architecture also results in a client interface that is coupled loosely with the business logic. This loose coupling makes it possible to reuse component functionality in various client implementations, which ultimately increases the flexibility and reusability of the system.

Other benefits of ActiveX components include:

- *Iterative Development:* An iterative development approach focuses on growing a system rather than packing everything into one big release. "Release early, release often" typifies the iterative lifecycle. The key is to focus on architectural concerns during the primary iterations and selectively add functionality during each successive iteration. Component development is a natural fit in the iterative lifecycle because new functionality can be added by creating new components or modifying existing components with minimal impact to the rest of the system.
- *Compatibility:* ActiveX components provide compatibility across all languages that support the COM interface. This includes programming languages such as C++, Visual Basic, Power Builder, Delphi, and Visual J++. (COM is in use on over 150 million systems worldwide.)
- *Productivity:* Products like Visual Basic 5 make it fast and easy to design, test, and deploy Visual Basic applications as ActiveX components. The large number of commercially available components (supported by a U.S. $670 million market — Giga Group) also can provide an alternative to custom development.
- *Maintainable:* Properly designed component systems can be easier to maintain because application logic is packaged into discreet units with well-defined interfaces. This reduces the impact of changes to the system and enables the system to adapt to new requirements. A component architecture also can simplify testing.

- *Reuse:* Properly designed components can be reused by any COM-compatible application or programming environment. Existing custom or commercial components can be extended to add custom behavior and specialized interfaces. This extension is based entirely on the interface of the base component to avoid breaking encapsulation. Components also can collaborate (interface) with other components to form complex application behaviors.
- *Performance:* ActiveX components created with Visual Basic 5 can be compiled to native binary code. In addition, components can be instantiated in-process to run in the application server's memory space. These features both contribute to fast execution, especially when running on a fast server.

Other uses of ActiveX components include the following:

- *Object-Oriented Language Extension:* Many of the application server programming environments do not support custom object creation directly. ActiveX component libraries can be used to extend the capabilities of the programming environment with custom-defined objects that are instantiated through a COM interface.
- *Wrapping:* Specialized components can be developed to wrap existing legacy applications with an object-oriented component interface.

VISUAL BASIC AND OO

Visual Basic 5 is not a true object-oriented language in the strictest sense of the term. Booch (see white paper: "Object-Oriented Development with Visual Basic") refers to the language as object-based because, although it supports the creation of classes and the principle of encapsulation, VB does not support true inheritance and polymorphism. Visual Basic 5 supports a form of inheritance called "interface inheritance," which uses object composition to simulated inheritance. As Gamma states (*Design Patterns — Elements of Reusable Object-Oriented Software Page* 19, Par 2), "Object composition is an alternative to class inheritance. Here, new functionality is obtained by assembling or composing objects to get more complex functionality. Object composition requires that the objects being composed have well-defined interfaces. This style of reuse is called black-box reuse, because no internal details of objects are visible. Objects appear only as black boxes."

In Visual Basic, object composition refers to the process of declaring or embedding an object in the class definition of another object. In this case, the containing object inherits only the interface of the parent object and does not have direct access to the internals of the parent object. Some would argue that the lack of true inheritance support in Visual Basic (such as one would find in C++) does not make it a viable option for truly leveraging the strengths of object-oriented development. Gamma goes on to say

(Page 25 Par 3) "Object composition in general and delegation in particular provide flexible alternatives to inheritance for combining behavior. New functionality can be added to an application by composing existing objects in new ways rather than by defining new subclasses for existing classes."

In Visual Basic 5, object composition applies both at the class level, when designing and programming the internal workings of a component, and at the component level, when combining components to produce complex system behaviors. In situations when Visual Basic is not sufficient to model complex business rules, components can be created using C++ and accessed via a COM interface.

Is VB the right choice? Ultimately, this will depend on the current development environment and the skills of the development team. It also may depend on the complexity of the business rules that one is trying to model. Is VB a good choice? With good OO development practices and a strong architectural vision, VB will enable one to develop component-based systems quickly and cost-effectively. VB is also an excellent choice for getting started with component-based development.

COMPONENT DESIGN AND DEVELOPMENT

On its own, a component-based development approach does not guarantee a successful system. Component-based systems are equally susceptible to poor analysis and design. Component-based systems also can involve large numbers of interacting objects — a situation that quickly can become unmanageable if not properly documented and understood.

In the Visual Basic environment, a consistent development approach is important on two levels: (1) object-oriented design and development of the internal workings (the guts) of components and (2) defining and scoping the interactions that will occur between components and groups of components that comprise the system as a whole.

Rational Rose is an object-oriented modeling tool from Rational Software corporation that provides the modeling tools necessary to produce high quality, robust component-based systems using Visual Basic 5. Rational Rose for Visual Basic also enables direct generation of Visual Basic code based on a class/component model.

High-Level Features of Rational Rose

Object-Oriented Modeling Features. Rose supports the UML (Unified Modeling Language) notation for creating detailed object models. Object models identify the class abstractions that are used to instantiate objects in the system, relationships between classes, class packaging, and component design. Rose also supports object interaction modeling and object state modeling.

505

Code Generation. Rose can generate Visual Basic code from a class model directly into a Visual Basic project. The generated project consists, initially, of the class skeleton definitions that contain declarations for all of the classes, class attributes, operations, and relationships that are necessary to implement the desired object behavior. The code generator is customizable.

Round-Trip Engineering. The initially generated Visual Basic skeleton project does not become functional until the developer adds the supporting logic to each of the generated class operations. To synchronize the logical class model with the generated VB project, Rose does two things:

1. The code generator creates protected code regions that separate the generated skeleton from the developer-added logic. This enables Rose to regenerate the project without impacting the custom implementation code.
2. The Rose environment also contains a code analyzer facility that can be used to integrate code level model changes back into the logical class model. Code level model changes can occur when a developer introduces a new class or modifies a class directly in the generated code. The code analyzer also can be used to completely reverse-engineer existing VB projects to create a logical class model.

Component Support. Rose/VB has direct support for component modeling. In Rose, a component in the object model corresponds directly to a VB 5 project (through code generation). The type of component can be any of the VB 5 supported component types including ActiveX DLL, ActiveX EXE, and ActiveX control. Existing ActiveX components (i.e. commercially developed ActiveX controls) also can be represented in the Rose component model. In fact, ActiveX components can be added to a Rose model by simply dragging them from the Windows explorer into the component view of the Rose model.

OOAD IN A NUTSHELL

The process used to discover and build a class model in Rose is entirely up to the user. Using an object-oriented approach, however, enables one to develop loosely coupled (reusable) components that accurately model the functional requirements of the system. Rose modeling techniques are designed to support a scenario-based approach to modeling the desired system/component behavior. Use case analysis provides a systematic approach to deriving objects and object interactions from system usage scenarios. Use case analysis focuses on the external (user) view of the system enabling the modeler to capture the desired system functionality more accurately.

What follows is a very high-level overview of some of the key object-oriented analysis and design (OOAD) techniques that Rational supports for developing object models in Rose.

Modeling System Behavior — Use Cases

Use cases are used to capture the functional requirements of the system. A use case model consists of the use cases that collectively describe the intended functionality of the system. Each use case is a text-based description of the series of events or transactions that a user of the system must complete to perform a particular system function. Users of the system (indeed anything that interacts with the system, including other systems) are referred to as actors. Rose supports the creation of use case model diagrams which represent, on a very high level, the use cases that exist for the system and the actors that initiate the use cases. The bulk of each use case (referred to as the use case report) usually is documented externally using Word or Requisite Pro. Rose allows users to attach use case reports to use cases icons in the use case model diagram. Linkages between Rose and Requisite Pro also are supported.

FINDING OBJECTS AND CLASSES

Objects and classes in the system being modeled are discovered by analyzing use case scenarios. A use case scenario is a particular instance of a use case flow that involves specific object references. For example, part of a use case flow could be an event such as "the user enters his/her PIN number ..." One corresponding scenario might be: "Bob enters his PIN number — 1234 ..." Objects in use case scenarios are identified by repeatedly filtering nouns that appear in the scenario text (e.g., "Bob," "PIN number," "1234"). The filtering process is designed to eliminate nouns that do not correspond to actual objects in the system. Many scenarios must be analyzed in this way to create a comprehensive list of potential system objects.

Once candidate system objects have been identified, classes can be created to represent the common abstractions shared between groups of objects. Classes are named and added to the class model diagram.

OBJECT INTERACTION

Object interaction refers to the interactions that must be supported between objects in the system to produce the functionality described in the use case model. In Rose, object interaction is modeled using a message trace diagram. A message trace diagram shows the sequential series of messages that are exchanged between objects to support the events that occur in a particular use case scenario.

RELATIONSHIPS

Relationships describe the connections or links that must exist between objects to support the message passing that is discovered in the object interaction diagrams. Relationships (also referred to as associations) can be unidirectional, bidirectional, by value (containment), or by reference. Relationships also have multiplicity attributes that indicate the relative number of related objects (e.g., 1 to 1, 1 to many).

OPERATIONS AND ATTRIBUTES

Operations and attributes are assigned on the class level to represent the behavior and state-of-object instances of the class. Class operations ultimately are derived from object interaction modeling and represent the operations that must be available via the object's interface to support interaction with (provide services to) other objects. Attributes are defined to capture the internal state of an object. Attribute values can be modified only through an object's interface (encapsulation).

OBJECT BEHAVIOR

An object's state is represented, at any time, by the combined values of its attributes and the relationships it has to other objects. In Rose, object behavior is modeled using state diagrams. A state diagram shows the discrete states that an object can be in during its lifetime. It also indicates the transitions that can occur when an object changes from one state to another and the events that cause the transitions to occur. State diagrams are useful for understanding the internal behavior of complex objects. One typically does not need to create a state diagram for each object in the model.

ARCHITECTURAL CONSIDERATIONS

Rose VB directly supports a three-tiered architecture for creating component-based systems. In this architecture, the basic building blocks of the system are components. Components are organized into three distinct service layers:

1. *User services:* User interface-related components that enable the user to interact with the system. Those can include GUI applications, browsers, and ActiveX controls.
2. *Business services:* Commonly referred to as the "middle tier," the business services tier houses components that encapsulate business rules and system functionality. This is the tier in which Internet server-based components are deployed. In many cases, this tier is accessed by the user services tier via an application server of some sort.

3. *Data services:* Components responsible for retrieving and updating persistent data. Persistent data usually is managed by an RDBMS or object-oriented database.

The three-tiered architecture takes full advantage of the reuse benefits of component-based development. It is also a good match for an iterative development approach because system functionality can be added incrementally to each layer as new components are developed.

PERSISTENT COMPONENTS

A use case-driven OOAD approach to modeling components focuses on the external behavior of the system. The emphasis is on designing user-centric component interfaces that accurately implement the behavior described in the use case scenarios. This differs from the typical client/server approach in which a great deal of emphasis is placed on first designing a data model that efficiently will store the data that is manipulated by the system. A client front-end then is created to work with the specific database design. This data-centric approach can result in a system that may not meet the user's needs because it has been adapted (compromised) to work with a specific database design.

In the OOAD process, persistent storage is not considered until the design phase. During that phase, key mechanisms are added to the class model to facilitate the storage and retrieval of entity objects. In a component-based system, persistent components encapsulate business entity objects that can exist independently of the component. This usually is accomplished by storing the attributes of the entity component in a database. When a persistent component is created or destroyed, the associated database attributes are loaded from or saved to the database respectively. During the design activities one must decide where in the component model to place persistence mechanisms. The two main choices are

1. Persistence mechanisms in each persistent component. This approach can simplify the class/component model because very few new classes need to be introduced. Persistence mechanisms become available through the interface of each entity component. The downside is that the persistence logic must be implemented in each persistent component, resulting in redundancy and code bloat. Persistent components also will be coupled very tightly with the storage mechanism resulting in a system that is not easily transportable.
2. Persistence mechanisms in a secondary component that is designed specifically for storing and retrieving one or more entity components. This approach will increase the complexity of the class/component model because new classes/components will be introduced to encapsulate the persistence mechanisms. However, by placing all

persistent storage mechanisms in separate classes/components, the entity components are not coupled directly to the storage mechanism. This increases overall reusability. In some cases, it may be possible to combine persistence mechanisms into a single group (layer) of classes/components that can support persistence for any of the entity classes/components in the system.

ACTIVE DATA OBJECTS

Components developed in Visual Basic 5 can use a number of database access technologies that are supported by Microsoft. These include the DAO (Data Access Objects) and RDO (Remote Data Objects) programming models, which can support both ODBC and native driver connections.

Active data objects (ADO for short) is Microsoft's latest data access technology, which is based entirely on ActiveX and designed specifically for Internet-based applications. Microsoft describes ADO as a technology that

> "enables you to write an application to access and manipulate data in a database server through an OLE DB provider. ADO's primary benefits are high speed, ease of use, low memory overhead and a small disk footprint."[Source: Microsoft®]

According to Microsoft, OLE DB is "... a specification for a set of data access interfaces designed to enable a multitude of data stores, of all types and sizes, to work seamlessly together... OLE DB goes beyond the simple data access by partitioning the functionality of a traditional relational database into logical components, and the events needed for those components to communicate." [Source: Microsoft®]

ADO provides an excellent key mechanism for persistence in a component object model. Because ADO itself is components-based, it enables the designer to abstract data stores into database components that interact with entity components for storage and retrieval. In addition, OLE DB gives users the flexibility to create data providers for nonrelational data sources such as spreadsheets and flat files.

OTHER BENEFITS OF ADO

- Easy to use. With ADO, Microsoft has encapsulated complex API-based logic into a simplified component object model.
- Consistent Interface. ADO is based on ActiveX and provides a consistent programming interface, regardless of the type or location of the data store being accessed.
- Language neutral. ADO is based on ActiveX enabling it to work with a variety of languages, operating systems, and databases that support the COM interface.

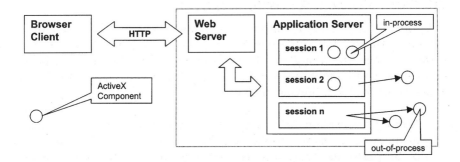

Exhibit 38.1. Web-based application server architecture.

- Easily integrated. Finally, as with any ActiveX component, ADO components may be integrated easily into the Rose modeling environment. This provides the designer with full access to all the component interfaces and classes that are supported by the ADO object model.

COMPONENT DEPLOYMENT

The task of component deployment is the process of making components available to other components or applications in a controlled, stable, and scalable way. For Internet server-based components this task is simplified somewhat because these components usually are deployed on a single server supporting the data services tier (also referred to as the middle tier). Furthermore, if a COM-compatible application server is used, the creation and management of component object instances can be controlled by application code executed on the application server. Exhibit 38.1 shows a Web-based application service architecture utilizing components.

REGISTERING ActiveX COMPONENTS

ActiveX components must be registered before they can be used by other applications or components. The act of registering an ActiveX component places a serverwide reference to that component in the NT server registry. Component-specific configuration information also can be stored in the registry. When an application attempts to instantiate a component, it uses the registry to locate the required component implementation files (binary files: .dll, .exe, or .ocx) and configuration information. Windows NT provides command line services for registering components with the operating system. VB5 also has a setup wizard that enables one to create a Windows setup program that automatically will install the component support files and register the component on the server.

CHOOSING THE ActiveX COMPONENT TYPE

Choosing the correct component implementation type is critical in determining the run-time characteristics of a component instance such as memory usage, threading, multiuser support, and performance. The recommended component type for server-based components is ActiveX DLL, which provides the following benefits:

- *In process execution:* An ActiveX DLL component executes in the same memory space as the application that instantiates it. This results in better performance because the data exchanged with the component (via the component's interface) does not have to be marshalled across a process boundary.
- *Multithreaded support:* This ensures that multiple instances of the same ActiveX DLL component run in their own memory space (also called thread apartments). This is necessary to avoid contention issues such as blocking in a typical multiuser Internet application environment.
- *Application Server Integration:* ActiveX DLL components integrate seamlessly with application servers that support COM.

MANAGING COMPONENTS ON THE MIDDLE TIER

Component management on the middle tier is required to ensure that the system is scalable and reliable.

Scalability is especially significant in an Internet environment where service requests to the middle tier could be very high. A scalable component architecture should have the ability to dynamically adjust to variations in request loads, manage the creation and destruction of component instances, and optimize available server resources.

Regarding reliability, as the number of components in the system grows so does the complexity of component interaction and collaboration. In many cases, complex business transactions are based on the interaction of groups of middle-tier components. For mission-critical applications it is necessary to guarantee that component collaborations are transaction-based; that is, they either finish completely or roll back completely.

For simpler component systems, a COM-compatible application server usually will provide the basic capabilities necessary to manage components. The Hahtsite application server, for example, manages server resources and allocates memory on a per user-session/request basis. The VB-compatible Hahtsite programming environment can be used to control the creation and collaboration of components available on the server through the development of custom code.

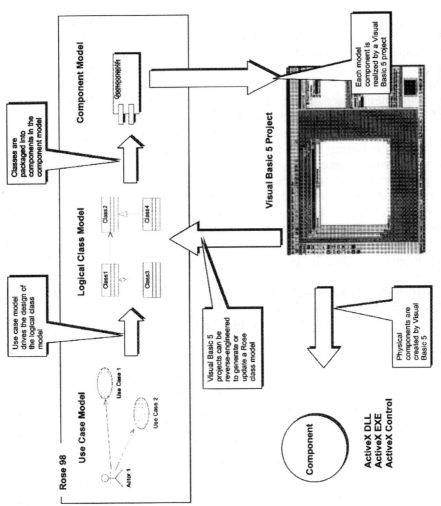

Exhibit 38.2. Component development with Rational Rose 98 and Visual Basic 5.

For more complex systems, a transaction monitor such as Microsoft Transaction Server can be used. Microsoft Transaction Server is a comprehensive solution for managing ActiveX component systems on the middle tier. It offers the following features to address directly the problems of scalability and reliability: automatic thread and process management, object (component instance) management, component packaging, database connection pooling, and automatic (component) transaction support.

CONCLUSION

As the popularity and importance of Internet-based applications increases, organizations will be forced to develop robust applications that are usable across many environments and able to adapt to changes quickly. Component-based applications (Exhibit 38.2) that encapsulate business logic on a centralized server have the potential to deliver on these goals. Microsoft's distributed object standard, COM, is a proven and widely used technology on which to build a component architecture. Together with systematic object-oriented analysis and design techniques, Rational Rose 98 provides the modeling tools necessary to develop reusable, stable components and component systems designed to meet or exceed user expectations. Visual Basic 5 offers an implementation and programming environment that makes component development fast and easy. Finally, server-based component systems must be scalable and able to handle the potentially high transaction volumes that are typical of the Internet environment. Most COM-compatible application servers will support simple approaches for dealing with these issues, whereas transaction servers such as Microsoft Transaction Server provide the infrastructure and resource control mechanisms that promise to support truly mission critical applications on the Web.

Chapter 39
A Technical Primer for Getting Started with JavaBeans

Charles Dow

SOFTWARE ENGINEERS ALL OVER THE WORLD ARE TIRED OF WRITING THE SAME CODE over and over again. They want to be able to reuse with ease the bulk of the code required to build the plumbing of an application, then be able to concentrate on the business rules and data. To accomplish this, tested and reliable building blocks that can be plugged together using a common protocol are needed.

JavaBeans provides a key piece of the technologies needed for these building blocks. The fact that JavaBeans is simple to develop, uses a modern object-oriented (OO) language, and handles the Internet and its associated security issues, makes its appeal unquestionable.

JavaBeans technology is very much like all OO technology; it has rich layers that need to be peeled away like an onion. This chapter is designed to show readers a few of its layers and how easily they can be peeled. Remember, one does not need to know all of the layers to reap the rewards of this remarkable innovation of the recent past. More importantly, by applying a few coding standards, the benefit of using JavaBeans can be obtained without requiring additional effort by developers. JavaBeans are not just for GUI widgets. They can provide far more business value. Components at runtime can be nonvisual (i.e., they do not have a graphical user interface).

SOME HISTORY

JavaBeans 1.0 has been available in JDK 1.1 since February 1997. Apple, Baan, Borland, CI Labs, Corel, Informix, IBM, JUSTSYSTEM, Lotus, Microsoft, Netscape, Novell, Oracle, ParcPlace, Silicon Graphics, SunSoft, Sybase, Symantec, Texas Instruments, Visual Edge, plus many external reviewers, participated in its development. JavaBeans is a Core API, which means one can expect it to be available on all the VMs.

TOOLABILITY

A key design goal for the JavaBeans technology was to provide components that could be manipulated visually by tools. JavaBeans allows developers to create reusable software components that then can be assembled together using visual application builder tools, such as Sybase's PowerJ, Borland's JBuilder, IBM's Visual Age for Java, SunSoft's Java Workshop, Symantec's Visual Cafe, and many, many others. Visit the Website, http://java.sun.com/beans/tools.html for a current listing of tools (available at the time of publication).

SIMPLE BEANS ARE FREE

Wouldn't it be nice to be able to concentrate only on writing the code needed to solve a particular problem and then be able to turn it into a component for others to use? That is possible in Java by following a few simple rules (a.k.a. design patterns) when writing code.

Before learning the name for those rules, follow some steps that will illustrate the process of bean-building.

Step 1. Write a Class

```
// A very simple example
// Time Bean class
// Time.java

import java.text.*;
import java.util.*;
import java.awt.Color;

public class Time {
Date currentDate;
SimpleDateFormat formatter;
String dateString;

public String getDateString () {
currentDate = new Date();
formatter = new SimpleDateFormat ("EEE, MMM d, ''yy");
```

```
dateString = formatter.format(currentDate);

return dateString;

}

public void setDateString (String newString) {

dateString = "No date as yet";

}

}
```

Note: A JavaBean does not have to be an applet or an application. It is a Java class, no more, no less. (Java classes do not have to be simple.)

Step 2. Compile the Class

D:\MyJavaSource\Time javac Time.java — javac is the compiler supplied with the JDK. One can download the JDK from http://java.sun.com/products/jdk/1.1/ (Web address accurate at time of publication). Do not forget to add a source directory to the CLASSPATH before compiling. Once that is done, execute javac from the source directory, as shown above.

Step 3. Create a JAR File for a Bean

A JAR file is the standard archive for Java code. There is one little twist that has to be applied if it is to contain a JavaBean. A manifest should be added. The manifest is a text file that needs to have at a minimum:

```
Name: Time.class

Java-Bean: True
```

Enter a command such as:

```
D:\MyJavaSource\Time jar cfm Time.jar Manifest.txt
Time.class
```

Note: Type jar by itself for a listing of the switches jar will accept. After running the command, you will have Time.jar.[1]

Step 4. Test the Bean

If one does not have the JavaBeans Development Kit (BDK), it can be downloaded from the following site: http://java.sun.com/beans/software/bdk_download.html (Web address accurate at time of publication).

Copy the new *Time.jar* file to the jars sub-directory of the BDK (...*\BDK\jars*).

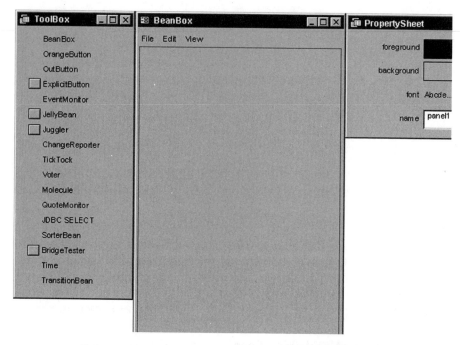

Exhibit 39.1.   ToolBox, BeanBox, and PropertySheet.

Using the BeanBox[2] supplied for free by JavaSoft (part of the BDK), launch the BeanBox. On Windows NT, use the batch file provided ...\BDK\beanbox run.bat. On other operating systems, please read the documentation that came with the BDK.

The three windows (namely ToolBox, BeanBox, and PropertySheet) shown in Exhibit 39.1 appear on the screen.

The toolbox contains sample beans provided by JavaSoft. Ignore them at this time. Notice the Time bean is one of the options in the list provided by the Toolbox. This one will be used. Left mouse click on the Time entry in the Toolbox; crosshairs will appear. That signifies that the cursor is loaded. Move the cursor over the BeanBox and Left mouse-click. A button-like shape entitled *Time* will appear. Left mouse click on it to select it. Then choose *Edit, Report* from the menu. A report similar to the one shown in Exhibit 39.2 will appear.

The *setDateString* is the method to set the DateString property or attribute.

The *get DateString* is the method to get the DateString property. A *get without a set* is a read-only property and vice-versa.

```
C:\WINNT\System32\CMD.exe

H => Hidden
E => Expert
I => Indexed Property

Properties:
    class                 class java.lang.Class     getClass/
    dateString            class java.lang.String    getDateString/setDateString

Event sets:

Methods:
    public final native void java.lang.Object.notifyAll()
    public final native void java.lang.Object.wait(long) throws java.lang.InterruptedException
    public final void java.lang.Object.wait(long,int) throws java.lang.InterruptedException
    public java.lang.String java.lang.Object.toString()
    public void Time.setDateString(java.lang.String)
    public final native void java.lang.Object.notify()
    public boolean java.lang.Object.equals(java.lang.Object)
    public java.lang.String Time.getDateString()
    public native int java.lang.Object.hashCode()
    public final native java.lang.Class java.lang.Object.getClass()
    public final void java.lang.Object.wait() throws java.lang.InterruptedException
```

Exhibit 39.2. Report 1.

Then a list of Event sets:

We have none at this time.

Then a list of Methods:

Notice, the above will appear for the class and all that it inherits. (This can be turned off.)

HOW DOES THE BEANBOX KNOW?

The BeanBox uses Introspection. Introspection simply put says, "If I know it is a bean (from the Manifest), then I will use the Java Core Reflection API that the JDK provides to allow us to dynamically obtain the fields, methods, and constructors of loaded classes from the class file."

The Introspection process can be assisted better by providing an associated BeanInfo class.

VOILA — OLD CODE INTO BEANS

But what if one did not know the few rules when writing your code? Modify the method names, as shown below (Essentially getting rid of the get and set portions that the Reflection API recommends).

```
// A very simple example

// Time Bean class

// Time.java


import java.text.*;
```

519

```
import java.util.*;

import java.awt.Color;


public class Time {

    Date currentDate;

    SimpleDateFormat formatter;

    String dateString;


    public String obtainDateString () {

        currentDate = new Date();

        formatter = new SimpleDateFormat ("EEE, MMM d,
''yy");

        dateString = formatter.format(currentDate);

        return dateString;

    }

    public void replaceDateString (String newString) {

        dateString = "No date as yet";

    }

}
```

If the above is compiled, and placed in a Jar with the same manifest file as above the report from the BeanBox that appears is shown in Exhibit 39.3.

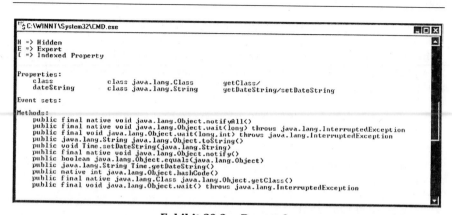

Exhibit 39.3. Report 2.

Note: The only property that can be seen by Introspection is the inherited read-only property. All methods are found.

ADDING A BEANINFO CLASS

To make a bean smarter, the BeanInfo[3] class is provided. Developers are encouraged to use this facility. The BeanInfo class will return instances of XxxDescriptor classes to describe the Bean, e.g., BeanDescriptor, EventSet-Descriptor, FeatureDescriptor and others when sent the appropriate messages.

To allow one to only provide the information that he or she wants to specify, there is a helper class, SimpleBeanInfo class, that can be inherited from; it will provide appropriate defaults for any method not overridden. The PropertyDescriptor classes should be used so that the BeanBox can see the getter and setter. Following is the BeanInfo class used:

```
// The BeanInfo class that we associate with our Time
Bean


import java.beans.*;

public class TimeBeanInfo extends SimpleBeanInfo {


    public PropertyDescriptor[]
getPropertyDescriptors() {

        try { PropertyDescriptor aPropertyDescriptor =
        new

        PropertyDescriptor( "dateString," Time.class,

    "obtainDateString,""replaceDateString");

        PropertyDescriptor[] anArrayOfPropertyDescriptors =
        {

        aPropertyDescriptor};

        return anArrayOfPropertyDescriptors ;

            } catch (Exception e) {

                System.err.println("Exception occurred "+e);

                return null;

            }

        }

    }
```

```
C:\WINNT\System32\CMD.exe                                                    _ □ ×
H => Hidden
E => Expert
[ => Indexed Property

Properties:
      dateString          class java.lang.String        obtainDateString/replaceDateString

Event sets:

Methods:
      public final native void java.lang.Object.notifyAll()
      public java.lang.String Time.obtainDateString()
      public final native void java.lang.Object.wait(long) throws java.lang.InterruptedException
      public final void java.lang.Object.wait(long,int) throws java.lang.InterruptedException
      public java.lang.String java.lang.Object.toString()
      public void Time.replaceDateString(java.lang.String)
      public final native void java.lang.Object.notify()
      public boolean java.lang.Object.equals(java.lang.Object)
      public native int java.lang.Object.hashCode()
      public final native java.lang.Class java.lang.Object.getClass()
      public final void java.lang.Object.wait() throws java.lang.InterruptedException
-
```

Exhibit 39.4.   Report 3.

Compile as before and use the following command to create the Jar:

```
Jar cfm Time.jar manifest.txt *.class
```

Note: The manifest does not change, because only Time.class is a bean. Run the BeanBox and get the report.

The report from the BeanBox now appears as shown in Exhibit 39.4.

Note: A more complex bean will have three parts, as follows:

- Properties
- Methods
- Events

There are many other features that Beans could use. After this taste of Beans, readers are encouraged to explore these further. Please note that for illustration purposes the code sample was trivial and broke many of the rules of a well-mannered Bean. The best reference that the author is aware of for JavaBeans Guidelines is a document produced by IBM's WebRunner team http://www.ibm.com/java/education/jb-guidelines.html.

CONCLUSION

JavaBeans is a relatively easy-to-learn tool for building components that provide more functionality than mere widgets. Components provide both functionality and data management in reusable, easy-to-snap together, little pieces that are combined to build sophisticated applications. The World Wide Web can be mined for many of the tools for getting started with JavaBeans.

References

Tremblett, P., Java Reflection, *Dr. Dobb's J.,* Jan. 1998, 36.

Morrison, M., Weems, R., Coffee, P., and Leong, J., How to program JavaBeans, *JavaSoft's Beans Development Kit (BDK),* ZD Press, Indianapolis, IN, May 1977.

Notes

1. For those with Winzip, you can quickly snoop at the jar file and the manifest.mf file contained within.
2. According to the BDK documentation, "the BeanBox is intended as a test container and as a reference base, but it is not intended as a serious application development tool."
3. Look at the documentation for the BeanInfo class.

Chapter 40
JavaBeans™ and Java Enterprise Server™ Platform

David Wadsworth

A MAJORITY OF THE WORLD'S DATA RESIDES ON MAINFRAME SERVERS. This legacy poses many challenges to the information systems (IS) community as it struggles with the demands of business units for new and innovative solutions to business problems. Organizations need to adopt a flexible, secure, and cost-effective architecture that will enable them to remain competitive and enable breakaway business strategies. Adoption of Java™ computing realizes these benefits by providing key technology enablers.

JAVA TECHNOLOGY REVIEW

The Java programming language was introduced to the public in May, 1995. Key features of the language such as platform independence and ease of programming made it an instant success in the software development community. Other features such as safe network delivery and baked-in security have made the language the *de facto* standard for the development and deployment of Web-based applications.

Applications written in the Java programming language are compiled to bytecode that can run wherever the Java platform is present. The Java platform is a software environment composed of the Java Virtual Machine and the Java Core Application Programming Interfaces (APIs). Portability of applications is achieved because there is only one virtual machine specification, which provides a standard, uniform programming interface on any hardware architecture. Developers writing to this base set of functionality can be confident that their applications will run anywhere without the need for additional libraries. Core libraries include functional support for GUI development, I/O, database connectivity, networking, math, components (JavaBeans), multithreading, and many others.

Sun's Java computing architecture is an implementation framework that uses standard, currently available network protocols and services to deliver the power of Java applications to the widest possible base of Java platform-enabled devices and users. With this architecture, transactions can be moved transparently to the most cost-effective, appropriate support channel within a network owing to the portable, Write Once, Run Anywhere™ nature of Java applications.

JAVA PLATFORM COMPONENT ARCHITECTURES

Designing and developing applications by means of components has been available for many years. The challenge has been to embrace and extend existing technology with new technology. Until recently, such an approach has been proprietary and difficult to deploy. The Java computing environment with JavaBeans, a component technology and server architecture solution, Java Enterprise Server, enables organizations to simplify greatly access to business systems. What follows is a description of the JavaBeans component model and an overview of the Java Enterprise Server platform.

JAVABEANS

A JavaBean is a reusable Java software component that visually can be manipulated and customized in a builder tool. These application building blocks are constructed so as to communicate easily with each other in a common environment. They also have the ability to store their state on the shelf to be revived at a later date. Because they are written in the Java programming language for deployment on any Java platform, JavaBeans are the platform-independent components for the network.

JavaBean components can range from simple GUI elements, such as buttons and sliders, to more sophisticated visual software components, such as database viewers. Some JavaBeans may have no GUI appearance of their own, but still can be manipulated in an application builder.

The JavaBean API has been designed to be accessible by builder tools as well as manipulated manually by human programmers. The key APIs, such as property control, event handling, and persistence, can be accessed by both hand-crafted applications and builder tools. As well as event handling, property control and persistence, introspection, and customization are distinguishing features of all JavaBeans.

Property Control

Property control facilitates the customizing of the JavaBean at both design and run-time. Both the behavior and appearance of a JavaBean can be modified through the property features. For example, a GUI button might have a property named "ButtonLabel," which represents the text displayed in the button. This property can be accessed through its getter and setter methods. Once properties for a bean are configured, their state will be maintained through the persistence mechanism.

Persistence

The attributes and behavior of a bean are known as the state of the bean. The persistence mechanism within the JavaBean API supports storage of this state once the bean is customized. It is this state that is incorporated into the application and available at run-time. This externalization can be in a custom format or the default. A custom external format allows the bean to be stored as another object type such as an Excel document inside a Word document. The default is reserved for those instances where the bean's state needs to be saved without regard to the external format.

Event Handling

Event handling is a simple mechanism that allows components to be connected based on their production of and, often, interest in certain actions. A component or series of components can be sources of events that can be caught and processed by other components or scripting environments. Typical examples of events include mouse movements, field updates, and keyboard actions. Notification of these events generated by a component are delivered to any interested component.

The extensible event-handling mechanism for JavaBeans allows for the easy implementation of the model in application builder tools. Event types and propagation models can be crafted to accommodate a variety of application types.

Customization

Changing the appearance and behavior of a JavaBean is accomplished through the customization features of the JavaBean's API. Each JavaBean contains a list of exported properties, which an application builder can scan and use to create a GUI property editor sheet. The user then can customize the bean using this dynamically created sheet. This is the simplest form of customization.

Another layer of customization is possible by attaching to the bean a customizer class that acts as a properties wizard. This wizard will have a GUI that can be employed to tailor the properties for the related bean in a guided tour fashion. Such wizards are more likely to be found associated with complex beans such as calculator beans or database connection beans. Once customization is completed the properties will be stored using the persistence mechanism.

Introspection

The properties, methods, and events a JavaBean supports are determined at run time and in builder environments by means of introspection. Introspection is a prescribed method of querying the bean to discover its inherent characteristics. Introspection is implemented using the Java programming language rather than a separate specification language. Thus, all of the behavior of the bean is specifiable in the Java programming language.

One introspection model supported by the JavaBeans API provides a default view of the methods, events, and properties. This simple mechanism does not require the programmer to do extra work to support introspection. For more sophisticated components, interfaces are available for the developer of the bean to provide specific and detailed control over which methods, events, and properties are exposed.

Default, low-level reflection of the bean is used to discover the methods supported by the bean. Design patterns then are applied to these methods to determine the properties, events, and public methods supported by the component. For example, if a pair of methods such as setColor and getColor are discovered during the reflection process, the property color is identified by the application of the get/set design pattern for property discovery.

More complex component analysis can be built into the bean by the use of a BeanInfo class. This class would be used by a builder tool to discover programmatically the bean's behavior.

Security

JavaBeans are governed by the same security model as all other Java applets and applications. If a JavaBean is contained in an untrusted applet, then it will be subject to the same restrictions and will not be allowed to read or write files on the local file system or connect to arbitrary network hosts. As a component in a Java application or trusted applet, a JavaBean will be granted the same access to files and hosts as a normal Java application. Developers are encouraged to design their beans so they can be run as part of untrusted applets.

Run-time vs. Design-time JavaBeans

Each JavaBean must be capable of running in a number of different environments. The two most important are the design- and run-time environments. In the design environment a JavaBean must be able to expose its properties and other design-time information to allow for customization in a builder tool. In some cases wizards contained in the bean may be employed to simplify this process.

Once the application is generated the bean must be usable at run time. There is really no need to have the customization or design information available in this environment.

The amount of code required to support the customization and design-time information for a bean could be potentially quite large. For example, a wizard to assist in the modification of bean properties could be considerably larger than the run-time version of the bean. For this reason it is possible to segregate the design-time and run-time aspects of a bean so it can be deployed without the overhead of the design-time features.

JavaBeans Summary

JavaBeans are the component object model for the Java platform. These device-independent components can be customized and assembled quickly and easily to create sophisticated applications.

JAVA ENTERPRISE SERVER PLATFORM

As organizations adopt Internet technologies to enable new business strategies, they are faced with the task of integrating all of their legacy applications, databases, and transaction services with Web-based services. Traditional applications designed in the client/server model do not deploy well in an Internet/extranet environment. Although not new, multi-tier architectures for application development and deployment are best-suited for extending the reach of a company's infrastructure to partners, suppliers, customers, and remote employees. The Java Enterprise server platform provides such an architecture in an open and standards-based environment that it incorporates existing infrastructure while extending their reach to intranets, extranets, and even the Internet. An extensible architecture, the Java Enterprise server platform contains the API's products and tools necessary to construct new enterprisewide applications and integrate with existing systems.

Traditional mission-critical applications are written to the APIs of the underlying operating system, thereby tying the application to a single operating system. Porting of the application to a new operating system is both difficult and expensive. These same applications may rely on a service, such as a transaction monitor. Access to this service will be through the software vendor's proprietary APIs creating another platform lock and presenting a barrier to moving to a different service provider.

The Java Enterprise server platform is designed to address these platform-lock issues. It extends the notion of "write once, run anywhere" to include "and integrate with everything." Based on a layer and leverage model, the Java Enterprise server platform can be built on top of existing legacy systems such as transaction monitors, database access, system

529

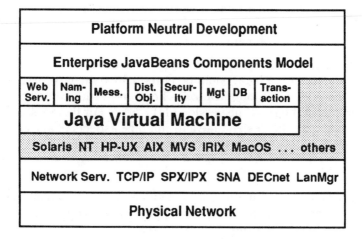

Exhibit 40.1.   Java Enterprise server platform architecture.

---

management, naming and directory services and CORBA (Exhibit 40.1). Interfaces to these services, as well as a component model that provides for application encapsulation and reuse, are integral to the Java Enterprise server platform. The component model includes JavaBeans, components for the client, and Enterprise JavaBeans (EJB's) components for the server.

All of the benefits of rapid application development, scalability, robustness, and security of the JavaBeans component architecture are extended to the Java Enterprise server platform. EJBs also have the ability to provide transactional services. Coupled with these benefits is an open architecture capable of providing ease of development, deployment, and management.

Enterprise JavaBeans, an extension of the JavaBeans architecture, provide a distributed component architecture for developing and deploying component-based, multi-tier applications. Business logic is encapsulated in the Enterprise JavaBeans promoting a high degree of reuse. Access to low-level services such as session management and multithreading is simplified such that developers building applications do not need to deal directly with these functions.

Distributed applications developed with Enterprise JavaBeans can be deployed on any other platform without modifications. Support for transactions and messaging integrate with existing legacy systems and middleware.

The heart of the Enterprise JavaBean platform is the Enterprise Java-Bean executive (Exhibit 40.2). This run-time executive is used to execute the components that provide the services required by an application.

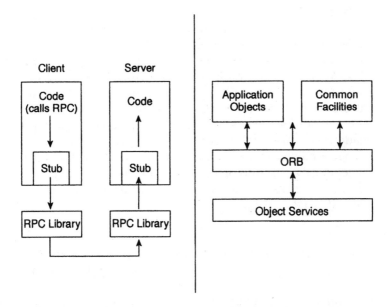

Exhibit 40.2.   Enterprise JavaBeans framework.

Through its components, the executive manages load balancing and handles multithreading, transaction management, security, and connection management. This frees programmers to focus on developing the components that contain business logic.

Communication between the client and server in an application does not need to rely on any particular protocol. Both client and server side of the application are coded using the Java programming language. At deployment time the underlying communication stubs are generated automatically. The Java programming language introspection of the application class files is used to generate the communication stubs.

Unlike JavaBeans which use the Java event model, Enterprise JavaBeans use the distributed CORBA event model. The event model supported by the Java programming language is well-suited for local, tightly integrated applications, but does not perform as well in a networked environment where high latency and insecure networks are common. Enterprise Java-Bean events are propagated across the network over CORBA's Internet InterORB Protocol (IIOP) to other components.

Enterprise JavaBeans can be configured automatically as CORBA objects, then accessed through IIOP by clients. These client applications do not have to be written in the Java programming language to access the components. EJB's also can function as COM/DCOM objects for Windows clients.

OBJECT TECHNOLOGY, OBJECT MODELING, AND OBJECT DATABASES

Access to several key services are offered as part of the Enterprise Java-Bean specification (Exhibit 40.2). These services are offered through specific Java platform APIs such as JavaIDL/RMI for accessing CORBA, DCE, or ONC services; Java Message Service (JMS) for access to messaging systems such as MQ Series; Java Naming and Directory Interface (JNDI) for accessing multiple naming and directory services such as LDAP and NDS; Java Database Connectivity (JDBC) for connecting to various relational and nonrelational databases; Java security API's providing for encryption and authentication; Java Transaction services (JTS) providing a Java programming language binding to the object transaction services (OTS) of CORBA; Java management API (JMAPI) providing for the management of networked resources such as workstations and routers; and Web services through the Java Server API. Each is detailed below.

JavaIDL

The Java Interface Definition Language (IDL) provides standards-based interoperability and connectivity with CORBA. Through these interfaces, Java applications are able to access existing infrastructure written in other languages. This is one of the key interfaces for legacy system integration. JavaIDL is part of the Java platform core API set and is, therefore, available across multiple platforms.

Java Message Service

Java Message Service (JMS) provides an interface to messaging systems that provide publish/subscribe and message queue services. This platform-independent interface also will support the emerging push/pull technologies.

Java Naming and Directory Interface

Many different kinds of naming and directory services exist in today's enterprises. Directory services such as LDAP, NIS, and NDS provide networkwide sharing of information about the users, systems, applications, and resources that exist on an intranet or the Internet. User information can include log-in IDs, passwords, security access, and electronic mail addresses. System information can include network addresses and machine configurations. The Java Naming and Directory Interface (JNDI) is independent of any specific naming and directory service implementation. Application developers can access multiple namespaces easily through JNDI. A single interface simplifies the access to composite namespaces as well as enabling an application to be portable across different platforms.

Java Database Connectivity

One of the earliest and now core APIs is the Java database connectivity API (JDBC). This is a SQL-based, database-independent API that frees developers from writing database vendor-specific code in their applications. JDBC supports the common database functionality such as remote procedure calls, SQL statements, database connection, and result sets. Because JDBC is implemented via a driver manager, which itself can be implemented in the Java programming language, applets can be delivered to the client with the database connectivity built in. Implementation drivers for all the major RDBMS are already available for JDBC, and a JDBC-to-ODBC bridge is standard in the Java Developer's Kit Version 1.1. JDBC drivers for object-relational DBMSs as well as IBM's IMS are also currently available.

Java Security API

Security is an integral part of the Java Platform and extends to the Java Enterprise Server architecture. There are four key areas that are supported by various security APIs: authentication, authorization, privacy, and integrity.

Authentication is the system's ability to verify or recognize a user. Typically performed at application access or system sign-on, authentication is the first line of defense present in a comprehensive security model. The JavaCard APIs allow smart cards to be employed as secure user authentication devices. These physical cards combined with a secure personal identification number (PIN) enable users to be recognized by the target system. Digital signatures, another authentication method, also are supported through the Java Virtual Machine.

Authorization is the means of determining which data, systems, and services a user can access. The Java Security APIs and access control lists (ACL) are available for managing who can access what. ACLs can be built for each Enterprise JavaBean and consulted whenever the bean is accessed. Based on the user's role some form of access can be given or denied. Transaction servers installed in the application enforce the ACL at run time. Because ACLs are not a static structure they can be moved around the network with an EJB object. These embedded ACLs then can be accessed by the application developer.

Privacy concerns are raised in the context of transmission of sensitive data across public networks. To protect data such as credit card numbers, encryption typically is employed. The Java language cryptography APIs provide application or session-level encryption. This interface can support any encryption implementation including DES.

As data passes through a network, be it private or public, there is a chance for malicious or accidental modification. To prevent such actions it is necessary to be able to guarantee the integrity of the transmission. The same mechanisms for insuring privacy can be used for maintaining integrity of network communications, namely session and application encryption.

Java Transaction Services

Java Transaction Services (JTS) within the Enterprise JavaBean framework are a low-level API not meant as an application programmer interface. JTS programming is targeted to the resource managers and TP monitor programmers. Currently available implementations include BEA Systems Jolt product for Tuxedo access or IBM's JavaCICS for access to mainframe CICS applications.

Java Management API

The Java Management API (JMAPI) is a set of interfaces for the development of distributed network, system, and application management applications. JMAPI is designed to be incorporated into a variety of devices, across diverse network protocols and numerous operating systems. With support for the Simple Network Management Protocol (SNMP), JMAPI can communicate directly with a variety of existing devices. In the future, device manufacturers will incorporate the JMAPI directly in their products. System administrators using applications developed on this foundation are able to easily manage their network, applications, or other systems from any Java platform located anywhere on the network.

Java Server API

The Java Server API is an extensible framework that can be employed to develop network-centric servers quickly. These servers are capable of providing network-based services, such as Web services, file and print services, proxy services, and mail services. To extend the functionality of a Java server a developer can create servlets using the Java Servlet API. Java servlets are programs that can be local to the server or downloaded across the network, then executed on the Java server. These servlets are perfect for processing form data from HTML pages, replacing the platform-dependent CGI-bin scripts in use by many organizations.

SUMMARY

The ability to integrate with legacy systems and extend enterprise services to the network with platform-independent technologies are key benefits of developing a Java Enterprise Server strategy. Enterprise JavaBeans, the component architecture for the Java Enterprise Server, provide a software- and hardware-independent method to access these systems and make them available to business components. These components easily can access services, such as transaction monitors and message systems, DBMSs, and naming services with the assurance of the Java Platforms "write once, run everywhere."

Chapter 41
Distributed Objects and Object Wrapping
Hedy Alban

ADVANCES IN SYSTEMS INTEGRATION OVER THE PAST DECADE have resolved connectivity issues at lower layers of the Open Systems Interconnection (OSI) network model. Solutions exist for connecting systems at the hardware level or the transport level. Communications networks, phone lines, cables, and fiber are available to connect systems to local area or wide area networks, hubs, and switches. Connectivity between most operating system platforms is similarly available.

Data sharing among disparate platforms and applications largely is resolved as well. The common architectural features among relational database management systems (DBMSs) enable middleware products to mix and match data from heterogeneous sources, and SQL Access interfaces allow nonrelational data architectures to participate as well.

A variety of replication techniques can enhance access. New and better solutions for data reconciliation among platforms come to market almost daily. A similar variety of approaches is available for preserving transaction integrity in distributed environments.

Although integration solutions are available in the lower layers of the OSI networking model, analogous interoperability at the application level remains elusive. Processing routines are locked into specific applications environments and cannot be invoked except through that specific application. Stored procedures are buried within the proprietary languages of DBMS products, uninvoked during heterogeneous data access, so that they cannot deliver on their promise of universality and consistency. Object-oriented programming fares no better; object systems are not compatible with one another.

As a result, a vast treasure of useful intelligence is trapped within specific contexts. Imagine that the fastest routine for cursor movement was devised for a vertical application that caters to a small number of users. Theoretically, such a function could revolutionize the user interface for

0-8493-9832-0/00/$0.00+$.50

other applications that are installed on the same machine or network; however, it may be trapped inside the specific vertical application and remain unavailable for use in other applications. Thus, the customer actually owns an outstanding capability but cannot put it to use except in a very small context.

Sometimes, the dependence of individual processing routines on the proprietary applications that contain them cripples the very mechanisms that have been built up over the years to impose consistency and administrative order at the application level. For example, stored procedures contain processing routines that consistently should be enforced each time a data element is accessed. They are a means for enforcing business rules such as maximum credit limits, ensuring consistent enforcement no matter what application accessed them.

Unfortunately, however, the language of stored procedures is proprietary to each DBMS. When a developer tries to write a multivendor DBMS application or a user tries to access multiple DBMSs through a query tool, the stored procedures fall by the wayside and consistent enforcement disappears.

For these reasons, then, application interoperability is regarded widely as the next step in the evolution toward enterprisewide networking capability. The requirement is for cooperation among heterogeneous equipment and software applications that are installed currently.

ACHIEVING MULTIPOINT CONNECTIVITY

At present, the remote procedure call (RPC) is the most common technology for application-level interoperability. RPC is the favored technique for implementing cross-platform DBMS stored procedures. It is the mechanism chosen for the Distributed Computing Environment (DCE) architecture promoted by the Open Software Foundation, and the basis for the Sun Solaris network file server (NFS). Currently, there is not a more robust approach than DCE for heavy production environments. It is not the best theoretical answer, but it is the most mature of the developed distributed approaches.

Nevertheless, RPCs are not optimal for many enterprise solutions because they are point-to-point solutions. They are able to connect an individual application with another. As the network becomes more complicated, however, a more comprehensive solution is required.

With a more comprehensive solution and with broad multipoint connectivity throughout the network, it will be possible to enforce business rules consistently, to locate data consistently, to reuse helpful routines in multiple contexts, and to consistently apply application routines to the data.

536

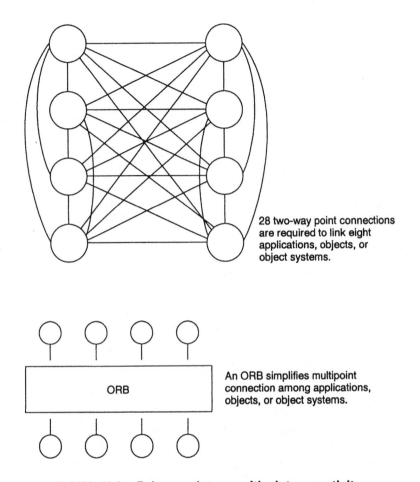

28 two-way point connections are required to link eight applications, objects, or object systems.

An ORB simplifies multipoint connection among applications, objects, or object systems.

Exhibit 41.1. Point-to-point vs. multipoint connectivity.

Many theorists and practitioners believe that distributed object technology provides the solution for these problems. Distributed object technology promises to overcome the current obstacles to enterprisewide client/server implementation. The object request broker (ORB), the engine of a distributed object environment, provides a universal layer for multipoint connectivity (Exhibit 41.1). The RPC mechanism and the object request broker are explained and contrasted in this chapter and in Exhibit 41.2.

WHAT ARE DISTRIBUTED OBJECTS?

Distributed objects represent the next generation of client/server facilities. In this context, an object is a chunk of code that represents a business

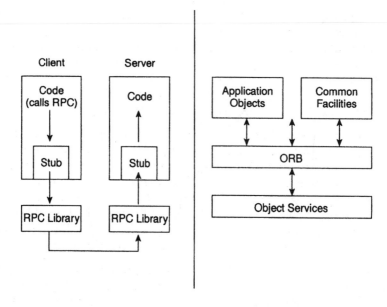

Exhibit 40.1. RPC vs. ORB

function. A distributed object is an object that can be accessed from anywhere on a network, across platforms, programming languages, and application systems.

Distributed object computing allows developers to build applications as a series of components or services that can be designed and stored across a network and brought together only when needed to perform a specific business function. Developers essentially snap together complex client/server systems simply by assembling and extending reusable distributed objects. A systems builder could select objects from several vendors and connect them as easily as audio components are connected at home today. Individual programming modules (objects) would exist independent of the application for which they were created, free for recombination with other modules in new contexts and for new applications. With distributed object computing, component developers and users can locate code without knowing its location in advance.

Outgrowth of Compound Document Applications

Distributed object technology appeared first in compound document applications. Compound documents contain more than one data format — for example, they may contain a combination of text, charts, and graphical material.

In early practice (which continues, for the most part, even today), each component was created in the tool most appropriate for it (e.g., text in a word processor, charts in a spreadsheet, and graphics in a drawing program) and then assembled into a single whole, usually in a desktop publishing package. To edit the document, users would access the appropriate component via its source application (i.e., the spreadsheet) and then reassemble the edited components into the complete document.

With the advent of distributed object technology, returning to the source application became unnecessary; each component of the document came with its own tools for editing and manipulating it. Thus, for example, the creator could edit a spreadsheet within the same environment that he or she edited the text or drawing. In Microsoft parlance, the compound document is created in a container application that accepts component processing modules from various applications; the function of the component modules appears to the user as selections in a menu bar.

For compound documents, the convenience to the end user of application integration is obvious and important. The significance of application integration goes far beyond this specific application, however. The true significance of application integration comes forth in a networked environment, where it comes into play for the administration and maintainability of the system. It also dovetails with other current practices, like business rules and stored procedures and maintaining consistency across the enterprise.

OBJECT-ORIENTED PROGRAMMING AND DISTRIBUTED OBJECTS

Object orientation is becoming increasingly popular for the benefits of code reuse, adaptability, and the ability to make the computer environment look and feel like the real world as never before. In the context of object-oriented programming, an object generally is defined as a software entity that contains both data and the processing code to manipulate that data.

By definition, classical software objects possess the qualities of inheritance, polymorphism, and encapsulation (although the details of these terms are irrelevant to this discussion). A distributed object, in contrast, is defined and evaluated in terms of its context independence — that is, its ability to function independent of the application (e.g., context) from which it was created.

Therefore, a distributed object need not possess the qualities of the classical software object; instead, it may be a standard sequence of coded statements that are isolated and enveloped in such a way as to become available for interaction with other objects. In modern parlance, a software module can be transformed into a distributed object by encapsulating it

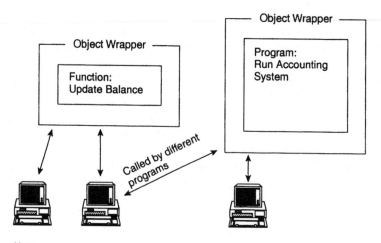

Note:
Large or small objects can be encapsulated in a "wrapper" for modular use.

Exhibit 41.3. Object with wrapper.

in a wrapper (Exhibit 41.3), thereby exposing it to other distributed objects on the network.

Once a software module is transformed into an object, it can be accessed and executed as if it were a primitive. Object programmers and users no longer view the module or its code. Instead, they view the object as a basic computing element. They manipulate the object itself, not its internals.

Object Wrapping

The chief mechanism for integrating legacy applications into the distributed object environment is wrapping. The simplest form of wrapper, with which most readers are familiar, is the Windows icon. A user can access a DOS application within a Windows environment simply by clicking on its icon. In this situation, the icon is the wrapper for the DOS application, permitting it to be treated like a Windows application; the internals of the application, however, function like a DOS program and not a Windows program.

Technically speaking, it is possible to convert an entire application into a single object by this means. All applications can be converted into distributed objects by this means. Optimally, however, conversion to distributed objects exposes individual application components in a more granular way.

Most applications require a better level of integration, where individual functions of an application are made universally available within the object environment. For example, a programmer might wish to integrate the data access routines of one application into the user interface of another application. The original access routine performs unchanged, but as a whole the routine will be merged into a second application. To accomplish this, the programmer must wrap the required routine and then make it accessible (i.e., expose it) to other objects in the environment.

Wrapping is possible only when clear boundaries exist between objects. In other words, the distributed object must contain all information required for the computer to execute it. In the previous example, if the original application were written in a modular fashion, then it will be easier to isolate the routine for integration into the new application. But even so, the process is not really a clean-cut one.

A typical application, even if it is well-written, modular, and well-organized, will still have dependencies among various portions of the code. At the very least, the definition of variables and working storage areas are defined outside a programming module. The wrapper must accommodate this to operate.

Bridging Legacy and Distributed Object Environments. An object wrapper serves as an interoperability bridge between the legacy system and the object environment. On one side of the bridge, the wrapper links up to legacy system's existing communication facilities. On the other side of the bridge, the wrapper defines the legacy system to the object environment, exposing it within the object environment and bringing specific services, such as security.

During the process of object wrapping, a development team may decide to perform other system enhancements at the same time. For example, an installation may collect metadata at the same time that it performs its analysis for object wrapping, preparing the system for future maintenance projects. Reverse engineering may be in order, or data migration into a more modern DBMS architecture. Sometimes, object wrapping may be used to subdivide a large project into modules with clear boundaries, for future enhancements on a component-by-component basis.

Each legacy system presents a unique integration problem with its own constraints. Some legacy systems may have no API at all, and others may have an extensive proprietary API. Access mechanisms can be sockets, RPCs, or something else. The object wrapper hides these idiosyncracies and presents a consistent and clear interface.

Object wrapping occurs when an organization migrates existing applications into a distributed object environment. During this process, it is wise to seek a path that avoids extensive software rewriting. It is also wise to keep the target environment firmly in mind, to choose wrappers that conform to a set standard so that objects will interoperate once the task is complete.

Wrapping Techniques. Wrapping greatly simplifies and empowers client/server computing. Individual objects within the system are inconsistent internally but, given a uniform interface, can interoperate seamlessly. Some techniques for wrapping include:

- *Layering:* Layering is a basic form of wrapping wherein one form of API is mapped onto another. For example, one can layer a CORBA-based interface over RPC services. This technique is applicable where the existing object already has a clearly defined API and well-defined services.
- *Encapsulation:* Encapsulation is a general form of object wrapping where the original code remains largely intact. An encapsulation is a black box where only the input and the output are revealed externally; underlying implementation is hidden. Encapsulation separates interface from implementation. Encapsulation is a convenient way to wrap legacy systems where source code is inaccessible or nonexistent.
- *Object gateways:* Object gateways implement the most generic form of encapsulation and are used in worst-case situations, where the legacy system provides no API, no access to code, and no scripting interface. With this form of wrapping, all processing occurs within the closed system using that system's menus, user interface, and toolset. The user interacts with the application using the facilities provided by the legacy system. Object gateways can be handy tools for quickly loading multiple legacy applications unchanged into the new object environment.

OBJECT REQUEST BROKERS

The object request broker (ORB) is the engine of the distributed object environment, enabling communication among objects both locally and across the network. ORBs can make requests to other ORBs and can process responses. They hide all differences between programming languages, operating systems, object location, and other physical information that is required for interobject and internetwork communication. All these processes happen behind the scenes, hidden from the user and the client/server application.

Common Object Request Broker Architecture (CORBA)

CORBA is a specification for an object-oriented universal middleware that supports application interoperability in three-tier client/server environments (Exhibit 41.4). CORBA-compliant tools permit objects to communicate with one another, even if they reside on different platforms and are written in different languages using different data formats. The CORBA

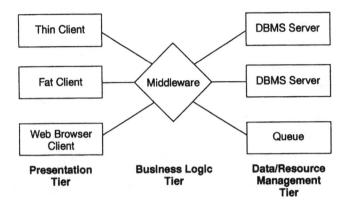

Note:
Three layers exist to separate presentation, business logic and data/resource management levels.

Exhibit 41.4. Three-tier client/server architecture.

specification provides a language for multiple object systems to communicate with one another.

CORBA Specifications and Implementation. CORBA-compliant products provide a uniform layer encapsulating other forms of distributed computing and integration mechanisms. CORBA can accept many different implementations.

The RPC, which is the basis for interprocess communication under DCE, is one implementation model. Message-oriented middleware (MOM) is another implementation. Some vendors, like Iona Technologies, are basing CORBA on Open Network Computing (ONC)-compatible RPCs. Other vendors, such as Hewlett-Packard, are using OSF/DCE; some others, like Sun-Soft, are bypassing the RPC layer and implementing CORBA at low layers. CORBA is designed to accept all of these models as well as future solutions that might arise. CORBA-compliant software completes the interoperability task through well-defined interface specifications at the application level.

CORBA defines a high-level facility for distributed computing, the object request broker (ORB). CORBA is a specification for creating ORBs. The ORB functions as a communication infrastructure, transparently relaying object requests across distributed heterogeneous computing environments.

CORBA also defines an Interface Definition Language (IDL), a technology-independent language for encapsulating routines. A universal notation for defining software boundaries, IDL, can be mapped to any programming language. Mappings to C, C++, and Smalltalk, as approved by the Object

Management Group (OMG), are currently available. The mapping is contained within the header files of IDL.

Finally, CORBA includes a set of specifications for common facilities, object services, and application objects. Common facilities define high-level services such as printing and e-mail. Object services define lower-level services such as object creation, event notification, and security. Application objects are all other software, including developer's programs, commercial applications, and legacy systems.

The Object Transaction Service (OTS) subspecification of CORBA is of particular interest to database programmers. OTS defines how atomic transactions can be distributed over multiple objects and multiple ORBs. OTS was designed to interact simultaneously with both ORB-based and traditional TP monitor-based transaction services. OTS can support recoverable nested transactions, even in a heterogeneous environment, that fully support ACID and two-phase commit protocols. OTS is based on technology developed by Transarc Corp., inventors of the Encina transaction processor, which usually functions on top of their DCE product.

Typically, commercial ORB products provide facilities for creating objects and wrappers. The developer first creates an object and defines its boundaries. The developer then submits this IDL code to the ORB product. The compiler in the product translates the IDL code into the target language (e.g., C++). The compiler generates the header files, stubs, and skeleton programs for each interface, exposing the object to other objects within the environment. In an environment where objects use OMG IDL interfaces and are otherwise CORBA-compliant, these objects discover each other at run time and invoke each other's services.

Note that CORBA is a specification, not an actual product. It does not deliver an accompanying reference implementation (i.e., source code) in the way that DCE and UNIX do. Furthermore, CORBA specifies only interfaces among objects; it does not define the object system itself.

Individual vendors build their own products and their own ORBs. CORBA-compliant ORBs interoperate with one another as long as they are referencing version 2 of the CORBA specification. (The various releases of version 1 are too general to guarantee interoperability.) Most object vendors provide developer support for implementing linked library code using OMG IDL interfaces.

Significance of the CORBA Standard. The significance of CORBA will grow as object-oriented systems gather critical mass within the corporate information resource. At present, many corporations already have begun pilot projects and small-scale systems using object technology. They may be working with VBX and OLE 2.0 in the context of their desktop workstations, exploring Internet and intranet applications using Java, and developing some applications with C++ as well. Right now these environments operate as discrete units, but dependencies among them are inevitable. What will bind them together?

Point-to-point solutions provide a quick fix but add complexity to the system. A standard such as CORBA is required if systems builders are to create a flexible, layered structure for connectivity between object systems and avoid point-to-point connectivity. In point-to-point connectivity, one object system requires a specific protocol to connect with, for example, Microsoft's DCOM (Distributed Component Object Model), another to connect with Java, a third to connect with IBM's System Object Model (SOM), and so on. True, it is faster and easier to create point solutions to satisfy immediate requirements, but the market must keep the long view in mind as well.

Fortunately, several of the products just mentioned do indeed comply with CORBA. The only way that a rational format for interoperability will take place is through market pressure. If customers insist on CORBA compliance, then vendors will deliver it; if not, then CORBA will die.

Distributed Computing Environment (DCE)

The Distributed Computing Environment (DCE) provides the means and the tools to transform a group of networked computers into a single coherent computing engine. It is a large and complex middleware product that enables communication among multiple heterogeneous platforms, masking differences among computer platforms. It enables the development of distributed applications that make optimal use of existing computer resources such as storage devices, CPUs, and memory.

DCE enables cooperation among these computer resources and, at the same time, provides tools to deal with such problems as data protection, time and event synchronization, reconciliation of data formats and file-naming schemes among platforms, and so on. An appropriately configured DCE environment allows end users to access multiple computers with a single log-on and to access remote data with the same ease that they access local data.

DCE can be described in terms of its benefits to the end user, the programmer, and the network administrator.

DCE's Benefits for the Network Administrator. DCE provides facilities for organizing an enterprise into administrative units (called cells) and then creating directory services to help programs locate resources within this organization. Following installation, network administrators can move files from one location to another without modifying programs or notifying users.

DCE delivers the following features:

- Multihost replication of files and applications, so that programs can continue to operate even when systems go down and servers are moved around.
- DCE Security Service for cross-system protection by means of authentication.
- DCE Distributed File Server (DFS) for tracking programs and data when they are moved from one computer to another, so that programs need not be recompiled with the new address and users need not be aware of the move.
- DCE Directory Service for look-up capability, so that users and applications can communicate with people and resources anywhere in the network without knowing their physical location.

Although not itself object-oriented, the Distributed Computing Environment can support interoperability among different object strategies. For example, DCE can provide a transport layer above which ORBs communicate with one another. In fact, DCE provides explicit support for ORBs through its DCE Common InterORB protocol.

DCE's Benefits for the Programmer. For applications developers, DCE provides the RPC and threads.

Remote Procedure Calls. The remote procedure call is a mechanism for interprocess communication that ties the client and server application code together. It handles the lower levels of interprocess connectivity, shielding the programmers from the details of that connection. It performs data conversion and manages all lower-level aspects of communication and, when programmed to do so, provides automatic recovery from network or server failure.

The RPC invisibly hides the differences in data formats between heterogeneous computers, reconciling differences in byte ordering, data formats, and padding between data items. It hides these differences by converting data to the appropriate forms needed by the destination system.

To integrate legacy applications into the DCE environment, the programmer can wrap the application with an interface definition. The wrapped application will be available within the DCE environment to all supported systems, but it must be rewritten into a client/server style (i.e., it must be rewritten in modular fashion or given a client/server interface through a DCE-compatible screen scraper or similar tool) to reap the benefits of distributed computing.

Threads. DCE threads enhance performance by allowing the programmer to specify threads for the purposes of task separation and task division. In task separation, the programmer can designate slow-moving tasks (e.g., routines that require user input or retrieval from a slow data storage device) to be performed in a separate thread, so that the flow of the application can continue simultaneously with the slow operation. In task division, a large task can be broken into several smaller tasks and assigned to different processors.

DCE's Benefits for the End User. The end user on a DCE system enjoys the benefits of distributed computing often without being aware of it. In a well-implemented DCE environment, the end user experiences better performance when the workload is better distributed among available resources. The end user also derives benefit from the client/server application that permits a more user-friendly interface and greater end-user autonomy in accessing corporate data. Finally, the end user experiences reduced downtime as a result of DCE's high-availability features. DCE permits access to the entire distributed environment with one log-on.

DCE and CORBA Contrasted

DCE and CORBA share a similar concept of the distributed enterprise, promising a seamless distributed computing environment with transparent interoperability among applications. They share concepts, some facilities, and even terminology. They are so similar, in fact, that many regard CORBA as the next generation of DCE.

In many ways CORBA and DCE are complementary. They are also remarkably similar in the way that they work. Both are developed by a consortium of vendors: DCE is promoted by the Open Software Foundation (OSF); CORBA is endorsed by the Object Management Group (OMG). Both depend on the consensus of their members, and both evaluate technologies that are submitted by their members for adoption. The overlap in membership between the two organizations could explain their remarkable similarity in concept.

Important differences exist as well, as summarized in Exhibit 41.5.

Exhibit 41.5. Differences between CORBA and DCE

CORBA	DCE
Object-based	Nonobject-based
Provides specifications for interfaces only	RPC provides complete specifications and source code for the network computing system
Not yet a fully implemented specification	High level of product maturity and robustness for large-scale, high-security, heavy-transaction systems
Addresses OSI application layer	Addresses OSI presentation and session layers

OSI Model Support. Most important, CORBA and DCE address different layers of the OSI model, and they express the application environment at different levels of abstraction. In fact, CORBA and DCE are considered complementary precisely because they address different layers of the OSI seven-layer mode.

CORBA addresses the application layer of the OSI model, whereas DCE addresses the presentation and session layers. Therefore, DCE contains a lot of the lower-layer information and processing that is necessary for system interoperability to take place.

CORBA, in contrast, does not deal with these low-level details at all. Instead, it specifies a mechanism by which objects can interoperate, even if they are built on disparate low-level processes. CORBA's aim is to provide interfaces between objects so that they can interoperate. CORBA works at the application layer, reconciling incompatibilities between two or more object-oriented systems so that the objects deriving from two or more development systems will interoperate.

A derivative benefit of this application-level interoperability is simplicity or, in analyst jargon, abstraction. CORBA specifications require programmers to examine applications and functions at a higher level of abstraction than any other tool for distributed computing. This high level of abstraction makes it easier for people to grasp the big picture. It insulates the programmer and user from technical details of the computer environment. The resulting applications are flexible, adaptable to change and new technologies, as well as to layering and a divide-and-conquer approach to applications development and reengineering.

Furthermore, CORBA adds a comprehensive layer of support for object-oriented programming. Specifically, it aims to provide interoperability among different object systems. Its primary purpose is to deliver interORB interoperability.

CONCLUSION

Many analysts have jumped on the object bandwagon, proclaiming object-oriented programming to be the breakthrough technology that will enable the industry to upgrade software as quickly as hardware. Like many technologies that are excellent in theory, however, the upfront effort for large-scale conversion is enormous. A golden rule is always to balance theory and practice.

To move from current information structure into the object paradigm requires a enormous rewrite of all code. Although object wrappers could provide a quick fix, wrapped objects do not provide the full benefit of more granular objects.

At the same time, object technology is penetrating every organization, at least to some degree. This is because the technology is infiltrating off-the-shelf applications software, especially at the client level. Similarly, object technology likely will become the norm for developing applications to run on the ubiquitous Internet, where upfront reengineering costs do not come into play and infrastructure issues are predefined largely.

Given the inevitably of object orientation, it is important for object systems to work together. A standard for interoperability at the application level, like CORBA, is a necessity.

Nevertheless, CORBA has traveled a rocky road. CORBA had a bad reputation from its initial release. OMG members with different interests slowed down consensus. Because of these delays, many vendors implemented their products ahead of the specification and later were reluctant to retrofit their work for the sake of compliance. In addition, the public was slow to understand the benefits of CORBA beyond DCE. Probably most important, CORBA's viability was shaky because Microsoft products, which account for 80 percent of the object market, are noncompliant.

Vendors and users seem, at last, to be rallying around CORBA. The growth of the Internet probably has a strong role here — as the market takes off, vendors perceive an opportunity and are more likely to cooperate. They also need the compliance to enhance their own marketability. CORBA has won Microsoft's support for moving its DCOM object infrastructure into compliance with CORBA.

In conclusion, object technology and distributed objects may not be the cure-all for distributed computing issues, but when combined with other integration strategies — most notably the Internet — it can become a practical solution for many specific applications. With a growing market for object technology and Microsoft support in hand, the outlook for CORBA looks better than ever.

Section VIII
Distributed Databases, Portability, and Interoperability

DISTRIBUTED DATABASES ARE FAIRLY COMMON IN CLIENT/SERVER APPLI-
CATIONS. The popularity of the Internet and the World Wide Web make
these even more common. This section looks at various aspects of distributed databases. It also examines system portability and interoperability.

Chapter 42, "The Next Step in DBMS Management," examines the need
for a common set of data sharing standards and how management tools
that comply with these standards will provide improved end-to-end system
performance.

Chapter 43, "Server-Based Computing Architecture," examines the
server-based computing architecture model by focusing on Citrix products. This model is also contrasted to thin client and fat client architecture.

Chapter 44, "Distributed Database Design," provides an overview of
distributed database system concepts, client/server technology, homogeneous distributed database systems, heterogeneity, architectural
aspects, and standards. In addition, the status of commercial products and
their limitations are discussed.

Chapter 45, "Managing Multiple Databases Across Heterogeneous Hardware and Software Systems," describes various factors that must be taken
into consideration in connecting disparate databases.

Chapter 46, "Mobile and Federated Database Interoperability," describes
the architecture and funtionality of interoperating mobile clients within a
federated database system.

Chapter 42
The Next Step
in DBMS Management
Paul Korzeniowski

ONE REASON WHY COMPANIES ADOPTED DATABASE MANAGEMENT SYS-
TEMS (DBMS) is these systems helped to integrate the autonomous nature
of corporate information. Previously, information was stored by application, which added a lot of processing overhead and increased the chances
of erroneous entries being generated. DBMSs enabled companies to store
information in a central place so applications viewed information collectively rather than autonomously.

A similar transformation is about to transpire in the enterprise management space. Because of the rapid acceptance of network computing and an
increasing reliance on the Internet, networks have become important to organizations. Not only do employees rely on them to exchange information,
but also customers and suppliers also need them to place orders or ship
goods.

As networks have become vital to daily operations, so to has the desire
to ensure that they remain up and running. Since it would be impossible for
a technician to examine each component on a worldwide corporate network, management tools been developed to automate the process. Unfortunately, they do not offer organizations as much functionality as desired.

A large part of the problem stems from the rapid expansion and growing
complexity of corporate networks. Even in a simple dial-up network connection, performance problems could stem from a variety of locations: a
desktop application, a communications package, a modem, a WAN link, the
receiving system's modem, a remote access concentrator, a corporate LAN,
a directory server, a backbone switch, a DBMS server, or a Web application.

Suppliers have delivered tools, called element management packages,
that test individual components, such as a DBMS. Corporations desire tools
that would examine all components and determine which one is slowing
down the connection. But suppliers have not been able to fulfill this desire

because their tools cannot consolidate the information coming from the element management packages.

This shortcoming does not stem from a lack of effort. Vendors, such as Computer Associates International Inc., Hewlett-Packard Co., and IBM, have pumped millions of dollars into the development of enterprise management frameworks that would be capable of gathering data from element management packages. Their tools included open Application Programming Interfaces so third parties could send management information to central consoles for processing. In theory, the enterprise management tools would solve integration issues but in reality this has seldom been the case.

The APIs (Application Programming Interfaces) are complex and difficult to use. Third parties were not terribly interested in helping framework suppliers promote their wares and have instead focused on adding new features to their packages. So, the onus fell on users to improve upon the rudimentary integration between element management and enterprise management systems. To complete the work, corporations needed skilled technicians, so demand—along with salaries—for such professionals grew. Corporations invested a great deal of time and effort in rolling out enterprise management systems, but many of the systems failed to deliver their promised levels of integration.

Standards would have helped the process. Starting in the middle 1980s, vendors forged several such initiatives. There was some progress: the Simple Network Management Protocol (SNMP) provided a common way of moving management information from a device to an element management package. Unfortunately, no easy way to ship information from several element management packages to an enterprise management console emerged.

Consequently, technicians were left tinkering with a hodgepodge of different element management tools. So now, corporations desire more from their management systems: more integration among applications, more ease of navigating from one element management application to a second, and more help in determining what may cause a performance slowdown.

THE WEB EMERGES AS NETWORK MANAGEMENT PANACEA

Soon, they may get it. Just as the Web dramatically altered the way companies build daily business applications; it is changing the way application, network equipment, DBMS, and systems vendors design their management applications. Rather than continue to be locked into proprietary APIs that hinder interoperability and increase development costs, suppliers are moving to open, Web-based systems.

World Wide Web technology has emerged as the dominant new development environment for a number of reasons. Web software is built on open standards that can significantly reduce development costs. Using standard

Web browsers to develop GUIs eliminates the bottlenecks inherent in traditional cross-platform application development and reduces engineering requirements. Web software tends to be less expensive than traditional commercial products.

Unlike previous network management initiatives, the move to Web-based management tools is in-synch with customers' desires. Corporations understand that browsers offer an inexpensive, easy-to-use alternative to proprietary and command-line user interfaces and are now demanding devices that they can access, monitor, and control. Soon, companies will no longer require the services of expensive specialists who understand difficult network management programs. Instead, they can choose from the large—and growing every day—pool of Web programmers.

Aware of customer desires, suppliers are embedding Web-server software in their products' firmware, a move that gives customers Web management capabilities without the high cost of traditional network management systems. Technicians can monitor, control, and configure products; obtain status and statistical data; and upload firmware updates and configuration files with standard Web browsers. They can perform these tasks via a wide range of Web-enabled devices: laptop computers, Personal Digital Assistants, cell phones, and pagers.

PUTTING THE PIECES IN PLACE

While the Web has the potential to solve outstanding enterprise management issues, not all of the pieces necessary are in place yet. The first set of Web-based management applications offered a browser-based view of static, simple, and proprietary pages. While this is a good initial step, it still does not fully address the problem of information integration. To take on these challenges, suppliers have to develop standards that will mask all data differences.

Standards are a place where network management suppliers have historically come up short. All of the groups formed to ease management chores have experiences varying degrees of success before splintering with one notable exception: the Desktop Management Task Force (DMTF).

pFounded in 1992, this consortium's first goal was to develop specifications for the collection of management information from desktop PCs. At the time, central technicians could not query remote system and learn fundamental issues, such as how much RAM was in the machine and what applications it was running. The consortium developed the Desktop Management Interface (DMI) specification, which provides hardware and software management information.

As the DMI specification started to gain acceptance, the Internet was beginning to become the computer industry's focal point. Hardware, software, and network equipment suppliers viewed it as a potential elixir to their long-standing management problems. In the fall of 1996, industry heavyweights BMC Software Inc., Cisco Systems, Inc., Compaq Computer Corp., and Microsoft Inc. outlined plans for the Web Based Enterprise Management (WBEM), specifications, which would leverage Internet standards and technology to solve enterprise management issues.

The companies turned development work over to the DMTF and WBEM became the umbrella under which the DMTF will fit its current and future specifications. The goal of the WBEM initiative is to outline standards based on Internet technology that provide for interoperable management of devices in an enterprise. The ultimate objective is to provide customers with the ability to manage all systems, regardless of their instrumentation type, using common standards.

THE MISSING ITEMS: CIM AND XML

After taking on WBEM development, the DMTF set out to develop the Common Information Model (CIM), an object-oriented information model that provides a conceptual framework within which any management data may be modeled. The model is not bound to a particular implementation and allows for the interchange of management information between management systems and applications, which can be either agent-to-manager or manager-to-manager.

In a CIM-compliant world, one can build applications using management data from a variety of sources and different management systems. The specification allows management data to be collected, stored, and analyzed using a common format while allowing vendors to add proprietary extensions for value added functions.

CIM includes two parts: the CIM Specification and the CIM Schema. The CIM Specification describes the language, naming, Meta Schema and mapping techniques to other management models such as SNMP MIBs. The Meta Schema defines the terms used to express the model and their usage and semantics. CIM offers a richer way of describing managed resources: originally developed for systems, it has been extended for describing network infrastructure, devices, and applications.

CIM was an excellent foundation to build standards that solve management data interchange problems. However, vendors have been using CIM as a data model, but retaining their own proprietary encoding and transport mechanisms for exchanging data between applications. This has limited interoperability and forced users to standardize on a single vendor's management software.

The DMTF had a couple of options for tackling data exchange problems. One possibility would have been to create a new application development standard. However, this approach would have continued to wedge network management issues into a narrow niche and drive up personnel and programming costs.

Instead, the group decided to adopt the Extensible Markup Language (XML). It is a metalanguage that describes information about information and describes how data is formatted and exchanged between servers and clients over an IP network.

XML is the more-powerful big brother of widely accepted HyperText Markup Language (HTML). XML is similar in concept to HTML, but whereas HTML is used to convey graphical information about a document, XML is designed to add structure and convey information about documents and data. XML provides more programming tags than HTML and can therefore be used to format and structure information more precisely.

XML provides a way of identifying structured management information exchanges so applications can trade CIM data. With XML, a programmer can specify details about elements through Document Type Definitions that provide a way to pass information between different vendors' products or send it directly to a Web browser.

XML provides an application with access to diverse data sources and the ability to manipulate them many times without a trip back to a database.

One plus in XML is emerging as a *defacto* data manipulation standard for all Web application development. In February 1998 after roughly a year and a half of evaluations, the World Wide Web Consortium (W3C) released XML 1.0 as an official recommendation. The XML Working Group defined a flexible language that is useful for representing a variety of data types on the Web. Support for the specification has come from all of the major database management system suppliers and Microsoft and Netscape, which are adding XML compliance to their browsers.

In October 1998, the DMTF announced its first version of XML and support came from a broad range of suppliers including Cisco, Computer Associates International Inc., Microsoft, and Tivoli Systems Inc. The first round of XML compliant management applications and devices should start to arrive this year.

THE FUTURE BECOMES CLEARER

Coupled with CIM, XML offer users the first realistic attempt at integrating management data and linking heterogeneous management systems and tools. The standards should gain widespread acceptance because they offer so many benefits to network equipment suppliers and their customers.

For suppliers, CIM and XML will ease element and enterprise management application development. The specifications work with a wide range of hardware, software, and applications and can scale from small to large networks. Rather than work with proprietary interfaces, applications will rely on common standards. Instead of porting software to a range of APIs, suppliers will be able to write software once and connect it to any compliant element or enterprise management system. Ultimately, suppliers will embed XML in a new generation of smart devices that will be simpler to configure and easier to manage than current devices because they are Web based.

Customers will be happy. The move to standards will provide them with a simple, standard based physical and logical interface to management data. The standards are flexible enough to cover all network management requirements: physical management, billing, and root cause analysis. So once implemented, the standards will enable them to examine end-to-end network performance rather than continue to work in a piecemeal fashion.

HOW THE WEB WILL SIMPLIFY ENTERPRISE MANAGEMENT

The move to CIM and XML will help companies identify network problems faster and more easily. Currently, network managers have to bounce from one element management to another to pinpoint a trouble spot. With the growth of networks, technicians may have to manipulate a dozen or more management applications. CIM will enable technicians to systematically test all potential trouble spots and identify the faulty device and CIM combined with the web makes this possible using only one interface: a Web browser.

For instance, the executive vice president of marketing, who works out of one of the firm's remote office's, calls the help desk and says he has been having problems accessing an Intranet application that lets employees place orders for computer equipment. The help desk technician must quickly examine each component along the link (the user's browser, his PC, his network connection, the local switch, the local router, the central remote access concentrator, the data center switch, the Web server's network connection, the server, the DBMS, and the application), pinpoint the malfunctioning equipment, and take the steps necessary to improve response time. With CIM, an enterprise management application will start at the lowest layer of the networking model and work its way up until the problem is identified, a process called root cause analysis:

1. First, the management tool will check the physical network connection (the local switch, the local router, the central office remote access concentrator, the data center switch) by sending a packet along the line.
2. Next, the management tool will examine the network layer (the user's network connection, the Web server's connection) and determine whether or not there is a protocol problem.

3. Then, the management tool will look at the server and determine how quickly it is processing information.
4. The manager can then move up to the DBMS and examine how quickly it is processing information.
5. Last, the management tool will examine the application layer (the browser, the Intranet application) and determine if they are hung up.

Root cause analysis offers companies two benefits. First, training requirements drop since a technician only needs to know how to operate a browser rather than a series of proprietary user interfaces. Second, suppliers can build more sophisticated management applications, ones that examine problems and recommend solutions on an end-to-end basis rather than a piecemeal fashion. Increasingly, companies want to examine system and network performance on an end-to-end rather than piecemeal fashion.

THE IMPACT OF CIM AND XML ON DBMS SUPPLIERS

When a user calls the help desk to report a response time problem, a technician would like to enter a few commands, quickly discover that the DBMS is having problems processing requests, drill down to examine why the problem is arising, and make any necessary changes. CIM and XML compliance would make such capabilities possible.

To move toward that goal requires that suppliers incorporate support for the emerging standards in their DBMS management tools. Currently, these tools rely mainly on SNMP to gather and transport management information. Moving to CIM and XML offers DBMS vendors a couple of benefits. First, these standards are more flexible and better able to gather DBMS performance data than SNMP, which was designed to oversee network equipment. Second, they are more in line with customers' desire to integrate all management data.

Because of the benefits, DBMS management suppliers are starting to line up in support of XML and CIM. BMC Software and Microsoft were two of the key supporters of the WBEM initiative and has stated it plans to back the emerging standards, and DBMS suppliers vendors Informix, Oracle, and Sybase see XML as an aid in easing customers' application development as well as system management.

CONCLUSION

The move to the new standards will take time. The enterprise management space has been evolving for more than 15 years so there is now a huge base of installed management tools. Corporations will only be able to justify the expensive and often difficult task of moving to new management tools in select cases. Consequently, the migration to CIM and XML will begin in 1999 but three to five years may pass before it is widely adopted.

DISTRIBUTED DATABASES, PORTABILITY, AND INTEROPERABILITY

While one may debate the timeline, there seems to be a consensus that movement to CIM and XML will occur and end-to-end management chores will eventually become simpler.

CIM, XML Websites

www.dmtf.org

Vendors Supporting the Standard

www.bmc.com

www.cisco.com

www.compaq.com

www.microsoft.com

www.tivoli.com

Chapter 43

Server-Based Computing Architecture

Bosco Cheung

THE ADVENT OF THE COMPUTER REVOLUTION GREATLY EXPANDED THE UNIVERSE OF INFORMATION AND PROCESSING POWER AVAILABLE TO THE END USER. The once simple standalone computer and the software that ran on it grew in complexity, creating a whole new set of problems for enterprise computing.

Faced with an ever-changing computing environment, IT professionals must improve the efficiency of business-critical application deployment. In order to reduce the total cost of computing ownership for their organization, they must also leverage everything in their current computing infrastructure-hardware, applications, networks and training. And all of this must be accomplished along with:

- Managing and supporting users in a timely and cost-effective manner.
- Extending access to business-critical applications to dispersed users-regardless of connection, location, or device.
- Ensuring exceptional application performance.
- Providing tight security for enterprise-level computing.

These challenges have made enterprisewide application deployment even more daunting because the products developed to this point have only addressed one, or possibly two, of the obstacles discussed in this section.

MANAGEMENT

From a management perspective, traditional enterprise application deployment is often time-consuming, expensive and difficult to maintain. Not only do administrators have to physically distribute applications to every client, but they also have to deal with version control issues, remote support, multiple system configurations and data replication. When confronted with thousands of users, the cost of application ownership can quickly spiral out of control.

ACCESS

Today's corporate computing landscape comprises a heterogeneous mix of desktop devices, network connectivity and operating systems. Access to vital Windows-based applications is difficult-or, in the case of Internet/Intranet computing, nonexistent-and often involves costly upgrades, problematic emulation software and complete application rewrites.

PERFORMANCE

Most corporate applications today are designed for high-bandwidth networks and powerful desktop computers. This type of application design puts tremendous strain on congested corporate networks and yields poor performance over lower-bandwidth, remote connections. Because of this, many users simply avoid using the vital applications and data to get their work done. When this happens, redundant work and significant decreases in productivity are often the result.

SECURITY

Security is also a challenge, because in traditional client/server architectures, business-critical applications and data live on both the server and the client desktops spread throughout the world. Not only does this increase the risk of unauthorized access, but it also increases the risk of lost or stolen information.

A BETTER APPROACH: SERVER-BASED COMPUTING

Server-based computing is a model in which applications are deployed, managed, supported and executed 100 percent on a server. It uses a multiuser operating system and a method for distributing the presentation of an application's interface to a client device.

With server-based computing, client devices, whether "fat" or "thin," have instant access to business-critical applications via the server-without application rewrites or downloads. This means improved efficiency when deploying business-critical applications. In addition, server-based computing works within the current computing infrastructure and current computing standards, and with the current and future family of Windows-based offerings. This means improved returns on computing investments-desktops, networks, applications and training. The end result: Server-based computing is rapidly becoming the most reliable way to reduce the complexity and total costs associated with enterprise computing.

How Does Server-Based Computing Work?

The server-based computing model employs three critical components. The first is a multi-user operating system that enables multiple concurrent users to log on and run applications in separate, protected sessions on a single server. The second is a highly efficient computing technology that separates the application's logic from its user interface, so only keystrokes, mouse clicks and screen updates travel the network. As a result, application performance is bandwidth-independent. The third key component, centralized application and client management, enables large computing environments to overcome the critical application deployment challenges of management, access, performance and security.

Server-based computing is made possible by two Citrix technologies: Citrix Independent Computing Architecture (ICA®) and Citrix MultiWin. A *defacto* standard for server-based computing, the ICA protocol shifts application processing from the client device to the server. MultiWin, the technology licensed by Citrix to Microsoft to jointly create Terminal Server, enables multiple users to simultaneously access applications running on a server.

WHAT IS INDEPENDENT COMPUTING ARCHITECTURE (ICA)?

Independent Computing Architecture is a Windows presentation services protocol from Citrix that provides the foundation for turning any client device-thin or fat-into the ultimate thin client. The ICA technology includes a server software component, a network protocol component, and a client software component.

On the server, ICA has the unique ability to separate the application's logic from the user interface at the server and transport it to the client over standard network protocols—IPX, SPX, NetBEUI, TCP/IP and PPP—and over popular network connections-asynchronous, dial-up, ISDN, Frame Relay and ATM. On the client, users see and work with the application's interface, but 100 percent of the application logic executes on the server.

The ICA protocol transports keystrokes, mouse clicks and screen updates over standard protocols to the client, consuming less than 20 kilobits per second of network bandwidth.

Role of ICA

ICA is highly efficient—it allows only keystrokes, mouse clicks and screen updates to travel the network. As a result, applications consume just a fraction of the network bandwidth usually required. This efficiency enables the latest, most powerful 32-bit applications to be accessed with exceptional performance from existing computers, Windows-based terminals, network computers, and a new generation of business and personal information appliances.

With over two million ports in use worldwide, Citrix ICA is a mature, reliable technology and is fast becoming a *defacto* industry standard for server-based computing.

Server-Based Computing Compared to Network Computing and Traditional Client/Server Computing

While all three computing models have a valid role in today's enterprises, it is important to note the differences between them. In traditional client/server architecture, processing is centered around local execution using fat, powerful hardware components. In the network computing architecture as defined by Sun, Oracle, Netscape, IBM, and Apple, components are dynamically downloaded from the network into the client device for execution by the client. But with the Citrix server-based computing approach, users are able to access business-critical applications—including the latest 32-bit Windows-based and Java™ applications—without requiring them to be downloaded to the client. This approach also provides considerable total cost of application ownership savings since these applications are centrally managed and can be accessed by users without having to rewrite them.

Basically, the server-based computing approach delivers all the benefits of both host computing and personal computing as follows:

- Host computing benefits
  - Single-point management
  - Physically and technically secure
  - Predictable ownership costs
  - Mission-critical reliability
  - Bandwidth-independent performance
  - Universal application access
- Personal computing benefits
  - Thousands of off-the-shelf applications
  - Low-cost and fast-cycle application development
  - Standards based
  - Graphical, rich data, and easy to use
  - Wide choice of device types and suppliers

WHAT IS A WINDOWS-BASED TERMINAL?

A Windows-based terminal (WBT) is a thin-client hardware device that connects to Citrix server-based system software. Because the applications it accesses are installed on the server, a Windows-based terminal is not the equivalent of a computer with its operating system and array of local applications. Nor is it interchangeable with a network computer or NetPC, because these devices download and run applications off the network.

The key criterion that distinguishes Windows-based terminals from other thin-client devices, such as NCs or NetPCs, is that there is no downloading of the operating system or applications, and there is no local processing of applications at the client. All execution of the application logic occurs on the server.

Defining Characteristics of a Windows-based Terminal

Windows-based terminals have the following characteristics:

- An embedded operating system such as DOS, Windows CE, or any real-time operating system.
- ICA and/or Microsoft Remote Desktop Protocol (RDP) presentation services protocol to transport keystrokes, mouse clicks and screen updates between the client and server.
- 100 percent server-based execution of application logic.
- No local execution of application logic at the client device.
- A Windows-based terminal may incorporate third-party emulation software such as X, 3270 and 5250 for connection to other host systems.

Fitting the Windows-based Terminal Within the Enterprise

The "thinness" of a Windows-based terminal and the many benefits of server-based computing make these thin clients ideal for certain types of workers and market segments. For example, task-based employees who primarily work with line-of-business applications, such as order entry, would be ideal candidates for a Windows-based terminal. Retail organizations operating point-of-sale terminals, and branch locations of banks and stores, are markets that are also rapidly adopting these thin clients. Windows-based terminals are also well suited for existing "green-screen" terminal users moving to a Windows environment.

SERVER-BASED COMPUTING KEY FEATURES AND BENEFITS

While other approaches for deploying, managing, and supporting business-critical applications across the extended enterprise have been introduced, only the server-based computing model developed by Citrix provides today's growing enterprises with the tools and capabilities they need to be successful. This innovative software enables enterprises to:

- Bring server-based computing to heterogeneous computing environments providing access to Windows-based applications—regardless of client hardware, operating platform, network connection or LAN protocol.

- Offer enterprise-scale management tools to allow IT professionals to scale, deploy, manage and support applications from a single location.
- Provide seamless desktop integration of the user's local and remote resources and applications with exceptional performance.

MIS rarely has the luxury of deploying mission-critical applications in a homogeneous environment, let alone from a centralized location. Instead, the enterprise network usually includes a wide variety of servers, client workstations, operating systems and connections. The user base can include from dozens to thousands of local, remote and mobile users.

Heterogeneous Computing Environments

Heterogeneous computing environments are a fact of life in the enterprise, comprising an installed base of many client devices, operating systems, LAN protocols and network connections. However, for the enterprise interested in making Windows-based applications available to all users, server-based computing enables an organization to leverage its existing infrastructure, yet still provide the best application fit for both users and the enterprise. This type of approach supports all types of hardware, operating platforms, network connections and LAN protocols. As a result, organizations can deliver the same set of applications to virtually any client device, anywhere, with exceptional performance.

ENTERPRISE-SCALE MANAGEMENT TOOLS

Organizations building application deployment systems will want the added benefits of server-based computing system software to gain robust management tools that help scale systems and support applications and users enterprisewide. With these tools, administrators will be able to significantly reduce the costs and complexities of deploying, managing and supporting business applications across the extended enterprise.

SEAMLESS DESKTOP INTEGRATION

With server-based computing, end users of both Windows and non-Windows desktops gain an enhanced computing experience through broadened application access with exceptional performance that is bandwidth-independent, as well as complete access to local system resources—even though applications are running remotely from the server.

SERVER-BASED COMPUTING SOLUTION SCENARIOS

With server-based computing, customers can increase productivity and develop a competitive advantage by gaining universal access to the business-critical applications they need to operate successfully, regardless of the connection, location, or operating systems they may be using.

The following solution scenarios demonstrate how server-based computing can help customers overcome the challenges of enterprisewide application deployment.

Branch-Office Computing

For manageable, secure application deployment and access over corporate WANs.

Problem: To better serve and support customers, many enterprises are opening branch offices. However, this is creating many difficulties for administrators who do not have the resources to adequately staff these new offices. One such problem is database replication. Many times, individual LANs are built for each branch office. Configuring and managing these branch-office LANs—and the information on them—creates numerous management challenges. Another problem is application performance. Since most branch offices are connected by WANs to headquarters, vital data and applications must travel back and forth across the network. This type of setup creates numerous user delays and unacceptable application response. Previously, the only option was a bigger WAN connection, which meant increasing costs, not just once, but on an ongoing basis.

Solution: Server-based computing is a better solution because it minimizes network traffic, even for Windows-based, 32-bit applications. This approach allows applications to be deployed, supported and managed from a central location.

Cross-Platform Computing

For Windows-based application deployment to non-Windows desktop users.

Problem: In today's era of global consolidation, many enterprises are buying and/or merging new companies into their organizations, as well as adding their own new employees and locations around the world. Typically, this has resulted in a widely diverse set of client devices, operating systems, processing power and connectivity options across the enterprise.

For IT professionals, trying to leverage existing technology investments while deploying business-critical applications—especially the latest 32-bit Windows-based applications—to all users has become more and more difficult. As a result, organizations have had to resort to using problematic emulation software, purchasing additional hardware, investing in costly application rewrites.

Solution: Server-based computing is a better, more cost-effective solution because it enables virtually any existing device in the enterprise to access Windows-based applications without special emulation software, changes in system configuration or application rewrites. This means that enterprises can maximize their investment in existing technology and allow users to work in their preferred computing environments.

Web Computing

So remote users can access full-function Windows-based applications from Web pages.

Problem: Web computing is taking off. But to deploy interactive applications on an Intranet or the Internet, application development is required. The Java applet "download-and-run" model is not an extension of any current computing technology. New software and often new hardware are required to successfully deploy these solutions. Every time the application changes, the Web-based application needs to change as well.

Solution: Server-based computing enables administrators to launch and embed corporate Windows-based applications into HTML pages without rewriting a single line of code. Plus, it eliminates the need to manage and maintain two separate sets of code.

Remote Computing

To give high-performance, secure access to business-critical applications over remote, dial-up connections.

Problem: The changing work environment is allowing more and more employees to work away from the office—at home, hotels, customer locations, etc. This means that a wide variety of network connections are being used to access corporate applications. Unfortunately, the lower the bandwidth, the lower the application performance. Because of this, many remote users are avoiding corporate applications altogether, as they'd rather work than wait.

Another factor is application management and support for remote users. Administrators are forced to spend excessive amounts of time trying to diagnose and correct problems over the phone. Unfortunately, the problems are usually not resolved the first time.

Solution: Server-based computing works better for remote users because it keeps all application processing on the server, meaning less traffic is sent across the network. Plus, it's optimized for low-bandwidth connections so users can get LAN-like performance over analog or ISDN modems, WANs, wireless LANs and even the Internet. By eliminating the need for on-site staff, server-based computing also makes it easier for administrators.

Thin-Client Device Computing

Windows-based applications can be extended to newer, low-cost devices.

Problem: Traditional mini- and mainframe computing deliver some of the same "centralized computing" benefits as server-based computing. The problem is that these types of machines weren't designed for the thousands of GUI-based Windows applications that are available today. Furthermore, users on these types of machines are familiar with the text-based interface and are typically slow to adopt new operating systems.

Also, many of today's new devices—like Windows-based terminals, PDAs, wireless tablets, and information appliances—are not compatible with the Windows-based, business-critical applications being used in the enterprise unless rewrites are performed.

Solution: With server-based computing, the latest Windows-based programs can be extended to these thin devices without application rewrites. This enables users to work in their preferred environments and still access the Windows-based applications they need to work successfully. Plus, organizations can reap the benefits resulting from reduced overhead, lower acquisition costs and fewer moving parts.

CONCLUSION

The server-based computing architecture model offers any size organization an alternative enterprise computing solution that reduces the total cost of computing ownership, leverages components of their current computing environment, and reduces the development and support hardships normally associated with implementing an enterprise solution.

Chapter 44
Distributed Database Design

Elizabeth N. Fong
Charles L. Sheppard
Kathryn A. Harvill

A DISTRIBUTED DATABASE ENVIRONMENT ENABLES A USER TO ACCESS DATA residing anywhere in a corporation's computer network without regard to differences among computers, operating systems, data manipulation languages, or file structures. Data that are actually distributed among multiple remote computers will appear to the user as if they resided on the user's own computer. This scenario is functionally limited with today's distributed database technology; true distributed database technology is still a research consideration. The functional limitations are generally in the following areas:

- Transaction management
- Standard protocols for establishing a remote connection
- Independence of network technology

Transaction management capabilities are essential to maintaining reliable and accurate databases. In some cases, today's distributed database software places responsibility of managing transactions on the application program. In other cases, transactions are committed or rolled back at each location independently, which means that it is not possible to create a single distributed transaction. For example, multiple-site updates require multiple transactions.

CURRENT DBMS TECHNOLOGY

In today's distributed database technology, different gateway software must be used and installed to connect nodes using different distributed database management system (DBMS) software. Therefore, connectivity among heterogeneous distributed DBMS nodes is not readily available (i.e., available only through selected vendor markets).

0-8493-9832-0/00/$0.00+$.50
© 2000 by CRC Press LLC

In some instances, distributed DBMS software is tied to a single network operating system. This limits the design alternatives for the distributed DBMS environment to the products of a single vendor.

It is advisable to select a product that supports more than one network operating system. This will increase the possibility of successfully integrating the distributed DBMS software into existing computer environments.

In reality, distributed databases encompass a wide spectrum of possibilities, including the following:

- Remote terminal access to centralized DBMS (e.g., an airline reservation system).
- Remote terminal access to different DBMSs, but one at a time (e.g., Prodigy, CompuServe, and Dow Jones).
- Simple pairwise interconnection with data sharing that requires users to know the data location, data access language, and the log-on procedure to the remote DBMS.
- Distributed database management with a generic data definition language and a data manipulation language at all nodes.
- Distribution update and transaction management.
- Distributed databases with replication that support vertical and horizontal fragmentation.
- "True" distributed DBMSs with heterogeneous hardware, software, and communications.

The definition of distributed DBMSs lies anywhere along this spectrum. For the purpose of this chapter, the remote terminal access to data as discussed in the preceding list is not considered a distributed DBMS because a node on the distributed DBMS must have its own hardware, central processor, and software.

Limitations of Commercial Products

Some of the problems that currently frustrate managers and technicians who might otherwise be interested in exploring distributed data solutions include the following:

- A distributed database environment has all the problems associated with the single centralized database environment but at a more complex level.
- There are no basic, step-by-step guidelines covering the analysis, design, and implementation of a distributed database environment.

A distributed DBMS offers many benefits. However, there are also many architectural choices that make the applications design for distributed databases very complex.

To ensure an effective and productive distributed database environment, it is essential that the distributed environment be properly designed to support the expected distributed database applications. In addition, an effective design will depend on the limitations of the distributed DBMS software. Therefore, implementing today's distributed database technology requires identifying the functional limitations of a selected commercial product. Identification of these limitations is critical to the successful operation of an application in a distributed database environment.

DISTRIBUTED DATABASE DEVELOPMENT PHASES

Effective corporationwide distributed database processing is not going to happen overnight. It requires a carefully planned infrastructure within which an orderly evolution can occur. The four major development phases are planning, design, installation and implementation, and support and maintenance.

The Planning Phase. The planning phase consists of high-level management strategy planning. During the planning phase, an organization must consider whether it is advantageous to migrate to a distributed environment. This chapter assumes that migration to a distributed environment is desirable and feasible and that the corporate strategy planning issues and tasks have been identified. The result of this phase is the total management commitment for cost, resources, and a careful migration path toward a distributed database environment.

The Design Phase. The design phase is concerned with the overall design of the distributed database strategy. The overall design task involves the selection of a distributed DBMS environment in terms of the hardware, software, and communications network for each node and how these elements are interconnected. The design of the distributed database environment must incorporate the requirements for the actual distributed database application. The overall design divides into two main tasks: the detailed design of the distributed database environment and the detailed design of the initial distributed database application. In certain cases, the initial application may be a prototype that is intended to pave the way for the full-production distributed database application.

The Installation and Implementation Phase. This phase consists of the installation and implementation of the environment that provides basic software support for the distributed DBMS application. The task of developing the distributed database application could occur in parallel with the installation of the environment.

The Support and Maintenance Phase. The support and maintenance phase consists of support for the distributed DBMS environment and the support and maintenance of the application. Although these support and maintenance tasks can be performed by the same people, the nature of the tasks and responsibilities are quite distinct. For example, the distributed application may require modification of report formats, whereas the distributed environment may require modification to add more memory.

CORPORATION STRATEGY PLANNING

The main task during the strategic planning phase is to obtain the commitment of senior management. The measure of this commitment is the amount of resources — both personnel and equipment — necessary for the development of a distributed DBMS. The factors that must be considered during the strategy planning phase are as follows:

- What are the objectives of the organization's next 5-year plan?
- How will technological changes affect the organization's way of doing business?
- What resources are needed to plan for the development of, and migration to, a distributed DBMS?
- How will outcomes be measured relative to the impact on the organization's competitive position?

The corporate strategy plan must include detailed specifications of the total system lifecycle. It must also include a realistic timetable of schedules and milestones. Important consideration must be paid to the allocation of cost for new acquisitions, training personnel, physical space requirements, and other tangible items.

During the strategic planning phase, information must be gathered on the organization's business functions and goals, related constraints and problem areas, and the organization's user groups. Only after the needed information has been gathered is it possible to develop high-level information categories and their interrelationships.

The process of developing the distributed database plan is iterative. The activities involved are performed by IS managers. Although these individuals often have the vision to recognize the long-term benefits of a distributed DBMS environment to an organization, they must rely on the participation and input of those in the organization who are directly involved with the business functions and use information to make decisions and manage operations. There must be considerable interaction among many different people in the organization, each of whom provides feedback to validate and refine the plans.

Strategic planning must first provide a sufficient justification for the expenditure of resources necessary to migrate to a distributed environment. Only after this justification has been accepted and fully approved by senior management can the task of initiating projects to design, develop, and implement a distributed DBMS environment and application start.

OVERALL DESIGN OF DISTRIBUTED DATABASE STRATEGY

A distributed database environment consists of a collection of sites or nodes connected by a communications network. Each node has its own hardware, central processor, and software, which may or may not include a DBMS. The primary objective of a distributed DBMS is to give interactive query and application programs access to remote data as well as local data.

Individual nodes within the distributed environment can have different computing requirements. Accordingly, these nodes may have different hardware and different software, and they may be connected in many different ways. Some of the variations possible in the distributed database environment are discussed in the following sections.

Client/Server Computing

The most basic distributed capability is remote database access from single users at a node. A node may be a mainframe, a minicomputer, or a microcomputer (personal computer). The node that makes the database access request is referred to as a client node, and the node that responds to the request and provides database services is referred to as a service node. The association is limited to the two parties involved — the client and the server. Exhibit 44.1 represents several different configurations available under a client/server computing environment. The following are descriptions of the different configurations shown in the exhibit.

Client Single-User Node. The operating environment of an individual can be single user or multiuser, depending on the operating system of that node. In a single-user operating environment, a node can be only a client. Such a node may or may not have databases. For non-database client nodes, the software typically consists of front-end application programs used to access remote database server nodes. This front-end software is generally in the form of end-user interface tools (e.g., a query language processor, a form processor, or some other application-specific program written in a third-generation language).

DESIGNING AND MANAGING DATABASES

The front-end software formulates and issues user requests. It processes user requests through its established links with appropriate communications software. The front-end software only captures a user's request and uses communications software to send that request to a remote database node requesting its DBMS to process the request. In addition to the capabilities outlined, single-user nodes with databases allow local data to

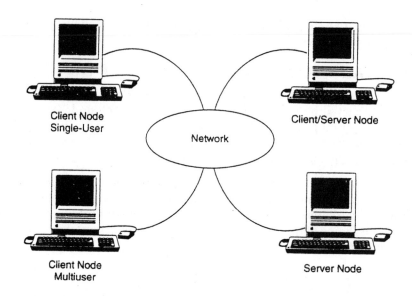

Exhibit 44.1. Client/server computing.

be included in the same query operations specified for remote data. Therefore, operationally, the query results will appear as if all data are coming from a central database.

Client Multiuser Node. The functional capabilities outlined for the client single-user node are expanded in the client multiuser node because of the presence of a multiuser operating system at the user node. Such a configuration generally has several user processes running at the same time. At peak use time, the presence of several user processes can cause slower response time than is experienced in a client single-user node. The client multiuser node is more cost-effective, however, because it can allow multiple remote database access at different sites by different users at the same time. This is made possible through an identifiable list of remote server node locations. In addition, as with the client single-user node, the client multiuser node can include local database access in conjunction with access to remote databases.

Server Node. The server node is capable of providing database services to other client requests as well as to itself. It is a special multiuser node that is dedicated to servicing remote database requests and any local processes. This means that incoming requests are serviced, but it does not originate requests to other server nodes. The functional capabilities of a server node are as follows: this node must be included in the server list of some remote client node, there must be an operating DBMS, and there must be a continuously running process that listens for incoming database requests.

Client/Server Node. A node with a database can be a client as well as a server. This means that this node can service remote database requests as well as originate database requests to other server nodes. Therefore, the client/server node can play a dual role.

Homogeneous Distributed DBMS Environment

A completely homogeneous distributed DBMS environment exists when all the nodes in the distributed environment have the same DBMS but not necessarily the same hardware and operating system. However, the communications software for each node must use the same protocol to send or receive requests and data.

Design and implementation of a homogeneous distributed DBMS environment need involve only a single vendor. Any data request issued at a client node does not require translation because the database language and data model are the same across all nodes in the network.

Heterogeneous Distributed DBMS Environment

In a truly heterogeneous distributed DBMS environment, the hardware, operating systems, communications, and DBMSs can all be different. Different DBMSs may mean different data models along with different database languages for definition and manipulation. Any database request issued at a client node would have to be translated so that the server node responding to the request would understand how to execute the request.

Various degrees of heterogeneity can exist. For example, within the distributed environment, different DBMSs can still be compatible if they all support the relational data model and understand SQL, a relational query language that is an ANSI and ISO standard. Presently, however, even among SQL-conforming systems, there is no general communications software that will accept generic SQL statements from any other SQL-conforming DBMS. This is an area in which the pending remote data access standards are needed.

DISTRIBUTED ENVIRONMENT ARCHITECTURE

The design of a distributed database environment can be evolutionary — by incremental interconnection of existing systems, or by developing a totally new distributed DBMS environment using the bottom-up approach. Some of the design issues in adopting either approach are described in the following sections.

Interconnection of Existing Systems

Not all organizations have the luxury of developing the distributed database environment from scratch. Already-existing database management applications are costly investments that are not likely to be replaced all at once by new distributed systems. The existing environment, including hardware, software, and databases, can be preserved by providing a mechanism for producing federated systems (i.e., systems composed of autonomous software components).

The federated approach is a practical, first-step solution toward a distributed database environment. It accommodates a legacy of existing systems while extending to incorporate new nodes. Therefore, it is important to select distributed DBMS software that supports existing computer hardware and allows for expansion. Within a federated system, pairs of nodes can be coupled in ways that range from very loose (i.e., each node is autonomous) to very tight (i.e., each node interacts directly with the other). The various forms of coupling affect the design, execution, and capability of the distributed applications.

The mode of coupling affects the number of translations required to exchange information between each site. Zero translations are needed when both components use the same representations. Some systems may choose to translate the data produced by one site directly to the format required by the other site. A more common method is to translate the data into a neutral format first, and then translate into the target format.

Loose Coupling. Loosely coupled systems are the most modular and in some ways are easier to maintain. This is because changes to the implementation of a site's system characteristics and its DBMS are not as likely to affect other sites. The disadvantage of loosely coupled systems is that users must have some knowledge of each site's characteristics to execute requests. Because very little central authority to control consistency exists, correctness cannot be guaranteed. In addition, loosely coupled systems typically involve more translations that may cause performance problems.

Tight Coupling. Tightly coupled systems behave more like a single, integrated system. Users need not be aware of the characteristics of the sites fulfilling a request. With centralized control, the tightly coupled systems are more consistent in their use of resources and in their management of shared data. The disadvantage of tight coupling is that because sites are independent, changes to one site are likely to affect other sites. Also, users at some sites may object to the loss of freedom to the central control mechanisms necessary to maintain the tight coupling of all the systems.

Cooperation Between Sites

For a truly distributed DBMS environment, a variety of methods are available to specify cooperation between sites. One way of classifying the distributed environment is to define the amount of transparency offered to the users. Another way is to define the amount of site autonomy available to each site, and the way sites interact cooperatively.

Degrees of Transparency. Transparency is the degree to which a service is offered by the distributed DBMS so that the user does not need to be aware of it. One example of transparency is location transparency, which means users can retrieve data from any site without having to know where the data are located.

Types of Site Autonomy. Site autonomy refers to the amount of independence that a site has in making policy decisions. Some examples of policy decisions include ownership of data, policies for accessing the data, policies for hours and days of operation, and human support. In addition, all modifications to the site's data structures must be approved by the cooperating federation of data administrators.

Interconnection of Newly Purchased Systems

An organization will have much more freedom if it decides to establish a distributed database environment from scratch. Currently, vendors are offering homogeneous distributed DBMSs with a compatible family of software. This approach, however, can lock the organization into a single vendor's proprietary products.

Other distributed architecture choices are as follows:

- Identical DBMS products at each node, with possibly different hardware environments but a single proprietary communications network to interconnect all sites.
- Standard conforming DBMS products at each node that rely on standard communications protocols.
- Different DBMSs, using the same data model (e.g., relational), interconnected by a single or standard communications protocol.
- Different DBMSs, using different data models (e.g., relational or object-oriented), interconnected by a single or standard communications protocol.

Some distributed DBMS vendors offer a bridge (gateway) mechanism from their distributed database software to any foreign distributed database software. This bridge (gateway) may be obtained at additional development cost if it has not already been included in the vendor's library of available software.

In the design of a totally new distributed DBMS product, it is advisable to consider a mixture of standard conforming DBMSs and communications protocols. Because the technology and products are changing quickly, the designed architecture must be continuously reviewed to prevent it from being locked into an inflexible mode.

CONSIDERATION FOR STANDARDS

As the trend toward distributed computing accelerates, the need for standards, guidance, and support will increase. Application distribution and use will be chaotic unless there is an architectural vision and some degree of uniformity in information technology platforms. This is particularly true in client/server and workstation environments. To achieve this goal, a systems architecture incorporating standards to meet the users' needs must be established. This architecture must isolate the application software from the lower levels of machine architecture and systems service implementation. The systems architecture serves as the context for user requirements, technology integration, and standards specifications.

The benefits of standardization for both the user and the vendor are many. The number and variety of distributed DBMS products are increasing. By insisting that purchased products conform to standards, users may be able to choose the best product for each function without being locked into a specific vendor. Therefore, small to midsize vendors may effectively compete in the open marketplace. For effective planning and designing of a distributed DBMS environment, it is important for the designers to consider what standards already exist and what standards will be emerging to be able to incorporate standardized products.

There are many areas of distributed DBMS environment in which standards should be applied. Some of the standards relevant to the design of a distributed DBMS include communications protocols, applications programming interfaces, data languages for DBMSs, data representation and interchange formats, and remote data access.

Communications protocol standards are necessary so that systems from different products can connect to a communications network and understand the information being transmitted. An example of a communications protocol standard is the Government Open Systems Interconnection Profile (GOSIP).

The application programming interface (API) standard is directed toward the goal of having portable applications. This enables software applications developed in one computing environment to run almost unchanged in any other environment. An example of an application programming interface standard is the Portable Operating System Interface for Computer Environments (POSIX).

The data languages commonly supported by a DBMS are the data definition language, the data manipulation language, and the data control language. An example of a standard data language for the relational DBMS model is SQL.

To exchange data among open systems, a standard interchange format is necessary. The interchange format consists of a language for defining general data structures and the encoding rules. An example of a standard data interchange language is Abstract Syntax Notation One (ASN. 1).

An important standard for the distributed processing environment is the remote access of data from a client site to a database server site. A specialized remote data access protocol based on the SQL standard is currently under development.

SUMMARY

To start the overall design process, a review of the organization's existing facilities should be conducted. This review is done to determine whether the new distributed database environment can use some or all of the existing facilities. In the decision to move into a distributed environment, requirements for additional functionalities must be identified. Such organizational issues as setting up regional offices may also be involved. The distributed architecture must take into consideration the actual application operating, the characteristics of the user population, and the workloads to be placed on the system. Such an architecture must also incorporate standardized components.

Chapter 45

Managing Multiple Databases Across Heterogeneous Hardware and Software Systems

James Woods

A FUNCTIONAL BRIDGE BRINGS TRANSACTIONS FROM ONE DATABASE TO THE OTHERS, so that there is a single update path for all data items. The databases, though physically separated, thus function as one. This chapter reviews, step-by-step, the planning and design decisions related to the communications infrastructure and the designation of the database master. The techniques recommended will work with two or more separate databases.

THE GOAL: A SINGLE FUNCTIONAL DATABASE

Corporate IS management is often challenged when it finds that it must control multiple databases that may reside on separate and disparate systems. However, the cost of not harnessing these multiple databases into a coherent whole is very high.

First, there is the problem of data redundancy. The data that designates a single fact is represented multiple times in the organization. Apart from the obvious storage requirement considerations, there is the problem of inconsistent information. Because the databases each have their own update paths, the data items are likely to have conflicting values. Even if the updates pass along the same value to each data item, it will most likely not be in the same time frame. This leads to information that is out of sync with the other data items. However, more than just one data item is involved in this problem; the problem is widespread — probably tens or hundreds of data items. Some of those items will be used for critical business decisions.

When the information is summarized and reported to top management, conflicts in the information will become obvious, though it will not be obvious which specific data items differ, only that the information from one department does not square with another. Confidence levels in the integrity of all the databases will drop and the decision support results will be minimized.

Although a single, central database is preferable, the reality is that multiple databases exist. They come into existence for any number of reasons:

- *Independent purchases.* A user department buys and uses a separate system because it believes that is the best answer to its needs or that IS cannot address its informational requirements within an acceptable time frame.
- *Legacy systems.* The system has been in place for some time while IS attended to more urgent matters. Eventually, the need for some form of technical management of the data becomes evident.
- *Acquisitions.* The company has just acquired a new division that has its own database system.

All the problems cited can be avoided if the databases, although physically separate (and possibly residing on different hardware and software platforms), are made to function as a single database. In other words, the update path for one database is the update path for the others. This minimizes all the problems except for data redundancy. Exhibit 45.1 illustrates, from a user's perspective, how multiple databases can be physically separated yet conceptually linked together.

The remainder of this chapter addresses how to build the bridge from one database to another so that they function as one. Although the scenario described thus far considers two databases, more may be involved. The techniques suggested in this chapter will also work with multiple separate databases.

THE MANAGERIAL CHALLENGE

Although there are substantial technical considerations, the primary challenge is managerial. The reasons are threefold:

- *Departmental and functional areas will cross in the formation of the solution.* Without senior management involvement, turf lines may be drawn and the entire project risks becoming mired in political infighting.

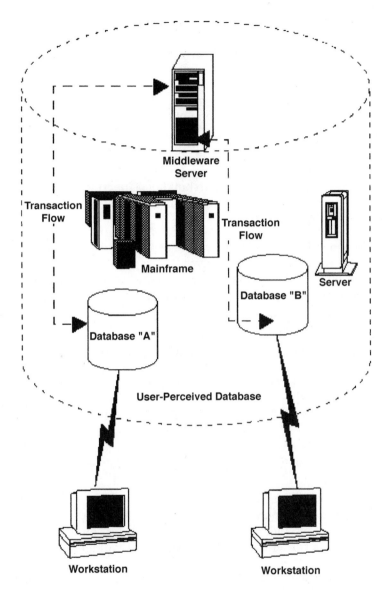

**Exhibit 45.1. Physically separated but conceptually linked databases
(user's perspective).**

- *The lack of detailed data definitions can cause the cost of the project to
  go up and the effectiveness of the solution to go down.* This activity is
  not primarily technical but rather managerial. The organization must
  decide who has what rights to the data and what, exactly, the data
  represents. As any database administrator can attest, this activity can

585

be hampered by departmental disputes. Senior management support and involvement can help minimize these disputes. An attempt to harness two (or more) databases without a serious data definition effort will produce enough confusion to endanger the entire project.

- *Because the ramifications of project failure can materially affect the organization's bottom line, senior management must be involved.* Management must recognize data as one of the most important assets of the organization.

EVALUATING ALTERNATIVES

Early in the project, alternatives to building a functional bridge might be evaluated. The alternatives fall into two main classes: incorporation versus consolidation of databases.

Incorporation. This technique involves expanding one database to cover the functions of the second. Data items that represent those not currently in the main database are added. New software must be created that provides the functional capabilities of the old system.

Although neither a small nor simple project (depending on the complexity of the replaced system), incorporation of databases does have the advantage that it eliminates the data redundancy problem.

Consolidation of Databases. This alternative involves combining the two databases on the same platform. The databases remain separate but reside on the same hardware and under the same software. A functional bridge must still be built, but the communications aspect is greatly simplified and replaced by internal computer processes. However, as in the incorporation technique, the replaced system's functional capabilities must be replaced with new software.

In each of the alternatives, considerations should be given to the current system load, the number of added users to the primary database, among other factors. Incorporation is technically less ambitious than consolidation and is therefore the preferred of the two methods. However, both of the alternatives are generally more expensive to implement than the functional bridge.

THE FUNCTIONAL BRIDGE SOLUTION: STEP BY STEP

A functional bridge is a method to bring transactions from one database to the other so that there is a single update path for all data items.

Planning the Functional Bridge

The first step, of course, is to plan the bridge. There is a great deal more documentation and planning work required than technical implementation effort in building the bridge. If inadequate planning is performed, it is almost certain that no amount of technical prowess will compensate. There are two main initiatives in the planning phase of the functional database bridge:

- *Evaluations of the existing communications infrastructure, available expertise, and commercial middleware.* These evaluations are primarily technical in nature, although management will have some influence because new capabilities may be indicated. For example, if the current communications infrastructure is deemed inadequate, management must approve the building of the new abilities.
- *Designations of master databases, update frequency, and data ownership.* These designations, although influenced by technical considerations, are primarily management decisions and represent points that could materially alter business practices.

Evaluating the Communications Infrastructure. An evaluation of the existing communications infrastructure should establish the following information:

- *The available communications paths between the databases.* This may be a LAN, WAN, T1 line, batch tape, queuing system, or any other way to move the information between systems.
- *The security of the communications paths.* Because there will now be transaction flow from one database to another, security considerations are important. For example, if the proposed communications channel is a T1 line from another city, it can be considered secure. If, however, the proposed channel is over a UNIX system that is connected to the Internet (without a firewall), then steps should be taken to qualify all incoming transactions before an update (or any other action, for that matter) is applied.
- *The stability of the communications paths.* How reliable is the channel? How often does it go down?
- *The current load on the communications channel.* Is there enough bandwidth to accommodate the new transaction load? This evaluation necessitates an estimate of transactions per unit time.
- *Failure analysis of the communications channel.* What are the ramifications if the communications carrier should fail? And how long can that failure continue before there are serious ramifications?
- *Communications protocols.* Some smaller (or older) systems do not natively possess modern communications protocols. The choices in this case are either to custom-build an interface to the database, perhaps with vendor assistance (though adding a modern communications protocol to a system can be complicated), or to drop back to a less ambitious communications protocol — for example, batch tape transfer instead of TCP/IP transfer.

Designation of the Database Master. With multiple databases, one database must be considered the master database. That is, the values of the data items in the master database are considered to be the final word. This designation as master, however, is on a data basis. For example, the database on the corporate mainframe may be considered the master for customer name and address, whereas the shipping database (which also contains the customer name and address) is considered the master for the shipping date for a customer's order.

In the determination of the master database, the following criteria should be considered:

- *Stability.* How stable is the database? How much maintenance is required?
- *Vendor support.* How effective is the vendor support for this system/ database? How promptly does the vendor respond to support calls?
- *In-house expertise.* Who within the organization knows the system/database well enough to answer routine questions and solve performance problems?
- *Available consultant expertise.* If in-house expertise does not exist or should disappear, is there a pool of consultant expertise upon which to draw?
- *Volume of data.* What is the current volume of data on the database? If data fields are added, what are the ramifications?
- *User load on the host system.* How will the transactions affect system performance? Batch updates, for example, can almost negate online response while it is running. Again, an estimate of transaction volume should be made.

Making Critical Design Decisions

Overall Data Architecture. The design phase of the project should not be entirely end-user driven. The end-user maintains a biased view of the data and often requires data items that are actually derived information and not necessarily stored as fields (e.g., average customer order size). A database administrator (DBA) view, in this case, is required.

The DBA should obtain information about the data items in question from the end-users because they know the data. However, the DBA should then take that information and put it into the context of the overall database structure.

For example, the users tell the DBA about a data item called Last_Contact. The DBA is required to find out the context of this field (i.e., contact by whom?). This may be different from the data item in the main database with a similar name.

Database Linkage. A determination should be made of how tightly linked the databases are — that is to say, how often should the cross-communications occur? This factor is, of course, substantially affected by the communications infrastructure available.

Insofar as technically possible, this consideration should be made for business reasons. The update frequency of names and addresses will likely require no more than a batch update, whereas the update frequency of a medical chart location (in a hospital), for example, would require nothing less than a real-time update. The creation of additional communications ability may legitimately be driven by this design decision.

Data Item Map. The organizational aspects of generating the data definitions required for building the functional bridge were mentioned previously. The actual elements of that definition include:

- The name of the data field in both databases.
- The form of the field in both databases.
- The source of the data. It is not unusual for essentially different data to have the same or similar names across databases.
- The update path of the data. Where does the data originate? Is it original data (i.e., someone keys the data) or is it derived from other items in the database? Who audits the data, and who has the authority to change it?

Update Paths. The data definitions now become an essential ingredient to the design of the update paths. Without the documentation of the existing update paths for each data item involved, and the proposed new update paths, it will be impossible to create an effective transaction flow between the databases.

Changes in the update paths will undoubtedly change departmental procedures. This requires the full cooperation of that department's management and, of course, senior management support.

Communications Back-flow. In some cases, it will be necessary to send transactions in more than one direction. Communication in two or more directions is termed back-flow.

For example, names and addresses may originate in the corporate mainframe and it is considered the master. However, there could be a requirement that the data be updated from the satellite database at a customer service center, for example. Transactions must flow from the master to the satellite for a new customer, but also flow from the satellite to the master to ensure quality customer service. Again, these are not technical decisions (although they have technical ramifications). These decisions should be made for business reasons, not solely technical ones.

Ensuring Positive Feedback. No communications path is error free or fully functional 100 percent of the time. Good communications design requires a positive feedback. The receiving system must tell the sending system that the data it received was acceptable. This requirement is different from the standard acknowledgement/negative acknowledgement (ACK/NAK) code of a communications systems protocol. This feedback is done at the data application level. It must be known not only that all the bits of the address were received (ACK/NAK), but also that the customer number pointed to a real existing customer.

Sometimes, the positive feedback and the back-flow communications can be combined, thus reducing the network traffic. For example, a medical master database that is adding a new patient sends a transaction giving the demographic data. The satellite database reports back the local contract number assigned to the patient, which is added to the master as an alternative key. Thus, both functions are served with a single transaction.

Preventing Feedback Loops. Like a public address system, transaction systems can suffer from feedback. Transactions are usually triggered when a data field is updated. When this transaction arrives at the satellite database, the associated data field is updated as well. If the satellite database also reports changes in the data item, it would, of course, send a transaction to report the change just made. The result is a feedback loop that causes an endless chain of updates.

To avoid feedback loops, the triggering mechanisms must be aware of the source of the update. If the update came from the master database, the satellite database must recognize that fact and prohibit the change from being reported back to the master database.

Split Transactions. Occasionally, more than one satellite database must be updated with the same data from the master. It is good design to split the transaction rather than have the master send two transactions. Middleware software is usually used in this case. The transaction is received by the software and two (or more) transactions are forwarded to the satellite databases. The transactions may not have the same format (or even the same communications protocol), even though they convey the same information.

Recovery. What happens if the satellite system sends a transaction and the communications channel is down? An important feature of the network should be that it is not possible to lose a transaction. Therefore, if the communications channel is down, the software must wait and retry the transaction later. This recovery feature is inherent in some middleware and some gateways. Regardless of where it exists or whether it was bought or built, it must be present in the functional bridge in order to have a reliable communications path.

Common Ground: Constructing the Bridge

Once the above design has been completed, the actual bridge can be constructed. The bridge consists of five parts: transactions, transaction carriers, gateways, middleware, and trigger events.

Transactions. At this stage of design, the data required and the associated update paths should be fully known and documented. Because multiple transaction systems are not unusual, the content of the transactions must be designed so that coherent sets of information are available during update.

Transaction Carriers. This is the protocol of the transactions. There are multiple levels of the communications protocol. The low level is usually handled by the software employed (multiple communications protocols could be involved, however, and ways of translating one protocol to another may be required). On another level, the transaction must have ways of identifying itself to the update software. This requires transaction identification within the transaction itself. Routing information may also be required for complex environments.

Gateways. The software that actually updates the database is typically known as a gateway. In some database systems, the gateway comes as an internal part of the database itself; with others, it must be added.

In extreme cases, it will be necessary to create the gateway. This kind of gateway is likely to be the most difficult to test and debug, since all combinations of data must be tested — a substantial task even for a moderate set of transactions.

Middleware. Early in the project, evaluations of existing commercial middleware should be undertaken. There are several products on the market with a range of capabilities, some better than others. This software can substantially reduce the technical development and support aspect of the project and provide significantly better control than could (or would) be produced in-house.

Middleware is a generic name that refers to software that accepts and sends transactions between disparate clients and servers, usually converting communications protocols along the way. Better commercial versions also offer transaction reformatting and splitting.

Middleware is very effective in larger client/server systems, but requires an initial commitment to infrastructure creation. Middleware capabilities range from basic queuing support to full distributed computing management environments.

The control and statistical aspects of the software are also important because these features give the user the ability to shut down portions of the network and to keep track of the number, size, and status of the transactions.

Trigger Events. These are the events that cause a transaction to be sent or received. The trigger can be as simple as a command at the console (in the case of batch), the act of receiving a TCP/IP transaction, or a relational database stored procedure designed to act as a trigger.

In any case, the trigger event controls the flow of transactions over the bridge. Usually, these triggers must be coded in the database itself because it is at that point that the transaction originates.

SUMMARY

This chapter presents an overall view of the elements required for the successful management of multiple databases. The recommended approach is the construction of a functional bridge that allows the multiple databases to function as a single database.

The construction effort is largely one of management and definition, rather than a challenge of technical implementation. Failure to implement an integration strategy, such as a functional bridge, for databases that contain related data will inevitably result in inaccurate information being supplied to the organization's management.

Chapter 46
Mobile and Federated Database Interoperability
Antonio Si

WIRELESS NETWORKS AND MOBILE COMPUTING HAVE OPENED UP NEW
POSSIBILITIES for information access and sharing. The need to interoperate
multiple heterogeneous, autonomous databases is no longer confined to a
conventional federated environment.

A mobile environment is usually composed of a collection of static servers and a collection of mobile clients. Each server is responsible for disseminating information over one or more wireless channels to a collection
of mobile clients. The geographical area within which all mobile clients
could be serviced by a particular server is called a cell of that server.

In this mobile environment, databases managed by database servers of
different cells might be autonomous. Information maintained in a database
will usually be most useful to clients within its geographical cell. In this respect, information maintained by databases of different cells might be disjoint or might be related. A mobile client, when migrating from one wireless
cell to another, might want to access information maintained in the database server and relate it to the information maintained in its own database.
Such an environment is termed a mobile federation, to distinguish it from a
conventional federated environment. The database managed by a mobile
client is termed a mobile database, while the database managed by the
server is a server database. Using similar terminology, the database system
managed by a mobile client is referred to as a mobile component and the
database system managed by a server is referred to as a server component.

It is not clear if existing techniques can address interoperability in this
newly evolved computing environment. This article presents a reference
architecture for a conventional federated environment, proposes a set of
functional requirements that a federated environment should support, and

0-8493-9832-0/00/$0.00+$.50
© 2000 by CRC Press LLC

examines existing techniques for a federated environment with respect to each functional requirement in the context of the newly evolved mobile federation.

A WORKING SCENARIO

A tourist would like to discover information about attractions and accommodations within a certain area. With a portable computer equipped with a wireless communication interface, each mobile client (tourist) can receive travel information from the server over a wireless channel. Such an application might be called an Advanced Traveler Information System (ATIS).

In practice, each server database would maintain traveler information restricted to its own cell. For example, a server database serving the city of Los Angeles might provide vacancy information in all hotels within the Los Angeles area, such as the Holiday Inn near the Hollywood freeway. A user might query the server database to obtain all hotels that have vacancies. Information maintained by different server databases might, to a large extent, be disjoint in this application domain, but there might still be some information overlap among different server databases.

For example, a Holiday Inn within the Los Angeles region might decide to maintain partial information on Holiday Inns in other regions, such as Pasadena. It is also important to note that different server databases will, in general, be autonomous, employing different database management tools and even different data models to manage its own information. Exhibit 46.1 illustrates a snapshot of the information maintained in different server databases and a mobile client who accesses information via a wireless channel.

It would be useful to have a high-level capability that allows structured units of information to be identified from a server database and incorporated into a local database managed by a mobile client. For example, a client might want to maintain information on all hotels in cell 1 and cell 2, since it travels to these two areas the most. A client visiting cell 1 (as shown in Exhibit 46.1) might issue a query to obtain all hotel information. When the client visits cell 2, the hotel information incorporated into his or her database will have to be interoperated with the existing information that the client previously incorporated from the server database in cell 1. This allows a mobile client to query the information using its own familiar database management tools. These various server databases, together with the local database of the mobile client, form a mobile federation. It is interesting to note that the local database maintained in a mobile client is, in effect, a data warehouse since its data is constructed by integrating data from various data sources.

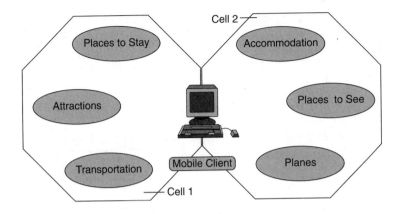

Exhibit 46.1. Snapshot of ATIS databases.

The objective of a mobile federation is similar to a conventional federated database environment. Both environments are trying to share information among multiple autonomous databases. In a mobile federation, the sharing of information is implicit; the information is shared within the context of a mobile client. In a conventional federated system, the information is shared among the databases themselves. Obviously, the server databases of various cells could also share information among themselves, in which case the server databases form a conventional federated environment as well.

FEDERATED ENVIRONMENT ARCHITECTURE

Exhibit 46.2 illustrates a typical federated environment. As the exhibit shows, a collection of independent database components is interconnected via a communication network. Each component consists of a database and a schema. A database is a repository of data structured or modeled according to the definition of the schema, which can be regarded as a collection of conceptual entity types. (The implementation of an entity type, of course, depends on the database model employed by the component; it may be a relation in a relational model, or it can be an object class, if an object-oriented model is employed.)

Information Sharing Techniques

Sharing of database information in this federated environment could be achieved at three different levels of granularity and abstraction:

- Entity types belonging to the schema of individual components could be shared such that modeled real-world concepts could be reused.

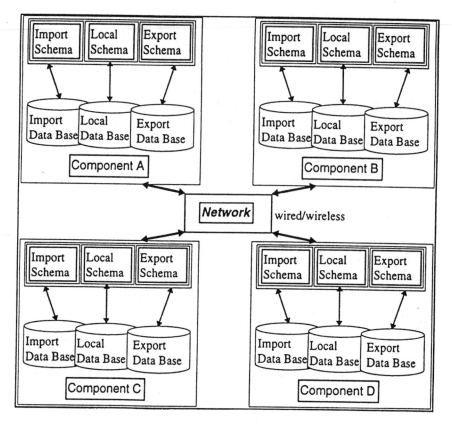

Exhibit 46.2.   Reference architecture for a federated environment.

- Data instances stored in individual components' databases (the implementation of which also depends on the database model employed) could be shared such that information of modeled real-world entities could be reused.
- Applications developed on a component's database could be shared among any other components. For example, if the server database in cell 1 in Exhibit 46.1 develops a pathfinder application that allows a mobile client to search for the shortest route to a destination, it could be reused by a mobile client in searching paths within cell 2 as well.

The simplest way to achieve information sharing in a database federation is for a component to simply browse through the content of a nonlocal (i.e., remote) component's database. In this respect, an explorer should be provided. Alternatively, a component could integrate remote information into its local database. The newly integrated information could be reused by the component in the future. To support such reuse of information, the database of a component, say X, is logically partitioned into three different subsets, as shown in Exhibit 46.2:

- *Local database.* The local database (LD) refers to the set of data instances originally created by X.
- *Import database.* The import database (ID) refers to the set of remote data instances that X retrieves from the export databases of remote components.
- *Export database.* The export database (ED) is a subset of the union of the local database and import database, which represents the set of data instances the component is willing to share with other components. In other words, a component should be able to export its imported data instances if the access privilege constraints specified on the imported instances are not violated.

Similarly, from the reference architecture in Exhibit 46.1, the schema of a component X is also partitioned into three different subsets. The local schema (LS) refers to the entity types originally created by X and is used to model the local database. The import schema (IS), which refers to the entity types X retrieves from the export schema of remote components, is used to model the import database. Finally, the export schema (ES), which is the subset of the union of LS and IS, is used to model the export database.

Integrating a remote application belonging to a remote component, say Y, into X's local system is difficult because X's local computer system might be different from that of Y. One possibility (proposed by D. Fang, et al.) is to integrate the signature of the remote application into X's local system. To execute the application, X's local data is passed to component Y; the application is run on the remote component using X's data and the results are returned back to X. The Java virtual machine could make application sharing easier.

CHARACTERISTICS OF A FEDERATED DATABASE ENVIRONMENT

Each component within a federation is usually heterogeneous and autonomous in nature. Heterogeneity is a natural consequence of the independent creation and evolution of autonomous databases; it refers to the variations in which information is specified and structured in different components. Autonomy means each component is under separate and independent control.

Heterogeneity

In general, a spectrum of heterogeneities of different levels of abstraction could be classified.

Database model heterogeneity. Each component may use different database models to describe the structure and constraints of its data.

Conceptual schema heterogeneity. Each component may model similar real-world concepts in different ways, such as the different schema used by the different database components of the multiple ATIS databases depicted in Exhibit 46.1. This is also referred to as semantic heterogeneity. This conceptual schema heterogeneity could be further divided into three discrepancies, each of which can be explained as follows:

- *Naming mismatch.* Two entity types from different components modeling the same real-world concept might use different naming conventions in representing the attributes. In the ATIS database in Exhibit 46.1, the ranking of a hotel might be modeled by an attribute called "rank" of Places to Stay in component A, while the same information might be modeled by an attribute called "number of stars" of Accommodation in component B.
- *Domain mismatch.* The same attribute of two entity types from different components might be represented in different domains. For example, both Attractions and Places to See of components A and B, respectively, in Exhibit 46.1 might have an attribute "zip code." However, component A might represent the attribute as an integer, while component B might represent it as a string.
- *Schematic discrepancy.* Data in one database might be represented as entity types in another database. In Exhibit 46.1, entity type Planes of component B might be represented as an attribute of Attractions in component A.
- *Data specification heterogeneity.* Each component may model similar real-world entities in different units of measure. One component might represent the distance of an attraction in meters, while another component might represent it in miles.
- *Update heterogeneity.* Since each component is under separate and independent control, data instances modeling the same real-world entity in different databases might be updated asynchronously. When the daily rate of a hotel is updated, databases A and B in Exhibit 46.1 might be updated at different times.
- *Database tools heterogeneity.* Each component may use different tools to manipulate its own database. For example, different components might use different query languages.

Types of Autonomy

Orthogonally, each component can exhibit several different types of autonomy.

Design autonomy. This refers to the ability of a component to choose its own design on the data being managed, the representation of the data instances, the constraints of the data, and the implementation of the component's database system.

Association autonomy. This refers to the ability of a component to decide to what extent the component would like to participate in the interoperability activity. A component is free to share its schema, data, or applications with other components; a component can even decide not to participate in the sharing activity at all.

Control autonomy. This refers to the ability of a component to control the access privileges of any remote component on each of its exported information units (entity types or instances). In general, four types of access control privilege could be granted by a component to a remote component on each of its exported information units:

- Read (R) access to the database instances
- Read definition (RD) access to entity types
- Write (W) access to database instances
- Generate (G) access for creating database instances

These four access privileges form a partial order such that $W > G > RD$ and $W > R > RD$. Neither G nor R dominates each other. For instance, if component X grants W access privilege to remote component Y on one of its exported entity types, component Y is allowed to read the instances of the entity type as well. By contrast, if X only grants R access privilege to Y on the entity type, Y is not allowed to modify any instances of the entity type.

If an exported unit of a component, say X, is imported from another component, Y, the capability of X to control the access privileges on the exported unit will depend on whether the unit is imported by copy or imported by reference from Y.

Execution autonomy. This refers to the ability of a component to execute local operations without interference from external components. If, for example, component X might run an application on behalf of remote component Y. This autonomy implies that X can run the application as if it is a local execution (i.e., X can schedule, commit, or abort the application freely).

FUNCTIONAL REQUIREMENTS OF A FEDERATED DATABASE ENVIRONMENT

From the perspective of a component, X, several functional capabilities need to be supported in order to be able to participate in the interoperability activity with other components.

Information Exportation

Component X must be able to specify the information it is willing to share with other components. Such a facility should allow the component to specify the export schema, the export database, or any application that the component would like to be sharable. Furthermore, X should be able to specify the access privileges of each remote component on each of its exported information units.

A mobile federation is comparatively more dynamic than a database federation, connecting and disconnecting from the wireless network frequently. A mobile component also enters and leaves a cell frequently. It is difficult for a server component to keep track of which mobile components are currently residing within the cell under its management. Furthermore, a cell can potentially have many components visiting at any moment. Therefore, it is not possible for a server component to indicate the access privileges of each mobile component. An access control mechanism that is scalable with respect to the number of mobile components is necessary. Due to the dynamic nature of a mobile component, it is not always possible to incorporate information from a mobile component.

Information Discovery

Before component X can access or use any remote information, X must be aware of the existence and availability of the information in which it is interested. A facility must be provided to allow X to discover any remote information of interest at various granularity or abstraction, including schema, data, or applications.

In general, there are two ways information could be discovered by component X. One possibility is that X can formulate a discovery request for its interested information, in which case a facility must be provided to identify the components containing information units that are relevant to the request. Another possibility is for component X to navigate or explore the exported information space of each remote component and look for the interested information. An explorer must then be provided for such a navigation purpose.

Information Importation

Once interested information units from remote components are discovered, component X can import the information units into its local database. Through importation, component X can reuse the discovered information in the future. In general, three importation capabilities are required: schema importation, data importation, and application importation.

Schema importation. This refers to the process of importing remote export schema into X's local schema. This process is further composed of two activities — heterogeneity resolution and schema integration. Heterogeneity resolution is the process of resolving any conflict that exists between X's local schema and the remote schema.

Since different components might use different database models to specify the data, a facility must be provided to translate the remote schema from the remote database model to the one used in X's local system. Furthermore, since different components might model similar real-world concepts differently, another heterogeneity that must be resolved is to identify the relationship between X's local schema and the remote schema.

Referring back to the ATIS federation in Exhibit 46.1, two entity types belonging to two different schema might model the same real-world concept, such as the Attractions information of component A and the Places to See information of component B. Alternatively, two entity types might model related information, such as the Transportation information of component A and the Planes information of component B. Finally, two entity types might model different concepts, such as the Attractions information of component A and the Planes information of component B.

Data importation. Similarly, data importation refers to the process of importing remote export database information into X's local database. This process is composed of two activities — instance identification and data integration.

Instance identification refers to the process of identifying the relationship between the remote database and the local database. Two data instances from different databases might model the same, related, or different real-world entities. This process is complicated because, on the one hand, instances from different databases cannot be expected to bear the same key attributes; on the other hand, merely matching non-key attributes may lead to unsatisfactory results because data instances modeling different entities may possess the same attribute values. This process is further complicated by possible update heterogeneity that might exist between the two instances.

Once the relationship between the remote database and X's local database is identified, the remote database can be integrated into the local database. Again, the remote database should be integrated such that its relationship with the local database is reflected.

There are two different paradigms for integrating a remote data instance from a remote component, Y, into X's local database: imported by copy and imported by reference.

When a remote instance is imported by copy, the data instance is copied into the local database. The copied data instance becomes part of the local database. Any access to the imported instance is referred to its local copy.

When a remote instance is imported by reference, a reference to the remote instance is maintained in the local database. Any access to the imported data instance requires a network request to Y for up-to-date data value. When a remote data instance is imported by copy, the local component, X, has complete control on the local copy of the imported instance and is allowed to specify the access privileges of other remote components on the local copy of the imported instance. However, when a remote data instance is imported by reference from component Y, Y still maintains its control over the imported instance. Component X is still free to export the imported instance; however, X cannot modify the access privileges specified by Y on this imported data instance.

Application importation can only be achieved to a very limited extent due to the possible differences in the computer systems of the different components. However, with the advent of Java mobility code, this could soon become a reality.

In a mobile federation, communication between a mobile component and a server database is usually over an unreliable wireless channel. It is more efficient for a mobile federation to import an instance by copying since a component does not need to rely on the network to obtain the data value of the instance. A mobile component, in general, has less storage space than a federated component. A mobile component, therefore, might not be able to import all data instances and will have to maintain only those instances that it accesses most frequently.

Information querying and transaction processing. Component X should be able to operate its imported information in its local system. The operation on the imported information should be transparent in the following manner:

- *Functional transparency.* All existing local tools of component X, such as its query language and DBMS software, should be operational on the imported information units in the same manner as they operate on the local information units.
- *Location transparency.* Users and tools operating on the imported information units should not be aware of their original locations and remote nature.

Very often, there is a conflict between supporting the described functional capabilities in a component and preserving the autonomy of the component. To preserve the autonomy of a component, modifying any component of the DBMS software is not recommended.

TECHNIQUES FOR DATABASE SHARING

To support database sharing functional capabilities, data model heterogeneity must be resolved. This is usually addressed by employing a common canonical model, which provides a communication forum among various components. Schema and instances represented in the local data model are required to convert to the canonical model. Most research prototypes use an object model as the canonical model because of its expressive power. Most corporations, however, use relational models. ODBC from

Microsoft and JDBC from Sun Microsystems are generally considered the industry standards.

Information Exportation

Information exportation can be easily achieved using database view mechanisms. Exhibit 46.3 illustrates the management of exported information. A sub-hierarchy rooted at class Exported-Classes is created under the root of the class hierarchy (i.e., OBJECTS). To export a class, O, a class name E_O is created as a subclass of Exported-Classes. To export an attribute of O, the same named attribute is created for E_O; this allows a component to specify exported information at the granularity of a single attribute.

Each exported instance is handled by a multiple-membership modeling construct of the object model, relating the original class to which the instance belongs to the E_ counterpart. In effect, classes belonging to the sub-hierarchy rooted at Exported-Classes represent the export schema, and the instances belonging to the sub-hierarchy represent the export database (depicted by the shaded region in Exhibit 46.3).

In Exhibit 46.3, only class Places to Stay is exported because only Places to Stay has a corresponding E_Places to Stay class. All attributes of Places to Stay have the corresponding ones defined on E_Places to Stay. Furthermore, two instances of Places to Stay are exported, relating via a multiple membership construct to E_Places to Stay. A component employing a relational data model could use a similar tech-

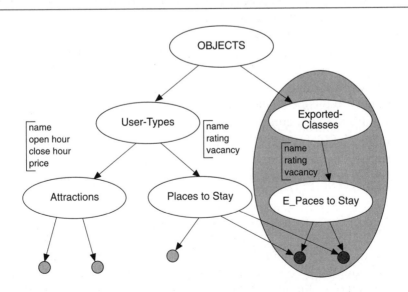

Exhibit 46.3. Information exportation via object view.

nique to specify its exporting information units since the export schema and database are, in effect, a view of the database.

Access control mechanisms for exported information are limited and especially difficult to achieve in a mobile federation. It is difficult for a server component to keep track of which mobile components are within the cell under its management and specify their individual access privileges. A multilevel access control mechanism is more applicable in this domain.

In a multilevel system, database information units are classified into privilege levels. The privilege levels are arranged in an order such that possessing a privilege level implies possessing all its subordinate levels. For example, a typical multilevel system contains four privilege levels: top secret (TS), secret (S), confidential (C), and unclassified (U). A typical database system could have an arbitrary number of privilege levels. To access an information unit, the user needs to obtain a clearance at least equal to the privilege level of the unit. In a mobile federation, a mobile component could join a privilege level that will inherit the database information units that it could access from the server database.

Information Discovery

Information discovery can be achieved by exploring the exported information of a database component. A typical device that explores the content of several databases is depicted in Exhibit 46.4. This explorer is implemented on the Netscape Navigator, providing a platform-independent browsing capability because of the availability of Netscape in UNIX workstations, Macintosh computers, and PCs.

The explorer in Exhibit 46.4 allows a component to explore multiple databases at the same time. It employs a relational model as the canonical model. Exported information units are viewed as relations. The explorer has windows to browse four separate databases of remote components and a window to the local database of a component.

An alternate approach to discovering remote information units that are interesting to a particular component is to specify the requirements of the interested information units. Remote information units that are relevant to the discovery specification will be identified. Specification could be initiated in an ad hoc manner. Following are three different types of discovery requests:

- A component can request remote entity types (instances) that model the same real-world concept (entity) as a local entity type (instance).
- A component can request remote entity types (instances) that model a complementary view of a local entity type (instance).
- A component can request remote entity types (instances) that model an overlapping view of a local entity type (instance).

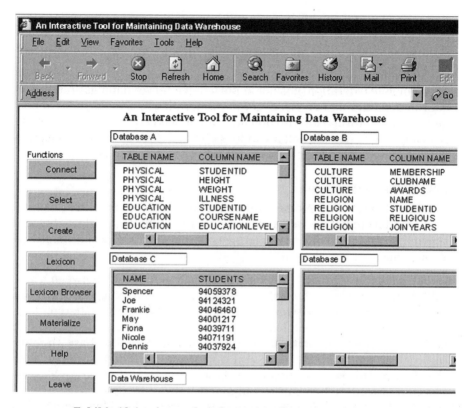

Exhibit 46.4.   A sample information discovery explorer.

To support these three types of discovery requests, one approach is to use a probability model to determine the extent to which two entity types (instances) from different databases modeled the same real-world concept. The probability model is based on two heuristics derived from the common attributes of the two entity types: intra-concept similarity indicator and inter-concept dissimilarity indicator.

Intuitively, an intra-concept similarity indicator refers to the probability that the common attributes will be modeled in related entity types. Inter-concept dissimilarity indicator refers to the probability that the attributes will be modeled in unrelated entity types. Two entity types from different databases will have a high probability of similarity if their overlapped attributes have a high intra-concept similarity indicator as well as a high inter-concept dissimilarity indicator. The use of these heuristics is based on the observation that different databases might model complementary or even disjointed views of the same concept; on the other hand, different databases might model different concepts similarly.

A more general specification could be achieved using first-order logic like language. Each component will thus require a mediator that understands the specification language and identifies information units relevant to the specification.

In a mobile federation, it is not important if a server database returns all information relevant to a discovery request; rather, it is much more important that the returned information units are indeed relevant because of the typically low bandwidth on a wireless channel. One approach to ensure this is to create a profile capturing the interests of each component.

Information Importation

Schema importation. As mentioned previously, a component, X, can import (partial) remote schema from a remote component, Y, into its local schema by first resolving any heterogeneity between X's local schema and Y's schema.

One common approach to resolve schema heterogeneity between X's local schema and Y's remote schema is through a common knowledge base that contains various real-world concepts. Entity types from different databases are required to match with the concepts in the knowledge base. If both entity types map to the same concept in the knowledge base, they are regarded as modeling the same real-world concept. The knowledge base also provides instructions that define how a remote entity type could be integrated into the schema of a component's local database. The instructions could be specified in the form of rules or in a logic-like syntax. The former is easier to understand, but is less flexible. The latter is more flexible, but is less user-friendly.

In a mobile federation, it is difficult to specify a knowledge base that is applicable to all mobile components because there is a potentially unlimited number of mobile components visiting a wireless cell. It is perhaps more appropriate for a mobile component to provide its own knowledge or its personal profile, containing its own view for integrating remote schema into its own local schema.

Instance importation. To identify the relationship between instances from two databases, one needs to address the data specification heterogeneity and the update heterogeneity problems. Data specification heterogeneity is usually resolved, again, via a knowledge base, indicating how the representation of a remote instance could be converted into the representation of the local database.

Exhibit 46.5 illustrates the importance of update heterogeneity in identifying the relationship between instances from various databases. In Exhibit 46.5, valid time denotes the time in which a fact was true in reality,

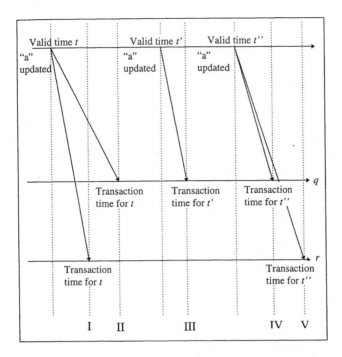

Exhibit 46.5. Updated heterogeneity in a database federation.

while the transaction time denotes the time in which a fact was captured in a database.

One approach to addressing update heterogeneity is to use historical update information on the instances to determine their degree of similarity. The historical update patterns of each instance represent the changes of states of the instance since its creation, inherently capturing its behavioral properties. This allows the instance identification to be performed based on behavioral property in addition to their structural property, as is done traditionally. The historical update information of an instance could be easily obtained through a transaction log.

As mentioned previously, instance integration could be performed via import by copy or import by reference. Using an object model as a canonical model, it is quite easy to support these two integration paradigms within one general framework. Exhibit 46.5 illustrates the partial conceptual schema of two components, A and B, of the ATIS databases from Exhibit 46.1. Instances x and y of component B are imported from class Accommodation of component A. The class Remote-Classes is created in component B to hold the object instance of definitions (OIDS) of the imported instances and the address of components from which the instances are imported (i.e., address of component A in the example). These two types of information are placed in the attributes r_oid and r_host , respectively. A class called R_Accommodation is created in component B as subclass of Remote-Classes to model the imported instances.

In effect, the sub-hierarchy rooted at Remote-Classes represents the import schema and the instances belonging to the sub-hierarchy represent the import database; this is depicted by the shaded region in Exhibit 46.6. Notice that the import sub-hierarchy has a mirror structure as the export sub-hierarchy mentioned previously.

Attributes of classes belonging to the Remote-Classes sub-hierarchy are user-defined methods. To obtain the attribute value for attribute "a" of an imported instance, x, the method "a" will obtain the "r_oid " of x and initiate a remote request to the remote component, whose address is specified in "r_host " of x, to obtain the attribute value for the instance. This achieves the effect of imported by reference. To support import by copy, the imported instances are added to a local class via multiple-membership construct. The additional inherited attributes could be used as placeholders for the copied attribute values of the imported instance. This is illustrated in Exhibit 46.6. The obtained value of an attribute of an instance returned from the corresponding method could be stored in the additional attributes inherited.

In a mobile federation, the connection between a mobile component and the server component could be disconnected at any moment, either due to the unreliability of a wireless channel or due to the movement of a mobile component to another cell. It is, thus, more appropriate for a component to import an instance by copy rather than by reference. This also has an effect of caching the instance into the local database of a mobile component. In this respect, one could regard the local database of a mobile component as a data warehouse since the local database is derived from multiple database sources.

Information discovery and importation could be provided within a uniform framework or interface. This allows discovered remote information units to be imported into the local database of a component. The explorer in Exhibit 46.4 also provides functions for information importation as well. In this particular system, a relational model is employed as a canonical model. The integration of information units from several databases is basically achieved via the "join" operation in this explorer. A component could also create a lexicon containing relationships among attributes of different databases. This resolves the conceptual heterogeneity. This lexicon acts as a localized profile of the component, capturing the perspectives of the

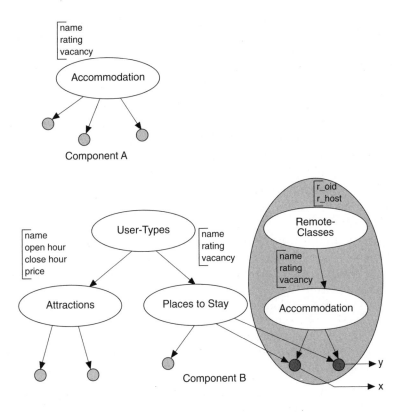

Exhibit 46.6. Data integration.

component on the relationships among information units from different databases.

Information Querying and Transaction Processing

The notion of transaction is supported weakly in existing database federation prototypes. The reason stems from the fact that it is very difficult to support all the properties of transaction processing in a federated database system without seriously violating the autonomy of individual components and without rewriting the DBMS software of individual components.

Consider a situation in which a component X submits a transaction T to a remote component Y. The transaction T, when executed in component Y, is simply a local transaction of component Y. Component Y is free to abort the transaction without notifying component X. Component X, thus, might obtain inconsistent data.

CONCLUSION

This article has presented a reference architecture and functional requirements for a federated database environment. Techniques for addressing each functional requirement have been presented. Limitations of existing techniques in the domain of a mobile federation have been discussed, and proposed solutions have also been briefly illustrated. Experiences with real applications in a mobile federation are necessary to further pinpoint additional problems that require research.

ACKNOWLEDGMENTS

This work is supported in part by the Hong Kong Polytechnic University Central Research Grant Number 351/217. Part of the materials in this chapter are the results of the Remote-Exchange project at the University of Southern California.

Section IX
Data Replication

DATA REPLICATION COMMONLY SATISFIES SEVERAL REAL WORLD RE-
QUIREMENTS. This includes data backup, data sharing, and performance
improvement. Data warehouses, data marts, and reporting systems also
rely on accessing replicated data stores. This section contains three chapters that describe tools, techniques, and processes relating to data replication.

Chapter 47, "The Power of Transformational Data Replication," shows
how replication software can be used to simplify the task of moving data
between heterogeneous computer systems and database software, with
extensive programming.

Chapter 48, "Database Replication: Appliation Design and Deployment
Issues," discusses the benefits of replication, including data availability,
performance, data integration, application integration, and application migration. The chapter also describes other issues related to replication,
such as architectural considerations, heterogeneous replication, managing
replication, and design.

Chapter 49, "Secure Information Through a Replicated Architecture," describes how replicatoin could provide multilevel security. The idea is to
replicate the data based on security levels. Each node stores data at or below the security level designated; that is, a confidential node stores unclassified and confidential data, while a secret node stores unclassified,
confidential, and secret data. This means that unclassified and confidential
data are replicated at both nodes. The chapter then describes a prototype
system based on this approach.

Chapter 47

The Power of Transformational Data Replication

Jason Weir

BUSINESS SOLUTIONS TODAY ARE NOT BUILT BY CONCRETE AND STEEL but rather by data or information. Fast access to data in a format conducive to query and analysis activity by decision-makers and knowledge workers offers companies significant competitive advantages.

Commonly, answers to critical business decisions are hidden away in data collected from various departments or corporate operation centers. For many organizations, accessing and analyzing that data is next to impossible. Production data is often stored in formats not readily interpretable by those who need it. Obscure naming conventions and database codes make extracting the required information a lesson in cryptography.

On top of this, in a business climate where change is the only constant, the proliferation of mixed-system environments is staggering. Rapid corporate mergers and acquisitions often leave IS managers with a variety of computing platforms and database technologies. Further, end users demand better data availability and the freedom to choose from today's variety of powerful front-end access tools, which offer a rich, robust computing experience. To complicate things more, many companies harness the power of distributed computing applications, enterprise resource planning systems (ERP), and continue to tap valuable legacy data housed on mainframe systems.

With the introduction of new operating systems, database software and computing platforms, IS managers face momentous obstacles. Traditionally, solutions would require significant investment of time, resources, and money. Programmers, consultants, new equipment, and support staff would have been necessary to get the job done, not to mention a good deal of time, which many companies hold as a rare commodity.

For businesses facing the challenges outlined by the above scenarios, as well as those looking to implement many of today's distributed data applications such as data warehousing, electronic business, and high systems availability, data replication may be the solution.

WHAT IS TRANSFORMATIONAL DATA REPLICATION?

Historically, sharing corporate data enterprisewide has involved using one of several options. Companies could copy data to physical storage media, such as tape or disk, and deliver it to remote sites, or rely on batch copy or disk mirroring software. Alternatively, custom applications were built to duplicate local databases and distribute them to other systems.

However, these methods had drawbacks. They were slow, inefficient and, because they all depended on some form of straight data copy, delivered data in the same and, often times, confusing format. With data replication software, businesses can not only move data from where it is, to where it needs to be, but also ensure that it is presented in the required format for decision support, query, and analysis.

Data replication involves selecting and filtering data from production databases, moving it among similar or disparate operating systems, computing platforms, and database technologies, and transforming it so that it is in desired and standardized formats.

Businesses can harness the power of data replication tools for such solutions as data distribution and synchronization, loading and replenishing data marts and data warehouses, high systems availability, and electronic business. Another key use is in integrating enterprise resource planning systems (ERP) like SAP, Baan, and PeopleSoft with relational databases such as Oracle and Sybase.

As with many sectors of the computer software market, the replication space is highly competitive. Several companies focus exclusively on data replication and transformation software and most major database vendors, including Oracle, Sybase, and Microsoft, all offer replication solutions. The various replication solutions built by these vendors vary in approach but outlined below are some basic characteristics every good replication tool should have.

ASYNCHRONOUS REPLICATION

Some replication software packages use asynchronous architecture, meaning that synchronization can occur while other processes continue. This is in contrast with the two-phase commit logic inherent in distributed database management systems (DBMS). Distributed DBMSs involve placing pieces of a database on different systems and accessing data as though it exists on one system.

Two-phase commit architecture guarantees that all database copies are synchronized, regardless of location, but any update failure can cause a transaction to be *rolled back*. This necessitates a complete database refresh, or resynchronization, which can be extremely time consuming. Moreover, as the number of nodes within a DBMS increases, two-phase commit logic becomes unworkable as all subsequent updates are frozen until the commit process is completed for the current transaction. Essentially, system usage comes to a halt each time an update occurs.

Asynchronous replication, on the other hand, provides reliable delivery of data while preventing any possible transaction deadlock between multiple database engines. Asynchronous architecture also allows data recovery in case of communication failure and offers replication on a predetermined schedule to avoid network or resource interruption.

SELECTIVE FILTERING

An effective replication tool should let users distribute database updates based on row and column criteria. Rather than copying an entire database periodically to synchronize remote systems, the software should be able to distribute database changes on a *net-change* basis. That is, the replication tool should send only those records in a database that have changed since the last update rather than sending every record even if it is redundant. It should also let users distribute changes conditionally, based on critical column updates or row selection criteria.

A good example of the benefits gained by the ability to replicate data by row and column selection can be drawn from human resources databases. With sensitive data, such as that stored in human resources systems, many companies want to exclude particular elements or enhance them for easier analysis. For instance, salary figures could be deselected from the replication process or filtered out so that only salaries exceeding a set amount are distributed to data marts or decision support systems. Another example involves replicating location specific data. For example, data could be selected dependent on department or business unit and replicated to specific remote systems for local use. Selective filtering ensures that only relevant data is sent to target systems and avoids decision support systems from becoming unworkable and inefficient.

FLEXIBLE DATA TRANSFORMATION AND ENHANCEMENT

As mentioned, many replication methods simply copy entire databases from one system to another. This may be desirable in some instances, but most companies require the ability to transform and enhance data. This is especially important for businesses with mixed system environments that do not have standardized data formats.

DATA REPLICATION

With some replication tools, custom applications have to be developed and extensive programming may be necessary to accommodate the task of data transformation. Robust replication software, on the other hand, has built-in data transformation and enhancement functionality.

A simple example of the power of data transformation involves multilocation businesses or companies that have merged with or acquired other interests. Branch offices within organizations often adopt different database conventions for such elements as inventory databases. Dissimilar codes and abbreviations for product names, sizes, or colors present real problems when synchronizing data throughout the enterprise, especially for those basing critical decisions on this obscure information.

In short, transformation refers to the ability to alter the data being moved between databases. With transformational capabilities, replication software can remedy common discrepancies. For example, if one branch office uses the code "BI" to represent a "backordered item" and the head office uses the code "02" for the same value, transformation can consolidate the difference to represent a meaningful standard. Now, backordered items can be registered as a single, understandable value such as "Back_Order" on the target data warehouse or decision support system.

Another example of data transformation is value translations such as currencies, weights, and measures. This is extremely valuable for international organizations that want to maintain synchronized databases throughout various countries. International weight units can be converted to United States standards or Canadian dollars converted to British Sterling, for example. Another important data transformation involves the Year 2000 date issue. Many databases, especially those housed on legacy systems, have date formats such as 12/27/94 (December 27, 1994). Data replication software that incorporates transformational capabilities can convert two-digit dates to ISO standard, Year 2000 compliant date formats. The above example would be converted to 1994/12/27 at the target system.

HETEROGENEOUS PLATFORM SUPPORT

As discussed, rapid corporate mergers, acquisitions, and takeovers are commonplace. Often times, however, not a great deal of consideration is given to the compatibility of the technology infrastructure of the new entity. Many replication tools assist, to varying degrees, in delivering data across dissimilar computer hardware, databases, and networks.

Good replication software allows for a high level of platform or database independence and is "scalable." That is, not only should the tool be able to replicate data among existing systems and databases, but also be prepared to handle future introductions.

The level of ease with which replication software replicates data throughout mixed-system environments is also an issue. Many database vendors offer proprietary data replication functionality included as part of their software or as an optional component. The capabilities of such tools range from simple import and export functions to full heterogeneous replication.

Companies relying on these built-in database replication utilities would be wise to keep in mind that it is not in the best interest of database vendors to move data off of their own database, but rather to move data into it. This means that, although these types of tools will often readily and easily replicate another vendor's data-type to their own database, replicating data out of that database to another vendor's can be extremely challenging. To provide seamless replication among disparate databases and computing systems, extensive, time consuming and resource intensive programming of *agents* — components that link one application to another — or use of gateways may be necessary.

Comprehensive data replication packages enable seamless integration of multiple databases and hardware platforms. While they pose an initial expense, the savings of high programming costs and the drastic reduction in implementation time can easily justify the purchase.

Furthermore, some database vendor replication offerings require *data staging* — the movement of data into a temporary holding area prior to being transmitted to the target system. This slows the replication process and may necessitate the purchase of additional hardware as some data stages are housed on intermediary systems that sit between the source and target computers. Data replication software moves data directly from source to target, with no stage required. This enables real-time data replication. As transactions or other changes occur on the source database, they are immediately reflected on any target databases.

In short, while database vendor tools provide support for data replication among heterogeneous systems, the feasibility is limited by high custom programming costs, lengthy implementation processes and, in some cases, data staging logic. In contrast, data replication software provides transparent access to data on dissimilar systems and moves it point to point in real-time.

BI-DIRECTIONAL, REAL-TIME REPLICATION

Many companies, especially those with multiple locations, or autonomous business units, require replication for not only distribution of centralized data, but also for data collecting or consolidation from those sites. To enable synchronization of databases throughout the enterprise, data replication tools must have bi-directional capabilities. Additionally, in some applications, the ability to move data in real-time, as opposed to replicating data at scheduled times or even staging data, is critical. Real-time data movement allows access to up-to-the-minute information for more accurate reporting and analysis.

However, users should still have the option to choose among a variety of replication *modes*. That is, some applications may not demand real-time data delivery. Users should be able to schedule replication times or replicate data on an *on demand* basis as required. Regardless, the tool should, as mentioned, replicate only those records that have been added, deleted, or changed since the last update. This ensures that the process is carried out as quickly as possible and high communication costs, traditionally associated with refreshing remote databases, are minimized.

In sum, the replication tool should enable replication among a variety of popular databases, including Oracle, Sybase, Microsoft SQL Server, and DB/2, as well as legacy data from mainframe servers, to and from UNIX, Intel-based servers, and IBM AS/400 systems.

REPLICATION ARCHITECTURE

There are several architectures that data replication tools use to deliver functionality. Brief summaries of each are provided below.

Log-Based vs. Trigger-Based Replication

In log-based replication, changes are captured from a journal or system log and then transmitted to the target system. Log-based replication operates asynchronously and, therefore, has the least effect on system performance. Trigger-based replication, on the other hand, relies on database *triggers* — small event-based functions — that are fired with each database change on the main system. Updates are captured directly from the database and then replicated. If many simultaneous updates occur, trigger-based replication has a greater impact on performance than does log-based replication as triggers require system resources to work.

Push vs. Pull Replication

Replication involves either *pushing* or *pulling* data from the production database. With push replication, replication software on the source computer decides what needs to be transmitted and when to send it. Data is then pushed from the source database as it changes (or at specified time intervals) to the target system(s). As a result, users can use push replication to maintain current copies, or snapshots (time-stamped version of data in the database), of source data on as many systems as required.

With pull replication (also known as the gateway method), user queries at target sites pull data directly from the source database via a communication "gateway." Data is never completely current with this method; and that may be adequate in some situations. Instead, updates are pulled based on time intervals specified by the data administrator when setting up the copy requests. E-mail is a basic analogy of both push and pull methodology. Users can ask the server to deliver their mail by logging on and executing a "send and receive" from their mail program. On the other hand, if users are continuously connected to the server, mail can be pushed by the server to the user at specified intervals like every ten minutes or hourly.

Push and pull replication both let users schedule their data transfers at specific intervals or to coincide with off-peak periods. Users can schedule replication to suit end-user update requirements and system availability. For example, with query databases, a daily or twice-daily update schedule may be sufficient; while database changes may need to be available as soon as they occur on the source system. Using log-based or trigger approaches, replication tools recognize when database updates occur and then, using their defined methods, replicate the updates to the target system(s).

Mixed-mode replication, which involves a combination of push and pull methods, is also possible. Mixed-mode replication usually involves periodically pushing data to an intermediate database and then pulling it from that database at predetermined intervals. You may recall the previous discussion of data staging. This intermediate database is also referred to as a data stage. The mixed-mode architecture has some advantages over straight pull methods as it reduces the performance impact on the source system and allows for some data summarization at the intermediate database. Unfortunately, mixed-mode replication does not provide data concurrency because the target system pulls data only periodically. The required intermediate stage database also results in increased processing load and disk storage to work. A data stage does not necessarily require a separate system, but if it resides on the source system, resources could become strained.

Master/Slave vs. Two-Way Replication

Master/slave replication is the least complex of all data replication architectures. Under this model, there is one master data source, typically a production database. Users or batch jobs make production updates to the master database. The master database then replicates updates to the slave database(s), which accepts updates only from the master. Users can then use slave databases for queries, reporting, and any other processing in which data is not updated.

Two-way replication has some beneficial uses. For example, companies could use two-way replication for *workload management* (also referred to as workload balancing). One system could run interactive processes that update and maintain core data and have data replicated to another system which would run batch processes that maintain totals and other summary data. Companies could then use replicated databases for offline batch processing without interrupting online production transaction processing on the main system.

Two-way replication is also a better solution than two-phase commit logic, in which the update process is synchronous. As noted earlier, failures cause update transactions to roll back to the source database. With large-scale distribution of changes through many servers, multi-level rollbacks could cause considerable processing delays.

Cascading Replication

Some form of cascading replication, in which the target computer replicates data to subsequent targets, may be the only way to broadcast data over large client/server installations. Cascading replication reduces the load on the originating machine and creates a multiplier effect that distributes changes quickly to many targets.

APPLICATIONS

With data replication architecture and core functionality outlined, we can now discuss some of the business solutions that it helps enable.

Data Warehousing

Data warehousing as a tool for business intelligence has gained wide acceptance in the last few years. It is estimated that over 90 percent of Fortune 1000 corporations will have data warehouses or data marts (departmental data warehouses) by the end of the current year. The reasons for this trend are many. Undoubtedly, the data warehouse offers businesses a significant competitive advantage with important benefits that allow companies to:

- Monitor sales activity in order to make fast, informed decisions based on up-to-the-minute information.
- Deliver product to market faster using inventory and manufacturing elements of the data warehouse.
- Predict and understand trends to make better business decisions.

An important part of the data warehouse is the software that loads and replenishes the data that is stored there. This component, namely data replication software, involves constructing an information database from production data in a format that is beneficial to knowledge workers and decision-makers. It also includes regularly updating the informational database as changes to production data occur.

Again, most companies implementing data warehouses require the ability to select, filter, transform and enhance raw production data so that only relevant information, stored in appropriate formats for query and analysis, is transmitted to the data marts or warehouse. It is essential to keep these needs in mind when setting up a data warehouse. The right replication software should not require programming to set up the process of delivering data to the warehouse, should be easy to administer, and offer flexible data conversion, enhancement, and transformation capabilities. Additionally, depending on the technology environment, support for cross-platform, cross-database data replication may also be required.

High Systems Availability

With the growing dependence on data as a competitive weapon and, in some cases, the lifeblood of the organization, few companies can afford even a few hours of total system downtime, let alone days or weeks. Without access to production data, business loses momentum or, worse still, stops altogether. Even if companies can avoid the disaster of unplanned downtime, they still have scheduled outages for hardware and software upgrades and routine maintenance. To avoid the loss of data, or the loss of access to that data, companies implement high systems availability solutions.

In most cases, organizations elect to transfer business-critical applications and data to a failsafe system located offsite. The ideal situation is to switch to the failsafe site when needed and have any changes that occur during downtime replicated back to the production machine when it is brought back online. That is, if the main system is down for 2 hours, and no original data is lost, then only the changes that occurred on the failsafe system during the outage should be replicated back — not the entire database. However, if data is lost on the primary system due to corruption or natural disaster, then companies should have the ability to resynchronize it with the failsafe machine.

Solid data replication tools transfer data from primary system to failsafe machine in real-time, as changes occur, or entire databases on a predetermined schedule. This means companies can opt to refresh the failsafe machine nightly or weekly as required, or have replication software move changes to databases in real-time so that the most current data is available in case of planned or unplanned outages.

Ultimately, when the production system comes back online following downtime, the replication software should intelligently resynchronize the database, replicating only the changes to the data that occurred during downtime or, in case of data loss, completely refresh the primary database using the failsafe data.

Data Distribution

Data distribution allows companies to move data from one source system to multiple target systems. With the proper replication software, organizations can distribute entire databases from the source machine to targets or replicate location specific data, such as daily price updates, to branch offices or retail sites. For example, parts of centrally administered files could be replicated to remote locations for local query and analysis purposes. Replication software that allows users to select, filter, and enhance data permits this type of distribution environment. To reemphasize the point, users should be able to select between real-time data replication or scheduled, periodic updates.

Whatever options are selected, only changes to data should be replicated in order to maintain efficient operations and avoid unnecessary redundant data transfer that ties up system resources. Additionally, data distribution across like or heterogeneous environments should be attainable without extensive custom programming. The ability to replicate data using the cascading replication model mentioned previously ensures the highest level of efficiency, especially when distributing data across large area networks or between many sites.

Electronic Business

Electronic business, or *e-business,* is changing the way companies interact with suppliers, alliances, and customers. It is changing business models, streamlining supply chains, increasing efficiency and productivity, and bringing collaborative applications to unprecedented levels. Data replication software, especially if it handles cross-platform, cross-database content delivery, can prove invaluable to companies implementing e-business solutions.

For example, companies may want to share data with suppliers and business partners via a corporate *extranet* — a private Internet site or application accessible by password. To do this, the company could harness the power of replication software to select subsets of data to share beyond the firewall. That is, the company could have the security of knowing that only the data that they choose is accessible and that no threat of intrusion exists. Through e-business, companies can allow customers to check order status, allow suppliers to monitor inventory levels, dealers to access information and run queries on select data for their own reports, and much more.

The ability to move data among disparate systems and databases is critical as many production databases are housed on midrange systems like UNIX and AS/400, while Microsoft Windows NT-based Web servers are rapidly becoming the standard. Being able to replicate corporate data to the safety of a Web server kept beyond a firewall is crucial, but many organizations face the obstacle of how to get it there (Exhibit 47.1). Replication software enables rapid, secure content delivery among heterogeneous systems and databases (Exhibit 47.2).

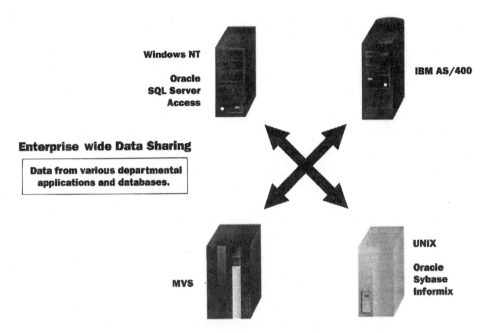

Exhibit 47.1. **Illustrates capability of replication tools to share, synchronize, and distribute data across dissimilar computing platforms and databases for business solutions such as data warehousing, application integration, and electronic business.**

CONCLUSION

Regardless of which data replication architecture or type — either database vendor or third party tools — companies explore, they will soon realize the benefits that the software offers. Data replication software enables a diverse range of applications, while reducing costs and increasing efficiency levels of traditionally expensive, time-consuming projects. By allowing cross-platform data delivery, replication software offers companies unparalleled flexibility. It provides the freedom to choose which software and hardware tools run their business and the comfort of knowing that, as they grow, any introduction of dissimilar computing systems or software can be easily and seamlessly integrated.

Chapter 48
Database Replication: Application Design and Deployment Issues

Jagdish Mirani

REPLICATION IS NO LONGER THE EXCLUSIVE DOMAIN OF INNOVATORS AND EARLY ADOPTERS; it has moved into the mainstream and is perceived to be the obvious solution to a large class of problems. Often, however, the application design considerations and deployment issues are overlooked until the last moment. This chapter describes the benefits of replication, the requirements that must be considered, and application design issues.

As a point of clarification, within this chapter, the term *replication* is used to describe the continuous dissemination of changes to data, as opposed to *copy management*, which is a term that is often used to describe the periodic movement of bulk data.

BENEFITS OF REPLICATION

Data Availability

Replication removes the vulnerability to system and network failures. If a remote system fails, and a replica of the same data is stored locally, then local users can still have access to the data.

In a disaster recovery scenario, the user population connected to the failed system can be rerouted to a remotely located replica. Similarly, network failures are less consequential — if the network fails, local users can access the local replica. Hence, replication provides data availability locally for environments in which the participating systems are mostly accessible, but sometimes inaccessible because of system or network failure.

Mobile Implications. As an extension of this concept, replication can also provide enhanced data availability for mobile users who are only occasionally connected to a central consolidated database. In this case, the mobile users are treated as replicate sites, with their own replica of data residing on laptop computers. These users can access and modify their local copy of data and occasionally connect to the central consolidated database, at which point the remote user is resynchronized with the consolidated database through a process of bidirectional replication of changes.

Performance

Replication can partition a large user population across various replicas of data. Without partitioning, when a large user population tries to access the same copy of data, inevitably there is poor response time. In addition, significant performance gains can be realized by customizing the local replica to the local applications.

A common example is the separation of online transaction processing (OLTP) and decision support system (DSS) processing, and accordingly, optimization of the local schema for either OLTP or DSS. Most performance enhancements are realized by moving some of the performance burden away from runtime. Examples of local customization include removal of extraneous data (through horizontal and vertical partitioning), consolidation and denormalization tables from multiple sources, or schema transformations based on the needs of local applications.

Data consolidation is usually required for decision support applications in which a consolidated view of the business is required before decision support analysis can be performed. Although it might be possible to consolidate these data "on-the-fly" at query runtime, preconsolidating these data by means of replication can shift the performance burden away from runtime.

Data Integration

In special cases involving data consolidation, performance is not the prime motivation, yet "on-the-fly" consolidation is simply not practical, even if the performance penalty is tolerable. In the construction of an operational data store, for example, integration of data from various sources can be exacerbated by semantic differences in the source data models and by "dirty" data. Sophisticated replication schemes can support in-flight transformations of data and transactions to reconcile such discrepancies.

Application Integration

Replication allows multiple applications (or multiple instances of the same application) across multiple systems to share the same data. This capability also encourages the deployment of small and targeted applications rather than large and monolithic applications.

Application integration can occur across disparate environments, such as legacy systems, relational systems, and groupware. Data replication then becomes the "information distribution backplane" through which these applications can be integrated. This integration can even extend to process automation and workflow, in which a new generation of distributed applications can be built by replicating application data and control information.

Application Migration

Replication offers a mechanism through which older applications running on legacy platforms can be gracefully retired, while new or replacement applications can be built on new platforms. Data can be shared between the old and the new platforms through replication, until the old applications have been completely replaced or retired.

ARCHITECTURAL CONSIDERATIONS

Of the numerous design decisions made by vendors of replication products, several have major consequences that affect the performance and applicability of the product. Although these different design points do not completely preclude diversity in the uses of the product, they do optimize the products for a subset of the uses.

Trigger-Based Capture vs. Log-Based Replication

One key difference is in the way in which different products capture information at the source. Some products take advantage of database triggers for capturing information into a staging area from which replication can commence. Although this method is easier for vendors to implement, it involves a substantial performance overhead because the trigger code competes for processing cycles with applications using the database.

External replication schemes take advantage of database logs for capturing changes. These schemes take advantage of normal database processing (logging for recoverability offered by modern relational databases) in order to capture changes. External replication schemes also allow greater architectural extensibility through easier implementation of heterogeneity at the source. In supporting replication from another vendor's database, they simply provide a customized capture component for the database in order to incorporate the foreign source into their replication environments.

627

In some cases, however, the source may not support logging, or the log structure may not be conducive to log-based replication. In these cases, alternate approaches, like trigger-based capture, need to be adopted. Other schemes might involve actively identifying and selecting (via SQL selects) changed data from the source. However, these schemes are difficult to implement and can require enhancements to the data model and applications at the source.

Push and Pull

Some replication schemes were primarily designed for continuous replication and suboptimally support scheduled (or periodic) replication, whereas other schemes were primarily designed for periodic replication and suboptimally support continuous replication.

Periodic replication schemes often involve an architecture in which a process at the receiving site periodically "pulls" the changes from a staging area. In these implementations, continuous replication can be simulated by constantly polling the staging area and pulling changes frequently. However, this solution produces considerable overhead, especially when the data at the source are not changing frequently and the constant polling and pulling of changes are not necessary. Other architectures are more conducive to continuous replication because they "push" the changes out to all the subscribers as they occur.

On the other hand, so-called pull architectures are more appropriate for supporting occasionally connected mobile users because the mobile computer can pull changes and initiate replication when it is connected. In this instance, a so-called push architecture would incur the overhead of delivering changes to a large population of mobile users, of which only a small subset of users is actually connected.

HETEROGENEOUS REPLICATION

Most large enterprises deploy databases from multiple vendors. Departmental purchasing decisions are made autonomously, with the selection being based on the optimization of departmental requirements. Very rarely are large enterprises able to standardize on a single vendor's database solution. Therefore, large enterprises typically encounter the challenge of implementing replication between multivendor databases.

There are two sides to this challenge:

- Supporting replication *from* multivendor databases
- Supporting replication *to* multivendor databases

Vendor solutions can differ significantly in this respect. Some vendors view replication as an extension of their databases and are therefore focused on enhancing their replication schemes within the domain of their own database products. Other vendors take a broader view of replication and are inclined to promote replication as database-independent middleware.

Support for heterogeneous replication is much more than a checklist of multivendor database sources and targets supported by the vendor. Key questions for customers to ask in the evaluation of a replication solution include:

- Does the architecture easily support the incorporation of heterogeneous replication, or is it case-by-case force fit? Even in cases where a significant amount of heterogeneity is offered, performance, flexibility, and manageability can differ significantly, depending on the specific configuration.
- Can the vendor support bidirectional replication between multivendor databases? Is performance sufficient in this scenario?
- Which of the features in the replication management utility are extensible to heterogeneous environments?
- What are the future directions of the product that will address some of these usability issues in a multivendor environment?
- Are there any automated conflict detection and resolution schemes that support heterogeneous environments?

FLEXIBILITY

Replication is applied as a solution to a broad set of problems. In addition, there is a high degree of variability in the conditions that must be reconciled in a replication environment. This variability precludes any simple turnkey approach to replication, with the implication that an efficient replication scheme must offer enough flexibility for users to customize a solution.

Support for Different Topologies

The replication scheme must support various topologies and usage modes. These topologies range from a one-source-to-one-target topology for disaster recovery, or one-to-many data distribution from a single consolidated site to several subscribers, or many-to-one data consolidation from several distributed sites to a single consolidated site. Alternatively, this could be configured using a bidirectional one-to-many/many-to-one topology, as in a consolidated site servicing several mobile users. One-to-one configurations resembling a workflow topology are also starting to become more common.

In the most general case, replication can be configured in a bidirectional many-to-many data-sharing configuration. An adaptable replication scheme must support any of the topologies that might be required.

Even in a single-vendor environment, replication forces the resolution of differences between databases that participate in replication. Typically, departmental databases are designed and implemented autonomously and end up with differences in the data models and data definitions. Data formats, naming conventions, and schemas often differ between databases. It is important for the replication scheme to support in-flight transformations of transactions so that an efficient replication scheme can be implemented without compromising local autonomy.

More advanced replication schemes offer event notification features, with logic that is automatically invoked in one location, based on an event that was raised at another location. These schemes are beginning to resemble more generalized messaging solutions. Such event notification schemes are of interest to users who are interested primarily in data replication but also want extensions like asynchronous event notification.

REPLICATION MANAGEMENT

Manageability is the Achilles' heel of replication. On the one hand, the management of the various replication components often adds another dimension to an already monumental management challenge; on the other hand, a replication scheme's manageability is important because it can help users mitigate some of the inherently high-touch aspects of replication.

The manageability of a vendor's solution is often overshadowed by elegant product features in search of a problem, yet the lack of manageability can either become a show-stopper to deployment or make a replication solution very expensive when all maintenance costs are factored in. A workable solution must allow administrators to monitor all the components of replication, manage the environment, and troubleshoot when problems occur.

Monitoring

Administrators must be able to monitor components in a way that maps to the specific topology and set of activities being performed via replication. Administrators should be able to monitor objects as groups, defining groups to present a hierarchical view of the components if desired. If replication subscriptions are distributed across several systems, then the administrator should be able to drill-down and view subscriptions at any location. Exception logs must be easily viewable and manipulated if necessary.

Administrators will often need to look for orphaned or skipped transactions in the exception logs. They must then be able to either purge transactions or manually commit them from the log. Much of this work can be automated via custom filters that can extract information or purge transactions from the exception logs. In addition, administrators need to monitor the status of replication queues, including queue size and performance.

Good replication monitoring products allow administrators to automate by providing thresholds that the system uses to raise events when these thresholds are exceeded. Latency events can be raised when a latency threshold is exceeded, or queue events can be raised when a transaction stays in the queue beyond a specified threshold, or the queue size exceeds a specified threshold. In some cases, it is desirable to specify a duration of time a set of conditions can exist before an event is raised.

Management Interfaces

Management interfaces must aid in the task of setting up and initializing the replication environment. In particular, the management interface must allow administrators to create, drop, alter, suspend, activate, or validate subscriptions, database connections, or routes. A drag-and-drop graphical interface can collapse multiple steps into a few visual and intuitive operations.

In large-scale replication environments consisting of many databases, many of these operations need to be carried out on groups of components. For example, if the same change is required to a large number of subscriptions relating to a large number of target databases, it should be possible to carry out this change as a single group operation. For setup and initialization, manipulation of a one-shot default configuration is often a quicker path to the end result, rather than defining the configuration from the ground up.

Administrators need to be able to perform many such operations and perform configuration changes dynamically, especially in mission-critical environments. Schema changes should be possible through the replication management interface so that corresponding replication subscription changes can also be made.

Troubleshooting

The management interface should allow administrators to issue troubleshooting commands that report status and recommend actions if the commands fail. Special commands can help administrators diagnose various components, including replication definitions and subscriptions.

Integrated Management

Finally, administrators usually prefer a replication management facility that integrates well with database, system, and network management. The ideal solution provides all the necessary components within a single open framework so that the components can interoperate and be integrated using shared components and messaging conventions.

APPLICATION DESIGN CONSIDERATIONS

With replication, success is often measured by the amount of time spent up-front in the design phase. Users who are apprised of the various application design considerations can reduce the risk of false starts and overblown expectations.

Data Latency Considerations

The first fact that users must confront is the data latency that is inherent in asynchronous replication. For the data associated with the user's portfolio of applications, the user must determine the degree of latency that is acceptable for each application.

Synchronous vs. Asynchronous Updates. For applications in which no data latency is tolerable (e.g., transactions involving large funds transfers), a two-phase commit protocol for maintaining replicated data may be most appropriate. However, there is a tendency to overestimate the need for data concurrency, and the population of applications that really require perfect concurrency is limited.

On the other extreme, if a data latency period of hours or days is tolerable (e.g., as in many data warehousing applications), bulk data movement or copy management products that are invoked periodically can provide the required degree of concurrency. Asynchronous replication is best suited for the case in between the two extremes — cases in which the data latency must fall within a few seconds.

Application designers should be able to specify thresholds for a tolerable data latency period, and then have the application determine at runtime whether to access the local replicate data or to access the primary instance of the data over the network. The problem, however, is that there usually is no way of determining the age of a particular data item.

In an update scenario, the application designer may want to set a threshold for deciding between a synchronous or an asynchronous update. Distributed application designers must evaluate vendor support for making decisions at application runtime about which version of the data to access and whether to perform updates synchronously or asynchronously.

Peer-to-Peer Replication. In the case of asynchronous replication, users can choose one of two topologies for handling updates to data. Peer-to-peer topologies allow direct updates to local data, which are then replicated to the subscribing sites. Although this approach reduces data latency at the site initiating the update (local updates are immediately available), there are a number of perils associated with peer-to-peer replication (some of which are discussed later in this chapter).

Master-Slave Configurations. Some vendors advocate a master-slave approach in which the database tables or table partitions are assigned ownership, and any update to data elements must first clear through the owner and then be replicated to the subscriber. With this approach it is slightly easier to handle update conflicts; the tradeoff is a small degree of data latency.

However, even in master-slave configurations, there are techniques for minimizing data latency. For example, local updates can be saved in a "pending transaction table" so that they are immediately available to the applications accessing the data. Then, when the owning site performs the update and replicates back to the subscribers, the transaction can be removed from the pending transaction table after the update is performed at the replicate site. This technique, however, requires additional work in designing the application.

Automated Conflict Detection and Resolution

If the distributed application requires bidirectional replication, users must also confront the issue of update conflicts. These perils must be carefully considered in any application that has automated conflict detection and resolution.

Even in master-slave approaches, conflicts can still occur at the owning site, especially in the process of reconciling large volumes of transactions that may have occurred at multiple locations during a network failure. Although a master-slave configuration does not eliminate conflicts, it clearly identifies the owning site as the site at which conflicts can be detected and resolved.

Business Rule Violations. A large class of replication conflicts are manifested as business rule violations, in which the conflict does not pertain to the update of the same table but to interacting tables. In these cases, it may be unclear whether a referential integrity rule (reflecting a business rule) is being violated or a replication conflict has occurred.

Example. For example, there may be an employee table that is related to a department table through a foreign key. As a business rule, the designer may have placed a referential integrity constraint that disallows departments without employees. But what if a department has only one employee and the tables are available at two replicate sites? At one site, the employee is removed from the department — requiring a removal of the department based on the referential integrity rule. At the other site, an employee is added to the department. Each transaction is replicated to the other site.

At the site where there is no department record, a violation is detected (adding employee to a nonexistent department). At the other site, there is an attempt to remove a department with employees — another business rule violation. In effect, each system will end up with an orphaned transaction. If there is a third system receiving updates from the two conflicting systems, the state of the third system will be determined purely by the order in which it receives the updates.

Although there are schemes to detect conflicting updates to the same row, in this case the conflict is manifested through the rejection of two transactions, even though the updates involved two different tables that interact through a parent-child relationship.

Real business applications are replete with such relationships that exacerbate the challenge of conflict detection and resolution. To automate the resolution to this type of conflict, it is necessary to first identify such conflicts (e.g., an integrity rule that is being violated because of a replication conflict) and then take corrective action that maintains the intent of the business rules and corresponding integrity constraints.

"Compensating" Transactions and Business Practices. Even when all conflicting transactions are easily detected, automating the resolution to the conflicts can be challenging. Several schemes are commonly used for automating conflict resolution, such as earliest change wins, last change wins, and designated-site always wins.

These schemes can often leave a database with either inconsistent copies or internal transactional inconsistencies. Any conflict resolution scheme based on time stamps, for instance, can be problematic because each system has its own clock and all the system clocks are not perfectly synchronized.

Conflict resolution based on a message-arrival sequence is also problematic because the asynchronous nature of the system will affect arrival sequences. Different delays in wide area networks will cause transactions to arrive in a different sequence at each location.

Even in a perfect world, in which all conflicts can be successfully detected and resolved, users must confront the fact that committed transactions will be backed out at all the losing sites. This can be disconcerting to application designers who are use to the notion of database integrity resulting from the ACID — atomicity, consistency, isolation, durability — properties. There is now way of avoiding the window of vulnerability from the time at which a transaction is committed to the time at which it is backed out because of a replication conflict.

Inventory examples are often used to illustrate this vulnerability. If the inventory of a particular item is down to one, and the same item is sold to two customers in different locations because the same time is shown as being available in multiple replicate databases, then one of the two customers must be recompensed for a false sale. In the case of airline reservation systems in which the last remaining seat is often sold to multiple customers, the issue is dealt with through policies that provide additional restitution to customers in these situations (e.g., an additional free ticket or frequency-flyer miles for taking a later flight). In fact, the airlines have institutionalized the practice of overbooking through a set of policies that try to restore customer satisfaction in these situations.

Often, a business policy, or adaptation of a business process, can provide the recourse for problems introduced by distributed applications. Thus, all transactions are handled regardless of conflict, and conflicting transactions actually trigger compensating transactions at certain points in the business operations.

In some situations, however, there may be dependencies caused by a ripple effect and a series of transactions may need to back out to truly undo the effects of the conflicting transactions. Obviously, the consequences can be serious if this situation occurs in an environment of financial applications involving large sums of money.

Additional Overhead. In the case of peer-to-peer updates, automated conflict detection and resolution introduce significant performance overhead and complexity. In peer-to-peer configurations, every site must monitor all the incoming traffic looking for conflicts. There is further complexity resulting from the introduction of support tables. These factors can severely limit scalability and manageability.

Conflict resolution in a peer-to-peer configuration also introduces significant disk space utilization overhead. Every site must temporarily save all incoming transactions in order to monitor for conflicts. If one of the replication sites becomes unavailable, the overhead is extreme — for the duration of the failure, every single site must save on disk all incoming transactions to resolve potential conflicts with the unavailable site.

In a peer-to-peer environment, backup and restore operations also become extremely complex. Because there is no official value for each piece of data at any point in time, there is no fast way to restore the entire replication system in case of failure. Data may be floating between writes for hours until conflicts are resolved.

Conflict Avoidance. In many cases, the nature of the application is such that transaction conflicts are not even an issue. In a human resources example, every site can have access to the records relating to every employee in the company. But if the branch office to which the employee reports is the only location that will change the records relating to that employee, then there is no possibility of conflict. In other cases, transaction sequence is inconsequential because the updates are cumulative, in which the end result will be the same regardless of the order in which the transactions are performed (as with some debit/credit transactions, or transactions involving inserts that are unique).

It is also possible to address the concurrency control issues within the application design itself by designing the application to avoid conflicts or by compensating for conflicts when they occur. Conflict avoidance ensures that all transactions are unique — that updates only originate from one site at a time. Schemas can be fragmented in such a manner as to ensure conflict avoidance. In addition, each site can be assigned a slice of time for delivering updates, thereby avoiding conflicts by establishing a business practice.

Special Considerations for Disaster Recovery

One of the most common uses of replication is to replicate transactions to a backup system for the purpose of disaster recovery. However, users are advised to pay close attention to several issues relating to the use of replication for disaster recovery.

In a high-volume transaction environment, many transactions that have occurred at the primary system may be lost in flight and will need to be reentered into the backup system. When the primary fails, how will the lost transactions be identified so that they can be reentered? How will the users be switched over to the backup? The backup system will have a different network address, requiring users to manually log in to the backup and restart their applications.

Is there a documented process for users and administrators to follow in the event of a disaster? Once the primary is recovered, is there a clean mechanism for switching users back to the primary? In the best-case scenario, it should be possible to switch the roles of the systems, making the backup the new primary and making the primary the new backup once it is recovered. This practice eliminates the need to switch all users back to the original configuration.

Special Consideration for Network Failures

Although the availability of data is enhanced through replication because there is a local copy of data, users must understand the implications of extended network failures. Network failures can cause replicate databases to quickly drift apart because local updates are not being propagated. If the application is sensitive to the sequence of transactions originating at various replicate sites, then extended network failures may cause local processing to shut down, nullifying any perceived benefit to data availability through replication.

In addition, once the network is available again, a carefully reconciliation of all the replicate databases must be performed, paying close attention to the sequencing of transactions originating from different systems. This process of reconciliation can encounter many replication conflicts and is subject to all the caveats associated with conflict detection and resolution.

Replication and Triggers at the Target System

Replication can interfere with the normal operation of database triggers used to enforce business rules and integrity constraints. Consider a situation in which a transaction at a primary site causes trigger scripts to be invoked. The direct effect of the transaction is replicated — but so are the effects of the trigger scripts. At the replicate site, if the same trigger scripts exist, they are invoked again as a result of the changes caused by the transaction. Hence, the trigger scripts actually affect the replicate site twice, leading to an unpredictable outcome.

To avoid this integrity issue, the target database must provide a mechanism for suppressing trigger scripts in the case of replicated changes.

SUMMARY

Replication is appropriately used for various problem areas. However, success with replication depends heavily on up-front work done toward resolving department issues and application design considerations. In particular:

- The implications of data latency must be carefully considered.
- Conflict avoidance is the safest way to implement replication, averting numerous perils associated with conflict detection and resolution.

Careful consideration of these factors can lead to the expected levels of payback from the benefits of replication.

Chapter 49
Secure Information Through a Replicated Architecture

Judith N. Froscher

INFORMATION TECHNOLOGY AND AUTOMATION PLAY A MAJOR ROLE in all aspects of an enterprise's business and operations. Computing cycles are cheaper, and computational capability has increased, although the costs of reengineering legacy information processing systems and business processes have delayed the benefits that many enterprises hope to realize.

Nevertheless, investment in the enterprise's information infrastructure and migration to open, distributed access to information have begun. Once these reengineering hurdles are overcome, everyone in the enterprise will have access to consistent information from many heterogeneous data sources, and the enterprise can realize the benefits of its investment and achieve a technological advantage. Modern data management systems play a major role in this endeavor and depend on replication for distributed data access, fault tolerance, availability, and reliability.

Every enterprise has secrets. Global access poses a significant threat to enterprise secrets. For example, aspects of personnel, payroll, finances, planning, marketing, new products, product liability, production problems, research results, test results, and efficiency are sensitive information and need to be protected. Conventional approaches to protecting this information are not effective in environments that are open and seek to provide global access.

This chapter explores these issues of secrecy and how replication can help to provide strong protection against compromise. In particular, the Secure INformation Through the Replicated Architecture (SINTRA) project has demonstrated this approach through various prototypes. Application of SINTRA to an operational application is described, the benefits of the approach examined, and plans for research and development discussed.

639

CONSEQUENCES OF OPENNESS

An assumption for this discussion is that the information systems supporting an enterprise have migrated to client/server computing environments, and that the enterprise is reengineering its internal processes to make better use of its resources and available information to improve its effectiveness. However, everyone may also have access to critical data needed to achieve the goals of the enterprise, and thus expose the enterprise itself to unnecessary risk.

This migration process is the most difficult part of the enterprise's transition, yet is necessary to take advantage of new technology that can advance the goals of the enterprise. The migration and reengineering problem is not only a technology issue, but also affects what jobs are needed and which personnel can most effectively perform those jobs. Data protection is part of the enterprise reengineering problem as well.

Everyone has access to all the data needed for a given job. However, everyone may also have access to all the critical data needed to achieve the goals of the enterprise and thus places the enterprise at risk. During the reengineering process, an enterprise is especially vulnerable to both insider threats and attacks from competitors, suppliers, and other outsiders.

The Challenge: Protect Data Yet Make It Accessible

The enterprise must protect its secrets. Prior to more open computing environments, these secrets were probably safe because few people accessed the systems containing them and the systems were not connected. Perhaps the data was not even electronically stored.

As a first step, the enterprise must identify secrets and how critical these secrets are. Some secrets will be more important than others and will be sensitive for different reasons. For example, competitors must not be able to access research results that can lead to the development of new products and markets. Employees should not be able to change their own performance data. The requirement to protect data managed by an information processing system is not new; however, the need to protect data and at the same time allow authorized users access to data they need in a distributed computing environment challenges earlier solutions.

Deciding which data is sensitive and to what degree is a difficult task because objective criteria for deciding secrecy are often unavailable. Identification of secrets for each major process of an enterprise can simplify this exercise and is necessary to determine who needs access to which data. However, the major processes identified at the beginning of the reengineering process may change as the enterprise itself changes. Hence, making decisions about data sensitivity and who needs access are continuing aspects

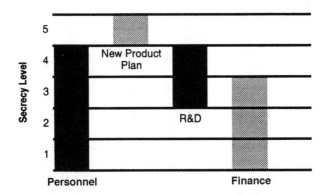

Exhibit 49.1. Enterprise data organization.

of information technology itself and need to become part of the data management process.

Data Engineering. Data engineering plays a primary role in the migration process. To migrate to client/server computing architectures, the data needed to support major operational or task areas of the enterprise must be identified. Servers are developed that manage and manipulate data to support the enterprise. Data may then become available to other task areas. Task areas themselves may change because of improved data access. Secrecy is another organizing criteria for enterprise data and is orthogonal to the task area organization. Exhibit 49.1 depicts some example task areas and secrecy levels for an enterprise.

Identifying Authorized Users. Once the data has been organized so that it is accessible and its consistency can be maintained, users authorized for access must be identified. Certainly, users must have access to the data they need to do their jobs. However, the users who need to access more secret data should be minimized and the enterprise should have some confidence that those users will not compromise the more sensitive data. The enterprise needs a means to determine whether an individual employee can be trusted. A person's past employment and personal history is one indicator of character. Background investigations and length of service with the enterprise can be used to establish the trustworthiness of employees.

Creating Computing Enclaves. Enterprise secrets and users authorized for their access can be grouped into a computing enclave. The most secret enclave is physically separate from enclaves containing less sensitive data.

Within enclaves, employees working on closely related tasks can form smaller groups or work domains. Work domains cross secrecy enclaves, and work domains in higher enclaves may need access to work domain data in lower enclaves. High-level users may send requests to lower-level work domain servers to access the data they need. This seemingly innocent communication poses a threat to enterprise secrets, however. A disgruntled employee could pass information protected in the high enclave to the lower work domain server making a request. Worse yet, rogue software could reside in the high enclave and could send information to lower work domain servers, where many more, less trustworthy people have access.

Some enterprises may never connect their information systems outside the enterprise. However, other enterprises must protect their secrets from insider/outsider threats and malicious code, which can encode sensitive information in a query or send information directly to less sensitive information servers as part of a message. All software is vulnerable to these kinds of attack.

Data replication allows users access to information at remote sites and provides fault tolerance in the event that another site becomes inoperable. For quite similar reasons, replication of data in low enclaves to higher enclave servers provides users in high enclaves access to the information they need to do their job without compromise. Because users in different enclaves access only their copy of data at different levels of secrecy, replication thwarts rogue software and attempts by malicious users to leak secrets. Hence, replication used as part of a protection approach enables tolerance of malicious software or users.

Physical separation and replication do not solve all security problems. Each component of an enclave must provide its own authentication and audit mechanisms. To ensure privacy, encryption may be used to pass information through the communication infrastructure. Within enclaves, different work domains may enforce different access policies. If compromise occurs, the effects are confined to the enclave, where everyone is equally trusted. Further attempts to gain unauthorized access can be detected and monitored.

Exhibit 49.2 illustrates a possible computing environment with three levels of secrecy. Each server represents a different work domain; the upward arrows represent a means by which low data is replicated to more secret enclaves.

MULTILEVEL SECURE (MLS) APPROACH TO DATABASE SECURITY

This discussion of protecting secrecy demonstrates the vulnerability of information systems to rogue software. If a business relies on software to preserve secrecy, then it must be convinced that the reliance is justified.

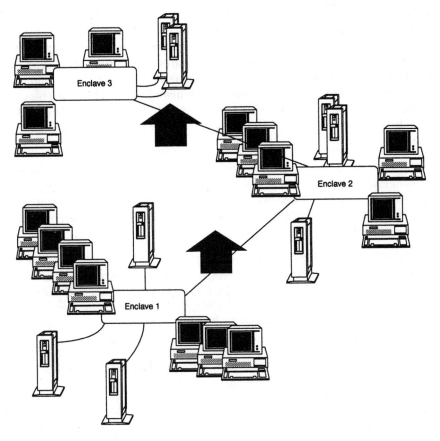

Exhibit 49.2. Enterprise enclave processing.

Formal methods, rigorous software engineering, testing, peer review, independent adversarial evaluation, and penetration testing contribute to assurance that software is dependable. Once the software is declared dependable, the vigil to protect the software against the introduction of any malicious code begins. However, assurance that software can be trusted and its trustworthiness maintained is quite expensive.

The SINTRA project exploits declining hardware and software costs to avoid the development of costly, high-assurance software and provide a high-assurance, multilevel secure (MLS) database service. Multilevel secure refers to a mechanism that allows users of varying degrees of trust to have access to computerized data and programs for which they are authorized, yet prevents them from gaining access to those for which they are not authorized.

DATA REPLICATION

Replicating Low Data to High Databases

The philosophy of protection for SINTRA is strongly influenced by the need to minimize the amount of software, both trusted and untrusted, that runs on a high-assurance, painstakingly crafted, trusted product while at the same time preserving full database capability without introducing security vulnerabilities. No protection mechanism is more effective than absolute separation; however, the need to provide access to low data for more trustworthy users led to the notion that low data be replicated to high databases.

The strength of the approach lies in the simple observation that if low data enclave users do not have access to the same copies of low data that high data enclave users access, then malicious code cannot be effective in signaling high information to low users. Hence, the replicated architecture can tolerate malicious code attacks.

In the SINTRA approach, a database exists for each hierarchical security level and contains all data at that level and below. Because each database contains only information to which a user has legitimate access, untrusted database management systems can be used. Each database resides on a separate data server. The authentication procedure for each server controls whether the user can access the data stored in that database.

When the low database is modified, the update must be propagated to higher-level databases securely and consistently. The only information flow required by this approach is from low to high — an inherently secure flow. In this way, SINTRA limits opportunities for malicious code in untrusted applications to exploit system vulnerabilities. The technical difficulty with this approach is to ensure the consistency of the replicas without introducing a vulnerability that could be exploited.

Once an update is made in a less secret data server, it cannot be rolled back because a more secret server is unable to make the update. If the rollback were allowed, rogue software could manipulate the completion of these updates to signal more secret information to less secret servers.

This read-at-high, write-at-low channel is a problem for all data separation mechanisms and impacts database schedulers in all approaches to database security. A primary objective of this project has been to discover a transaction management scheme that does not require modification of the commercial data management systems on each server. The approach, how the replica control problem was solved, and the prototype are documented in numerous reports. SINTRA research results suggest that accepting the replica consistency problem in return for a virtually free high-assurance, strong protection mechanism is a choice well made.

644

Controlled Propagation

Because each data server contains data from less secret servers, update queries have to be propagated to more secret servers to maintain the consistency and currency of the replicated data. If the propagation of update queries is not carefully controlled, inconsistent database states can be created among the distributed servers.

Consider two lower-level update transactions T_i and T_j that are scheduled with serialization order $<T_i, T_j>$ at the less secret data server. Because these two transactions are update transactions, they have to be propagated to the next more secret data server. If these two transactions are scheduled with serialization order $<T_j, T_i>$ at the next more secret data server, an inconsistent database state between these two servers may be created by the execution of conflicting operations at the more secret server.

Even the serialization order of nonconflicting transactions has to be maintained to preserve one-copy serializability. This is a parallel result that has been reported in the context of multidatabase systems. Hence, the serialization order introduced by the local scheduler in the commercial data management system where the update was initiated must be maintained in the more secret servers.

Earlier SINTRA prototypes depended on a trusted replica controller that used either a read-down or write-up capability and a Naval Research Laboratory (NRL) implementation of a global scheduler on a high-assurance trusted product. The spirit of the SINTRA approach is to be able to use commercially available products. When Sybase introduced a replication server that used such a scheduling scheme, it became part of the prototyping effort. However, both forward and backward communication exists between the primary site database and the replicate database with the commercial product. The trusted replica controller also requires a one-way communication device that must satisfy two equally important kinds of requirements:

- Security requirements (e.g., no information flow from high to low)
- Database replication requirements for functional capabilities (e.g., reliability, recoverability, and performance)

A Trusted Replication Component and Buffer. Even though blind write-up and read-down methods may satisfy the security requirements, they do not satisfy the database replication requirements. The NRL Pump is a device that balances these conflicting requirements (Exhibit 49.3).

The Pump places a nonvolatile buffer (size n) between low and high data enclaves and sends acknowledgement code (ACK) to low data enclaves at probabilistic times, based on a moving average of the past m high ACK

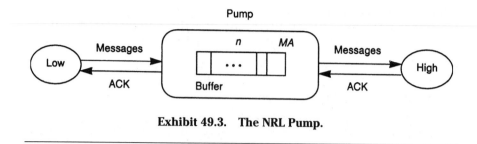

Exhibit 49.3.   The NRL Pump.

times. A high ACK time is the time it takes for the buffer to send a message to high and for high to return an ACK. By sending ACKs to low data enclaves at a rate related to high data's historical response rate, the Pump provides flow control and reliable delivery without unduly penalizing performance.

It is important to emphasize that ACKs are not passed through the Pump from high to low data enclaves. In fact, the Pump can acknowledge receipt of messages from low data before high data receives them because of the Pump's buffering capability. Each ACK sent to a low data enclave is generated internally by the Pump only in response to a message from low. The average rate at which these ACKs are sent from the Pump to a low data enclave reflects the average rate at which a high enclave acknowledges messages from the Pump.

The rate of the ACKs from the Pump to low data enclaves represents a downward flow of information. However, the algorithm controlling the rate at which acknowledgments are returned is parameterized to allow the capacity of the timing channel to be made as small as may be required.

Several prototypes of the NRL Pump have been developed to support SINTRA applications, and the basic concept has been expanded to address the complications of fairness and denial of service in a network.

A BUILDING BLOCK FOR SECURE SYSTEMS ENGINEERING

In a cooperative, distributed computing environment, the Pump becomes a building block for secure systems engineering. In effect, security can be integrated without the organization having to worry about whether some feature of the desired system is protection critical, because the protection mechanisms are completely separated from the system's conventional features.

The security engineering and assurance techniques required to develop such a high-assurance building block are affordable in this approach because a Pump can be used with commercial replication products and data management products. The most difficult technical aspect of the SINTRA approach to database security is the development of the interfaces or wrappers needed between the Pump and the commercial products. Wrapper development has become an essential skill for building distributed systems.

A Sample Application

The development of wrappers to permit the use of the SINTRA approach for the Joint Maritime Command Information System (JMCIS) has been the focus of one prototyping activity. JMCIS is an integrated Navy C4I system used for tracking ships and planning missions. Most JMCIS installations have two systems: a less classified (low) JMCIS system and a more secret (high) JMCIS system.

The low and high systems each include its own copy of the Central Database Server (CDBS). Users at each level update their local CDBSs independently, although updates to the low system are provided periodically to the high-level system using tape. The current mode of operation does not permit users of highly secret systems to use less classified CDBS updates promptly or consistently.

The SINTRA approach offers an automated solution for this problem. The conventional solution for this problem is the installation of a bidirectional guard processor between the high and low systems. These guard systems typically require a human reviewer to monitor traffic that is passed, since information moves in both directions. The SINTRA approach does not require any alterations in the basic operation or the computing platforms of the systems. Instead, a small set of untrusted software, the Pump, and the Sybase replication server automatically replicate selected data from low databases to high databases as low updates are made, while preserving the secrecy of the high data.

This application of the SINTRA approach illustrates how strong protection can be obtained without changing the database design, the data servers, or applications. As long as transactions can be defined for any legacy systems, the application of the SINTRA approach results in a secure confederation of legacy system enclaves. Enhanced availability of data can be achieved by assigning labels to a finer granularity of data. For example, secrecy labels can be assigned to each element of a tuple in a relation. This fine-grained labeling is a capability that can be obtained in the SINTRA approach and has been demonstrated in prototypes.

BENEFITS OF THE REPLICATED ARCHITECTURE

SINTRA offers many benefits over conventional approaches to database security.

Resistance to Rogue Software. The architecture is resistant to rogue software attacks because authorized users access only their copy of less secret data. The trusted replication component, the Pump, is analogous to encryption for secure communication: the Pump allows any enterprise to take advantage of readily available information technology while still protecting the secrecy of their information. This is unlike conventional approaches that require the development of a trusted version of the desired technology. Under the best conditions, untrusted mission-critical applications must be modified to satisfy the constraints of the product, and both the trusted product and the application software must be placed under constant vigil to protect against the introduction of rogue software, which can leak protected information. Any software that runs on these platforms can be infected and can pass data through information channels available in every trusted product.

(Relatively) Uncomplicated Database Distribution. SINTRA does not solve all the issues associated with database distribution and heterogeneity. However, it does not make distribution and heterogeneity more complex.

Unlike conventional database security approaches, SINTRA distributed data management can use solutions found for conventional databases primarily because these solutions can be applied level by level. The lifecycle costs of the SINTRA approach to database security are similar to conventional database lifecycle costs. The lifetime vigil to protect against the introduction of malicious software is not required for a SINTRA solution. There are minimal trusted components, and upgrades can be made to the data management technology without disturbing the trustworthiness of the system.

Ability to Meet Security and Operational Requirements. Probably most important, however, the SINTRA approach allows the secure use of current advances in information technology. The use of trusted replica controllers for connecting components securely allows users and developers to concentrate their information technology resources on implementing systems that satisfy operational requirements rather than focusing on security. The approach easily scales to accommodate new data servers and can be inserted without disruption to the operation of an organization.

FUTURE PLANS

The operational need for a high-assurance MLS database management system has resulted in the use of the SINTRA approach in the Global Transportation System, a joint service data management system that tracks all the platforms in the Services. The relative ease with which security can be integrated into an operational solution has prompted several DoD organizations to initiate SINTRA implementations of their operational systems. In particular, DoD's maps and images will become available to users at different security levels through this approach. Several pilot programs that will use a SINTRA implementation for major command and control and tactical combat systems are underway at present.

SUMMARY

Enterprises that rely on distributed computing require software that can be trusted to enforce multilevel security requirements. The SINTRA approach to database security relies on physical separation to provide strong protection and replication to allow users with different security authorizations access to data created at a less restricted security level.

Because this approach exploits distribution and replication to provide a secure data management service, it allows critical information systems to exploit commercial advances in data management technology and to protect sensitive information at the same time. Each node in a SINTRA confederation is a commercially available data management system, but the confederation itself is secure. A simple, strong, reliable store-and-forward device provides the protection-critical component and is reusable with other transactional systems. The SINTRA approach provides an affordable, strong approach to the protection of critical information and allows both government and commercial enterprises to take advantage of the commercial investment in information technology.

Section X
Data and the Internet, Intranets, and the Web

THE POPULARITY OF THE INTERNET, INTRANET, AND THE WORLD WIDE WEB has created the need to access databases through these architectures. This section contains five chapters that explore techniques for connecting data stores to the Internet, intranet, and the World Wide Web.

Chapter 50, "Developing Client/Server RDBMS Applications Using Java Servlets and JDBC," demonstrates how to develop and deploy a three-tier application using Java Servlets.

Chapter 51, "Knowledge Management on the Internet: The Web/Business Intelligence Solution," discusses how to use technologies such as CORBA, IIOP, Java, XML, and Web-enabled intelligence tools to leverage the Internet infrastructure to build Web/business intelligence solutions.

Chapter 52, "Building Database-Enabled Web Applications with IDC," provides a substantial example for creating Web pages that are refreshed directly from live databases and database servers. This technique uses basic SQL statements and a minimal amount of HTML coding. Internet Database Connector (IDC) provides the toolset for doing this.

Chapter 53, "Intranets: Notes vs. the Internet," examines notes-based intranets, browser-based intranets, and a hybrid environment in the context of information dissemination.

Chapter 54, "Web-Enabled Data Warehouses," describes data warehouse access through the Web. Some of the unique aspects of Web-enabled data warehouses include special access controls, integrating the architecture with browsers, and infrastructure issues. This chapter describes design and implementation considerations for such warehouses. With the emergence of the Web, there will be a great need for this technology.

Chapter 50

Developing Client/Server RDBMS Applications Using Java Servlets and JDBC

Jonathan Held

CLIENT/SERVER COMPUTING IS BY NO MEANS A NOVEL CONCEPT; it has been around nearly as long as the computer. What is new, however, is how the rise of the World Wide Web (circa 1992) impacted this computing concept. Client/server computing, given this venue, has reached new ground and its popularity is indelibly tied to the astounding success that the Internet has seen. What makes the Web so attractive, in part, is the price — client software is free. Using Netscape's Communicator or Microsoft's Internet Explorer (or any other capable browser), one can get a multitude of information on virtually any subject. The information has to be stored somewhere, and, in most cases, it is kept in a relational database management system (RDBMS), with which the browser (translate as client) interacts.

What is needed:

- •Some prior knowledge of the Java programming language and Structured Query Language (SQL)
- •Java Development Kit (JDK) 1.2
- •Microsoft Access (MSACCESS)
- •Sun's Servlet Software Development Kit (SDK)
- •Web server software

If you think Web-based databases haven't caught on, you might want to reconsider. Consider the Web search sites (Lycos, Yahoo, Excite, Metacrawler, Webcrawler, or Hotbot, to name a few); where do you think the "hits" come from?

If you are as much of an Internet junkie as I am, you may even go so far as to check online to see what movies are playing in your local area. Two online sites offer such information http://www.movielink.com and http://www.moviefinder.com   Enter zip code, click the mouse a couple of times, and find out what movies are playing at local theaters and their show times. Why pick up the phone, call the theater, and get a recording that you can barely hear? If you would rather stay at home and park yourself on the couch with a bag of potato chips, try http://www.tvguide.com and you can choose the television listings available by cable company. So, if you were purchasing the Sunday paper just for the *TV Week* magazine that came with it, cancel your subscription, and save yourself some money.

These examples all have several things in common. The first is that the Web browser is the client application. As a developer, you can now breathe a sigh of relief knowing that you can completely concentrate your programming efforts on the server-side interface to the data repository.

So how does it all work? Well, the short (and extremely simplified) answer is that the client, you and your browser, initiate a process that somehow interacts with the back-end database. This process is also responsible for returning content back to the browser, although what it returns may vary on what action was being performed. If you are merely submitting personal information about yourself or making an entry into a guest book, the response might simply consist of a confirmation that the information was successfully entered into the database.

As you can probably well imagine, there are a number of technologies available today that would allow us to accomplish such tasks. We could opt to adopt Common Gateway Interface (CGI) scripts, but this option is replete with security risks, making it an unattractive solution to even experienced programmers. Active Server Pages (ASP), a Microsoft technology designed to operate in conjunction with that company's Internet Information Server (IIS) 4.0, is another possibility, but it locks us into an operating system and a Web server that our Internet service provider (ISP) might not be using. Of course, there are a number of other options available, but perhaps one of the better but less explored ones is made possible by Java servlets and JDBC™.

THE JAVA INCENTIVE

There are two key requirements for database programmers:

- They must have intimate knowledge of the language construct used to manipulate databases.
- They need to be cognizant of what means are available for invoking these constructs from external applications.

Of course, the syntax for performing the former task is accomplished by a data query language that is now universal across different computer systems — Structured Query Language (SQL). SQL is neither difficult to learn nor use; rather, it is the means of using SQL in programs that, until recently, presented the greater challenge.

At first, many database applications were developed by making Open Database Connectivity (ODBC) Application Programming Interface (API) calls. But despite all that Microsoft's ODBC allowed you to do, it wasn't without its own problems. Chief among these were the following:

- ODBC was written exclusively in the C programming language, so there was no concept of objects or methods. The logical organization that is intrinsic to Object-Oriented Programming (OOP) was nowhere to be found, resulting in a great deal of frustration when you were trying to find the right procedure or function to call.
- The API was extremely large, hard to follow, and required a fair amount of knowledge on the part of the programmer.

These shortcomings were noted and Microsoft proceeded to create several object models that programmers could use instead. These new collections of objects and methods were ODBC wrappers; they encapsulated calls into the ODBC API and hid the implementation details from the programmer. They exist today in the form of Data Access Objects (DAO), Remote Data Objects (RDO), and the more recent ActiveX Data Objects (ADO), as illustrated in Exhibit 50.1.

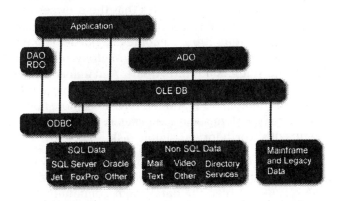

Exhibit 50.1.   Comparison of ADO, DAO, and RDO.

Then came Sun Microsystems and the rise of Java. Java made many new promises, but what made it so attractive was that it was designed to offer a secure (or more secure) programming environment and could run on any platform regardless of the operating system being used. Now, if one could create a Java database application, the days of porting programs from one machine to another were all but gone. The only problem was that Java, like all new things, was extremely immature and no part of the core language had database-enabled applications. That shortcoming was noticed and fixed with the subsequent release of the *java.sql* package, which contains the JDBC™ object model. The JDBC™ API became the mechanism by which programmers bridged the gap between their applications and databases. It defines a number of Java classes that allow programmers to issue SQL statements and process the results, dynamically learn about a database's schema etc. It is by far one of the easier to understand object models, and it is nearly effortless to incorporate it into Java applications.

THE PROJECT

So what is it that we're going to set out to do? Let's suppose we wanted to create a fortune/quotation server that interacts with a Microsoft Access database and returns an entry and five lucky, random numbers back to the client's browser. We're going to create this application and support this functionality using Java and JDBC™, but one more thing is needed that requires us to make some development decisions.

We could create an applet that is downloaded by the browser and provides a user interface enabling information retrieval from the database. However, this solution has some notable drawbacks. First and foremost, to use an applet and interact with a database requires a JDBC™ driver. There are many types of commercially available drivers, but they are prohibitively expensive and a project of this scope does not justify the expense. Another disadvantage to using these drivers is that they typically consist of a large number of class files. The more files that the browser has to download over a slow connection, the more irate clients will get at using the system, eventually abandoning it if it becomes to burdensome (i.e., time-consuming) to use. We could opt to use Sun Microsystem's JDBC™-ODBC bridge, which is free, but it is not thread-safe. And unfortunately, incorporating this driver into an applet requires that we take some additional steps to make it a trusted component. So now we have to explore how we can manipulate the browser's built-in security manager so it works, and this is far more trouble than it's worth for our simple task.

A final disadvantage of using applets is that they can only make connections back to the machine from which they were downloaded. This means that if we use a JDBC™ driver, the database it communicates with must be co-located with the Web server. It is possible to use a proxy server to circumvent this restriction, but, short of doing this, we should see if an easier solution exists (after all, why make more work for ourselves than is necessary?)

The solution we'll use that enables us to get around all of these potential pitfalls is the Java servlet. The servlet concept was first introduced in April of 1997, in conjunction with the first all-Java Web server. Servlets are protocol and platform independent server-side components. You can think of them as an applet for a server. They are almost identical to their CGI counterparts, and they can do anything that CGI can do. But servlets differ in several ways: they are easier to write than CGI programs/scripts written in C++ or PERL, and they are noticeably faster and much safer. There are four important reasons why we'll turn our attention to the servlet solution:

- *Performance:* Servlets do not require a new process for each request (CGI does, and if a server fails to load-balance or put a limit on the number of concurrent requests, it can easily be brought to its knees). The servlet *init()* method allows programmers to perform resource-intensive operations common to all servlet invocations once at startup. For example, by having the *init()* method establish a database connection, this process can be done once. Consequently, the slowest performance occurs the very first time the servlet is executed; subsequent invocations occur much more rapidly.
- *Portability:* Because Java is platform independent, so are servlets. We can move our compiled servlet code from one machine to another without having to recompile, and we can use our code with many different types of Web servers.
- *Security:* Servlets have the Java advantage — memory access and strong typing violations are simply not possible. By default, all servlets are untrusted components and they are not allowed to perform operations such as accessing network services or local files unless they are digitally signed and accorded more freedom by manipulating Java's security manager.
- *Flexibility:* Although servlets are written in Java, their clients can be written in any programming language. Servlets can be written as clients to other services that are written in any programming language. For example, we can use them with JDBC to contact a RDBMS. They can process data submitted via an HTML form, allow collaboration between people by synchronizing requests to support systems, such as online conferencing, and pass requests to other servlets to load-balance the amount of work that a system or servlet is performing.

With all these good things going for us, we should be convinced that servlets are a viable option for our project. The only part that remains now is to put this thing together, but that is where the fun begins.

THE BACK-END DATABASE

Creating the database for this project was by no means a difficult process, but it was time-consuming to populate it with 700 fortunes/quotations. Fortunately, should you decide to put this project together on your own personal computer, you can just download the Microsoft Access database. To give you an appreciation of what was done and how, we'll briefly outline the database's schema, and how we used and configured the control panel ODBC applet.

The fortune database has only one table. This table has two fields:

- a *Fortune_ID*
- a *Fortune*

The *Fortune_ID* is a unique, self-generated autonumber that is indexed and serves as the table's primary key. The *Fortune*, as you might expect, is a text entry of up to 200 characters that holds all the wise adages we'll be delivering to the client. Exhibit 50.2 is a screen capture of the database design view as it appears in Microsoft Access, and Exhibit 50.3 shows you the datasheet view.

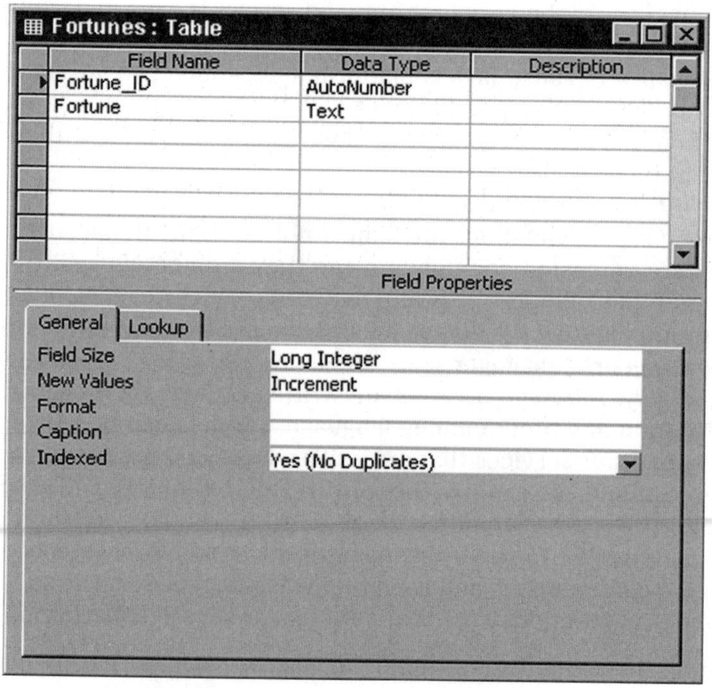

Exhibit 50.2.   The *Fortunes* table schema.

▦ Fortunes : Table	_ □ ✕
Fortune_ID	**Fortune**
► 93	It is unwise to be too sure of one's own wisdom. It is healthy to be re
94	In the attitude od silence the soul finds the path in an clearer light, a
95	Adaptability is not initation. It means power of resistance and assum
96	It is the quality of our work which will please God and not the quanti
97	Honest differences are often a healthy sign of progress
98	A keen sense of humor helps us to overlook the unbecoming, under
99	Hot heads and cold hearts never solved anything.
100	Most of us follow our conscience as we follow a wheelbarrow. We p
101	The test of a preacher is that his congregation hgoes away saying,
102	Comfort and prosperty have never enriched the world as much as a
103	Abstaining is favorable both to the head and the pocket
104	Fame usually comes to those who are thinking of something else.
105	Common sense is very uncommon
106	Journalism will kill you, but it will keep you alive while you're at it
107	Fame is vapor, popularity an accident, riches take wings. Only one

Record: ⏮ ◀ 1 ▶ ⏭ ▶* of 700

Exhibit 50.3.   The *Fortunes* table datasheet view.

We now need to decide where to place the Access database in the file system. Because we intend to use our database from the Web, We might be inclined at first to move it to where all our other Web files are located. A better solution, though, is to place the *.mdb* Access file in a directory named *Internet Databases* (or whatever name you choose) that resides entirely elsewhere. This is a good practice in general, especially for security reasons (we don't want someone downloading our database, do we?).

To do this, create your directory. Once this is completed, open the Windows Control Panel and double click on the ODBC icon as shown in Exhibit 50.4.

ODBC

Exhibit 50.4.   The ODBC control panel applet (also listed as ODBC data sources [32-bit] in Windows 98).

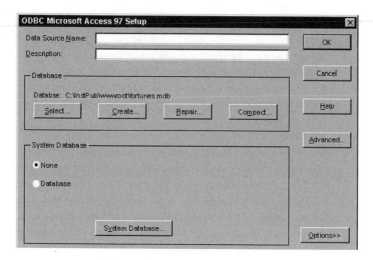

Exhibit 50.5. Configuring the ODBC data source.

This should display a tabbed dialog box appropriately titled *Data Source Administrator.* We use this program to inform the system of data source names and locations; we'll use it in our servlet programs to refer to the database we wish to manipulate with SQL statements. Once you have placed the fortune database in a directory, select the *System DSN* tab and click *Add.* You'll be prompted for the type of driver for which you want to set up a data source. Since we're using an Access database, we want the Microsoft Access driver. Click *Finish*, and you should then be directed to a new dialog titled *ODBC Microsoft Access Setup.* Here, there are two pieces of information which we have to provide:

- The name of the data source
- The location of the database

In Exhibit 50.5 above, the data source name is *Quotation_DB*, and it is located on the C drive, in the *wwwroot* subdirectory of the *InetPub* directory. You indicate this path by clicking the *Select* button and manually locating the *.mdb* file. With this step of the process successfully completed, you are one third of the way in creating the client/server application.

THE HTML FRONT-END

We now need to provide a Web interface through which the client will interact with the database we have set up. The easiest and quickest way to do this is by using a form on an HTML page. Forms enable page authors, such as us, a means of requesting and then processing user input. Every form is submitted to the server via a method specified by the *ACTION* attribute. This attribute can have one of two values:

- *GET:* This operation sends name/value pairs for each form element appended to the end of the URL. Each name/value pair is encoded and separated by an ampersand before being sent to the server.
- *POST:* Data are transmitted to the server via the standard-input, i.e., via HyperText Transfer Protocol (HTTP) headers. Information can be posted only to files that are executable, e.g., CGI scripts.

To demonstrate how this works, we'll create two forms — one that uses the *GET* method to get a fortune/quotation and five lucky numbers, and one that uses the *POST* method to search the database for a particular keyword. The HTML source code is displayed in Exhibit 50.6, and Exhibit 50.7 illustrates what you should see in your browser.

THE MIDDLEWARE

In a two-tier client/server system, the business logic is either contained in a user interface like an applet, or it resides within the database on the server (e.g., a set of stored procedures). Alternatively, it can be in both locations. Two-tier systems are slightly more complex to manage because they are not as modular as systems which successfully separate the application and business logic from each other and the data. Our servlet project is a three-tier example that does just this. Here, the application logic (user interface) we don't even need to worry about — Microsoft, Netscape, and others have done the work for us. The servlet is the business logic which is going to mediate access between the client and the RDBMS. The servlet can be considered middleware, a vague term that refers to all the software needed to support interactions between clients and servers.

The first thing we're going to do before we even write a servlet, however, is to concentrate on the Fortune/Quotation server. The code for this project component is shown in Exhibit 50.8.

How Does the Server Work?

Let us examine the code and get a general idea of what's going on here, and how this component can be used in conjunction with servlets to complement our project. First, notice that the *FortuneServer* class is a subclass of *Thread*. This means that it has all of the *Thread* methods and data members, and the methods will remain as written unless we explicitly override them by redefining their behavior. The server is going to be a multithreaded process so it can capably handle many concurrent requests.

The *FortuneServer* begins by executing code contained in its *main()* method. It is here that we simply create a new *FortuneServer*, and then start

Exhibit 50.6.   Raw HTML source code.

```html
<html>
<head>
<meta http-equiv="Content-Type"
content="text/html; charset=iso-8859-1">
<title>So you want a fortune?</title>
</head>
<body bgcolor="#000080">
<CENTER><font color="#FFFFFF" size="6">700 Quotations/Fortunes as of
    10/19/98!!!</font></p></CENTER><BR>
<form action="127.0.0.1:8080/servlet/FortuneClientServlet" method="GET">
<CENTER><font color="#FF0000" size="5"><strong>So you want a
    fortune/quotation, huh? Don't we all... <br>
We got good ones and bad ones, so take a chance and grab one (or
    many)...</strong></font></CENTER><BR>
<CENTER>
<input type="submit" name="B1" value="I'm daring enough to push this
    button!">
</CENTER>
</form>

<form action="127.0.0.1:8080/servlet/QuoteSearch" method="POST">
<table border="0" width="100%">
    <tr>
        <td><CENTER><font color="#FFFF00" size="5"><strong>ADDED 10/20/98:
            SEARCH THE QUOTATION DATABASE BY KEYWORD!!!!<br>
        </strong></font><font color="#FF00FF" size="3"><strong>(Be patient,
            as the search may take some time.)</strong></font></CENTER>
        </td>
    </tr>
    <tr>
        <td><table border="0" width="100%">
            <tr>
                <td><CENTER><font color="#FF8040" size="5">Text you want to
                    search for:</font></p>
                </td></CENTER>
                <td><input type="text" size="38" name="keyword">
                </td>
            </tr>
        </table>
        </td>
    </tr>
    <tr>
        <td><CENTER><input type="submit" name="B1" value="Search!"></CENTER>
        </td>
    </tr>
</table>
</form>
</body>
</html>
```

the thread that the application just spawned. We should briefly look at the class constructor to see what happens when we create a new *FortuneServer* object. Here, the variable *queries*, a 700-element integer array, is created and its contents are initialized to 0. We're going to use this variable to keep track of how many times a particular fortune was displayed. In this manner, we can examine our logfile later to determine if we're really getting a

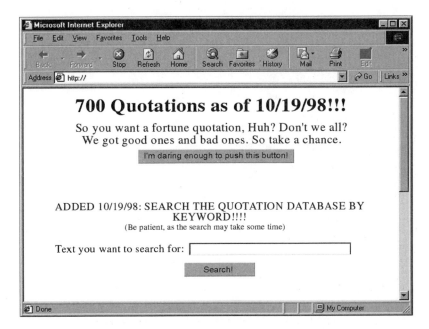

Exhibit 50.7.   Visual representation of the HTML displayed in Exhibit 50.6.

random, distributed return of fortunes. Once the array has been initialized, we need to get the server to bind to a port. We do this by creating a new *ServerSocket* called *fortuneSocket* and binding it to port 8888. If all is successful, you should see the message "Fortune server successfully bound to port 8888" when you run the program.

Of course, the next important step the server needs to make is to connect to the database. We could leave this task to the servlet, and do it once and only once in its *init()* method; however, it's just as appropriate for the *FortuneServer* to do this job on its own. This is exactly what happens in the *try/catch* block that follows. We load the *sun.jdbc.odbc.JdbcOdbcDriver* and then use a JDBC™ *Connection* object to connect to our remote data source. Notice that we specify what data source we want to use with a string. In our example, the string is set to "jdbc:odbc:Quotation_DB", where *jdbc* is the protocol, *odbc* is the subprotocol, and *Quotation_DB* is the name of the data source. Because the server is going to run on the same machine as the data source, there is no need for a host name or Internet Protocol (IP) address to let the application know where the database is. If this were not the case, i.e., there was physical separation between the server and the database, you would need to use a different driver and syntax.

This brings us to the *run()* method, where most threads contain the specialized code they are going to perform during their lifetime. Our *run()*

663

Exhibit 50.8.   The *FortuneServer* Java code.

```
import java.net.*;
import java.io.*;
import java.sql.*;
import RequestProcessor;
import WriteToFile;

/**
 * The FortuneServer object binds to port 8888 and waits for clients to
 * connect. When it receives a connection, it interprets this as a request
 * for a fortune and starts a  RequestProcessor thread to handle the
 * request.
 * Created October 15, 1998.
 * @author Jonathan S. Held
 * @version 1.0
 * @see RequestProcessor
 */
public class FortuneServer extends Thread {

    java.net.ServerSocket fortuneSocket = null;
    java.net.Socket clientSocket = null;
    java.lang.String url = "jdbc:odbc:Quotation_DB";
    java.sql.Connection con = null;
    java.sql.Statement stmt = null;
    static long numberOfRequests = 0;
    final int DB_SIZE = 700, DATA_DUMP = 50;
    static int queries[];

    /**
     * Class constructor
     * Creates a socket on port 8888 and binds to it. Attempts to load the
     * Sun bridge driver which is used to talk to the MSAccess database.
     * Enters into the log file fortune.log the date on which the log file
     * entries that follow were created.
     * @param none
     * @exception ClassNotFoundException thrown if the FortuneServer is
     * unable to load the Sun Jdbc-Odbc bridge driver
     * @exception SQLException thrown if the database url is unaccessible
     * @exception IOException thrown if unable to bind to port 8888 (e.g.,
     * the port is already in use by another process)
     */
    FortuneServer(){
        try {
            queries = new int[DB_SIZE];
            fortuneSocket = new ServerSocket(8888);
            System.runFinalizersOnExit(true);
            System.out.println("Fortune server successfully bound to port
                8888.");

            try {
                Class.forName("sun.jdbc.odbc.JdbcOdbcDriver");
                con = DriverManager.getConnection(url, "sa", "");
                stmt = con.createStatement();
                System.out.println("Established connection to database.");
                System.out.println("Awaiting client requests...");
                java.util.Calendar ts = java.util.Calendar.getInstance();
                java.lang.String info = new String("Log file created on " +
                    ts.getTime().toString());
                (new WriteToFile(info)).start();
```

Exhibit 50.8.   *(continued)*

```
        }
        catch (java.lang.ClassNotFoundException e1) {
            System.err.println(e1.toString());
        }
        catch (java.sql.SQLException e2){
            System.err.println(e2.toString());
        }
    }
    catch (java.io.IOException e3){
        System.err.println("Unable to bind to port 8888.");
        System.err.println(e3.toString());
        System.err.println("Hit any key to continue.");
        try {
            System.in.read();
        }
        catch (java.io.IOException e4){
            System.out.println(e4.toString());
        }
    }
}//end FortuneServer() constructor

/**
 * Uses the socket.accept() method to wait for an incoming request. The
 * server indicates how many requests it has processed, determines if
 * it needs to dump statistical information to the log file (currently
 * done after every 50 requests), and then starts a new
 * RequestProcessor thread to handle the request. The RequestProcessor
 * object is passed the client's socket information as well as a JDBC
 * statement object that is used to query the MSAccess database.
 * This method is run in a while(true) loop and can only be terminated
 * by system shutdown or CTRL-C.
 * @param none
 * @see RequestProcessor
 * @exception IOException thrown if unable to accept incoming client
 * requests
 * @return none
 */
private void runServer(){
    while (true){
        try {
            clientSocket = fortuneSocket.accept();
            System.out.println("Processing request number " +
                (++numberOfRequests));
            if (numberOfRequests % DATA_DUMP == 0)
                writeStatistics();
    (new RequestProcessor(clientSocket, stmt)).start();
        }
        catch (java.io.IOException e){
            System.out.println("Unable to fulfill fortune request.");
            System.out.println(e.toString());
        }
    }
}//end runServer()

/**
 * Creates a new FortuneServer object and calls the thread's start
 * method. @param args[] a series of command line arguments stored in
 * array; not used.
 * @exception none
```

(continues)

Exhibit 50.8. *(continued)*

```
 * @return none
 */
public static void main(String args[]){
    //start a new FortuneServer
    (new FortuneServer()).start();
}//end main()

/**
 * Called when the thread is started; calls the private utility method
 * runServer
 * @param none
 * @return void
 */
public void run(){
    runServer();
}//end run()

/**
 * responsible for creating a new WriteToFile object and writing
 * information to the  logfile fortune.log.
 * @param none
 * @see WriteToFile
 * @return void
 */
private void writeStatistics(){
    java.lang.StringBuffer statistics = new StringBuffer("Data Dump for
        " + Long.toString(numberOfRequests) + " requests: ");
    for (int ix=0; ix < DB_SIZE; ix++){
        statistics.append(Integer.toString(queries[ix]) + " ");
        if ((ix !=0) && (ix % 25 == 0))
            statistics.append(" | BREAK | ");
    }
    (new WriteToFile(statistics.toString())).start();
}//end writeStatistics()
}//end class FortuneServer
```

method is called *runServer()*, which waits for a client to connect. The *fortuneSocket accept()* method is a blocking call which keeps the program waiting here until that connection is made. Once a client binds to the port the server is listening on, another message appears that indicates what request number is being processed. A data dump of the *queries* variable into our logfile occurs every 50 requests (by making a call to *writeStatistics()*), and execution continues by turning over control to the *RequestProcessor* component. This allows the server to continue its job of waiting for requests, while some other part of the system processes the actual request and responds to the client. The *RequestProcessor* code is shown in Exhibit 50.9.

What Does the RequestProcessor Do?

The *RequestProcessor* is itself a thread, and the server spawns a new *RequestProcessor* thread for each new client request. Notice that this class does not have a *main()* method; rather, the object's *start()* method is called

Exhibit 50.9.   The *RequestProcessor* Java code.

```java
import java.net.*;
import java.io.*;
import java.sql.*;
import FortuneServer;
import java.util.Random;


/**
 * The RequestProcessor object is used by the FortuneServer to handle
 * client requests. This thread is created when the server needs to get a
 * quotation or fortune from the MSAccess database, generate five lucky
 * numbers, and send the information back to the FortuneClientServlet.
 * Created October 15, 1998.
 * @author Jonathan S. Held
 * @version 1.0
 * @see FortuneClientServlet
 */
public class RequestProcessor extends Thread {

    java.net.Socket cs = null;
    java.sql.Statement statement = null;
    final int MAX_FORTUNES = 700;
    final int LUCKY_NUMBERS = 5;
    final int LOTTERY_NUMBER_MAX_VALUE = 50;

    /**
     * Class constructor
     * @param clientSocket the socket the client attached from
     * @exception statement a JDBC Statement object associated with a
     * database connection; these parameters are passed from the
     * FortuneServer at the time a new RequestProcessor object is created
     */
    RequestProcessor(java.net.Socket clientSocket, java.sql.Statement
        stmt){
        cs = clientSocket;
        statement = stmt;
    }


    /**
     * Called when the RequestProcessor thread is started; run generates a
     * random number, selects the quotation from the database based on this
     * number, then makes creates random numbers; this information is sent
     * back to the FortuneClientServlet, which will then process it and
     * send it back to the client's browser.
     * @param none
     * @return void
     * @exception IOException thrown if an outputstream cannot be created
     * to the client @exception SQLException thrown if an SQL error occurs
     * when trying to query the database
     */
    public void run(){

        try {
            Random generator = new Random();
            int random = Math.abs(generator.nextInt() % MAX_FORTUNES) + 1;
            int num[] = new int[LUCKY_NUMBERS];
            java.lang.String query = new String("SELECT * FROM Fortunes WHERE
                Fortune_ID = " + random);
            FortuneServer.queries[random-1] += 1;
```

(continues)

667

Exhibit 50.9. *(continued)*

```
            java.lang.String response = null;
            java.sql.ResultSet rs = statement.executeQuery(query);
            while (rs.next()){
                rs.getInt(1);
                response = new String(rs.getString(2));
                response += "<BR><BR><font color='#004080'>Your lucky numbers
                    are: </font>";

                for (int ix=0; ix<LUCKY_NUMBERS; ix++){
                    int number = Math.abs(generator.nextInt() %
                        LOTTERY_NUMBER_MAX_VALUE) + 1;

                    if (ix !=0){
                        boolean check = true;
                        while (check){
                            for (int jx=0; jx <= ix; jx++){
                                if (num[jx] == number)
                                    number = Math.abs(generator.nextInt() %
                                        LOTTERY_NUMBER_MAX_VALUE) + 1;
                                else {
                                    check = false;
                                    num[ix] = number;
                                }
                            }
                        }
                    }
                    else num[ix] = number;
                }
                response += "<font color='#FF0000'>" + num[0] + ", " + num[1]
                    + ", " + num[2] + ", " + num[3] + ", " + num[4] +
                    "</font>";
                if (response != null){ break; }
            }
            java.io.BufferedWriter out = new java.io.BufferedWriter(new
            OutputStreamWriter(cs.getOutputStream()));
            out.write(response, 0, response.length());
            out.flush();
            out.close();
            cs.close();
        }
        catch (java.io.IOException e1){
            e1.printStackTrace();
        }
        catch (java.sql.SQLException e2){
            System.out.println(e2.toString());
        }
    }//end run()
}//end class RequestProcessor
```

and control is eventually routed to the *run()* method. When one of these objects is created, two vitally important pieces of information are needed — the client's socket and an initialized JDBC™ *Statement* object. We retain the information about the client because it is to this port number that we are going to transfer information. The *Statement* object is initialized from the *Connection* object, so whenever we perform SQL operations (which is why we want it), the *Statement* object inherently knows what data source it is tied to.

The SQL statement we're going to use is

"SELECT * FROM Fortunes WHERE Fortune_ID = " + random

This object's *run()* method generates a random number which corresponds to the fortune/quotation we are going to return. The SQL statement is executed by using a *ResultSet* object. The net effect of the line that reads

rs = statement.executeQuery(query)

is to execute the SQL string specified by the variable *query* and to return a reference of the results back to the *ResultSet* object that invoked the method. In this case, we expect to get only one tuple (or row) back from the database. The *getXXX()* methods of the rs object allow us to pick off the values contained in each column (or field). Without any real reason, we make a call to rs.getInt(1) to illustrate how to retrieve the *Fortune_ID* number. It is the next part that we make use of — rs.getString(2) returns the text of the fortune/quotation to the *response* string. To this, we append our five lucky numbers (which includes a little algorithm for ensuring all numbers are unique), and generate some HTML code that is sent back to a servlet via a *BufferedWriter* object.

The only part that remains is somehow to tie the browser and the server together. We do this with the *FortuneClientServlet*. This component will be invoked by the HTML form and will connect to the server on the client's behalf. Once this is done, all of the actions that were described above take place. Let us turn our attention to this project's centerpiece, the *FortuneClientServlet* code (see Exhibit 50.10) — without it we'd be unable to make any of this happen.

Creating the Client Servlet

The *FortuneClientServlet* is a subclass of *HttpServlet*. It contains one and only one method — *doGet()* — that redefines the behavior the superclass provided. When we click the button "I'm daring enough to push this button," on the HTML form, a program called *servletrunner* (part of the servlet SDK) is executing on the target machine, takes the form request and any information the form contains, and acts as a proxy by directing it to the appropriate servlet. Our *FortuneClientServlet* gets called, and code execution begins in the method *doGet()* — *doPost()* if this were a *POST* action. Notice that the *FortuneClientServlet* attaches to the port the server is listening to; the server delegates the task of getting a fortune to the *RequestProcessor*, and this last component returns the fortune to the servlet. The servlet has initiated a chain of events that effectively limits its participation in this system to receiving a fortune, then forwarding it to the client that requested it. The culmination of this part of the project is shown in Exhibit 50.11.

Exhibit 50.10.   The *FortuneClientServlet* code.

```java
import java.io.*;
import java.net.*;
import javax.servlet.*;
import javax.servlet.http.*;
import WriteToFile;

/**
 * FortuneClientServlet creates a·new socket and attaches to the
 * FortuneServer object. The connection to the fortune server generates a
 * request for a fortune, and FortuneClientServlet waits until its request
 * has been fulfilled before returning the fortune and five lucky numbers
 * to the client that invoked it. Please note that this is not like a
 * regular object (there is no constructor). Creation of the
 * FortuneClientServlet is done by the servletrunner utility program,
 * which is part of the Servlet Software Development Kit (SDK).
 * Created October 15, 1998.
 * For more information, please see <a href="http://jserv.java.sun.com/
 * products/java-
 * server/servlets/index.html">the Servlet SDK.</a>
 * @author Jonathan S. Held
 * @version 1.0
 */

public class FortuneClientServlet extends HttpServlet
{
    /**
     * doGet() - Overridden from HttpServlet to handle GET operations.
     * @param request HttpServlet request object encapsulating
     * communication from the client
     * @param response HttpServletResponse object encapsulating means of
     * communicating from the server back to the client
     * @return void
     * @exception IOException thrown if the servlet cannot create a socket
     * to the server on port 8888
     * @exception ServletException handled by the superclass
     * This method implements a GET operation called from an HTML form's
     * ACTION URL. HTML is sent back to the client via the response object.
     */
    public void doGet (HttpServletRequest request, HttpServletResponse
        response) throws ServletException, IOException
    {
        java.lang.String fortune = new String();
        java.io.PrintWriter out;
        String title = "Your lucky fortune/quotation...";
        response.setContentType("text/html");
        out = response.getWriter();
        out.println("<HTML><HEAD><TITLE>");
        out.println(title);
        out.println("</TITLE></HEAD><BODY>");
        out.println("<body bgcolor='#FFFF00'>");
    try {
        java.net.Socket socket = new Socket("127.0.0.1", 8888);
        java.io.BufferedReader in = new BufferedReader(new
        InputStreamReader(socket.getInputStream()));

        for (int ch = in.read(); ch > 0; ch = in.read())
        fortune += (char)(ch);

        socket.close();
```

Exhibit 50.10. *(continued)*

```
    }
    catch (java.io.IOException e){}

    out.println("<CENTER><font color='#000000'><H1><B><I>" + fortune +
        "</I></B></H1></font><BR></CENTER>");
    out.println("</BODY></HTML>");
    out.close();

    java.util.Calendar ts = java.util.Calendar.getInstance();
    java.lang.String info = "On " + ts.getTime().toString() + " received
        request from " + request.getRemoteAddr();
    System.out.println(info);
    (new WriteToFile(info)).start();
    }//end doGet()
}//end class FortuneClientServlet
```

Searching the Database

Surely one of the more popular tasks today is being able to perform searches against databases. For that reason, we've developed a *Quote-Search* servlet. The client can enter a keyword, then exhaustively search all 700 fortunes/quotations, and, if the keyword is found, the entry is returned. This servlet is no more difficult to develop than the former; however, it does illustrate some things we haven't talked about, e.g., how do we capture form input from a servlet and how do we use the *init()* method to our benefit? Before we continue, take some time to examine the code in Exhibit 50.12.

Much of the code we see here should look familiar — the process of connecting to the database and working with SQL statements remains the same. We perform the initial resource-intensive operation of connecting to the database only once — in the *init()* method. The *servletrunner* proxy, which listens for servlet requests, ensures that each servlet's *init()* is executed just once.

After the client enters the keyword and clicks the Submit button, a *POST* operation is performed. For this reason, we override the *doPost()* method and tailor our response to the client's action with any code we place in here. Notice that we have an *HttpServletRequest* and an *HttpServletResponse* object. If it wasn't previously mentioned, we should say that these objects contain a number of methods that allow us to learn information about the request that was generated (such as where it came from, information that was passed in the request via HTTP headers, etc.) and a means for responding to the request as we see fit.

We use the *HttpServletRequest* method *getParameter()* to retrieve values from forms. This method takes a string that represents the name we assigned to the HTML text control. If the client tries to submit the form without entering a keyword, which we explicitly check for, no action is taken

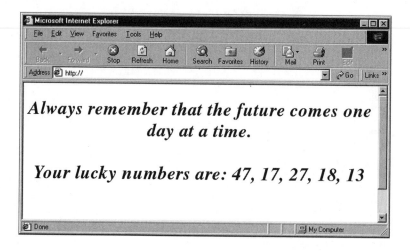

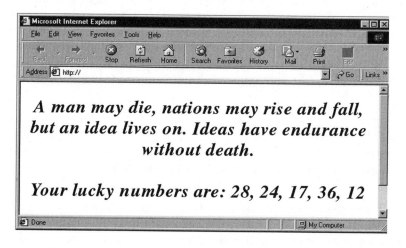

Exhibit 50.11. Random fortunes and quotations as seen by the client.

(although a white screen will appear). We could later customize this servlet to return an error message, if we were so inclined. If a keyword is entered, we make a call to *goFindIt()*, which requires two parameters: the keyword being searched for and the *HttpServletResponse* object which is used to communicate back with the client.

Some HTML is immediately generated and sent back to the client, so when you run this servlet you'll get a maroon screen that informs you a

Exhibit 50.12.   The *QuoteSearch Servlet* code.

```
import java.io.*;
import javax.servlet.*;
import javax.servlet.http.*;
import java.sql.*;

/**
 * QuoteSearch is a Java servlet created to allow a client to search the
 * database for a keyword.
 * Created October 15, 1998.
 * For more information, please see <a href="http://jserv.java.sun.com/
 * products/java-server/servlets/index.html">the Servlet SDK.</a>
 * @author Jonathan S. Held
 * @version 1.0
 */
public class QuoteSearch extends HttpServlet
{
    static java.sql.Connection con;
    static java.sql.Statement stmt;
    static final java.lang.String url = "jdbc:odbc:Quotation_DB";
    static final int INITIAL_SIZE = 20;

        /**
         * init() - Servlet method invoked only once by the servletrunner
         * utility; this is a good method to include code for resource-
         * intensive operations, such as connecting to a database
         * @param response ServletConfig object
         * @return void
         */
    public void init(ServletConfig config) throws ServletException {
        super.init(config);

        try {
            Class.forName("sun.jdbc.odbc.JdbcOdbcDriver");
            con = DriverManager.getConnection(url, "", "");
            stmt = con.createStatement();
        }
        catch (java.lang.ClassNotFoundException e1) { }
        catch (java.sql.SQLException e2){ }
    }//end init()

    /**
         * doPost() - Overridden from HttpServlet to handle POST operations.
         * @param request HttpServlet request object encapsulating
         * communication from the client
         * @param response HttpServletResponse object encapsulating means of
         * communicating from the server back to the client
         * @return void
         * @exception ServletException handled by the superclass
         * This method implements a GET operation called from an HTML form's
         * ACTION URL. HTML is sent back to the client via the response
         * object.
         */
    public void doPost (HttpServletRequest request, HttpServletResponse
        response) throws ServletException, IOException {
        java.lang.String keyword = request.getParameter("keyword");
        if (keyword.equals(""))
            return;
        else goFindIt(keyword, response);
    }
```

(continues)

Exhibit 50.12. *(continued)*

```
/**
 * goFindIt() - Searches for a keyword in a fortune/quotation.
 * Returns the fortune/quotation with the keyword highlighted to the
 * client.
 * @param response whatToFind a string representing the keyword to
 * find
 * @param response HttpServletResponse object encapsulating means of
 * communicating from the server back to the client
 * @return void
 */
private void goFindIt(java.lang.String whatToFind, HttpServletResponse
    response)
{
    java.lang.String query = "SELECT Fortune FROM Fortunes";
    int number_found = 0, total_quotes = 0;
    java.io.PrintWriter out;
    java.lang.String title = "Matches...";

    try {
        response.setContentType("text/html");
        out = response.getWriter();
        out.println("<HTML><HEAD><TITLE>");
        out.println(title);
        out.println("</TITLE></HEAD><BODY>");
        out.println("<body bgcolor='#800000'><font color='#00FF00'
            size='5'>");
        out.println("<H1><I>Searching... Matches appear
            below:</I></H1>");
        out.flush();
        java.sql.ResultSet rs = stmt.executeQuery(query);
        while (rs.next()){
            java.lang.String quote = rs.getString(1);
            total_quotes++;

            if (inQuote(whatToFind, quote)){
                number_found++;

                int index =
                    quote.toLowerCase().indexOf(whatToFind.toLowerCase());

                out.print("<img src='http://127.0.0.1/images/speaking.gif'
                    width='25' height='25'>");

                for (int ix=0; ix < index; ix++)
                    out.print(quote.charAt(ix));
                out.print("<B><I><font color='#FFFF00'>");

                int match_length = whatToFind.length();
                for (int jx=index; jx<index+match_length; jx++)
                    out.print(quote.charAt(jx));
                out.print("</font></B></I>");

                int start = index+whatToFind.length(), end =
                    quote.length();
                for (int kx=start; kx < end; kx++)
                    out.print(quote.charAt(kx));
                out.println("<BR><BR>");
                out.flush();
            }
        }
```

Exhibit 50.12. *(continued)*

```
        out.println("</font><font color='#FF0080' size='4'>");
        out.println("Number of quotations is " + total_quotes + "<BR>");
        if (number_found == 0)
            out.println("Sorry... Your keyword was not found in any " +
                "quotations/fortunes.");
        else
            out.println("Your query resulted in " + number_found + "
                matches.");
        rs.close();
        out.println("</font></BODY></HTML>");
        out.close();
    }
    catch (java.io.IOException e) { }
    catch (java.sql.SQLException e) { }

}


/**
    * inQuote() - Returns a boolean value indicating whether the
    * keyword being looked for is anywhere in the fortune/quotation;
    * this is a case insensitive search
    * @param lookingFor the keyword string
    * @param quote the text to be searched
    * @return boolean indicating whether lookingFor is in the quote or
    * not
    */
private boolean inQuote(java.lang.String lookingFor, java.lang.String
    quote)
{
    boolean found = false;
    if (quote.toLowerCase().indexOf(lookingFor.toLowerCase()) != -1)
        found = true;
        return found;
    }
}
```

search is in process. All quotations are retrieved from the database, and *in-Quote()* determines if the keyword is found. If it is, the quotation is returned (with the keyword portion highlighted in yellow), and the search process goes on until the entire database is examined. Meanwhile, the client gets the perception that the page is still loading. When the servlet is done executing, some summary statistics are returned. I promise not to scrutinize the code any further (you can examine it as well as I can). Suffice it to say that this search is slow and could be significantly improved in a couple of ways: if a keyword appears as part of word, the keyword portion is highlighted; if it appears twice in a fortune, only the first occurrence is highlighted. These are areas for improvement that I'll leave as an exercise for the reader. Exhibit 50.13 shows two screen captures of what you should expect the *QuoteSearch* servlet to return.

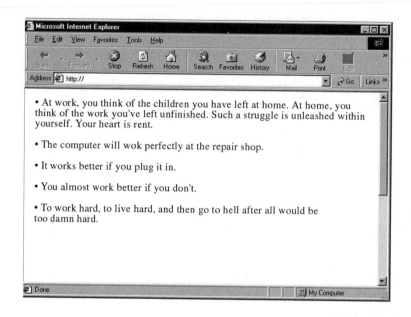

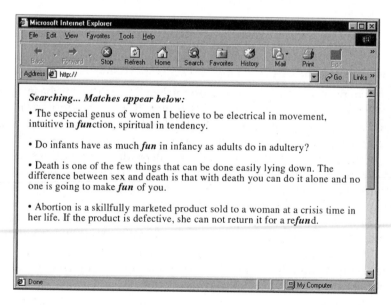

Exhibit 50.13. *QuoteSearch* **servlet results for the keywords "Fun" and "Work."**

QUICK SETUP

Installation of the servlet SDK will create a JSDK2.0 directory and subdirectories for documentation (*doc*), executable programs (*bin*), library files (*lib*), and source code (*src*). You'll find the *servletrunner* utility in the *bin* directory. You configure this program, i.e., associate a servlet name and its compiled class file, by modifying the *servlet.properties* file in a text editor. Examples of how to use this file are illustrated in Exhibit 50.14.

Exhibit 50.14. The *servlet.properties* file.

```
# @(#)servlets.properties 1.86 97/11/14
#
# Servlets Properties
#
# servlet.<name>.code=class name (foo or foo.class)
# servlet.<name>.initArgs=comma-delimited list of {name, value} pairs
#        that can be accessed by the servlet using the
#        servlet API calls
#

# simple servlet
servlet.simpleservlet.code=SimpleServlet

# survey servlet
servlet.survey.code=SurveyServlet
servlet.survey.initArgs=\
   resultsDir=/tmp

servlet.FortuneClientServlet.code = FortuneClientServlet

servlet.QuoteSearch.code = QuoteSearch
```

Writing your own servlets requires two more things: all your programs must import the *javax.servlet* and *javax.servlet.http* packages, and you must start the *servletrunner* utility after you've edited the *servlet.properties* file. The easiest way to import the packages into your programs is by modifying your *CLASSPATH* setting as follows:

SET CLASSPATH = %CLASSPATH%;C:\jsdk2.0\lib\jsdk.jar

This will allow you to use the *javac* compiler without error, and the only thing left to do is to start the *servletrunner* utility. You can do this by simply typing the name of the program at a DOS command prompt, or you can append a number of parameters to customize its configuration. Exhibit 50.15 shows you what command-line parameters are available.

CONCLUDING REMARKS

Servlets are a useful extension to the Java programming language that have almost the identical functionality and utility of CGI programs, but unlike the latter, they are not as prone to security risks and are much easier

Exhibit 50.15. *Servletrunner* **command-line parameters.**

```
C:\JSDK2.0\bin>servletrunner /? >t
Usage: servletrunner [options]
Options:
    -p port        the port number to listen on
    -b backlogthe  listen backlog
    -m max         maximum number of connection handlers
    -t timeout     connection timeout in milliseconds
    -d dir         servlet directory
    -s filename    servlet property file name
java.exe: No error
```

to write. This chapter has demonstrated how you can rapidly develop and deploy a three-tier client-server RDBMS application using this technology. If you have specific questions that you cannot find answers to after consulting the resources listed below, you may contact the author via e-mail at jsheld@hotmail.com.

RESOURCES

1. JDK1.2:
   http://www.javasoft.com/products/jdk/1.2
2. Servlet 2.1 SDK:
   http://www.javasoft.com/products/servlet/index.html
3. Servlet 2.1 API:
   http://www.javasoft.com/products/servlet/2.1/html/
   servletapiTOC.fm.html
4. JDBC™ 2.0 API:
   http://www.javasoft.com/products/jdbc/jdbcse2.html

All Java code (source and compiled class files) and the MSAccess database for the project described in this chapter can be obtained from this magazine's Web site.

Chapter 51
Knowledge Management on the Internet: The Web/Business Intelligence Solution

Jason Weir

IN THE 21ST CENTURY, YOU WON'T BE ABLE TO TELL WHERE YOUR ENTERPRISE ENDS AND THE WORLD WIDE WEB BEGINS. What's more, you won't really *care*—any more than you care now about which tabular scheme your computer's operating system uses to store and retrieve data on your hard drive. That's because the Web promises to transform the enterprise so that concepts like *local storage* and *remote access* will be so obsolete as to seem quaint. The Web will be so tightly integrated with the methods people use to access, analyze, and present corporate information that it'll become increasingly inaccurate to talk about business intelligence *applications*. Rather, people will manipulate enterprise data in a rich business intelligence environment.

Like a natural ecological system, a business intelligence environment will feature a variety of processes working in harmony to ensure the growth and enrichment of the system as a whole. In more concrete terms, business intelligence will evolve away from a model in which functionality is dumped on every desktop whether the user needs it or not, and where widely used data is needlessly duplicated across several personal hard drives when it could be shared and updated centrally. Users will gain access to server-based business intelligence services according to their needs. And crucial data in the environment—from full-fledged reports to simple executive buttons—will be stored and shared out centrally.

The Web will not be just another networking pipeline; it'll be an actual application platform on par with — indeed, seamlessly integrated within — major operating systems. Applications that run over the Web in this way are called *thin clients*. Microsoft's next-generation operating system already incorporates the Web look and feel into its desktop interface so that everything — locally stored files, programs, and external Web sites — appear as links do in Web pages, and the globe-sprawling Web itself appears as an extension of the desktop.

And what we now call *fat* business intelligence applications — feature-rich, flexible, muscular programs that require at least some logic to reside on the desktop — will nevertheless use Web technology (like Java *applets*) and access Web-based resources as just another part of the enterprise *view*.

That's what's coming in the 21st century. The question now facing the enterprise is simple — How do we build a business intelligence environment for the Web that will get us there?

THE ENTERPRISE AND BUSINESS INTELLIGENCE

To understand just what the Web means for business intelligence, you have to first look at how enterprises access, analyze, publish, and distribute corporate information. The complex task of extracting meaningful information from relational databases, multidimensional databases, and Relational Online Analytical Processing (ROLAP) servers into a point-and-click affair has been greatly simplified by modern technologies from a variety of vendors. For many Fortune 1000 companies, these business-oriented, high-performance repositories — deployed as *data warehouses* or, more recently, *data marts*, in the case of departmental repositories — have become the standard method of organizing data from an enterprise's operations. They rely on these business intelligence systems to help cut costs, find new revenue opportunities, or change the enterprise and its processes to meet new challenges.

CHALLENGES OF THE WEB

While the Web's promise for revolutionizing the enterprise is now well recognized, so too are some of its challenges. From a business intelligence perspective, Web technology is still evolving. Unaided, it can't deliver the kind of functionality or performance required by the enterprise. From the standpoint of Information Technology (IT) professionals, the Web is a new frontier very different from the client/server landscape they know so well. Web technologies are still in flux, yet the onus is on IT to choose a Web/business intelligence solution that employs technology most likely to be relevant years down the road. In short, IT has to pick a winner when the picking is tough. Research has shown that concerns about business intelligence over the Web break down into roughly three key themes:

- The *security* of mission-critical (and expensive) corporate information systems.
- The *scalability* of Web-based systems when large volumes of information are exchanged between databases and Web clients.
- The burden of *administration* that may come with adopting Web systems that operate separately from existing business intelligence environments and may create a separate "stream" of Web-specific materials (reports and so on) that duplicates work done in the fat-client environment.

SECURITY

When it comes to security, the Web suffers from a largely unjustified image problem. Because it was developed around open standards, the Web is thought to be wide open to all manner of electronic larceny—wiretapping, hacking, spoofing, and other security-compromising activities. Although such vulnerabilities may apply to poorly managed Web sites, a robust Web security toolkit exists nevertheless, consisting of public-key encryption, digital certificates, user-specific security "cookies," secure sockets, and so on.

However, these security measures were developed largely for uses of the Web—electronic commerce, for instance—that have nothing to do with business intelligence. In a typical, secure electronic-commerce transaction (the online purchase of a book using a credit card for example), the security measures applied are short-term and session-bound; once the customer sends an encrypted message containing his credit card number and the order is logged, the relationship between buyer and seller is over as far as the Web server is concerned.

But in business intelligence environments, users aren't customers who encounter corporate information on a one-time basis. Rather, they have an ongoing relationship with the enterprise's data sources; they are individual *users* of data as well as members of one or more *user groups*, and they may fulfill organizational *roles* that cut across these groups. In a business intelligence environment, a marketing strategist is a single user but is also a member of the Marketing group, with full access to Marketing-specific reports, data tables, and data models. She may also be a manager, with access to financial data appropriate for this organizational role. In other words, she has a *user, group*, and *role* security profile that reflects her various responsibilities within the organization. With its emphasis on encryption, Web-specific security cannot account for such continuous roles and relationships to enterprise data.

SCALABILITY

This is one concern about the Web that's justified, at least where data-intensive, high-volume business intelligence requirements are concerned. Enterprise Web servers were really designed only to dole out Web pages—and when there are too many users knocking at their doors, even this simple task proves too much for most of them. Asking a Web server to handle a complex query with a results set of 5,000 records is like pumping data through a pinhole.

What's more, a Web server alone doesn't have the smarts to handle something like a simple SQL query; it can hand off data processing to secondary processes using the Common Gateway Interface (CGI), but it then promptly forgets about the job until that secondary process returns results. This *occasionally connected session* is at odds with the needs of a business intelligence environment, which requires a *persistent* connection among client applications, processing services, and data sources.

Persistence is key for any business intelligence session because the user needs an unbroken connection to services handling connectivity, query processing, security, and the like. A persistent session means faster performance of business intelligence tasks and much less chance of losing data. Conversely, data in an occasionally connected session is slowed and may even be lost as it's passed from secondary processes through the Web server to the client. It's rather like being served by absent-minded waitstaff who have to be constantly reminded who you are, where you're sitting, and what you ordered.

ADMINISTRATION

From the point of view of many IT professionals, it looks like deploying business intelligence capabilities over the Web means reinventing the wheel. They've invested a lot of time and resources making the client/server model work for a sizable community of users. Now they have to use different technology—some of it pretty new and risky—to reach an even larger audience. Worries over administration break down into three categories:

- *Managing two environments*—Just because the enterprise is serving a wider audience of users over the Web doesn't mean it's going to dump its fat-business intelligence clients. Many users will continue to need the expanded range of functionality that only resident client applications can provide. So if the Web/business intelligence solution isn't compatible with the fat clients, IT now has *two* environments to manage, each with its own particular challenges, foibles, and infrastructure requirements. And if a fat-client user wants to use the Web as well, IT has to set up and maintain a second security profile.

- *Managing two streams of content*—If the environments are separate, so too are the materials created and stored in those environments—different report formats, different semantic layers, different query formats, and so on. This perpetuates the gap between fat-client users and the rest of the enterprise because it precludes sharing content among users with differing business intelligence needs and access privileges. From the point of view of the enterprise, a report is a report, and Web and fat-client users alike must view, interact with, and share the same content if the environment itself is to be enriched.

- *Installing and maintaining plug-ins*—One way a vendor can really woo a crowd at trade shows is to build browser-specific plug-ins. These plug-ins look and feel like fat desktop applications because they *are* fat desktop applications, only they're running inside a Web browser instead of within a normal desktop window. While such products make great parlor tricks, they suffer from some fatal flaws:
  — They're big—in thin-client terms, 1.8 megabytes is the size of an aircraft carrier.
  — They're platform-specific, meaning that you have to buy different plug-ins for different operating systems and even different versions of those systems.
  — They're Web browser-specific, meaning the plug-in you buy for Netscape Navigator doesn't work on Microsoft Internet Explorer.
  — Finally, and what's most important, these plug-ins *must be installed individually on each desktop.*

Theoretically, you could ask your enterprise's 2,000 users to install the plug-ins themselves. However, most IT professionals know that their user audience has different levels of technical sophistication—and they also know to whom the job of installing the plug-ins will fall. It'll fall squarely on themselves. This type of desktop-centric deployment is a fat-client requirement: what's gained by making it a Web client requirement too?

What Does the Enterprise Need in a Web/Business Intelligence Solution?

Clearly, it needs a Web solution that addresses the three crucial concerns discussed above. Such a Web solution must use a security model that promotes users' ongoing relationships with corporate data as well as with other users, other teams, and other departments within the organization. It must be scalable, circumventing as much as possible the bottlenecks inherent in Web server technology. It must be seamlessly integrated with its fat-client counterpart and must serve users—regardless of platform—the same business intelligence content. Finally, such a Web solution must be able to balance these concerns about security, scalability, and ease of administration with Web users' needs for powerful, meaningful access to the organization's business intelligence resources. In short, what is needed is a well-managed Web/business intelligence solution.

So exactly what is needed to bring about such a solution? A discussion of some basic principles and emerging technologies that will enable a robust and effective Web-based business intelligence solution will help outline this.

FIRST PRINCIPLES

If it's going to succeed, a complex endeavor like a Web/business intelligence environment must start from first principles. These should be few in number but be applied without wavering. So before we get into all the technology, here are some first principles:

- *No gaps or stovepipes*—The enterprise is an unbroken continuum of needs. A business intelligence environment should reflect this, leaving no gaps among user communities. In fact, Web functionality and fat-client functionality should overlap, so that learning and experience are applicable when users gain new levels of access.
- *Tight integration*—Many organizations have spent the last five years re-engineering their business processes, eliminating organizational stovepipes in favor of tightly integrated ones. Why should business intelligence vendors set back the clock by delivering technologies that separate users arbitrarily?
- *Common services, common data*—The business intelligence systems that service this spectrum of needs must be holistic; Web (or thin) clients and fat clients should merely be different outlets for the same data. And as much as possible, thin and fat clients should be administered by the same logic and processing services.
- *Standard technologies*—Budgets aren't bottomless, and resources aren't infinite. Technologies that become obsolete within two years are useless to the enterprise. So any Web-enabled business intelligence solution should employ technologies that are most likely to become industry standards with lasting value.

With these first principles defined, a brief discussion of the technologies that enable Web-business intelligence is necessary.

THE BASIC ELEMENTS OF A WEB/BUSINESS INTELLIGENCE SOLUTION

First, what elements are involved in a Web/business intelligence solution? In other words, what is the architecture of the environment? While vendors in the business intelligence space offer a variety of different packages, comprised of various components, most share the following services as part of their solution.

Web/Business Intelligence Server

This is a server dedicated to housing the business intelligence solution for the enterprise. It may be completely dedicated to remote or occasionally connected users accessing the system via the Internet, or "balanced" with in-house activities. It houses the database and related applications required for the Web/business intelligence solution.

Session Management Services

These services control a Web client's access to the server, track the use of various other services, detect whether the session has been discontinued, and clean up after the Web client has moved on. These services also monitor the performance of the session.

File Management Services

These include directory management, file naming, and file transfer services used by Web clients. For example, the directory management service maintains a list of materials (for example, reports and data models) that a Web user sees in their business intelligence "portfolio."

Scheduling, Distribution, and Notification Services

These services allow a Web user to schedule reports, queries, and information refreshes at a given time. Some tools enable event-based triggers, such as reports generated when inventory levels of a particular product drop below a certain level, or when sales of a specific product line increase to a given value. Notification can be sent via e-mail, by "push," or channel, technologies, or by way of proprietary solution.

Load Balancing Services

Depending on the number of users, organizations may find it necessary to offload activity to alternate servers. That is, as more users share the same resource pool on a single server, the need to create duplicate, or mirrored, systems arises. Load balancing services manage the entire resource pool in a manner similar to what is called as a "clustered" environment. A cluster is two or more systems that essentially act as a single unit. Clusters are transparent to both end-users, and, for the most part, even administrators.

Application Services

These services are the brains of the operation. They enable simple Web browsers to become powerful front-end query and analysis tools. Some business intelligence vendors offer complete Web-enabled solutions that include browser plug-ins for end-user query, analysis, and reporting while others rely on proprietary applications to perform these tasks.

SUPPORTING TECHNOLOGIES

Now that the basic elements of the Web-business intelligence solution have been discussed, a brief introduction to some of the technologies used to enable robust and effective solutions is useful.

The Plumbing—CORBA, IIOP, and the Business Repository

Consider all the different "audiences" to which the Web/business intelligence solution has to "play." A typical enterprise has a mixture of Windows platforms (Windows 3.1, Windows 95, Windows NT) and perhaps some AS/400 and UNIX systems as well. To complicate matters, there are popular Web browsers offered by Netscape and Microsoft, with several different versions of each.

Obviously, there cannot be a separate copy of information formatted for the different versions of end-user tools on each platform. Somehow, the server has to be able to talk to all of these clients and give them what they need in a format they can use. It's rather like asking an interpreter at the United Nations to translate for several delegations at once—a daunting task even for the most accomplished linguist. What would make that beleaguered interpreter's life a lot easier would be a universal translator. In essence, this is what CORBA does.

CORBA

The Common Object Request Broker Architecture (CORBA) is a specification that allows applications to:

- Communicate with one another even though they're running on different platforms. For instance, a UNIX version of the business intelligence server can service a Windows 95 desktop.
- Move commonly used services, or *objects*, from the desktop to another location on a network—in this case, onto the business intelligence server. This is the heart of the *distributed computing systems* model that's fast becoming adopted in enterprise software.

Overseeing CORBA is the mandate of the Object Management Group (OMG), a coordinating body with a membership of over 750 companies. Established in 1989, the OMG promotes "the theory and practice of object technology for the development of distributed computing systems." The group's CORBA specification (now at 2.0) forms the standards by which Object Request Broker (ORB) vendors create their products. More specifically, the OMG defines the Interface Definition Language (IDL) and the Application Programming Interfaces (APIs) used to keep ORBs talking to one another.

686

Think of the ORB as middleware; but instead of mediating a connection between, say, a desktop client and a database, it sets up connections between the client and the application objects it needs located on a network. Thanks to the ORB, the client does not actually have to have that application object running on the desktop, nor does it need to know where the object actually *is* on the network. All the client needs to know is where the ORB is; the ORB in turn takes care of finding the object, passing on the client's request, and returning the results of the object's work to the client. All of this is transparent to the user.

IIOP

In a distributed object environment, ORBs need a robust, persistent pipeline through which to communicate. The Internet Inter-ORB Protocol (IIOP) is that pipeline. Adopted in 1994 as part of the OMG's CORBA 2.0 specification, IIOP is designed for *interoperability* among objects. This means that if an object meets CORBA 2.0 specifications, it can by definition speak to any other CORBA 2.0-specified objects, even if they are made by different vendors.

What's more important to Web-enabled business intelligence, IIOP is a persistent communications protocol, a stark contrast to the HyperText Transfer Protocol (HTTP), the impersistent method Web servers use to take in and serve out data. Throughout a Web query session, the ORBs keep in constant touch with one another, exchanging user requests, returning results, and handling other background processes. Unlike a Web server, ORBs never hang up on one another as long as there's a job to be done. In other words (going back to our plumbing metaphor), IIOP provides a robust pipeline in an environment where a user needs continuous access to services like database access or query processing.

Java and XML

Originally developed by Sun Microsystems as a platform-independent programming language for consumer electronics devices, Java has quickly become the *defacto* standard for extending the capabilities of the Web beyond the confines of HyperText Markup Language (HTML). Based loosely on C++ (the object-oriented programming language in which most desktop programs are coded), Java programs—called applets—are designed to run in any environment that supports a Java Virtual Machine (JVM). Microsoft and Netscape have fully integrated JVMs into their Web browser products.

For Web/business intelligence purposes, Java provides:

- A method of deploying application interfaces (data models, for instance) that are identical to the ones used by in-house applications.
- The means to render data (results sets from queries, reports, and so forth) in much more flexible ways than is possible using HTML.

687

- A way to circumvent the impersistence of the Web server; Java applets can be "carriers" for ORBs, thus helping establish the IIOP pipeline between the Web client and the business intelligence server.

This use of Java and XML means that Web/business intelligence solutions can be freed from the limited presentation abilities of HTML. For instance, HTML cannot deliver the WYSIWYG control required for reports because it cannot handle X–Y positioning, the ability to put a particular object (a graphic, chart, or block of text) in one precise spot on the page. Java and XML handle X–Y positioning perfectly so that reports look exactly the same whether viewed over the Web or in a fat client.

CONCLUSION

In summary, by combining emerging technologies like CORBA, IIOP, Java, and XML with robust Web-enabled business intelligence tools, Web/business intelligence solutions offer organizations a superior weapon in today's competitive global economy. Companies can gain real competitive advantage by moving and transporting the proven effectiveness of in-house decision support systems to the Web.

Chapter 52
Building Database-Enabled Web Applications With IDC

Ido Gileadi

THE WORLD WIDE WEB (THE WEB) HAS BEEN PRIMARILY CONSTRUCTED FROM STATIC HTML PAGES. These pages generally contain text, graphics, and hyperlinks that give Net users the ability to search and view information easily with the click of a mouse. The static page always displays the same information regardless of individual user selections or personal preferences. Furthermore, the static page displays the entire range of information available to it without consideration of the specific requirements of unique, busy individual users accessing the Web site.

In recent years, there has been a strong movement toward a more dynamic approach for Web page design. Web pages can now be created on the fly, customized to an individual viewer's requirements, and linked with database servers to provide accurate, up-to-the-minute data. There are many techniques for creating dynamic Web pages. Some of the technologies available involve creation of a Web page on the fly, based on selections a viewer makes in previous pages. Active pages and CGI scripting can easily achieve these tasks.

In many cases, creating dynamic Web pages that contain subsets of data based on the viewer's selection of a query is the ideal. A simple example of this type of application is a telephone directory publication on the Web. Such an application requires the ability to select and display one or more entries from the database, based on a selection (query) the user makes on the screen. Most likely, the selection will involve a last name and/or first name combination.

The traditional way of creating a database-enabled Web application, such as the telephone directory, is to use CGI scripting. The CGI script is a program that is referenced by the selection screen. It is invoked by the submission of the selection criteria (last name and first name) and receives the selections as input parameters. Once invoked, the CGI script works like any other program on the server and can access a database server to retrieve the information that is required. It then builds the dynamic Web page based on the retrieved data and presents it back to the user on the Web page.

This approach is lacking in execution speed and requires programming knowledge in Perl or some other computer language that is used to construct the CGI script. This article describes a database-enabled application using the Internet Database Connector (IDC) technology. Building this application will require no traditional programming skills and relies only on minimal coding statements.

INTERNET DATABASE CONNECTOR (IDC)

IDC is a technology developed by Microsoft to allow the execution of an SQL statement against a database and represents the results in an HTML page format. This technology works only with an Internet Information Server (IIS), which is a Microsoft Web server offering. Any browser can be used to access database information using IDC; the only requirement is that the browser be able to interpret HTML pages. Exhibit 52.1 depicts the way in which IDC operates.

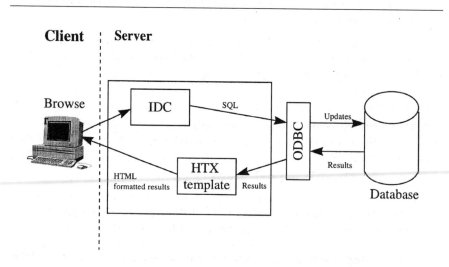

Exhibit 52.1.   IDC operation.

In this example, a client machine (e.g., a PC) is running a Web browser. The browser requests an IDC page, which happens to be a text-based page. The server intercepts the request and sends the SQL statement included in the IDC file to the ODBC data source defined in the IDC file. The database returns a result set or performs the insert/update operation. The data returned is formatted, using the format specified in the HTX template, into a valid HTML stream that is then sent back to the requesting client to be displayed by the browser.

In the following sections of this article, this functionality will be demonstrated by building a simple telephone directory application.

DEVELOPING THE TELEPHONE DIRECTORY APPLICATION

Requirements

This is a small sample application designed for the sole purpose of demonstrating some principles of database access over the Web. The requirements are identified in terms of the required functionality and access. The functionality required is as follows:

- Store first name, last name, and telephone number of multiple individuals.
- Allow the user to search for a specific directory entry using a part or the whole of the last name and first name.
- Display a list of all matching entries as the results of a search.
- Allow the users to add a new entry to the directory.
- Allow users to access the telephone directory through a Web browser and their Internet connection.

The preceding requirements are sufficient to begin developing the application. The following sections provide a guide that can be used on a step-by-step basis to develop the application.

The Database

An access database will be used to support this sample application. Any database with an ODBC-compliant driver can be used. A new database that contains only one table will be created to contain the directory entries. The structure of the table is shown in Exhibit 52.2.

IDC requires an ODBC data source to communicate with the database. Here, an ODBC data source is created for the access database that has just been created using the 32-bit ODBC manager in the control panel.

Programming Tip: The datasource must be defined as a system datasource for the Web server to be able to access it.

691

Exhibit 52.2. Example Database Structure

Field Name	Description	Type	Comments
id	The directory entry unique id	Counter	This is an automated counter that will be incremented every time a new record is inserted into the database
LastName	Last name	Text	
FirstName	First name	Text	
tel	Telephone number	Text	

The datasource will be named Tel_Directory and pointed to the newly created access database. Security will not be added to the database for the purpose of this example. In a real-life application, one will most likely want to create a user ID and a password for the users accessing the database over the network and have them key it in at runtime. Another alternative is to create a user ID and a password with very limited permissions and include the login parameters in the IDC file to avoid the extra step of logging in.

Warning: The IDC file is a plain text file and can be easily viewed by anyone with access to the Web. When storing the login parameters in this file, one must execute great caution to restrict the user access to the very minimum required.

The Application Directory

Any directory that will be accessed by the Web server (IIS) has to be defined in the administration section of the Web server. This allows the Web server to know about the directory and allows the developer to set some parameters for each directory. The parameters of interest in this discussion include the access rights. There are two access parameters:

- *Read* access allows the server to read the files in the directory and send their contents to the requesting browser. This is sufficient for regular HTML files.
- *Execute* access allows the server to execute the program stored in the files in the directory. This is required for CGI scripts as well as IDC files.

For the application here, one directory will be created that contains all the files needed to run the application, with the exception of the database file. Both read and execute permissions will be granted to this directory.

Programming Tip: Create the directory under the Web server's home directory (typically .../wwwroot) and make sure to grant read and execute

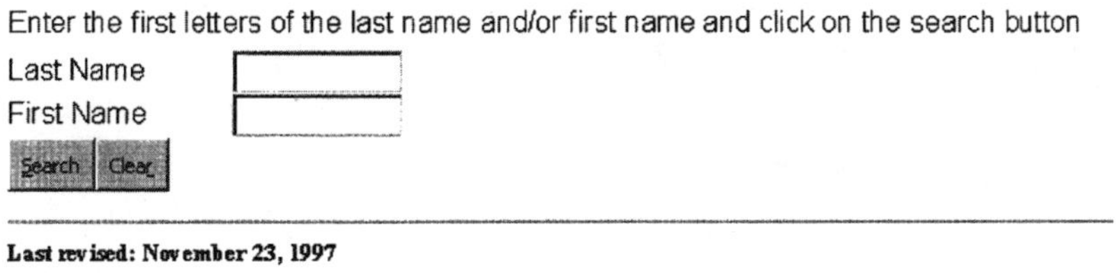

Enter the first letters of the last name and/or first name and click on the search button

Last Name [   ]

First Name [   ]

[Search] [Clear]

Last revised: November 23, 1997

Exhibit 52.3.   Search screen.

---

permissions to the home directory. The home directory is marked in the directory property window of the Web administration section.

The Search Screen

As defined in the requirements, a search is allowed by a combination of first and last name. Defining the search screen as an HTML form will allow for passage of the user's selection as parameters to the IDC script. Exhibit 52.3 shows the search screen as it will display on the browser.

The HTML code for the screen in Exhibit 52.3 was created using Microsoft Front Page, and it consists of the following:

```
<!DOCTYPE HTML PUBLIC "-//IETF//DTD HTML//EN">

<html>

<head>

<meta http-equiv="Content-Type"

content="text/html; charset=iso-8859-1">

<meta name="GENERATOR" content="Microsoft FrontPage
2.0">

<title>Search Directory</title>

</head>

<body>

<h1>Search Directory</h1>

<hr>
```

```
<p>Enter the first letters of the last name and/or first
name and click on the search button</p>

<form action="Search.idc" method="POST">
    <table border="0">
        <tr>
            <td>Last Name</td>
            <td><input type="text" size="20"
            maxlength="20"

            name="lname"></td>
        </tr>
        <tr>
            <td>First Name</td>
            <td><input type="text" size="20"
            maxlength="20"

            name="fname"></td>
        </tr>
    </table>
    <p><input type="submit" value="Search"> <input
    type="reset"

    value="Clear"> </p>
</form>


<hr>


<h5>Last revised: November 23, 1997</h5>
</body>

</html>
```

The HTML code is a standard form with fields that are arranged into a table for cosmetic reasons. Highlighted are the names of the input fields that will be passed as parameters to the IDC script.

The Search IDC Script

The general format of an IDC script is as follows:

```
Datasource: <Name of a system ODBC datasource>
Username:
Password: <Password for the user>
Template: <A URL of the HTML template file *.HTX>
SQLStatement:
+<Lines of the SQL statement>
+<Lines of the SQL statement>
```

There may be more than one SQL statement in the file. This feature will be revisited in the following sections.

The IDC script used with the search screen is as follows:

```
Datasource:Tel_Directory
Username:
Password:
Template:Directory.htx
SQLStatement:
+SELECT id,FirstName,LastName,Tel from Directory
+WHERE LastName like '%lname%%' and FirstName like
'%fname%%'
```

A username or password has not been included for this sample. In a production environment, one would definitely include a user ID and password, or prompt the user for one using a login screen.

The SQL statement containing the SELECT statement will typically return a result set. The result set may be empty or contain one or more rows. The HTML template file will have to handle the display of multiple rows. The field names in the SELECT section reflect the names of the columns in the database, and the parameter names in the WHERE clause reflect the field names on the search HTML form. The parameters coming from the HTML form are enclosed in percent signs (%). In this case, the percent signs (%), are enclosed in single quotes so that the WHERE clause will contain the correct syntax for a text field. In addition, it was desirable to allow the user the flexibility of keying only the first few letters of the name. Also included is an additional percent sign (%) that acts as a wild card character, indicating that any string of characters can replace it. The final SQL statement may look like:

```
SELECT id,FirstName,LastName,Tel from Directory

WHERE LastName like 'Smi%' and FirstName like '%'
```

This will return all the entries where the last name starts with 'Smi,' regardless of the first name.

The Search Result Screen

The search results are displayed using the HTX template. The HTX file is a regular HTML file and can contain any codes included in an HTML file. In addition to the standard HTML codes, it contains the following construct:

```
<%BeginDetail%>

    Any valid HTML code <%FieldName1%><%FieldName2%>

    Any valid HTML code <%FieldName3%><%FieldName4%>

<%EndDetail%>
```

Anything contained between the <%BeginDetail%> and the <%EndDetail%> will be repeated in the constructed HTML file for each row of results coming from the database. The <%FieldName%> parameters are the field-names as they appear in the database, and will be substituted with the values returned from the database.

The following is the listing for the search results HTX file. The name of this file is stated in the IDC script; it is 'Directory.htx'. This template was created using Microsoft Front Page. Highlighted in the following example are the important construct elements, including begindetail, id, Last-Name,FirstName, Tel, enddetail, if CurrentRecord EQ 0, action="AddEntry.idc," and endif:

```
<!DOCTYPE HTML PUBLIC "-//IETF//DTD HTML//EN">

<html>

<head>

<meta http-equiv="Content-Type"

content="text/html; charset=iso-8859-1">

<meta name="GENERATOR" content="Microsoft FrontPage
2.0">
```

```
<title>Directory Listing</title>
</head>

<body bgcolor="#FFFFFF">

<p><font color="#0000FF" size="5"><em><strong>Telephone
Directory
Listing</strong></em></font></p>
<table border="2" cellpadding="2" cellspacing="3">
    <tr>
        <td><font color="#0000FF"><em><strong>Entry
        ID</strong></em></font></td>
        <td><font color="#0000FF"><em><strong>Last
        Name</strong></em></font></td>
        <td><font color="#0000FF"><em><strong>First
        Name</strong></em></font></td>
        <td><font color="#0000FF"><em><strong>Tel
        Mumber</strong></em></font></td>
    </tr>
<%begindetail%>
        <tr>
            <td><%id%></td>
            <td><%LastName%></td>
            <td><%FirstName%></td>
            <td><%Tel%></td>
        </tr>
<%enddetail%></table>

<p> </p>
<%if CurrentRecord EQ 0%>
<table border="0" cellpadding="0" cellspacing="4">
    <tr>
        <td><form action="AddEntry.idc" method="POST">
            <p><input type="submit" name="B1" value="Add
            Entry"></p>
```

```
            </form>
            </td>
        </tr>
    </table>
    <%endif%></body>
    </html>
```

In the preceding listing, there is an additional conditional construct that looks like <%if CurrentRecord EQ 0%> any HTML code <%endif%>. This conditional construct allows for better control over the creation of the HTML code. In the example, the construct is used to add an AddEntry button that will activate the add entry screen.

Tip: The conditional construct can also contain the element <%else%>, which will allow the creation of a completely different HTML code based on the result set.

Warning: The conditional construct will not work if used before the <%BeginDetail%>.

The CurrentRecord is one of the built-in variables that can be used in the template. It indicates the current record being processed. If used after, the <%BeginDetail%> <%EndDetail%> construct will hold the last record number. The record number relates to the sequential number within the result set.

The Add Entry Screen

The Add Entry button will appear on the search results screen only when there are no records in the result set. Having no records in the result set will indicate that the entry was not found and therefore may be entered into the database. The Add Entry button is a submit button within an HTML form that points to the AddEntry.idc script.

The AddEntry.idc script will fetch the total number of entries in the database and invoke the HTML template named AddEntry.htx. Following is the listing for the AddEntry.idc script:

```
Datasource:Tel_Directory
Username:
Password:
Template:AddEntry.htx
SQLStatement:
+SELECT count(id) as NumRec from Directory
```

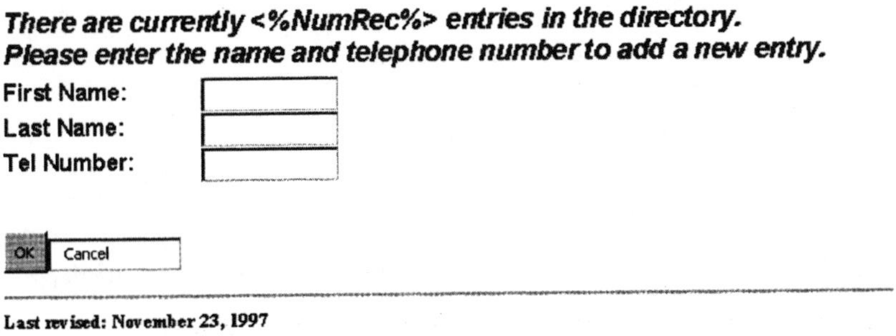

There are currently <%NumRec%> entries in the directory.
Please enter the name and telephone number to add a new entry.

First Name: [   ]
Last Name: [   ]
Tel Number: [   ]

[OK] [Cancel]

Last revised: November 23, 1997

Exhibit 52.4.   Add entry screen.

The AddEntry.htx template is different from the search result template previously seen. The user only expects one record to be returned to this screen. That record will contain the total number of records in the database. The rest of the template is an HTML form that will allow the user to enter the details of the new directory entry and submit them to the database. Exhibit 52.4 shows the add entry screen.

The following example is the AddEntry.htx HTML listing supporting Exhibit 52.4: Add Directory Entry Screen:

```
<!DOCTYPE HTML PUBLIC "-//IETF//DTD HTML//EN">

<html>

<head>

<meta http-equiv="Content-Type"

content="text/html; charset=iso-8859-1">

<meta name="GENERATOR" content="Microsoft FrontPage
2.0">

<title>Add Entry</title>

</head>


<body>

<h1>Add Directory Entry</h1>


<hr>

<%BeginDetail%>
```

699

```
<p><font size="4"><em><strong>There are currently

&lt;%NumRec%&gt; entries in the
directory.</strong></em></font></p>

<%EndDetail%>

<p><font size="4"><em><strong>Please enter the name and
telephone

number to add a new entry.</strong></em></font></p>


<form action="Add2DB.idc" method="POST">
    <table border="0">
        <tr>
            <td><strong>First Name:</strong></td>
            <td><input type="text" size="20"
            maxlength="20"

            name="fname"></td>
        </tr>
        <tr>
            <td><strong>Last Name:</strong></td>
            <td><input type="text" size="20"
            maxlength="20"

            name="lname"></td>
        </tr>
        <tr>
            <td><strong>Tel Number:</strong></td>
            <td><input type="text" size="15"
            maxlength="15"

            name="tel"></td>
            </tr>
        </table>
        <blockquote>
            <p> </p>
        </blockquote>
        <p><input type="submit" value="OK"> <input
        type="button"

        value="Cancel"> </p>
```

```
</form>

<hr>

<h5>Last revised: November 23, 1997</h5>
</body>
</html>
```

In the preceding listing, note the <%BeginDetail%> and <%EndDetail%> around the <%NumRec%> variable, without which the %NumeRec% variable will not be assigned a value. Also note the form action is referencing yet another IDC script named Add2DB.idc. The Add2DB.idc script contains the SQL INSERT statement that will insert the new record into the database. The listing for the Add2DB.idc script is as follows:

```
Datasource:Tel_Directory
Username:
Password:
Template:Directory.htx
SQLStatement:
+INSERT INTO Directory (FirstName, LastName, Tel)
+VALUES ('%fname%', '%lname%', '%tel%')
SQLStatement:
+SELECT id, FirstName, LastName, Tel FROM Directory
```

Careful examination of this script reveals that it has an SQL INSERT statement that takes as parameters the values that had been entered in the HTML form. The INSERT statement is not the only statement in the script. There is a second SQL statement that selects all the records in the telephone directory. The second select statement will populate the Directory.htx template, which was seen previously. This script performs the insert action and then displays all records in the directory, including the newly inserted record.

Tip: Results returned from the database must match the template.

Each result set returned from the database will correspond with a single <%BeginDetail%> <%EndDetail%> in the template. There may be more than one <%BeginDetail%> <%EndDetail%> in the template. If one SQL statement does not return a result set it will be skipped and the next result set will be matched to the <%BeginDetail%> <%EndDetail%> in the template. In this example, the INSERT statement does not return a result set. The second SQL statement does return a result set and will therefore be used by the <%BeginDetail%> <%EndDetail%> in the template.

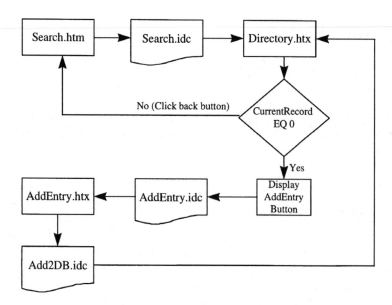

Exhibit 52.5.   Web telephone directory application.

Organizing the Application

The application directory was created previously. All the HTML, IDC, and HTX files should now reside in the same directory. They are all built to reference each other in a cyclic fashion. Exhibit 52.5 depicts the relationships between the various screens and scripts.

CONCLUSION

The sample application created in this article demonstrates the principles of accessing a database through a Web server. The task is accomplished without the need for traditional programming. All the developer needs to know are basic SQL statements and some HTML coding. With this basic knowledge, an application has been created that can be useful and provide value.

The IDC technology is compatible with a Microsoft Internet Information Server. The personal Web server version was used to test this application. Users accessing the telephone directory can do so with any browser that can read and interpret HTML code (e.g., Netscape or Microsoft).

There are many ways to access data through the Web; IDC is the simplest and quickest way of doing so. If the requirements for specific applications can be met with this method, it will be a convenient and low maintenance solution.

Chapter 53
Intranets:
Notes vs. the Internet

Brett Molotsky

A BUYER IS LOOKING FOR SOME NEW TRANSPORTATION and a friend recommends a dealer who specializes in many different types of vehicles. The dealer suggests either a car or a tractor, based on the logic that the vehicles are essentially the same; both have engines, drivetrains, steering and braking mechanisms, and both will transport the driver from one location to another.

Although the similarities between the two vehicles may be strong, there are also strong differences. The vehicles are designed and built for different purposes and different environments, and will work differently on different types of terrain. The reasons for choosing one over the other depend entirely on what the driver's transportation needs are and how those needs are affected by the environment in which the vehicle will be operated.

This metaphor can be applied to a current trend in corporate IS strategy. Companies are starting to question how Lotus Notes as a groupware product may fit into a corporate technological infrastructure that seeks to exploit the current rush toward the corporate intranet. Many managers are wondering why they should implement or continue to use Lotus Notes when a World Wide Web browser and a Web server can do the job.

But like the differences between the car and the tractor, there are significant differences between Lotus Notes as a corporate technology and the Web as a corporate technology. They are not the same vehicles, and they each have strengths and weaknesses in different environments.

This chapter points out those differences and raises some of the key issues related to using either or both of these tools in a company's Internet and intranet initiatives.

Some people believe that Web technology will supplant the need for products like Notes in the very near future, and others feel that Notes and

0-8493-9832-0/00/$0.00+$.50
© 2000 by CRC Press LLC

products like it offer features that Web technology will never be able to provide on its own. The reality, however, may fall somewhere in between.

THE CONCEPT OF THE INTRANET

The basic premise of the whole Internet is founded on the idea that the computers that are connected to each other need not share the same operating system, platform, or software. All that they need in order to communicate is a common networking protocol, such as Transmission Control Protocol and Internet Protocol (TCP/IP), physical connections, and software capable of displaying and retrieving files in specific formats. By providing each node on the network with the proper tool to access information, the source and/or location of the information becomes secondary.

Managing Distributed Information

As more companies move toward TCP/IP as their standard networking protocol, they have the opportunity to begin exploiting this concept of distributed information within their own organizations. Like the Internet, information will be placed on distributed servers within the company in a standard format (in this case, hypertext markup language [HTML]), and users across the organization will be able to view, print, and give feedback regardless of their hardware/software configuration. As long as they have a Web browser on their workstation, corporate information will be accessible.

Extending this model through a large corporation has tremendous appeal, mainly because browser software is very inexpensive (if not free), and no other client-side tool is required to access data. Coupled with new products emerging for the back-end of the equation, including products that allow HTML publishing of database data, companies see an opportunity to provide client/server computing solutions to all users at a fraction of their originally estimated costs.

The intranet is the collection of servers and workstations connected to each other using the same paradigm as the Internet: the workstations are connected via TCP/IP and browser software to various information stores that may be simple HTML documents or complex database applications using powerful back-end database tools. All of this functionality comes at a low cost per workstation, is generally platform independent, and does not have to disrupt current development projects using standard database development tools.

LOTUS NOTES IN THE ENTERPRISE

Many companies have already found all of this functionality and more by installing Lotus Notes within their organization. Notes, with server and workstation software for all of the major operating systems and platforms, provides exactly the same basic functionality as an intranet: the ability for low-cost client software to access a wide variety of information and database applications using the existing corporate network. Notes also allows users to provide feedback and input into databases, as well as develop sophisticated applications within its own development environment.

Lotus Notes is almost as pure a client/server environment as exists today for the PC platforms. A server task runs on a file server in the network and the Notes client software makes requests for information from that server task. The information is fed to the client, where all the processing is done. Any changes made to the information on the client are submitted back to the server on request.

Companies have implemented Lotus Notes for a variety of reasons. Notes provides a secure, monitored environment for the management of information, has built-in messaging and e-mail features, and allows groups of users to share and exchange information in a controlled environment. Coupled with the development tools built into the product, Notes provides a stable environment for developing and distributing applications in which groups of users need to move, share, or store information.

Costly Implementation

All of these benefits come at a cost, however. There are costs associated with the software, but that is only the beginning. Notes generally requires close administration and management on the server side, and database management on the application side. As the size of the Notes network grows, the administration tasks become more critical to the overall performance of the network.

In the past, Notes has been criticized for the lack of flexibility of its development tools and the overall cost of implementation. Lotus has repositioned Notes with the release of version 4.0. The client software now retails for as little as $70 per workstation (which is not much more than the license for a standard browser tool like Netscape) and $750 per server. Steep discounts exist for volume licensing and members of Lotus' special purchasing programs.

This pricing policy has put Notes right into the mix among companies looking to either leverage their existing Notes infrastructure into a companywide intranet or extend Notes' influence to build new standards for computing within the organization.

NOTES VS. INTRANETS

There is a pervasive feeling among IS managers that Notes and intranets are somehow mutually exclusive. According to popular opinion, the rise of the intranet means the demise of Lotus Notes as a useful information platform, simply because Web technology coupled with an intranet provides all the functionality of a Notes installation at a fraction of the cost.

For many IS managers, supporters of Notes technology fail to see the bigger picture and the advantages of Web technology that reaches across database platforms and client workstation issues. For managers in organizations using Notes, the reverse is often the case; the benefits they have realized by using Notes cannot be replaced simply by installing a browser on every desk. IS professionals at all levels may wonder why they must make an "either/or" choice with respect to intranetworking and the tools that support it.

If the two approaches are considered opposite technologies as diverse as the car and the tractor, with Web technology at one pole and Notes at the other, the true area of opportunity and possibility lies in the middle. The questions that IS managers should be asking when considering the implementation of an intranet in their organization is not whether Web technology or Notes technology should be used.

Instead, an organization needs to look beyond the technical limits of both technologies into how each might function within the organization. Instead of either/or, the question may become: where are the areas of synergy among these technologies and how can that synergy be used to build the most effective intranet solution for the organization?

Browser-Based Intranets

Netscape, Microsoft, and others already ship or have announced cross-platform versions of their browser tools. Netscape has even stopped calling its tool a browser, preferring instead to call it "an environment." The implication is that the tool used to view HTML content on the network is not just a viewing tool, but with the use of add-in programs, it allows users to execute sophisticated client/server applications from within the tool itself.

The browser, in Netscape's view, becomes the front-end to everything — content on the Internet, content on the corporate network, client/server applications, e-mail, and groupware applications. Because the interface is standard across all platforms and the basic functionality never changes across applications or information types, the focus returns to the information being presented to the user, and not the effort typically required to design and build a comfortable user interface for every application. Because this approach requires only that the user have a compatible browser installed, there is no inherent reason to choose a single browser from a single manufacturer.

Currently, several companies offer low-cost, commercially available browser tools that run on a variety of platforms. The key feature they share is the ability to retrieve and display information from any hypertext transfer protocol (HTTP) server. Minor differences among platforms are accounted for by the browser without the user or the programmer having to deal with them. Font differences, screen resolution differences, even interface object rendering differences (i.e., the way buttons and form fields are drawn by the operating system) are removed from the responsibilities of the programmer.

IS managers may welcome a degree of standardization that is possible by using a browser tool in the context of a corporate client/server computing strategy, especially when coupled with the types of HTTP server software now available. The HTTP server is the backbone of the corporate intranet. Many of the most respected enterprise database software companies have announced products or plans to incorporate HTML document publishing into their database architecture. What this means for the corporate IS strategy depends on which tools are used in the company.

All of the major database vendors have either released or intend to release products that will incorporate the information stored in their databases into Web-compatible content. The features of these new products vary, but most will allow the retrieval and display of information via live queries into the database, as well as allow dynamic updates of information in the relational database via the browser.

Notes-Based Intranets

Notes performs the same basic functions as an intranet installation — the ability to access information in a friendly, comfortable format tied with the ability to generate and store large amounts of data in a database format. The Notes client software is cross-platform in nature, allowing users across the organization to share and update information.

Notes' built-in database development tools set it apart from the browser market; any user with an appropriate license may become an applications developer in Notes simply by invoking the Design menu on the toolbar. The development environment is simple enough for novices to grasp quickly and robust enough for some sophisticated development to take place.

However, it is the inclusion of InterNotes tools, released by Lotus in 1995 and to be upgraded this year for the new release of Notes, that places Notes squarely in the realm of a practical intranet solution. Using InterNotes, a standard Notes workstation can become a browser tool.

THE HYBRID ENVIRONMENT

A hybrid environment can be created in which Notes may function for certain users as their primary interface to both workgroup solutions as well as the corporate intranet. For other users who may not need the applications or information currently stored in Notes, a standard browsing tool may be all that is required.

Using InterNotes, users of a standard browser are not kept out of Notes-based information. The InterNotes Web Publisher, a component of the InterNotes tools, allows Notes databases to be published, searched, and updated via Web technology. Regardless of the front-end tool being used, the Notes-based data is just as accessible as other types of information.

Administrative Benefits

Using the standard Notes administration and database development tools, an organization can implement and manage Web-based information. The Web Publisher can publish any Notes database into HTML documents and refresh those documents on a scheduled basis.

This means that users do not have to learn HTML codes in order to generate or update Web information. Much of the cost related to managing Web information comes with maintenance and upkeep of the documents themselves. By using the Notes Web Publisher, that administrative task can be reduced significantly. Because all of the changes are made using Notes, editing and publishing of the HTML information can be greatly simplified.

Drawbacks

The biggest disadvantage to the hybrid approach is that it requires an investment in Lotus Notes. For organizations that have already made this investment for other reasons, there is a logical extension to the Notes environment. Leveraging existing experience with the Notes interface and environment reduces the learning curve and provides seamless integration with corporate information on an intranet. However, the desire to build an intranet or to extend the company's reach to the Internet is not justification for building a Notes infrastructure.

INTRANET IMPLEMENTATION ISSUES

Regardless of the approach a company decides to take — browser-based or Notes-based — there are issues relating to the implementation of the technology that must be addressed.

Fit with Existing Technology

Decisions already made for workstations, servers, and the network play a key role in deciding which directions the organization will take in the future. Platform decisions, standardization of desktop applications, and decisions related to workgroup computing environments all play a part. IS must consider how the new environment will take advantage of the best features of the existing one, and determine which tools will be the most useful when the intranet is in place. IS planners should also determine internal and external workgroup computing needs. As the new infrastructure takes shape, IS may find an opportunity to reshape how the corporate computing environment should be put together.

How Is It Connected?

The current state of the corporate network must be factored into the plans. If an organization is already using TCP/IP, then it already has in place the communication layer necessary to extend an existing Notes network to an intranet or onto the Internet. Otherwise, a network protocol upgrade will need to be planned for the entire corporate network. If the network needs to be upgraded, or if the standard protocol needs to be changed, then the company will have an opportunity to change the fundamental paradigm related to how users interact with the information on the network.

Learning and Training

There is a significant learning curve involved in training someone to develop and manage Internet content. This education extends well beyond the IS staff to the people who will be charged with building individual Web pages. These are the people who, if they are not using a tool like Notes to manage content, are going to have the longest learning curve.

Once the intranet is in place, training will have to be conducted for each end-user on browser techniques, basic Internet protocols, and the use of the intranet itself. With Notes, the standard training on the workgroup computing environment is simply mapped onto the corporate intranet. The tool is already in place from the users' perspective.

Management

If, for example, it is 4:00 p.m. on Friday and a ten-page press release needs to go online immediately, someone must be responsible for putting this content on the company's Web page — be it an IS employee, a Webmaster, or a public relations agent. Once a company Web site is running, there is a daily need to watch and administer the activity. Allowing end-users to manage this content through a standard interface like Notes can reduce production and development time and allow IS to monitor the activity in the site.

SUMMARY

IS staff and managers can use the following questions as general guidelines when setting a corporate strategy for information management and the development of workgroup applications:

- What are the company's strategic information goals?
- Do the goals, in general, include the use of workgroup computing tools such as Notes or Microsoft Exchange?
- Is the organization interested in gaining specific expertise in the management and implementation of the intranet?
- Is the company interested in making the producers of the intranet content experts in HTML and Web technologies, or should those technologies be as hidden and seamless as possible for these users?
- Who is going to administer and manage intranet Web sites?
- Where is the Web site expertise going to come from?

Existing Investments

The following questions can help IS evaluate the existing corporate technology investment:

- Does the company have an existing investment in Notes?
- What are the strategic directions for workgroup computing in the organization?
- Have standards been set for the use of browsing tools or client/server database applications to be used on the corporate intranet?
- Given the direction in the industry toward a more distributed form of information dissemination, how do the company's existing database investments and database systems (i.e., Notes, DB2, Sybase, or Oracle) fit into an overall corporate strategic plan for client/server and workgroup computing?

Long-Term Thinking

IS may want to consider the following questions to plan more efficiently for the future:

- What are the company's long-term plans for integration of all database and non-database content on a corporate network?
- Given the integration of workgroup computing tools into the basic structure of the corporate intranet, are there standards and guidelines in place for the construction, implementation, and maintenance of the enterprise workgroup computing environment?

Chapter 54
Web-Enabled Data Warehouses

Mary Ayala-Bush
John Jordan
Walter Kuketz

DELIVERING DATA WAREHOUSE ACCESS VIA WEB BROWSERS HAS A VARI-
ETY OF BENEFITS. Inside a corporate intranet, Web-enabled data warehouses can increase ease of use, decrease some aspects of training time, and
potentially cut costs by reducing the number of proprietary clients. Upgrades can also be accelerated given a standard client, and data warehouses can more easily integrate with other applications across a common
platform. Extended to corporate trading partners via a so-called extranet
(a secure extension of an intranet outside a firewall), the information contained within a data warehouse may be of sufficient value to become a revenue source. While such internal and external benefits may be appealing,
they do not come without complicating issues.

In these traditional implementations, data warehouses have been used
by a small population of either highly trained or high-ranking employees
for decision support. With such a small audience having the warehouse application on their desktop, access control was straightforward: either the
end-user could access a given table or not. Once the warehouse begins to
be accessed by more people — possibly including some outside of the
company — access may need to be restricted based on content. Security
concerns also change as the user population increases, with encryption
over the public Internet being one likely requirement. Because Web-based
access to a data warehouse means expanding the community of people
who will access the data, the types of queries will most likely be more varied. Better business intelligence may thereby be derived, but once again
not without complications.

In addition to security, performance (and therefore cost) issues become
immediately relevant, dictating reconsideration of everything from replication patterns to log-in requirements. This article explores how Web-enabled

data warehouses change the strategy, architecture, infrastructure, and implementation of traditional versions of these applications

STRATEGY

Business Relationships

The strategy for a Web-based data warehouse should answer at least two questions:

- Who is being granted access?
- Why are they being granted access via the Web model?

Answering these two questions will supply important information for the cost justification of broader access. Possible justifications might include getting better service from vendors, facilitating better relationships with customers, shortening time of products in the supply chain, and receiving revenues from an internal application. The implications of broader access include having to design an architecture flexible enough to allow for new audiences with needs and requirements that may not be well identified. In addition, going into the information business can distract a company from its core focus: how are pricing levels determined? How does revenue derived from a potentially unexpected external source change payback and ROI models? What are the service level agreements and how are they determined? Who becomes the customer service liaison, especially if the IS organization is already running at full capacity for internal constituencies?

Access Control and Security

Security is a primary consideration when contemplating Web access to sensitive corporate information. Authentication can be required at three separate stages, allowing administrators to fine-tune who sees what when, while encryption (typically through the use of the secure sockets layer, or SSL) protects both queries and responses from being compromised in transit. Initially, the Web server can require either name and password log-in or the presence of a certificate issued by the data warehouse administrator. This grants access to the site and triggers the SSL encryption if it is implemented. Once inside the data warehouse, the user might also be required to authenticate himself at the query server, which allows access to the appropriate databases. This might be a dedicated data mart for a vendor, for example, that precludes vendor A from seeing anything pertaining to vendor B, whose information is held in a logically (and possibly physically) separate data mart. Finally, authentication may be required by the database to limit access within a given body of data: a clerk at vendor A can see only a selected portion of the A data mart, while A's president can see that company's entire data mart.

The logistics of security can be extensive. Maintaining certificates requires dedicated resources, while planning for and executing multitiered log-ins is a nontrivial task. At the same time, limiting access can imply limiting the value of the data warehouse, so security must be designed to be flexible and as friendly to legitimate users as possible.

New Components

Broader access to a data warehouse introduces a number of new elements into the traditional application model. What happens to the query engine vendor's pricing model as its proprietary desktop clients are no longer required? Where are the skill sets and hardware to implement Web servers and connect them to the query engine? How much will data be transformed (and by whom) if it is moved out of a central data warehouse into data marts for security, performance, or other reasons?

ARCHITECTURE

If strategy is concerned with goals and objectives, architecture is the unifying conceptual design or structure. It defines a system's component parts and relationships. Good architectures ensure that the component hardware and software pieces will fit together into an integrated whole.

A Web-enabled data warehouse introduces additional components within a system architecture, which must be expanded to include:

- The Web server component.
- The components that connect the Web server to the query engine.
- The component that formats the results such that they are viewable by a Web browser.

The system architecture may also need a component for integrating data marts.

Even given these elements, the architecture must be flexible enough to change rapidly, given both the pace of innovation in the Internet arena and the evolving place of data warehouses in contemporary business. The warehouse components may change due to increasing numbers of people using it, changing aggregations based on security or performance requirements, new access paths required by technological or organizational evolution, etc.

New design considerations are introduced by each of the above components. Web servers introduce new complications, particularly in regard to scalability issues. Secure transactions over a dial-up connection can be painfully slow, but detuning the security at either the firewall or the Web server can expose the corporate network to risk. Middleware between the Web server and the query server can dramatically affect performance, particularly if common gateway interface (CGI) scripts are used in place of APIs. Database publishing to HTML is reasonably well advanced, but even here some of the newest tools introduce Java programming into the mix, which may cause implementation problems unless the skills are readily available. Java also presents the architect with new ways to partition the presentation layer and the application logic, with implications (for the network and desktop machines in particular) that are only beginning to be experienced in enterprise computing.

The system architecture must support competing enterprises accessing the data sources. One challenge is to support competing vendors where access control is data dependent. Both vendors can query the same tables; for example, by product, by region, by week. If a given retail outlet sells both vendors' products, and people from the sales outlet are allowed to query the data warehouse, they will need access to both vendors' history.

A good system architecture must include the facility for access control across the entire Web site, from the Web server through to the database. If a mobile sales force will be given access while they are on the road, the architecture must have a component to address the types of connections that will be used, whether they are 800 dial-up services, local Internet Service Providers (ISPs), or national ISPs such as CompuServe or AOL.

INFRASTRUCTURE

The infrastructure required to support the Web-enabled data warehouse expands to include the Web site hardware and software, the hardware and software required to interface the Web server to the query server, and the software that allows the query server to supply results in HTML. The corporate network may have to be altered to accommodate the additional traffic of the new data warehouse users. This expansion increases the potential complexity of the system, introduces new performance issues, and adds to the costs that must be justified.

The Web-enabled warehouse's supporting infrastructure also introduces new system administration skills. Because the warehouse's DBA should not be responsible for the care and feeding of the Web site, a new role is required — the Web site administrator, often called the Web master. This term can mean different things to different people, so clarity is needed as the position is defined. Depending on the context, corporate Web masters may or may not be responsible for the following:

- Designing the site's content architecture.
- Writing and editing the material.
- Designing the site's look and feel.
- Monitoring traffic.

714

- Configuring and monitoring security.
- Writing scripts from the Web server to back-end application or database servers.
- Project management.
- Extracting content from functional departments.

The amount of work that may have to be done to prepare for Internet or intranet implementation will vary greatly from company to company. For example, if the warehouse is going to be accessible from the public Internet, then a firewall must be put in place. Knowing the current state of Web-based application development is essential: if organizational factors, skills, and infrastructure are not in place and aligned, the data warehouse team may either get pulled from its core technology base into competition for scarce resources or be forced to develop skills largely different from those traditionally associated with database expertise.

Web Site

Web site components include the computer to run the Web server on and the Web server software, which may include not only the Web listener but also a document manager for the reports generated from the warehouse. One of the Web protocols, called the Common Gateway Interface, allows the Web browser to access objects and data that are not on the Web server, thereby allowing the Web server to access the data warehouse. The interface used does not access the warehouse directly but will access the query engine to formulate the queries; the query engine will still access the warehouse. The CGI has been identified as a bottleneck in many Web site implementations. Because the CGI program must incur the overhead of starting up and stopping with every request to it, in high-volume systems this overhead will become pronounced and result in noticeably slow response times. API access tends to be faster, but it depends on the availability of such interfaces from or in support of different vendors.

Application Query Engine

The infrastructure must support the application query engine, which may run on the same computer as the data warehouse or on a separate computer that is networked to the data warehouse computer. This component must be able to translate the query results into HTML for the server to supply to the browser. Some of the query engines will present the results in graphic form as well as tabular form. Traditional warehouses have supported relatively small user communities, so existing query engines will have to be monitored to see how their performance changes when the number of users doubles, triples, or increases by even larger multiplers. In addition, the type and complexity of the queries will also have performance implications that must be addressed based on experience.

Data Warehouse

The infrastructure for the data warehouse is not altered simply because Web browsers are being used; instead, the expanded number of users and new types of queries this may need to be executed will likely force changes to be made. When a data mart architecture is introduced for performance or security reasons, there may be a need to change where the mart will be located: on the same machine as the warehouse, or on a separate machine. The infrastructure will have to support both the method of replication originally specified and new patterns of replication based on DASD cost considerations, performance factors, or security precautions.

Security

Web server access. Access to the Web server can be controlled by: 1) requiring the user to log into the Web site by supplying a user name and password, 2) installing client certificates into the browsers of the clients to whom access is granted, or 3) specifying only the IP addresses that are allowed to access the Web site. The client certificate requires less interaction on the user's part because they will not have to supply a user name and password to access the system. The client's certificate is sent to the Web server, which will validate the certificate and grant the user access to the system. (Part of the process of enabling a secure Web site is to install a server certificate. This must be requested from a third party, called a certificate authority, which allows one to transmit certificates authenticating that someone is who they say they are.) A less secure strategy is to configure the Web server to allow connection from a selected number of computers, with all others being categorically denied access. This scheme will allow anyone from an authorized computer — as opposed to authorized persons — to access the Web site. Because this method is based on IP address, DHCP systems can present difficulties in specifying particular machines as opposed to machines in a particular subnet.

Communication transport security. Both the query and especially the information that is sent back to the browser can be of a sensitive nature. To prevent others along the route back to the browser from viewing it, the data must be encrypted, particularly if it leaves the firewall. Encryption is turned on when the Web server is configured, typically via the Secure Socket Layer (SSL) protocol.

Query server application. To access the query server, the user may be asked to supply a user name and password. The information supplied by the certificate could be carried forward, but not without some custom code. There are various approaches to use to for developing the user names and passwords: one can create a unique user name for each of the third parties that will access the system (allowing the log-in to be performed on any machine), or create a unique user name for each person who will access the warehouse. Each approach has implications for system administration.

Database access. Database access can be controlled by limiting the tables users and user groups can access. A difficulty arises when there are two competing users who must access a subset of the data within the same table. This security difficulty can be solved by introducing data marts for those users, where each data mart will contain only the information that particular user is entitled to see. Data marts introduce an entirely new set of administrative and procedural issues, in particular around the replication scheme to move the data from the warehouse into the data mart. Is data scrubbed, summarized, or otherwise altered in this move, or is replication exact and straightforward? Each approach has advantages and drawbacks.

IMPLEMENTATION

The scope of implementing a Web-enabled data warehouse increases because of the additional users and the increased number of system components. The IS organization must be prepared to confront the implications of both the additional hardware and software and of potentially new kinds of users, some of whom may not even work for the company that owns the data in the warehouse.

Intranet

Training will need to cover the mechanics of how to use the query tool, provide the user with an awareness of the levels (and system implications) of different queries, and show how the results set will expand or contract based on what is being asked. The user community for the intranet will be some subset of the employees of the corporation. The logistics involved with training the users will be largely under the company's control; even with broader access, data warehouses are typically decision-support systems and not within the operational purview of most employees.

Implementing security for the intranet site involves sensitizing users to the basics of information security, issuing and tracking authentication information (whether through certificates, passwords, or a combination of the two), and configuring servers and firewalls to balance performance and security. One part of the process for enabling a secure Web server is to request a server certificate from a certificate authority. Administratively, a corporation must understand the components — for example, proof of the legal right to use the corporate name — required to satisfy the inquiries from certificate authority and put in place the procedures for yearly certificate renewal.

Monitoring a Web-based data warehouse is a high priority because of the number of variables that will need tuning. In addition, broader access will change both the volume and the character of the query base in unpredictable ways.

Intra/Extranet

In addition to the training required for internal users, training is extended to the third parties that will access the warehouse. Coordination of training among the third parties will likely prove to be more difficult: competing third parties will not want to be trained at the same time, and paying customers will have different expectations as compared with captive internal users. In addition, the look and feel within the application may need more thorough user interface testing if it is a public, purchased service.

Security gets more complex in extranet implementations simply because of the public nature of the Internet. It is important to keep in mind the human and cultural factors that affect information security and not only focus on the technologies of firewalls, certificates, and the like. Different organizations embody different attitudes, and these differences can cause significant misunderstandings when sensitive information (and possibly significant expenditures) are involved.

Monitoring and tuning are largely the same as in an intranet implementation, depending on the profiles of remote users, trading partner access patterns, and the type and volume of queries.

In addition, a serious extranet implementation may introduce the need for a help desk. It must be prepared to handle calls for support from the third parties, and combine customer service readiness with strict screening to keep the focus on questions related to the data warehouse. It is not impossible to imagine a scenario in which the third-party employees will call for help on topics other than the warehouse.

CONCLUSION

Because Web browsers have the ability to save whatever appears in the browser, in Web-enabled data warehouses, information that appears in the browser can be saved to the desktop. Protecting information from transmission into the wrong hands involves a balancing act between allowing for flexibility of queries and restricting the information that can potentially move outside corporate control. Legal agreements regarding the use of information may need to be put in place, for example, which tend not to be a specialty of the IS organization. Pricing the information can be another tricky area, along with managing expectations on the part of both internal and third-party users.

By their very nature, however, data warehouses have always been more subject to unintended consequences than their operational siblings. With changing ideas about the place and power of information, new organizational shapes and strategies, and tougher customers demanding more while paying less, the data warehouse's potential for business benefit can be increased by extending its reach while making it easier to use. The consequences of more people using data warehouses for new kinds of queries, while sometimes taxing for IS professionals, may well be breakthroughs in business performance. As with any other emerging technology, the results will bear watching.

Section XI
Data Warehousing, Decision Support, and OLAP

DATA WAREHOUSES SUPPORT ONLINE ANALYTICAL PROCESSING REQUIRE-
MENTS. This includes time series analysis, slicing and dicing information,
and answering "what if" scenarios. Taken together, these offer decision support. Data warehousing are growing in size all the time. Where a 100 MB data
warehouse was once considered to be quite large, the new upper end data
warehouses are in the terrabytes. Data Warehouses store highly summarized data, generally drawn from an OLTP application through a translation
routine that runs on a regular basis, and stores data in a multidimensional
data model format. This section contains five chapters.

Chapter 55, "Developing a Corporate Data Warehousing Strategy,"
shows how organizations can improve the efficiency of data warehousing
initiatives from the start.

Chapter 56, "Business Rules for Time Variant Dimensions," examines approaches for processing gradual changes that are made to contextual information that is contained in a data warehouse in order to reflect the
operations against a live data store.

Chapter 57, "Implementing a Hybrid Online Analytical Processing
(HOLAP) Solution," shows how to combine the Multidimensional OLAP
model and the Relational OLAP model to produce a Hybrid Online Analytical Processing (HOLAP) model. HOLAP solutions allow typical business users to retrieve data in summary MOLAP format, and then to optionally
"reach through" to the relational database to retrieve underlying detail.

Chapter 58, "A Framework for an Enterprise Data Warehousing Solution," provides a five-stage framework that is designed to accommodate
the common challenges encountered by project teams when building
enterprise data warehousing solutions.

Chapter 59, "Why Dimensional Modeling is Right for Decision Support," focuses on the star schema and demonstrates how it can be used to satisfy the requirements of business managers. This chapter aligns the dimensions of the model with the manner in which real world questions are asked. This makes it a powerful communication tool.

Chapter 55
Developing a Corporate Data Warehousing Strategy
Manjit Sidhu

As RECENTLY AS THREE YEARS AGO, DATA WAREHOUSING WAS THE DO-MAIN OF A FEW LARGE ORGANIZATIONS WITH DEEP POCKETS. In these early initiatives, data warehousing projects took two to three years to implement. The hardware costs alone were measured in the millions. The software and human resource cost to implement these warehouses were at least as much again if not more. A generally acceptable implementation strategy was to implement a data warehouse in an iterative-phased approach with each phase taking from four to nine months for completion.

As the tools and technologies matured and improved in performance, data warehousing became available to the mainstream. Many organizations have started to implement data warehouses and mini-data warehouses in the form of data marts. Individual business units have started implementing these solutions by themselves or with the help of consultants who are independent of the corporate IT groups. This was done without due regard for the overall needs of the enterprise as a whole. Before long, a multitude of data mart implementations with disparate technologies, uncoordinated data models, and metadata have sprung up in organizations. In the rush to implement applications, organizations are not taking the time to first develop a well thought out data warehousing strategy and architecture, which can subsequently be used to guide the development of data-warehousing initiatives within the organization.

723

Data Warehousing Concepts

● Data Warehousing
- *Data Warehousing* is a discipline which results in applications that provide decision support capability, allow access to business information, and create business insight.

● Warehouse Structures
- A *data warehouse* is a (mainly) read-only time variant database in which data is transformed, integrated, summarized and organized by subject area to be used effectively for decision support.

- A *data mart* is a smaller data warehouse with a limited focus. The focus can be limited functionally (financial analysis, fraud detection, etc.) or it can be cross-functional, but limited in scope (by line of business, by region, etc.).

Exhibit 55.1. Data warehousing concepts.

DEFINING A DATA WAREHOUSE

For the purposes of this paper we will use the terms "Data Warehousing," "Data Warehouse," and "Data Mart" as described in Exhibit 55.1.

Although much debate has raged over the differences between data warehouses and data marts, for the purpose of this paper we will use the term "data warehouse" or "data warehousing" to include data marts. Where a distinction needs to be made between warehouses and marts we will state that:

1. Data is sourced from multiple independent operational "legacy" systems and possibly from external data providers (e.g., Dunn and Bradstreet, Nielsen, and Census data).
2. This data is then cleansed (bad data corrected) and homogenized (codes and values made consistent, e.g., one system may have 'M' for male and 'F' for female while another may have '0' for male and '1' for female).

3. It is then loaded into data structures to produce a consistent integrated view of the data allowing for *insight* and analysis through 'query' processing.
4. This data is generally not updateable except through a predefined update cycle to keep it synchronized with the source systems that feed it.
5. Metadata, that is data that describes the data is created and maintained throughout the process.

The major components of a data warehousing process are shown in Exhibit 55.2.

There are different information requirements at various levels of an organization. Executives require very concise highly summarized information whereas those running the day to day operations require detailed transactional level information. Middle management requires information that is summarized to a level between the transactional and the highly summarized levels.

Exhibit 55.3 shows the various levels of information requirements that exist in a typical organization.

Data Warehousing Process Overview

Source Data
Both internal data (mostly transactional) and external competitive data.

Load & Scrub Facilities

Middleware products to extract and transform data from sources using "load-side" metadata.

Data Warehouse & Metadata

Metadata is "data about data," which describes how to load and scrub it ("load-side"), and how to find and use it ("client-side").

End-User Applications

Tools or complete applications (depending onuser needs) for getting at and analyzing data.

A data warehouse is more than just a repository. We must also consider source data, extraction, transformation, "scrubbing", loading, storage, and end user tools.

Exhibit 55.2. Data warehousing process overview.

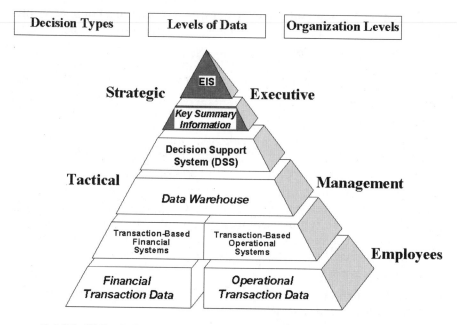

Exhibit 55.3. Information requirements and delivery approaches.

DEVELOPING A DATA WAREHOUSING STRATEGY AND ARCHITECTURE

A data warehousing strategy is a blueprint for the successful introduction, ongoing support and enhancement of data warehousing in an organization, i.e., for the provisioning of information to users at all levels of an organization. This information is used primarily for decision making and is generally sourced from operational data used for the ongoing operations of the organization.

The strategy serves to provide a common vision for availing information aligned with business objectives, strategies, and goals. It provides a platform for common definitions and an understanding of data and business terms and for ensuring a consistent approach amongst the many initiatives that will arise. The strategy also serves to focus IT and the business towards specific, long-term business objectives and away from purely technical considerations, while providing a robust and flexible foundation for meeting these evolving needs.

The development of a data warehouse strategy can be thought of like planning a journey. It describes where you want to go, why you want to go there, and what you will do when you get there. The strategy acts as an itinerary and roadmap for getting there. It also describes the means (the technology and tools) that will be required for getting there safely and expediently.

Just as a travel plan does not require the need to define internal technical specifications for all vehicles required on the journey, a strategy and architecture describes the important characteristic of the technologies but not the specific 'nitty-gritty' details. The details are left for subsequent technology selection projects.

There is no single definitive strategy on how to implement data warehousing in an organization. Decisions about data warehousing strategies need to be based on the specific needs of an organization.

A data warehousing strategy needs to take into consideration an organization's vision, structure, and culture. Therefore it is important to keep in mind that the strategy needs to address not only information and technology considerations but what will work in the organization from the organizational, skills, infrastructure, cultural and political perspectives. In particular, the cultural perspective should not be underestimated. Many technically sound strategies have failed because of the cultural and political environments within an organization.

It is important that all of the individuals involved in implementing data warehousing projects work with the same goals in mind. Part of understanding the goals involves ensuring that there is consistent use of terminology such as the difference between a data warehouse and a data mart, the meaning and purpose of an operational data store and the definition of metadata. The strategy should define how information should be organized in data marts versus a data warehouse and the level of detail that needs to be stored. The strategy should also provide a glossary of terms for data warehousing.

FRAMEWORK FOR A DATA WAREHOUSING STRATEGY AND ARCHITECTURE

Exhibit 55.4 is a pictorial representation of a framework for the development of a data warehousing strategy and architecture.

The significance of presenting the framework as a pantheon is that built correctly, the strategy should survive change occurring in a business for a long time, just as pantheons survive generations.

The steps of the pantheon represent the foundation required as the base for the strategy. It establishes a baseline understanding of the business and technology that the data warehousing strategy needs to support.

The columns represent individual components of the strategy. The 'Information Delivery' column represents how information will be delivered

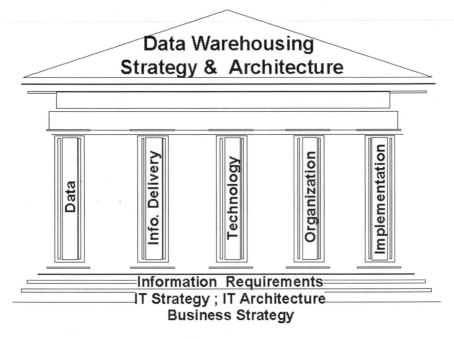

Exhibit 55.4. Framework for data warehousing strategy and architecture.

to the organization and the implementation component defines how the strategy will be implemented.

PROJECT STRUCTURE

The data warehousing strategy and architecture project should be conducted by two to three individuals with data warehousing experience. The team lead should possess solid data warehousing experience and have participated in a previous strategy and architecture development project. All members of the team should have practical experience in the design and implementation of data warehouses.

The team members should be knowledgeable about the business to know the informational needs of that type of business. The informational needs of a high technology manufacturer, for example, are significantly different than a government branch. The team should be augmented on at least a part-time basis with industry-specific subject matter experts who bring expertise on where the industry is headed and other future considerations that the team may not always be able to glean from interviews with users from the business community. The team should also have access to technical staff from the organization that can provide information on current and planned technology, systems, and data.

The project typically lasts between one to three months depending on the size of the organization, the scope of the mandate (enterprisewide or for a specific part of the organization or subject area) and the level of detail required. There is a danger that a longer project could lose focus and executive interest. Besides, there is no need to go into deep levels of detail at the strategy level.

The strategy usually does not delve into specific details behind tools and technology selections although certain recommendations around tools and technologies need to be made, especially if the choices are clear. For example, if the organization has already selected a DBMS and that DBMS is clearly sufficient for the data warehouse project then that recommendation can be made. The mandate of the strategy is to provide rules and guidelines around the selection of tools and technologies.

ESTABLISHING A BASELINE UNDERSTANDING

At the outset of the strategy a baseline understanding of the situation needs to be established. This provides an overall context of the environment for which the strategy is being developed and helps to quickly establish an understanding of the "as is" situation, so that a "to be" can be defined.

Understanding Business Objectives

At the beginning of the process, relevant documents should be obtained and reviewed to gain a baseline understanding of the business mission, vision, goals, and objectives. The strategy must be supported and support these business goals and objectives of the organization. This baseline understanding should be used as a reference point to ensure that the requirements and strategy are aligned with business objectives. If a major deviation is detected or there is a lack of clarity as to how data warehousing will support the business objectives then the project should be paused and a quick review conducted.

Understanding Existing Technical Strategy and Environment

The data warehousing strategy team should also gain a baseline understanding of the technical strategy of the organization. This includes the current or evolving technical standards and technologies employed at the organization and how they are meant to support the business strategy. This should be used as a reference point to ensure that the strategy and architectural recommendations resulting from the work are in compliance with and support the technical strategy.

The technology component of the data warehousing strategy should support and comply with the technical architecture of the organization. We say "should" as it is sometimes possible that the architecture development process may discover that the technology architectural standards employed are not adequate to support the data warehousing initiative and need adjustment. This sometimes happens when a particular platform standard, such as the Data Base Management System (DBMS) or server standard for operational systems, may not be adequate to support the very large data volumes and complex queries that the data warehousing solution may require. In such cases an alternative DBMS or server technology will need to be introduced.

Understanding Current and Planned Initiatives

The data warehousing strategy team should gain an understanding of current or planned initiatives underway that will impact the strategy. This information is sometimes not as straight forward to obtain as the other baseline information mentioned earlier. Some digging may be required and it is not unusual to discover some hidden "skunk-work" projects of which management was not aware. It is important to determine the scope of these projects, subject areas covered and technologies used. This information can serve three purposes:

- It can be an eye opener for management as to what is really going on and it can provide an added impetus to develop and enforce a coherent strategy.
- It serves to demonstrate the plethora of technologies that may have "sneaked in" and need expensive licensing and support to maintain.
- It can show how the overlapping of subject areas across these independent initiatives may be leading the organization down the path of silos of data warehousing data.

Understanding Organizational Readiness

An assessment should be conducted on organization readiness to implement, support, and use data warehousing. The assessment should consider whether the organization has the mind set to use and leverage the data warehouse, uses common data definitions and has the skills and readiness to implement, use, and support the data warehouse.

BUSINESS REQUIREMENTS

Once a baseline understanding has been achieved around the business and technical strategies, the requirements gathering phase can begin.

The business requirements phase involves the interviewing of key business users of the data warehouse and should involve individuals from across all areas of the organization. The "business-discovery" phase as it has been characterized in some methodologies is followed by "data discovery" whereby the data required to support the informational needs is determined and assessed for availability and quality.

There are a number of techniques for requirements gathering. This can range from individual interviews to joint application development (JAD) group sessions where users or 'stakeholders' from various areas are brought together to define and prioritize requirements. The requirement identification phase should include senior management as well as middle management.

Sometimes it is not a good idea to include people from different levels of the organization in the same meeting for fear that feelings of intimidation may lead some people to withhold their opinions and experiences. Power and casual users who will use the information on a day-to-day basis as part of their jobs should also be involved. Sample reports currently used should be obtained and analyzed.

The strategy at this point should clearly lay out the business requirements and gain agreement from key stakeholders and sponsors of the project before proceeding on to the next phase.

BUSINESS BENEFITS

One of the most difficult tasks in the development of a data warehousing strategy is the identification of business benefits. Business benefits are the core of a business case that management looks for in order to judge the merits and value of proceeding with the data warehouse.

Traditionally, management looks to the business case to identify tangible benefits and costs for the data warehouse. This requires clear identification and quantification of benefits and costs. Although the costs are relatively easy to assess, the benefits are much harder to quantify.

The data warehousing project by definition is one whose exact nature and usage is unpredictable. There are a lot of 'soft' benefits that accrue from its usage that are not easily quantifiable; for example, what is the dollar value of making faster decisions because the information will now be readily available? To determine the benefit of having accurate consistent data for making informed decisions, one must estimate the cost to the organization of making all the bad decisions that are being made with bad data! And no one will own up to that!

One of the difficulties with developing a business case is that the business community understates the benefits they can achieve. There are three reasons for this:

- They will have to take accountability for delivering on those benefits once the data warehouse is implemented. If they don't deliver, they look bad.
- Their budget may be adjusted based on the benefits they identified. For example, if they identified two clerks spend much of their time

731

gathering information that could be readily available in the data warehouse, then they may lose those clerks when the data warehouse is implemented.

- They may look bad if they claim they have had all this inefficiency in their organizations and have not done anything about it until now.

There are a number of approaches for analyzing benefits and some consulting companies have developed methodologies to do this.

Whatever approach is used in the final analysis, the benefits must be documented and an agreement must be obtained from stakeholders and sponsors before moving on to the next stage.

DATA STRATEGY

Data strategy is concerned with defining the highlevel data architecture to support business requirements. This includes the following:

- Determining subject areas that will be part of the data warehouse and the order in which they should be implemented.
- The granularity or level of detail stored.
- The placement of data at various locations with the topology.
- The modeling constructs used, i.e., entity-relational modeling, dimensional modeling, or a combination.
- Identifying the main types and sources of the data from a high level, with the details being left to the data warehouse development projects.

Subject Areas

Subject areas are broad categorizations of an area of interest to the organization. Some examples of subject areas include the following: Customer, Product, Supplier, Expenses, Assets, and Organization. An analysis of requirements will determine the subject areas to be included in the data warehouse and the order that these subject areas should be implemented. Subject area data is often spread amongst many different applications and data stores in operational systems and the data warehouse brings data for a subject area together from these sources. Subject areas and their relationships to one another can be represented schematically in a high level E–R (Entity Relationship) type model. (See Exhibit 55.5.)

Granularity

Data granularity refers to the level of detail that will be stored in the data warehouse. Data can be stored from an individual atomic (transactional) level through to lightly summarized to highly summarized. It is important to establish the level of granularity required at this stage since the implications on the architecture can be profound. Storing detailed 'atomic' data

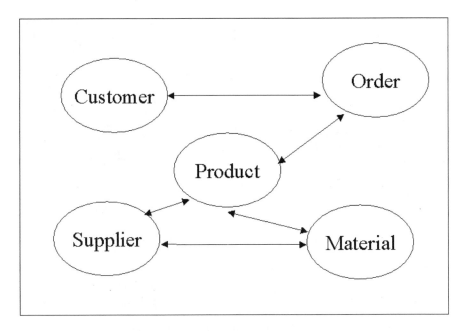

Exhibit 55.5. Subject areas map.

can magnify the size of the warehouse exponentially and require changes in the topology and architecture, i.e., where to place detailed data, how and when to summarize data for physical access by various levels of usage.

The level of granularity can only be established by careful examination of requirements. It is important at this stage to separate the real needs from the wants. It is quite common for users to answer "I want all the details" when asked what data they need and at what detail to do their job. There can be orders of magnitude difference in disk-storage requirements between storing detailed or summarized data, resulting in the difference between success and failure of the project.

In addition the level of detail depends on the particular manner in which the data will be used. Exhibit 55.6 shows the various levels of detail at which data needs to be stored for various analytic purposes.

History

One of the distinguishing characteristics of a data warehouse is the "time-variant" element of the data. The time variant nature naturally leads to the need for storing historical data in the data warehouse, which can cause an explosion in terms of volumes of data. The impact of this is not only on the larger storage space required to house the data but more

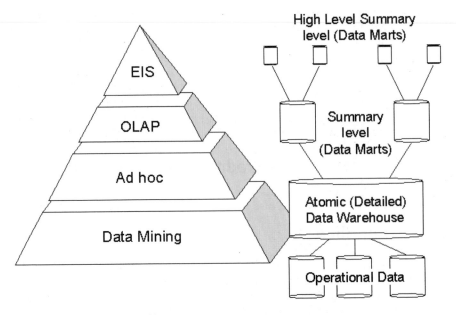

Exhibit 55.6.   Data granularity and usage.

significantly on the negative impact on performance as queries will need to plough through larger and larger volumes of data. The requirements gathering should clearly draw out the real historical needs of the organization, again, separating the needs from the wants.

The strategy should provide direction on how much history should be loaded into the data warehouse.

Time Element

The time elements stored in a data warehouse differ significantly from the time elements stored in transactional systems. Transactional systems usually "time-stamp" transactions in terms of date, hours, minutes and seconds. This is mostly for tracking exactly when an event occurred and for the purpose of sequencing transactions. Time characteristics in a data warehouse are defined and used differently. It is common for the time element to be stored at the date level with characteristics such as day of week, weekday or weekend, holiday, and season. This allows for analysis such as "how do sales volumes of a product compare within a week of a major holiday to a week following the holiday?"

Data Model

In the data warehousing arena, a debate has been raging for a long time on whether a data warehouse should contain normalized or denormalized data. The debate centers around the use of normalized entity-relationship type of model to a heavily denormalized dimensional model. Vendors of hardware and software products favor one over the other, often based on how well their product handles one type of model over the other.

The issue is one of balance between flexibility and performance. The strategy needs to address this and define what type of modeling will be employed at the various locations within the data warehouse and where data will be stored. This may include an operational data store, an enterprise data warehouse, data marts or any combination of the above. There is usually room for both types of constructs within the data warehouse.

The strategy must clearly address this and provide guidance for a consistent development approach for data warehousing within the organization.

Data Quality

The data quality issue is of paramount importance to data warehousing and many a data warehousing effort has resulted in failure for one simple reason — failing to realize the poor data quality of the source systems and not having implemented programs in advance to do something about it.

The strategy is not the place to assess detailed data quality, but it is a place for defining data quality policies and metrics. The strategy should include policies on the necessary evaluations that must be conducted before data can be introduced into the data warehouse. Various techniques ranging from statistical sampling through complete analysis can be deployed and there are many tools on the market to assess as well as cleanse data.

Data Extraction, Transformation, Transportation, and Loading

The data extraction, transformation, and loading (ETL) tools support the capturing, transferring, receiving, cleansing, transforming, and loading of data from operational and, frequently, external data sources into the data warehouse. This is the most complex and time-consuming process in the development of a data warehousing project. It is estimated that 60 to 70 percent of the effort and cost of building data warehouses is the extraction and transformation of data. It is also an area where data warehousing projects typically fail.

To be successful, it requires the adoption of a proper strategy and consistent approach and set of tools. The tools and processes required to support this must be tightly integrated with the entire data warehouse and will need to interface with many of the source systems and technologies within a typical environment.

The lack of a coherent strategy can create the risk of individual business units sourcing and "staging" data independently of each other leading to inconsistencies in the way business rules are implemented and how the data is loaded into the data warehouse environment. It can also add to the load on the source system platforms as the source systems are being accessed multiple times instead of in a coordinated fashion.

The strategy should clearly layout the process that needs to be followed to minimize "going to the well" too often and ensure the enterprise uses tools that can be integrated within the overall environment.

Data Staging

Data warehousing architectures typically employ some form of data staging strategy where an image of the data is copied to an intermediate location after being extracted from source systems and before being loaded into the data warehouse tables where it will be accessed by users.

The reasons for staging data include:

- Centralizing the data before it is 'homogenized' in terms of standardization of structures and codes.
- Ensuring a low impact on production process windows
- Providing the ability to audit 'raw' data before it is altered during transformation

The techniques that can be employed for staging data depend on a number of factors including the frequency and the location of the data. The project should take these and additional considerations into account and define an overall data staging strategy. This includes rules around the need for staging, the length of time staged data can be retained, access to the staged data and possible archiving of the 'raw' staged data for audit purposes.

Information Management

The successful implementation and long term success of the data warehouse depends on effective management of the data through information management policies, procedures, and practices. These practices are usually established, maintained, and enforced by an Information Management Function within the organization. The strategy needs to define information management roles, responsibilities, and accountabilities within the organization and ensure the following data characteristics, which are of paramount importance to the successful implementation of data warehousing, are promoted and maintained:

- *Data Integrity and Accuracy*—the usefulness of the data warehouse is dependent on the accuracy and completeness of the data and confidence that the data is what it is represented to be. The level of data accuracy and quality must be ascertained, published and be understood by the user community.

- *Data Consistency*—there is enterprise wide semantic and syntactic consistency of data definitions. The definitions must be available to all who need them in a consistent, coherent, easy-to-use format.
- *Managed Data Redundancy*—unmanaged data duplication leads to reduced accuracy, questionable integrity and increased costs. The goal should be to have as few copies of data as possible.
- *Data Accessibility*—there is significant value in data and in it's shareability across the organization. Data should be easily accessible to anyone who requires it for the purpose of executing their job function except where privacy or legal implications prohibit it.
- *Manage Data as an Asset*—data is an important corporate asset and should be managed as such including it's creation, usage, retention, security, and final disposition. Roles and responsibilities for the usage and management of data should be defined, understood, and accepted by both the systems groups and business users. All data must have an "owner" defined for the purpose of having functional accountability for the definition and management of the data.

Information Management includes the following points:

- Creating and communicating the corporate data strategy;
- Creating, enforcing, and monitoring adherence to data standards;
- Developing and publishing metadata management standards;
- Developing and publishing a high-level enterprise information model to be developed to more detailed levels through systems development efforts;
- Monitoring data for consistency and accuracy and publishing data quality assessments;
- Implementing and monitoring a data management "roles and responsibilities" model within the organization.

Metadata Management

A strategy to support the proper capture, management and provision of metadata, "data about data," is essential for the successful implementation of data warehousing.

There are three types of metadata that need to be managed:

- Technical metadata which describes the technical characteristics of the data within the warehouse, for example, the length of a particular data item and its format.
- Business metadata which describes data in terms of business understanding and usage, for example, the definition of net profit and the formula for calculating it.
- Operational metadata, which describes operational aspects of the warehouse such as the last time the data was refreshed.

The metadata strategy needs to address how the metadata will be managed and provide high level policies and guidelines for a follow on project to develop. The strategy should provide direction for the selection of metadata management tools.

Methodology

Traditional systems usually employ a "waterfall" methodology to implementation where requirements can be accurately defined so that an action and the result of that action is both predictable and repetitive. Decision Support systems by their very nature are not predictive in the sense that often the questions or queries posed to the system are of an ad hoc type and not easily predictable. The formulation of the next question usually depends on the results from a previous question, leading to what's often described as "drilling down" to more detailed levels for answers to findings obtained at a higher level of summarization.

Managers charged with overseeing the development of the data warehousing are often comfortable with working with a rigorous and "safe" systems development methodology, where exact requirements are clearly documented and 'frozen' before development begins. They are sometimes uncomfortable with the system being developed in small pieces where the data content and capability of each phase isn't precisely known and open to change from one iteration to the next. They feel a lack of control in not knowing "exactly" what they will get at the end of the "deliverable."

Data warehousing projects are most successful when implemented in an iterative manner, with each iteration taking four to six months, and the deliverables subject to change during the follow on iteration.

The strategy should address the methodology issue carefully and recommend an iterative approach to implementation. A particular methodology should be recommended if possible or at least a follow on methodology selection project should be identified and scheduled.

CONCLUSION

This article examined key components and approaches for assembling a data warehousing strategy for an enterprise.

Chapter 56
Business Rules for Time Variant Dimensions
R. Michael Pickering

DATA WAREHOUSES CAPTURE HISTORICAL DATA ON A COMPANY'S BUSI-NESS. When built on a dimensional data model (star schema), the warehouse is well positioned to provide useful information for analysis by decision makers. The fact tables in the data model store a time series of measurements that are the subject of the warehouse. The dimensions in the data model provide characteristic, descriptive information about the measurements. Dimensions provide context for the facts, which make up the content of the warehouse. The fact table can be thought of as the "what" of the warehouse, while the dimensions represent who, where, when, and how. In performing analysis on the warehouse, the user strives to understand the "why."

Over the course of time, changes to the company's business environment have an impact on the context of the warehouse. What's more, as the data warehouse may store five years or more of historical data, this type of change may happen many times within the lifetime of the data in the warehouse.   .

There are many types of context changes that can impact the data warehouse. Some are changes to the internal environment, that is, changes that are under the company's direct control. The company may reorganize its sales regions, promote an employee, create a new general ledger account, discontinue a product, or even acquire or merge with another company. Other changes result from the external environment, for example, a customer may move one of their offices or expand their operation into a new area, or a competitor may merge with, acquire, or be acquired by another company.

Regardless of whether the context changes are to the internal or external business environment, they must be dealt with appropriately in the data warehouse. This article discusses the appropriate handling of context changes in a data warehouse.

DIMENSIONS IN A DATA WAREHOUSE

A star schema is a data warehouse data model that organizes the data that is the subject of the warehouse so as to facilitate ad hoc querying and analysis (also known as Online Analytical Processing—OLAP). The metrics or measures that are important to the business are collected and related ones are stored as records in fact tables. Descriptive, characteristic and classifying information is grouped together into dimension tables. Fact tables contain primarily quantitative information, while dimension tables contain mainly qualitative information. The records in the fact tables are linked by foreign keys to the related records in dimension tables.

One dimension table that should appear in every star schema is time. This is because the measures that are recorded in the fact table have some kind of effectivity. The metrics in the fact table are a time series: they take on discrete, measurable values which change over time. In this sense, the fact table is time variant—it stores sets of content measurements as their values vary over time. The time dimension groups together those measurements that were taken at the same interval. By using the time dimension, we know when the measurements were taken, we can compare the content values as at one time interval to another, and get some understanding of trends of change over time.

Of course, different metrics may have different measurement frequencies. In typical business processes, this is generally one day or longer. Content measurements may be made weekly or monthly, although a daily measurement interval is most common. This is typically the finest granularity required for business processes.

The time dimension itself is unique among the dimensions in the star schema because it does not change. It grows uniformly, day by day and week by week as time passes, and it may shrink from time to time as old data is dropped from the warehouse, but time itself does not change. The values of a record in the time dimension, once inserted, remain constant. This is because everyone has a completely common frame of reference for understanding what a day is, and what a year is. It just does not happen that someone will decide to change the number of days in a year. Time is essentially an invariant.

Most other dimensions in the data warehouse exhibit an aspect of time variance. Like the content of the warehouse, the context changes over time. The dimension tables must somehow capture the time series of context values. However, unlike the content of the warehouse, the context changes much more sporadically, and asynchronously. In most cases, only one or two records change at one time. Also, context changes typically occur on a much longer time scale (more slowly) than the content changes in the fact table. Thus, the term "slowly changing dimension" (SCD) is often used to describe the phenomenon.

How should we depict slowly changing dimensions in a data warehouse? The simplest answer, of course, is to ignore all the changes. With this strategy, we pretend the dimension is time invariant. Once each dimension record has been populated from the source system, it is not changed in the warehouse. Obviously, this will lead to the data warehouse and the source system getting increasingly out of synch, as changes actually do occur on the source system, and fail to be reflected in the data warehouse. For this reason, ignoring the changes is a very bad answer.

Ralph Kimball has described three possible answers, which he refers to as Type 1, 2, and 3 Slowly Changing Dimensions. (The simplest answer, ignoring changes, can be referred to as Type 0.) A Type 1 Slowly Changing Dimension is implemented by keeping the dimension in the data warehouse synchronized with updates in the source system. This is much better than implementing a Type 0 SCD, as the data warehouse will correctly reflect changes made in the operational system. However, like Type 0, Type 1 SCDs are not truly time variant. They reflect the most recent update only, but do not capture any history of changes. This means that all facts linked to the dimension for the entire duration of the warehouse reflect only the current version of the dimension attributes, which is not necessarily the way the dimension attributes would have looked when each fact record was originally created.

It is this weakness of Type 1 SCDs that becomes the focus of Type 2 SCDs. With Type 2, the dimension is kept in synch with the operational systems, like Type 1, but the history of changes over time is tracked. A Type 2 SCD is truly time variant. This is implemented by creating a new version of the dimension record each time any of its fields are changed. The previous version of the changed record, with all field values as before the change, remains in the database, and is referenced by all fact records that reflect those field values. Fact records that reflect the new field values (those created after the time of the change, but before the next change is recorded in the warehouse) reference the new dimension record.

Using Type 2 SCDs partitions history, such that each fact record is connected to the dimension record with the characteristic attribute information effective for its time. The partitioning happens naturally, just as the events and measurements recorded in the fact table occurred when their respective dimension attributes were effective. The fact records match up correctly with the SCD records because the world was the way it was when the facts were recorded. Queries against such a data model will return the

741

right answer because the data model accurately depicts the world as it changes over time.

Sometimes the users of the data warehouse only want to see some of the changes to a dimension over time. They may want to see only the latest value and the next latest value (the current value and the immediately previous one). A Type 3 Slowly Changing Dimension implements this behavior. This is done by duplicating the field(s) in question, and calling one the 'current' and the other the 'previous.' This approach can be further extended to track the last 'n' changes by creating 'n' versions of each field. However, this extension gets awkward to implement and work with for any value of 'n' much larger than two or three. Furthermore, if users really need to be able to query on the last 'n' changes, is it not possible they might soon need to query on the last 'n + 1' changes? Unfortunately, the same argument holds no matter how many changes are included.

Also, a Type 3 Slowly Changing Dimension, like Types 0 and 1, is not truly time variant. Only the most recent changes are visible, and their effectivity is unspecified. We do know that the latest one is currently effective, but in general have no information on when it or previous versions became effective. In practice, it may be better to take the Type 2 approach and track all changes through the duration of data in the warehouse.

EXTENDING THE DIMENSIONS

In some cases, rather than needing to query the last few changes, the users may need to query the current version and the original version. This may be important for analysis of the eventual outcome of some process under study compared to how the process started. For example, if we are working in a sales business, we may want to calculate the estimate of the eventual value of a customer to the business. Once we can do this, we may want to understand where our most and least valuable customers come from. Do our valuable customers first call our toll free number or connect to our internet site or walk into our store? Did they respond to a TV ad, follow an internet link, or were they referred to us by another customer?

If knowing the original values for some fields is important, but carefully tracking all changes over time as with Type 2 is not, we could simply add an 'Original' or 'First' version of each field to the dimension. These would be kept invariant as changes occur to the operational system, as in a Type 0 implementation. The other fields would be updated in step with changes to the operational data, as in a Type 1 implementation. We might call this a Type 4 Slowly Changing Dimension.

This gives us a total of five different answers (counting Types Zero through Four) to what started out as a seemingly simple question: 'how do we handle gradual changes of contextual information in a data warehouse?'

Unfortunately, all of these answers may be either right or wrong, depending on the underlying business requirements. Furthermore, if you ask a business person if they want to see only the current information, track the history of all changes, or track only previous or original values, they may say yes, they want to be able to do all these things. In fact, it is likely that at one time or another, all these types of questions may need to be asked for very legitimate business reasons. None of the approaches discussed so far can provide this much flexibility.

SELECTING A METHOD FOR HANDLING CHANGING DIMENSIONS

The approach implied by our names for the choices for handling slowly changing dimensions discussed above is that one must choose only one of the five approaches. This is sort of a multiple choice quiz, where we must choose our answer from one of five options presented. Even if more than one answer seems viable, or none does, we must decide which one is best, and choose only that. We've all written this type of test, so this situation is very familiar to us. However, when it comes to handling slowly changing dimensions, our assumption that we must choose only one answer is not correct. It is possible to choose all or some of the approaches to changes to dimensions, according to the business requirements in each case.

To understand how to do this, we must consider how we could combine the different answers together. In fact, we've already done this to a certain extent with our Type 4 answer. This combines Type 0, ignoring changes, with Type 1, propagating changes from the operational system into the warehouse directly. As it turns out, we can fully generalize this approach and, according to the business rules, allow a single dimension to take on the characteristics of all types of slowly changing dimensions.

To avoid confusion, let's call the fully generalized slowly changing dimension a Time Variant Dimension (TVD). Recall that a Type 2 Slowly Changing Dimension must have a surrogate key assigned for use in the warehouse—it's primary key in the data warehouse cannot be the operational key. The operational key is invariant as the entity attributes change over time. For the data warehouse, each Time Variant Dimension needs a Time Variant Key. Each time an attribute value of a record in the operational system changes, a corresponding new record, with a new primary key, is created in the Time Variant Dimension.

In the operational system, entities have exactly one primary key, which is unique for all time. Each record in the data warehouse has exactly one primary key also. However, many unchanging records in the Time Variant Dimension correspond to one changing record in the operational system. In this way, the Time Variant Dimension is exactly analogous to a Type 2 Slowly Changing Dimension.

The difference is that the data acquisition process for the Time Variant Dimension must be somewhat more sophisticated. For each field in the TVD the data acquisition process must implement specific procedures corresponding to the business rule that governs the management of changes to the field on the operational system.

There are three possible business rules that may be implemented depending on the type of field in the TVD. A field that never changes, a time invariant field, must be loaded with the initial field value, and never subsequently changed. If all the fields in a TVD used time invariant fields, the TVD would be a Type 0 SCD. Note, however, that a time invariant field can be used to record the original value for the dimension record, even if other fields in the TVD are managed differently.

A field that is kept synchronized with the operational field, in other words, a time synchronous field, should be updated to track the field in the operational system. If all the fields in a TVD are time synchronous fields, the dimension is a Type 1 SCD. Also, if some fields are time invariant and some are time synchronous, we have implemented a Type 4 SCD. Further, we can produce a Type 3 SCD by creating duplicate time synchronous fields but introducing a lag in the update process.

Finally, a time variant field can be implemented by creating a new version of the dimension record, with new surrogate key, and recording the changed value of the field in the new record only. If all the fields in a TVD are time variant, it is equivalent to a Type 2 SCD.

Exhibit 56.1 describes the actions that must be implemented in the data acquisition process for the different business rules.

Exhibit 56.1. Data acquisition process.	
Business Rule	**Action**
Time invariant field	no action
Time synchronous field	update TS field of all TVD records which correspond to the operational record
Time variant field	create new record in TVD with new field value

The beauty of Time Variant Dimensions is that the different field types can be mixed and matched as needed. In fact, just as one record in the operational system can correspond to more than one record in the TVD, one field in the operational system can correspond to more than one field in the TVD record. This was already suggested as a way to implement a Type 3 SCD. Better than that, though, creating multiple copies of the operational field in the TVD and making one time invariant, one time synchronous, and one time variant, can satisfy the business person who asks for all the types of Slowly Changing Dimension. If there is a business need, potentially all fields in the TVD can be implemented this way, allowing all possible types of analysis.

CONCLUSION

The key to unlocking the benefits of Time Variant Dimensions is in creating and managing primary keys that are distinct from the operational keys for all dimensions in the warehouse. This allows the freedom to treat any fields in the dimension as time variant. Only if it is absolutely impossible that a dimension would ever contain time variant fields should the operational key be used as the primary key for the dimension. Of course, it is difficult to know for certain whether this will be the case, so in almost all cases, it's better to assign and manage separate keys for the warehouse.

For the same reasons, it may be better to hedge one's bets and track all dimension fields as both time variant and time synchronous. This can be easily done by keeping two versions of each field in the warehouse—one of which is maintained as a time-variant field, the other of which is maintained as a time synchronous field. If this is done from the beginning, and a need arises to have a time-invariant field based on any of the time-variant fields, the time-invariant field can be constructed from the historical record of changes captured by the time-variant field.

It is possible that three copies of each operational field would be maintained in the data warehouse. This would satisfy any possible business rule for tracking changes on the operational system. This proliferation of fields can be made transparent to end users by defining the fields appropriately in the ad hoc query tools, and possibly hiding fields which are not yet necessary. In this way, as a new way of handling slowly changing dimensions is dictated by changing business requirements, the required answer is already available in the warehouse.

Chapter 57

Implementing a Hybrid Online Analytical Processing (HOLAP) Solution

Diane Johnson

FRONT-END SOLUTIONS CAN MAKE OR BREAK YOUR DATA WAREHOUSE PROJECT. In all the implementation of front-end solutions to meet the business needs of today and for the future is the most difficult challenge. Online Analytical Processing can help navigate the treacherous waters.

Online Analytical Processing (OLAP) is a process that supports the analysis of business trends and projections interactively using computer-based tools. There are two main technical solutions to support OLAP: Multidimensional OLAP (MOLAP) and a Relational OLAP (ROLAP). The main difference between these two solutions are the databases: MOLAPs database is a proprietary multidimensional database; ROLAPs database is a relational database.

A third technical solution has emerged: Hybrid OLAP (HOLAP). HOLAPs are a combination of MOLAP and ROLAP. The typical configuration of a HOLAP is a MOLAP solution with a ROLAP back end. The reason for being is to extend the data depth of the MOLAP solution while keeping the speed and rich calculations of a MOLAP. HOLAPs store detail data in a relational database. The business user reaches the end of data in summary format in the MOLAP, then they may "reach through" to the relational database to get the underlying detail.

GETTING STARTED

An evaluation of business functions is necessary before choosing a technical solution. Typical profiles for HOLAP solutions are:

0-8493-9832-0/00/$0.00+$.50
© 2000 by CRC Press LLC

- Large amounts of data
- Requirement of advanced analytics
- Summary data to provide quick response time
- Small number of users that require the details

Timing is an issue when selecting front-end solutions. Typically a tool evaluation begins after gathering business requirements. The tool list should focus on three to five vendors that suit the needs of the business users. That selection may take as long as one month to complete, so work on the back end needs to continue during the selection process. Most companies already have a relational database that can be used to store the data for the data warehouse regardless of solution. The work on the database can be leveraged in all types of solutions.

There are a number of implementation factors that need to take place before a HOLAP solution is developed. The main considerations are:

- Architecture
- Data threshold
- Replication path
- Rules
- Metadata

ARCHITECTURE

HOLAP solutions implement a three-tier environment. The main goal is to support a highly scaleable environment. The relational database sits on the back end server, a MOLAP application server in the middle-tier and on the front end the client (Exhibit 57.1). There are three areas for scalability—data, model, and users. Main scalability features include a multithreaded architecture, shared metadata, caches, and database connections to avoid bottlenecks.

DATA THRESHOLD

In HOLAP solutions the relational database provides the basis for information but the decision needs as to where best to store the data. There are three types of storage in a HOLAP solution: user defined, persistent and transient. It is through the persistent, and transient that the window to the relational database is defined. Typically, up to ten gigabytes are stored persistently in the MOLAP portion of the HOLAP solution. The relational database and hardware limit the transient storage. User defined variables are kept within the MOLAP solution and are not fed by the operational systems.

Drawing the line between what is considered summary data and detail is not an easy choice in any front-end solution. Data volume can be one determinant for summary data. I prefer making the decision with the business user with the key of how they are going to use the data. Yearly,

HOLAP

Exhibit 57.1   A three-tier environment.

quarterly, and monthly are all good candidates for summary data. As well as the top levels in all dimensions depending on volume. For example, in a HOLAP solution that was just implemented in the insurance industry, the certificates were deemed detail and the product groups (traditional non-dividend, traditional dividend, universal life, etc) were summary.

REPLICATION PATH

Once the line is chosen for summary data and detail data, data delivery becomes an integral part of the operations. The detail data flows into the relational database. The summary data may flow into the relational database or directly into the multidimensional database. The path that the summary data should follow from the operational systems into the HOLAP solution depends on the number of sources, cleanliness of data, and volume of data. A distinct group of HOLAP tools store the data in a multidimensional model in memory. In that case, all of the data needs to reside in the relational database regardless of the factors above.

Write Back

A rich calculation engine is one of the benefits of an HOLAP solution. Once a value is calculated through analysis or 'what-if' scenarios, the value may be written back to the operational system or relational database. The action of writing a value back to the operational systems is known as closed loop decision support. For example, a product manager can analyze the inventory of a product and implement necessary production changes.

RULES

Exceptions and changes are a part of any business that the rules in a HOLAP application need to handle seamlessly. In the insurance industry, different countries have different products and roles up the hierarchy differently depending on what country you are in. Overall the product profits from each country roll up into the overall profit for the company. Flexible rules are essential in these cases where the rule may be applied to the leaf, parent or ancestor.

METADATA

Metadata is an often overlooked, but important component in data warehousing efforts. The product that is chosen may not give you a choice as to where to store the metadata in the multidimensional or relational database. Some products need the metadata stored in the multidimensional database so that it may recognize the data in the relational database. That solution may be a problem if the data in the relational database is constantly changing. Dynamic, real-time access to relational data may be another alternative. Other products choose to store the metadata in the relational database and access it through the MOLAP.

Stored in either location, the metadata catalog needs to contain reusable data mappings, dimensions, hierarchies, calculation logic, business rules, reports and queries, and data management functionality. Metadata is also used to store personal preference information. That means that anyone can logon anywhere and access all their reports and have the application customized to their personal preferences.

CASE STUDY: HOLAP IN A LIFE INSURANCE COMPANY

The main goal of this large life insurance company was to improve their valuation process. The valuation process is regulated by government.

Guidelines set out the amount of reserves a company must hold on a policy in the event of paying out today for the company to remain solvent. The reserves for life insurance companies are the largest dollar amount on the balance sheet.

Currently, it took five months to extract, cleanse, and gather the data from a number of different systems. Their new requirements were to produce valuations quarterly, three weeks after the end of a quarter. As well the data was never used again after the results published. Their secondary objective was to improve their reporting and analytical process like year-to-year comparisons.

The first step was to implement a data mart to extract, cleanse, integrate and store the data in a week time frame from month or quarter end. The data needed to be at the policy transaction level, the lowest gain in an insurance company. The data then needed to be exported to a sophisticated data mining application that would calculate the reserves and other information for each policy. Once the assumptions and results were desirable, the data was then brought back to the data mart for reporting and analytics.

Analytics included year to date historical information for trend analysis, profitability analysis, movement analysis, experience studies, premium persistency, and various model predictions against actuals for risk and investment return. This company turned to a product named WhiteLight, from WhiteLight Systems, Inc. WhiteLight enables companies to interactively build, analyze and scenario test analytic applications in areas such as risk management, profitability and customer relationship management. WhiteLight 1.5 shatters the ROLAP barrier with integrated write-back, cell-based security, unparalleled modeling and what-if analysis for enterprise-scaleable "closed-loop" analysis applications.

For this customer, WhiteLight was able to build simple reports like a balance sheet, but also do year on year comparisons for profitability analysis. More importantly for the experience studies like mortality studies and lapse studies calculate exposure-to-risk. Exposure to risk is defined as the amount of time that each policy is in-force during a specified time period. For example if the time period is 12 months and a policy is issued 3 months into this period and is in force at the end of the period, the exposure-to-risk is 9 months. This exposure-to-risk can be used for any experience study in the following equation: the sum observed experiences during the time period divided by the sum of the exposed-to-risk for the time period.

The following elements in the exposure-to-risk may be selected:

- Start date and end date of the investigation period.
- Policies included in the investigation, based on either where they live, or the type of policy they hold.

- Duration of policies investigated.
- Premium or total sum insured band.
- Smoker / non-smoker status.
- Gender.

Using HOLAP techniques, this company translated their business challenges into automated and repeatable solutions where the parameters are flexible. The parameters may be stored with the results for later comparison reducing the need for guesswork and apples to apples comparisons. The group is more informed and share information and knowledge with each other effortlessly. Another benefit is that they can now explain variances easily to upper management instead of guesswork.

SUMMARY

HOLAP solutions are another alternative to solve a business problem. The business user does not care about the architecture of the solution. They care about the functionality and whether the product meets their needs. Standards for products nominating themselves as HOLAPs are still emerging. (See Exhibit 57.2 for a listing of HOLAP vendors.) HOLAPs offer yet another bullet to shoot at the data warehousing bulls eye. Implementing a HOLAP depends on the skill of shooter, the weapon used and the distance from the target!

Exhibit 57.2. HOLAP vendors.

Product	Company Name	Web Site	Phone Number	Database	HOLAP Capabilities (Y/N)
Arbor Essbase Analysis Server	Hyperion Software	www.hyperion.com	(800) 286-8000	MDDB	Yes
BrioQuery	Brio Technology	www.brio.com	(800) 879-2746	MDDB	Yes
Business Objects	Business Objects, Inc.	www.businessobjects.com	(800) 379-4330	Relational	No
Decision	Comshare Inc.	www.comshare.com	(800) 922-7979	MDDB	No
Seagate Info	Seagate Software	www.seagatesoftware.com	(800) 877-2340	MDDB/Relational	Yes
DB2 OLAP Server	IBM	www.ibm.com	(800) 426-2255	Relational	No
DSS Agent	MicroStrategy	www.microstrategy.com	(800) 927-1868	Relational	No
Express Server, Objects	Oracle	www.oracle.com	(617) 768-5600	MDDB/Relational	Yes
Gentia	Gentia	www.gentia.com	(303) 794-8701	MDDB	Yes
Hyperion OLAP	Hyperion Software	www.hyperion.com	(800) 286-8000	MDDB	Yes
InfoBeacon	Platinum Technology, Inc.	www.platinum.com	(800) 442-6861	Relational	No
Pilot Decision Support Suite	Pilot Software, Inc.	www.pilotsw.com	(800) 944-0094	MDDB/Relational	Yes
Media	Speedware Corporation	www.speedware.com	(416) 408-2880	MDDB/Relational	Yes
BI Query, BI Anaylzer	Hummingbird Communications, Ltd	www.hummingbird.com	(613) 548-4355	MDDB/Relational	Yes
PowerPlay	Cognos Corporation	www.cognos.com	(800) 426-4667	MDDB/Relational	Yes
SAS/MDDB	SAS	www.sas.com	(919) 677-8000	MDDB	No
Whitelight Server	WhiteLight Systems, Inc.	www.whitelight.com	(650) 321-2183	Relational	Yes

Chapter 58

A Framework for Developing an Enterprise Data Warehousing Solution

Ali H. Murtaza

THE DECISION TO BUILD A DATA WAREHOUSE IS NOT FOR THE FAINT OF HEART — many critical issues must be understood early, or the project will fail. An enterprise data warehousing project is generally a huge, time-consuming investment. In many cases, the benefits are not immediately quantifiable and require a leap of faith to justify. While there are many reasons to build a data warehouse, the two most common reasons are to optimize control of current operations or to gain significant competitive advantage. For instance, a complex, geographically distributed organization may decide that they need to identify their most profitable customer segments for target marketing programs. This is accomplished by extracting customer data from multiple production systems into a single, consolidated data warehouse. On the other hand, a niche company may architect a data mart as the first stage of a large data mining effort — revealing insightful purchasing patterns that could be leveraged for additional revenue. In both cases, the data warehouse defines itself as an integrated, non-volatile catalog of organizational data that is convertible into actionable information for strategic decision-making.

There are numerous advantages to maintaining such a central perspective over the business that allow the end user to monitor both departmental and corporate performance, access all customer account information, increase managerial control, make proactive business decisions, and

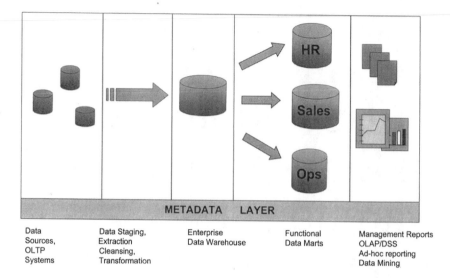

Data Sources, OLTP Systems	Data Staging, Extraction Cleansing, Transformation	Enterprise Data Warehouse	Functional Data Marts	Management Reports OLAP/DSS Ad-hoc reporting Data Mining

Exhibit 58.1. Enterprise data warehouse model.

create sales opportunities. Although an IDC study reported an average data warehousing implementation cost of $3 million, this expensive investment also produces a three-year average return-on-investment (ROI) of 401 percent. Exhibit 58.1 shows a standard enterprise data warehouse architecture.

CONSIDERING THE CHALLENGES

An enterprise data warehousing initiative is one the most daunting projects an organization can tackle; a typical effort requires high levels of executive sponsorship, close cooperation between the business and IS communities, cross-functional expertise, and significant time and capital investments. In fact, the high risk of failure prompts experts to depict unsuccessful data warehousing projects as characteristic rites of passage for new project managers; experts state that approximately one out of every five DW projects actually run to completion. This can easily make a project manager's decision to develop a data warehouse a risky move — often the key to success is the simple ability to neutralize the negative elements that could otherwise sabotage the project.

Before embarking on any data warehousing journey, a clearly defined enterprise strategy with specific goals and objectives must be presented to the project sponsors and stakeholders. Also, the project's objectives must align with those of the organization, or the project will fall short; the main driving force of any data warehousing effort is to assist decision making in achieving corporate objectives. Any project that focuses on achieving strategic objectives that differ significantly from the parent organization will be rejected by senior executives, and teach a painful lesson to the project manager.

A data warehousing venture differs from most technology projects in having a high level of executive involvement. There should be no misconceptions about which group is driving a data warehouse project: the business users. Business users define the information requirements, validate the enterprise data model, and access the data for queries and reports. If the business user cannot easily navigate or understand the detailed, summarized, and historical data stored in the warehouse, the benefits are minimized. Frequent communication between the business and IS communities is mission-critical during all project phases to ensure that both groups are aligned and that the development plan meets the original business objectives.

Furthermore, the overall project structure and individual responsibilities must be clearly identified from the start to prevent any confusion among team members. If appropriate technical expertise is not available within the organization to staff the desired roles, the project manager should consider external consultants to fill in the skill gaps. Often, these consultants can provide valuable industry knowledge and vendor relationships important during the data modeling and tool selection stages. Regular meetings should be scheduled at all levels to keep everyone up-to-date and to uncover any potential roadblocks. A mandatory high level of sponsorship ensures political support and reduces resistance from any of the business units. As the project progresses, the project manager must be aware of all organizational or resource issues, and raise them immediately to the project sponsor. Clear communication among the different project teams maintains high morale and strong levels of commitment to project objectives. Many data warehousing projects last over 18 months — albeit in manageable three-to-six month iterations — but their benefits are realized even later, and maintaining the executive commitment and sponsorship becomes a serious challenge. The project manager must be aware of any cultural sensitivities to sharing data among the different functional units. Any political vendettas, power struggles, or personal conflicts should be identified early and handled quickly before they can become destructive. The key to success is constant involvement — business involvement in generating user requirements, creating the logical data models, and choosing the end-user tools, and IS involvement for the hardware/software selection, data extraction, physical implementation, and performance tuning.

A typical driving factor behind data warehousing projects is competition within the industry. As competitors take the lead in implementing their own corporate data warehouses and start to make sizable gains in market share and improvements in their bottom line, many companies naturally follow and expect dramatic results in performance and significant gains in competitive advantage. Consequently, it becomes critical to understand the stability of the organization's industry — potential acquisitions or mergers could leave behind a lot of unfinished work, greater confusion surrounding corporate data, and wasted capital expenditures for both organizations. Today, many vendors are offering vertical solution sets for data-rich industries such as financial, telecommunication, and health care services. These solutions are sought desperately by organizations for common business requirements and data models essential for effective analysis to be done. External consultants are also being leveraged for their vertical expertise and familiarity with vendor tools in addition to their project-related experience.

STAGE 1 — BUSINESS REQUIREMENTS

In the first stage of a data warehousing project, business requirements for enterprise information are gathered from the user community. This process generally consists of a series of interviews between the end users and the information technology teams in order to understand the informational needs and gaps in the organization. The consolidated results of these interviews drive the content of the data models and establish specific objectives for the new data architecture. The selection of business facts, dimensions, aggregations, level of granularity, historical depth, hierarchies, predefined queries, and standardized reports are all driven by the business users. Once the final version of the information requirements is approved by both the business and IS functions, functional data models are created with the granularity, historical detail, and summarization needed to allow end users access to the data while minimizing the performance effects of common table joins and complex queries. Specific vertical knowledge is most valuable here in customizing the data model to handle industry-specific analysis. Every piece of data in the target data model should have some business value attached to it, or it is useless to the business and should be dropped from the model. Lack of trust in the data raises a red flag and severely hinders the success of the project. However, the users must have realistic expectations of the kind of information that will be available to them in the new world. Sample reports or vendor demonstrations can help in this stage to train inexperienced users to visualize the types of querying results and analytical capabilities of the data warehouse front-end tools.

The degree of summarization and size of the data being retained determines whether the data should be stored in a relational or multidimensional database. While the relational DBMS is well-established, commonly understood, and can support very large databases, the multidimensional DBMS is growing in popularity by offering quicker access to pre-aggregated data and multidimensional analysis capabilities. Multidimensional hypercubes are memory-intensive but reduce the number of physical joins for queries, and take advantage of hierarchical and historical information in the schema to roll-up through dimensions. Many organizations are discovering the need for a hybrid schema; both technologies are used by loading the data first for longer term retention into "near normal" relational models subsequently used to build specific views or dimensional models. All external feeds that are required for additional information must also be mapped into the enterprise model in this phase.

STAGE 2 — DATA SOURCING

Companies with data-intensive businesses typically have great difficulty in accessing their operational data. Somewhere in the depth of the multiple legacy systems, lie valuable nuggets of business information that can never be capitalized upon because of generally poor data quality and integrity. Consequently, this second stage, which involves extracting, cleansing, and transforming the data from the multiple sources to populate the target data warehouse, is vital and often tends to be the most time-consuming part of the project. Further compounding this problem is the possible discovery that the technical resources supporting these legacy systems are no longer employed in the organization, so that cryptic data definitions and programs are left to be deciphered for extraction when they are required. The task of cleaning up enterprisewide data from different functions and departments is often underestimated and can add significant delays to the project timelines. Increased complexity of the data makes the extraction process all the more difficult and laborious. Also, another issue to consider is the capacity of the transactional systems to scale in order to capture larger data volumes or external feeds that might be required in the target warehouse. Tool selection in this data staging layer must be well-researched to integrate well with the proprietary systems and the target warehouse.

STAGE 3 — TARGET ARCHITECTURE

The initial IS task to design a target architecture for the data warehouse can create religious, ideological wars among the architects; debates have raged over the tactical deployment of data marts and operational data stores as compared to the complete vision of an enterprise data warehouse. Some organizations will not take the risk of a failed project that could consume three years of their best resources. The scope of the business vision can also dictate the architecture approach: a short-term vision would require a lower budget, quick ROI implementation with small resource requirements offered by data marts, while more strategic objectives of long-term gain and full organizational control would necessitate the full-blown, enterprise data warehouse architecture. The most popular architecture choices outside the enterprise data warehouse model are the operational data store, virtual data warehouse, DSS data warehouse, and the data mart.

An operational data store is a rudimentary data store that provides a consolidated view of volatile transactional data from multiple operational systems. This architecture often provides real-time operational data that removes the redundancy and resource costs of creating a separate data warehouse. Analysis can be done with basic querying and reporting without impacting the performance of the production systems. This architecture also offers a shared view of the data, with regular updates from the operational systems. It contains current-valued data which is volatile yet very detailed. Unfortunately, operational data is not designed for decision support applications and complex queries may result in long response times and heavy impact on the transactional systems.

A virtual data warehouse is quick to implement and usually less risky than a traditional data warehouse. It involves data access directly from operational data stores without creating a redundant database. This method gives the user universal access to data from any of the multiple sources; however, the extensive process of cleaning up the data to transform it into actionable information cannot be avoided. There are obvious time and cost savings from not having to consolidate the data or introduce infrastructure changes, but the tradeoff exists in the reduced usability of the data from the multiple systems. If there is a lot of data duplication in the various systems, this will easily confuse the end user and remove any confidence they have in the information. Also, if the data distribution across the legacy systems requires cross-functional information between non-SQL compliant data sources, the load, complexity and access time will be impacted on the OLTP systems and network, even if the query can be performed. This architecture also requires more intelligent analysis from the end user to understand the results of multiple queries instead of just one. Distributed query processing software must be in place to decide where and when the queries should be performed in the transactional systems. Once results are obtained, significant data validation may be required to make sense of the business information that was not cleansed or integrated. Also, the end user will not have access to historical snapshots which are one of the most valuable strategic decision-making tools offered by a data warehouse. Finally, the results will not be repeatable as the data is continuously changing.

The decision support data warehouse architecture simply consists of snapshots of corporate information consisting of low-level or highly summarized data. This method has the advantages of minimal infrastructure costs, access to non-volatile data, quick deployment time, and no repetitive data stores. However, the main flaw of this architecture is its inherent lack of flexibility to handle complex decision support analysis expected from a fully architected data warehouse; the data structures are not changed, merely stored periodically as snaphots for comparative analysis. This technique provides good historical information but fails to optimize access to the data. In fact, the snapshots of data are ideal for independent business intelligence and data mining approaches to unearthing customer patterns and trends.

Another potential architecture is the popular data mart or functional data warehouse that captures a subset of the enterprise data for a specific function, business unit, or application. Data marts require less cost and effort to deploy, and provide access to functional or private information to specific organizational units. They are suited for businesses demanding a fast time to market, quick impact on the bottom line, and minimal infrastructure changes. Data marts are essentially mini-data warehouses without the huge cost, long-time investment, high risk of failure, and high level of corporate approval; they are ideal for a rapid, iterative, prototype deployment. Data marts store non-volatile, time-variant, and summarized information used to serve the information needs of the business unit. However, data marts should not be used as a cheaper solution to a data warehouse; they should simply represent an initial step towards an enterprise data warehouse. If data marts are introduced first, they should be designed to integrate with a future enterprise data warehouse, or much rework will have to be done over the long term. As other business units notice the benefits, data marts must not be allowed to propagate freely throughout the organization, or the situation will spell disaster when attempting to integrate them into a single corporate warehouse. When data marts are introduced after the successful implementation of a data warehouse, they can be deployed quickly by replicating required subsets of the corporate database.

STAGE 4 — ACCESS TOOL SELECTION

The level of sophistication of the intended user should be a main driver in the reporting tool selection process. Exhibit 58.2 illustrates the many levels of query, reporting, and OLAP tools in the marketplace with functions ranging from basic management reporting to complex, drill-down, pass-through analytical processing. It is crucial that the user be comfortable in navigating through the newly consolidated data. Otherwise, this huge capital investment will result in the same scenario the organization started with; namely, lots of data with no perceived method to access it. Sample reports and demonstrations are good aids in assessing the results and the capabilities of the business intelligence tool.

In fact, careful training should be provided for the end users to ensure that they understand the various capabilities of the tools. Instead of

Exhibit 58.2.   User access tools.

producing monthly management reports, they should be encouraged to make ad hoc queries and "slice and dice" through the multiple dimensions and navigate throughout the available information to isolate the specific set of information they require. Once the user taps into the metadata layer (see Exhibit 58.1) and understands the type of data and relationships that exist in the warehouse, he or she is better equipped to perform meaningful analysis and extract valuable information about the business. Newly evolved data mining technologies promise to bring even greater benefits by performing complex statistical analysis on historical records to uncover business patterns, customer trends, organizational inefficiencies, and even potential fraud.

STAGE 5 — DATA WAREHOUSE ADMINISTRATION

One of the most commonly neglected issues is the administration of the data warehouse after it is built. The appropriate technical resources must be assigned to monitor query load and performance, to handle dynamic changes to the data structures, and to ensure platform scalability with increased user demands. External data may be needed (e.g., stock feeds, Web downloads) and so the architecture must have an open interface to incorporate these new requirements. As users become more sophisticated in their use of the decision support tools, the frequency and complexity of the queries and reports will significantly impact the query performance. A "query from hell" can destroy perceived levels of performance if not identified and managed carefully. Consequently, a dedicated administrator is needed to maintain constant supervision of the query performance and to prevent the data warehouse from grinding to a halt.

Generally, data warehousing projects use the prototype approach to development, and much of the initial success of the prototype will determine the overall success of the project. The data model should be designed against an extensive range of end-user queries and target reports showing enhanced analytical business information, and should be designed to maintain buy-in from the executive sponsors during the pilot demonstration. Most importantly, the information must be accurate, or at least more accurate than the pre-data warehouse data to increase the user's confidence in the information. If the user has unwavering faith in the data, the project has a greater chance to succeed.

CONCLUSION

A common point of debate arises when measuring the overall investment impact of a particular project — the added value of business information is hard to translate into cost savings or generated revenue. The difficulty in quantifying these benefits is one of the most problematic issues facing the project manager in keeping corporate buy-in and team commitment. How can one measure business value? As shown in Exhibit 58.1, an answer lies in a well-developed metadata repository that allows the business user to easily understand and navigate through the large amounts of corporatewide data contained in the new warehouse. Each piece of data selected for the new data model should be clearly defined in the metadata and perceived as adding business value. If the end user sees no value in it, he or she will not use it and it should be omitted from the new data model. The remarkable change in the business analyst's job is represented by the drastically reduced time needed to gather organizational data — much more time is dedicated to garner meaningful information that will drive the sustained growth and operational efficiency of the corporation.

The designed architecture of the metadata and data warehouse must be scalable enough to support future changes to information needs and analytical requirements (e.g., Web-based delivery). Ongoing management of the data warehouse with minimal adjustments to the data architecture, and business users excited about their data are true indicators of project success. Business value is reflected by the enhanced corporate control, lowered costs, increased revenue, strong market share, and new opportunities that are all direct results of the information delivery architecture called the data warehouse.

References

Bachteal, P., Data warehouses: professional management key to successful implementation, *Can. Man.*, 22: 22, 20-21, Summer 1997.

Barquin, R. C., *An Introduction to Data Warehousing,* Barquin and Associates, The Data Warehousing Institute, 1997.

DATA WAREHOUSING, DECISION SUPPORT, AND OLAP

Benson, B. and Von Hollen, C., *Case Study III: Strategies for a Successful Data Warehouse*, May 28, 1997.

Bischoff, J. and Alexander, T., *Data Warehouse Practical Advice from the Experts,* Prentice-Hall, New York, 1997.

Evans, J., Need for analysis drives data warehouse appeal, *Health Man. Tech.*, 18: 11, 28-31, Oct. 1997.

Foley, J., Data warehousing pitfalls, *Inform. Week,* May 19, 1997.

Hackney, D., *Understanding and Implementing Successful Data Marts*, May 28, 1997.

Stedman, C., Turning to outside warehousing help," *ComputerWorld.*

Waltner, C., Ready-made warehouses," *Inform. Week,* 655, 100-108, Nov. 3, 1997.

Chapter 59
Why Dimensional Modeling is Right for Decision Support

R. Michael Pickering

A DECISION SUPPORT SYSTEM (DSS) IS USED TO STORE AND RETRIEVE INFORMATION needed by a company's managers and executives for use in performance tracking and decision making. Unlike an Online Transaction Processing (OLTP) system, where the primary purpose of the system is usually to store, update, and maintain operational data, the primary purpose of a DSS is to provide answers to business questions. A DSS is used to help manage a business that is run on one or more OLTP systems. The different types of systems are complementary, but designed to serve fundamentally different purposes.

The focus of an OLTP system is usually on getting data into a system. This is often extremely critical to the business because earning revenue may depend, for example, on being able to record orders as they are received. Recording an order requires capturing and storing various related bits of data that make up the order, such as who is making the order, exactly what is being ordered, where and when it is to be sent, and so on. Getting data into OLTP systems quickly is so important that this criterion has been taken up above all others in the generally accepted process for designing them.

NORMALIZATION

There are several variations on the generally accepted process for designing OLTP systems for implementation on relational databases. All the major ones involve the use of normalization, so named because it depends on a series of normal forms defined using the mathematical theory of functional dependencies. Normalization provides a systematic process for ensuring that the size of each record (or bit of data) stored in each table in the system is as small as is reasonably possible. In fact, normalization ensures that each data record is the smallest it can be, while still making sense in the context of the system as a whole. This is the best way to get data into a system quickly. Storing data in small records allows each new record to be processed quickly. In this way, very many small OLTP transactions (updates, inserts, and deletes) can be processed concurrently. However, it also means that the system is made up of very complex and interrelated set of tables.

Because normalization has a sound basis in theoretical mathematics, it has been taken up with great fanfare in academic circles and is taught at the undergraduate level in computer science programs. It has been so successful in designing real OLTP systems that have become a critical part of so many businesses that it is very highly regarded by IT practitioners and business managers alike. It has become almost a religion in that so many people believe in it without question. Normalization has become such a basic part of the design of OLTP systems that people forget it is primarily a tool used to solve the problem of getting data into a system quickly. This just is not a big problem in the design of decision support systems.

DECISION SUPPORT

A decision support system (DSS) is about information. Information is made up of data, but that data must be organized and processed into a form that is appropriate for the situation. In a sense, information can be thought of as data viewed at a higher conceptual level. The data must be organized and processed so that it is meaningful and useful to its intended audience. The intended audience or users of the information provided by a DSS are business analysts and managers. They are concerned primarily with seeing the big picture — trends and variations from expectations (information), rather than all the details (data) of the business. For example, knowing that there were 1000 orders received this month is more meaningful if compared to what was expected. Expectations typically are based on past experiences, so how many orders were received last month or in the same month last year must be known. The fact that 1000 orders were received is data, but knowing that orders are up 10 percent over last year is information.

Another important thing to remember about a DSS is that users do not care how quickly data gets into it, as long as it gets there. What is important is that they can get the information out when they need it. A DSS must be designed with this essential difference of purpose in mind. It must be built from data, but it must deliver information. The DSS also must be flexible in the way it delivers this information. As has been seen, normalization helps to get data into systems quickly, but this is not particularly important in a DSS. Thus, normalization is not critical to building a DSS. To implement a successful DSS, consider what is important for its audience.

DIMENSIONAL MODELING

A technique called dimensional data modeling has proven very successful in DSS design. Dimensional modeling is based on understanding the nature of information requirements of the DSS.

Dimensional data modeling produces a simple but powerful and flexible database schema, commonly referred to as a star schema. This way of designing the schema for a DSS focuses on the requirements of the target audience. Business managers tend to need to know about certain essential measures that determine the success of the business. They need a way to look at these measures in different ways. For example, it is always important to know how the measures are changing over time. Knowing that sales are high is good, but knowing that sales are high and rising over recent weeks is better. Other breakdowns are typically important to managers also. For example, if the company sells more than one type of product or if the sales of some products are not increasing as quickly as others, the manager may want to know if sales are high for all products. If the business sells to the same customers repeatedly, it may be important to know which customers are increasing vs. which customers are reducing their buying. The business managers need to be able to pick out the contributions to the important measures along whichever axis are important. This often is called *slicing and dicing*.

There are often hierarchical relationships along one or more measurement axis. For example, there may be different classes of products and, within each class, there may be different brands and, within each brand, there may be different colors, and so on. The business manager wants to be able to look at the contribution to the important measures at any level of the hierarchy or by adding in categories from a different measurement axis. This is known as *drilling down*.

In dimensional modeling, unlike the general relational model, there are different types of tables. This is an important logical concept of dimensional modeling intended to help align the data model of the DSS with the business being supported. The different types of tables correspond to the way business people do analysis. This helps the dimensional modeler understand the business the way a DSS user does and helps the DSS user understand the dimensional model. This mutual understanding is crucial toward ensuring that the DSS user gets whatever he or she needs from the warehouse.

The concept of business metrics, also known as key performance indicators (KPIs), is virtually universal across the business world. It is easy to find discussions of business measures in any business textbook or magazine. An obvious example in any business is the bottom line or amount of profit earned or loss incurred by the business for the year. This is a very high-level measure of the success of the business, which is determined by adding up the contributions of all the various operations and processes of the business over the course of the year.

A star schema is a way to capture the important business metrics and store them with all the common business categories and conditions for analysis. The metrics are stored in a fact table, which forms the center of the star, and the categories and conditions (the measurement axes and hierarchies) are stored in dimension tables, which form the points of the star.

The star schema is a very good way to satisfy the requirements of business managers. The model itself clearly shows the important business measures and the dimensions along which they can be analyzed. It corresponds very closely to the way they need to ask questions. This is important not only because it allows the questions to be answered almost directly from the model, but because the model itself can be used as a communications tool. The designer can talk through the model with the users to help them understand what business analysis they will be able to perform using the system. This is a significant difference between a star schema and the much more complex schemas for OLTP systems. A typical OLTP schema is difficult to explain to the users of the system. In fact, many designers refrain from even trying. Due to the inherent simplicity of a star schema, it is much easier for a user to understand.

Most real OLTP schemas are denormalized to some extent — they do not conform to the (theoretically best) highest order normal form. This is the result of a conscious decision on the part of the designer, made typically for performance reasons, or sometimes because the designers did not think that normalization was something that needed to be applied too rigorously. Normalization is a tool that, when used properly, generally produces an OLTP schema to which data can be added and updated quickly. However, normalization is at best a heuristic rather than an algorithm, in that it is not guaranteed to produce a schema that will yield the best possible performance for OLTP systems in all possible cases. The fact is that normalization does not guarantee good performance for OLTP systems and does nothing at all to help produce a correct and complete schema — one that will satisfy the user requirements.

PERFORMANCE CONSIDERATIONS

One of the principle criticisms against star schemas is that they lead to poor database performance. This is largely a fallacy contributed to by practitioners more familiar with OLTP systems. They expect to normalize the data model for performance and think that the two terms are synonymous. In fact, databases designed with star schemas for business analysis can provide excellent performance.

Consider a simple star schema consisting of one fact table and several dimensions. At the logical level, the only difference between the fact table and the dimension table is that the fact table is a dependant entity, although all the dimension tables are independent entities. In some variations on simple stars, the fact table itself may be an independent entity. In addition, at the physical level, fact tables typically contain many more rows of data than dimension tables.

There may be a difference between the fact tables and the dimension tables in a dimensional model at the physical implementation level, depending on the available data structures in the RDBMS on which it is implemented. Typically, the fact table is indexed more heavily than the dimension tables. However, the reason fact tables and dimension tables are thought of differently in dimensional modeling is that they will be used in queries differently. A typical business query set will use certain attribute values of the dimension tables to choose only a small number of rows from the fact table for any given query. Ideally, the RDBMS' query optimizer will be able to benefit from this typical access pattern in choosing a query-processing strategy. Because the fact table contains very many rows, doing a table scan of the fact table would be very time-consuming — this is a very important difference between fact tables and dimension tables. This leads to a reason there is often a difference between fact and dimension tables at the physical level. The indexing scheme needs to be much more sophisticated for a fact table than for a dimension table, due to their very significant size difference. Most dimension tables are easily small enough to fit in memory on most hardware used to store data warehouses, so in many cases, they require only a primary key index to ensure unicity of primary keys. By contrast, fact tables are extremely large, so scanning the entire fact table is usually a disaster. It is important to create any indices that could be used to provide fast access to the target rows in the fact table. Specifically, some kind of index should be created on every foreign key in the fact table, at the very least.

Because the differences between fact tables and dimension tables are confined primarily to the physical design level, one can think of dimensional modeling as a special case of relational modeling. However, to design an appropriate star schema, it is essential to consider fact tables and dimension tables explicitly as part of the design process. In a dimensional design, not all tables are created equal.

Typical business analysis involves very complex queries, which often include aggregations of large numbers of database records, summarized at a high level. For example, a typical query might request the total sales in a region for a year, which could require summing the sales amounts from thousands of sales detail records. To answer this query, the RDBMS query processor also must find a way to retrieve only the records from the requested region. Consider the schema for this query. It is a star schema with at least two dimensions, geography (including regions) and time (including years). There also must be a fact table containing the sales amounts in dollars, along with other significant facts and metrics, plus the foreign key to each dimension table. In forming her query, the analyst browses the time dimension table and chooses the nonempty set of rows that corresponds to the current year. She also selects the nonempty set of rows that represents the region in which she is interested (note that the actual number of rows in each set depends on the form and number of hierarchies in each dimension). She then forms an aggregate query to calculate the total sales for the region for the year. This typically would be done using a query tool with a graphical front end, so that the query could be posed by the user without having to know SQL. The query tool would generate a query that might look something like this:

```
SELECT sum(sales_amount)

FROM sales_facts f NATURAL JOIN time d1 NATURAL JOIN
geography d2

WHERE d1.year = '1998' AND d2.region = 'Great Lakes';
```

Although most real decision support queries would be more complex, this simple example shows the primary characteristics of such queries. It involves an aggregate function computed over a numeric field. It is a join of the fact table with two dimension tables from the star. And it uses the dimension tables to restrict or filter rows from the fact table. (Note that this query is written to the ANSI SQL-92 standard in its use of the natural join operator. Natural join performs an equi-join over common columns of listed tables. This syntax is a good way to separate the table relationships, specified in the FROM clause, from the business criteria, which are specified in the WHERE clause. Not all real query tools or relational databases will support this syntax, but it was used in this example because it is the best way to communicate the meaning of the query.)

As discussed previously, the fact table in a star schema is typically very much larger than the dimension tables, so assume that such is true for this example. This means that the joins of the fact table to the dimension tables would be very time-consuming if the joins were evaluated first, then the restrictions. If possible the restrictions should be evaluated first, and the join done only on the rows of the dimensions that satisfy the restrictions. This should be possible if there are appropriate indices on the foreign keys in the fact table. In this case, because there are restrictions from two different dimensions, it may be necessary to guess which one will give the smallest answer set, create that answer set, and then evaluate the other condition on that intermediate result. This strategy processes queries against the star schema from the outside in.

Many relational database systems are providing combined indices to assist in processing multiple joins in just one step. If they are available, their use generally will improve performance significantly for such queries.

Some relational databases may attempt to process a query from the inside out, starting from the fact table. This usually results in queries that do not return. In these cases, the main tuning strategy is to diagnose the problem and figure out how to get the queries processed from outside in. Tweaking the foreign key indices may help in this process.

During the physical design phase of the project, and particularly during implementation of the data warehouse, it is important to consider the potential for running queries in parallel. Most relational database systems allow spawning multiple processes to run a single query, which is particularly beneficial for complex decision support queries when the host server has multiple processors. To maximize the benefits of parallelism, the physical disk configuration on the host server must be taken into consideration, and database files allocated accordingly. By spreading database files across many physical disks, parallel server processes can access data effectively and concurrently.

The final tuning tool in the data warehouse bag of tricks is to create prebuilt aggregates. Typical business analysis usually looks at information at a high level. For example, the user may start by requesting the sales revenue metric for a given year (restricting using the time dimension table), broken down by product category (part of the product dimension). If anomalies are discovered, further queries are constructed to further zero in on the problem area. Most of the queries involve some form of aggregation, either to exclude some dimensions from the star, or to roll up data within a hierarchy in one dimension. By precomputing one or more commonly used aggregates, much of the work to answer this type of query is done up front, so the answer comes back more quickly. This does come at a cost of increased data warehouse maintenance and schema complexity, so appropriate administration and user query tools should be used to help mitigate this.

COMMUNICATIONS GAP

This leads to the normalization communications gap. The designer of an OLTP system must use normalization to ensure that the system will meet performance requirements (it could be argued in some cases, that the actual performance requirements are not so onerous as to warrant the degree of normalization that is done as a matter of course in OLTP system design). This leads to a large and complex schema that is difficult for the prospective users to understand. Although normalization helps in the design of such a schema, it is not much help in explaining such a complex schema to the system's intended users. Explaining normalization and functional dependencies to business people is almost as difficult as explaining the schema itself — and can chew up more time than it is worth. If the prospective users of the system do not understand the schema, it is unlikely that they will be able to effectively draw on their own depth of business knowledge to point out errors or omissions in the design. The designers talk the language of normalization, but the users talk the language of business, and neither group can understand the other effectively.

This is a significant advantage of dimensional modeling for designing decision support systems. The actual schema for the system can be used effectively in the communication and design process. Because getting data quickly into OLTP systems is important, normalization is unavoidable in OLTP design. As has been seen, though, a DSS is not an OLTP system. Although normalization plays an important role in the design of OLTP systems, it has no part in the design of decision support systems.

BRIDGING THE COMMUNICATIONS GAP

Using dimensional modeling in the design of a DSS helps bridge the communications gap. It allows the designer to talk more like a business person and is approachable enough that business people can learn something about how to talk like designers.

The key to this process is to focus on the important business issues that must be dealt with, without getting too deeply into the gritty technical details. The data warehouse designers must succeed at getting the essence of the business needs into the design. Bringing business people into the design process is critical to the success of the project, as they are the only people with the relevant business knowledge. Fortunately, dimensional modeling helps bridge the communications gap between the designers and the business people.

To form the footings of the bridge, try taking the business perspective; the business people have questions they need to be able to answer. Discuss the questions for which they have trouble getting answers and the ones they cannot even ask. It is sometimes surprising how many important questions cannot be answered at all.

What would be the value to the business of providing a better methodology for answering questions? The business value of data warehousing is that it is intended to be just that: a better methodology for answering business questions. It is successful because it is focused on doing just that. That is why, in telling the story of data warehousing to business people, it is necessary to start at the end — with the business questions. Answering business questions is what is important to business people. Business people do not so much as care that the data model for the warehouse system is a star schema, but they care very much about what they can do with a star schema. A star schema is particularly well-suited to, for example, slicing and dicing and drilling down. These concepts generally will be understood easily and embraced enthusiastically by business people, because they are naturally effective in business analysis. Therefore, though being able to do this comes only after the design process is complete, it is a good place to start discussions with business people. Describe how slicing and dicing and drilling down work, using terms like categories and metrics, or whatever terms make sense to them. If possible, show them what is meant, and work through examples that are relevant to the business. In this way, ease them into discussions of star schemas by starting them out on solid, comfortable ground.

Section XII
Data Mining

DATA MINING IS THE PROCESS OF EXTRACTING INFORMATION, OFTEN PRE-VIOUSLY UNKNOWN, FROM DATA SOURCES. The data sources may be data-bases, collections of data, or even warehouses. A warehouse often prepares the data so that it can facilitate mining. Various technologies, concepts, and algorithms have to be integrated for effective data mining, including data-base management, statistical analysis, machine learning, and information retrieval. Parallel processing techniques improve the performance of data mining. Furthermore, visualization techniques facilitate data mining by pro-viding a better picture of the contents of a database. This section consists of five chapters devoted to aspects of data mining.

Chapter 60, "Is Data Mining Merely Hype," discusses reasons why data mining brings new and exciting opportunities for organizations to leverage their corporate information. This chapter also shows how data mining for-malizes and facilitates the analytic process to provide tangible business advantages to the organization.

Chapter 61, "Discovering Knowledge in Corporate Databases," discuss-es techniques and opportunities for leveraging information that is stored in corporate databases.

Chapter 62, "Data Mining: Exploring the Modern Corporate Asset," shows how companies, with very large and complex databases, can lever-age discovery-based data mining approaches to realize the complete value of their corporate data.

Chapter 63, "When a Business Abandons a Data Mine: A Case Study," ex-amines the corporate expectations, conduct, and reactions towards a data mining project. This case study takes a unique twist by focusing on the con-sequences to an organization that abandoned such an effort.

Chapter 64, "Multimedia Databases and Data Mining," provides an over-view of multimedia database systems—data models, query processing, storage issues, and distribution are discussed. The chapter goes on to pro-vide an overview of data mining, and shows how it can improve multimedia data retrieval, especially from the World Wide Web.

Chapter 60
Is Data Mining Merely Hype?

David Yeo

The term "data mining" seems to be appearing virtually everywhere. But what, exactly, is data mining? Everyone answers this question differently; and herein lies the problem. For by virtue of its inherent vagueness, data mining can become anything and everything, its scope running from data access to predictive modeling. Is data mining merely just another evocative catch phrase introduced for promotion and profit, or does it really offer something truly unique and valuable?

Many of us can recall the marketing frenzy surrounding similar overused constructs, terms such as "user-friendly" and "artificial intelligence," which although they may once have had real meaning, were exploited into disrepute. Will data mining prove as suspect? We already see a number of online analytical processing (OLAP) vendors claiming that they offer data mining. Is this just a marketing strategy, i.e. jumping on the data mining bandwagon, or is there a sincere confusion at work here? And what about the claim that data mining is simply statistics repackaged? Are statisticians, in fact, right when they, rather pejoratively, suggest that data mining brings nothing new to the table? These are just a few of the fundamental issues this paper examines.

WHAT IS DATA MINING?

Perhaps the most consistent definition is that data mining is a process. As an example, at SAS Institute, Data mining is defined as "the process of selecting, exploring and modeling large amounts of data, to uncover previously unknown patterns, for business advantage." This definition is far reaching. First, it is claimed that data mining applies mainly, if not wholly, to the domain of large databases. Ignoring for a moment the thorny issue of what qualifies as large, one might immediately ask why the uncovering of unknown patterns does not apply equally well to databases of any size. The simple answer is that it does — at least within certain statistically defined limits. The determination of these limits is a non-trivial exercise, involving the calculation of something called a power curve. Unfortunately a discussion of power curves takes us well beyond the scope of this piece of work. Suffice it to say that, in general, recommended minimum sample size is dependent on such things as the amount of variability within the sample as well as the size of the difference we wish to detect. That said, however, the point of the emphasis on large databases in the aforementioned definition is not so much to restrict the range of possible data mining applications, as to underscore the reality that massive data sets are now a fact of life for most organizations. In other words, the *raison d'etre* of data mining is to enable organizations to productively sift through these massive data stores.

The proposed definition identifies three key components of the data mining process: selecting, exploring, and modeling. The seemingly benign notions of selection and exploration belie the huge conflict they evoke. For selection and exploration span a wide range of traditional data management activities — activities not typically thought of as part of data mining such as data access, data cleansing, querying, static, and *ad hoc* reporting, statistics, and data visualization. Does this then imply that data warehousing, OLAP, and even SQL are now to be considered components (i.e., a subset) of data mining?

The answer to this question very much depends on whom you ask. At one extreme are the "purists" who maintain that the term data mining should be reserved for discovery. In particular, they seek to limit the term to the application of advanced machine learning techniques such as neural networks. At the other extreme are those (e.g., Mattison, 1996) who view a data mining tool as any product which allows end-users direct access and manipulation of data without the intervention of customized programming activity.[1] The truth, no doubt, lies somewhere in between. Clearly data mining requires data. And in data mining, as elsewhere, the old adage "garbage in, garbage out" holds. So whether data mining is viewed as the exploitation of data which has been previously extracted, scrubbed and stored (usually in a data warehouse), or if the process of data mining is extended downstream to the legacy system is, in many ways, a moot point. Data sources must be identified and accessed, data quality examined, inconsistent domains and missing data resolved, outliers detected, and so forth, before reliable models can be constructed. To arbitrarily specify some point in this process as data mining is, well, arbitrary.

What is more interesting, and arguably more relevant, in the proposed definition is implied by the phrase "to uncover previously unknown patterns." This may sound good, but it begs the question: "What is a pattern?" Surprisingly, this is not an easy question to answer. Take, for example, the pattern implied by the series: 1212121212É. I suspect that most of us would unhesitatingly complete this series with 1. But what of the series: 12123_1212É ? If the single occurrence of number 3 in this series is merely an aberration, then, as before, the correct continuation of the series is 1. If the series is to be taken literally, however, and if a single sample suffices, then the proper continuation would be 3. In fact, the distinguished philosopher and logician Ludwig Wittgenstein argued that it is possible to make a sound case for, literally, *any* continuation of the series (or any series). We begin to see just how tenuous the notion of pattern really is.

The attentive reader may also have noticed how intimately pattern detection and statistics are intertwined. Specifically, the frequency with which the pattern occurs is a strong determinant of the confidence we have that the pattern really exists. Thus, if the series 121231212É is ultimately found to continue with a 3, the second occurrence of 3 increases the certainty that the core pattern segment is 12123. The problem is further exacerbated by the fact that, for any given data set, it is possible to identify many more patterns than there are data elements (Fayyad, 1998). Since many of these patterns are likely to be rather uninteresting (e.g., all husbands are male), the final task of data mining is to detect which of its discovered patterns to enumerate. Here we come full circle; for the current state of data mining is such that detection of meaning necessarily remains a human task. This is where data visualization methods, as well as data summarization tools like OLAP, prove indispensable. When guided by the tenets of what constitutes a sound scientific hypothesis, i.e., novelty, validity, utility, simplicity, and understandability, these methods allow the business end-user to evaluate the machine selected patterns in order to determine which ones, ultimately, lead to business advantage.

WHY DO I CARE?

Marketing departments were among the first to realize the "business advantage" promised by data mining. In the simplest case, *descriptive* models of the organization's customer base are constructed (often using a technique known as "clustering"). These descriptions are then used to select, or avoid, prospects matching the profile. In a more sophisticated variant of this scenario, the data miner would construct a *predictive* model of the event of interest. Guided by past cases, say those who did and did not respond to past campaigns, a model is generated and used to score prospects on their similarity to those who, in past, responded. The targeted mailing is then preferentially sent out to those who, according to the model, are most likely to respond. This typically substantially reduces mailing costs. Similar models can be generated to predict which customers are more likely to switch to a competitor (attrition or churn analysis), which customers would be likely to purchase a related product (cross-sell and up-sell opportunity identification), and so forth.

Credit risk departments are now also realizing substantial benefits from data mining. Again predictive models are leading the charge. Application "scorecards" (i.e., models) assess applicants on their likelihood of defaulting on their credit payments. Behavioral scorecards act as a delinquency early warning system for those already extended credit. And collection scorecards maximize the creditor's chance of recovering their investment once the account has gone delinquent (typically for 90+ days).

Ultimately the application opportunities are as diverse as the industry segments they address. For instance, telephone companies use mining to optimize network throughput and, thus, maximize capacity; retailers use it rationalize store and inventory placement; and the resource sector use it to guide exploration, to name but three possibilities. No doubt it will be these and similar applications of mining, applications yielding tangible returns, that will most effectively answer the question "Is data mining merely hype?"

IS DATA MINING JUST STATISTICS REPACKAGED?

The contention that data mining is just statistics repackaged, i.e., that statistics and data mining are synonymous terms, at first brush might seem rather difficult to refute. After all, statisticians have been in the business of "uncovering previously unknown patterns" for years. Moreover, they have developed a formidable arsenal of mathematical techniques and methodologies to assist them in extracting information from raw data. So exactly what is it that data mining offers which distinguishes it from statistics?

There are at least two ways to answer this question. The simplest, but in some ways least satisfactory, reply focuses on the issue of ease of use. Because data mining effectively automates the statistical process, it empowers business end-users in much the same way as the spreadsheet did in the late 1970s (Berson and Smith, 1997). That is to say, the promise of data mining is that the predictive power of statistics is no longer exclusively the purview of analysts. Unfortunately this claim of simplicity of use is often overstated. True, the top mining packages offer an extremely rich set of defaults, enabling less statistically sophisticated users to develop and implement useful decision support models. But even the most powerful data mining packages assume at least a certain degree of familiarity with statistical concepts, e.g., sampling, correlation, data type (i.e., nominal, ordinal, interval, ratio), and variable distributions. And if one wants to optimize model performance, *substantial* statistical expertise may be required. That said, with data mining the turnaround time for model development has gone from weeks and months to days and, sometimes, even minutes. The resulting gains in productivity alone often enough offer enough competitive advantage to justify data mining.

The second, and in my view more definitive, distinction between statistics and data mining reintroduces the problematic issue of the scope of data mining. Simply put, *data mining is multidisciplinary*, drawing extensively from a wide range of fields including database theory, statistics, artificial intelligence, machine learning, pattern recognition, genetics, and even neurophysiology. As a result, a rich new set of tools with names like genetic algorithms, self-organizing feature maps, and multi-layered perceptrons, have been added to the analytic toolkit. Add to this the fact that data mining also incorporates a number of classic decision support techniques like decision trees (CART, CHAID), and one quickly comes to realize that statistics is merely a component of data mining.

IS A DATA WAREHOUSE A PREREQUISITE TO DATA MINING?

In order to properly answer this question it is first necessary to define precisely what we mean by the term "data warehouse." Unfortunately, as was the case with data mining, we immediately run aground. For as Mattison (1996) succinctly put it:

> Coming up with a good definition for a data warehouse is actually going to be pretty difficult. Certainly not because of lack of information about what people think it is, but more so because of an abundance of it. (pp. 4–5)

Perhaps the closest we can hope to come to agreement is Inmon's well-known formalization: a data warehouse is a subject-oriented, integrated, time-invariant, and non-volatile collection of data in support of management decisions. While this definition clearly shows that data warehousing and data mining are directed toward one and the same goal — decision support — it in no way constrains data mining. That is, no necessary progression from data warehousing to data mining is implied. In truth, *much of the data mining today is done from flat files extracted from operational data stores.* In fact, there is growing evidence that data mining can as readily be seen to be the driving force behind data warehousing, as the other way around. This may not be the optimal state of affairs, but it is often today's reality. I would even be willing to go so far as to suggest that one reason that an estimated 52 percent of warehousing initiatives fail is because, to parody a famous movie line, *when you build it they don't come.* The rationale for the data warehouse is the business advantage it provides. And data mining, because it implies an identified business problem with tangible benefits, is one way to realize this advantage. Data mining carries with it an implicit justification for the warehouse to support it. On the other hand, the business advantage of a data warehouse is solely a function of the power of the analyses it facilitates. Not to mention the fact that there is a growing awareness that data mining can be used to build and refine a data warehouse. One of the fundamental difficulties in constructing a data warehouse is determining which data is relevant to the majority of business questions. Data mining can guide the construction of the data warehouse by identifying which columns in the original data store should become dimensions in the data warehouse. Thus to claim that data warehousing is a prerequisite to data mining may, in fact, be putting the cart before the horse.

CONCLUSION

So is data mining "hype?" If the most pervasive definition of data mining carries the day, unless one is willing to say that data warehousing, OLAP, and the like are also hype, the answer is clearly "no." But even under more restrictive interpretations of the term, data mining shows itself to differ from classical analytical methods in meaningful ways. Most important, these differences translate into tangible business advantages. Herein lies its strategic value. Mining's tactical value is that it formalizes and facilitates the analytic process, making the formerly "mystical art" of decision support widely accessible. Still, care must be taken not to succumb to the temptation to oversell data mining. For as the Gartner Group warns, as the fanfare over the potential of data mining grows so, too, does the opportunity for unscrupulous vendors to position non-mining technologies as data mining in order to take advantage of market enthusiasm.

Notes

1. Actually, Mattison restricts the term to access and manipulation of data from *within a data-warehousing environment*. Thus legacy system access, for example, is not data mining under his definition. But OLAP, spreadsheets, SQL querying, and report writers, all fall under this umbrella definition of data mining.

References

Berson, A. and Smith, S. J., *Data Warehousing, Data Mining, & OLAP*, McGraw-Hill, New York, 1997.

Fayyad, U., "From Giants to Monsters: Mining Large Databases for Nuggets of Knowledge," *Database Programming and Design*, March 1998.

Mattison, R., *Data Warehousing: Strategies, Technologies and Techniques*, McGraw-Hill, New York, 1996.

Chapter 61
Discovering Knowledge in Corporate Databases

Younghoc Yoon

ALTHOUGH DATA CAPTURES INFORMATION ABOUT CRITICAL MARKETS, COMPETITORS, AND CUSTOMERS, raw data rarely generates direct benefits. Its real value is realized when one extracts information and knowledge useful for decision support or exploration to understand the phenomena governing the data source. Knowledge discovery and databases (KDD) is a process for discovering patterns that help turn data into knowledge. Data mining (DM) is a particular activity of KDD that applies a specific algorithm to extract patterns. DM combines techniques from machine learning, pattern recognition, statistics, databases, and visualization to extract concepts, concept interrelations, and interesting patterns automatically from large corporate databases. Its primary task is to extract knowledge from data to support the decision-making process. The use of DM systems alleviates the problem of manually analyzing the large amounts of collected data which decision makers currently face.

This article examines the steps that make up the knowledge discovery process as well as the algorithms that are commonly used in data mining. By better understanding the components of KDD, IS managers can apply these processes more effectively for meeting overall corporate strategies.

PROCESSES OF KNOWLEDGE DISCOVERY

Extracting knowledge from databases is a five-step process, as shown in Exhibit 61.1. The five-step process of knowledge discovery should not be interpreted as linear, but as an interactive, iterative process through which discovery is evolved.

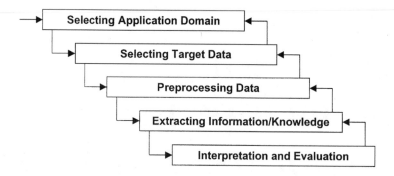

Exhibit 61.1. Steps involved in data mining.

Step 1: Selecting Application Domain

The first task for knowledge discovery is to select an appropriate domain area. When choosing an application area, developers should assess whether the DM is a most viable alternative to solve the problem. The availability of sufficient, quality data is another important criterion in choosing an appropriate domain. Once a domain area is selected, the goals of DM application must be clearly defined. Detailed discussion on selecting an appropriate domain is presented in a later section.

Step 2: Selecting the Target Data

The second step is to select the types of data to be used for discovery in a chosen domain. Although a target data set has been created for discovery in some applications, DM can be performed on a subset of variables or data samples in a larger database.

Step 3: Preprocessing Data

Once the target data is selected, the data is then preprocessed for cleaning, scrubbing, and transforming to improve the effectiveness of discovery. During this preprocessing step, developers remove the noise or outliers if necessary and decide on strategies for dealing with missing data fields and accounting for time sequence information or known changes. In addition, the data is often transformed to reduce the effective number of variables under consideration by either converting one type of data to another (categorical values into numeric ones) or deriving new attributes (by applying mathematical or logical operators).

Step 4: Extracting Information/Knowledge

The fourth step of DM refers to a series of activities in the process of discovering knowledge hidden in the data. These activities, listed in the order performed, are as follows:

1. Decide on the type of DM operation.
2. Select the DM technique.
3. Choose the DM algorithm.
4. Mine the data.

First, the type of DM operations must be chosen. The DM operations can be classified as classification, regression, segmentation, link analysis, and deviation detection. The next section explains these five operations in detail. Based on the operation chosen for the application, an appropriate data-mining technique is then selected. A classification model is often developed by supervised neural net and induction techniques. Link analysis is supported by association discovery and sequence discovery techniques. Clustering techniques are used to segment the database, and deviation detection is done by statistical as well as visualization techniques. Once a data-mining technique is chosen, the next step is to select a particular algorithm within the DM technique chosen. For example, the DM algorithm called ID3 uses an inductive technique to develop a classification model for the qualitative variables, whereas another DM algorithm called Backpropagation uses a supervised neural net technique that can be employed for quantitative variables with continuous values. Choosing a data-mining algorithm includes a method to search for patterns in the data, such as deciding which models and parameters may be appropriate and matching a particular data-mining technique with the overall objective of data mining. After an appropriate algorithm is selected, the data is finally mined using the algorithm to extract novel patterns hidden in databases.

Step 5: Interpretation and Evaluation

The fifth step of DM process is the interpretation and evaluation of discovered patterns. This task includes filtering the information to be presented by removing redundant or irrelevant patterns, visualizing graphically or logically the useful ones, translating them into understandable terms by users. In addition, the result interpretation determines and resolves potential conflicts with previously found knowledge and/or decides to redo any of the previous steps. The extracted knowledge is also evaluated in terms of its usefulness to a decision maker and to a business goal. Then extracted knowledge is subsequently used to support human decision making such as prediction and to explain observed phenomena.

DATA-MINING OPERATIONS

The goal of data mining is to unearth information and knowledge useful for making decisions by building a real-world model from the data collected from various sources such as customer histories, transactions, and credit bureau information. The model is built to discover novel patterns and relationships in the data set. Such models are useful in providing knowledge that can assist users in making predictions and understanding latent patterns to determine appropriate actions.

There are five types of DM operations: classification, regression, link analysis, segmentation, and deviation detection. Classification and regression are useful for prediction, whereas link analysis, segmentation, deviation detection are for description of patterns in the data. However, a DM application typically requires the combination of two or more DM operations.

Classification

The goal of classification is to develop a model that maps a data item into one of several predefined classes. Once induced, a model is used to classify a new instance into one of the classes. Examples include the classification of bankruptcy patterns based on the financial ratios of a firm and of customer buying patterns based on demographic information to target the advertising and sales of a firm effectively toward the appropriate customer base.

Regression

This operation builds a model that maps data items into a real-valued prediction variable using the databases. Models have traditionally been developed using statistical methods such as linear and logistic regression. Both classification and regression are used for prediction. The distinction between these two models is that the output variable of classification is categorical, whereas that of regression is numeric and continuous. Examples of regression are the prediction of change in a rate between the yen and the Government Bond Market and of the crime rate of a city based on the description of various input variables such as populations, average income level, education, and others.

Link Analysis

Link analysis is used to establish relevant connections between database records. Its typical application is market-basket analysis to which the technique is applied to analyze point-of-sales transaction data to identify product affinities. The use of scanners has enabled a retailer to analyze the transaction that makes link analysis possible. A retail store is usually interested in what items sell together — such as baby's diapers and formula —

so it can determine what items to display together for effective marketing. Another application could find relationships among medical procedures by analyzing claim forms submitted to an insurance firm. The link analysis is often applied in conjunction with database segmentation.

Segmentation

The goal is to identify clusters of records that exhibit similar behaviors or characteristics hidden in the data. The clusters may be mutually exclusive and exhaustive or may consist of a richer representation such as hierarchical or overlapping categories. Examples include discovering homogeneous groups of consumers in marketing databases and segmenting the records that describe sales during "Mother's Day" or "Father's Day." Once the database is segmented, link analysis is often performed on each segment to identify the association among the records in each cluster.

Detecting Deviations

This operation focuses on discovering interesting deviations. There are various types of deviation: the unusual patterns that do not fit into previously measured or normative classes; the significant changes in the data from one time period to the next; outlying points in a dataset — records that do not belong to any particular cluster; and discrepancies between an observation and a reference. Detecting deviations is usually performed after a database is segmented to determine whether they represent noisy data or unusual casualty. Deviation detection is often the source of true discovery since deviations represent anomaly from some known expectation and norm.

DATA-MINING TECHNIQUES AND ALGORITHMS

A variety of DM techniques are available to support the five types of DM operations presented in the previous section. Classification models are developed by induction techniques, neural nets as well as other example-based methods. Regression models are created by induction methods, neural nets, and statistic techniques. Link analysis is done by association discovery and sequence discovery techniques, database segmentation by clustering techniques. Deviation detection is performed by statistics as well as visualization methods. Although visualization methods are useful in detecting deviations, this technique itself is more often used in conjunction with the other DM techniques to augment their utilities and functionality, and to help the user to better understand information extracted by other DM techniques. Exhibit 61.2 presents the five DM operations, various techniques supporting these DM operations, and specific DM algorithms in each category.

Induction Technique

This technique develops a classification model from a set of records — the training set of examples. The training set may be a sample database, a data mart, or an entire data warehouse. Each record in the training set belongs to one of many predefined classes, and an induction technique induces a general concept description that best represents the examples to develop a classification model. The induced model consists of patterns that distinguish each class. Once trained, a developed model can be used to predict the class of unclassified records automatically. Induction techniques represent a model in the form of either decision trees or decision rules. These representations are easier to understand, and their implementation is more efficient than neural network and genetic algorithms.

Over the years, researchers in machine learning have developed many induction algorithms including ID3[1] and Version Space.[2] Independent studies in statistics have also developed similar induction algorithms such as CART[3] and AID. Unlike other induction algorithms, CART can be used to develop a classification model as well as a regression model predicting the continuous output value of a dependent variable. Among the many inductive algorithms, ID3 has been most widely used in many applications. Its objective is to develop a decision tree that requires a minimum number of attribute tests for a set of examples. To minimize a decision tree, ID3 chooses the attribute whose discriminating power is largest among them and splits the examples into subsets according to the chosen attribute. Each subset is then classified by the attribute with the largest discriminating power among the remaining attributes. The process is repeated until all examples are appropriately classified and, often, until no other attribute is available to be used for classification.

Neural Nets

Neural net methods can be used to develop classification, regression, association, and segmentation models. Neural net technique represents its model in a form of nodes arranged in layers and weighted links between nodes. There are two general categories of neural net algorithms: supervised and unsupervised. Supervised neural net algorithms such as Backpropagation[4] and Perceptron require predefined output values to develop a classification model. Among the many algorithms, Backpropagation is the most popular supervised neural net algorithm. It uses a gradient descent approach by which network connection weights are iteratively modified to reduce the difference between the output of the model and the expected output over all examples. Backpropagation can be used to develop not only a classification model, but a regression model. Other groups of supervised neural net algorithms like BAM are useful for detecting the associations among input patterns.

Operations   **Techniques**   **Algorithms**

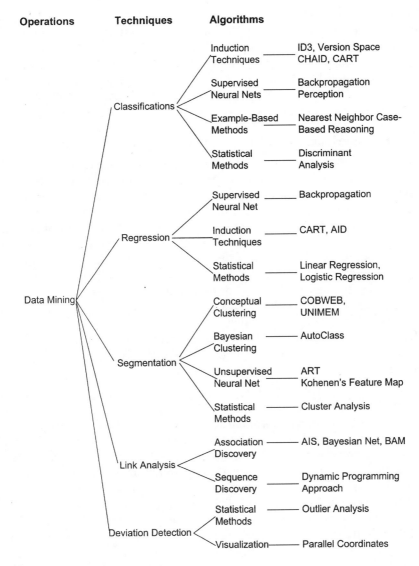

Exhibit 61.2. Types of DM operations, supporting techniques, and algorithms.

Unsupervised neural net algorithms such as ART[5] and Kohonen's Feature Map[6] do not require predefined output values for input data in the training set and employ self-organizing learning schemes to segment the target data set. Kohonen's Feature Map is a two-layered network that performs clustering through a competitive learning method, called "winner take all." In the competitive learning method, the output node with the largest activation value given an input pattern is declared the winner in the competition, and the weights of the link connected to this output node are modified to encode its association with the input pattern presented. Once trained, the weight vector of each output node encodes the information of a group of similar input patterns. Although the neural net technique has a strong representational power, interpreting the information encapsulated in the weighted links can be very difficult.

Other Example-Based Methods

There are other types of example-based methods such as nearest-neighbor and case-based reasoning. The nearest-neighbor technique uses a set of examples to approximate a classification model that decides which class to place a new instance by measuring similarity — counting the number of matches for each instance. The technique identifies the number of instances with the highest degree of match, called nearest neighbors, and assigns the new instance to the class to which most of the identified neighbors belong. It requires a well-defined distance metric for evaluating the distance between the instances. The number of neighbors to use for prediction is a parameter of the model to be estimated. Case-based reasoning stores training cases or experience in memory, called case base, and retrieves the cases relevant to a new case. Its power depends largely on the indexing method to store the cases and the matching method used to retrieve relevant cases.

Associated Discovery

Given a collection of items and a set of records containing some of these items, association discovery techniques discover the rules to identify affinities among the collection of items as reflected in the examined records. For example, 65 percent of records that contain item A also contain item B. An association rule uses measures called support and confidence to represent the strength of association. The percentage of occurrences, 65 percent in this case, is the confidence factor of the association. The algorithms find the affinity rules by sorting the data while counting occurrences to calculate confidence. The efficiency with which association discovery algorithms can organize the events that make up an association or transaction is one of the differentiators among the association discovery algorithms. There are a variety of algorithms to identify association rules such as AIS and BAM. Bayesian Net can also be used to identify distinctions and casual relationships between variables.

Sequence Discovery

Sequence discovery is very similar to association discovery except that the collection of items occurs over a period of time. Sequence is treated as an association in which the items are linked by time. When customer names are available, their purchase patterns over time can be analyzed. For example, it could be found that, if a customer buys a tie, he will buy men's shoes within one month 25 percent of the time. Dynamic programming approach-based on the dynamic time warping technique used in the speech recognition area is available to identify the patterns in temporal databases.

Clustering

Clustering techniques are employed to segment a database into clusters, each of which shares common and interesting properties. The purpose of segmenting a database is often to summarize the contents of the target database by considering the common characteristics shared in a cluster. Clusters are also created to support the other types of DM operations, i.e., link analysis within a cluster.

The database can be segmented by traditional methods of pattern recognition techniques; unsupervised neural nets such as ART and Kohonen's Feature Map; conceptual clustering techniques such as COBWEB[7] and UN-IMEM; and the Bayesian approach like AutoClass.[8] Conceptual clustering algorithms consider all the attributes that characterize each record and identify the subset of the attributes that will describe each created cluster to form concepts. The concepts in a conceptual clustering algorithm can be represented as conjunctions of attributes and their values. Bayesian clustering algorithms automatically discover a number of clusterings that are maximally probable with respect to the data using a Bayesian approach. The various clustering algorithms can be characterized by the type of acceptable attribute values such as continuous, discrete, qualitative; by their presentation methods of each cluster; and by their methods of organizing the set of clusters, either hierarchically or into flat files.

Visualization

Visualizations are particularly useful for detecting phenomena hidden in a relatively small subset of the data. The techniques are often used in conjunction with other DM techniques to augment their utilities. For example, features that are difficult to detect by scanning numbers may become obvious when the summary of data is graphically presented. Visualization techniques can also guide users when they do not know what to look for to discover the novelty. Also, this technique is useful in facilitating end users' comprehension of information extracted by other data-mining techniques. Specific visualization techniques include projection pursuit and parallel coordinates. Projection pursuit successively displays two-dimensional graphs showing the structures between different variable pairings. Parallel coordinates translate N-dimensional space to a two-dimensional representation through a series of parallel vertical axes representing different variables. This algorithm enables users to analyze the hypergeometrical structure of multidimensional data by displaying the patterns and trends in multivariate data.

APPLICATION SELECTION

For a successful implementation of DM techniques, an organization should carefully select its application. There are a number of characteristics to consider when selecting an application suitable for DM techniques — both technical and nontechnical issues. Although it is unlikely that any application will meet all desirable characteristics, missing characteristics frequently indicate weak points of the application, which developers should attempt to minimize, eliminate, at least to monitor carefully for successful implementation.

Nontechnical Criteria

The success of a newly developed system is measured by the benefits generated. A desirable application is a task whose solution has large potential benefits and payoffs. The benefits of DM applications are measured by the novelty and quality of the discovered knowledge in terms of producing greater revenue, lower costs, higher quality, or savings in time. The benefits can be either tangible, such as profits or savings in cost for the company, or intangible, such as increasing product quality and the level of customer loyalty and improving corporate image. Also the development of a DM application requires the investment by an organization in resources. The payoff of the discovered knowledge is large enough to justify the costs and generate a high return in investment. Another nontechnical consideration is that there exist no good alternatives. The solution is not easily obtainable by other standard traditional approaches so that end users have vast interest in pursuing the DM venture. Organizational support for an application is another important consideration. Support from upper management is crucial for the project success, especially as an initial DM project. Therefore, it is necessary to select an application where top management has strong interest. Also, for the application itself, there should be a cooperating domain expert who is available to define a proper measure for that domain to evaluate the goodness of discovered knowledge. Finally, selection criteria should include the potential for privacy and legal issues. Some kind of knowledge discovery may be inappropriate and actually illegal, i.e., discovering patterns that possibly raise legal, ethical, as well as privacy issues.

Technical Criteria

In addition to the nontechnical criteria for the desirable DM application, there are many important technical attributes to be included when evaluating the appropriateness of an application. First, for any DM application, there must be a sufficient amount of data. Although the amount of data necessary for knowledge discovery significantly varies depending on the DM operation pursued and the techniques adopted, the more attributes used, the more instances required. Second, there must be data attributes pertinent to the discovery task. A large amount of data does not guarantee the quality of discovered patterns. Attributes must encapsulate the information required to discover the novel patterns. Third, the data available must be of high quality — having lower noise levels and few data errors. Data mining with poor data is unreliable and often infeasible, if not impossible. Noise in the data makes it difficult to discover knowledge unless a large number of cases can alleviate random noise. Fourth, although there are debates about the utility and pitfall of using prior knowledge in data mining, it is often useful to have prior knowledge regarding the domain, such as the pertinent attributes, the likely relationships between attributes, the user utility function, and previous patterns. Some application problems are so large that the use of prior domain knowledge is necessary to limit the search space. However, the developers should note that the use of prior knowledge might limit the patterns they can find.

CONCLUSION

There is a growing gap between powerful massive storage retrieval systems and the ability to analyze the collected data effectively to extract useful knowledge for decision-making processes. In response to the demand for a technique assisting end users in unearthing knowledge hidden in the massive amount of data, DM has been emerging as an interdisciplinary field combining techniques from machine learning, statistics, databases, and others. Since its birth in the early 1990s, there has been a rapid growth in new research results and applications. The technique has demonstrated its potential for addressing real problems in various areas, including finance, insurance, market data analysis, astronomy, diagnosis, manufacturing, biology, and other areas. Its viability is also being recognized by business as well as by government organizations. To help IS professionals better understand this important emerging technique, this article has presented an overview of DM technique, including its overall process, the types of DM tasks, and a survey of DM techniques and algorithms. This article also attempted to provide to IS professionals a guide for applying DM by presenting application areas and domain selection criteria. Despite the challenges which DM currently faces as a young field, DM is a promising technique to increase the ability to mine useful information and knowledge implicitly encoded in large corporate databases.

Notes

1. J.R. Quinlan, "Induction of Decision Trees," *Machine Learning* 1 (1983): 81–106.
2. T. Mitchell, "Version Spaces: An Approach to Concept Learning," Ph.D. Dissertation, Stanford University, December 1978.
3. L. Breiman, J.H. Friedman, R.A. Olshen, and C.J. Stone, *Classification and Regression Trees* (Belmont, CA: Wadsworth, 1984).

4. D.E. Rumelhart, G.E. Hinton, and R.J. Williams, "Learning Internal Representation by Error Propagation," in *Parallel Distributed Processing*, ed. by Rumelhart, D.E., McClelland, J.L., and the PDP Research Group (Cambridge, MA: The MIT Press, 1986), 318–362.

5. G. Carpenter and S. Grossberg, "The ART of Adaptive Pattern Recognition by a Self-Organizing Neural Network," *IEEE Computer*, 21, no. 3 (March 1988): 77–88.

6. T. Kohonen, *Self-Organization and Associative Memory,* 2nd ed. (Berlin: Springer-Verlag, 1988).

7. D. Fisher, M. Pazzani, and P. Langley, *Concept Formation: Knowledge and Experience in Unsupervised Learning* (San Mateo, CA: Kaufmann, 1991).

8. P. Chessman, "Bayesian Classification (AutoClass): Theory and Results," in *Advances in Knowledge Discovery and Data Mining*, ed. by Fayyad, U., Piatetsky-Shapiro, G., Smyth, P., and Uthurusamy, R. (Menlo Park, CA: AAAI Press/The MIT Press, 1996), 153–180.

Chapter 62

Data Mining: Exploring the Corporate Asset

Jason Weir

COMPANIES TODAY GENERATE AND COLLECT VAST AMOUNTS OF DATA that they use in the ongoing process of doing business. Transaction data such as that produced by inventory, billing, shipping and receiving, and sales systems is stored in operational or departmental data stores. It is understood that data represents a significant competitive advantage, but realizing the full potential of it is not simple. Decision makers must be able to interpret trends, identify factors or utilize information based on clear, timely data in a meaningful format. For instance, a marketing director should be able to identify a group of customers, 18 to 24 years of age, that own notebook computers who need or are likely to purchase an upcoming collaboration software product. After identifying them, the director sends them advance offers, information, or product order forms to increase product presales.

Data mining, as a methodology, is a set of techniques used to uncover previously obscure or unknown patterns and relationships in very large databases. The ultimate goal is to arrive at comprehensible, meaningful results from extensive analysis of information.

HOW IS IT DIFFERENT FROM OTHER ANALYSIS METHODS?

Data mining differs from other methods in several ways. A significant distinction between data mining and other analytical tools is in the approach they use in exploring the data. Many analytical tools available support a verification-based approach in which the user hypothesizes about specific data relationships and then uses the tools to verify or refute those presumptions. This verification-based process stems from the intuition of the user to pose the questions and refine the analysis based on the results

0-8493-9832-0/00/$0.00+$.50
© 2000 by CRC Press LLC

of potentially complex queries against a database. The effectiveness of this analysis depends on several factors, not the least of which being the ability of the user to pose appropriate questions, the capability of tools to return results quickly, and the overall reliability and accuracy of the data being analyzed.

Other available analytical tools have been optimized to address some of these issues. Query and reporting tools, such as those used in data mart or warehouse applications, let users develop queries through point-and-click interfaces. Statistical analysis packages, like those used by many insurance or actuarial firms, provide the ability to explore relationships among a few variables and determine statistical significance against demographic sets. Multidimensional online analytical processing (OLAP) tools enable fast response to user inquiries through their ability to compute hierarchies of variables along dimensions such as size, color or location.

Data mining, in contrast to these analytical tools, uses what are called discovery-based approaches in which pattern matching and other algorithms are employed to determine the key relationships in the data. Data-mining algorithms can look at numerous multidimensional data relationships concurrently, highlighting those that are dominant or exceptional. In other words, true data-mining tools uncover trends, patterns and relationships automatically. Earlier in the chapter was mentioned the fact that many other types of analytical methods rely on user intuition or the ability to pose the right kind of question. To sum things up, analytical tools — query tools, statistical tools, and OLAP — and the results they produce, are all user-driven, but data mining is data-driven.

THE NEED FOR DATA MINING

As discussed, traditional methods involve the decision maker hypothesizing the existence of information of interest, converting that hypothesis to a query, posing that query to the analysis tool, and interpreting the returned results with respect to the decision being made. For instance, the marketing director must hypothesize that notebook-owning 18- to 24-year-old customers are likely to purchase the upcoming software release. After posing the query, it is up to the individual to interpret the returned results and determine if the list represents a good group of product prospects. The quality of the extracted information is based on the user's interpretation of the posed query's results.

The intricacies of data interrelationships as well as the sheer size and complexity of modern data stores necessitates more advance analysis capabilities than those provided by verification-based data-mining approaches.

The ability to discover automatically important information hidden in the data and then present it in the appropriate way is a critical complimentary technology to verification-based approaches. Tools, techniques, and systems that perform these automated analysis tasks are referred to as discovery-based. Discovery-based systems applied to the marketing director's data store may identify many groups including, for example: 18- to 24-year-old male college students with laptops, 24- to 30-year-old female software engineers with both desktop and notebook systems, and 18- to 24-year-old customers planning to purchase portable computers within the next 6 months. By recognizing the marketing director's goal, the discovery-based system can identify the software engineers as the key target group by spending pattern or other variable.

In sum, verification-based approaches, although valuable for quick, high-level decision support, such as historical queries about product sales by fiscal quarter, are insufficient. For companies with very large and complex databases, discovery-based data-mining approaches must be implemented to realize the complete value that data offers.

THE PROCESS OF MINING DATA

Selection and Extraction

Constructing an appropriate database to run queries against is a critical step in the data-mining process. A marketing database may contain extensive tables of data from purchasing records and lifestyle data to more advanced demographic information such as census records. Not all of this data is required on a regular basis and should be filtered out of the query table. Additionally, even after selecting the desired database tables, it is not always necessary to mine the contents of the entire table to identify useful information. Under certain conditions and for certain types of data-mining techniques, for example, when creating a classification or prediction model, it may be adequate first to sample the table and then to mine the sample. This is usually a faster and less expensive operation.

Essentially, potential sources of data (e.g,. census data, sales records, mailing lists, demographic databases) should be explored before meaningful analysis can take place. The selected data types may be organized along multiple tables. Developing a sound model involves combining parts of separate tables into a single database for mining purposes.

Data Cleansing and Transformation

Once the selected database tables have been selected and the data to be mined has been identified, it is usually necessary to perform certain transformations and cleansing routines on the data. Data cleansing or transformations are determined by the type of data being mined as well as the data-mining technique being used. Transformations vary from conversions of one type of data to another, such as numeric data to character data, or currency conversions to more advanced transformations such as the application of mathematical or logical functions on certain types of data. Cleansing, on the other hand, is used to ensure reliability and accuracy of results. Data can be verified, or cleansed, to remove duplicate entries, attach real values to numeric or alphanumeric codes, and omit incomplete records. Dirty or inaccurate data in the mining data store must be avoided if results are to be accurate and useful. Many data-mining tools include a system log or other graphical interface tool to identify erroneous data in queries, but every effort should be made prior to this stage to ensure that it does not arrive at the mining database. If errors are not discovered, lower quality results and, due to this, lesser quality decisions will be the result.

Mining, Analysis, and Interpretation

The clean and transformed data subsequently is mined using one or more techniques to extract the desired type of information. For example, to develop an accurate classification model that predicts whether a customer will upgrade to a new version of a software package, a decision maker first must use clustering to segment the customer database. Next, they will apply rules to create automatically a classification model for each desired cluster. While mining a particular data set, it may be necessary to access additional data from a datamart or warehouse and perform additional transformations of the original data. The terms and methods mentioned previously will be defined and discussed later in this chapter.

The last step in the data-mining process is analyzing and interpreting results. The extracted and transformed data is analyzed with respect to the user's goal, and the best information is identified and presented to the decision maker through the decision support system. The purpose of result interpretation is not only to represent the output of the data mining operation graphically, but also to filter the information that will be presented through the decision support system. For example, if the goal is to develop a classification model, during the result interpretation step the robustness of the extracted model is tested using one of the established methods. If the interpreted results are not satisfactory, it may be necessary to repeat the data-mining step or to repeat other steps. What this really speaks to is the quality of data. The information extracted through data mining must be ultimately comprehensible. For example, it may be necessary, after interpreting the results of a data-mining operation, to go back and add data to the selection process or to perform a different calculation during the transformation step.

TECHNIQUES

Classification

Classification is perhaps the most often employed data-mining technique. It involves a set of instances or predefined examples to develop a model that can classify the population of records at large.

The use of classification algorithms begins with a sample set of preclassified example transactions. For a fraud detection application, this would include complete records of both fraudulent and valid transactions, determined on a record-by-record basis. The classifier-training algorithm uses these preclassified examples to determine the set of parameters required for proper identification. The algorithm then encodes these parameters into a model called a classifier or classification model. The approach affects the decision-making capability of the system. Once an effective classifier is developed, it is used in a predictive mode to classify new records automatically into these same predefined classes.

In the fraud detection case above, the classifier would be able to identify probable fraudulent activities. Another example would involve a financial application where a classifier capable of identifying risky loans could be used to aid in the decision of whether to grant a loan to an individual.

Association

Given a collection of items and a set of transactions, each of which contain some number of items from a given collection, an association is an operation against this set of records that returns affinities that exist among the collection of items. Market basket analysis is a common application that utilizes association techniques. Market basket analysis involves a retailer running an association function over the point of sales transaction log. The goal is to determine affinities among shoppers. For example in an analysis of 100,000 transactions, association techniques could determine that "20 percent of the time, customers who buy a particular software application, also purchase the complimentary add-on software pack."

In other words, associations are items that occur together in a given event or transaction. Association tools discover rules.

Another example of the use of association discovery could be illustrated in an application that analyzes the claim forms submitted by patients to a medical insurance company. The goal is to discover patterns among the claimants' treatment. Assume that every claim form contains a set of medical procedures that were performed to the given patient during one visit. By defining the set of items to be the collection of all medical procedures that can be performed on a patient and the records to correspond to each claim form, the application can find, using the association technique, relationships among medical procedures that often are performed together.

Sequence-Based

Traditional market basket analysis deals with a collection of items as part of a point-in-time transaction. A variant of this occurs when there is additional information to tie together a sequence of purchases. An account number, a credit card, or a frequent shopper number are all examples of ways to track multiple purchases in a time series.

Rules that capture these relationships can be used, for example, to identify a typical set of precursor purchases that might predict the subsequent purchase of a specific item. In this software case, sequence-based mining could determine the likelihood of a customer purchasing a particular software product to purchase subsequently complimentary software or hardware devices such as a joystick or video card.

Sequence-based mining can be used to detect the set of customers associated with frequent buying patterns. Use of sequence-based mining on the set of insurance claims discussed earlier can lead to the identification of frequently occurring medical procedures performed on patients. This then can be harnessed in a fraud detection application, also discussed earlier, to detect cases of medical insurance fraud.

Clustering

Clustering segments a database into different groups. The goal is to find groups that differ from one another as well as similarities among members. The clustering approach assigns records with a large number of attributes into a relatively small set of groups, or segments. This assignment process is performed automatically by clustering algorithms that identify the distinguishing characteristics of the data set and then partition the space defined by the data set attributes along natural boundaries. There is no need to identify the groupings desired or the attributes that should be used to segment the data set.

Clustering is often one of the first steps in data-mining analysis. It identifies groups of related records that can be used as a starting point for exploring further relationships. This technique supports the development of population segmentation models, such as demographic-based customer segments. Additional analyses using standard analytical and other data-mining techniques can determine the characteristics of these segments with respect to some desired outcome. For example, the buying habits of multiple population segments might be compared to determine which segments to target for a new marketing campaign.

Estimation

Estimation is a variation on the classification technique. Essentially it involves the generation of scores along various dimensions in the data. Rather than employing a binary classifier to determine whether a loan applicant, for instance, is approved or classified as a risk, the estimation approach generates a credit-worthiness score based on a prescored sample set of transactions. That is, sample data (complete records of approved and risk applicants) are used as samples in determining the worthiness of all records in a data set.

APPLICATIONS OF DATA MINING

Data mining now is being applied in a variety of industries ranging from investment management and retail solutions to marketing, manufacturing, and health care applications. It has been pointed out that many organizations, due to the strategic nature of their data-mining operations, will not discuss their projects with outsiders. This is understandable due to the importance and potential that successful solutions offer organizations. However, there are several well-known applications that are proven performers.

In customer profiling, characteristics of good customers are identified with the goals of predicting who will become one and helping marketing departments target new prospects. Data mining can find patterns in a customer database that can be applied to a prospect database so that customer acquisition can be targeted appropriately. For example, by identifying good candidates for mail offers or catalogs, direct-mail marketing managers can reduce expenses and increase their sales generation efforts. Targeting specific promotions to existing and potential customers offers similar benefits.

Market-basket analysis helps retailers understand which products are purchased together or by an individual over time. With data mining, retailers can determine which products to stock in which stores and how to place them within a store. Data mining also can help assess the effectiveness of promotions and coupons.

Lastly, fraud detection is of great benefit to credit card companies, insurance firms, stock exchanges, government agencies, and telecommunications firms. The aggregate total for fraud losses in today's world is enormous, but with data mining, these companies can identify potentially fraudulent transactions and contain damage. Financial companies use data mining to determine market and industry characteristics as well as to predict individual company and stock performance. Another interesting niche application is in the medical field. Data mining can help predict the effectiveness of surgical procedures, diagnostic tests, medication, and other services.

DATA MINING

SUMMARY

More and more companies are beginning to realize the potential for data mining within their organization. However, unlike the "plug-and-play," out-of-the-box business solutions that many have become accustomed to, data mining is not a simple application. It involves a good deal of forethought, planning, research, and testing to ensure a sound, reliable, and beneficial project. Another thing to remember is that data mining is complimentary to traditional query and analysis tools, data warehousing, and data mart applications. It does not replace these useful and often vital solutions.

Data mining enables organizations to take full advantage of the investments they have made and currently are making in building data stores. By identifying valid, previously unknown information from large databases, decision makers can tap into the unique opportunities that data mining offers.

Chapter 63

When a Business Abandons a Data Mine: A Case Study

Ronald A. Wencer

DATA MINING CAN INFLUENCE BUSINESS DIRECTION SIGNIFICANTLY, but inappropriate expectations may arise from a purely operational view of mining: endless strings of railroad cars brimming with ore, fed by machines and by relentless, back-straining labor, everything working together with assembly-line precision. Data mining requires prospecting — the exploration that must constantly guide mining operations. As in any discipline, one must test hard realities against hypotheses, objectivity against preconception. The template that sets directions for data mining must be validated repeatedly by a complementary analysis of what is being discovered.

The object of the study exhibited many characteristics of successful information systems projects, and none of the flaws usually associated with project failure. Yet, its early high-profile success decayed steadily into obscurity, with many perceiving its eventual conclusion as a predictable fate for a project gone awry.

An awareness of the decisions and misunderstandings that shaped the project may prove relevant to future undertakings. Certainly, if the same business culture were to attack the same problem again, a deeper appreciation of data mining concepts could avoid reliance on cultural perceptions, and could instead foster recognition of the true business problems at hand.

CORPORATE BACKGROUND

Building on decades of conservative growth, ABCBank was a widely respected organization. It was meeting challenges from larger, newly aggressive competitors by pursuing a strategic plan, which was to fundamentally change the bank's texture. ABCBank was edging upward; it was solidifying and enlarging its traditional customer base, yet also gaining footholds in new market niches.

The plan called for a quantitative study of the bank's relationships with its corporate clients, relationships that traditionally had been characterized by networking and informality. Personal knowledge, skills, and judgment played important roles, converging in a negotiation-centered process through which multimillion-dollar transactions were affected.

For many services delivered to commercial clients, bank costs were unknown. Working from uncoordinated bundles of operational data, staff had to rely more on intuition and experience than on information. Despite the bank's track record, executives felt compelled to monitor corporate client services more vigorously.

The information systems environment was an obstacle to the proposed quantitative study, because it focused on client accounts and transactions, ignoring overall relationships. During the years of cultural stability, it had provided a solid foundation, but it now proves brittle. With each application interacting with customers and staff on its own terms, there was little opportunity for synergy. Restructuring the corporate information resource would be critical to ABCBank's future.

BUSINESS FOCUS OF THE STUDY

Centralizing corporate/client dealings at a single bank office had hastened decision making, but it offered no meaningful feedback about the profitability of relationships — doing further business with a given client did not necessarily mean better, or even adequate, return on incremental exposure.

Commercial credit services (ongoing loan commitments, lines of credit, actual borrowings, etc.) were of special concern, because the impact of a single commercial transaction was great. Negotiated pricing bred complex, often unique terms that generally involved hierarchies of potential and actual borrowing agreements. In addition to the obvious, the formula for each agreement might encompass less expected variables — such as other institutions' lending rates, or client deposits (credit clients sometimes agreed to maintain deposit balances, which fluctuated according to repayments and borrowings).

The bank lacked quantifiable and objective models by which to evaluate such complexity, yet the financial climate demanded objectivity. With commercial loan rates at unprecedented levels, financial institutions and clients alike were reevaluating their positions. Sporadic but large defaults had become a notorious feature of the industry, seriously affecting some of ABCBank's peers. Concerned regulators were monitoring commercial lending more closely. Banks could no longer afford to make uninformed commitments in the credit marketplace.

Moreover, corporate client profiles had become quite intricate. Diversified clients used many unrelated services, traditionally administered by disparate bank units. Subsidiaries and affiliates sometimes dealt independently with different bank offices; sometimes they dealt as a body with a single contact. Interrelated clients might pool their respective credit or deposit accounts. As these factors increasingly muddied ABCBank's view of its biggest clients, loan officers could no longer determine whether deposit obligations were being met.

The bank could not evaluate its loan officers' negotiations with clients. Risk was increasing, but as things stood, achieving the bank's prime strategic objective in this arena — determining whether long-term relationships with given clients were in fact profitable — was not feasible.

INCEPTION OF THE PROJECT

Although it would be rebuilt eventually, the operational system for commercial loans was to remain in place for some time. Expanding business already demanded constant system maintenance. Except for highlighting important but obvious conditions (e.g., defaults), operational data could not directly support any decision to pursue or ignore a given client opportunity.

The lack of adequate aggregated information was clear. Management proposed a decision-support environment, built specifically to permit analysis of corporate/client relationships, to be created and managed by a team with no operational responsibilities. A key deliverable for this team would be a framework for viewing complex customer families.

Assessing client family relationships would enable these primary objectives:

- Leveraging profitable corporate/client relationships.
- Repairing or shedding unprofitable client relationships.
- Identifying extraordinary performance-linked characteristics and trends among client subset.
- Addressing any consistently poor performance by loan officer teams.

Anticipated secondary objectives were as follows:

- Disentangling client family obligations, allowing the bank to identify areas of noncompliance.
- Providing client families more comprehensive information about their banking.
- Promoting the bank's own compliance with regulatory obligations.

If the objectives were met, payback would be certain.

DATA MINING

Terms of Reference

With ABCBank's president expressed personal interest, the project was organized swiftly. Sponsorship was delegated to a senior vice-president (two levels below the CEO), and business and technical directors were chosen. The steering committee also included executives from information systems and commercial credit operations.

To free the decision-support environment from operational constraints, the steering body determined that:

- There would be an independent base of replicated data, collected by a quasi-operational application, to be accessed via highly flexible technology.
- The environment would feature new query and analytical modeling tools.
- New processes would replicate selected data from the disparate operational environments; in the new environment, it would be transformed in accord with strategic direction.
- Bank services and clients would be classified, and data aggregated appropriately.
- Association concepts would support the assessment of a client relationship's long-term profitability.
- In response to the periodic feed of operational data, the decision-support environment would return a high-level view of each client's compliance.

The following project constraints were accepted:

- No existing system process or data within the resource-intensive commercial loan environment could be modified. At the most, limited new processing could be injected at noncritical points. Replication and synthesis of the data to be mined would be made as external to the existing environment as possible.
- The mined data would have to be fitted to an effective model, which would feature uniform, readily understood measures by which to appraise phenomena that traditionally had been considered complex.
- Results had to demonstrate high integrity; neither internal management nor clients could question them.
- Because of resource concerns, the priority given to credit arrangements over other services, and expectations of significant benefits based solely on credit service analysis, analyzing non-credit services was deferred to a later project.

PROJECT ORGANIZATION

Three project teams were established:

- Three commercial loan experts, drawing on operational and executive resources as necessary, would develop the initial concepts and direction for the mining effort, including the principles for compiling views of client families. This team was credit from the bank's back-office credit unit.
- Four information systems professionals were to develop the mechanisms by which data was to be collected from the bank's operational environment and partially aggregated. This team was recruited externally; its members had extensive team-oriented experience at various competitors of ABCBank.
- Responsibility for housing the replicated data, and for more fully aggregating it, was outsourced to a vendor that offered appropriate technologies and skills. Vendor personnel were to work closely with the business team to determine classification principles. The vendor would also provide the business team with training and technology for conducting ongoing evaluation and analysis.

All team leaders were to participate as peers, from the onset of detailed project planning through delivery.

CONDUCT OF THE PROJECT

The project plan overlapped business-area and systems activities. It relied on an opening position — a template-like set of assumptions that would drive the initial phase of data selection and transformation. The business experts defined a draft analytical model that quantified profitability while still attempting to respect business complexities and variations. It suggested certain first-cut abstractions that guided the recognition of rudimentary classifications.

Armed with this opening position, the technical team affected a logical mapping of decision-support requirements to operational data structures and timings (Exhibit 63.1). Analyzing this mapping led to the determination of tactics by which data could be replicated effectively for transformation. Confident that both the logical decision-support view would have a sound foundation of operational data, and that it could evolve through the ongoing exercise of analytical tools, the team began designing bridges to the operational environment.

Simultaneously, the first-cut analytical model was validated through a prototyping exercise. The business and vendor teams mimicked the target environment, populating a bare-bones functional prototype with manually replicated data. Because this exercise refined, but did not significantly alter, the classification parameters of the draft analytical model, management was convinced that the project was on track, and that its objectives would be met readily.

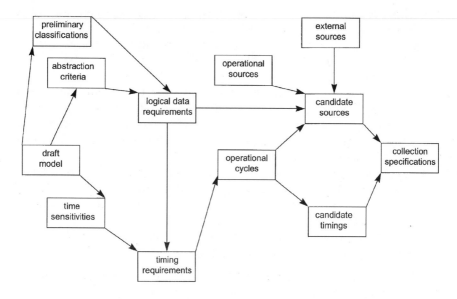

Exhibit 63.1. Determining sources for data collection.

By this point, the project team knew that the decision-support environment would have to sustain analysis of:

- 25,000 active corporate client accounts.
- 10,000 corporate families (multiclient families averaged about four accounts each, and might include many more).
- On average, two loan arrangements per account.
- As many as seven actual loans per arrangement at any moment.

At the start of data collection, the bank would have as many as 13 months of history for each family. Data would grow daily as new arrangements were made, terms were renegotiated, interest rates changed, and funds were deposited. Projections of these figures were used to validate the proposed architecture and resourcing for collection, aggregation, and evaluation activities.

Thereafter, the activities unfolded in a straightforward fashion, progressing as follows:

1. Using a representative sample chosen by the business team, clients were clustered, thereby refining the initial project scope (i.e., some clusters were deemed to be not of interest). The project team — and bank management as well — began to articulate the characteristics of corporate client relationships of different sizes.

2. The team elaborated its criteria for considering nominally distinct clients as parts of a single corporate family. Staff then began collecting data in order to identify families (a prerequisite for rendering certain aggregations meaningful).

3. A universal cost model was developed. Management could then envisage a consistent bottom-line comparison of different types of clients and credit services.

4. An expanded set of historical data was replicated from the operational environment. Aggregation was done in accord with the first-cut abstractions that had been posited for the analytical model.

5. The team defined a cyclical framework for managing the ongoing growth of data. It determined the timings for monitoring operational data, for replication and preprocessing, and for the creation of certain "standard" aggregations. These timings were chosen by balancing the need for complete, current data against the risk of overemphasis should spikes occur.

6. An automated process was built to detect potentially relevant changes to operational data. Rules determined whether or not a change was of analytical interest, identified to which client families it applied, and scoped the timeframe for which the change impacted analysis (impacts could be either prospective or retrospective). The replication cycle consolidated the results of this monitoring so that all aggregations remained current.

7. First-cut abstractions were embedded into a rigid automated process to be supplemented by tools that extended hands-on analytical capabilities. This prepackaging of abstractions supported preliminary criteria for the classification of loan officers' performance, for the comparison of clients' deposits against their obligations, and for the much-desired assessment of client relationships.

Thus, upon its first full-scale collection and aggregation of data, the project had achieved these strategic deliverables:

- A framework for analyzing interrelated corporate client accounts (focused on credit services, but intended to accommodate non-credit analysis as data and principles evolved).
- A mapping of all existing corporate credit clients to that framework.
- Complete and accurate aggregated data, which could support exercise and refinement of the first-cut analytical model.
- Operational links for ongoing maintenance of that data.
- Hands-on technology by which business experts could continually explore and refine the analysis of credit-based relationships.
- A high-level view of compliance for corporate client families.

The project had proceeded per plan, earning a reputation as an exemplary success. Having solidly positioned the bank as intended, the project team now started refocusing on the analysis of non-credit services to corporate clients. Per plan, custodianship for explorative data mining was transitioned to less senior business area resources.

RESULTS

Assessing credit relationships yielded immediate, dramatic results, due primarily to the bank's having (for the first time) comprehensive pictures of its client families. It uncovered numerous unfulfilled deposit obligations, which ABCBank rectified quickly, greatly increasing the bank's average available funds. Smaller gains were realized through financial penalties for clients who consistently failed to meet their obligations, and through the more accurate application of credit-pricing formula.

Of course, these benefits were essentially one-time corrections of long-outstanding deficiencies, and operational management soon would take them for granted. For the moment, however, the highly visible 8-digit increase in available funds was impressive, and it further enhanced perceptions of the project.

The shining success soon clouded over, as the bank turned its attention to other issues. Foremost among these issues were the daily challenges it encountered in the non-credit arena, which long had been neglected by operations management. Contrary to expectations, the requisite analytical effort was challenging. Furthermore, issues invariably spanned the full operational breadth of the organization; progress was arduous at best. The work persistently outgrew schedules and budgets, and it ultimately threatened realization of the strategic plan, all the while demanding far more executive attention than predicted.

Increasingly diverting critical resources to the non-credit work, senior management began to neglect further exploration of credit relationships. Having already seen one sizeable payback, far in excess of project cost, the custodians did not feel compelled to seek more. Responsibility for analyzing credit relationships was again shifted, now to operational management, who lacked the time and inclination to focus on strategic outlooks. The prospecting elements of data mining ceased abruptly. No one took the time to refine the first-cut analytical models or seek predictive associations. Rather than exploiting the hands-on analytical tools, which did not conform to operational norms, management simply codified the preliminary model's prepackaged analysis, hoping to discover any remaining compliance gaps.

Thus, the first-cut abstractions became enshrined and assumed the role of a fixed application. With this role came the final shift in perception: what had once been a robust data mining effort was now merely another "management information system" adrift in the bank's operational morass. Not a front-line source of bank revenue, it was treated as a frill.

Events continued to outstrip the plan. Resources for collecting new operational data, or for supporting the fixed application, were sometimes unavailable. It no longer mattered. The quasi-application lingered for a time, without visible benefit. Eventually, it was simply ended: the separate-site environment shut down, the replicated data left to wither. No announcement, recognition, or explanation was necessary. Its failure was as silent as its success had been prominent.

REASONS FOR FAILURE

Despite having the tools to rate, compare, and explore corporate credit relationships, ABCBank had not pursued these core project (and strategic) objectives. In large part, this lack of commitment was due to the resistance of key players: the commercial loan officers. Each was responsible for dealing with a given set of clients, and was mandated to maximize both bank business and profit with these clients.

From the start, loan officers had universally objected to the premises of the contemplated analysis, because:

1. Negotiated terms reflected the basic dilemma of a competitive market: higher pricing drove clients to competitors, while lower pricing increased business. The first-cut model had not accommodated this fundamental consideration.
2. Even with the new decision-support capability, the bank still could not accurately measure the profitability of an overall client relationship. A credit-only view of clients was a distorted picture, and (due to the many difficulties of integrating the analysis of non-credit services) the distortion was not to go away in the foreseeable future.
3. In-depth exploration of client relationships, good or bad, seemed irrelevant in the field. It seemed far more valuable to try to understand clients' lines of business, needs, plans, etc., in the context of economies' volatile credit markets. Again, the template had not encompassed such comprehensive factors.
4. Clients were too dissimilar to warrant meaningful comparison. The many complex factors at work within large corporations, and their respective histories of dealings with ABCBank, created unique factors for negotiating with each client.
5. Similarly, it was not meaningful to rank a loan officer's performance, as each dealt with a different client base. No matter how an officer was rated, the officer's response never varied — "I negotiated the best terms that I could at the time."

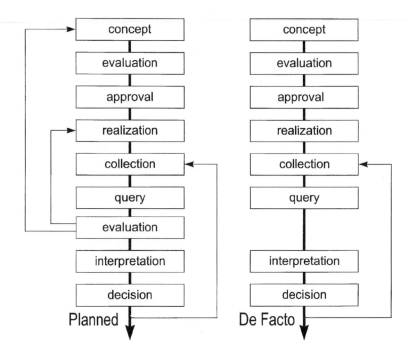

Exhibit 63.2. Comparison of planned and *defacto* standards.

Unprepared to counter these arguments, bank management allowed the project's real analytical objectives to languish. It effectively decided that the first-cut analysis and assumptions, which were based on intuition and some preproject prospecting, were adequate for more than just the moment. The bank was now merely content to excavate the mine's lode, and — as inevitably happens — the lode was finally exhausted.

If a business ceases to explore, it cannot expect to discover further benefits from a data mining exercise. At the end of the day, ABCBank's management viewed its continuing investment as a poor one — it saw an operational system that had already outlived its one-time yield.

Exhibit 63.2 illustrates the impact of this decision. The opportunities for using feedback to bring forward the vision in which the project had first been conceived, to refine the analytical model or to substitute a more robust one, or even to explore classifications, were negated by eliminating the left-most arrows on the diagram. Prospecting had been forsaken.

Although the compliance payback far offset project costs, the costs still seemed excessive — a planned throw-away effort with a narrow compliance focus would have been much cheaper. Yet, as costs had been recovered, no one felt compelled to analyze why work on the project ceased. No one thought it wise to comment on the failure to meet objectives, or to assess the consequent impact on ABCBank's strategic direction.

LEGACY: BENEFITS AND DAMAGE

In hindsight, the project did provide both strategic and operational benefits:

- After the initial recognition of widespread deposit noncompliance, wary loan officers and clients quickly learned to avoid ongoing compliance problems — an unforeseen benefit.
- Ultimately, the prolonged follow-up effort for non-credit services ended. Again, ABCBank had deferred data mining to an operational approach, but it nonetheless established a broader base of data about clients, which permitted some rudimentary assessments. This was largely built on the classifications and approaches to aggregation that had been developed earlier in the credit arena.
- Operational management began to appreciate the risks of dealing with large clients on diverse fronts (e.g., bank contact A, seeking to reinforce a client relationship, offers one service at a significant discount; bank contact B similarly discounts another service; C does the same, etc., so that the client relationship becomes uniformly unprofitable).

These benefits were balanced by negative impacts and uncertainties:

- The credit project's demise discouraged the spread of discovery-oriented practices. Non-credit "analysis" mutated into a purely operational system. Its success was attributed to the introduction of a new comprehensive client statement. Ironically, the new statement employed the client family concept to lever operational data to the client's advantage, not the bank's.
- Some key objectives of the strategic plan were never met. Clients and bank performance were not rated, nor was any additional discovery contemplated. In fact, the replicated, proto-warehouse nature of the original credit-services environment had more readily supported data mining than the new environment, which was constrained by production-world technologies.
  - After abruptly introducing more strict deposit compliance and penalizing clients, ABCBank did not contemplate the long-term impacts.
  - Had lax enforcement been an integral part of some client relationships?
  - Had foregoing full deposit compliance encouraged more profitable business with respect to other services?
  - Were relationships less or more profitable once strict enforcement was introduced?

The original data mining environment was poised to explore such questions, but the bank never asked them.

Lessons

Some of the apparent shortcomings of the project were inherent in the culture in which they were spawned:

- Years of success, bolstered by good performance in a changing marketplace, had bred complacency. Decision makers would have accepted anything related to the strategic plan, in which everyone had great faith. New phenomena, such as replicating data into an analytical framework, were accepted without being fully understood.
- The transitions demanded by the plan severely burdened executive visionaries. Sponsorship migrated steadily from exciting vision toward indifferent custodianship. Early project success aggravated this problem, encouraging management to neglect something that appeared to have its own momentum.
- With the bank overtaxed by the restructuring of its entire milieu, there was fierce internal competition for resources. A warehouse-like information environment was seen by many as a frivolous investment, and it became an easy political target.
- Rapid change permeated the organization, fostering the black-and-white mindset that was fatal to the project. Instead of taking the time to understand any effort's potential value, management focused on quick judgments of success or failure. In this case, the compliance payback offered management a political exit — even as they privately judged the project a failure, they could label it a success and quietly end it.

Other shortcomings stemmed from shortsighted project decisions and improperly managed expectations:

- While executives were making sweeping decisions about business direction, the commercial lending experts wanted to make black-and-white judgments about client relationships. Quantifying vague perceptions was a sound notion, but it led to a naive outlook. Executives were sold on the idea of rating clients and loan officers, not on the value of discovery.
- In hindsight, the initial prototype may have been biased in favor of the draft analytical model. Reinforcing that model early in the project served to further obscure the value of future prospecting.
- Deferring consideration of non-credit services seemed pragmatic to a steering body that had been selected for its expertise in the credit arena. People failed to appreciate the implications of not looking beyond their customary boundaries.

- Although sophisticated, the thinking that formed the original model was imperfect. Underlying the model was a substrate of traditional back-office concerns. The first-cut deliverables reflected this situation; instead of seeking a balanced client view across credit and non-credit engagements, operational questions were asked (Are clients complying? Which agreements are relevant?).
- Similarly, front-line questions (At what point will bank profitability drive clients to the competition?) were not addressed, although the collected data might have guided some vital investigations. When later faced with such business realities, the business experts lacked the ability and/or energy to revisit the model, despite being nominally prepared for such an evolution.

Ultimately, the vision that had conceived the project proved too limited to see the job through to the end.

CONCLUSION

Could the bank, or the project itself, have avoided all these shortcomings? Without previously enduring a strategic realignment of such magnitude, it does not seem likely. No one had anticipated all the exigencies that the strategic plan imposed. Management was simply too distracted. If the organization were to repeat the exercise now, it would be better prepared, and it might fare better.

On the other hand, certain problems were not unique to ABCBank, and are of interest to other data mining efforts. The project ought to have resolved or minimized them.

What could the project team have done to promote success?

- *Market exploratory data mining on its own terms.* Whereas business traditionally develops solution definitions for delineated problems, data mining targets unexpected insights that can lead to innovation. Thus, marketing the idea of data mining to potential sponsors may be difficult. The bank's project promised rigid queries that implied predefined paybacks. This approach sold the project, but it undersold data mining. The business bought the queries, rather than the process.
- *Find appropriate sponsors and educate them.* Visibility — the bank president actually participated in the early conceptualizations — proved to be a mixed blessing. The resulting impetus encouraged the unfortunate decision to defer non-credit analysis. A high-level study of this area could have been integrated into the project with little impact on the schedule; such a study probably would have alerted senior management to the problems that lay ahead. Moreover, although visionaries, the senior executives had very strong operational footings — they

could see far, but they all tended to stand in the same place. Committing to a process like data mining, as opposed to an operational solution, was a foreign concept. Under pressure, they relapsed into an operational perspective.

- *Manage expectations of technology.* Mining tools — parallel processing, very large databases, specialized tools for time-series analysis, and related phenomena — quickly acquire promising reputations. Their promise may do them a disservice, however, for it encourages businesses to seek quick remedies for complex situations. The promise may prevent the realization that unknowns make prospecting a continuing phenomenon. ABCBank overlooked this fact.
- *Secure lasting commitments and resources.* Competition for skills and expertise exists in any organization, threatening resource commitments. Because it is inherently open-ended, data mining may be particularly susceptible to such threats. The project team enjoyed conceptualization, construction, and initial discovery, but they disliked prolonged exploration of the same data (perhaps because it might lead to doubts about their preconceptions). They were happy to move on to new problems — as was their management — leaving behind an analytical vacuum.
- *Hear the concerns of all key players.* The business team was expert in the financial principles of commercial lending expertise, but it was blindly biased. There was little consultation with loan officers, and it never did appreciate some of their primary concerns. The team's first-cut model was deficient and did not deserve to be enshrined. Not improving the model precluded its acquiring necessary strategic value.

Perhaps this final point was the project's greatest failing. In retrospect, the very heart of the project — the idea that the back office would evaluate multimillion-dollar front-line decisions, based on incomplete data — was never practical.

Chapter 64
Multimedia Databases and Data Mining

Venkat N. Gudivada
Yongjian Fu

THE TERM UNIVERSAL SERVER IS FAST BECOMING ACCEPTED AS A GENERIC DESCRIPTION OF USER-CUSTOMIZABLE MULTIMEDIA ADD-ONS TO THE RDBMS MODEL. The use of data extensions to manage unstructured data is being implemented by the major DBMS vendors. This chapter explains the characteristics of multimedia data types and other approaches to database management that further expand on this universal technology strategy. A special area with very relevant application of the multimedia database approach is also discussed: data mining.

MULTIMEDIA CONTENT-BASED RETRIEVAL

Faster processor speeds, enormous increases in the capacity of secondary storage devices, and the emergence of CD-ROM and optical disks are contributing to the rise in the production of multimedia, which includes text, graphics, audio, and video, among other data types. More multimedia information sources are being made available for online access through the World Wide Web; with the proliferation of multimedia on the desktop, multimedia data will soon be as common to computers as text data.

Multimedia database systems are expected to coherently handle these disparate data types and provide content-based access to the data. Content-based multimedia information retrieval (CBMIR) means that the system retrieves information according to the textual, visual, auditory, and semantic contents of the media. This content is interpreted at suitable levels of abstraction, but transparently to the user. Relevance of retrieved data may be judged differently by different users, even if an identically formulated query is performed. The notion of relevance is thus subjective and

0-8493-9832-0/00/$0.00+$.50

dynamic, and depends on the particular user's retrieval need and context. Semantic correlation across media types is essential to CBMIR.

Tools and techniques for multimedia data organization, search, retrieval, and presentation comprise the enabling technologies of CBMIR. However, they have not kept pace with the insatiable quest for multimedia data generation. The severity of this problem can be seen in the limitations of current tools for searching the Web. Advances in CBMIR are essential to developing multimedia database systems because CBMIR constitutes the primary component of a multimedia database system.

CHARACTERISTICS OF MULTIMEDIA DATA MANAGEMENT SYSTEMS

In contrast to relational and object-oriented systems, multimedia data management systems are defined by the following characteristics:

- *Data model heterogeneity.* Each multimedia data type requires a data model and associated retrieval model that suit its intrinsic nature. However, these disparate data and retrieval models need to be integrated using a layer of abstraction.
- *Temporal nature of data.* Time dimension is intrinsic to image sequences, audio, and video. This has several implications, including the need for intra- and intermedia synchronization for presentation of media on output devices. This affects algorithms and protocols for multimedia servers and communications networks.
- *Feature extraction and semantics capture.* The ability to extract required features and semantics automatically or semiautomatically from multimedia data is necessary for developing large multimedia database systems.
- *Query processing and similarity measures.* Queries are processed and rank-ordered based on some notion of similarity. What features contribute to similarity and the degree of their contribution greatly affect the quality of retrieval.
- *Multimodal query language or specification scheme.* Content-based retrieval is characterized by various generic query operators (e.g., retrieval by color, shape, or spatial relationships). Each operator requires a specification scheme that is intrinsic to its nature. However, these schemes need to be integrated to provide a unified view of querying multimedia data. In contrast with conventional database systems, browsing is commonly used for exploitative querying of multimedia databases. Also, the display of query results is often required in the form of a multimedia presentation, and the query specification scheme is expected to provide this functionality.
- *Indexing structures for efficient query processing.* Not all multimedia data features are suitable for indexing using B-tree or R-tree based methods, especially those that represent spatial and topological

relationships in images and video. Mapping methods are required to transform complex multimedia features into ordered domains so that B-tree or R-tree–based indexing methods can be used.

- *User subjectivity in multimedia data interpretation.* A user's interpretation of multimedia data may differ from its stored interpretation. For example, in an image database of police mugshots, a feature named *nose length* may have one value — "long" — recorded in the database, whereas a system user may interpret this value as "normal." User queries tend to be subjective, imprecise, and uncertain.

- *Distribution issues.* Multidatabase solutions are a possibility for distributed multimedia data management. However, multimedia collections on the Web are not managed by database management systems, which is usually the case in multiple databases.

- *Tertiary storage management.* Because of the voluminous nature of multimedia data, it is not practical or economical to store all the data on secondary storage devices. For example, 30 minutes of high-quality uncompressed video requires about 50G bytes of disk storage. Data migration strategies between tertiary-secondary-primary memory assume paramount importance to meet temporal media synchronization and performance requirements. Compression algorithms are also vital to keep the storage requirements affordable for multimedia applications.

THREE VIEWS OF MULTIMEDIA DATA

Multimedia data management can be broadly categorized into approaches: (1) image processing and pattern recognition, (2) database, and (3) information retrieval. To better explain the distinctive characteristics of these approaches, they are considered in the context of the three views of multimedia data:

- *Structured data.* Structured data are usually managed by a relational data management system. These include character strings and numeric data types. Internal representations for and operations on these data types are well understood.

- *Semistructured data.* Semistructured data fall somewhere in between and includes, for example, e-mail messages, Usenet newsgroup postings, and tagged or markup text such as hypertext markup language (HTML) or virtual reality markup language (VRML). The tags or markup in the semistructured data are primarily intended to provide one specific function. For example, HTML is intended for authoring documents that can be rendered on a variety of output devices of heterogeneous computers dispersed in a global communications network. However, some of these tags can also be used for extracting terms that represent the content of an HTML document (e.g., title and heading tags).

- *Unstructured data.* Unstructured data is simply a bit stream. Examples include pixel-level representations for images, video, and audio, and character-level representation for text. Substantial processing and interpretation are required to extract semantics from unstructured data.

The Image Processing and Pattern Recognition Approach

The image processing and pattern recognition approach to multimedia data management views multimedia data as unstructured. This approach relies on various image processing and pattern recognition techniques to automatically extract features from unstructured data. In other words, the approach transforms unstructured data to semistructured data and uses it to process user queries. The features that can be extracted automatically are usually primitive and geometry based.

The Database Approach

The database approach views multimedia data as structured. Features are usually extracted manually or semiautomatically. The features, referred to as attributes, entail a high level of abstraction on unstructured data. The higher the level of abstraction in the features, the lower the scope for ad hoc queries.

The Information Retrieval Approach

The information retrieval approach views multimedia data as semistructured, which is primarily in the form of keywords, specially crafted captions, or free-form text. This semistructured data may naturally be associated with multimedia data or can be derived manually.

User queries are processed using information retrieval models that range from the simple Boolean search to sophisticated vector processing. Natural language processing techniques are often used to assign content descriptors to the text associated with multimedia data. Although visual and auditory information is reduced to textual form, this approach is widely used because it benefits from the extensive research on text retrieval. Also, this approach has special appeal — image, audio, and video data co-occurs with text, which is the predominant data type in many applications.

Vendor Strategies

Almost all major commercial database vendors are making claims that their products can manage multimedia data and support content-based queries. However, the reality is that most vendors have more work to do to fully support multimedia.

Many database vendors and their products — including CA-Ingres, DB2/6000 C/S, Informix/Illustra, ODB II, Odapter, Omniscience, Oracle

820

Corp., UniSQL, and Versant — do indeed provide functionality for integrated storage of multimedia data with conventional string and numeric data. Some systems have advanced to support content-based queries.

Datablades and Data Cartidges. Informix/Illustra packages a collection of user-defined data types, functions, and the access methods associated with them as *datablades*. Datablades encapsulate application-specific functionality transparently to the database users and application programs.

The notion of datablades is more general than the concept of an abstract data type (ADT). Datablades are an integral part of the database engine and are not opaque to the query optimizer. The query optimizer can use the user-defined access methods associated with the datablades in deciding an optimal plan for the execution of a query.

Furthermore, datablades and the database engine share the same type system and possibly execute in the same address space. In contrast, ADTs and the DBMS engine have separate type systems and execute in different address spaces. Though the ADT approach reduces the security risk, performance suffers.

Incorporating base type extensions into a relational or object-oriented DBMS is neither a simple nor straightforward task. The biggest challenge lies in making the query optimizer treat the base type extensions as native to the DBMS. Multimedia representations and associated operations for content-based retrieval vary widely across applications. Therefore, it is conceivable that a DBMS is required to support a large number of base type extensions. To provide the ability to add a new base type or an operation associated with the base type to the DBMS (without the need for system shutdown), as well as to contain the size of the DBMS, the DBMS should be capable of dynamically linking the user-defined base type extensions.

Incorporating base type extensions entails choices in the client/server architecture and has implications for system security. For example, where do the functions associated with base type extensions execute? There are two possibilities: client-side activation and server-side activation. Client-side activation is desirable when the function is computationally intensive, does not make frequent calls to the DBMS, and the bandwidth required to transfer data from the server to the client is insignificant. The security concern for client-side activation is not as serious as that associated with the server-side activation.

There are two options for server-side activation. First, the function can be activated in the same address space as the DBMS. The function call is then essentially a local procedure call with little overhead. However, this option has the potential for creating a grave security loophole since the function may accidentally or intentionally erase or modify the data in the database. Second, the function can be run in a different address space or on a different machine. Then a remote procedure call (RPC) must be used and the performance degradation of the DBMS depends on the overhead associated with the RPC.

DBMSs from the major vendors differ in their approach to content-based querying of multimedia data. The Informix Universal Server seems to be ahead of others (in fact, the term *universal server,* coined by Informix to label its new product line, is becoming widely accepted as a generic description of similar multimedia add-ons). Informix offers text, image, spatial (2D or 3D), visual information retrieval, and Web datablades; many more are being developed by independent software vendors. Similar functionality has been announced by Oracle, which refers to its offerings as *data cartridges.*

The real challenge to truly harnessing multimedia information lies in establishing cross-correlation among various data types (i.e., heterogeneous information integration). The current vendor approaches provide a piecemeal solution (based on the data type) to the multimedia data management. The development of datablades and data cartridges is only a beginning. It will be some time before all the defining characteristics described earlier in this chapter are featured in a multimedia DBMS.

DATA MINING

Data mining, a primary component of a larger process referred to as knowledge discovery in databases (KDD), is the effort to understand, analyze, and eventually make use of the huge volumes of the data that reside in databases.

There is a rapidly growing interest in data mining from both the academic and industrial communities. KDD is the process of identifying valid, novel, potentially useful, and ultimately understandable patterns in data. Steps in a KDD process include data selection, preprocessing, transformation, data mining, and interpretation/evaluation of the results, as shown in Exhibit 64.1. Because data mining is the central part of the KDD process, it is often used as a synonym for knowledge discovery from databases.

A data mining system includes a user interface, a search engine, and a data management component. The architecture of a typical data mining system is shown in Exhibit 64.2. A data mining session is usually an interactive process of data mining query submission, task analysis, data collection, interesting pattern search, and findings presentation.

Data Mining Tasks

Data mining tasks can be classified based on the kind of knowledge a user is looking for. The most common types of data mining tasks are:

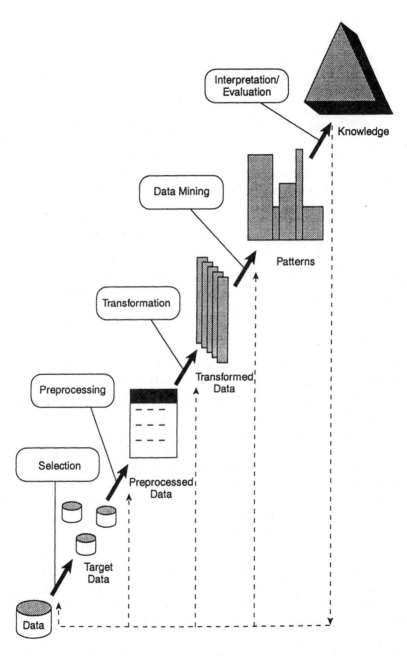

Exhibit 64.1. Steps of the KDD process.

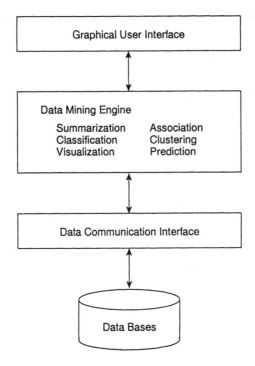

Exhibit 64.2. A typical data mining system.

- *Summarization.* A set of task-relevant data is summarized and abstracted, resulting in a smaller set providing a general overview of the data with aggregation information. A summarization table can be generalized to different abstraction levels and viewed from different angles. For example, the sales of a company can be summarized by product, region, or year and viewed at various abstraction levels in any combination of them.
- *Classification.* A set of training data (i.e., a set of objects whose class label is known) is given and analyzed. A classification model is then constructed based on the features of the training data. The model can be used to classify future data and develop a better understanding of each class in the database. For example, a classification model can be built for diseases based on symptoms as features that can be used to diagnose new patients.
- *Association rule mining.* An association rule reveals associative relationships among objects, especially in a transactional database. For example, an association rule, "call waiting® call display," says if a customer subscribes to the call waiting service, he or she very likely also has "call display" service. Databases are searched to identify strong

associations among objects and data. As another example, a retail store may discover that a set of commodities is often bought together with another set of commodities. This discovery can then be used to design sales strategies.

- *Clustering.* Clustering is the process of identification of classes (i.e., clusters) for a set of unclassified objects based on their attributes. The objects are clustered so that the intraclass similarities are maximized and the interclass similarities are minimized based on certain criteria. Once the clusters are decided, the objects are labeled with their corresponding clusters, and common features of the objects in a cluster are summarized to form the class description. For example, a company may cluster its customers into several categories based on the similarities of their age, income, or address, and the common characteristics of the customers in a category can be used to describe that group of customers.

- *Trend analysis.* Patterns and regularities in data-changing behaviors are discovered in time-related data (i.e., data that has the attribute *time*). Data is analyzed along the time dimension, and the data-changing tracks are compared and matched. Trends, such as increasing streaks or decreasing streaks, that happen frequently are reported. For example, a company's sales can be analyzed for every year, quarter, or month to discover the sales patterns and analyze the reasons behind them.

Data Mining Techniques

The three most prevalent data mining techniques are: 1) mathematical and statistical, 2) machine learning, or 3) database oriented.

- *Mathematical and statistical methods.* Usually, mathematical or statistical models are built from a set of training data. An optimal model, based on a predefined measure, is searched for, and rules, patterns, and regularities are then drawn from it. The most commonly used tools include Bayesian network, rough set, linear or nonlinear regression, and X^2.

- *Machine learning methods.* Cognitive models are used by most machine learning methods to resemble the human learning process. Like mathematical and statistical methods, machine learning methods search for a best model that matches the testing data. The most common machine learning methods used include decision tree induction, conceptual clustering, and inductive concept formation.

- *Database-oriented methods.* Database-oriented methods do not search for a best model, as is the case with the previous two methods. Instead, data model, or database-specific heuristics are used to discover the characteristics of the data. For example, transactional databases are scanned iteratively to discover patterns in customer shopping practices. Iterative, frequent pattern searching and attribute-oriented induction are two representatives of the database-oriented methods.

There are many other methods for data mining, such as visual exploration, neural networks, knowledge representation, and integrated methods. Most data mining systems use multiple methods to deal with different data mining tasks, kinds of data, and application areas.

Data Mining Applications

Successful data mining case studies can be found in many business application areas, as well as many scientific areas such as astronomy, molecular biology, and medicine. Following are descriptions of databases specific to different commercial industries:

- *Marketing databases.* Database marketing is the most successful and popular application of data mining. By mining historical customer databases, patterns and trends are extracted and customer profiles are built that can be used for more effective marketing.
- *Retail databases.* Retail databases consist of transactions that are lists of bar codes. Data mining can reveal customer shopping patterns that can be used, for example, in sales campaigns.
- *Stock market databases.* By searching stock market data for trends and patterns, stocks that have performed well can be identified. Better investment decisions can be made by selecting stocks that have a potentially high return.
- *Customer claim databases.* Customer claims can be analyzed to detect fraud in insurance claims, health care expenses, and tax returns.
- *Credit application databases.* Applications for credit and loans can be decided based on the applicant's information and the decision support model; the latter is constructed based on existing data.

DATA MINING FOR IMPROVED MULTIMEDIA RETRIEVAL

Multimedia is becoming increasingly available on the World Wide Web, which can be viewed as a large, distributed, multimedia database. However, the data is unstructured and heterogeneous.

Although SQL-3 allows constructs for querying multimedia data, the underlying assumption is that the data are structured abstract data types that are application-specific and can be constructed to transform semi-structured data into structured data. As browsing becomes the predominant mode for exploratory querying of multimedia data on the Web, data mining techniques can be applied to research the traversal paths of users accessing data, so frequent paths can be determined and data can be reorganized to reduce the time it takes to access it. Data mining techniques can also be used to learn about user behavior and subsequently develop user models to improve the retrieval effectiveness of a system.

Another area where data mining techniques (especially classification) can prove valuable is in extracting features from new image instances. Feature values for images in the training set are extracted manually to train the classifier. Then the classifier can be used to derive features from new image instances automatically. Although this has long been a topic of interest in the pattern recognition area, the number of classes are relatively few compared to the number of classes that arise in the data mining context.

Because of inherent difficulties in feature quantification and subjective interpretation of multimedia data by users, it is not possible to precisely characterize database contents as well as user queries. This often leads to poor retrieval effectiveness. Only a small fraction of retrieved objects are relevant to a user's query.

Relevance feedback techniques — used successfully in the text retrieval area — can be used to improve retrieval effectiveness in multimedia databases as well. The user specifies relevance judgments on a subset of the retrieved data by labeling them as relevant, somewhat relevant, or not relevant, for example. Inductive learning techniques can be used on this data to improve precision in the user query and to resolve subjectivity.

SUMMARY

The data mining discipline simply draws on well-established techniques in machine learning, probability and statistics, pattern recognition, visualization, and databases; however, synergistically employing these techniques is not an easy task. Data mining addresses the most important aspect of these techniques — scalability. Because multimedia databases are usually enormous, the potential impact of data mining techniques for multimedia data management deserves attention.

Section XIII
Document Management

DOCUMENT MANAGEMENT OFFERS A STRONG ALTERNATIVE TO OTHER METHODS OF DATA MANAGEMENT. Document management solutions are suited to situations where rich-text documents require storage under a small set of access conditions. However, the text within a document cannot be as readily searched as those contained in a relational database. However, traditional relational databases are not well suited for manipulating the same type of information that is stored in document management systems. As a general rule, document management systems can store more information in a problem domain, but with limited lines of accessibility than other storage mechanisms. A whole suite of tools, including Lotus Notes and Intranets, are available to support document management systems. This section contains five chapters that focus on different aspects of document management.

Chapter 65, "Evolution in Systems Development and the Parallels in Document Management," shows how to avoid repeating the risks of traditional document management development projects by defining enterprise platforms from the start of the initiative.

Chapter 66, "A Practical Planning Guide for Lotus Notes/Domino," discusses concepts for preparing an organization for the introduction of Lotus Notes/Domino into the corporate environment. This chapter provides a practical planning guide.

Chapter 67, "Terms of Reference: The Foundation for Implementing Document Management Systems," provides the instructions for properly constructing a Terms of Reference document for an Enterprise Document Management System (EDMS) for increased project success.

Chapter 68, "Strategies for an Archive Management Program: The Digital Preservation of Corporate Information" shows how to plan, design, and contruct an "Archives Repository" so that an organization can avoid suffering from "corporate amnesia" — the loss of corporate memory.

DOCUMENT MANAGEMENT

Chapter 69, "Integrating EDMSs and DBMSs," describes how to combine the strengths of a Database Management System and an Electronic Document Management System to support rich and diverse information sources and datatypes, while supporting the quick access and search capabilities offered by relational databases.

Chapter 65

Evolution in Systems Development and the Parallels in Document Management

Charles Banyay

THIS CHAPTER DISCUSSES THE EVOLUTION OF BUSINESS SOFTWARE DEVEL-OPMENT FOR MANAGING STRUCTURED DATA. Furthermore, the chapter explores some of the parallels between the development and evolution of the software for managing structured data, and the evolution which is currently underway for managing unstructured data or to use more familiar terminology—document management systems. The starting point is to explore the initial attempts at building business systems using flat file structures and custom built software. An examination of the first database management systems and the packaged applications built on top of these tools follows, ending with an examination of the enterprise resource planning application systems of today. The parallels in the development of document management systems are then examined under the same phases of evolution.

THE EARLY YEARS OF DATA PROCESSING

The 1960s were probably the decade where modern business systems development became a pervasive concept. Most application systems initially were designed with a flat file structure. The concept of the flat file i.e. having a single dimension, containing one or more records which in turn contained one or more fields as the lower level elements, was the basic construct for data management for early business systems. This early construct for electronic data management, the file with records containing fields was originally popularized by IBM.

Business systems of this era were characterized by the construction of custom applications designed to solve a specific business problem. The data repository, the flat file, was designed, optimized, and constructed, to address this specific business problem. The business problem was analyzed and the basic entities within the problem domain were identified. A record was assigned to each entity. A flat file was designed for each entity type containing the records for that entity type. The data fields within each record, were designed to contain all of the data, but only the data, required for that particular business problem. It was common to have a number of flat files supporting an application with one of the files generally being designated as the "master" file.

The important aspect of this design philosophy is that the files, records, and fields were designed, optimized, and constructed from the original perspective of the solution to the original business problem domain. The files were designed for optimal access by the application, which owned them. The records were also designed with the same objective in mind. The fields within the records were designed to contain the data only from the perspective of the application. For example, if the first five characters of the surname field was the only data which was required by the business solution, then that is all that was designed into the record.

The application of business rules such as editing and validation of each data field were also limited to the perspective of the business problem at hand. The business rules became hard-coded into the application. The application system was designed around the data structure. The data structure in this way became embedded within the application and the application was dependent on the data structure. During the first decade of business system development, applications designed using this philosophy, solving specific business problems, proliferated throughout the enterprise.

At a certain level of technology integration within the business environment, this design philosophy was acceptable and may even have been preferable. If one is only considering the solution of the business problem at hand, then this design philosophy has merit. It does limit the application development activities to those required by the solution of the business problem. The application is optimal in its access of the data because it owns the data files. However, as these custom application systems grew in numbers within enterprises and as changes within the enterprise and within the associated business environment necessitated changes to the data definitions embedded within the application systems, the weaknesses inherent within this design philosophy became evident.

Part of the justification behind this design philosophy, just like the justification behind the original two digit year in the date field design, was optimal processing speed and minimal storage and memory requirements. As the date field design turned into a monumental problem for information systems organizations, popularly called theY2k bug, the solution specific application design turned into an even bigger problem called the application silo.

As enterprises evolved to a new level of technology integration which required a holistic view of enterprise data, the long term impacts of the weaknesses inherent within the solution-specific application design philosophy became acutely evident, and began to outweigh the immediate benefits of discreet information technology solutions.

The application perspective on data means that the same data element may be within multiple files in different applications. Any change to the data structure for any reason means that changes are required to every application that references the data element. Multiple conversion programs may be required. This results in significant duplication of effort. The effort involved at times prevented enterprises from adopting more optimal business processes, if these processes mandated changes to the data structure.

Reuse of application code was almost impossible. Thoughts of reuse or the concepts of enterprise applications were not common. Even when reuse was attempted it was usually far more complex than originally conceived. New applications had to be developed "from scratch" without the benefits of any development, which had preceded them.

Having the same data located in different applications with possibly different formats and different application of business rules such as editing or validation, meant that the same data elements would frequently have different values in different repositories. Data integrity issues such as this caused the credibility of the underlying technology, and its value to the enterprise to be questioned. Very often, this hindered the further acceptance and adoption of any new technology.

As enterprises entered a new level of technology integration within their business operations, a more holistic view of the data was required. The use of technology for decision support purposes requiring enterprise information retrieval capability, became as important as its use for the solution to discreet business problems at the operational level. This holistic approach to data required access to the enterprise information in one logical repository, which was not possible in the environment of fragmented, silo, application systems.

DATA DRIVEN DESIGN AND DEVELOPMENT

By the mid- to late-1970s, the weaknesses and the disadvantages of custom systems development based on the flat file, solution specific design philosophy, made it painfully obvious that a new and different approach was required for utilizing information technology within the business enterprise. Thanks to the likes of James Martin, Ed Yourdon, Gane and Sarson and their contemporaries, a new and different approach to the application of information technology within business computing did indeed develop.

The fundamental difference in the new approach was the recognition that a base of enterprise data existed as a collection of entities with a multitude of different processes acting on the same data. Systems exclusively for the management of data or the database, were developed. Whether the database management system was hierarchical, networked, or relational is not relevant to this discussion. The recognition that a base of enterprise data existed as a whole, independent of the processes which acted on the data, was a critical, important step in the evolution of the application of information technology.

The data-driven perspective on information means that the same data element never appears within multiple files in different applications. Data redundancy is at a minimum. Any change to the data structure, means that changes are required to the database management system which manages the data elements. Only a single conversion program is required. There is minimal duplication of effort. The enterprise is free to adopt new and more optimal business processes even if these processes involve changes to the data structure. The effort to change is not prohibitive.

Reuse of application code is by definition. The database management system is used by every application system, which acts on the data. Concepts of enterprise applications are common because the underlying data is enterprise data as opposed to application specific data. New applications can benefit from any development which had preceded them through the reuse of components.

Data exists only once. The same data is not located in different applications. There is no possibility of different formats. Business rules such as editing or validation are consistent. Data integrity is ensured.

The data-driven approach to enterprise data management was definitely an evolutionary step in the right direction. There were further steps required, however, before arriving at today's model for the application of information technology within the business enterprise.

THE ADVENT OF PACKAGED APPLICATIONS

Probably somewhat earlier if not in parallel to the evolution of data driven design and development, began the evolution towards packaged application systems. Most application systems until the early 1970s were developed as custom applications. This means that all of the code was developed as a "one of" or custom solution to a business problem or a custom automation of a business process. Estimates have shown that up to 70 percent of the total cost of ownership of an application is in the development and ongoing maintenance of code. Any savings in this area would ultimately reduce the total cost of development and ownership of application systems.

At least to some degree, many business problems and processes share common elements such as data fields and process flows for example, between various enterprises. Systems developers recognized this early on after consistently redeveloping the same or similar applications or application components. Two unrelated situations further facilitated the move towards packaged applications.

By the mid-1970s, many IT groups had reached the limits of their budgets. Maintaining existing applications and technology infrastructures consumed between 80 to 90 percent of most IT budgets. There was not much left over to build new applications yet the demand for application development was at an all time high. Most IT organizations faced multi year application backlogs. IT leaders were looking for better ways in which they could further the adoption of information technology within their organizations, without the responsibility of a lot of custom manufactured code.

In parallel to the IT budget challenge, and as the market became more receptive to packaged applications, a number of reputable vendors such as Management Sciences of America (MSA), and Information Sciences Incorporated (InScI), were bringing solid packaged applications to the business community. These applications addressed areas from accounting to manufacturing and human resources.

For packaged applications to become an accepted approach to reducing the application backlog required one final hurdle to be overcome. One of the tenets of systems development was that applications should be modified rather than business processes. Until the mid-1970s this was unquestioned. The large volume of the application backlog coupled with the availability of good application packages started many business leaders to question whether they could afford to continue to spend on extensive computer software modifications and the associated ongoing maintenance just to preserve the sanctity of existing processes.

The acceptance of packaged applications was a natural evolution in the software industry. The adoption of best of breed packaged applications still left IT groups with the challenge of developing code to integrate these applications. This at times represented a considerable challenge especially when the packaged applications were from different vendors.

ENTERPRISE RESOURCE PLANNING SYSTEMS

The acceptance of the packaged solution and the associated acceptance of modifying existing processes to fit the industry accepted application, was the beginning of the move to entire application suites. Escalating IT budgets and the increasing complexity of integrating "best of breed" applications, the rapidly changing business environment, the Y2k bug, and the re-engineering tidal wave of the late 1980s, took application systems development one step further towards industry accepted common application suites.

Enterprise Resource Planning (ERP) applications are a natural extension of the move towards packaged applications except that ERP applications are already integrated suites of application components. ERP applications have been developed not just to support discreet components of a business function but to support the entire function with integrated components of automation. Some of the larger ERP applications such as those from SAP, are designed to automate multiple business functions. The key ingredient to these ERP applications is integration! Integration of "best of breed" applications proved to be far more complex both initially and on an ongoing basis, and far more resource intensive, than most IT shops had anticipated. An application suite, which already provided the integration "out of the box," was more than welcome.

Market leading ERP applications include industry best practices representing years of accumulated experience with re-engineering. Business executives bitten by the reengineering bug, frustrated by years of IT's inability to meet the expectation of the user community saw in ERP applications more than just the solution to their Y2k problems. They are expecting a solution to many of their ongoing challenges with IT in general.

PARALLELS IN DOCUMENT MANAGEMENT APPLICATIONS

In approach, technique, and methodology, the management of unstructured data i.e. documents, is approximately 25 to 30 years behind the management of structured data. Since 80 to 90 percent of business information is contained in documents, the management of documents could conceivably be more important than the management of structured data. Unfortunately, technology did not evolve to the point where it made economic sense to use it to manage unstructured information i.e., documents until approximately the late 1980s.

A few of the first document management systems found their origins in the imaging boom of the late 1980s and early 1990s. Information technology, in the form of high-speed local area networks, low cost yet high volume mass storage devices, and low cost yet high-resolution monitors had evolved to the point where it became cost effective to manage large volumes of relatively large-sized content i.e., documents, in electronic format.

Independent of imaging, came the proliferation of desktop tools, which enabled the creation and sharing electronically, of many of the documents

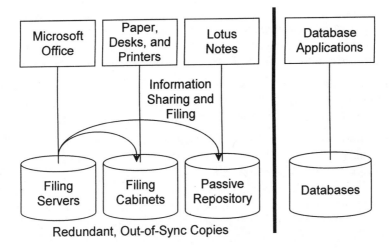

Exhibit 65.1. Without document management.

used within an enterprise. As the creation and sharing of electronic documents became easier, documents multiplied throughout the enterprise. These documents eventually ended up in multiple locations, with various versions, annotations, and changes. Even though most documents existed as multiple copies or versions, they were difficult to find when needed, and even when found it was difficult to determine which was the most recent authorized version. Exhibit 65.1 shows a view of the world without document management.

A number of creative software vendors recognized the acute need to develop an environment where any document, not just images of paper documents could be managed.

The first document management systems provided nothing more than basic library functions. Library functions consist of a logical centralized repository with check-out and check-in functionality, document versioning, secured access, and search capability both on metadata and document content (full-text indexing). As document management systems evolved they developed additional functionality such as integration to varying degrees, with the desktop software which ultimately operates on the documents. Today's industry leading document management applications offer complete document lifecycle management with virtual or compound document functionality, and comprehensive workflow.

MANAGING DOCUMENTS IN A SILO

One would think that IT practitioners would learn from the past and not repeat the mistakes, the effects of which we live with today. As discussed in the previous sections, IT practitioners learned that taking an application specific approach to data can lead to duplication of effort, silo applications, lack of data integrity, an inability to have access to critical data throughout the enterprise, and possible prohibitive costs to change.

With this history so well known today, why then are IT practitioners travelling the identical path with the management of unstructured data as they did with the management of structured data?

Even though the systems development for documents did not begin until the advent of ERP applications to manage structured data, there are remarkable similarities between document management systems development today and early systems development efforts for structured data. Document management systems are being developed in the same manner, with the same weaknesses as the custom developed application systems of the 1960s with the possible difference that the basis is not a flat file system.

The document management applications today are being developed as custom, solution-specific applications. Rather than building these applications on an enterprise platform, many document management applications today are being created on a solution-specific basis. Many ERP vendors as well as vendors of customer relationship management applications, and vendors of solution-specific application software, are providing their own solution-specific repositories for document management. Even Internet solution providers are busy developing their solution-specific document management systems.

Exhibit 65.2 shows that the silo document management systems of tomorrow are being developed today. These applications will suffer from the same or similar weaknesses as the earlier application systems, which were developed to manage structured data in a solution-specific manner. It must never be forgotten that the metadata associated with documents is structured information. Treating it in a solution-specific manner will have similar consequences as treating any other structured data in that way.

Multiple copies of documents will lack integrity just as multiple copies of data did. It will be effort intensive and expensive to change the same documents in multiple locations. When enterprise information is required one should not have to search multiple repositories. Imagine the scenario of having product documents managed in a Siebel document management system, having engineering drawings managed in SAP and a drafting document management system, customer correspondence in the customer support system, and on and on. Trying to access documents from an enterprise perspective would be impossible under these circumstances.

Data was duplicated from application to application in the flat file era not because it was stored in a flat file, but because it was viewed from a

Marketing
Product Manuals,
Drawings

Development
Specs, Product
Plans, Drawings

Manufacturing
Drawings,
SOP

Customer
Support
Product Manuals

Legal
Contracts,
Product Manuals

Drafting
Policies,
Drawings

Exhibit 65.2. Document silos.

solution-specific application perspective. The application in a sense owned the data. Application ownership of data can occur using a relational database management system just as it can under a flat file construct. Many application systems of the early 1970s retained the application ownership model even when the base file access method was switched from flat files to a DBMS.

It is irrelevant that document management applications today use an RDBMS to house the metadata. The associated document management system can still become a silo if it is developed from a solution-specific perspective. As shown in Exhibit 65.3, what is needed is an enterprise document management architecture, which is scalable and which will grow as the needs of the enterprise grows. Focus on a specific solution is good as long as the solution is developed on an enterprise architecture.

Only a few of the document management applications on the market today offer an enterprise scalable architecture. Fewer still are the vendors behind these systems, with the vision, foresight, and the financial wherewithal to continually evolve their product in the right direction.

PACKAGED DOCUMENT MANAGEMENT APPLICATIONS

One of the more promising evolutionary directions of industry leading document management systems today, and one that has a direct parallel with the applications which manage structured data, is the evolution away from custom development and towards packaged application solutions. There are document types or classifications such as engineering drawings, standard operating procedures, material safety data sheets, just to name a few, which characterize an industry and exist across numerous enterprises.

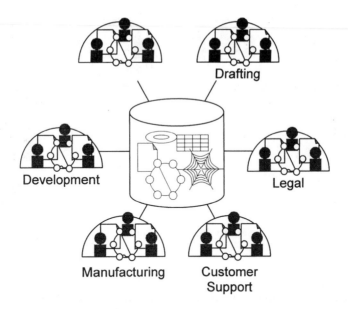

Exhibit 65.3.   Enterprise document architecture.

Each document type or classification of documents has its own lifecycle, as shown in Exhibit 65.4, which may not differ greatly between different enterprises. These document types or classifications can to some degree, have a solution set developed around them which could constitute a document management packaged application. These document types or classifications generally share similar attributes or metadata, they have similar software which operates on them, they have similar workflows with appropriate status and promotion criteria for approval associated with them, and they share similar requirements around distribution and publishing.

As did the systems developers in the early 1970s, some document management system vendors and some systems integrators who use the tools provided by the document management vendors have recognized for some time now that they are re-developing the same code over and over. A few document management system vendors have recognized the opportunity to develop this code once, and provide systems integrators with the tools to be able to configure and to fine tune these packaged solution sets to meet specific client needs. Some of these packaged solution sets have just recently arrived on the market. It is hard to say at this time whether they will be successful, and it is difficult to determine which are the major hurdles which will need to be overcome.

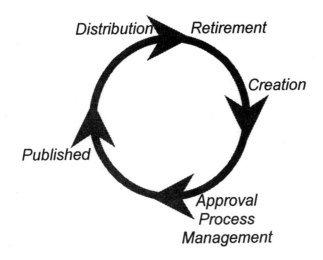

Exhibit 65.4. Document lifecycle.

ERP APPLICATIONS AND DOCUMENT MANAGEMENT

Whether document management will ever see the evolution of its equivalent of the enterprise resource planning application is difficult to say. There is a convergence of systems which manage unstructured data i.e., documents, with those systems which manage structured data within an enterprise. Some call this the journey to managing enterprise knowledge.

As organizations evolve into truly knowledge-based enterprises, they create a pressing need to manage the knowledge capital within the enterprise. Because of this, it is probable that the convergence between applications which manage structured data with those which manage unstructured data, will happen sooner than any other evolution within the document management environment.

Once this convergence is complete, the distinction between document and data management could become meaningless.

SUMMARY

The evolution of business computer systems development has progressed far during a relatively short period of time. There are different categories of business systems, two of which are data management applications and document management applications. The two have evolved quite independently, with document management just coming into its own, during the previous ten years. As can be seen there are interesting parallels between the two.

Chapter 66
A Practical Planning Guide for Lotus Notes/Domino

Michael Simonyi

EVERY ONCE IN A WHILE, A PRODUCT EMERGES IN THE INFORMATION TECHNOLOGY INDUSTRY that captures the imagination of the community as a whole. Lotus Notes/Domino, a product that fits this description, is actually a set of products encased in a well-designed and integrated chassis. This chassis provides a wide array of functionality and opportunity for the Information Technology department to utilize in providing a service-oriented infrastructure for the organization as a whole. The Notes environment provides the following functionality:

- Communications (e-mail and C&S).
- Groupware.
- Workflow.
- Applications development (macro level, Lotus Script, and Java tools).
- World Wide Web services (SMTP and NNTP).
- Document management.
- Security.
- Integration (for attaching to new or older legacy systems).

Each of the preceding functions provides the basis for the construction of a corporatewide knowledge center. Although it is possible to construct such a knowledge base with individual tools and products, the general consensus dictates that the time involved in integrating dissimilar products and tools can best be suited to customizing the Notes environment for one's business needs. Often, varied tools and products increase the overall cost of ownership at all levels in an organization, rather than lowering them.

Having multiple options of information delivery at one's disposal is paramount in today's ever-changing business environment, and Lotus Notes/

Domino is a product that can deliver that information to every crevice of an organization with efficiency and security.

Although Lotus Notes/Domino is a very powerful product, there are areas for which it is not intended, for example, a transaction processing system. However, it can be utilized to complement an existing transaction processing system by emulating the workflow environment of an organization or perform reporting functions and deliver critical information to key stakeholders. This article presents a walk-through of the required steps that are necessary to plan for and implement a Lotus Notes/Domino solution, including the following activities: planning the knowledge-based architecture, organizational acceptance, rollout (including pilot phase), follow-up projects, and future projects. These form the basic framework for the solution.

DEFINING THE OVERALL FRAMEWORK FOR LOTUS NOTES

In approaching the overall project for a Lotus Notes/Domino-based solution, the following areas require detailed analysis:

- Hardware platform and operating system platform
- Load requirements (number of users and desired system intent)
- Training requirements (user and systems)

PLANNING THE KNOWLEDGE-BASED INFRASTRUCTURE

One of the key requirements for introducing Lotus Notes into an organization are the initial planning activities. The number of users to be supported by the system, offices and geographical layout of the organization, and corporate requirements and security will all be paramount in making decisions for building the Lotus Notes infrastructure. For example, although Lotus Notes/Domino is operating system independent, the choice of operating system for deployment depends on the number of users supported by the system, overall growth of the system, system response, and availability. In general, a rule of thumb is to double or triple mass storage requirements up front in an effort to cap reconfiguration and maintenance issues in the future. This is primarily due to the fact that as Notes rolls out into the organization, more uses are found to capture data, knowledge, and business processes. An SMP platform should be considered wherever medium to heavy document search and retrieval functions are to be performed, heavy security and encryption will be required, or expected growth is projected to double within two years. Memory requirements should also be increased up front for future growth potential as well as for maintaining optimal performance when additional load is placed on the server. It is far better to grow into a system than to outgrow it during the rollout.

Exhibit 66.1. Operating system requirements for a Notes-based solution.

Requirement	Operating System	Hardware
<100 users	Windows NT/UNIX	Midrange Intel server
<200 users	Windows NT/UNIX	High-end Intel server, entry level UNIX server
>200 users < 1000 users	UNIX, AS400, Windows NT*	Entry level UNIX server — low-end enterprise UNIX server, multiple high-end Intel server
>1000 users < 20,000 users	UNIX, AS400, S390, Windows NT*	Mid–high-end enterprise UNIX server, Multiple high-end Intel servers
>20,000 users	UNIX, AS400, S390	Clustered UNIX enterprise servers, High-end System 390

* This exhibit assumes single-server capacity unless otherwise noted.

Exhibit 66.1 presents a table showing the operating system requirements for a Notes-based solution. The platform, as mentioned previously, depends on a large set of criteria. However, should the system require mission-critical status in a 24 × 7 environment, the choice of operating platform will become apparent. In addition, an organization's hardware standards will also affect the choice of platform. When deciding on the operating system and its configuration, plan for at least two to four weeks of configuration and testing time to make sure the system will perform as expected. Prior to performing any work, it is prudent to collect any and all materials regarding the hardware, operating system, and Notes configuration FAQs for the platform. This will let one gage the amount of time and effort that will be required for this phase of the project.

DOCUMENTATION STRUCTURE

The outline for documentation of the system follows a hierarchical pattern (see Exhibit 66.2). At the top lies the overall high-level description of the environment. This layer is designed as an executive summary and master reference. Underneath are the highly technical guides for the environment's construction. There are three technical guides: one each for the hardware, the operating system, and Lotus Notes.

The guides are laid out in step-by-step fashion. The style promotes the ability to capture all essential details for the construction of the hardware environment, operating system configuration, and Lotus Notes configuration. It is advisable that as the documentation undergoes revision, that each member of the installation team be given the opportunity to install the system from scratch and verify the accuracy of the documentation. This technique allows the members of the team to gain a full understanding of the system and enhance their ability to support the system when moved

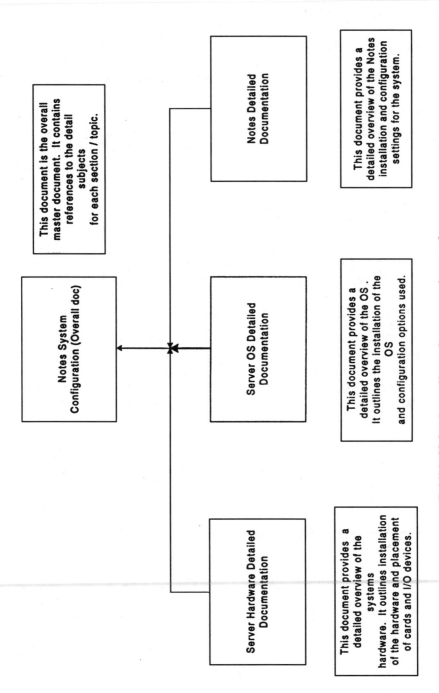

Exhibit 66.2. Lotus Notes documentation road map.

into production. The added benefit of using this type of installation approach directly affects disaster recovery. The system documentation built during the installation process is, in effect, disaster recovery documentation that has been thoroughly compiled for accuracy. When completed, the documentation and copies of the software are sent to the recovery site where they can be utilized in disaster recovery testing. These materials, together with a regularly scheduled backup cycle, will provide the basis for a strong disaster recovery process.

Exhibit 66.3 presents a table showing a table of contents for the System Hardware Reference, System OS Reference, and the System Lotus Notes Reference guides. The specific contents will vary according to the hardware and OS requirements selected for the Lotus Notes installation.

SAMPLE PROJECT PLAN

Exhibit 66.4 shows a sample project plan that can be used as a starting point for a Lotus Notes/Domino-based initiative. The project plan includes activities for research, system management, configuration, installation, and training. The plan can be customized for specific projects.

PLANNING FOR ORGANIZATIONAL ACCEPTANCE

Unlike the current file-based systems that have been available for over a decade and the attachments that everyone has become accustomed to, the Lotus Notes/Domino operating environment utilizes no drives, drive letters, or file systems. Although these elements still exist underneath Notes, they are irrelevant to the Notes operating environment. With Lotus Notes, there are fields, which are part of documents, and documents reside in databases. The paradigm shift can be extreme for some users who are accustomed to opening up their word processor, creating a file, saving it into a directory or a nested series of directories, and then sending the document for review (or whatever the case may be). With Lotus Notes, one would create a document within a document library, providing a title for the document and additional details and then creating the word processing document directly within the context of the Notes document. The document libraries allow for review cycles and document distribution by utilizing the underlying e-mail architecture of the product. It is also possible to have full-text indexes to search these documents for words or phrases or create spanning indexes that search multiple databases of documents.

This is an extreme example; however, the point to understand here is that sufficient training must be provided for in making the transition to Lotus Notes/Domino. The training must span not only the user community but also the systems community. Lotus Notes/Domino is an effective tool in delivering information within and outside of an organization. Understanding the utility of the product and how it can be used effectively will directly

Exhibit 66.3.   Table of contents for sample reference guide.

System Hardware Reference	System OS Reference	System Lotus Notes Reference
1.General hardware overview	1.OS software installation overview	1.Software installation notes
1.1 Hardware components	1.1.Initial software installation process	1.1.Preparations checklist
2.Hardware overview	1.2.Interactive installation process	2.Security standards
2.1I/O system setup	1.3.Package installation process	2.1.Corporate database security standards
2.2Memory setup	2.OS revision patch overview	2.2.Network security
2.3Network setup	3.OS Y2K-ready analysis	2.3.Lotus Notes security
2.4Processor setup	4.OS disk setup	2.4.Encryption security
3.Diagnostics information	5.Operating environment specifics	2.5.Maintaining security
3.1System configuration revision	5.1.Profile and environment configuration	3.Lotus Notes systems management
3.2System diagnostics revision	5.2.File systems configuration	3.1.Notes directory structure
4.Initial installation CMOS configuration	5.3.Administration configuration	3.2.User/departmental group naming conventions
4.1Preliminary setup	5.4System logging configuration	3.3.Name and address book configuration
4.2System hardware design diagram	5.5.User accounts and groups	3.4.Performance management
4.3System burn-in test results	5.6.Security configuration	3.5.Server administration
Appendices system	5.7.Remote admin configuration	3.6.Domino server administration
Diagnostics output	5.8.Pre Notes installation configuration requirements	3.7.User administration
System configuration	5.9.Post Notes installation configuration requirements	3.8.Client desktop/laptop configuration
Output OS HCL OS HCL	6.Fault recovery testing process	3.9.Application distribution
Test results for system	6.1.Mirrored drive tests	3.10.Server partitioning
	6.2.Array drive tests	3.11.Notes cluster setup
	6.3.System power interruption test	4.Communications
	6.4.Other tests	4.1Mail topology
		4.2.Managing mail

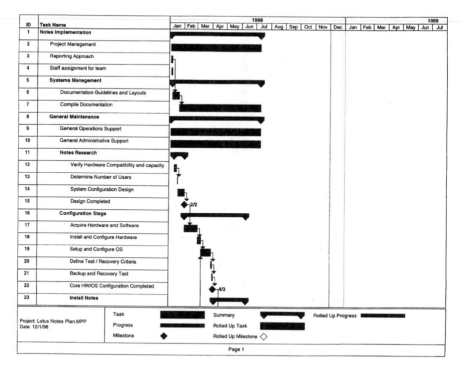

ID	Task Name	1998												1999						
		Jan	Feb	Mar	Apr	May	Jun	Jul	Aug	Sep	Oct	Nov	Dec	Jan	Feb	Mar	Apr	May	Jun	Jul
1	Notes Implementation																			
2	Project Management																			
3	Reporting Approach																			
4	Staff assignment for team																			
5	Systems Management																			
6	Documentation Guidelines and Layouts																			
7	Compile Documentation																			
8	General Maintenance																			
9	General Operations Support																			
10	General Administrative Support																			
11	Notes Research																			
12	Verify Hardware Compatibility and capacity																			
13	Determine Number of Users																			
14	System Configuration Design																			
15	Design Completed	2/2																		
16	Configuration Stage																			
17	Acquire Hardware and Software																			
18	Install and Configure Hardware																			
19	Setup and Configure OS																			
20	Define Test / Recovery Criteria																			
21	Backup and Recovery Test																			
22	Core HW/OS Configuration Completed	4/3																		
23	Install Notes																			

Project: Lotus Notes Plan.MPP
Date: 12/1/98

Task		Summary	Rolled Up Progress
Progress		Rolled Up Task	
Milestone	◆	Rolled Up Milestone ◇	

Page 1

Exhibit 66.4a.   Sample project plan.

relate to the product's acceptance by the organization at large. If more than a simple e-mail system is required, then Lotus Notes/Domino is the product of choice.

The training must effectively transmit the concepts of what Lotus Notes/Domino is and what it can do in relation to the organization. This will involve the cooperation of the IT areas, departmental heads, and the training team to assess the needs to achieve an effective course outline and useful accompanying materials. The most effective training plan constitutes an in-house approach for reasons of familiarity with the environment and practical exposure to the technology within the organizational boundaries. The key concept here is to make sure that all the key players are involved in the project from day one. This provides a stake in the project for each player and a means for establishing benefits for them on an individual basis.

Selecting projects for the Lotus Notes/Domino environment will also provide a base for its introduction into the organization. Applications that can be deployed should include Help Desk, Human Resources, corporate directories, and daily bulletins. Some other applications, such as departmental or group level discussion and document libraries, will provide

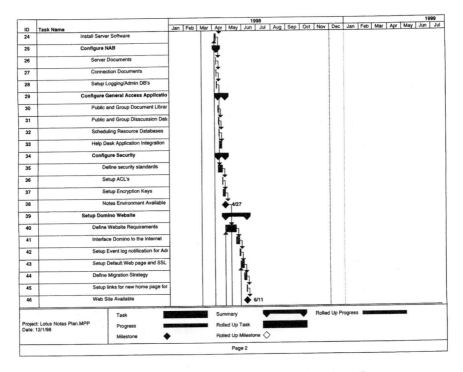

Exhibit 66.4b. Sample project plan. *(continued)*

additional areas for collaboration of information. Discussion databases offer unique opportunities to document minutes of meetings and allow for
authorized access to these minutes during and after their compilation.

Ideally, development scenarios for the development teams should begin
by encompassing relatively small- or medium-sized projects that will utilize
a broad range of Lotus Notes-rich development areas. This will, in turn,
provide enough developmental exposure to varying streams and degrees
of Lotus Notes/Domino development and instill core aspects of the overall
development environment.

ROLLOUT INTO THE ORGANIZATION

Once the applications base has been determined for the Lotus Notes/
Domino rollout, the selection of a pilot group or department will need to be
determined. The key components for the pilot group should be (1) fairly
unbiased to existing environment and the future environment, (2) a good
mix of casual and power users, and (3) a reputable department or group.
To set up a pilot within the systems area is not a good idea, although perhaps they would be the first group of individuals using the system. A user

851

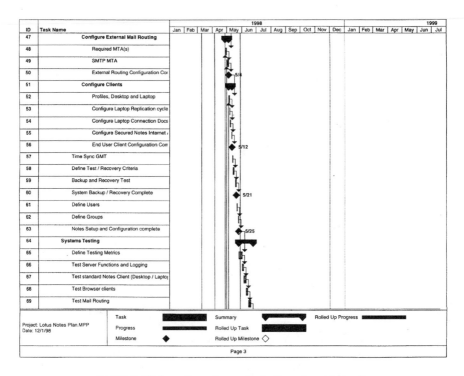

ID	Task Name	1998												1999						
		Jan	Feb	Mar	Apr	May	Jun	Jul	Aug	Sep	Oct	Nov	Dec	Jan	Feb	Mar	Apr	May	Jun	Jul
47	**Configure External Mail Routing**																			
48	Required MTA(s)																			
49	SMTP MTA																			
50	External Routing Configuration Cor					5/4														
51	**Configure Clients**																			
52	Profiles, Desktop and Laptop																			
53	Configure Laptop Replication cycle																			
54	Configure Laptop Connection Docs																			
55	Configure Secured Notes Internet /																			
56	End User Client Configuration Con					5/12														
57	Time Sync GMT																			
58	Define Test / Recovery Criteria																			
59	Backup and Recovery Test																			
60	System Backup / Recovery Complete					5/21														
61	Define Users																			
62	Define Groups																			
63	Notes Setup and Configuration complete					5/25														
64	**Systems Testing**																			
65	Define Testing Metrics																			
66	Test Server Functions and Logging																			
67	Test standard Notes Client (Desktop / Laptop)																			
68	Test Browser clients																			
69	Test Mail Routing																			

Project: Lotus Notes Plan.MPP
Date: 12/1/98

Task | Summary | Rolled Up Progress
Progress | Rolled Up Task
Milestone ◆ | Rolled Up Milestone ◇

Page 3

Exhibit 66.4c.   Sample project plan. *(continued)*

department or group will provide more constructive feedback during the pilot phase.

Once the pilot phase has been completed, any and all feedback from the experience should be acted upon. In any case, there may be action items that can be utilized by all areas of the organization that should be applied if possible. These should be prioritized in order of enhanced functionality, performance tuning, or specific departmental requirements. The departmental requirements should be collected and prioritized for development projects or subprojects after the initial rollout period has expired. These types of requests are usually more complex than they first appear, and will require analysis to develop the solutions.

FOLLOW-UP PROJECTS

Once the rollout of Lotus Notes/Domino has been successfully carried out, it will be necessary to bring the management team back together to discuss the projects highlights and mistakes. These are learning experiences that will help identify areas that can be used to streamline future

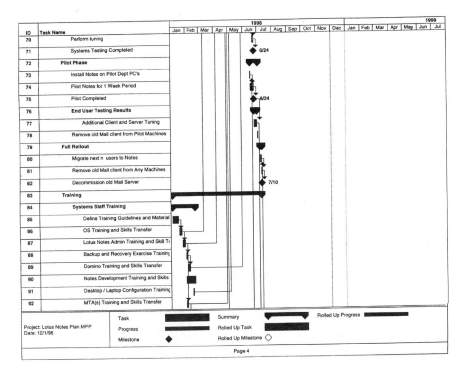

ID	Task Name
70	Perform tuning
71	Systems Testing Completed
72	**Pilot Phase**
73	Install Notes on Pilot Dept PC's
74	Pilot Notes for 1 Week Period
75	Pilot Completed
76	**End User Testing Results**
77	Additional Client and Server Tuning
78	Remove old Mail client from Pilot Machines
79	**Full Rollout**
80	Migrate next n users to Notes
81	Remove old Mail client from Any Machines
82	Decommission old Mail Server
83	**Training**
84	**Systems Staff Training**
85	Define Training Guidelines and Material
86	OS Training and Skills Transfer
87	Lotus Notes Admin Training and Skill T
88	Backup and Recovery Exercise Training
89	Domino Training and Skills Transfer
90	Notes Development Training and Skills
91	Desktop / Laptop Configuration Training
92	MTA(s) Training and Skills Transfer

Project: Lotus Notes Plan.MPP
Date: 12/1/98

Task — Progress — Milestone — Summary — Rolled Up Task — Rolled Up Milestone — Rolled Up Progress

Page 4

Exhibit 66.4d. Sample project plan. *(continued)*

development projects and offer insight to problem areas and how to handle them in the future.

FUTURE PROJECTS

Once the rollout of Lotus Notes/Domino has been completed and it is well established within the organization and operating optimally, additional development can begin. The primary areas of development should begin with information dissemination applications, workflow processes, and business process improvement functions.

Information dissemination applications are used to deliver data and knowledge to individuals who require up-to-the-minute information to perform their job function or make decisions. These types of applications require careful analysis of the individual requirements and most likely will require the design of a security framework that allows only authorized individuals to gain access to this type of information. Information bases such as sales forecasting, corporate health, and corporate planning will fall into this category.

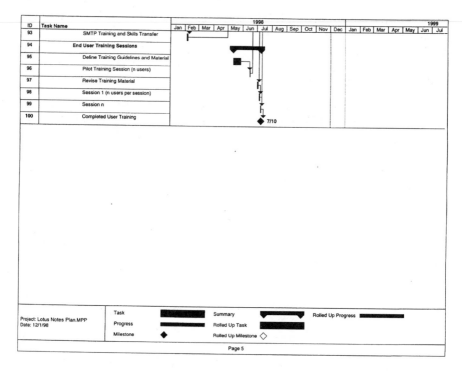

ID	Task Name	1998	1999
		Jan Feb Mar Apr May Jun Jul Aug Sep Oct Nov Dec	Jan Feb Mar Apr May Jun Jul
93	SMTP Training and Skills Transfer		
94	**End User Training Sessions**		
95	Define Training Guidelines and Material		
96	Pilot Training Session (n users)		
97	Revise Training Material		
98	Session 1 (n users per session)		
99	Session n		
100	Completed User Training	7/10	

Project: Lotus Notes Plan.MPP Date: 12/1/98	Task		Summary		Rolled Up Progress	
	Progress		Rolled Up Task			
	Milestone	◆	Rolled Up Milestone	◇		

Page 5

Exhibit 66.4e.   Sample project plan. *(continued)*

Workflow processes are business-specific functions that follow a defined path toward completion. Such processes as purchase orders, expense reporting, and change management fall into this category. These are applications specifically designed to follow a defined path in order to complete a process wherein proper signoff and approvals are required.

Business process improvement functions are those that can be designed to streamline otherwise manual intensive reporting tasks or information processing and delivery tasks. These are typically intensive functions that undergo a large degree of hand-holding to accomplish a given task and can be categorized under workflow if necessary. Other areas that fall under this category would include any business processes that have evolved over time and become uncontrollable or unintelligible. These are usually processes that follow an ill-defined path to completion.

Other areas of development may focus around the World Wide Web or Internet in the pursuit of commerce applications that may become a priority within the organization to enter a different market place and continue to compete with rivals. The ability of Lotus Notes/Domino to perform dynamic information translation into HTML and present it on the Web in real time is unparalleled. To be in a position to save time and money in quick "get to" market situations is increasingly becoming the norm, and to be able to present product information or other data to the Web as it is required is a strong requirement these days.

Along with many other attributes, Lotus Notes/Domino provides the basis for the construction of a strong, reliable, and secure communications infrastructure for enterprise.

Chapter 67
Terms of Reference: The Foundation for Implementing Document Management Systems

Michael J.D. Sutton
Pierre J. Lemay

WITH PURPOSE AND GUIDANCE, MANY MANAGERS HAVE NAVIGATED THROUGH NUMEROUS PROJECTS, PROJECT TEAMS, SUCCESSES, AND FAILURES in the area of Enterprise Document Management. During those initiatives, the project manager continually refers back to project terms of reference (TOR). Why? Because the terms of reference is the manifesto — the mission statement. Without it, an electronic document management system (EDMS) manager can experience significant pain. A set of guidelines on the satisfactory ingredients to the TOR is presented for the sake of those project managers and project leaders coming on new and ever-increasing EDMS initiatives. The Terms of Reference is one of the most important communication documents in your leadership toolkit.

BASIC CONCEPTS
Definitions

Terms of Reference. The sustainable agreement (manifesto) for a complex project containing the mission statement, governance outline, and project control structure for accountability, responsibility, and authority.

EDMS. A system of overseeing an enterprise's official business transactions, decision-making records, and transitory documents of importance.

0-8493-9832-0/00/$0.00+$.50
© 2000 by CRC Press LLC

The repository for an EDMS contains representations of an object loosely termed a "document." (The medium of the business transaction [electronic, photographic, audio, or paper] is irrelevant.)

Need for Terms of Reference

The Terms of Reference is the manifesto. Why does one need a manifesto? One needs a manifesto because the EDMS initiative about to be embarked on is nothing like anything previously experienced. The territory is not well defined or clearly mapped. The initiative is generally 1 to 2 years in length, has an average team size of 7 to 10 for an enterprise of 1,000 client users, and is primarily comprised of individuals from groups such as information management, information technology, security, training, records and archives management, and the actual business units. The tools used within an EDMS project are the same as a generic information management project: collaborative, project management, e-mail, scheduling, presentation graphics, and office automation software. The same sources of information that were used for traditional project management are applicable for updating an EDMS project schedule.

Individuals in the information management profession have worked for almost 30 years to automate less than 15 percent of the enterprise's information assets and intellectual capital. Many authorities have pointed out that these individuals have not exactly been stellar performers. Today's project managers have the opportunity to cut their teeth on a project associated with documents. The project bears very little relationship to the data and databases with which they are familiar. In fact, it is significantly more than just data.

Project managers are now responsible for one of the largest and highest impact projects for the enterprise. It will deal with the most critical information asset of the organization — documents. The manifesto is the public declaration of intention and objectives. It just makes good "business sense" and complements traditional, good, project management approaches and methodologies. The manifesto will frame the motives and opinions about the boundaries, constraints, and assumptions of the project. By the end of the project, management or customers will have to "take it out of the manager's cold, dying hands" before he or she will give it up.

Nonetheless, before one can write about something, one must be able to understand, describe, and reconstruct the concepts and principles of that particular something. In this case, the project manager will want to speak intelligently about a "terms of reference." Historically, a "terms of reference" was a sustainable agreement between management and the leader of a project. This did not always include the client or customer in the organization, just a representative of the management.

The project was planned as a set of steps that would change, improve, or somehow alter the "status quo" of an organization. The agreement was reached as the discussion before a decision became formalized into the implementation plan that followed the decision. The sustainable agreement for a complex project became crystallized into a formal document called a Terms of Reference. The Terms of Reference was imbued with accountability, responsibility, and authority. It was now in writing, and it was supposed to have "teeth"!

TERMS OF REFERENCE COMPONENTS

There is no such thing as a "standard" project. The starting point, resources, and approach can differ for every project initiated. However, it is useful to have a standard set of stages or components to describe the Terms of Reference. The standard components of a Terms of Reference generally include:

- Scope and context
- Goal
- Objectives
- Assumptions and constraints
- Critical success factors
- Suggested approach in implementation
- Transition strategies

In this way, the project manager can make informed choices about what to include, exclude, and defer.

Scope and Context

The project scope and context answer the simple questions of:

- WHO?
- WHAT?
- WHEN?
- WHERE?
- WHY?
- HOW?
- HOW MUCH?

This scope and context should contain several simple paragraphs that describe in a conversational style the "playing field" within the organization or client area where the project manager will maneuver.

The scope statement should outline specific areas that are included, excluded, and deferred. The first section specifies: WHO will be involved (business units), WHO will do the work (project team business unit participants), WHO will make the decision that the implementation has been a success (the project authority), WHO may put up obstacles, and, finally, WHO will gain from the initiative. Keep it succinct — there is no need to name everyone by title and telephone number.

The second section indicates: WHAT is needed to manage and deliver the project, WHAT resources (in terms of tools, information, people, and facilities) will be required, and WHAT will the cumulative key deliverables looks like to the client. The third section describes: WHEN the project begins and ends, WHEN the major milestones will be complete, and WHEN the significant resources will be available for the project.

The fourth section outlines: WHERE the EDMS application will be delivered, WHERE the training and conversion will take place, and WHERE the technological tools will be maintained. The fifth section stipulates: WHY the problem exists, WHY the project is important to solve, and WHY the enterprise is investing in this project.

The sixth section states: HOW the project should be organized, HOW the project will be measured as completed or successful, HOW the project team will communicate with the project authority and the remainder of the organization, and HOW often the total project committee/team will meet. The seventh and final section qualifies: HOW MUCH the project is estimated to cost, WHERE the financial resources will come from to pay for this project, and WHAT the cost-benefit, ROI, or payback is estimated to be.

Thus, the scope and context consists of four to five paragraphs that concisely define the scope of the project and the management and execution context.

Goal of an EDMS

Following the scope and context statement is a very clear specification of the goal of the EDMS initiative. This is very difficult to express, so do not be fooled into thinking that this step will only take a few minutes. First, what is a goal? A goal is the statement of the business intent toward which the project is being directed. The goal must be measurable by means of a qualitative assessment criteria. The project authority must be able to unambiguously state that the goal has been achieved. The initiative should have only one project goal, but it may encompass a number of objectives.

Some sample goals to choose from might be:

- Enable the client business unit staff and managers to quickly and effectively "file and find" their working documents, official documents, and the shared documents of others stored in the EDMS repository.
- Prove that the storage of important official records can be more efficiently administered within the protection and control of an EDMS repository.

- Eliminate the need for shared network drives or individual workstation drives of managers, staff, and officers.

Note that quickly and effectively are subjective but measurable indicators mentioned in these goals. The team or project leader should take a baseline measurement before the initiative is underway. The measurement will make it possible for the project authority to assess whether the documents are now stored and retrieved "quicker or more effectively."

Objectives of an EDMS

Once the overall goal has been identified, the project manager then selects measurable objectives. The objectives are statements of business intent that can be measured quantitatively. Targets can be set and specific measurements can be taken at a milestone to see if the objective has been achieved.

Sample objectives to choose from might include:

- Increase the speed for authoring, publishing, and disseminating documents within the individual's scope of control by 15 percent.
- Decrease duplication of documents by 25 percent in the repository by making the author of a document accountable for its addition to the repository.
- Increase the volume of documents that can be reused and recycled from less than 10 to over 50 percent by optimally storing documents in a centrally accessible repository instead of on shared network directories.
- Increase speed and precision of retrieval from 5 days to less than 1 hour through consistent use of a records management classification system when indexing documents for retrieval.

Additional objectives to choose from might comprise:

- Decrease continued reliance on legacy paper documents by quickly scanning and making retrievable paper documents when they are initially requested.
- Increase access control restrictions by appropriately securing documents to the relevant ownership group.
- Preserve a decision and accountability trail for documents by creating an audit trail of all users who accessed a document or series of documents.
- Decrease the backlog volume of paper and electronic documents that are scheduled for review and disposal by bringing forward this information to record administrators faster when they have reached their retention review stage.

Please note that any of these objectives should be easily and unambiguously measurable because of the quantification inherent in their narration.

Assumptions and Constraints

An assumption is a fact or statement "taken as true." As a project begins, there are numerous assumptions. On the other hand, a constraint is an inhibiting factor that restricts the possible success of the project, its resources, deadlines, milestones, volume of deliverables, etc.

Sample assumptions a project manager can choose from may include:

- Forecast of the estimated volume of users and document objects over a particular time period.
- Special situations for mobile/remote users.
- Any use or special circumstances for APIs.
- The applicable conversion subset of the current legacy documents.
- Certain document types that will not initially be accommodated.
- Shared and personal hard drives will no longer be used by clients.
- The access control and security restrictions matrix for users and groups.
- Assigned responsibility for the first tier of support.
- The estimated number of trips required to remote sites.
- Expected interaction and behavior with other, unrelated but integrated software products.
- The expected metadata that will or will not be captured.

Sample constraints a project manager can choose from may include:

- Specific configurations of all office automation software, network, and hardware.
- The status of the current File Classification Scheme.
- Acceptability of initial loss of time by a business unit.
- The EDMS team's development, test, and systems integration environment.
- New or revised policies and procedures that will be required.
- The client language for GUI implementation and documentation (i.e., Spanish, French, English, etc.).
- The method used for storing e-mail and its attachments in the repository.

All assumptions and constraints must be explicitly cataloged for later protection as the project progresses. Most executives and sponsors will remember the project manager's promises, but they seldom remember the assumptions and constraints that went into the calculation of the commitments to promise the goal and objectives.

Note that many constraints are actually assumptions that will inhibit the project; for example, "workstation configurations will remain as 80486-based processors with 8 MB of RAM storage." Other constraints may be more obvious, such as the adaptability to change within the organization, or the planned vacation schedule. Thus, assumptions and constraints are somewhat interchangeable, depending on the inhibition factor.

Critical Success Factors

Critical Success Factors (CSFs) are any factors, events, or circumstances that are regarded as critical to the success or failure of the project. A CSF must refer to those factors that, if not present, will make the project fail. There are numerous CSFs in an EDMS project.

Sample CSFs to choose from may include:

- The executive sponsor and champions must be identified and committed.
- The executive sponsor must be able to commit adequate resources and funding.
- The champions must actively participate and help celebrate the successes.
- The champions must effectively resolve business policy issues as they arise.
- The champions must decide and articulate the accountability, responsibility, and authority issues.
- The managers and staff must recognize the value of document management and accept the organizational changes in their processes.

Other useful CSFs may include:

- A useful and continuous marketing and communications strategy must be put in place.
- An EDMS project team information technology and management infrastructure must be immediately available and sustainable.
- A continuous training strategy must be implemented.
- The scalability and complexity of the application and its applicability to an EDMS must be evaluated.
- The network must accommodate sufficient bandwidth for the document traffic.
- The application, hardware, and network platform configurations must remain stable throughout the prototype and pilot periods.
- The EDMS project manager must be permitted to build a relationship based upon peer respect with other managerial and executive participants.

For example, there are very few successful EDMS projects without a committed and involved executive sponsor. Starting a project without an executive sponsor is a guarantee of failure, because so much change takes place during the project. Without a senior individual backing the requirements for change and aligning these to the business objectives of the enterprise, the project will be shelved or sabotaged by others who see it eroding their power.

Suggested Approach in Implementation

Specify what approach will be used to roll out the EDMS. Also, specifically define each stage in the approach. For example, will the system be rolled out and implemented as a turnkey application (the "clobber them while they're asleep approach") in all business units overnight, or will the application be rolled out on a business-unit-by-business unit basis? Explain which business units should go first, and why. If staging the application instead of "clobbering the client users," then some unambiguous sample definitions for this approach can be suggested:

1. Prototype: a mock-up of the proposed system interface, with very little functionality implemented (like a cardboard cut-out of an airplane).
2. Pilot: incorporates feedback about the prototype into a basic, functional system that can be used by a limited number of people (like an operational plane, with a motor and instrumentation but limited visibility and petrol).
3. Operational system: evolves from feedback about shortcomings, deficiencies, and benefits of a pilot (like the roll out of a new airplane, complete with operating, training, and technical support manuals).

Start with a prototype, refine it, and then reimplement it in a few business units as a pilot application. Then, refine it again based on feedback from the client user community, and finally implement it on a business-unit-by-business unit basis. Regardless of whether the product is off the shelf or customized, this staged approach has saved many project managers from disaster. The project manager must have a chance to test and recover before everyone has a chance to see the weaknesses (and with hope, the strengths) of a particular software product.

Transition Strategies

The transition strategies are just that — strategies. There are generally six strategies worth mentioning in the Terms of Reference:

- Communications strategy
- Data and document take-on strategy
- Training strategy
- Delivery and acceptance strategy
- Installation and support strategy
- Post-pilot follow-up strategy

Do not try to develop the entire project plan within the strategies. Describe the strategies in terms of what "should be" taking place. Nonetheless, the identification of these strategies guarantees that someone must address them in the project plan.

Communications Strategy

The communications strategy is very important because the project is ever changing. As one moves through a period of implementation, there will be:

- New people
- New constraints and assumptions
- New applications
- New technologies
- New methods and designs
- New data models
- New concerns and issues
- New ways of doing business

All of these "new" things must be communicated to both the project team and client community. The project manager will need to establish briefing sessions and ways of broadcasting the project status. The evolving roles of team members must be described to both the team and the client groups.

A familiar situation is one in which the project team entered a new business unit that had been selected for installation and training 6 months previous. Once they arrive, they find out that no one kept them informed and they were not ready to begin. In fact, the business unit thought the project had been canceled because they had heard nothing about it since it was initiated. The executive sponsor and management champion had claimed that all business unit managers were being kept informed. Alas, the channels of communication had remained closed because people were too busy to communicate.

Data and Document Take-On Strategy

The activities here can include loading the File Classification System, identifying the different metadata tables and the required table validation, and most importantly, identifying the specific legacy documents (paper and electronic) that must either be scanned or moved from shared network directories to the EDMS repository.

Training Strategy

Many organizations omit a training strategy. Executives often feel that an EDMS should be so easy to use that zero investment in training is required. This never works. Staff and managers have a difficult enough time with learning the interface and concepts of a new application that demands discipline. The staff must get help to "jump start" into the EDMS environment.

Activities that should be identified include responsibility for instructors, course design and delivery, training location and equipment, training tutorials, training accounts, course duration, and dummy document bases.

Delivery and Acceptance Strategy

This is often omitted in a TOR because the project manager has a challenging time trying to identify and get the commitment of any project authority. The executive sponsor may not yet have committed to their level of involvement. A client project manager may not have been selected, and client champions may not have stepped forward yet to take responsibility for their business units. So, the EDMS project manager is faced with trying to find out who will confirm the completion of the project. Only when the User Requirements have been matched in some manner to the delivered application, will the project authority sign off its delivery.

Installation and Support Strategy

The installation and support strategy ensures the day-to-day operation of the application as it moves from prototype to pilot, and then from pilot to operation system. Without a strategy, there is an ad hoc response to problems as they arise, a very difficult approach to manage successfully.

Activities included here are training support (how and when are new staff trained when they arrive in the business unit after the initial training has been given?); help desk support (are coaches or superusers trained in each business unit to solve the immediate problems before they are referred to the help desk? How do problems get escalated from the internal help desk to the external product vendor if they are not immediately solvable?); backup and recovery actions during pilot (do staff automatically lose what they were doing when the system goes down, or can a rollback be put into place, and over what time period — 1 hour or 1 day?); and finally, technical configuration and upgrades (how does the project manager address the implementation of the new version of the word processor in the middle of the implementation?). The technical support strategies ensure the routine operation of the application.

Post-Pilot Follow-Up Strategy

Finally, the strategies must reflect an evaluation period after the application has been in use for approximately 6 months. First, the project manager needs to schedule an impact assessment on Policies and Procedures of the business. There is a requirement to collect data about volumetric and performance testing, as well as integrity testing of the metadata databases and the document base. Several other activities include a review of the GUI, monitoring of any subsystems and APIs, a security audit, the potential redesign of staff and management roles and responsibilities, the impact on operational support and the network, and an assessment of the adequacy of hardware, application software, and network client/server operating systems.

The follow-up strategy will prove the success or failure of a project manager and project team.

CONCLUSION

Descriptions of the components of a TOR and suggestions for a number of issues that must be addressed in each component have been discussed.

The components were:

1. Scope and context
2. Goal
3. Objectives
4. Assumptions and constraints
5. Critical success factors
6. Suggested approach in implementation
7. Transition strategies

With a fully articulated TOR, the project manager stands a chance of defending and maintaining control over the project. This is the best the project manager can expect, other than thanks from the champion or sponsor. The project manager can now carry this TOR as his or her manifesto. Hopefully, the following Latin words will help the project manager reflect on the situation he or she is now at: *animus opibusque parati* — "(you are) prepared in minds and resources."

Chapter 68

Strategies for an Archives Management Program: The Digital Preservation of Corporate Information Assets

Michael J.D. Sutton

FEW PROFESSIONALS HAVE NAVIGATED THROUGH FEW ARCHIVES MANAGEMENT (AM) PROJECTS, TEAMS, SUCCESSES, AND FAILURES. Why? Because there have been few successes to point to, and because there has been no poignant business reason to proceed with such initiatives, (at least until recently). Nonetheless, many corporations and public sector organizations are now experiencing significant pain and financial liability from loss of their corporate memory. The lack of an AM strategy is holding back "well-intentioned" but untrained project directors and managers from coming to grips with the issues, concerns, problems, and obstacles associated with an Archive Repository (AR). The overall strategy outlined here could be an important reference document for your next initiative.

FOUNDATIONAL CONCEPTS

Why do you need a strategy? You need a strategy because the AM initiative you have been asked to embark upon has no anchors to hold you and

0-8493-9832-0/00/$0.00+$.50
© 2000 by CRC Press LLC

Exhibit 68.1.   Key business drivers and potential benefits of an AM initiative.

Even though there is little to go on at this time to justify an AM initiative, there is anecdotal material that points to business drivers and benefits. There are **key business drivers** that can justify an AM initiative:

- An antiquated or traditional records management system which cannot cope with the emerging challenges and requirements of a digital workspace.
- Increasing on-line space requirements for current, operational databases, data marts, and data warehouses.
- Short-term and long-tern technological obsolescence.
- An enterprises drive to harmonize all systems onto an heterogeneous environment.
- An inability to find, locate, catalogue, and use current or historical digital information objects.
- New uses for 'old' data from sales, human resources, marketing, facilities, engineering, and financial databases.

There are numerous **potential benefits** of implementing an Archives Management Program that may apply to your organization:

- Decreased corporate exposure during audits or legal inquiries.
- Increased compliance with various levels of laws and regulation: international, federal, state/province, county/region, and city/municipal.
- Improved records management and control.
- Appropriate retention and timely destruction of business records.
- Streamlined and rationalized processes where business owners do not have to be concerned with archiving information objects from their current systems.

---

your team to the *present*. AM is about *time* and the effect time has upon artifacts we create in the *present*. AM is, paradoxically, about the *future*, (which most of us cannot see unless we profess to be prophets); but only when that *future* has become the *past*. AM does not incorporate in its conceptual model a classical linear timeline. It presents a reverse timeline where the *past* only becomes valuable again when it is many years old.

You have been asked to plan an archives repository in such a way that information objects created in the *present* can be "read" (or at least understood) in the *future*, within their original, rich context. However, someone (or some automated system) in the *future*; must at its *present* moment, contend with information objects from the *past*. The information objects at that point in the *future* never seem to have enough context or content to permit their proper understanding.

Archives Management, especially as it is defined in digital terms, is a very young discipline. The key business drivers and benefits are not yet well defined or clearly mapped (see Exhibit 68.1). The project director has no means of testing whether information objects created as an output to an AM initiative will be usable in the future, other than through simulated testing. This testing cannot take into account software product or system evolution over a 5 to 10 year period, or even worse, over a 25 to 100 year period! The best the project director can do is make an educated guess, and hope when five or more years have passed, he may have been a prophet in his own land.

Take, for example, the Year 2000 issues and problems we are currently contending. These were a significant AM problem. As automated systems grew in the 1960s and 1970s, no one could predict how memory costs would fall or how software would handle date-related information. In fact, most of us who worked on such systems never expected COBOL, PL/I, RPG, or even assembler compilers to last more than five years. Alas, here we are in the *future*, and we are trying to cope with our professional inability to plan for legacy applications that were just too poorly documented to rewrite, and too integral to our business to throw away.

An AM initiative differs substantially from a contemporary information system project. The AM initiative can be described by a number of characteristics:

- Generally five to seven years in length.
- An average team size of five members for an enterprise of 1,000 client users.
- Historical focus on record and file structures that are not currently in vogue.
- Primarily concerned with the disposition of the digital records of the enterprise after they are at least seven years old.

Let's contrast this with the characteristics of a contemporary information system project:

- Generally less than two years in duration, (and preferably less than one year).
- An average team size of 7 to 10 members for an enterprise of 1,000 client users.
- Avant-guard focus on record and file structures that are just currently in use.
- Primarily concerned with the creation and use of digital records of the enterprise created in the *present*, less than two years from their date of creation.

There is a significant difference in the business goals and objectives of the two projects. In addition, the owners and technology supporters of the current system projects have been allocated no time or budget to worry about or plan for the eventual retirement or disposition of the systems, data, or documents. These *present-focused* business and technology leaders are incented with bonuses, dividends, or stock options based upon what they help the company accomplish *today* or *tomorrow*, not 5 to 7 years from now!

The tools used within an AM project must contend with both old and new technologies, software, media devices, methods, file structures, record formats, etc. The tools of an AM initiative are Janus-like in their employment. (Janus was the classical Roman god who had two faces, one looked into the past while the second looked into the future. He was identified with doors, gates, beginnings and endings). The AM project team must contend with having one foot in the *past* and one in the *future*, while at the same time the *present* passes them by.

Information management professionals—at the behest of private and public sector leaders—have worked for over 40 years to automate (digitize) less than 20 percent of the enterprise's information assets and intellectual capital. Regretfully, in doing so, we have forced most enterprises to be short-term in their vision of the value of information objects and systems, to rely too heavily on the digital nature of the information. Thus, many organizations almost ignore the digital as well as the hardcopy storage and long-term retrieval value of information. These enterprises may not have "lost their minds;" but they have lost their corporate memory. When an audit or legal discovery process tries to contend with digital information that is 5 to 10 years old, (or even 3 years old), there are significant problems in reconstructing these information objects and their context. And for many enterprises today, this "corporate amnesia" results in hefty legal costs, fines, and lost revenue.

Archives Management Problem Statement

Most organizations that wish to survive in today's aggressive business climate must continually improve, evolve, and reposition its market, products, and services; and aggressively maintain its profitability. The enterprise must create and achieve short-term business goals, objectives, and strategies. Many businesses have invested heavily in automated legacy systems. These systems may be nearing or have already passed their retirement date. The valued corporate memories in these systems may be incorporated into new, emerging corporate systems; or, alternatively, the digital information objects may be stored off-line to comply with legal and regulatory requirements. The worst case is that these "out-of-date" systems, data and document objects are ignored until it is too late to determine how they could be migrated to a physical media or logical format to be useful.

All enterprises are facing a challenge to preserve digital systems, data, and documents over short-term, medium and long-term periods of time. Some companies have lost significant income from audits because substantiating data and documents (stored digitally) were lost years earlier; but not discovered until it was too late. The business owners of current, operational information systems are generally pre-occupied with operational challenges, issues, and concerns surrounding an applications performance and availability. Managers are asked to contend with short-term

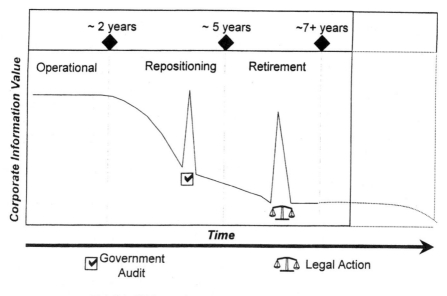

Exhibit 68.2. Information preservation stages.

business objectives and present problems, not with hypothetical problems that could emerge in the distant future.

The oversimplified diagram displayed in Exhibit 68.2 might help to illustrate the preservation challenge we face. Current information systems create or acquire information objects that have immediate corporate value. This is the Operational Stage of a Corporate Information Value Lifecycle. The **Operational Stage** may encompass 1 to 2 fiscal years. The requirement during this stage for instant retrieval dictates that the information objects are stored on-line. This stage might also encompass data marts and data warehouses that require relatively quick access and retrieval response times.

The corporate value of the information will decrease over time because it simply is no longer current; and current information is very important when generating profits or increased stock price value. The information objects migrate to the **Repositioning Stage** of the Corporate Information Value Lifecycle. The Repositioning Stage may incorporate 3 to 5 fiscal years of information objects. The use of near-line or off-line storage media (optical discs, CD-ROMs, QIC tapes, etc.) generally applies at this stage, and may continue for up to 5 or 6 years. Instantaneous retrieval is not as critical at this juncture in the lifecycle. Nonetheless, during this period of time external audits by regulatory or tax agencies may take place. This creates a peak in the perceived corporate value of the information where its value may be as much or more than its original corporate value.

Generally, information objects during this period of time exhibit certain characteristics of aging:

- There is loss of the original information and its context.
- The original media may be unreadable or devices to read it no longer manufactured.
- The original file and record structure may be unknown, foreign, or undocumented.
- Any significant business rules stored in the software programs are unreadable, unusable, or unknowable.
- Any individuals who may have worked on the original system or database have moved on to other opportunities.

In short, we have *corporate amnesia.*

Finally, the corporate information moves into the **Retirement Stage** of the Corporate Information Value Lifecycle. Information objects can remain dormant here for 6 to 20 years, depending upon legal, historical, and archival requirements. The information objects are loaded onto off-line medium such as magnetic tapes, DAT (Digital Archive Tapes), or possibly CD-ROMs. Historians, social scientists, or lawyers are the expected users for these seldom-accessed information objects. Nonetheless, the information objects must retain enough content, logical structure and context to be useful as more than just an historical artifact.

A business framework or archival facility has rarely existed in present-day enterprises to accommodate the Corporate Information Value Lifecycle as described above. Thus, a **Digital Archives Repository** rarely exists or is available in today's public and private sector institutions to use as a model. A Digital Archives Repository is required to contextually preserve the database objects, document objects, business rules, system documentation, and other descriptive data (metadata). This repository must accommodate information objects over a medium to long-term period of time, (i.e., from 5 to 20 years), in a software and hardware platform-neutral format, [such as proposed in ISO Reference Model of the Consultative Committee for Space Data Systems White Paper, *Open Archival Information System (OAIS)*]. The Archives Management Strategy may help you to position this commitment to a repository.

Foundational Definitions

Before we describe an Archives Management Strategy, let us first introduce some terminology intrinsic to Archives Management. An Archives Management Program consists of specific information objects, facilities,

Exhibit 68.3.   Preservation characteristics.

Charles Dollar in *Ensuring Access Over Time to Authentic Electronic Records: Strategy, Alternatives, and Best Practices* proposes a number of preservation characteristics that help preserve the legal integrity of a business record while stored and archived.

- *Authentic:* the measure of the reliability of a record, i.e., its ability to remain unaltered, unchanged, and uncorrupted;
- *Encapsulated:* the measure of the self-referential linkage of logical components in a record;
- *Identifiable:* the measure of the specification of unique identification boundaries in a record;
- *Intelligible:* the measure of the integrity of the bit stream represented in a record;
- *Readable:* the measure of the integrity of the bit stream device processing of a record;
- *Reconstructable:* the measure of the quality of rebuilding the same structure and intellectual content of a record;
- *Retrievable:* the measure of the capability to locate objects and parts of a record; and
- *Understandable:* the measure of the quality of the context of creation of a record.

processes, and preservation domains. Let's start with the information objects.

At the fore of a good AMS is the ***business record***—a by product of a business transaction preserved for future use as evidence of transacting business. A business record must maintain a number of preservation characteristics (see Exhibit 68.3).

Business records are aggregated into files. An ***operational file*** is an information object that contains information of immediate, instantaneous interest to a reader. Digital copies of *operational files* are normally created in the course of data management procedures, and are referred to as a ***backup file***. A ***repositioned file*** is a specially formatted copy of an original *operational file* that can be retrieved through a near-line storage media instead of an online storage media. For longer-term storage, *repositioned files* are migrated to *retired files*.

A ***retired file*** contains information objects that would be the foundation for re-constructing an *authentic* instance of a file in its original format and context. A *retired file* can encompass system, data and document objects. The information content can be conveyed to the user or another computer as: audio data, bitmap data, data fragments and databases, spatial (geographical data), spreadsheets, text, vector data, and video data.

The files are managed by different facilities (as illustrated in Exhibit 68.4). An ***operational facility*** is accountable for managing the current information assets of an enterprise. The information assets are digital and are stored on-line for immediate access. A ***repositioning facility*** manages the nearly-current information assets, i.e., information that may be between 2 and 5 years old. The information objects are stored on near-line

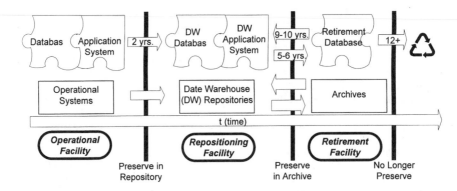

Exhibit 68.4. Time-based migration of information between current and successive stages.

media for near instant access. A ***retirement facility*** manages the dormant information assets, i.e., information that may be between 6 and 25 or more years old. The retirement facility may store the information objects in a hardware and software neutral format to diminish the problems of techno-logical obsolescence. All the facilities execute specific processes upon the information objects under their control (see Exhibit 68.5).

Finally, in our vocabulary, there is ***metadata***. This is specific descriptive data about particular data objects which increases the precision in recall-ing information objects from a search of a repository of data, document, or systems. *Metadata* can describe an information object with fields such as: author, business unit of the author, creation date, modification date, secu-rity classification, or subject. This overview of the emerging vocabulary of AM will serve as a foundation for our further discussions.

Strategies for an Archives Management Initiative

The following set of strategies and guiding principles are proposed for constructing a framework to design and successfully engineer an Archives Management Program.

Strategy # 1:   Develop a Repositioning Facility

Your *repositioning facility* will depend upon available budget as well as corporate technical resourcing, knowledge and support. In addition, your enterprise will require skills in data mart and data warehouse design, and an informed and experienced digital records management group. The *repo-sitioning facility* will ensure the availability of a corporate memory for be-tween 2 and 5 years. The *operational facility* feeds the *repositioning facility* after 2 or 3 fiscal years have elapsed for the operational data.

Exhibit 68.5. Archival management processes.

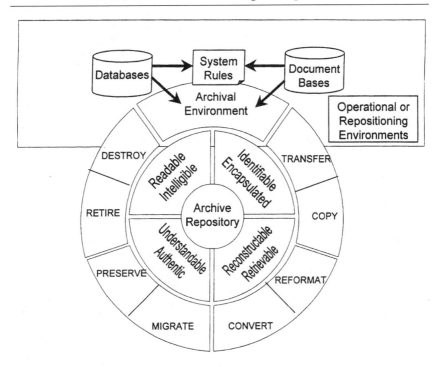

A number of specific processes may be executed upon the Operational and Repositioning Environments to move them into an Archival Environment:

- *Convert:* importing or exporting of records from one software dependent environment to another while ensuring the preservation of structure, content, and context.
- *Copy:* the creation of a digital binary twin of the original file.
- *Destroy:* physically disposing of the media and information objects so as to make them totally unreadable, i.e., degaussing, crushing, melting, etc.).
- *Migrate:* moving authentic electronic records from legacy information systems in on-line systems to another storage media, such as near-line or off-line storage while preserving the logical view of the original records.
- *Reformat:* transferring records from one media to another without alteration of the bit stream of a record, (e.g., with no change in appearance, content or logical structure).
- *Retire:* moving information objects to very dormant off-line storage to protect and preserve records from corruption and make them relatively inaccessible.
- *Transfer:* repositing electronic records from on-line or near-line storage to off-line storage for infrequent retrieval.

Strategy # 2:   Develop a Retirement Facility

Your *retirement facility* must construct a long-term program that most enterprises are not willing to fund. This *retirement facility* will need long-term financing so it is not cut from the budget during lean times. This is a corporate commitment to preserve the memory of the institution. This business unit will be responsible for the archival activities associated with appraisal, collection, migration, protection, reformation, retention, and finally the destruction of digital information assets. The *retirement facility* will warrant that valuable corporate memory is available and accessible. A Corporate Records Management Program may already handle many of these functions for hard copy records. But beware, most records management staff are ill-equipped to cope with managing digital records, especially over such a long-term. A new business unit may need to be defined in the organization.

Strategy # 3:   Employ Guiding Principles in Your Architecture and Design

The following guiding principles are proposed to jump-start the design and deployment of an AMS:

- ***Principle #1***: *Manage your long-term information assets in the same way you manage your short-term information assets.*   Most organizations ignore the problems and challenges of storing information assets over the long-term. This is metaphorically similar to the problems the industrial and manufacturing sectors are experiencing with pollution. If you ignore it in your planning and design, it will cost you 100 times as much to reconstruct information assets, or pay the fines and costs of mismanaged archival data.
- ***Principle #2***: *Business owners of the information assets are concerned with the present, not the future.*   Business owners should not be made responsible for ensuring medium-term repositioning and long-term preservation of their information objects. They hardly have enough time to keep their current, operational systems performing within acceptable operational limits and backed-up for disaster recovery. If the enterprise forces the operational facility to worry about repositioning and retiring, then these activities will never be done. (How many of you omitted backing up your hard discs when you first started on a PC?—my point exactly). A separate set of facilities (with their own goals and incentives) must be brought into play to relieve the stress and pressure exhibited in the operational facility. This can even be outsourced to companies that are starting to sell services for digital records and archives management facilities.
- ***Principle #3***: *Aggressively pursue the preservation of critical information assets.*   A digital *retirement facility* must be mandated to proactively collect and acquire the critical information objects that need to be preserved. Otherwise, we can guarantee corporate amnesia. We expect corporate amnesia to increase as companies expend incredible budgets on the Y2K problem instead of on more significant areas such as enterprise document management systems. Neglect and incompetence invalidate any warranty for corporate survival.

- ***Principle #4****: Destroy archived information assets in a timely manner.* Maintaining access and availability of all digital objects over a long-term period is both impractical and expensive. Assets must be categorized according to their records retention schedule to facilitate their timely destruction. Periodically evaluate the retention periods of archival information assets and destroy the records according to their legal requirements before they can be used against the institution in legal proceedings. The only thing worse than corporate amnesia is "photographic recall"—very risky in any court proceeding. Nonetheless, there may be corporate records of an historical nature that should be preserved longer than their normal destruction date. Make sure only the historical records are preserved.
- ***Principle #5****: Assess your compliance with all legal and statutory rules and regulations.* Some business unit must be made responsible for maintaining a comprehensive checklist of relevant laws, statutes, and regulations. Often the knowledge about retention is scattered amongst different business units. No one is really accountable for knowing or enforcing the legal and statutory requirements. This must change, and accountability must be assigned. There are too many financial liabilities that can cost of an institution if these requirements are ignored.

These guiding principles should help you create a firm foundation for your AM activities.

Recap

You were presented with a vocabulary, broad strategies and guiding principles for embarking upon an Archives Management Program. The strategies revolved around the creation and staffing of a *repositing facility* and a *retirement facility*. The existence of these two facilities will relieve the *operational facility* of the stress and pressure to try and find a short-term solution for a long-term problem. The solution is not really within their mandate or skill set to achieve. Separate business units must be appointed with these tasks.

Beware of the lack of funding and commitment when starting an AM initiative. Because of the short-term thinking prevalent in most organizations, these would be the types of facilities that would be cut from the organization when the times get tough. If the enterprise sees corporate value and the substantial benefits of an AM program, then they must be committed to keep it intact. An Archives Repository with gaps is a corporate memory with missing fragments—it may take a great deal of effort to understand; and there will be gaps that could leave out important data, legally required data. Can the enterprise afford that?

DOCUMENT MANAGEMENT

Bibliography

Barry, R., *Best Practices for Document Management in an Emerging Digital Environment*, http:/www.rbarry.com/UKRMS1/UKRMS1.html.

Barry, R., "Electronic Records And Objects Circa 2001," *University College London, School of Library, Archive and Information Studies Conference Proceedings — 75th Anniversary Celebration*, 1994 http:/www.rba rry.com /CON-PAP2/CON-PAP2.html.

Barry, R., "Electronic Document and Records Management Systems: Towards a Methodology for Requirements Definition," *Information Management & Technology*, Vol. 27, No. 6, 1994.

Beagrie, N., Greenstein, D., *A Strategic Policy Framework for Creating and Preserving Digital Collections*, Arts and Humanities Data Service: London, 7/14/98.

Bennett, J., *A Framework for Data Types and Formats, and Issues Affecting the Long Term Preservation of Digital Material*, British Library Research and Innovation Centre: West Yorkshire, UK, 1997.

Commission on Preservation and Access, Research Libraries Group, *Preserving Digital Information: Report of the Task Force on Archiving Digital Information*, Yale University, May 1, 1996.

Consultative Committee for Space Data Systems, *Open Archival Information System (OAIS) White Book*, CCSDS 650.0-W-4.0, 08/17/1998.

Dollar, C., *Ensuring Access Over Time to Authentic Electronic Records: Strategy, Alternatives, and Best Practices*, (Manuscript: Vancouver, BC: Nov. 1998), [Available soon as a digital book from http://www.cohasset.com].

Dollar, C., Williams, R., "New Strategy for Migrating Long-Term Electronic Records: Meeting Operational Needs with Less Risk and at Lower Cost," *Cohasset Associates, Inc. Managing Electronic Records Conference Proceedings*, 1995.

Getty Conservation Institute and Getty Information Institute, *Time & Bits, Managing Digital Continuity*, http://www.ahip.getty.edu/timeandbits.

Haynes, D., et. al., *Responsibility for Digital Archiving and Long Term Access to Digital Data*, (British Library Research and Innovation Centre: West Yorkshire, UK, 1997).

Hedstrom, M., "From Practice to Theory: Applying Archival Theory to Electronic Records Management," *Cohasset Associates, Inc. Managing Electronic Records Conference Proceedings*, 1996.

Jones, M., *Bibliography of Materials Relating to the Preservation of New Technology and Preservation Using New Technology*, (National Library of Australia: Canberra ACT, 1994), http://www.nla.gov.au/1/pres/pubs/bibmj.html.

Kahle, B, "Preserving the Internet," *Scientific American*, March 1997, http://www.sciam.com/0397issue/0397kahle.html.

Kelly, K, et. al., *Models for Action: Practical Approaches to Electronic Records Management & Preservation*, (Center for Technology in Government: Albany, NY, 1998), http://www.ctg.albany.edu/resources/pdfrpwp/mfa.pdf.

Kowlowitz, A, Kelly, K., *Functional Requirements to Ensure the Creation, Maintenance, and Preservation of Electronic Records*, (Center for Technology in Government: Albany, NY, 1998).

Long Now Foundation, *Clock/Library*, http://www.longnow.org/library/library.html.

MacCarn, D., Toward a Universal Data Format for the Preservation of Media, (WGBH Educational Foundation: Boston, undated), http://info.wbgh.org/upf/SMPTE_UPF_paper.html.

McGovern, T., Samuels, H., "Our Institutional Memory at Risk: Collaborators to the Rescue," CAUSE/EFFECT, Vol. 20, No. 3, Fall 1997, p. 19-21, 49-50.

Rasmussen, D., *Digitization - The Issues, Projects and Technology: A Selective Bibliography*, (National Library of Canada: Ottawa, 1995).

Ross, S., "Acting to Avoid Loss, But When Disaster Strikes–Relying on Digital Archeology," *Cohasset Associates, Inc. Managing Electronic Records Conference Proceedings*, 1998.

Rothenberg, J., "Ensuring the Longevity of Digital Information," *Scientific American*, Vol. 272, No.1, pp. 24-29.

Rothenberg, J., "Metadata to Support Data Quality and Longevity," IEEE Metadata Computer Conference Proceedings, 1996, http://computer.org/conferen/meta96/rothenberg_paper/ ieee.data-quality.html.

Shepard, T., "Universal Preservation Format Update," D-Lib Magazine, Nov. 1997, http:// www.dlib.org/dlib/november97/11clips.html.

Skupsky, D., "Legal Requirements for Optical Disk Records and Electronic Imaging Systems," *AIIM Show and Conference Proceedings*, March 31-April 3, 1996.

Sutton, M., *Document Management For The Enterprise: Principles, Techniques, and Applications*, (John Wiley & Sons: NYC, 1996).

Williams, R., "Managing the New Corporate Memory," *International Council on Archives–Section of International Organizations Workshop*, June, 1998.

Williams, R., "The Seven Key Legal Issues for Managing Electronic Records," *Cohasset Associates, Inc. Managing Electronic Records Conference Proceedings*, 1995.

Chapter 69
Integrating EDMSs and DBMSs

Charles Banyay

DATABASE MANAGEMENT SYSTEMS (DBMS) HAVE BEEN AN INTEGRAL PART OF INFORMATION TECHNOLOGY (IT) and the systems development lifecycle since the 1960s. The database, especially the relational database, has received ever-increasing visibility during the past decade due to the mass availability of very cost-effective PC-based DBMSs. As a result, the relational database has become ingrained as the natural metaphor for an information repository with most organizations who utilize IT.

With the advent of the electronic document or, to be more precise, the electronic document management system (EDMS), as a significant new metaphor for an information repository, it is useful to juxtapose the two approaches and to explore their relative advantages. First, it is necessary to discuss the traditional process of using a DBMS in managing data. Second, it is necessary to evaluate the unique properties of documents as opposed to structured data and the challenges associated with managing information using this metaphor. Having considered these two, it is possible to discuss how the DBMS can be used cooperatively with the new metaphor for information repositories — the electronic document or EDMS.

THE DATABASE MANAGEMENT SYSTEM

The majority of IT professionals would not consider developing even the most simple of applications without employing some kind of DBMS to manage the data. The traditional approach to utilizing database technology, regardless of the application, involves some form of data analysis. Data analysis generally consists of four stages called by different names, by the various methodologies, but they all involve some form of

- Data collection and normalization
- Entity-relationship mapping
- Transaction analysis
- Data modeling

At the end of this process, once the type of database management system to be utilized is determined, one has enough information with which to begin a physical and logical database design. The data analysis activities should provide enough information to enable a design which will have a high degree of predictability in terms of data access performance and data storage size.

Data collection and normalization within any organization begins with the analysis of the data as it exists currently. Various methodologies emphasize different approaches to this analysis. Some emphasize beginning with the analysis of source documents, while others advocate analyzing the data as it is presented to the users. For this discussion it is irrelevant where one starts a project, what is important is that a "functional decomposition" process is followed in all instances. Functional decomposition attempts to distill the relevant data from some source (e.g., data collection documents or presentation documents). As recently as 1 year ago, one could have safely assumed that the documents would have been on paper; however, today that may not necessarily be so. For the purposes of this discussion, however, the medium is irrelevant.

Once this distillation process or functional decomposition is finished, one proceeds with a truly data-driven approach to analysis. The next step involves grouping the data into logical groups called entities. Using a process called normalization, one then proceeds to remove as much data redundancy as possible from these entities, sometimes producing more entities in the process. There are many good references on data normalization techniques, and for the purposes of this article there is no requirement to go into any more depth than this.

Once the entities are in third normal form one generally proceeds to associate each entity with the other entities using some entity-relationship mapping technique. Entity-relationship mapping is, in general, an attempt to reconstitute the data back into something that is meaningful to the business where the data originated. A thorough understanding of the business functions and processes that use the data is crucial for creating meaningful entity-relationship maps. During this mapping process some form of quantification of the entities also occurs.

The next step in data analysis is the transaction analysis. Transaction analysis involves listing all of the business events that could trigger access to the information within the as yet undesigned database and mapping the flow of the transaction through the entities as it satisfies its requirement for information. The transaction flow is dependent on the entity relationships. Once all the transactions are mapped in this way and the quantity of each transaction is determined, one has a good idea of how the data should be ordered and indexed.

The final step in the data analysis activity is to construct the data model. Constructing the data model involves quantitative analysis. Using the structure from the relational map and the number of accesses identified in the transactional analysis, one derives a new structure for the model. This new structure may result in new entities that may reduce the number of entities that need to be accessed for certain high-usage transactions. The first data model generally proves to be inadequate. Data analysis is therefore an iterative process. As one proceeds through the iterations, one learns more about the data. The new information may indicate that decisions made earlier in the process may not have been optimal and may need to be revisited.

The ultimate database design will not only depend on the results of the data analysis activity but also on the choice of DBMS. Good design does not just depend on knowledge of the specific data requirements of a particular application or the general information requirements of an organization. These are critical elements of the design, but almost as important is a good understanding of the particular DBMS, its architecture, and its design constraints.

The critical aspect to understand about data analysis for the purposes of this discussion is the process of functional decomposition. Functional decomposition is a process that is extremely important to data analysis. It is the process by which reality or a body of knowledge is decomposed, summarized, or reduced into its most fundamental, elementary components. This decomposition is generally from the one perspective that is important to the particular application being considered. These elementary components are the data items that then ultimately make up the database, such as those shown in Exhibit 69.1.

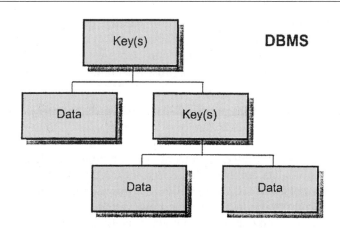

Exhibit 69.1. Elementary components.

An important consideration in Exhibit 69.1 is that any process of reduction or distillation results in a tremendous amount of other "stuff" that does not make it into the final version. This stuff is lost. Consequently, one advantage offered by functional decomposition is that the process reduces reality or a body of information to its elementary components that represent one or at least a very limited perspective on this body of information. This enables the construction of a database. The "bad" aspect of functional decomposition also relates to its strength, namely, that the process reduces reality or a body of information to its elementary components that represent one or at least a very limited perspective on this body of information. Much of the original body of information can be lost in the process.

THE ELECTRONIC DOCUMENT

Before comparing the DBMS with the electronic document management system as an information repository, it is useful to build a common understanding of the definition of a "document" in the context of this discussion.

The first thing that most people think of in any discussion of a document is paper. This is due to the fact that most of today's generations have grown up with paper as the most common medium on which documents have resided. A piece of paper or a collection of pieces of paper is usually referred to as a document, especially if it has a collective purpose. Paper, however, is very limiting and is just one method of representing a document. It is certainly not the only way. Even if one disregards the electronic medium for the moment, there is a myriad of ways that documents have existed and do exist. There are stone tablets, scrolls, hieroglyphics, paintings, carvings, and more recently film, just to mention a few. Even the scented letter is a document that is more than just scribbled words on a piece of paper. The scent can convey more information than the words.

If one includes the electronic medium, then a document can be much more than is allowed in the limited paper medium or in anything that has been described above. A document can contain voice-annotated video, with graphics, still images, and drawings with backup text. One can imagine the vast information content of a document of this nature.

The second feature that people think of when discussing documents is the concept of a page. This is also due, in all probability, to the association of documents with paper. People, in general, have an optimum quantum of information on which they can focus at any one moment. This is an aspect of what psychologists call bounded rationality. A page is probably an optimum quantum of information. Represented on paper, information could appear in the format that is most familiar; however, in some other form it could be quite different. The concept of a page is useful and will probably evolve as the understanding of documents evolves and as this understanding moves beyond paper as the common representation of a document. It will suffice for the purposes of this discussion to think of a page as a component of information and of a document as containing one or more pages or one or more quantums of information.

So, in summary, what is a document? The word *document* is both a verb and a noun. To document is to record (e.g., to record an event or to tell a story). It follows that anything that records an event or tells a story can be called a document. A document can and generally does contain many different types of entities. Generally there is either text or an image, but if people expand their horizon beyond paper, a document can contain voice, video, or, in the world of virtual reality, any combination of tactile stimuli. In the most general definition, a document is a representation of reality that can be reproduced and sensed by any combination of the five senses.

The preceding discussion may stretch human creative capabilities somewhat, so for the purposes of this discussion the definition of a document can be limited to a collection of images and textual information types. The information can be coded or uncoded. The essence of the definition of the document, as a representation of reality that can be reproduced and sensed, is really the crucial aspect of the definition that is most germane to this discussion. The representation of reality implies that a document captures information at a quantum level or quantum levels higher than simple data.

The best illustration of this is the well-known "A picture is worth a thousand words." A picture in one entity can represent a thousand data elements or more. An illustration may convey this idea better. Suppose one is creating a document describing an automobile accident report for a property and casualty insurance company. The document would begin with a notice of loss, which could be an electronic form, that is created initially by an agent within a call center. The agent would record all relevant information about the accident, including the name and policy number of the policyholder, the date and time of the accident, the date and time of the call, and all particulars of the loss, such as damages to the car, etc.

The agent then sends a compressed version of the document to the adjuster with some comments and instructions. The information to this point is in coded data format and could be through any traditional data system. The new capabilities of a document-based system allow the adjuster, when the document is received, to attach a few still photo shots of the automobile along with further comments and the detailed cost estimates supplied by the body shop. In addition, the adjuster can scan in the police report of the accident and attach it to the document. The claims document now contains a much more complete description of the entire event. This more complete description could produce a very different result by the end of the claims process. This more complete description is not possible through just simple coded data or traditional relational DBMS systems.

It is not necessary to describe the insurance claims process any further. What it illustrates is the wealth of information contained in a document-based approach to information processing. One needs to contrast this to an approach enabled by an application system containing only coded data in a relational format.

FUNCTIONAL DECOMPOSITION AND DATA DISTILLATION

The primary reason that traditional application systems oriented around a DBMS have sometimes failed to meet the expectations of the business community, and the reason that much of the business information today still resides on paper, is the failure of these applications to capture the entirety of the multifaceted information pertaining to an event. That is a real mouthful, but what it says is that if in capturing information electronically a business user only manages to capture the bare essentials focused on a certain perspective, and loses most of the other peripheral information which may be central to other perspectives, then the business user will, in general, not be completely satisfied. The business user is forced to keep other, nonelectrical repositories of information and continue to work with information in nonelectrical media. This generally adds up to a lot of paper and a lot of traditional, inefficient, and ineffective business processes.

As discussed at the end of the data analysis activity, in any process of reduction or distillation there is a tremendous amount of other peripheral information that does not make it through the process. Reality is reduced to a very limited perspective based on what is retained. This process may leave out information of interest to other perspectives. The result is a very narrow perspective on the information, general dissatisfaction, and alternative repositories of information within the organization.

THE DBMS AND THE EDMS

So why not just discard DBMSs and why not rely totally on documents as the new metaphor for an information repository. The above discussion seems to imply that database systems are bad and documents are good — far from the truth. Documents, despite having a tremendous capability of holding a great deal of multifaceted information, have their own weaknesses. Years ago one would have begun the list of these weaknesses with the fact that documents tend to take up vast amounts of storage space, require a great deal of bandwidth for transmission, and generally require expensive equipment for good presentation, such as large, high-resolution monitors and multimedia processors. Today, these weaknesses seem to be fading in importance, although not as quickly as one had hoped and would like. Bandwidth is increasing, storage costs are plummeting, and high-resolution monitors are dropping in cost.

The real weakness of documents, and this has little to do with storage or display technology, is that they are difficult to search. Because most of the information content of a document is uncoded and because there is very little in the way of search engines for uncoded data, documents are difficult to search. Once stored, they are difficult to find unless they have been indexed with exactly the criteria for which one is searching. Unfortunately, information is of little use if it cannot be found readily when needed.

It seems, then, that there is an impasse. On the one hand, a DBMS is a tool that has tremendous capabilities to search and reproduce information to which it has access, in the combinations that users generally require. The weakness of the DBMS, however, is that it generally has access to only a limited perspective on a small body of information. On the other hand, an EDMS is a tool that can house vast amounts of content about a body of information, from a multitude of perspectives. The primary weakness of an EDMS, however, is that once the information is stored it is difficult to find.

Neither one of the tools on its own seems capable of meeting the expectations for comprehensive information management. They do however have complementary strengths. With the DBMS, information is relatively easy to find, and, with the EDMS, information content is vast and rich. If one could successfully combine these strengths, then one would have a tool that might meet the expectations of the business community better. The combination might not meet all of the expectations, but would certainly be superior to either tool in stand-alone mode. The whole promises to be greater than the sum of the parts in this case.

The logical question arises, "Why use a DBMS to store data?" Why not use the EDMS to store the information, and use the DBMS to store the data about the EDMS or metadata? This would enable one to search the DBMS for the combination of information that one requires contained in the EDMS. This is exactly the approach that many leading vendors of document management applications, such as FileNet and Documentum, have taken. Both vendors use a relational database, such as Oracle or Sybase, to store the metadata that points to various data stores, such as magnetic or optical disk, that house the documents.

The DBMS in many of these document management systems has evolved beyond simple metadata which just houses pointers to content documents. These second-generation document management systems have developed the concept of the virtual document. The virtual document illustrated in Exhibit 69.2 is more than a collection of pointers to content documents. The metadata in second-generation document management applications also contains far richer information, such as a comprehensive

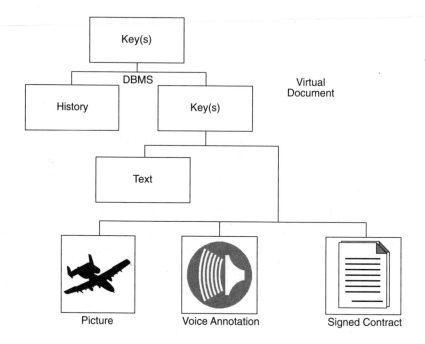

Exhibit 69.2. The virtual document.

---

history of the virtual document. The history may contain work-in-process information or information about each member document, such as the time each was added to the document collection, who entered it, and from which application.

CONCLUSION

The combination of DBMS and EDMS certainly offers advantages over either in stand-alone mode; however, the degree of the advantage can be deceptive. The metadata in the database is just that, data about the document and not about all of the information within the document. Here is the crux of the matter. What is metadata but distillation? If the only way to find a wealth of information is through the limited perspective of its metadata, then the information is not nearly as valuable as if one could find it from the multitude of perspectives contained within the information itself.

The challenge facing most document management application vendors today is how to minimize even this more expanded data distillation. The development of new search engines may be part of the answer. Development of such technologies as pattern-recognition applications, which can scan the uncoded components of documents, may be another part.

Whatever the solution to reducing the effects of data distillation, it is not something that will be totally eliminated within the near future. Combining the strengths of a DBMS and an EDMS, however, definitely provides better access to a larger volume of information than if either one is used alone. The combination is by no means a panacea, but it is a step or a number of steps in the right direction toward solving the information-processing problems that knowledge workers face every day.

As the marriage between the DBMS and the EDMS evolves further, there may be a new dawn for IT. This new dawn will be true electronic information processing rather than electronic data processing. The real payoff in this evolution and in developments of this nature is that it may eventually solve the seeming paradox of information processing in the office environment. This paradox is that, even though there has been a tremendous investment in information technology in the office, office productivity has not risen as dramatically as expected during the past 20 to 30 years.

Section XIV
Industry Specific and Package Solutions

RECENT TREND TOWARDS SPECIALIZATION AND RAPID DEVELOPMENT LEND THEMSELVES TOWARDS INDUSTRY SPECIFIC SOLUTIONS. The big question these days is the "build" versus "buy" debate. The "buy" includes package solutions like SAP, PeopleSoft and Baan. Business components and class libraries also offer "buy" solutions. This section contains five chapters that describe different types of reusable data solutions in different industries.

Chapter 70, "Choosing Your ERP Implementation Strategy," examines strategies for implementing ERP solutions within organizations that already have substantial infrastructures that need to be leveraged.

Chapter 71, "ERP Packages: What's Next," makes the case that CIOs need to shift their focus from "internal information processing" to "external information processing." The chapter argues that this shift will allow IT to capture meaningful business intelligence in the future.

Chapter 72, "Maximizing ROI by Leveraging the Second Wave of ERP," discusses an approach for maximizing the Return on Investement (ROI) by implementing a second wave of ERP.

Chapter 73, "Integrating Package Processes over Multiple Application Platforms," discusses business process integration over multiple application platforms, such as Baan, Peoplesoft, and SAP. This chapter shows how to utilize an additional layer, in the n-tier client/server model, to store common data between such package applications. This leads into a relatively new category of middleware, called ProcessWare.

Chapter 74, "Travel Insurance: Insurance and Information Technology on the Global Stage," discusses considerations, such as multiple currencies and languages, that organizations must consider in taking their operations global.

Chapter 70

Choosing your ERP Implementation Strategy

Marie Karakanian

THE ENTERPRISE RESOURCE PLANNING (ERP) PROJECT INTERFACES WITH ALL ASPECTS OF AN ORGANIZATION: people, process, technology, systems, structure, skills, culture, and definitely available technology funds. Executives responsible for such projects must develop a very clear understanding of the tasks they are about to undertake and ensure that all the relevant variables are accounted for in the planning process and time and effort are dedicated to them during and after the implementation. To be more specific, the strategy should focus on the following aspects of the project:

- Drivers
- Resources
- Visibility and profile
- Components of the ERP technology to be implemented
- Package functionality business fit
- Existing technology platforms, systems, and data
- Users
- Implementation logistics
- Budget and available funds

It is noteworthy to mention that although ERP implementations are categorized as projects, a one-time set of activities with a defined beginning and end, finite resources, and deliverables, in reality, they have become perpetual jobs in the current state of affairs. This is because of ongoing technology upgrades, technology change dependencies, mergers and acquisitions, de-mergers, and of course recycling of people from one project to another. Holding people down, to one job they have learned to become good at, has become a very difficult task to surmount in today's ERP labor marketplace. So an implementation strategy should also take into account project staff resourcing and retention strategy.

0-8493-9832-0/00/$0.00+$.50
© 2000 by CRC Press LLC

PROJECT DRIVERS

What instigated the project to start with? A proper understanding of the project, the reasons behind it and the demands on the organization must be understood very clearly by those who sponsor and run the project long before they initiate it. During the last four to five years, the following were among typical drivers for ERP projects:

- Lack of business systems integration.
- Multiple technologies requiring multiple sets, of tools, skill sets and vendors.
- Lack of shared corporate information.
- Inconsistency of data.
- Strategic information to executives.
- Data duplication and "multiplication."
- Lack of Year 2000 compliance of existing systems.
- Business globalization.
- Centralization of corporate data.
- Decentralization of regional or business unit data.

Today, as the Y2K scepter is quickly losing its punch, a large number of organizations still believe the demand for useful strategic information is greater than ever before in some business processes such as Human Resources. A recent survey conducted by Deloitte & Touche and Lawson Software discovered that 67 percent of the surveyed HR executives believe that the demand for HR to provide useful strategic information is greater than ever before. Previously downplayed corporate disciples of such disciplines continue on trying hard to play the strategic partner game with their corporate board members. Their challenge is converting the value of a not so easily definable asset, human resources, into palatable figures by the means of technology. The journey has been long, however, it continues.

While, most of the previous drivers still hold true for a number of organizations, more recent drivers such as shared services, employee self service and electronic commerce also impact your ERP projects or the systems that build upon them.

The nature of the driver will impact the formulation of the implementation strategy. For example, the need for Y2K compliance by Year 2000 can overrule a fundamental business process redesign, which can be undertaken at a later date.

RESOURCING

One key decision at the start of the implementation process involves project resourcing. The choice is between the acquisition of external consulting resources who have the required experience, skill sets, and the know-how versus internal resources who do not necessarily have the required expertise, but do have the promise of learning and internalizing a knowledge base that will remain within the organization following the conclusion of the project. Usually, resource selection is driven by the availability of project budgets, criticality of deadlines and the promise of knowledge transfer.

Recent experience that organizations have had varies significantly due to what appears to be high expectations from specialized consulting partners. The lack of true expertise is revealed fast and some organizations have had the sour taste of providing a learning platform to consultants who have professed prior expertise in a given ERP-package implementation. For this reason, organizations should conduct proper research and interviews before hiring their consulting partners.

An additional challenge organizations have faced and are still facing is the loss of their own staff to better paid jobs once the accumulation of new knowledge is at a level which is sought after in the labor markets. In some cases, organizations have rehired their own staff at much higher costs after they have defected into ERP consulting. Thus the "internalization" of the new knowledge base has been proven to be very shaky. Project executives should try and develop retention strategies that the organization can deal with which hopefully also has a certain level of internal equity.

VISIBILITY AND PROFILE

The ERP project needs to have its place among hundreds of concurrent projects it is competing with for executive attention. In smaller organizations, the champions of such projects are the executives themselves. The project should make sure that the appropriate communication plans and change management mechanisms are put in place right from the start of the project. Also, the project manager should ensure that time and budget are allocated to such activities within each phase of the project as the intensity for visibility heightens throughout the lifecycle of the project.

In large organizations, most executives, although accountable at the end, are detached from such projects until disaster time comes along. To prevent such occurrences, appropriate links and status reporting procedures should be established with at least the line executives to keep them informed of project progress, impact, risks, and challenges. Executive management should also be informed about the various alternative solutions and be part of the decision making process for the adoption of preferred solutions especially those that have critical impact on the operations of the organization.

COMPONENTS OF AN ERP PACKAGE

Before developing an implementation strategy, one focal area to concentrate on is the package itself and its components. Simplistically speaking, this can involve the following three areas at a minimum:

1. The various application modules included in the package, such as Financials, Distribution, Human Resources, and Payroll.
2. Various tools such as reporting, importing data, upgrades.
3. Various APIs that help integrate the package to various platforms of potentially different technologies such as scanners, interactive voice response systems.

The strategy should address the potential modularity of the implementation. Considering the number and variety of the business processes that these applications enable, as well as the legacy data conversion and legacy systems integration, it may simply be impossible to come up with a true big bang approach and attempt to implement all components concurrently. Normally, such implementations are staged based on a number of considerations including:

- The application dependencies within the new technology. Are there any mandatory modules that must be implemented before others?
- Optimization of the benefits of the new technology right from the beginning. Where can quick hits be identified that can start bringing some return on the technology investment?
- What currently manual business process can be automated to reduce high manual operation costs to the organization today?
- Are there internal resources available to the project to enable the concurrent implementation of some applications such as General Ledger, Payroll, Distribution, etc?
- Is the bundling of the package functionality suitable enough to replace and decommission some of the existing systems right away and stage the rest in a manageable manner? This will facilitate the decommissioning of the existing systems and potentially rid the organization of its maintenance costs.
- From package perspective, does it make sense to conduct a proper "proof of concept" of mission critical modules with a representative group of business units before charging ahead with complete implementation?

Finding and developing the answers to these questions are not necessarily easy and straightforward, however spending the effort up front will help understand the package and the organizational environment better and therefore, contribute to a more informed strategy.

PACKAGE FUNCTIONALITY BUSINESS FIT

The selection of an off-the-shelf package for an organization implies that this package is a reasonable fit for the organization and its business requirements. However, ERP clients generally come to realize during implementation that the way they do business is somewhat different from the way the package expects them to do them. This creates a conflict that must be addressed in one way or another during the implementation.

One option for addressing this gap is customizing the package to the client's requirements with the assumption that the package vendor also provides the customization tools. Another option would be changing the way the client conducts its business. This is easily said yet not so easily implemented. Apart from the challenges of managing change in organizations which have done certain things in specific ways for several decades, the potential impact of change can extend to collective agreements and union renegotiations which can take years to say the least.

Normally a compromise is reached with some customization and some process change. Some "flexible" ERP packages come bundled with their own proprietary tools that are used to perform the customizations. People-Soft is one good example that provides flexible and user friendly tools. The customizations, however, must be done with the longer term in view and consider the impact on upgrades and the basic application structure.

EXISTING PLATFORMS, SYSTEMS, AND DATA

This aspect of the ERP implementation project should never be underestimated. Often legacy data is not in good shape and requires purification or a clean up process. With respect to the data a number of decisions need to be made with a view to the implementation. History conversion is one aspect that needs to be thought of during strategy formulation in order to plan accordingly. Possibility for storing historical information in different ways as well as converting at a later phase should be considered with a view to the business requirements.

Although ERP implementations are expected to replace the existing platforms, it does not necessarily happen in all cases. And when it happens it doesn't take place in one shot meaning that the project needs to integrate the new technology with the old technology and therefore recruit resources to the project who have the right expertise. The total decommissioning of the existing platforms are normally driven by a of lack of Y2K compliance, however, projects may find that interfaces are required for various legacy mission critical systems not addressed by the new ERP. These systems may be in the process of being re-hauled or patched up for Y2K compliance.

USERS

As users are on the front line, it is crucial to know their numbers, evaluate their needs, profiles, skill sets, and orientation towards the project and the new technology. They are the targets for the training, communication and change management strategies of the project. An organization that is going to roll-out an ERP system for the first time to managers as end users will have a different approach than the one who is replacing an existing system from its current users such as Accountants or Payroll Data Entry clerks. A project team considering phased rollout will have a different training strategy than the one targeting for a big bang, one-time implementation approach.

An organization replacing a mainframe system with a client server, Windows-based system will need to consider training the users in Windows first if required before training them in the ERP system. Similarly, at the technical and operational user level, a client/server technology will introduce different challenges to operational staff who will require targeted and specific knowledge transfer plans and intensive sessions from the project team. Some of these training sessions may require one-on-one instruction for long periods of time or actual time done on the project.

IMPLEMENTATION LOGISTICS AND SCHEDULING

This could vary significantly from one organization to another. Usually, multi-location, multi-business unit organizations implement and roll out in a phased fashion. This could mean phased system hand over to the user community and/or phased functionality roll out. This strategy will support organizations that may have substantially decentralized and independent operations from each other, so that the phasing of the functionality and the roll-out schedule are negotiated and well-coordinated with other business unit specific projects.

If it happens that different units within an organization have different requirements in common areas such as payroll, than the system design and configuration timeline can be developed in coordination with the roll out strategy.

The timing and scheduling of the implementation should take into account not only the readiness of the project team and the user community but also the other corporate projects. The high profile of the project should not be stained with problems arising from inadequate scheduling of concurrent projects. Decisions and agreements should be reached at the executive levels to ensure a smooth implementation where the focus of all parties involved can be directed towards the ERP project at least for a temporary period of time.

BUDGET AND AVAILABLE FUNDS

The ERP project is one of the few winners among those competing for rare corporate resources. The size of the budget is a reflection of the expectations made from the project and its results. Therefore, it must be handled with extreme care and control.

The project manager should establish right from the start a budget monitoring process and a project reserve fund. Different budget buckets should be established including those for the consulting partner, independent contractors, implementation specific tools, project space, and team-building activities. He/she should make sure that the return on financial investment meets expectations and that budget gaps are highlighted and brought forward to executive attention on a timely basis.

CONCLUSION

As a last word, it is a good strategy to monitor and review the implementation strategy at each milestone of the project. Unfortunately, projects hardly ever finish as started. Changes occur constantly, project sponsors get reassigned, consulting partners move on, project resources depart, corporate priorities shift, and technology performance does not meet expectations. Therefore, a strategy review process should be built into the project plan especially for longer-term ERP projects.

Chapter 71

ERP Packages: What's Next?

Conghua Li

IN THE PAST DECADE, COMPANIES FROM ALL AROUND THE WORLD HAVE SPENT TENS OF BILLIONS OF DOLLARS in licensing, customizing, installing, maintaining, and upgrading enterprise resource planning systems. These systems have been applied in all conceivable industries, from banks and insurance companies to airlines and telecommunication companies, from manufacturing and utility companies to retail and hotel chains, from health care organizations and media companies to universities and government organizations, etc.

ERP packages, including those from SAP AG, PeopleSoft, Oracle, and Baan, have made a tremendous contribution to the world of business. They have made a wide range of businesses more efficient by providing them with much information they need. This information includes sales figures, financial results, information on the customer/client of the company, information on the suppliers of the company, inventory levels, distribution flow, production volumes, procurement volumes, and much more. This information gives businesses worldwide a clear overview and detailed understanding about their current performances almost anytime and anywhere. This information enables the management at all levels, from CEO to the lowest operational units, to make business and operational decisions efficiently and effectively.

However, this information is mostly limited to "internal information" only. It does not cover "the other half" of most businesses. It does not include information about the market, the competitors, the industry, the clients of the segment, the customers of the segment, and the distribution channels, for example. Is this information not important to the success of a business? The answer is clearly, "Yes, it is critical!" Why is it not included in the scope of the existing ERP/data warehousing initiative that has cost companies around the world tens, if not hundreds, of billions of dollars to date? Because, historically, it has always been this way.

The past decade has been an area of process reengineering. Emphasis has been on the internal efficiency and effectiveness of a business. As a result, the ERP wave has caught the interest and attention of businesses worldwide. CIOs have been required to play a key role in improving the internal efficiency. On the other hand, the millennium is rapidly approaching. The information systems developed in the early days cannot survive without significant restructuring and debugging. CIOs have also been wrestling with the Y2K problems for years now.

But, now that most of the businesses in the advanced world have already implemented ERP systems, or are at least in the process of implementing one, and the Y2K problems are mostly under control, the question inevitably turns to "What is next?"

WHAT IS NEXT?

The "next" will need to be "external focus." It will be for IT functions to take on the role of a Corporate Antenna. The intrinsic characteristic of doing business is like conducting warfare. In military operations, information technology has been applied not only to facilitate the internal communication and control but also, more importantly, to gather and process external information — like the antenna of an army. No army can win any battle or war if its information system is applied only to internal efficiency, e.g., to accurately indicate how much ammunition is available or how fast its troops can move. To win any battle or war, the army must accurately understand and in a timely fashion, the move of its opponents, the environment of the battlefield, and many other categories of external information.

Unfortunately, in the corporate world, IT has been mainly applied for internal-data gathering and processing only. Due to the development of technologies, including information technology, and the changing order of the global economy, today's industry and market is changing at an unparalleled rate of high speed. This requires businesses to continually monitor and make decisions against the changes in the industry and the marketplace. Historical approaches to strategic planning, which took place once every year or every couple of years, are dead. To enable businesses to compete effectively in the future, the interests and attention of CIOs of businesses around the globe will need and will be forced to shift from an internal focus to an external focus. The "next" may be called Total Information Solutions (TISs) or External Information Management (EIM).

Today's businesses need to understand, monitor, process, and apply information on their industry, their competitors, their customers, and a large volume of other information on an ongoing basis. The era is long gone in which strategic adjustments were done once every one to five years by the senior management only. And external information is collected, analyzed, and kept only by some strategists and senior management members.

The rise and fall of great companies is now proceeding at an unprecedented rate in corporate history. These ups and downs have hardly been due to how well companies have managed their internal information. Instead they are mostly due to how well they have managed and responded to the changes in their external conditions. No effort purely focused on internal efficiency can save an organization. The efforts to adapt to external conditions do. Peter Drucker, a father of modern management, recently said: "The forces that most influence organizations come from outside the organization, not from within." Today's businesses have to collect, process, and apply the external information on the fly. Otherwise, a great business will be landed in no time.

As a result, managing today's business organization is like flying a jet fighter. The jet fighter, with its complex internal operations controlled by sophisticated systems, needs to actively search, collect, and process external conditions and information on the fly. In fact, the information shown on the instrument panel concerning external conditions is so important that pilot needs only to operate based on what their instruments tell them instead of what their intuition or feelings tell them. Although managing a business is not exactly flying a jet fighter, the importance of collecting, processing, and using external information has increased to a previously unknown level.

Although many companies have made significant efforts in developing customer and supplier databases, but the companies were mainly focused on their direct customers and suppliers. Although these databases have contributed considerably to the companies, they limited them to a tunnel vision of their external interfaces.

The TISs will enable businesses to systematically monitor and collect data about broadly ranged external business conditions, integrate the external data with the internal data, and build or extract business intelligence for all adequate levels of management of a business.

The external data will cover, but will not be limited to, such data as the following:

- Consumer or customer trends of the target markets and their relevant segments.
  - Their changing preferences.
  - Their changing demand.
  - Their changing composition.
  - Their changing distribution.
- Trends of the relevant industries.
  - Technology adaptation — "The technologies likely to have the greatest impact on a company and its industry are technologies outside of its own field."

- – Industry economics.
- – Best practices.
- – Changing landscape of supply and distribution systems and mechanisms.
- Competitors.
  - – Key competitors.
  - – Their market positioning.
  - – Their competitive approaches.
  - – Their competitive results.
- Competitive product or services.
  - – Product or service innovations.
  - – The benefit of these innovations to the customers.
  - – Their competitive positions.
  - – The potential threat of these innovations to the company.

Traditionally this information was collected and processed by such corporate functions as strategic planning and marketing. By providing ongoing data collection and processing, the contribution and involvement of IT will bring a revolution to the ways in which external data is collected and processed as well as to the ways in which business decision-making processes are organized.

WHO NEEDS THE EXTERNAL INFORMATION?

Like in a military operation, almost every one in the army will need to access information and intelligence about the external conditions. In the past many companies prospered with only a small group of elite having access to some fragmented and discontinued external information, but businesses of the future will wonder how they can even conduct the most basic tasks without understanding the external context.

Although almost everyone in any business entity in the future will need to access external information and intelligence on an ongoing basis, the following are some of the most critical areas of people who need to have efficient and effective access to this information and intelligence:

- Strategy management
- Product development
- Product management
- Marketing
- Advertising
- Public relations
- Branding
- Distribution
- Sales
- Customer services

906

The wide range of people who need the external information will pose a great challenge to the data integration, distribution, and intelligence extraction. Covering external data will be far more challenging than covering internal data. TIS may well make "intelligent enterprise" come true, but of course, "intelligent-enterprise" decisions will still be made by human beings instead of computers.

For IT to take on some major responsibilities of collecting, processing, and distributing external information, it should not undermine the importance of corporate planning function. In fact, it is to reinforce the effectiveness of this function by providing a corporate antenna — the ongoing data collection, processing, and distribution.

WHAT ARE THE CRITICAL ISSUES IN DEVELOPING CORPORATE ANTENNA?

The critical issues of dealing with external data will focus on the following key areas:

- What data to collect
- Where and how to collect the data
- How to process the data
- To whom and how to distribute the data
- What are the organizational or process implications

What Data to Collect

The first and foremost critical issues will be identifying the relevant data that is needed by the enterprise. This will be determined by the industry and the company. All information necessary to "fly the jet fighter" will need to be collected. Of course, 20 percent of information will fulfill 80 percent of the need. The key will be to identify the 20 percent of relevant information, particularly in today's environment of over supply of information.

It is vital to understand that IT is not to completely take over the role of collecting external data from the functions that have traditionally bared the responsibilities, such as planning, marketing, etc. IT will focus on the data that can be effectively collected on an ongoing basis.

Where and How to Collect

Companies need to identify suitable sources and determine effective ways to collect the key information. There will be many sources possible for data collection, such as the following:

- Employees
- Customers
- Distributors
- Suppliers

- Strategic partners such as among Star Airline members
- Business information reporters such as Bloomberg, Reuters, Dow Jones
- Online information providers such as Yahoo Finance, E-Trade
- Business analyses from banks, brokerage houses, stock exchanges
- Business studies from associations, government organizations, and research institutes

While in most areas of today's business world team effort and partnerships are highly developed, the area of external information collection and processing team work and partnership approaches are still in the dark age. Team efforts and partnerships will be the keys for effectively establishing corporate antenna functions in the future.

It is also important to realize that collection and process of external data must be continuous and systematic. A jet fighter cannot fly without continuous collection of external data. Any interval in external monitoring may lead to catastrophe. Only structured data can be effectively integrated with the relevant internal data. And only effective integration of internal and external data can generate business intelligence that an enterprise needs to survive and to grow.

How to Process?

Integration of external and internal data will be the key. While an oversupply of data and information exists, a short supply of intelligence persists in today's business world. It is critical to extract intelligence out of the combination of the external and internal data. The speed of processing needs to be high. Results need to be clear. Intelligence needs to be effective. It will not fulfill the mission to put information simply on an intranet. The Internet phenomenon, in which people get billions of bits of data but can hardly find a relevant one, must be avoided.

As with data collection, the processing must be on an ongoing basis. Purpose-oriented processing needs to be emphasized. Miles Au Yeung, an IT expert with Deloitte Consulting, pointed out when reviewing this article recently, "Despite some companies are collecting external data today, they cannot turn data in real time into decision-making support. External data is not fed into operational systems for real-time adjustments. It still involves a lot of human effort in separating noise from useful data and processing the data into information."

Whom and How to Distribute?

It will be a significant challenge to determine what information will be accessible by whom and how intelligence will be extracted. Virtually every department, operational unit, and individual will need to extract intelligence from a wide range of information. The scope will be far larger than the context of the internal information. Also, the intelligence to be extracted will be far broader than the intelligence that has been extracted from the internal data only. But this will be the price a business will have to pay if it wants to survive in the next millennium.

Data distribution will be increasingly important. Only with effective data distribution can business intelligence be effectively extracted where and when it is needed.

What Are the Organizational or Process Implications?

In today's knowledge economy, information processes drive organizational structure. As the ways in which external information is collected and processed, and as the ways in which business decision-making shift, the organizational structures will be forced to change. This may well represent a new wave of worldwide corporate restructuring. This restructuring will go far beyond the simple change of IT organizational structures. It will cover most of the entire corporate organizations.

The change will be big. Challenges will be daunting. However, companies will have no other choice than to go through it, as this process will select the future winners and determine the future losers.

WHAT WILL BE THE ROLE OF CIOS?

Although CIOs will need and will be forced to shift their interests, attentions, and roles, the process will not be smooth.

CIOs will not only need to be more business-oriented in their future approach, but they will also need to help the company transit to new ways of doing business. They will need to assist the next wave of process reengineering and corporate restructuring. This wave of process reengineering and corporate restructuring will be focusing on building "intelligent enterprises." Like any other significant changes that happened in the corporate history before, tremendous resistance will occur.

Are today's CIOs prepared to take on these challenges? How much do they understand about strategic positioning? How much do they understand about business processes? How much do they understand about corporate organizational structures? How much do they understand about change management?

What do they need to do if they are not yet equipped with the capabilities to take on these future challenges? Time will be of the essence. The challenges are already approaching. CIOs do not have much time left to get ready for it.

While accountants' and chief financial officers roles have matured, the true role of the CIO is just about to be born.

CONCLUSION

With the burden of the Y2K, ERP, and data warehousing out of the way, and with the new landscape of global competition, companies will have the resources and will be forced to start to deal with external information processing issues. "Growth and survival both now depend on getting the organization in touch with the outside world," warned Peter Drucker. What is after ERP will be external data focused. It might be TIS, EIM, or any other fancy term.

The corporate world has been talking about strategic IT for a long time. Now IT is going to put a conclusion on the strategic importance of IT for the first time in history by developing "Corporate Antenna," transforming decision-making processes, and hence establishing Intelligent Enterprises.

Chapter 72
Maximizing ROI by Leveraging the Second Wave of ERP

Judy Dinn

A SURPRISINGLY LARGE NUMBER OF COMPANIES WHO HAVE IMPLEMENTED ENTERPRISE RESOURCE PLANNING (ERP) SYSTEMS are not seeing the expected returns on their Information Technology (IT) investment. Many companies are actually experiencing an initial dip in performance and realizing that if they want to maximize their ROI they will need to stabilize the systems environment, optimize business processes and conquer lingering change management issues. These new initiatives are collectively called the Second Wave.

ROI ON IT EXPENDITURES

Realizing ROI on IT initiatives has come to be a difficult process. During the last decade, businesses have made significant IT investments either in implementing new supporting applications and infrastructure or adopting new technologies in hopes of creating new business opportunities.

In the 1990s, IT expenditures consumed a large percentage of corporate yearly budgets. To resolve Year 2000 compliance issues and to meet the growing informational demands of the business, companies throughout the world participated in the implementation of Enterprise Resource Planning (ERP) systems. Information technology and business project sponsors accepted full responsibility for creating organizational chaos firming believing that the countless opportunities would clearly be illustrated once they went 'live.' Now these sponsors are perplexed as they see that some benefits are coming to fruition while others are not even beginning to blossom. These project sponsors concede that in order to realize all the benefits they promised it will mean more money, more organizational change and more effort.

THE LIFECYCLE OF APPLICATIONS

The evolution of applications has been dynamic over the last three decades. Applications originated as custom-built systems that met the immediate needs of a unique business group. They matured, becoming large complex packaged systems supporting numerous enterprisewide business processes. The growth of the Application lifecycle is described in the following stages.

Stage 1: Isolated/Home Grown Systems

In the 1970s, each department was supported by custom-built applications. Each application was built specifically for an individual function: General Ledger, Accounts Payable, Accounts Receivable, among others. Users were isolated from having to include or consider other functional areas' requirements.

Stage 2: Integrated Functionality

The introduction of Business Process Re-engineering emerged in the 1980s and companies slowly attempted to adopt the notion of aligning their organizations by business processes as opposed to functional silo's. In support of this movement, applications were redesigned around functional processes including Financials, Manufacturing, and Distribution, etc. This was accomplished by building complex interfaces to existing applications or through the selection and implementation of Functional Package Applications.

Stage 3: Enterprise Applications

Throughout the 1990s, integration efforts continued and business processes were redefined to become end-to-end solutions, for example, Order-to-Delivery. IT environments consisted of a collection of complex interfaces and multiple platforms. The business, at this time, was asking for a single system to support end-to-end business solutions while IT was attempting to simply support efforts and achieve cost efficiencies. In response, the market introduction of a single integrated system.

An integrated system is defined as a single application that supports business wide end-to-end processes and utilizes a common database. The market's solution was a packaged application called an Enterprise Resource Planning (ERP) system. An ERP system is an enterprise-integrated system consisting of linked applications, which coordinate business activities and support the flow of information across the enterprise.

ERP systems focus specifically on integrating BackOffice functions (i.e. Finance, Procurement, Manufacturing, and Distribution) to achieve efficiencies across business processes. They minimized the complexity of IT environments, meet the requirements of the business and address the issue of Year 2000 compliance. Companies view ERP systems as the answer to a number of their organizational issues.

Stage 4:   Bolt-on/Decision Support Late 1990s

With the BackOffice completely integrated and data collect centrally, bolt-on applications are introduced to the market. Bolt-on applications satisfy those functions not supported by traditional ERP applications. Bolt-ons interface with ERPs to further collect and support business information in order to provide real-time decision support. Bolt-ons include front-office applications like Sales Force Automation, E-commerce, Production Planning etc.

Stage 5:   Integrated/Decision Support Late 1990s

Now that all business data is capture and collected centrally more focus and investment is spent on information analysis and decision-support tools. Information exchange is platform-independent throughout the geographically distributed enterprise via the Intranet.

WHERE IS THE ROI ON ERP INVESTMENTS?

Both technology and operational problems motivated companies to undertake ERP systems implementation. The most compelling reasons at the beginning of the decade included not only Y2K compliance, but also disparate systems, poor IT performance, and limited visibility and accessibility to business information.

A 1998 survey by Benchmarking Partners, Inc., the Deloitte Consulting Second Wave Survey set out to understand ERP post-implementation issues and trends. The respondents of the survey were manufacturing and consumer business, the two industries who are farthest along in the ERP implementation cycle. One of the more interesting survey questions asked of the 62 Fortune 500 Companies was, are companies realizing the expected benefits from their ERP investments?

The findings illustrated that only 37 percent of the respondents expressed that they had achieved or were on track to achieve the specific, quantified benefits they expected. Some of the more disappointing post-implementation situations include:

- Financial and operational returns are lower than expedited whereas project and maintenance costs are higher than expected;
- Many elements of the "as is" processes are still in place therefore 'best-practice' efficiencies are not being utilized;

- The ERP implementation triggered new operational issues and many users do not know how to use the system effectively;
- Y2K compliance is achieved but the value of the systems is unclear.

Given the size and visibility of ERP initiatives within an organization, it is easy to comprehend why its ROI is on the radar of executive management. Now that the system is 'live' and the immediate results are disappointing, when can we expect to see returns?

THE NEXT STEP: EXECUTING THE SECOND WAVE

The implementation of ERP systems is now being referred to as the First Wave of the ERP Journey. Companies are realizing that to capitalize on their ERP investments and realize business opportunities they need to embark on a Second Wave.

The Second Wave deals specifically with Process Optimization. Throughout the First Wave, ERP implementations were strained by aggressive deadlines or the organizations' inability to make aggressive changes and key decisions. The result, implementations adopted 'As-Is' processes instead of best practices, data was not properly sanitized and 'dirty' data was converted, training and change management was minimized therefore users take longer to accomplish normal tasks. The Second Wave deals specifically with these issues by revisiting people, process, and technology.

In executing a Second Wave initiative, the organization is maximizing ROI by aggressively pursuing and measuring benefits. This involves stabilizing the current environment, realizing efficiencies and engaging new opportunities made available by the ERP implementation. The Second Wave utilizes an organization's existing resource investment and knowledge and it is *not* about creating a new solution, it is simply reworking an existing solution to maximize an investment.

APPROACH

The Second Wave Initiative starts once a company goes "live" with their ERP solution. It analyzes the status of the system and attempts to manage the expected dip in performance after going "live." It identifies short-term stabilization needs (i.e., system tuning, support organization), quick-hit opportunities (i.e., conduct more training, modify process) and longer-term business benefits. The three stages for implementation described by Deloitte Consulting address each area of potential benefit.[2]

Stage 1: Stabilize; Secure the Base

Once the implementation is 'live' the next step is to stabilize the technology and people processes. Stabilization may need anywhere from three to nine months to secure and sustain the core ERP functionality. It is during this time that companies may experience a dip in performance. The challenge is to manage the dip by fine-tuning the new processes and mastering the change in the organization. The result is improvement in speed and cost reductions in handling routine business transactions. Without this stage the organization cannot progress in successfully achieving additional capabilities.

Stage 2: Synthesize; Build for the Future

Utilizing the stable ERP backbone, organizations can now start building new capabilities. During the next 6 to 18 months, non-ERP applications are brought into the mix, process improvements are engaged and addition education is deployed to further motivate people to undertake the next level of change. This stage deals with realizing effectiveness from the ERP Investment.

Stage 3: Synergize; Achieve Value in Use

This is the future state that the organization has envisioned achieving when they first made their investment. The organization has put in place an infrastructure, which can support dynamically new business strategies and competencies. The people, processes and technology are not only able but willing to adopt sweeping changes which benefit the companies success and allow the company to transform itself to meet market pressures and customer demands. This stage is expected to last from twelve to twenty four months.

CONCLUSION

When will technology cease to be an expensive support infrastructure tool? The boastful advantages that each era of technology speaks to never fully come to fruition before companies are pressured to move on the next trendy technology gadget. In the case of ERP implementation, companies are learning that the size and complexity of such a project is overwhelming. It is a quite an accomplishment for those organizations who have gone "live" but it is not surprising to find that not all parts of the implementation take advantage of all the opportunities available.

The next wave, Second Wave, is a necessary step in ensuring that the originally investment is fully realized. Executives should understand the quantitative and qualitative benefits that they are achieving now are just the beginning. Continual investment and re-work of the solution is needed if the organization is to utilize all the possibilities that ERP presents.

References

1. 1998 Survey by Benchmarking Partners, Inc., the Deloitte Consulting Second Wave Survey.
2. Deloitte Consulting, Second Wave Approach, 1999.

Chapter 73
Integrating Package Processes over Multiple Application Platforms

Ido Gileadi

COMPANIES AND PEOPLE ARE RELYING MORE THAN EVER ON COMPUTER-IZED SYSTEMS to run their businesses. Traditional computing tasks such as finance, human resources, and contact management now are extended to include additional areas where the business is seeking to gain a competitive advantage. Computerized systems are viewed by management as the primary tool for gaining advantage over the competition.

The introduction of multiple applications at all levels of the organization and the executive attention that these applications are receiving is highlighting a well-known problem. All applications must work in tandem, communicate with each other, and, most importantly, pass meaningful data that then can be rolled up for management reporting.

IT organizations have been integrating packages for many years. The integration programs of the past were created like bridges connecting disparate islands. Point-to-point connections transferred subsets of data, typically in ASCII file format, on a predefined schedule. This type of point-to-point integration required detailed knowledge of each application data and did not provide a satisfactory solution when real-time access to data and functionality was required.

With the introduction of ERP (Enterprise Resource Planning) systems came the promise of support for integrated business processes. The idea was that the ERP systems would cover most aspects of computerization in an organization. ERP, being one integrated package, will allow for a complete start-to-end business process integration. The reality is that ERP

0-8493-9832-0/00/$0.00+$.50
© 2000 by CRC Press LLC

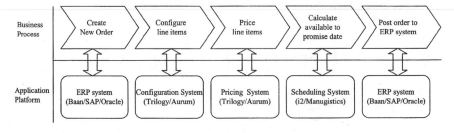

Exhibit 73.1. Order-taking process.

packages cannot address all of an organization's business requirements in a satisfactory manner. A combination of packaged software as well as legacy and custom-made software residing along side each other, therefore can be see each providing a solution to a portion of the business process.

Once again IT organizations are faced with the challenge of integrating multiple application platforms into one coherent business process.

THE CHARGE

An organization undergoing a major package implementation such as SAP, Baan, Oracle or PeopleSoft typically will start with identifying the scope of the project. The scope of the project may include a complete BPR (business process reengineering) that will result in new and improved business processes. The project may take the approach of implementing existing processes; this approach may minimize the benefits of implementing a new packaged software because a great deal of benefit is in the reengineering and tuning of existing processes.

The project's business team will be charged with redefining the business processes. The IT team will be charged with identifying the best application platforms to support the business processes and the integration of these various applications into one end-to-end seamless process.

An example of an integrated business process and the multiple application platforms that may support it is depicted in Exhibit 73.1.

Exhibit 73.1 describes a simplified order-taking process. Order header information first is created in the ERP system. Line-by-line information then is entered. As the lines are entered, the line items must be configured and priced. These tasks are accomplished by a configuration and pricing application. For each line and for the overall order, an available to promise (first date when this order can be manufactured completely) is calculated by the scheduling application. All of the data collected from the various applications is used to complete the order and submit all the order lines into the ERP system.

It is evident in Exhibit 73.1 that this is a process that is supported by multiple application platforms and that there is a need to integrate the applications in real time to support the process.

THE PERFECT WORLD

In a perfect world all applications would be on the same hardware and software platforms. The applications all would have well-defined APIs that provide all the functionality required for the business process. The applications all will be communicating using the same communication standards and using the same object models.

THE REAL WORLD

The real world is more complex than the imaginary perfect view. Applications can differ in the following areas:

- Hardware platform — the actual type of computer and processor that is used to run the application (e.g., Intel, RISK, MF);
- Software platform — the operating systems that the application is running (e.g., HPUX, NT, MVS, Solaris);
- Communication method — the way with which the application communicates with external applications (e.g., RPC, messaging, distributed objects);
- Object model — the definition of the common objects that all applications will adhere to for the purpose of communicating with each other (e.g., CORBA, COM/DCOM);
- Database — the database that the application uses to store the data (e.g., Oracle, Sybase, Informix); and
- Network protocol — the network protocol used on systems where the application is residing (e.g., TCP/IP, IPX).

Looking back at the example in Exhibit 73.1 we can now concentrate on the differences between the application environments. Exhibit 73.2 depicts these differences.

Exhibit 73.2 describes the different platforms used to support the applications that are required for the order-taking process. It is clear that the task of integrating all these applications is quite complex.

SELECTING AN APPROACH AND ARCHITECTURE

Once one has a clear picture of the applications to be integrated and the business process that should be integrated across the multiple application platforms, he or she is ready to select an approach and architecture for

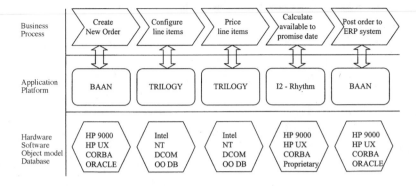

Exhibit 73.2.   Application differences.

integration. The following should be considered when selecting an approach and architecture:

- Platform information
  - Hardware platforms
  - Operating systems
  - Object models
  - Communication methods
- Real-time vs. batch processes
- Future software upgrades
- Future addition of new applications
- Ongoing management of integration code
- Error handling and transactions monitoring
- New skills requirements

The above considerations will help one to make a decision on the architecture and the integration objectives. This in turn will drive the selection of middleware software that will facilitate the integration between the applications.

The traditional approach of point-to-point integration will not deliver the required functionality for this process. An order entry clerk cannot wait for batch processes to kick in and perform file transfers while keying in an order. A real-time, processware approach is required. In an approach where the process is defined within a middleware/processware product and the applications act as servers, serving the required functionality is more appropriate.

Examining two approaches to processware implementation, the first approach is based on object definitions and a process definition that acts on these objects, and the second approach is based on event definitions

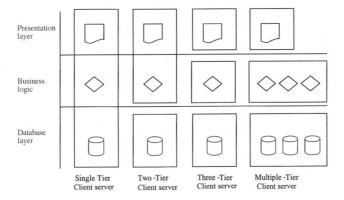

Exhibit 73.3.   Applications distribution.

and rules agents that trigger the events in a sequence related to the business process.

Stepping back, examine the various operating models of typical applications. A typical application can be divided into three layers:

- Presentation layer — the screens that the user interacts with to view and enter data
- Business logic layer — the processing logic that is triggered by user actions
- Database layer — storage and retrieval of persistent data over time

Most applications consist of all three layers. The primary difference between applications within the scope of this chapter is the degree of distribution of these layers. Exhibit 73.3 demonstrates the various options that are available for distributing the layers.

Exhibit 73.3 describes the most common models for application distribution. The single-tier model has all three layers residing on the same machine. The application can be accessed directly on the single machine or through multiple terminals. The two-tier (client/server) model has the database layer separate on a server designed and configured to run a database engine. The business logic and the presentation layers still are lumped together into what is known as a fat or thick client. The three-tier model separates each layer. The presentation layer can run on a Windows-based client or a browser; the business logic can run on an application server; and the database can run on a database server. The database server and the application server can be configured differently to accommodate the special requirements for running logic and database activities. The multi-tier model accommodates further distribution of the database

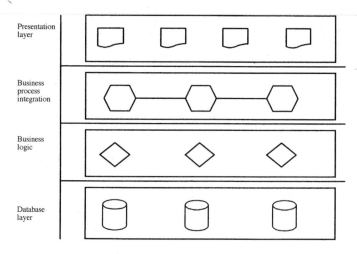

Exhibit 73.4. Processware integration.

and the application logic on multiple servers. Distribution of the computing layers allow for better load balancing.

The goal of business process integration over multiple application platforms is to create an additional business logic layer that contains common data structures that all applications can access and populate through a set of agreed-upon calls. The business logic layer can be implemented using distributed object models such as DCOM and CORBA or an event-based system where the common data can be implemented. Examine both approaches in Exhibit 73.4.

In Exhibit 73.4, observe that in addition to the familiar multi-tier architecture, there is a new layer for business process integration. This layer defines objects or events that contain common data structures. The business logic layer or the presentation layer can activate methods for these objects as well as access data contained in the objects. The objects data structures contain the data required to support the integrated business process. This layer may be implemented using events that can be published or subscribed to. Any application business logic or presentation layer may publish an event and populate all or part of the data structure for that event. Once an event is published, all the applications that subscribe to the event are notified and processing is triggered.

The preceding architecture supports the creation of an additional process logic layer. The key for successful business process integration over multiple applications platforms is to utilize this new layer for storing the common data between applications and implementing the business process using logic in the layer. Having achieved such an architecture, the business process and data from the applications have been managed, thereby making the integration easy to manage and monitor. It also will become easier to modify specific pieces of the integration; replacing applications or updating them to new versions becomes a much simpler task.

CONCLUSION

A new concept of processware has been introduced. Processware is middleware software that facilitates the creation of an additional computing layer called the business process integration logic. This layer can be implemented using distributed objects or events to encapsulate the common data structures and the business process. Among the benefits of this approach and architecture are

- Isolation of integration business logic from the applications
- Creation of common data structures to communicate information between applications
- Easy migration of integration code upon upgrade or replacement of any of the applications involved
- Ability to manage and monitor the integration of the various applications
- A set of tools that facilitates the creation of the integrated business process and takes care of the communication and networking layer, allowing the users to focus on coding the business logic

There are several products in the market that are in various stages of development that are suited to support processware. In some cases, portions of the products already have been released. Each of these products takes a somewhat different approach to implementation. Time will tell which of these products will thrive and become a major player in this new emerging market.

Chapter 74

Travel Insurance: Insurance and Information Technology on the Global Stage

Laura DiSisto

> Comes over one an absolute necessity to move. And what is more, to move in some particular direction. A double necessity then: to get on the move, and to know whither.
>
> —D.H. Lawrence

AS THE NORTH AMERICAN INSURANCE INDUSTRY MATURES TO A SLOW-GROWTH, highly competitive market, many insurers are choosing to explore global markets as a strategy to expand their operations and grow their customer base. Although many foreign insurers have long been pursuing this strategy, a majority of North American insurers are new to the global stage and are in for a few surprises.

On the surface, establishing global operations would seem to be a deceptively simple process: pick your country, apply for and obtain a license (if required), recruit a few employees, establish operations, start selling. However, many global markets, particularly underdeveloped ones, can differ significantly from those in developed countries. Implementing a traditional North American insurance operating model without considering country characteristics will impact the ability to achieve long-term success and profitability.

In the same way that a business strategy developed for domestic operations will not suffice for international operations, an Information and

Technology strategy developed to support domestic operations will fall short for meeting international requirements. An Information and Technology architecture established upon principles based purely on domestic considerations with the implicit belief that it will hold true on an international level is a recipe for failure.

While North American insurance companies aggressively pursue overseas expansion as a strategic objective, many CIOs find themselves scrambling to ensure that their information technology (IT) organization can support international operations.

The first steps when developing an Information and Technology strategy for international operations is to understand the key drivers of your strategy on a global level. When developing an information and technology strategy, a CIO must consider the international aspects of the organizations requirements and the questions that an information and technology strategy will need to address:

- How will your organization be able to make use of information managed globally to gain a competitive advantage on an international level?
- How will your IT organization support demands for global information?
- How can your IT organization support the business decisions made within your organization and ensure that they are based on high quality information from all relevant sources across the organization?
- How will your IT organization identify a common suite of information and technology products and services for the international organization?
- How can the sharing of information across the global organization enhance your organization's relationships with it's customers and suppliers worldwide?
- What technology investments will drive global competitive advantage over the next 5 years?
- How can your IT organization build an infrastructure that can change and adapt with the international needs of the business?
- How can your IT organization build an infrastructure that can incorporate new technology across all geographic locations as it adds value to the overall business?
- How can your IT organization best evaluate where to place the company's technology investments?
- How can your IT organization train international resources consistently and in a timely manner on concepts, techniques, and tools that keep changing?
- How can your IT organization evaluate and motivate the performance of all resources in a productive, consistent manner across all geographic locations?

- How can your IT organization provide incentives for people to contribute to the goals of the global company rather than the individual or the local operations?
- What organizational structure provides the best support for the business across all geographic locations?
- How can your IT organization ensure it is obtaining good value for its spending on Information and Technology?
- What attributes of information and technology does the global business value?
- In what ways can Information and Technology initiatives be linked to and described in terms of the value creating strategies of the business?
- How can your IT organization demonstrate the value contributions of Information and Technology to the global strategic objectives of the enterprise?

These questions are the first step towards understanding what the global needs are for a Information and Technology strategy. The difficulties in developing an information and technology strategy for global operations are often complicated by the uncertainty of which direction global expansion will happen. Licenses can often by granted sooner or later than anticipated, throwing a wrench in timelines and expectations. An architecture designed for global operations will need to be flexible enough to adapt to the demands of global operations without compromising the underlying principles of the architecture.

While adaptability is a basic principle of many information and technology architectures, the ability to adapt quickly to market changes is particularly crucial when dealing in overseas, untapped markets where regulatory and infrastructure changes happen almost daily. Insurers who can react quickly to these changes will find themselves better able to establish a competitive advantage within the market. In many cases, the ability to adapt will rely heavily on the speed with which the underlying information technology will adapt and a robust deployment strategy that will allow rapid deployment of a technology infrastructure for new global operations.

When developing or updating your information technology strategy, consider how your data and technology architecture will adapt to information operations. Key among the considerations for this are:

DATA INTEGRITY AND CONSISTENCY

Developing and managing a data architecture which spans multiple physical locations while ensuring integrity and consistency without redundancy is not an easy task. Add to this the possible regulatory laws restricting the location of data along with restrictions in communications capabilities and this becomes a primary consideration for global operations. When establishing a data architecture, frequently accessed data should reside locally and frequent replication should be kept to a minimum as this can be expensive and unreliable.

APPLICATION DEVELOPMENT AND DISTRIBUTION

Maintaining applications across geographic locations requires special consideration for application support and application distribution processes. Workflow support is of key importance if the workflow is spread among multiple geographic locations to ensure that operations are not disrupted. Design your workflow to avoid geographic difficulties by establishing shared services and regionalized processing where possible.

MULTI-CURRENCY

While this may seem an obvious one, supporting multiple currencies is more than just being able to enter and store transactions in differing currencies. Your architecture must consider the impacts of multiple currencies on consolidation and rollup capabilities, as well as analysis across multiple currencies if required. Will you be able to report on the total value of term life policies globally or within a region? Use your reporting and inquiry requirements as a driver for determining how to convert and store multiple currencies.

MULTI-LANGUAGE

In addition to obvious requirements of catering for language at input, consider the impacts of storing multiple languages to your data or the complexities of conversion at input. Storing multiple languages will impact your ability to search and analyze information across languages, while translation at input could prove costly and compromise data quality. You can reduce this considerably by standardizing on pick lists and drop-down selection for input as much as possible, but will still need to be developed, an approach to handle the cases where this does work.

REGULATORY LAW

Beware of local regulatory law that impacts information technology. For example, some countries require application servers to be physically located within their borders. In some cases, the impact of regulatory law on your architecture may not be immediately obvious. Laws that restrict where transactions or operations must occur may dictate where the associated technology is located. Be sure you have all the information you need on regulatory laws before making any architectural decisions and be prepared with alternative solutions should the regulatory restrictions of a new site cause difficulties.

COMMUNICATIONS

Robust communications infrastructures cannot be taken for granted. The reliability of communications will vary from country to country and the cost can also vary considerably. Consider these factors before developing an architecture that implies robustness and low cost communications. Avoid frequent long-distance transfer of high volumes or real-time cross border communications for your systems.

BACKUP AND RECOVERY

Your backup and recovery procedures will span multiple geographic locations and time zones and will involve infrastructures with varying degrees of robustness. This adds a level of complexity to the already challenging process of establishing reliable backup and recovery procedures. Take advantage of multi-country operations to provide alternate backup sites and coordinate your backup operations to take advantage of differing time zones.

BUSINESS CASE

Consider the traditional components of your business case, which may not hold true for international operations. For example, in many emerging markets, implementation of technology to reduce headcount will likely not result in cost savings; if this is a significant component of your business case it will not hold for global investments. Your business case model will need to consider global factors.

VENDORS

Vendor support and cooperation takes on new meaning when dealing internationally. Your vendors will need to have strong international experience and capabilities to support your global operations. Identify a list of preferred vendors who have an international network and can provide consistent quality support worldwide at reasonable cost.

IT ORGANIZATION STRUCTURE

Your IT organization structure must provide sufficient support and guidance at the local level. Recruiting, evaluation and compensation policies will need to be consistent across countries while considering any local regulations which impose restrictions. Develop a simple organizational structure which can be easily replicated or extended for new operations and considers the potential lack of skills or training available at the local level.

INFORMATION TECHNOLOGY STANDARDS

Any standards established must be easily accessible globally. When establishing standards for hardware, software, middleware, etc., ensure that these can be obtained and supported globally. Develop standards in conjunction with the identification of preferred vendors to ensure that these standards will be enforced and supported worldwide.

TIME ZONES

Your information technology infrastructure will likely cross multiple time zones. This can be good and bad: you can take advantage of this to provide better support for your operations—work to solve problems while users sleep—but you will also need to provide 7/24 support so that all time zones are covered.

This list is just the beginning; it is by no means definitive. You can ensure only that you consider and provide for all the key issues if you follow these primary principles when developing your information and technology strategy and architecture: develop an understanding of global markets and their differences; maintain as much flexibility and adaptability as possible; and align the information and technology strategy to the business strategy.

CONCLUSION

Establishing operations and supporting information technology can appear deceptively simple if looked at from a domestic perspective. Treating international operations as an extension of domestic operations can be a fatal mistake. Be aware of the issues and considerations that make developing an international information technology strategy and infrastructure a challenge. Be prepared to deal with the hurdles of data integrity, multiple currencies, languages, and time zones, application distribution, vendor alliances, regulatory restrictions, unreliable communications, and many more. Develop a strategy which will address these issues and map out the path to international success. As Yogi Berra once observed, "If you don't know where you are going, you might wind up someplace else."

Section XV
Linux Fundamentals

THE LINUX OPERATING SYSTEM HAS CAUGHT THE ATTENTION OF THE IN-DUSTRY in the past year as a potential end-user friendly replacement for UNIX and a new serious contender that can compete with NT. This section of the handback contains four chapters that examine Linux, the open source model, and applications that operate with Linux.

Chapter 75, "Gauging How Linux May Change the DBMS Market," examines Linux's promise as a reliable, standard-operating system that can fulfill some of the early promises made by UNIX. This chapter examines impacts on DBMS vendors and opportunities for organizations to get started in using this operating system.

Chapter 76, "Open Source Model of Software Development," describes the *Open Source* model of software development and assesses its implications on future software projects with an emphasis on Linux.

Chapter 77, "Linux and the Web," examines the architecture and design of Linux. This chapter also discusses applications that are available freely over the web to assist in building an infrastructure for E-commerce using this operating system.

Chapter 78, "Linux: Alternative Direction in Computing," discusses opportunites for using this new operating system as an alternative platform for a corporate computing environment.

Chapter 75
Gauging How Linux May Change the DBMS Market

Paul Korzeniowski

LINUX IS ONLY THE KERNEL OF AN OPERATING SYSTEM, the part that controls hardware, manages files, and separates processes. Third party companies can add multiple install methods, applications, and other add-ons, to the Linux systems they ship, which are called Linux distributions. The companies can combine utilities and applications to differentiate their offerings. However, between these products, the actual Linux kernel has remained almost completely the same.

LINUX HISTORY

Linux is the brainchild of Linus Torvalds, who created the operating system as a hobby while a student at the University of Helsinki in Finland in 1991. While studying, he developed an interest in Minix, a compact version of UNIX and set out to build a better variation of the operating system. In 1994, he delivered version 1.0 of Linux and the operating system has been gaining popularity ever since.

The reason for the rise is the way the Torvalds distributed the operating system. Linux does not really belong to any one company. Instead, the emerging operating system is available at no charge to developers who are encouraged to improve it (as long as any changes are available to all licensees) and then free to sell it to customers.

Because it's open-source software, a worldwide community of Linux engineers continually updates the operating system, and users can add modules as they choose. The result is the operating system is constant being upgraded and bugs are quickly fixed.

This model is antithetical to commercial versions UNIX or NT. In these cases, customers have little say about over the operating system since the vendors believe they understand the operating system best — knowledge they charge customers for.

The engineer community transformed Linux from a student's technical toy into an operating system with increasing appeal. The software is now available as a shrink-wrapped packaged, and many have found it to be reliable, simple to install, and easy to maintain.

The timing for Torvalds' new operating system model was fortuitous. The Internet changed the way large companies view and purchase software and offered the infrastructure needed to make Linux so accessible — and ultimately popular. Using technology via the Web isn't considered as big a risk as it once was; freeware, once a no-no in corporate IT departments, has become part and parcel of many companies' operations.

A stronghold for Linux is the Internet Service Provider market, where the freeware Web server Apache has proven to be very popular. Momentum is growing among small to mid-sized businesses. The new operating system has been used for applications, such as airplane design, firewalls, telescope control, and World Wide Web servers. A handful of small companies have been building new businesses based on marketing of their iterations of Linux with Caldera Inc. and Red Hat Software Inc. having two of the more popular versions.

International Data Corp., a Framingham, Mass. market research firm, reported that in 1998 240,000 Linux servers were shipped and that represents 6.3 percent of the total market. Because users can download the operating for free, there may be as much as ten times as many persons now relying on Linux.

Because of the growing level of support, the operating system is starting to attract attention from third parties, including top DBMS suppliers. One reason is the new operating system promises to deliver on past UNIX promises of application portability, which failed as various UNIX initiatives splintered. Supporting multiple iterations of an operating system can be an expensive proposition for vendors. The Linux Standard Base (LSB) defines a common core, which ensures that compliant applications will run on all distributions of Linux. Gradually, he UNIX operating system variation that doesn't cost customers a dollar is suddenly gaining respect from big companies. In addition to DBMS vendors, IBM, Intel, and Netscape have promised or delivered products that run under Linux.

LINUX ADVANTAGES

Corporations turn to new technology for two reasons: lower costs or increased functionality. Linux has the potential to offer companies both of those benefits.

Cost savings start with the fact that the operating system basically is free—although companies will have to make a modest payment from a third party that will deliver items, such as documentation and technical support. In addition, the operating system runs on the Wintel architecture so the underlying hardware requires a minimal investment.

Other savings are linked to the operating system's functionality. Like IBM's OS/2 and SCO's UNIXWare, Linux is an operating system that advocates view as technically superior to Microsoft's Windows product line, which has not been as reliable, stable, or easy to implement as corporations desire. Since its is more reliable, Linux should require less maintenance. While the difference in support requirements will vary by company, they can be great: rather than spend two to four hours maintaining a single Windows 95 machine per week, technicians may need to work for only 15 minutes per Linux machine.

Linux's distribution model helps to insure that the operating system will only get better with timely updates. Engineers can simultaneously work on needed enhancements and the only the best entries make their way into the operating system.

The emerging operating system also helps vendors cut costs. They no longer have to support an expensive research and development staff because any interested engineer is able to submit an enhancement. While building a business on contribution from unseen engineers may seem risky, to date, they have delivered high quality work. Engineers have focused on areas where they have expertise and have been able to add a wide range of functions to Linux.

LINUX WEAKNESSES

While Linux has made a great deal of progress since its inception, the operating system still has a long way to go until it meets supporters' expectations. The primary issues now revolve around support. With traditional operating systems, users have a clear idea of which vendor to call when an operating system fails. With Linux, the issue is not as clear, since anyone can download the software. While the Linux community exists and a company can get support on the Internet, it is not the kind of guaranteed 24-hour-a-day response an enterprise customer needs.

In select cases, this will not be a major concern. Large corporations have sophisticated in-house staffs and may be willing to take on the support chores in-house.

But in most instances, corporations are looking to offload support to third parties rather than add or find work for their in-house staffs.

Third parties, such as Red Hat and Caldera, offer companies documentation and technical support for a nominal fee. Because Linux suppliers are small and have smaller than average research and development staffs, corporations may be leery of adopting the operating system: IT managers worry about on-going enhancements, and the legal department is concerned with who sue if the operating system fails.

Recently, established PC suppliers have started to assuage these fears. In January, IBM announced it would support Linux on its NetFinity servers alongside Microsoft's Windows NT. If more well known vendors follow the same course, Linux use may spread.

Another issue is long term developments for the operating system. Since, no single vendor is in charge, companies have no assurances that Linux will deliver on its write-once, run everywhere portability claims. Currently, Torvalds—who founded Transmeta Inc., a Santa Clara, California start-up working on its first product—determines which enhancements will be incorporated in the operating system. While it has worked to date, there are concerns that this approach will be viable if acceptance grows in the future.

Proponents promote the operating system as simple to use, but that is the case only to those already familiar with Linux. The operating system is much different than Windows NT and getting Linux up and running can be a challenge. There are many differences from Windows starting with the jargon (hard drives aren't "C:" or "D:;" they're "hda" or "hdb") to the operating system's underlying concepts (Red Hat Linux is based on packages, a particular way of delivering and installing software).

Manually setting up hardware in Linux can be as arcane as it was in the old days of Microsoft's MS-DOS. To install Linux, a company needs to create anywhere from one to nine hard drive partitions. Red Hat recommends new users read its 300-page manual before starting. Also, application installations present speed bumps.

As much as Linux supporters would like it to be, the general consensus is the operating system is not strong enough or mature enough for the enterprise. Scalability is an issue. The emerging operating system has not proven that it can it can support large complex applications on multi-processing machines.

To make inroads into broader markets, operating systems need attractive applications. While thousands of commercial products operate on Windows, only recently have a few established software vendors shown any interest in Linux. In addition to DBMS supplier interest, Corel ported its WordPerfect suite to Linux and Netscape is working on versions of its Communicator browser, messaging server and directory server to the new operating system. But support is still lacking from key players, such as enterprise application vendors like Baan, PeopleSoft, and SAP.

The same holds true with Linux hardware. While IBM has moved to offer hardware support, most PC vendors are still sitting on the sidelines. To get into the corporate mainstream, Linux needs to have a few leading PC hardware vendors step up to the plate and deliver products optimized for it.

Add-on components support is also an issue. Linux has only a fraction of the video, printer, sound card and network card support of Windows. The Red Hat setup offers some plug-and-play support, but it's spotty.

LINUX' IMPACT ON THE DBMS MARKET

Microsoft's shadow hovers over DBMS vendors. Through a series of product enhancements, the firm now offers a robust DBMS application server, its SQL Server. To increase its market share, the company has been bundling the product as part of its Back Office suite and increasing the level integration with other top selling products. The strategy has been working well so now the firm is vying to become the market's top supplier.

Competitors would like to differentiate their wares and Linux offers them that opportunity. While Microsoft has said little about any plans to support the operating system, it would be surprising if the company moved quickly to port SQL Server to that platform. Historically, the company has left non-Windows development work to partners. So, there is an opportunity for another supplier to emerge as the leading Linux DBMS vendor and many are moving into that space.

In March 1996, Software AG became the first major DBMS vendor to line up in support of Linux. The company tailored its ADABAS D to run on Caldera's Network Desktop, a version of Linux augmented with client and server Internet and network tools, backup utilities, and a Graphic User Interface shell.

Other vendors were slower to make their move. In the summer of 1998, Informix outlined plans to develop a version of the Informix Dynamic Server for Linux. The company made the change because its international user group listed Linux support as its No. 1 priority. In keeping with the Linux's roots, the company offered free user licenses, free technical support, and free e-mail support through a "Try and Buy" evaluation period. The Informix Dynamic Server, Linux Edition Suite is comprised of Informix Dynamic Server, Linux Edition; Informix Client Software Development Kit which offers customers a single package of several application programming interfaces, including Open Database Connectivity and Java Database Connectivity needed to develop applications for Informix servers; Informix-Connect, a runtime connectivity product; and an Apache integration document since approximately 75 percent of all Apache Web servers run on Linux.

In July, Oracle Corp. announced that it would port Oracle8 and Oracle Applications to Linux. The products will be available on Intel server platforms and Oracle positioned its wares as an alternative to those running on Windows NT. The database vendor said that in addition to being so easy to maintain, Linux will catch up to the functionality in commercial UNIX over the next few years.

InterBase Software Corp., a division of Inprise, started off offering a freeware version of its InterBase version 4.2 DBMS for Linux in May of 1998. In August, the company announced the availability of InterBase 5 for the operating system.

At the end of 1998, Computer Associates unveiled Ingres II Linux Edition. The DBMS features a complete copy of the Ingres II database engine along with core database functions, such as variable page size; row-level locking; support for binary large objects (BLOBs); interfaces for C; compatibility with IngPerl (database access from the Perl scripting language); and Internet publishing capabilities that allow for application development using the Apache Server. The Ingres II Linux Edition is also compatible with other versions of Ingres II so code written for the Ingres II Linux Edition will be fully portable to other platforms.

LINUX QUICKFACTS

Websites of some vendors selling Linux software is:

- Caldera: www.caldera.com
- MkLinux (Linux for Apple machines) www.mklinux.apple.com
- Red Hat Software: www.redhat.com
- SuSe: www.suse.com

Other general Linux related Websites are:

- General Linux Information: http://metalab.unc.edu/LDP/links.html
- Linux BBS Service: http://www.komm.hdk-berlin.de/~rasca/linux-bbs.html
- Linux Users Group: http://lugww.nllgg.nl/

Supported Hardware configurations: Intel 386SX/16 with 1 MB RAM and can scale to work with more than 1GB of RAM. The operating system has been ported to run on 386/486/Pentium machines with ISA, EISA, PCI and VLB busses; Motorola 68020 with an MMU, a 68030, 68040, or a 68060; Compaq Alpha CPUs; and Sun Microsystems Inc. SPARC stations. (**Note:** There is no difference between client and server configurations. Developers have tailored the operating system to work on a number of chips but the work is free, so there are not the speeds and feeds that come with commercial packages).

CONCLUSION

Linux is the latest in a long list of emerging technologies with the potential to loosen the vice-like grip Microsoft now holds on desktop computers. Proponents claim that the operating system's technical superiority, ease of distribution, and ongoing enhancements will lead to mass market acceptance.

In addition, many network and systems administrators do not like monopolies, which Windows NT is threatening to become. With the IBM's OS/2 no longer a major player on the market and Apple Computer Inc. sputtering during the past few years, they see a need for another alternative to Microsoft's products.

However, the freeware operating system is far behind the market leader: Linux has at most 5 million users worldwide while companies and consumers have purchased more 200 million copies of Windows.

History has not been kind to those that have tried to battle with the Goliath. After severing its relationship with Microsoft, IBM tried to win the desktop with OS/2, Novell attempted to defeat Windows with UNIXWare, and Netscape tried to bypass the operating system and make the browser the focus of application development. Each of these initiatives failed.

Linux supporters understand the challenge: Microsoft may be the 20th century's greatest marketing firm and will not surrender any of its business without a fight. To fulfill its grandiose potential, Linux will need to gain corporate and consumer acceptance during the next two years. To date, the emerging operating system has garnered only niche acceptance. While techies have been promoting it, most IT managers still have yet to fully bless it. Many corporate cultures dictates that companies choose big, viable system vendors for IT solutions and that isn't likely to change soon with uncertainties around the year 2000 problem and global market fluctuations.

In addition, there is also the feeling that the Linux supporters are bonded more by an aversion to Microsoft than the operating system's benefits. The key backers have been companies with antipathy for Microsoft: Netscape, Oracle, and IBM.

Rather than dethrone Windows, a more realistic scenario has Linux overtaking SCO's OpenServer or UNIXWare 7 as the leading UNIX operating system on Intel platforms. The emerging operating system could make a push into data centers and battle with IBM's AIX, HP's HP-UX, and Sun's Solaris.

Because of its progress and potential, Linux should be a technology that companies monitor and maybe trial for select applications. Once Linux has equal market share to what Apple Macintosh enjoys at the desktop market, then the talk about it overtaking Windows may be justified. For now, the operating system is an interesting product that IT managers should track rather than rush out and deploy.

Chapter 76
Open Source Model of Software Development

Srinivas Padmanabharao

OVER THE COURSE OF THE PAST FIVE YEARS THE PHENOMENAL RISE OF LINUX, a UNIX-based operating system, has brought into sharp focus the entire model of software development as we know it. A look at the history of the development of this amazing piece of software (and the many applications that have now been written for it) shows the utter lack of respect for any known development model. At no time, after Linus Torvalds gave away the initial version of the kernel free, was any one person/organization responsible for its design, development and testing. In a collaborative effort, that would have been the envy of every organizational consultant, this team of self-motivated "hackers" has delivered a near bug-free piece of code that is today rivaling the mighty Microsoft. And, if you didn't already know — it's available for free. This paper is an attempt to understand the methodology that has emerged from this exercise and assess its feasibility as a model for future software projects.

WHAT IS *OPEN SOURCE*?

The label *Open Source* was contributed by Chris Peterson of the Foresight Institute, in February 1998, during a strategy session held in reaction to Netscape's announcement that it was giving away its browser free. While a more complete definition of what constitutes *Open Source* can be found elsewhere,[1] in essence it stands for software that is available without charge in binary and source code formats to all who wish to possess it. In addition you are free to enhance, debug, modify or make changes as you wish as long as all your changes are also subject to the same terms as the initial software.

The label *Open Source* is not the same as freeware, shareware and the other terms usually used in referring to software available on the Internet without charge. A comparison of these various terms can be found in the, now infamous, "Halloween memo,"[2] by Vinod Vallopil of Microsoft. Software complying with the guidelines of the CopyLeft or General Public License (GPL) classifies for use under the *Open Source* label. There are other licensing agreements such as the Artistic License, Mozilla Public License (MPL) and BSD style licensing which vary in the restrictions they impose on re-use and profit-making from the use of the original source code.

ALTERNATIVE MODELS OF DEVELOPMENT

In a paper[3] first released in April 1997, Eric Raymond coined the term "Cathedral" and "Bazaar" to refer to the traditional and open source models of development. In describing his own experiences, trying to duplicate Linus Torvalds' model, during the development of a "fetchmail" utility, Eric derived rules which could be exploited in future projects.

The Traditional Model

The "Cathedral" model of software development refers to the entire class of traditional software development models. Under this model, a single person/team of persons, usually belonging to the same organization, working under the guidance of a project manager would be responsible for the entire development lifecycle of design, develop, test, fix-bugs and repeating this cycle as often as necessary. The team would receive (hopefully) a clear definition of the requirements of its customers and would then rely on the skill and brilliance of the team members to implement the solution. As is often the case, time and resources are both in short supply. In addition the developers of the piece of code are rarely the end-users of software. Anybody who has been on such development teams will have a lot to say for the morale of the developers and way such projects are managed. The result is usually software that is unreliable, buggy and most importantly does not do all that its customers want it to do.

The *Open Source* Model

The "Bazaar" model of software development stands the above model of development on its head. Its central idea is that anyone who uses a piece of software is best suited to playing a key role in its development. The old adage "Stay close to your customer" is what this model of development revolves around. The development in this model starts when somebody in the wide world solves an immediate problem he is facing and decides to share the solution with the rest of the world. At this stage he can't be concerned if anybody else in the world is interested in his work. (I wonder what all the marketing folks would think of this approach!). Somebody else who faces the same or similar problem finds this work and modifies and enhances it for his own personal use. And the cycle continues.

Since each user of the software is also usually a developer, the quality of code is constantly enhanced through usage (much better than writing test cases) and additional features are constantly being added as each user works to solve his own particular problem. This cycle can continue forever without ever producing the kind of results it has but for another key element in the scheme of things — a central leader. He, while not necessarily always the first person to start this cycle and not necessarily the one with all the bright ideas and great programming skills, is the person who recognizes the best of the many ideas amongst his peers. He takes a best-of-breed approach, throwing out old ideas/designs for new ones and constantly motivates his users (who are also his co-developers). If at any point during the cycle this leader finds his interest/ability waning he finds another competent champion and hands it off to him (if he doesn't, the most democratic of media — the internet, will ensure the same) thus keeping the cycle going.

Critical Success Factors

The critical success factors in an *Open Source* endeavor will be:

- An idea that solves, or promises to solve, some problem for its users.
- The ability to attract and retain, competent people to help in the endeavor.
- The capacity to communicate with vast audiences rapidly (i.e., the Internet).
- The presence of a central figure, who motivates and leads the development exercise.

THE ADVANTAGES OF *OPEN SOURCE*

Was Linux a one-off success? Was Netscape's decision to give away its browser free a mistake? What promise does the *Open Source* model hold for future projects and especially in delivering software for mission-critical applications in large business houses? In this section we will examine how the *Open Source* model can consistently deliver high-quality software at a lower cost than has ever been possible.

Reliability

Since the 1960s, when the software industry as we know it began, reliability of software products has always been a thorn in the flesh of developers and users alike. A sampling of many of the popular products today will convince even the most skeptical person that the software industry has a long way to go in this regard.

The *Open Source* model revolves around the development of software that is at all times subject to the highest quality of review, testing and debugging because your peers/users/co-developers are the people involved in the exercise. The fact that all these people are working for free (in monetary terms) and still have the commitment to deliver quality on their piece of work is an idea that is radical to most businessmen. The idea that if you are the user of something you are building you will do a good job, somehow seems to have been missed in the past models.

An often-quoted example in support of this idea is the Internet. Much of the infrastructure behind today's Internet is the result of a model of development where the developers were driven by motivations other than money. If these tools were to disappear today the results could be catastrophic.[4] The fact that there may be hundreds of people using and testing your software, each in his own special way, will on an average guarantee that most bugs will be ironed out. And those that dont't get ironed out, are possibly bugs in features of your software that nobody uses anyway.

Higher Speed of Development

The *Open Source* model is capable of mustering resources of the highest quality in the shortest possible time. The key driver however, is the ability of the initiator to garner the interest of his peers and keep their motivation going.

Since there are many developers involved in the effort the situation can be likened to a massively parallel computing machine each doing its part in helping improve the overall quality of the software. History shows that the first mover has a distinct advantage over his rivals. It is no different here. The person who first begins a project in any particular niche will stand the greatest chance of attracting the best people. In addition the fact that most of these developers work from their homes, at their own leisure/time and do so for no obviously tangible monetary benefit greatly reduces the overhead costs of the project. For small software shops trying to grow big this is a great boon.[5]

Giving Customers What They Want

The *Open Source* model keeps the users of the software at the center of the development process, thus constantly gaining feedback from them. "Release early. Release often. And listen to your customers."[3]

The voluntary involvement of users spread over the entire globe combined with their access to the source code makes it possible for the release-feedback cycle to be completed much faster than previously thought possible. In fact Linus Torvalds was releasing versions of Linux at a rate of more than one a day during the initial phases.

Exhibit 76.1. Costs of software product

Software Product	Price (US $)
Windows 98	177.95/ 89.95*
Office 97	444.45/ 181.45*
BackOffice Server for Windows NT	2243.00
Linux	49.95

* Cost of upgrades

Source: http://www.beyond.com for Microsoft products.

The access to the source code also means that customers can choose which version of the software they want to use. Since there is usually one version labeled 'stable' and many subsequent versions which are undergoing changes/testing one can choose what is appropriate to him depending on the need to be at the cutting edge of technology. Also such a model of development is far more capable of quickly incorporating new technological advances and providing customers the best tools to use in their businesses.

The Cost Factor

The General Public License mandates that all software subject to this agreement must give away both the binary and source codes for no charge—that's right *for free*. Exhibit 76.1 compares the cost of Linux with other commonly used software products.

The results are obvious — *near-free software costs less*. Add to this the cost of support, of tracking the versions you presently have, making sure you have the appropriate licenses and the legal costs if you are caught without one — it sure adds up to a neat sum. And if you forgot — all this for software that is essentially unreliable.

DON'T SELL OFF YOUR TECHNOLOGY STOCKS — JUST YET

If you have been frightened by everything that you have read thus far and are considering calling your broker to sell off the Microsoft's, the SAP's, etc., you hold — stop. Even in this era when everything seems to change faster than you can utter "*change*" the *Open Source* model will take its time to establish itself as the preferred model of software development. While the success of companies such as Red Hat demonstrates the possibility of success in the *Open Source* model it still remains to be seen how the near future shapes up. In any case, the fact that you are giving away your most prized asset — the intellectual capital invested in developing the software code — for free means that businesses will need to develop alternative business models to take advantage of this model of development. Frank

Hecker of Netscape in his paper[6] "Setting-up-shop" discusses alternative business models for *Open Source* based organizations.

A key decision that any company that decides to pursue the open source strategy must make is the kind of licensing under which it will release the source code. The GPL which the most liberal of the many licenses mandates that any part of code released under this license is also under GPL i.e., you cannot take any part of this code and build your own proprietary software. Also any other product you release that uses this code must also be under GPL. The Artistic License allows users to create proprietary programs using the original source code as long as the work is embedded "invisibly" into the proprietary programs. It also allows input and output data from such a program to be used in creation of proprietary programs. The Mozilla Public License under which Netscape released its browser allows the integration of the basic source code with proprietary programs through defined *Open Source* APIs. The distinction is made at the source code level. A developer has the freedom to write code, that need not be released, which interfaces with the original source code through publicly available APIs.

However that still does not address the task of converting the code to revenue. Some of the models are:

- *Support sellers:* Companies like Red Hat Software, Caldera Software who sell the media, documentation and technical support for *Open Source* software like Linux
- *Loss leader:* Companies like Netscape which give away the source free to gain a set of customers who can then be sold other services/products for profit.
- *Widget frosting:* Companies such as Corel Computer that use the *Open Source* model to develop interfaces and drivers for its hardware. Revenue is usually generated from hardware sales.
- *Accessorizing:* Companies such as O'Reilly & Associates that publish books on *Open Source* software like Linux.
- *Sell it, free it:* Companies can release certain portions of their software under a BSD-style licensing and can incorporate the enhancements from the developer community into its other proprietary products whose licensing fees can reflect the cost of developing the original software. The challenge in this model will be the ability of the originator to enthuse developers to contribute to the enhancement of the source base. Developers must not get the impression that they are being taken for a free ride. A free license to the contributors is a possible option.
- *Brand-licensing:* Companies can give away the source code free but retain the rights to the brand, logos and other trademarks which they can license to others for a fee.

GETTING STARTED

The amazing ease of setting up a Linux system can be surprising. On the hardware side anything greater than a 386-based machine with 8 MB RAM will suffice for version 2.x of Linux. The binaries and source code for the Linux along with the installation instructions can be downloaded from the internet for free from web sites[7] or to further ease the process of installation and setup one can purchase a commercial Linux distribution from vendors such as Red Hat (U.S. $49.95). These distributions come complete with all the utilities required for configuring a fully functional system such as hardware drivers, TCP/IP support, a whole host of tools for development and documentation. The development of the source code for the Linux kernel is coordinated by Linus Torvalds and there are many newsgroups on the internet for those who wish to post queries or join the discussion.

Any company that wishes to pursue the open source route can do the following:

1. Set up a website and provide an option for users to download the source code.
2. Designate a single point of contact who is responsible for maintaining the "official" version of the source code and whom users can contact to submit their patches, enhancements etc.
3. Setup a discussion group and actively encourage and foster discussion amongst the user community.
4. Keep users informed at all times of any changes, enhancements, proposed developments, etc.
5. Share the latest versions of code through the Web site.

The apparent ease of starting an open source endeavor can be deceptive. It takes commitment and an ability to inspire others to join in the effort that would ultimately determine the success of such an endeavor.

CONCLUSION

The *Open Source* model is here to stay. It offers certain undeniable advantages that are absent in the traditional models of software development. While the success of Linux and the increasing support it is gaining in the business community is an indication of the potency of the *Open Source* model, it remains to be seen how the giants of today react to this very definite threat. It is clear that the alternative models hold the promise of a new structure emerging in the software industry. I believe that generic applications such as operating systems, word-processors, accounting packages, etc., will all eventually go *Open Source* and be available for free to its users. Most of the revenues in the software industry will come from the ability of software companies to develop vertical industry/company specific customizations of freely available software source code. As we move into the new millenium the success of Linux has shown that there is an alternative to the traditional models of software development. It remains to be seen whether this would become the defining model of development in the next century. I believe it stands a good chance.

ACKNOWLEDGMENTS

The author is thankful to all the pioneers of the *Open Source* concept whose work has been a source of inspiration and knowledge. My friends Sanjay Verma and Shashi Shekar have been invaluable allies in this endeavor.

References

1. http://www.opensource.org/osd.html
2. http://www.opensource.org/halloween1.html
3. http://www.tuxedo.org/~esr/writings/cathedral-bazaar
4. http://www.netaction.org/articles/freesoft.html
5. http://www.zope.org/Information/BusinessDecision
6. http://people.netscape.com/hecker/setting-up-shop.html
7. ftp://sunsite.unc.edu/pub/linux/distributions/slackware or http://www.debian.org

Chapter 77

Linux and the Web

Srinivas Padmanabharao

A REAL THREAT TO MICROSOFT'S DOMINANCE OF THE DESKTOP OPERAT-
ING SYSTEM WORKSPACE could come from the creation of a Finnish student
Linus Torvalds in the form of a freely available operating system — Linux.
Linux was originally developed by Linus and then enhanced, debugged,
and completely rewritten by thousands of programmers around the world
and today poses a credible threat to the domination of Microsoft. While
Linux is still a few years away from appearing on every desktop around the
world, its use as a server operating system has shown remarkable increase
over the past year. International Data Corporation (IDC) estimates that
shipments of Linux for use on servers rose by about 212 percent in 1998
capturing about 17.2 percent of the market compared to Windows NT's
35.8 percent. This paper presents a look at the world of Linux.

LINUX — THE OPERATING SYSTEM

Linux is a UNIX-clone operating system. It is a freely available implementation of the published POSIX standards and does not use any of the UNIX
source code. Linux traces its roots to another free operating system for the
x86 architecture called Minix developed by Andy Tanenbaum. Linus Torvalds, inspired by the desire to create a better Minix, took this code-base,
modified the kernel, added a driver for keyboard and screens and released
it as Linux under the General Public License (GPL) in 1991. Since then thousands of users have contributed to and enhanced the basic Linux kernel
and code. The latest stable version of Linux is 2.2. IBM and HP among others have announced that they will begin shipping & supporting Linux with
their machines.

In essence Linux is just a kernel and needs to be packaged with lots of
applications, drivers and tools to make it into a complete usable operating
system. However 'Linux' is commonly used to refer to the kernel along with
all other pieces of software that are needed to make the kernel useful.

Obtaining Linux

The two most common ways of obtaining Linux are:

- *By FTP over the Internet:*   Linux is usable under the General Public License. It means that Linux is available, free of charge, in both binary and source code forms and may be used without the need for any agreements, etc., by as many users as your system will support. There are many mirror sites over the internet from where one can download Linux[1] and choosing the site nearest to you is usually better. First time users are better off downloading a 'stable' version of the system and a version x.y.z where y is an even number (including zero) is a stable version.
- *Through a commercial distribution:*   Though Linux is itself free one is allowed to charge a fee for packaging it into an easy to install product usually referred to as a 'distribution.' Such 'distributions' come with all the other associated software needed to make it useful like desktop interfaces, network management tools etc., and documentation. They are made available via a CD-ROM. Examples of such companies are Red Hat (Version 5.1 costs U.S. $49.95), Caldera and Slackware. It must be remembered, however that all software found on the CD-ROM can also be obtained free over the internet and might be a worthwhile exercise to go through, for the adventurous types.

Hardware Requirements

If you bought your PC anytime during the last five years you probably already have a machine that is ready for Linux. (If you haven't, then it is probably time you called the nearest museum to inform them that you have an antique relic in your possession). While Linux was initially written for the PC, versions are available for other 'bigger' machines. IBM is porting Linux to its RS6000 machines if you needed proof of its growing popularity.

Linux supports Intel processors 386 and higher along with their clones. It also supports many DEC Alphas, Sun SPARC's and Power PC's to varying extents. On the memory side, Linux will function reasonably on anything greater than 8MB of RAM. However if you are using the X-windowing system and plan to use a lot of programs then a single user system will perform satisfactorily with 32 MB. You might want to consider adding more memory, around 8 to 16 MB per additional user of the system. Linux can support up to 1 GB of RAM. The falling price of storage makes it affordable and sensible to have at least about 4 GB of hard disk space, though the base Linux kernel can be installed in less than 15 MB.

Drivers for most types of peripherals like a mouse and sound card, video card, network card, and modems can be found. Most distribution vendors maintain a more complete and updated list of supported hardware. If you do not find a driver for your, very special, piece of hardware you are welcome to write one and contribute to the Linux effort.

Installing Linux

Linux has come a long way from the days when it was a "hacker's" operating system. If you are installing Linux off a commercial distribution then you will also usually get installation support for the price you paid. Documentation is also available along with the distribution. If you are installing Linux off the downloaded code from the net, then you can also get a guide on installation from the same site. Linux HOWTO documentation is a good source.[2] Instead of going into the gory details of a screen by screen description (OK, I mean a command by command description) I will emphasize on the need for planning for the installation. Answer at least the following questions satisfactorily before jumping ahead:

1. *What are hardware specifications on my machine?* Get all details of the hardware on your system. This will let you install the needed drivers and prevent many a headache later on.
2. *What is this system going to be used for?* If you are installing it on your machine at home and intend to use it for your personal pursuits then you might want to make sure you also install the Xfree86 to provide a graphical user interface. If you intend to use it as a Web server ensure that you have enough space to hold the Web-server software (like Apache), space for all the Web pages you will host and any HTML editors you wish to use.
3. *Do I want to use two operating systems?* It is not unlikely, especially if the system is at home, that you will want to retain the other operating system that is already present like MS-DOS or some flavor of the Windows family. In that case you might want to provide yourself with the option of a 'prompt' i.e., Linux will ask you which system you wish to use at bootup time. Of course, you can access your other files from the Linux environment by mounting it appropriately.

Some Features of Linux

If you went through the installation ordeal successfully, rest assured you have become the owner of a system that runs one of the best operating systems available. Here are a few of the features of the operating system that you now have:

- *Multi-tasking and multi-user:* Like any UNIX system Linux supports many users, each running many programs simultaneously. Linux also supports "virtual consoles" — this feature allows you to have multiple sessions and login as two users simultaneously (use ALT-F1 to switch between sessions). Use the feature judiciously — determining your current status can get pretty confusing, which is why you have commands like *whoami*.
- *Multi-threading:* Linux has native kernel support for multiple independent threads of control within a single process memory space. It runs in

protected mode on the 386, implementing memory protection between processes, so that one program can't bring the whole system down.

- *Memory management:* Linux demand loads executables i.e., it reads only those parts of a program that are actually used. Linux increases speed by using shared copy-on-write pages among executables. This means that multiple processes can use the same memory for execution. When one tries to write to that memory, that page is copied some where else. Linux uses a unified memory pool for user programs and disk cache, so that all free memory can be used for caching, and the cache can be reduced when running large programs.
- *Multiple file systems:* Linux supports several common filesystems, including minix, Xenix, and all the common system V filesystems, and has an advanced filesystem of its own, which offers filesystems of up to 4 TB, and names up to 255 characters long. It provides transparent access to MS-DOS partitions (or OS/2 FAT partitions) via a special filesystem. VFAT (WindowsNT, Windows 95) support and FAT-32 is available in Linux 2.0. A special filesystem called UMSDOS is also available which allows Linux to be installed on a DOS filesystem. Linux supports a CD-ROM filesystem which reads all standard formats of CD-ROMs.
- *Compatibility:* Linux is compatible with UNIX and most applications that have been written for UNIX can be recompiled to run on Linux with little or no modification. Linux is highly interoperable and can co-exist in a diverse environment with Netware and Windows NT.
- *Networking support:* Linux supports TCP/IP networking, including ftp, telnet, etc., that makes it ideal for use on a web server.

A comparison of Linux with most of today's popular operating systems can be found,[3] which can be used to compare the performance of Linux with other operating systems.

LINUX APPLICATIONS

An operating system by itself provides very limited functionality for end-use. It is the applications like databases, word-processors, and development tools that determine the ultimate success of any operating system. It is in this respect that Linux has had an amazing success story. Since the Linux source code has been freely available, it has provided developers around the world with the freedom to develop applications for this operating system without the need for acquiring expensive licences from any vendor. This freedom has led to the development and free availability of a wide variety of software applications such as:

- Development tools including compilers, assemblers and debuggers
- Text editors and word processing software
- A whole host of internet applications like usenet news readers, and e-mail agents

- World Wide Web development tools, web servers and browsers
- Graphics creation and manipulation tools
- Databases

A complete list of all applications that are available is maintained under the Linux Software Map (LSM).[4] The Linux Documentation project[5] is an excellent source of documentation for all Linux related material including applications for Linux.

ENABLING E-COMMERCE

In the Internet crazy times we are presently in, one of the key objectives of any company is to prepare itself for E-commerce. Today, companies are moving beyond the realm of providing static information on their Web sites and actively enhancing their Websites to provide opportunities for interaction with the customer. In this context the key enabling technologies that a company must consider are:

- A database to store information.
- A web server software to present a front end to the world.
- A tool to connect between the two and provide a mechanism for actively updating the database with customer details or provide customer requested information.

Keeping with the spirit of *free*dom in Linux, we will review the Apache Web server which runs on over half the servers on the internet, a database called PostgreSQL and an inter-connection tool called PHP.

PostgreSQL

PostgreSQL originates from a research project in Prof. Michael Stonebraker's group at Berkeley. It is a high-performance, Robust Object Relational DBMS. It provides a full-featured API for development of client/ server or n-tier applications. Also via PHP/FI it can be easily integrated with any Web site as a high performance back end. PostgreSQL is freely available under the GNU public license and a copy of the PostgreSQL database can be obtained from its Web site (http://www.postgresql.com).

Key features:

- Web/Apache interface
- Graphical interface
- APIs - C, C++, TLC, Perl, Python and Java
- ODBC
- JDBC
- Online backup
- Regression testing package included to ensure reliability

PHP

PHP is a server-side, cross-platform, HTML-embedded scripting language. Rasmus Lerdorf conceived PHP sometime in the fall of 1994. It was initially known as Personal Home Page Tools. PHP Version 3.0 is an HTML-embedded scripting language. Much of its syntax is borrowed from C, Java and Perl with a couple of unique PHP-specific features thrown in. The goal of the language is to allow Web developers to write dynamically generated pages quickly. PHP can be obtained free of charge from its Web site (http://www.php.net).

Key features:

- HTTP authentication: The HTTP authentication is available only when PHP is running as a module in the Apache server
- GIF creation
- File upload support
- HTTP cookie support
- Database support: This is probably the most powerful feature of PHP with its ability to connect to both commercial databases like Oracle and Informix and free databases like PostgreSQL
- Regular expressions for complex string manipulation
- Error handling
- Connection handling
- PHP source viewer

Apache Web Server

One of the key pieces of software that is needed on a Web server is the HyperText Transfer Protocol (HTTP) server. When an end-user enters a URL in order to view the Web site at the server end it is this HTTP server that processes his request and sends the required information back for formatting and displaying by the browser. One can download Apache free of charge from its Web site (http://www.apache.org).

Key features:

- A powerful, flexible, HTTP/1.1 compliant Web server
- Implements the latest protocols, including HTTP/1.1 (RFC2068)
- Is highly configurable and extensible with third-party modules
- Can be customized by writing 'modules' using the Apache module API
- Provides full source code and comes with an unrestrictive license
- Runs on most versions of UNIX without modification
- DBM databases for authentication: It allows you to easily set up password-protected pages with enormous numbers of authorized users, without bogging down the server.
- Customized responses to errors and problems
- Allows multiple DirectoryIndex directives

- Unlimited numbers of Alias and Redirect directives
- Content negotiation
- Multi-home servers facility which allows the server to distinguish between requests made to different IP addresses (mapped to the same machine).

CONCLUSION

The world of Linux and its applications offer great promise to developers and IT managers alike. Following the open source model of development, a number of diverse and reliable applications have been written which are available free of cost. Picking and choosing between them can enable an IT manager of today to enable his company's presence on the internet in an easy, quick and cost efficient manner. These offer even greater promise to those small businesses, who are cash strapped.

Acknowledgments

I am also thankful to all supporters of the *Open Source* concept and who are involved in developing such wonderful applications. My friend Sanjay Verma has been very helpful in this endeavor.

References

1. ftp://sunsite.unc.edu/pub/linux
2. http://metalab.unc.edu/LDP/HOWTO/Installation-HOWTO.html
3. http://www.falconweb.com/~linuxrx/WS_Linux/OS_comparison.html
4. http://www.execpc.com/lsm/
5. http://metalab.unc.edu/LDP/

Chapter 78

Linux: Alternative Directions in Computing

Michael Simonyi

What is Linux anyway? To make a long story short, Linux is a derivative UNIX-type Operating System that was developed by Linus Trovalds during the early 1990s. The Operating System is based on similar design patterns of the UNIX operating kernel. The Operating System is compact and efficient in its design. In fact, since it is an open source Operating System it has been criticized and scrutinized by scores of computer experts and systems professionals from all over the world. The high regard for quality, functionality, and robustness has led to a well defined, tested and implemented Operating System that is able to drive server applications in today's computing environment and paves the way to drive tomorrows enterprise server applications. Apart from server side uses the prospect of an end user computing platform looms on the horizon with the advent of commercial desktop suites being developed for the platform.

REQUIREMENTS

Most IT managers are worried about keeping their shops up and running at all times. Increasingly it is becoming more and more difficult to strike a balance between operational maintenance and complexity. Just a few short years ago, when Microsoft released the first version of its popular Windows NT Operating System, it was simple and easy to use, but lacked the wealth of applications to introduce it into the majority of computing environments. Today it is a serious contender for replacing some legacy systems. However, the cost and complexity associated with its adoption have caused some IT managers to rethink its deployment in the computing environment.

Linux is at the crossroads where Windows NT was when it was introduced. However, now the biggest players in commercial computing are porting and introducing product lines to support this new platform and propel it into the realm of enterprise computing. With vendors such as IBM, Lotus, Oracle, SUN, Sybase and others throwing their weight behind the promise of this new operating system new opportunities will evolve to allow IT managers to restructure their environments. To be able to implement new solutions or migrate existing systems using common tools that were previously only available on commercially available platforms, the IT community will be able to reduce costs in adopting the new platform to solving business problems.

THE PAYOFFS

The momentum of the industry behind Linux will give corporate IT managers the leverage to construct bullet proof systems that don't necessarily require the constant upgrade and investment in new hardware and software just to keep pace with new product features and have the ability to implement them. But not only for the corporate market, the smaller commercial market can also tap into this new spring to maintain and stabilize costs in running an operation. Recurring development and operations maintenance does not have to undergo a continual overhaul of the environment to make things work. The low cost of acquisition for Linux makes it a very attractive alternative to other options for all levels of business computing environments.

Although the initial cost of acquisition is low, one must evaluate the time and training requirements for its adoption also. Yes, the operating system is simple to use, if you are evaluating it for commercial development adequate training and experience with the platform must be cultivated. The perceived notion that Linux is a hobbyists platform or techies paradise has some merit, it's openness does provide the capability to tap the entire operating system for ones development efforts. This opportunity can alleviate a great deal of complex development and debugging effort as applications can be constructed and monitored to track its interaction with the operating system at the code level. This alone can give a development community greater control over its applications and remove the limitations of operating system dependencies.

The ease of Linux installation and product navigation is also a bonus factor in its adoption in the computing industry as well as end user communities. Commercial versions of the operating system were modeled with the concepts of rapid, simple and intuitive installation processes. Commercial product such as that provided by Red Hat and others are designed in a modular fashion so that even the novice can navigate the installation process without fear of being overwhelmed. The modular installation mechanics allow the user to select bundled application software easily in an effort to bring a system up with minimal knowledge.

YOU ARE NOT ALONE

If you are concerned with the lack of support available in the industry or commercially, rest assured that the big players are ramping up to become support centers to provide every means of support available to make the success of Linux a reality. IBM, HP, and Sun have all committed to provide the corporate customer with a means of support for endeavors on this platform. Investments in the existing software houses that offer Linux support have also been growing. Usenet groups, universities and graduates with skills in Linux are plentiful and becoming more so every day. In fact the openness of the Operating System (OS) has allowed exceptionally skilled IT developers to excel in creating applications for the platform. The ability to understand how the OS works and reacts with applications is extremely beneficial to the development process.

The breath of supported hardware and driver availability is also quite remarkable. A vast majority of hardware platforms are supported from Intel, Sparc, Alpha, and MIPS platforms. This provides the ability to scale between hardware manufacturers is an excellent means to right size a system for ones particular needs. As more hardware manufacturers embrace the Linux Operating System, companies such as HP and IBM are porting Linux to run on the PA-Risc, Merced, and Power PC chip sets. There even exists the capability to support the Operating System on top of older hardware systems that have long been obsoleted by the so-called new generation of Operating Systems. Exotic hardware drivers are also available, and if not available for your specific flavor of hardware they can be developed rapidly internally or externally by querying the user community or outsourcing its development.

Although the platform is still in its early stages, it is showing a great deal of potential for becoming a serious contender in the entry level and midrange server market. As a proliferation of new server and desktop application suites from commercial software vendors become available the question of its enterprise capability are becoming a reality. Linux on the desktop is only a stone's throw away from deployment. The cost effectiveness of the operating system and licensing will make the platform a very desirable alternative in the face of more expensive commercial computing platforms.

THE PRACTICAL AND COST EFFECTIVE USE OF LINUX

The Linux Operating System has many practical and cost-effective uses. Since Linux does not impose extraneous requirements on hardware, it is quite practical to use an older Intel 486 machine to perform relatively simple tasks. By using cast-off hardware it is possible to allow your IT staff to test drive the OS and thereby gain confidence and experience in the OS without imposing strain on the operating budget.

LINUX FUNDAMENTALS

The Linux Operating System was designed with the intention to keep things simple. Linux has applied what most IT professionals learn early on in their careers, the KISS principle. The kernel is compact, very well designed and does not require a hardware upgrade with each new generation of the OS.

Some of the practical uses for Linux are as a Network Domain Name Server (DNS), Mail Server, Firewall, Packet Router, File/Print Server, Application Server, or Web Server. Each of these applications can be introduced into a computing environment with a minimal amount of cost and effort. Although, setting up a Firewall or Packet Filter Router would be fairly complex and on par with most other products available commercially due to the nature of their application.

Setting up any of these applications under Red Hat is as simple as selecting an option from the package installation screen. Most of these types of applications use can actually be accomplished within one half-hour of an installation process. To begin the discovery phase in your environment you may want to setup a secondary DNS Server. This is a relatively simple use of Linux and will allow your IT staff to get use to the platform. Setting up a mail server would be another practical use of Linux. In fact this is one of Linux's more practical applications and is in wide spread use by ISPs around the globe.

The use of Linux as a Firewall or even as a packet filter router is perhaps a more complex use of the product. However, a very sophisticated Firewall can be constructed for proxying with ipfwadm or FWTK. With the 2.0 release kernel it is possible to configure the system to boot and automatically halt prior to loading the userspace. With no available userspace to crack it is virtually impossible to penetrate.

File and Print services under the Linux Operating Systems are very easy to configure and Print Server software such as HP's Jet Admin is available under Linux as well. By using Samba, one can configure a Linux server to participate as either a Windows NT Domain controller, Backup Domain controller, or standalone member server. The offerings at this level are only limited by the lack of a GUI for administration. Over time this too will be remedied. The Samba configuration options are similar to those that were offered By Microsoft Lan Manager and IBM Lan Server under the OS/2 environment and which can be found in the registry of NT Server today. With the introduction of Windows 2000 around the corner, Samba will continue to provide the functionality to participate with Windows based Networks.

Perhaps the "piece de resistance" is the ability to construct a fully functional and scaleable Web Server. The ability to setup and install Linux with the Apache Web Server under relative ease and minimal cost allows even a small business entity to setup their own intranet or internet presence. The available tools sets that can be used to create interactive sites of serious complexity are available by using Sun Microsystems Java language tools. By using common universal tool sets such as Java and JDB interface one can build front end systems that can interface with backend databases to extend the reach of your sales force, products or whatever you need to do. The remainder of this article provides a walk through of building a sample Web Server using Apache and the Linux Operating System using the Red Hat distribution of Linux version 5.2. If you wish to obtain a copy of Red Hat you can point your Web browser to www.redhat.com and download the installation, order it, or if you want you can even install it via ftp from the Red Hat site.

BUILDING A WEB SERVER USING RED HAT LINUX WITH APACHE

The preparation for the server will require the installation of Red Hat Linux and will require approximately seven steps to complete. From start to finish the entire process outlined below will take approximately one half-hour to an hour depending upon the speed of your machine. It is recommended that you get a valid IP address from your Network Administrator that you can use while testing this installation procedure.

You will need a valid IP address: in this exercise we will use 200.200.200.xxx. You will need a valid domain name, in this exercise we will use yourdomain, please substitute this name with your own.

RED HAT LINUX SOFTWARE INSTALLATION OVERVIEW

Creation of Boot Diskettes

If diskettes are not available, they can be created by using the RAW-RITE.EXE program in the \DOSUTILS folder on the Linux CD.

To make a diskette under MS-DOS, use the rawrite utility included on the Red Hat Linux CD in the dosutils directory. First, label a blank, formatted 3.5-inch diskette appropriately (e.g., "Boot Diskette," "Supplemental Diskette," etc). Insert it into the diskette drive. Then, use the following commands (assuming your CD is drive d:):

```
C:\> d:
D:\> cd \dosutils
D:\dosutils> rawrite
```

Enter disk image source file name: d:\images\boot.img
Enter target diskette drive: a:
Please insert a formatted diskette into drive a: and
press –ENTER– [Enter]

```
D:\dosutils>
```

Rawrite first asks you for the filename of a diskette image; enter the directory and name of the image you wish to write (for example, . . \images\ boot.img). Then rawrite asks for a diskette drive to write the image to; enter a:. Finally, rawrite asks for confirmation that a formatted diskette is in the drive you've selected. After pressing [Enter] to confirm, rawrite copies the image file onto the diskette. If you need to make another diskette, label another diskette, and run rawrite again, specifying the appropriate image file.

Initial Operating System Boot Up

1. Insert the Red Hat Linux 5.2 boot disk into the floppy drive.
2. Power on the machine.
3. Insert the Red Hat Linux 5.2 CD-ROM into the CD-ROM drive as the systems boots up.
4. After a short delay, a screen containing the boot: prompt should appear.
5. Press [Enter] to boot.

Interactive Operating System Installation Process

1. The welcome screen appears. Press [**ENTER**] to continue.
2. Select **English** as the language and continue.
3. Select **US** as the keyboard type and continue.
4. Select **Local CD-ROM** as the installation method and continue.
5. When asked whether to install or upgrade, select **install** and continue.
6. You will be prompted to specify an installation class. Select **custom** and continue.
7. You will be asked if you have any SCSI adapters. Select **no** and continue.
8. In the disk setup window select **Disk Druid** and continue.
9. You will be presented with a GUI screen allowing you to create file system partitions. There should be no existing partitions on this system (Note: we are assuming this is a *new install*, not an upgrade). If any partitions exist, delete them.
10. Choose **add**. Enter "/" as the mount point, a size of 3500M (assuming a 4GB hard disk), and a partition type of "Linux Native." Select OK.
11. Choose **add**. Leave the mount point blank, enter a size of 500M, and select a type of "Linux Swap." Select OK.
12. You should now see the newly created partitions on the screen. Choose **OK** to confirm. **Save** changes.
13. You will then be asked which partitions should be used for swap. You only created one, so only one choice should appear. Enable bad block checking and select **OK**. Swap space is formatted.

14. You are asked which partitions you would like to format. Format all partitions. Enable bad block checking and select **OK**. You are offered a list of components to install. Please select the bolded items in Exhibit 78.1.
15. **Confirm** your selection.
16. **Acknowledge** the install log message. **Continue**.
17. The installation then creates the file system. After a while, the various packages that were previously selected are installed.
18. The installation process should detect your mouse. **Accept** the mouse that is detected and continue.
19. If the PCI probe detects the video adapter correctly. **Accept** the selection and continue.
20. The monitor type window is displayed. **Choose** the appropriate selection and continue.
21. X Window probing will now begin. **Acknowledge** the message on the screen. After the probe completes accept the default screen configuration.
22. Choose **yes** to configure the LAN.
23. If the network interface is correctly detected. **Acknowledge**.
24. **Configure** the machine to use a **Static** IP address, as shown in Exhibit 78.2.
25. You are then asked to specify the time zone. Select the approprate one and continue.
26. The screen prompts you to specify the services you want to automatically start. Simply leave the **defaults** and **continue**.
27. When prompted to configure a printer, select **no** and **continue**.
28. You will now be prompted to specify a root **password**. **Set** the password.
29. When prompted to **create** a **boot disk**, insert a blank, formatted floppy and create the boot disk. Label the disk appropriately. Continue.
30. You will be asked where you would like to install the boot loader. Specify the **master boot record** and **continue**.
31. When asked to specify additional boot line parameters, **leave** the boot command line **blank** and **continue**.
32. You're done the OS installation.

SAMBA (SMB) CONFIGURATION

Perform the following file modification/creation actions in order using the vi editor.

Create the SMB shares needed. It is important to note that for a Microsoft NT user to make use of SMB shares, the registry must be edited. See Microsoft TechNet article PSS ID Number: Q166730.

Exhibit 78.1.

Printer support	**SMB (Samba) connectivity**
X-window system	IPX/Netware connectivity
Mail/WWW/News tools	**Anonymous FTP server**
DOS/Windows connectivity	**Web server**
File managers	DNS name server
Graphics manipulation	Postgres (SQL) server
X Games	Network management workstation
Console games	TeX document formatting
X multimedia support	Emacs
Console multimedia	Emacs with X Windows
Networked workstation	C development
Dial-up workstation	Development libraries
News server	C++ development
NFS server	X development
	Extra documentation
	Everything

Exhibit 78.2.

Field	Example Value
IP Address	200.200.200.003
Netmask	255.255.255.0
Default Gateway	200.200.200.200
Primary Nameserver	200.200.200.001
Secondary Nameserver	200.200.200.002

Next Screen

Field	Example Value
Domain Name	yourdomain.com
Hostname	host.yourdomain.com

For the purposes of this document, there is only one example that will be provided, and that will be the creation of a share called 'myshare.'

1. Change to the /usr directory

```
cd /usr
```

2. Create a new directory called 'myshare'

```
mkdir /usr/myshare
```

3. Change permissions on the directory

```
chmod 777 /usr/myshare
```

4. Edit the /etc/smb.conf file to contain the following settings:

```
Workgroup = NTDomain

Server string = Linux Samba Server
```

- Configure the myshare share by adding the following lines to the end of the /etc/smb.conf file:

```
[myshare]
        comment = Testing share
        path = /usr/myshre
        valid users = admin Mike
        public = no
        writable = yes
        printable = no
        create mask = 0777
```

5. Refresh the Samba configuration. Enter 'ps ax' at the command line to find out the pid (process id) of the smbd -D (Samba daemon). Once you have discovered the pid you can then refresh the Samba configuration with the kill command.

```
ps ax
kill -HUP pid
```

Apache Web Server Configuration

1. Edit the /etc/httpd/conf/httpd.conf file to contain the following settings:

```
ServerAdmin admin@yourdomain.com

MaxClients 50

ServerName host.yourdomain.com
```

2. Create a directory link to /usr/myshare from the web hosting directory.

```
cd /home /httpd/html

[root@host html]# ln -s /usr/myshare myshare
```

3. Set up basic security to require users to belong to a group called "Mygroup" (see the .htgroup file in /etc/httpd/conf). The htgroup file should read as follows:

```
Mygroup: Mike root admin
```

4. People in the Mygroup group have passwords in the .htpasswd file. To add a password use htpasswd.htpasswd username.

5. Edit the /etc/httpd/conf/access.conf file to contain the following settings:

```
# Controls who can get stuff from this server.

AuthName Mygroup_Only

AuthType Basic

AuthUserFile /etc/httpd/conf/.htpasswd

AuthGroupFile /etc/httpd/conf/.htgroup

<Limit GET POST>

order deny,allow

deny from all

allow from 200.200.200

require group Mygroup

</Limit>
```

This says that to access this server a user must provide a name and password of a member of the Mygroup group and must originate on your network. You will have to add to this if you wish other originating site to access this server directly.

6. Also in access.conf uncomment (and change domain to yourdomain.com) in the section:

```
# Allow server status reports, with the URL of
http://servername/server-status
# Change the ."your_domain.com" to match your domain to
enable.
<Location /server-status>
SetHandler server-status
order deny,allow
deny from all
allow from.yourdomain.com
</Location>
```

User Accounts and Groups

To create accounts from the command line you will need to use the useradd and passwd commands. Useradd adds the user account to the server, passwd prompts you to enter a passwd for a particular user.

```
useradd admin [Enter]
passwd admin [Enter]
useradd Mike [Enter]
passwd Mike [Enter]
```

When prompted enter an eight character password for the user and then re-enter it for confirmation. After performing these steps, verify that the admin and other accounts are fully functional by logging in with that user account.

Post Web Files

Copy any html files you have into the /usr/myshare directory.

Point your Web browser to the machine and there you go.

CONCLUSION

The commercial implications of Linux are becoming more apparent as time rolls on. The openness of the Operating System, tools available for it and embrace of it from the industry will only continue to nurture it and mature it. Its enterprise prowess is lingering in the not-too-distant future, as is its distinction for becoming a contender for the desktop.

Section XVI
Emerging Practices and Directions

THE INFORMATION TECHNOLOGY (IT) PROFESSION is defined by constant change and unpredictability. This section contains three chapters that focus on some current trends in the industry.

Chapter 79, "Business to Business Integration Using E-commerce" shows how to build a completely integrated supply chain solution by utilizing the Internet and various E-commerce applications.

Chapter 80, "Domestic Control Over a Global Phenomenon," discusses whether domestic public policies should be directed to promoting and developing the Internet as a whole, instead of focusing on domestic web content.

Chapter 81, "Ensuring Call Center Quality: A Case Study," presents the experience of a large bank in establishing training programs to increase the efficiency and quality of Call Center's as a central point to collect and disperse an organization's information.

Chapter 79

Business-to-Business Integration Using E-commerce

Ido Gileadi

NOW THAT MANY OF THE FORTUNE 1000 MANUFACTURING COMPANIES have implemented ERP systems to streamline their planning and resource allocation, as well as integrate their business processes across the enterprise, there is still a need for integration with the supply chain.

To reduce inventory levels and lead times, companies must optimize the process of procurement of raw materials and finished goods. Optimization of business processes across multiple organizations includes redefining the way business is conducted as well as putting in place the systems that will support communication between multiple organizations each having their own separate systems infrastructure and requirements.

This type of business to business electronic integration has been around for some time, in the form of Electronic Document Interchange (EDI). EDI allows organizations to exchange documents (e.g., purchase orders, sales orders etc...) using a standards such as X.12 or EDIFACT and Value Added Networks (VANs) for communication. The standards are used to achieve a universal agreement on the content and format of documents/messages being exchanged. EDI standards allow software vendors to include functionality in their software that will support EDI and communicate with other applications. The VAN is used as a medium for transferring messages from one organization to the other. It is a global proprietary network that is designed to carry and monitor EDI messages.

The EDI solution has caught on in several market segments but has never presented a complete solution for the following reasons:

- High cost for setup and transactions—smaller organizations could not afford the cost associated with setup and maintenance of an EDI solution using a VAN.

- EDI messages are a subset of all the types of data that organizations may want to exchange.
- EDI does not facilitate an online access to information, which may be required for applications such as self-service.

With the advance of the Internet both in reliability and security and the proliferation of Internet based E-commerce applications, E-commerce has become an obvious place to look for solutions to a better and more flexible way of integrating business to business processes.

The remainder of this article will discuss a real life example of how internet and E-commerce technologies were implemented to address the business to business integration challenge.

BUSINESS REQUIREMENTS

The business requirements presented to the E-commerce development team can be divided into three general functional area categories:

- General requirements.
- Communicating demand to the supply chain.
- Providing self-service application to suppliers.

General requirements included:

- 100 percent participation by suppliers—the current EDI system was adapted by only 10 percent of suppliers.
- Minimize cost of operation to suppliers and self.
- Maintain high level of security both for enterprise systems and for data communicated to external organizations.
- Utilize industry standards and off the shelf applications wherever possible. Minimize custom development.
- Supplier access to all systems through a browser interface.

Demand requirements included:

- Send EDI standard messages to suppliers
  - –830: Purchase Schedule
  - –850: Purchase Order
  - –860: Purchase Order Change
- Provide advance notice of exceptions to demand through exception reports.

Exhibit 79.1 describes the flow of demand messages (830,850,860, exceptions) between the manufacturer and supplier organization. The demand is generated from the manufacturer ERP system (Baan, SAP etc...), it is then delivered to the supplier through one of several methods we will discuss later. The supplier can load the demand directly into their system or use the supplied software to view and print the demand on a PC. The supplier

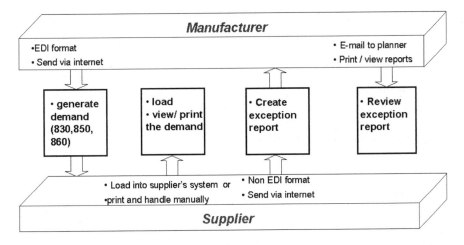

Exhibit 79.1. Demand flow.

can then produce an exception report, indicating any exception to the excepted delivery of goods. The exception report is sent back to the manufacturer and routed to the appropriate planner. The planner can view the report and make the necessary adjustments.

Self-service application requirements included:

- Ability for suppliers to update product pricing electronically thereby ensuring price consistency between manufacturer and supplier.
- Provide online access with drill-down capabilities for suppliers to view the following information:
  –Payment details.
  –Registered invoices.
  –Receipt of goods details.
  –Product quality information.

TECHNICAL REQUIREMENTS

The technical solution had to address the following:

- Transport EDI messages to suppliers of various levels of computerization.
- Provide complete solution for suppliers that have no scheduling application.
- Support small and large supplier organization seamlessly.
- Provide batch message processing and online access to data.
- Provide security for enterprise systems as well as data transmission.
- Utilize industry standards and off the shelf products.

Once again we can divide the technical requirements into three categories:

- General requirements.
  - –Low cost
  - –Low maintenance
  - –High level of security
  - –Industry standards
- Batch message management.
- Online access to enterprise information.

Reviewing the three main categories of technical requirements it is apparent that we will need a product to support message management (EDI and non-EDI) and same or other product to provide on-line access. The selected products will have to poses all the characteristics listed under general requirements.

E-COMMERCE PRODUCT SELECTION

Selection of E-commerce products to construct a complete solution should take the following into consideration:

- What type of functionality does the product cover (on-line, batch, etc...).
- Is the product based on industry standards or is it proprietary.
- Does the product provide a stable and extensible platform to develop future applications.
- How does the product integrate with other product selections.
- What security is available as part of the product.
- What are the skills required to develop using the product, and are these skills readily available.
- Product cost (Server, user licenses, maintenance)
- Product innovation and further development.
- Product base of installation.
- Product architecture.

The E-commerce team selected the following products:

- **WebSuite and Gentran Server** from Sterling Commerce—This product was selected for handling EDI messages and communication EDI and non-EDI messages through various communication mediums. This product provides the following features:
  - –Secure and encrypted file transfer mechanism.
  - –Support for EDI through VANs, Internet and FTP.
  - –Browser operation platform using ActiveX technology.
  - –Simple integration and extendibility through ActiveX forms integration.

–Simple and open architecture.

–Easy integration with other products.

–EDI translation engine.

- **Baan Data Navigator Plus (BDNP)** from TopTier—This product was selected for on-line access to the ERP and other enterprise applications. The product has the following main features:

    –Direct online access to the Baan ERP database through the application layer.

    –Direct online access to other enterprise applications.

    –Integration of data from various applications into one integrated view.

    –Hyper Relational data technology allowing the user to drag and relate each item data onto a component thereby creating a new more detailed query providing drill down capabilities.

    –Access to application through a browser interface.

    –Easy-to-use development environment.

Both the products were just released at the time we have started using them (Summer, 1998). This is typically not a desirable situation as it can extend your project due to unexpected bugs and gaps in functionality. We have chosen to select the products above for their features, the reputation of the companies developing the products and the level of integration the products provided with the ERP system we had in place.

E-COMMERCE SOLUTION

Taking into account the business and technical requirements we put together a systems architecture that provided a business and technical solution.

On the left side of Exhibit 79.2 are the client PCs located at the supplier's environment. These are standard Win NT/95/98 running a browser capable of running ActiveX components. Both the applications (WebSuite and Top-Tier) are accessed through a browser using HTML and ActiveX technologies. As can be seen in the diagram, some suppliers (typically the larger organizations) have integrated the messages sent by the application into their scheduling system. Their system loads the data and presents it within their integrated environment. Other suppliers (typically smaller organizations) are using the browser based interface to view and print the data as well as manipulate and create exception reports to be sent back to the server.

Communication is achieved using the following protocols on the internet:

- http, https—for delivery of on-line data.
- Sockets (SL), Secure Sockets (SSL)—for message transfer.

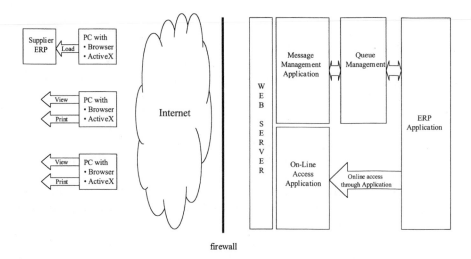

Exhibit 79.2.   Technical architecture.

All traffic enters the enterprise systems through a firewall for security. Security will be discussed in the following section.

On the Enterprise side, the client applications first access a Web server. The Web Server handles the http/https communication and invokes the server side controls through an ASP page.

The online application (TopTier) intercepts the http/https communication address to it and interprets the query. It then provides a result set and integrates the result set with an HTML template to be sent back to the client PC as an HTML page. The online access application communicates with the ERP application through the application API or through ODBC.

The message management application (WebSuite) communicates to the message queue using server side ActiveX controls and ftp to send and receive files between systems. The message management application communicates with the ERP and other enterprise applications using a set of processes that can read and write messages to a shared mounted disk area.

The above system architecture supports a mechanism for transferring messages in a secure and reliable fashion as well as providing online access to data residing in the enterprise systems. All through a browser interface with minimal requirements from the supplier and minimal support requirements.

SECURITY

The are two categories of security that must be handled:

• Enterprise systems security from outside intrusion.
• Data security for data communicated over the Web.

Security for the enterprise is intended to prevent unauthorized users from accessing data and potentially damaging enterprise systems and data. This is handled by various methods that are far too many to have a meaningful discussion in this article. We would review the steps taken to secure the system on this project, these are by no means the only or the complete set of measures that can be taken. In addition each organization may have different security requirements. On this project we have done the following:

• Use a firewall that provided the following:
  –Limitation on IP and PORT addresses.
  –Limitation on protocols allowed (http, https, IP).
  –User Authentication at the firewall level.
  –Abstraction of Server IP address.
• Authentication
  –Front office application layer.
  –Back office application layer.
  –Operating system layer.
  –Firewall layer.
• Domain settings
  –The Web server machine is not part of the enterprise domain.
  –The Web server machine has IP access to other servers.

Data Security is required to protect the information that is transferred between supplier and manufacturer over the public domain of the Internet. The intent is to secure the data from unauthorized eavesdrops. The are many methods to protect the data, these methods can be grouped into two main categories:

• Transferring data through a secure communication channel (SSL, https). This method utilizes:
  –Authentication.
  –Certificates.
  –Encryption.
• Encryption of data. This method is typically used in conjunction with the previous method, but can be used on its own. There are various encryption algorithms available. The encryption strength (cipher strength) which could be defined as how difficult it would be to decrypt encrypted data without the keys can vary and are designated

in terms of number of bits (i.e., 40bit, 128bit, etc...). For our project we have selected to use Microsoft Crypto API that is supported both by the Web Server (IIS 4) and by the client browser (IE 4). The cipher strength selected was 40bits to allow non U.S. and Canada access to the application. 128bit cipher strength is not available for browsers used outside of the U.S. and Canada.

CONCLUSION

Manufacturing organizations striving to reduce inventory levels and lead times must integrate business processes and systems with their supply chain organization. E-commerce applications utilizing the Internet can be used to achieve integration across the supply chain with minimal cost and standard interfaces.

When implementing E-commerce applications it is recommended to select application that can be used as an infrastructure to develop future business solutions to address new requirements. Selecting applications that provide technology solutions with a development platform rather then applications that provide an integrated business solution will provide a platform for development of future business applications as the use of E-commerce proliferates through the organization.

Chapter 80

Domestic Control over a Global Phenomenon

Elisabeth Ostiguy

THE INTERNET IS SAID BY MANY TO BE THE ULTIMATE COMMUNICATIONS VEHICLE. Touted as the communication path to the world, it is growing beyond chat lines and a research tool to provide a potential competitive alternative to traditional communications media.

At the present time, you can make a phone call over the Net or send e-mail to a friend or relative around the world. A favorite hockey team's performance can be monitored on radio broadcasts over the Web. You can participate in a discussion of your favorite cooking recipe with the host of a television cooking show. You can view a cartoon show over your Internet access.

The reality is that the Internet may become a competitive threat to traditional communications service providers, operating under terms and conditions of their domestic markets. In Canada, as in other parts of the world, providers of traditional communication services must provide social and cultural benefits to their domestic systems in return for the right and privilege to provide the basis of their business raison d'être.

Recently in Canada, the federal regulator, the Canadian Radio, Television, and Telecommunications Commission (CRTC) undertook a comprehensive review of the role of new media in light of existing legislation. They created a forum for a comprehensive dialogue to better understand the impact of this global phenomenon on the domestic obligations tied to the Broadcasting and Telecommunications Act, which define the world for Canadian broadcasters and telecommunications service providers.

During this review, the thoughts of the wise were gathered on fundamental issues such as does the new media fit any definitions within the legislation that would in turn require regulatory supervision. It explored in detail the growth of broadcasting and telephony delivery over the Internet. And it came down to a discussion of whether a domestic control could be put in place to protect national interests.

The whole process was a valiant effort, which attempted to freeze in time an amorphous entity that is growing exponentially on a local, national and most importantly on an international basis.

The critical element to whether Canadian Internet activities should be regulated centered on the reality of broadcasting over the Internet.

VISION OF THE FUTURE

WebTV has captured the attention of the journalists as a first step towards a new role for the television set. Regularly, there are articles espousing the notion that television will move beyond its traditional role of being the "boob" tube to a vehicle exciting the couch potato to use digital dexterity to interface with advertisers, television shows and communicate to the world.

Interactive television is the next step we are told.

The television set will become a two-way communications apparatus used to provide a means to communicate with the world, to conduct business electronically and to go beyond being a receptacle for entertainment programs to providing an interplay between viewer and broadcaster.

The television set will become a smart box, loaded with computer chips that will allow a viewer to opt for a more detailed version of a news story, or specify which car you would like to get more information on during the advertising break.

The basis for all the advancement is digital technology. The move from analogue signals to bits and bytes will allow for the delivery of all kinds of services that are currently unavailable.

Digital technology will allow the downloading of CD quality music right to your stereo. It will provide a wealth of in-depth information that you currently do not have access to. For instance, as the local announcer report on the major fire in the downtown area, you are being provided in a corner of the screen with alternative traffic routes.

As you turn to your favorite movie, you are able to inquiry on the length, the biographies of the stars and even information on its production. The producers may even include a contest to promote upcoming movies—a chance to win free tickets, by responding to a quiz about the movie. All this made available at a click of the remote. Sometime in the future, you may even be able to select the actors to play selected roles.

Digital technology will allow advertisers to target messages and products. The audience will be in control of what messages they receive. It will be no more difficult than a click of the remote to find out information on the product and where it can be obtained. However, there may not even be a need to move from your comfortable armchair to make the purchase. The next click could take you into an encrypted system that allows you to make the purchase from your home.

The move to digital technology is well entrenched in the United States, where the federal regulator (Federal Communications Commission) has mandated the transition to digital by all television stations to be completed by the year 2003. In Canada, industry lobby is pushing for federal commitment to ensure the smooth transition to digital for radio and television broadcasters is also completed in a timely fashion. Trials deploying digital radio transmission are already underway in major centers such as Toronto, Vancouver, and Montreal.

REALITY CHECK

Vision of electronic sugarplums dance in the heads of the futurists. However, for the many that have to implement the deployment of digital technology and the associated high speed bandwidth access, the reality is that it will happen later than sooner.

The major hiccup is that these new services are too expensive and that the high-capacity networks needed for the transmission of interactive technology are just not there yet.

Despite major efforts by cable, telephone and wireless companies to build high-speed digital networks, progress has been slowed down by the lack of widespread availability of the digital set top boxes.

Microsoft Corporation's efforts to establish a stronghold in digital television with its early introduction of WebTV have not been the panacea that the company expected. Its own marketing strategies and the growth of competitive alternatives to their software have thwarted their efforts. The cable TV industry objected to the Microsoft being cut into the deal regarding transaction fees. The company is now repositioning itself as a neutral technology supplier. It has also been hampered by the lack of delivery of the audience it had projected. Early in 1998 Craig Mundie, senior Microsoft executive, predicted WebTV would have one million subscribers by years end. Going into 1999, they had garnered only half that many.

But what drives it all is the technology. Until recent times, all communications, including the early days of Internet traffic, were transported over the ubiquitous Public Switched Telephone Network. This network was optimized for voice communications. It has also been combined with overlay networks to transport different types of data traffic.

The new emphasis is now on dealing with the exponential growth of data traffic and digital content. New network infrastructures are being developed to accommodate new applications protocols, such as IP and provide increased speed and throughput that the higher bandwidth services require. There is a growing migration on the technical side from circuit-switching technology to packet switching with its greater abilities to deal with the downloading of video input. Broadcast quality images require a far greater bandwidth than normal data streams.

At the moment, the Internet content is predominantly alphanumeric text supplemented by graphics. This is changing as rapidly as technology will permit. Audio and video applications are still in their infancy. Audio transmission is providing acceptable quality. Video transmission quality is still rudimentary. It is still not time to sit back and watch your favorite television program on the your computer.

Technology experts do not consider that the Internet can be considered a serious threat to the traditional broadcast quality video programming coming into your home via cable or satellite distributor. However, developments in streaming video technology continue to push forward. Within the next five years, on-demand programming may become common place. Traditional broadcasters will not be put out of business for some time to come.

COMPLEMENT OR COMPETITOR

So will the relationship between viewers and their television change? Will they want a service that provides relaxation and entertainment or will they jump at the chance to actively control the images coming into their homes?

Mainstream broadcasters express concern that the Internet is emerging as a major competitor for viewers' time and attention and for advertising dollars — their lifeblood.

Despite the growth in alternative interests, such as video games and Internet access, the hours spent in front of the television have hardly changed over the last decade. In Canada, the average television viewer spends 23 hours per week in front of the tube. Time and flat screen televisions will soon see the term "tube" replaced with plasma screen. It would seem likely that the draw away from the television would not negatively impact on traditional broadcasters.

However, the area, which may be of more concern, is the growing advertising market developing on the Internet. Traditional broadcasters rely heavily on advertising revenue. There is some growth in the area of subscription revenues as more Specialty Services reached the screens.

According to a report issued by SIMBA Information Inc,[1] in July 1996, the Web advertising market is dominated by a growing number of advertisers. Companies such as computer and car companies are early users of online advertising. Car manufacturers have long been a mainstay for national advertising buys on traditional broadcasters.

Broadcasters are not standing idly by while new media erodes their advertising base. Some have adopted the Internet and their Web sites as complementary to the advertising packages they offer their clients. Web ads are sold in conjunction with television advertising. A major sponsor may benefit from an additional advertising window as a bonus for their support of the traditional television service.

The Internet can provide an interesting ally as well. Broadcasters offer a on-line guide to television programming on their Web sites. Some go as far as to allow viewers to personalize their television schedule. You can quickly locate when your favorite gardening show is on, rather than having to search through the complete listing. Some offer search mechanisms providing reminders about specified interest programming and can go far as to warn you when the program is available for taping.

Some broadcasters use the Internet to take their programming a step further than general information. They will complement their line up with in-depth databases. Weather conditions for special interest groups can be instantly available, providing key information for crop management, allergy sufferers or for that crucial golf game. It also can a be an interactive resource providing the latest scores and statistics for a hockey series or to provide the standings during a major athletic competition.

Revenue opportunities are being developed through E-commerce applications. In some cases, the opportunity to buy props and costumes no longer in use are made available for purchase.

Most importantly, the broadcasters Web site has become for some and integrated expansion of the broadcasting component. More than just providing information on the programming, they actually draw the viewer into an interactive relationship with program hosts.

As with the competitive threat, the full potential of the Internet as a complement to television is at least ten years away and is limited to most likely a break even economic outlook.

REGULATING THE UNREGULATABLE

A fundamental determination is now being discussed and decided upon by the Canadian regulator. They must determine whether the potential threat of the Internet on the Canadian broadcasting sector and its cultural obligations merit their intrusion into regulating the Internet.

Many have argued that CRTC does not have the jurisdiction to apply its rules to an international phenomenon. Others argue that, due to the position taken by the U.S. government in applying taxes to Internet services, if it can be taxed it can be regulated.

Extensive discussions surrounded the application of legal definitions. This was the basis for many to conclude that new media, e.g., Internet content, would not constitute broadcasting as defined in the Canadian Broadcasting Act. The view was put forward that the Internet acted as an electronic hydro pole where bills are posted. Content on the Internet is nothing more that the information found on poles throughout our cities.

There is also the question as to the desirability to regulate. Much has been discussed at the limitations of a regulatory environment on a nascent industry. Industry leaders were quick to underline the restrictive nature of regulation. Regulation, in their view, would limit the development of this high-technology industry in Canada, driving talented Canadians outside its borders to continue their Internet business.

Fundamentally, what drove the whole debate was whether there is a perceived need to promote the development of Canadian content on the Internet. In the early years of television, Canadians received their programming from their American neighbors. The Canadian government, responded to a domestic need, establishing the Canadian public broadcaster to ensure that their citizens could see themselves and their stories on the television screens. From this basic premise grew the Canadian Broadcasting System which delivers 50 percent of its programming from Canadian sources. The balance for the most part is programming from the United States.

Many of the Canadian Internet providers argued against regulating Canadian content levels for the Web on the basis that quality content from Canadian sources was available and this due to consumer demand for Canadian information rather than from regulatory pressures. They believe that this is a better approach, leaving it to market forces to ensure a Canadian presence.

The protectionist camp argued that the form of the content was all that was needed to determine that it should be captured by regulation. A film, is a film, is a film according to traditional broadcasters. It doesn't matter whether it is viewed on television, in the theatre or on the Internet. If the cultural policies address the need to ensure certain levels of domestic film production, then this guarantee must also be applicable in the interactive new media.

Many industry experts contend that adding a level of interactivity to content and by specifying the delivery, content is taken out of the realm of broadcasting. This argument was accepted by government pre-1991 revisions to the Broadcasting Act. At that time, video-on-demand was excluded from the definition of broadcasting. However, in the 1991 Broadcasting Act this exclusion was removed, bringing on-demand content under the definition and the legislation.

From a protectionist standpoint, new media should be captured under the potential for regulation. But as the industry is new and growing, then regulation should be limited to exempting new media from any specific obligations and responsibilities.

Free marketers and broadcasters feel that rather than moving to even an exemption order, that the traditional obligations and responsibilities tied to the cultural objectives of Canadian government policy should be removed from the traditional players. This would remove burden from them to allow them to compete more fully against what they see as an impending threat.

At heart of the issue is whether the domestic public policy in Canada will emphasize the promotion and development of the network evolution rather than use a traditional constrictive and binding approach to motivate the production of Canadian new media services.

Ensuring its unique identity and being one of the most connected countries in the world may best be achieved for Canada though free market forces that have so far benefited from the talents of Canadian entrepreneurs, developing world class products and services.

CONCLUSION

Print and film evolved from heavily censored controls to near complete freedom of expression. The broadcast media remains one of the most restricted. The basic model of government control of broadcasting is the same now as in the early days, founded on the dispersal of a limited resource—the public airwaves.

The Internet was born as free as print is today. It does not depend on a scarce resource to provide its communications path. Governments should respect the freedom of expression that exists today on the Web and not try to capture the illusive beast in a net of confining regulations.

Note

1. SIMBA Information Inc., "online Advertising Will Hit Nearly $2 billion in 2000," July 1996.

Chapter 81
Ensuring Call Center Quality: A Case Study
Michelle Burgess

CALL CENTERS ARE A KEY POINT OF CONTACT FOR ENSURING THE EFFECTIVE CAPTURE AND SHARING OF INFORMATION between a business and its clients. At the Canadian Imperial Bank of Commerce's (CIBC), National Support Line, the New Employee Training Program lays the foundation from which superior telephone agents are built.

CIBC, one of the largest Canadian Banks in the country, has 32 separately managed call centers across Canada in 8 major business areas. These call centers are located in 10 major cities and vary in size from 6 to 353 telephone agents.

One of these call centers is the National Support Line at CIBC, which is an inbound Call Center. There are approximately 150 agents located in Toronto and 15 in Montreal, which cater to French and English speaking customers. NSL supports all CIBC branches in Canada, CIBC Head Office Staff and a select group of external clients.

NSL provides support in six specialized areas, which include:

1. *Automated Banking Machines (ABM)*—Provides procedural and technical support for all CIBC Automated Banking Machines located in Canada.
2. *Personal Computer (PC) Assistance*—Provides support for all computer software, hardware, and application support that is available in the branches and selected Head Office areas.
3. *CIBC Online Information Network System (COINS)*—Provides support for CIBC's mainframe of account information (called COINS). This also provides support regarding products that are being offered at the branches and assistance with branch procedures and systems.
4. *Commercial*—Provides support for all commercial and business loan services offered at the branches.

5. *CLASS*—Provides support for all personal loan and credit services offered at the branches.
6. *Centrex*—Centrex is CIBC's main switchboard.

THE AGENT

The agent provides specialized support by telephone in the above-defined areas to their customers. The overall purpose of the job is to:

Respond to inquires or requests from internal and/or external customers, typically through the telephone, regarding one or more of the following: products, services, technology, benefits procedures and policies.

This is done while in conjunction with providing superior customer service. A customer's first and sometimes only contact is with the telephone agent. For this reason, it is essential to ensure that agent has the required skills to do the job, to the best of his ability, and access to real-time information or data.

In National Support Line the Learning Program is a two-week training curriculum that is provided to all new agents.

National Support Line Call Center—New Employee Training Program

The program consists of six workshops — Orientation, Achieving Extraordinary Customer Relations, Team Building, Call Control, Handling Difficult Customers and a Day in the Life of an Agent. The training program is focused on enhancing the following attributes:

1. Service-oriented
2. Communicator
3. Analytic/systematic thinker
4. Adaptable
5. Team builder
6. Results oriented

Orientation

This session is approximately one day in length. The objective of this workshop is to:

- Understand the culture and strategy.
- Maximize external/internal customer satisfaction by the close of a call and accomplishing this in way that is aligned with CIBC and NSL goals, vision, and values.
- Understand the roles and the expectations of the Call Center Agent and Team Leaders.

The learning objective of this workshop is to:

- Describe the CIBC group of companies.
- Describe the vision, values and strategy of CIBC overall and tie these to key performance drivers.
- Describe how service quality applies to all aspects of this job.
- Describe the security guidelines for the employee's personal computer, confidentiality guidelines for customer and bank information, and personal security measures to take, when working various shifts.
- Describe the learning environment and adult learning principles.
- Understand Call Center technology and terminology.
- Understand the job expectations.
- Explain the relationship between Team Leaders and Agents.
- Explain how diversity and sensitivity can build a stronger team and enhance customer relationships.
- Explain how to maintain a healthy and safe work environment.

The workshop is delivered using a classroom approach with extensive group interaction.

Achieving Extraordinary Customer Relations Workshop

Achieving extraordinary customer relations will provide agents with proven techniques for every call to build a positive relationship with customers. This is a two-day external classroom course. This course is a foundation for customer service, a model for customer relationships and a method for creating positive outcomes through the review of seven modules.

The objective of the workshop is to:

- Identify customers within the organization.
- Learn how to handle potentially unproductive interactions.
- Create positive, memorable experiences for all customers.

The learning objective of this workshop is to:

- The foundation for customer service.
- How to give caring customer service.
- A model for customer relationships.
- Their impact on the customer.
- How to reduce stress.
- How to build rapport.
- How to create positive outcomes.

Module 1—Foundations for Customer Service
The learning objective of this workshop is to:

- Identify internal and external customers.
- Identify specific behavior that creates a 'positive, memorable customer experience' (PMCE).

- Identify the two levels of an interaction with customers.
- Describe how quality core service affects customer service.
- Describe "caring customer service."
- Explain the customer report card.

The method of delivery for this module includes presentations, reading, video and group exercises.

Module 2—Caring customer service.

The learning objective of this workshop is to:

- Identify different kinds of customer contact.
- List several policies that are difficult to handle.
- Demonstrate and use Caring Response.
- Create a positive memorable experience by using a series of caring responses.

The method of delivery for this module includes presentations, reading, video, group exercises and role-plays.

Module 3—A model forcustomer relations.

learning objectives, of this workshop are:

- Distinguish among the six parts of customer service.
- Identify voice tones and body language used by the six parts which can cause unproductive interactions.

The method of delivery for this module includes presentation, reading, video, group exercises and role-plays.

Module 4—Your impact on the customer.

The learning objective of this workshop is to:

- Identify ways in which one may unknowingly create unproductive customer interactions.
- Demonstrate and use expected customer courtesy rituals.

The method of delivery for this module includes presentations, reading, video and group exercises.

Module 5—Reducing stress.

The learning objective of this workshop is to:

- Identify actions that lead to negative feelings.
- Identify techniques to reduce stress and stay out of unproductive interactions.

The method of delivery for this module includes presentations, reading and group exercises.

Module 6—Building rapport.
The learning objective of this workshop is to:

• Demonstrate and use several defusing skills.
• Demonstrate and use techniques to lead your customers to business.

The method of delivery for this module includes presentations, reading, group exercises and role plays.

Module 7—Creating positive outcomes.
The learning objective of this workshop is to:

• Demonstrate and use escalated concern and selective agreement.
• Demonstrate and practice using techniques for saying 'no' to customer requests.
• Identify ways to explain policies and procedures to customers in a customer-friendly manner.

The method of delivery for this module includes presentations, reading, video, group exercises and role playing.

Call Control

Call Control introduces the agent on understanding the importance of keeping the call focused. This is a one-day session.

The learning objective of this workshop is to:

• Listen to others, interpreting tone (what is being said and what is not being said).
• Diffuse emotions, respond calmly and guide the conversation to end on a positive note.
• Use effective listening techniques (e.g., reflective, passive, active).
• Remain objective and keep personal feelings under control when dealing with conflict between oneself and others.
• Communicate respect for the views or positions of others that differ from your own.
• Respond promptly to customer needs or requests an exhibit interest in being helpful to others.
• Show patience and respect when dealing with customer complaints and difficult customers.
• Listen closely to others and respond in ways that communicate clear understanding of what they have said.

The method of delivery for this session includes presentations, group discussions, discovery exercises, practice sessions and role-plays.

Handling Difficult Customers

Handling difficult customers introduces the agent to turn difficult situations into positive outcomes.

This is a one-day session.

The learning objective of this workshop is to:

- Identify relevant alternatives and evaluate the potential consequences of each before taking action.
- Identify and follow effective, step-by-step approaches to analyze and solve problems.
- Apply criteria, standards, tools or methods appropriately and systematically to a situation or problem.
- Listen attentively to others and respond in way that communicates clear understanding of what they have said.
- Communicate with others clearly, concisely and directly.
- Communicate clearly in one-on-one discussions, using good examples of illustrations to explain things.
- Respond promptly to customer needs or requests and exhibit interest in being helpful to others.
- Show patience and respect when dealing with customer complaints an difficult customers.
- Remain objective and keep personal feelings under control when dealing with conflict between oneself and others.
- Communicate respect for others views or positions that differ from one's own.
- Use effective listening techniques (e.g., Reflective, Passive, Active).
- Listen to others, interpreting tone (what is being said and what is not being said).
- Diffuse emotions, respond calmly and guide conversation to end on a positive note.

TEAM BUILDING

Program Goal

This is a two-day session that is dedicated to understanding the importance of successful teams and being a member of that team. This session is conducted in a classroom environment. There are two modules that are reviewed.

Module 1—Elements of Successful Teams.

(Method of Delivery—Classroom Estimated Time = 45 min to 1 hour)

The class is divided into small groups and is asked to flipchart the elements of a successful team. They are asked to envision the most successful team in history and list what that team possessed that made them so successful. The groups are then asked to create an agreed upon list of required elements of a successful team. The objective of this exercise is to have a list that consists of all or part of the following list.

Elements of a successful team:

- Tradition of excellence.
- Common goal.
- Professionalism.
- All members understand their role.
- All members accept their role.
- Treat other with respect.
- Make yourself approachable.
- Treat others fairly.
- Diversity.
- All members are talented.

Module 2—"Marooned" produced by HRDQ.
(Method of Delivery—Classroom Estimated Time—3 to 4 Hours).

"'Marooned' is a unique group exercise because it involves participants in an exploration of alternative courses of action that have the power to affect their survival. 'Marooned' allows teams to solve problems related to their survival in an unusual, but plausible environment. At the same time, participants may explore the dynamics of group operation including consensus decision making, effective influence techniques, interpersonal skill development and the potential for synergy in a diverse group."

Goals of the Exercise:

- To provide a new team with a non-threatening opportunity to work together.
- To allow a team to practice consensus decision making.
- To provide an opportunity for a team to practice interpersonal skills, such as active listening, probing, and confronting behaviors in a realistic setting.

Reinforcement

Upon the completion of each day, the agents are asked to sit in a circle so that they are facing each other. They are then asked to share two new ideas or tips that they have learned. This process reinforces the agents' learning, and also enables them to listen to other perspectives that are provided during the round table. The process has proved to be the most successful method in reviewing that day's learnings.

EXPERIENCING A DAY IN THE LIFE OF AN AGENT

New agents are scheduled to sit with existing agents to experience a typical day in the life of an agent. This is also known as shadowing. This is offered for three days of the two-week training program. Upon completion of the orientation workshop, the agent will have a better understanding of CIBC and more specifically NSL. Providing them with the opportunity to sit with an agent at this time will enhance their understanding of the business and the customers at NSL.

The second day that they are scheduled to shadow occurs after the two-day customer service-training program (AECR). Upon completion of this course they will understand what an excellent level of customer service should look like and how it should be executed. Shadowing at this point, will enable the agent to see the hands-on approach to customer service and how it is being provided in a live environment.

The third day that they are scheduled occurs at the end of the program. At this point the agent will have participated in all the workshops and be able to see, with existing agents, all the components of the program at work dynamically.

On the final day, a program recap is provided to review all the workshops and the major learning objectives from each session. At this point, a ten-question quiz is administered that reviews the basic components of Customer Service, Call Control, Dealing with Difficult Customers and Team Building. This checkpoint will provide the facilitator with a measurable score to determine if the foundation has been built. If the agent is not able to communicate these basic principles, they are deemed unsuccessful for this program and are released from the position.

CONCLUSION

This training program has been in effect since September of 1998. It has provided the foundation for agents to "hit the ground running" and along with other Service Quality programs, has contributed significantly to the 92 percent customer satisfaction rating of NSL for 1998.

At CIBC, National Support Line, the New Employee Training Program does indeed lay the foundation from which superior telephone agents are made, thus affecting a major gateway of information into and out of the bank.

About the Consulting Editor

SANJIV PURBA holds a bachelor of science degree from the University of Toronto and has over 14 years of relevant information technology experience. He is a senior manager with Deloitte Consulting and leader of the object-oriented practice in Canada.

Mr. Purba has extensive industry experience, with a focus on the financial and retail industry sectors. As a consultant, Mr. Purba has also gained relevant experience in other industries, such as telecommunications, travel and tourism, ticketing and reservation systems, and manufacturing. He has served in a variety of roles in large organizations, including developer, senior developer, business analyst, systems analyst, team leader, project manager, consultant, senior architect, senior manager, and acting vice president.

Mr. Purba is the author of five information technology (IT)-related text books published by John Wiley & Sons. He is also the author of over 75 IT articles for *Computerworld Canada, Network World, Computing Canada, DBMS Magazine*, and the *Hi-tech Career Journal (HTC)*. Mr. Purba is a past editor of *ITOntario*, a publication of the Canadian Information Processing Society (CIPS). Mr. Purba has also written fantasy and science-fiction graphic novels.

Mr. Purba is a regular speaker at industry symposiums on technical and project management topics. He has also lectured at universities and colleges for the past 13 years, including Humber College, the University of Toronto, and Ryerson Polytechnic University. He recently hosted an IT Forum for a television program in the Toronto area.

Prior to joining the Deloitte Consulting, Mr. Purba ran his own computer consulting business, Purba Computer Solutions, Inc., during which time he consulted with Canadian Tire, Sun Life Assurance Company of Canada, and IBM in a variety of roles, including senior architect, facilitator, and project leader.

Mr. Purba also served as a Senior Architect and Senior Consultant with Flynn McNeil Raheb and Associates, a Management Consulting firm, for five years prior to owning his own business. During this time, he consulted with such organizations as IBM, ISM, The Workers Compensation Board, Alcatel, and The Ministry of Education.

Index